TELEPEN
80 7707436 6
DILEWYD O STOC
WITHDRAWN FROM STOCK

D0121505

14. JAN. 1994

PRIMITIVE HERITAGE

PRIMITIVE HERITAGE

An Anthropological Anthology

EDITED, WITH AN INTRODUCTION, BY

Margaret Mead AND
Nicolas Calas

VICTOR GOLLANCZ LTD

First published in Great Britain in 1954

Printed by Lowe & Brydone (Printers) Limited, London, N.W.10

ACKNOWLEDGMENTS

For permission to reprint the copyrighted items in this volume, the editors are indebted to the following authors and publishers:

George Allen and Unwin Ltd. for "What the Native Thinks of Pictures, Names, and Dreams" from *How Natives Think* by Lucien Levy-Bruhl; "The Primitive's Sense of Death" from *Primitive Mentality* by Lucien Levy-Bruhl

The American Anthropological Association for "Configuration of Culture" by Ruth Benedict; "A Native Account of the Meeting with LaPerouse" by G. T. Emmons

The American Museum of Natural History for "Shasta Puberty Ceremonies for Girls" by Roland B. Dixon; "The Mischievous Society of Boys" and "A Pawnee War Party" by James M. Murie; "Arapaho Marriage" by Alfred L. Kroeber; selections from *The Chukchee* by Waldemar Bogoras; "Ceremonial Bundles" by Clark Wissler

Appleton-Century-Crofts, Inc. for "A Non-Religious Individual" from *Primitive Man As Philosopher* by Paul Radin. Copyright, 1927, by D. Appleton & Company

Australian National Research Council for "Marriage Classes: Diagrammed" from *The Social Organization of Australian Tribes* by Alfred R. Radcliffe-Brown

Gregory Bateson for "The Naven Ceremony in New Guinea" from *Naven* by Gregory Bateson

Estate of A. A. Brill for "The Totemic Feast" from *Totem and Taboo* by Sigmund Freud

Burrows, Cleveland, Ohio, for "Hiroquois Cruelty" and "Killing the Old Mother" from *Jesuit Relations*

A. & C. Black Ltd. for selections from *Savage Childhood* by Dudley Kidd

Ruth Bunzel for "Psychology of the Pueblo Potter" from *The Pueblo Potter* by Ruth Bunzel

Cambridge University Press for "Andaman peacemaking" from *The Andaman Islanders* by A. R. Radcliffe-Brown

Jonathan Cape Limited for "Last Night at Teyma" from *Arabia Deserta* by C. M. Doughty

Cassell & Company Ltd. for "The Beauty of the Congo Huts" from *Travels in the Congo* by André Gide

The Clarendon Press, Oxford, for "The Character of the Nuer" from *The Nuer* by Edward E. Evans-Pritchard

Crown Publishers for selections from *Magic and Mystery in Tibet* by Alexandra David-Neel

J. M. Dent & Sons Ltd. for "The First Societies" from *The Social Contract* by Jean Jacques Rousseau

Department of Public Printing and Stationery, Ottawa, Canada, for "Abnormal Types of Speech in Nootka" by Edward Sapir

Dodd, Mead & Company for "The Iroquois' Faith in Treaties" from *League of the Iroquois* by Lewis H. Morgan

Executors of C. M. Doughty for "Last Night at Teyma" from *Arabia Deserta* by C. M. Doughty

E. P. Dutton & Co., Inc., for "Sailing on the Sea-Arm of Pilolu," "Launching a Canoe" and "The Kula" from *Argonauts of the Western Pacific* by Bronislaw Malinowski; "Betrothal by Mother-in-Law" and "How to Become a Sorcerer" from *Sorcerers of Dobu* by R. F. Fortune, copyright, 1932, by E. P. Dutton & Co., Inc.; "The First Societies" from *The Social Contract* by Jean Jacques Rousseau (Everyman's Library)

Farrar, Straus & Young, Inc. for "The Jealous Father and Couvade" from *Ritual: Psycho-analytic Studies* by Theodor Reik. Copyright, 1946, by Theodor Reik

Fisk University for selections from *A History of Ancient Mexico* by F. B. de Sahugun

Peter Freuchen for "Burying the Mother Alive in a Snow House" from *Eskimo* by Peter Freuchen

Victor Gollancz, Ltd. for "Bush Telegraph" and "The Hebridean as Artist" from *Savage Civilization* by Tom Harrisson

Geoffrey Gorer for "Dahomeyan Sacrifice of the Bull" from *Africa Dances* by Geoffrey Gorer

Harper & Brothers for "Causes of War in Australia" from *A Black Civilization* by W. Lloyd Warner

Hogarth Press Ltd. for "The Jealous Father and Couvade" from *Ritual: Psychoanalytic Studies* by Theodor Reik

International Publishers for "The Gens, Its Simplicity" from *The Origin of the Family* by Friedrich Engels

International Universities Press, Inc. for "Childhood Trauma in Australia" from *Journal of a Psychoanalyst* by Geza Roheim

The Johns Hopkins Press for "Mohave Homosexuality" from *Human Biology* by George Devereux

The Journal of Philosophy for "Being and Value in Primitive Society" by Dorothy Lee

Alfred A. Knopf, Inc. for "The Beauty of the Congo Huts" from *Travels in the Congo* by André Gide; "Bush Telegraph" and "The Hebridean as Artist" from *Savage Civilization* by Tom Harrisson. Copyright, 1937, by Tom Harrisson

Mrs. Frieda Lawrence and William Heinemann Ltd. for "The Australian Scene" from *Kangaroo* by D. H. Lawrence

Methuen & Co. Ltd. for "The Undifferentiated Character of the Primitive" and "Eating in Privacy" from *The Mystic Rose* by Ernest Crawley

Macmillan and Company, Ltd. for "Initiatory Ordeals" from *The Native Tribes of Central Australia* by B. Spencer and F. J. Gillen

McGraw-Hill Book Company, Inc. for "The Bush Negro Family" from *Rebel Destiny* by Melville Herskovits. Copyright, 1934, by Melville J. & Frances S. Herskovits

Margaret Mead for "Re-creation" from *Balinese Character* by Margaret Mead

William Morrow and Company, Inc. for "Early Influences That Mould the Arapesh Personality" from *Sex and Temperament in Three Primitive Societies* by Margaret Mead. Copyright, 1928, 1930, 1935, 1939 by Margaret Mead; "A Day in Samoa" from *Coming of Age in Samoa* by Margaret Mead. Copyright, 1928, 1930, 1935, 1939, by Margaret Mead

John Murray (Publishers) Ltd. for "Animism" from Primitive Culture by Edward B. Tylor

Museum of the American Indian, Heye Foundation, for "Zuni Breadstuff" by Frank Hamilton Cushing

The New York Academy of Sciences for "People with Two Souls" from *A Study of Bagolo Ceremonial, Magic and Myth* by Laura W. Benedict; "Re-creation" from *Balinese Character* by Margaret Mead and Gregory Bateson

W. W. Norton & Company, Inc. for "The Yurok Salmon Fisherman" from *Childhood and Society* by Erik H. Erikson. Copyright, 1950, by W. W. Norton & Company, Inc.

David Nutt for "Sermons by Natives Converted to Christianity" from *The Life of a South African Tribe* by Henri Junod

Open Court Publishing Company for "Interpretation of the Sacrificial Ceremony" by Henri Hubert and Marcel Mauss

Oxford University Press for "The Individuality of the Primitive" from *Anthropology* by R. R. Marett

Oxford University Press (in co-operation with the International African Institute) for "The Dead City of Bida" from *A Black Byzantium* by S. F. Nadel

Oxford University Press (Bombay) for "The Two-sex Dormitories of the Muria" from *The Muria and Their Ghotul* by Verrier Elwin

G. P. Putnam's Sons for "Troglodytes" from *Geography* by Strabo; "Blood and Cruelty as the Foundation of All Good Things" from *The Genealogy of Morals* by Friedrich Nietzsche

Routledge and Kegan Paul Ltd. for "Sailing on the Sea-Arm of Pilolu," "Launching a Canoe" and "The Kula" from *Argonauts of the Western Pacific* by Bronislaw Malinowski; "Pig-Giving at Funerals" and "Graded Associations and Secret Societies" from *Malekula* by Arthur B. Deacon; "Speaking to Tigers but Not to Bears" from *Psychomental Complex of the Fungus* by S. M. Shirokogoroff; "Killing and Eating One's Enemy in Sixteenth-Century Brazil" from *The True History of His Captivity* by Hans Staden; "The Death and Burial of a Sudanese King" from *A Sudanese Kingdom* by Charles K. Meek

St. Martin's Press, Inc. for "Initiatory Ordeals" from *The Native Tribes of Central Australia* by B. Spencer and F. J. Gillen; "Initiation Ceremonies of the Kiwai Papuans" from *The Kiwai Papuans of New Guinea* by Gunnar Landtman; "A Marriage in Borneo" from *Natural Man* by Charles Hose; "The Conduct of Oronn Warfare" from *Life in Southern Nigeria* by P. A. Talbot; "Human Beings Killed to Invigorate the King" from *The Baganda* by John Roscoe

Smithsonian Institution (Bureau of American Ethnology) for "The Head Trophy of the Jibaro Indians" from *Blood Revenge, War and Victory Feasts among Jibaro Indians of Eastern Ecuador* by Rafael Karsten; "Precautions during Pregnancy in Guiana" by Walter E. Roth; "Childbirth Ceremonies of the Sia Pueblo" by Matilda Stevenson

Thames & Hudson Ltd. for "The Goddess of Lust" from *Divine Horsemen* by Maya Deren

University of California Press for "The Unconscious Patterning of Behavior in Society," "Abnormal Types of Speech in Nootka" from *Selected Writings* by Edward Sapir

The Viking Press for "The Australian Scene" from *Kangaroo* by D. H. Lawrence. Copyright, 1923, by Thomas Seltzer, Inc., 1951, by Frieda Lawrence. Reprinted by permission of The Viking Press, Inc., New York

Yale University Press for "Cheyenne Marriage" and "The Society of Contraries" from *The Cheyenne Indians* by George Bird Grinnell

CONTENTS

* The dates in brackets immediately following the titles refer to the year of publication.

PART THREE
Theoretical Approaches

PART FOUR
The Scene

PART FIVE

Children

PART SIX

Puberty

PART SEVEN
Marriage

PART EIGHT
Art, Thought and Sport

PART NINE
The Daily Round

PART TWELVE

Extreme Changes in the Body Image and in Interpersonal Relations

PART THIRTEEN

Feasts and Sacrifices

PART FOURTEEN

War and Peacemaking

PART SIXTEEN
Immortality

INTRODUCTION

1. *The Restoration of Wonder*

This anthology will surprise many modern readers who have carefully kept themselves contemporary with the findings of modern anthropology. The last fifty years have been devoted to the task of bringing the most remote, the most savage peoples within the narrowing range of the human family. Geographically, with modern methods of communications, we have penetrated into the jungle hearts of continents, and conceptually, we have learned that there is no reason to believe that the newborn child of any people is incapable of learning the language and ways of behaving of any other people—though one group be naked head-hunters subsisting on feasts of tree grubs, the other group Americans drinking pasteurized, homogenized milk. Any savage baby could grow up to take the subway—if brought young enough into the subway-taking world. Exceptional savages may be able to learn the intricate machinery of civilized life at any age. Even the obverse statement—that any civilized baby can learn to be a hunter who whistles up his quarry by exactly imitating a young bird crying for its mother or can tolerate a life in which one woman is shared amicably by three men—has become a partial, less cherished part of the intellectual equipment of the educated. Savages are as contemporary as we are, we have learned. They are non-literate because they lived too far from the sources of human civilization; the ancient Britons, though fully as savage, were more accessible to Rome. Savages, being non-literate, lack also many of our other more prized traits, but this lack is social and can be repaired.

In the ethic of the mid-twentieth century, which has insisted upon a democratic relationship among the ways of men as well as among individual men, savages are the inhabitants of "underdeveloped areas" lacking technological know-how. Audio-visual methods of teaching literacy and agriculture to adults will soon, we believe, set that right, especially if we take cultural differences into account, have careful studies made of customs and beliefs, proceed slowly enough to give the leaders of each people a chance to assimilate and adapt the changes brought by the Western world.

All this is admirable, and no one of us would have it otherwise. Who is there among us who if asked for bread would give a stone? We have called the new version of human democracy our greatest good and are pledged to aid those who wish to share it—and within one generation. But there is danger that this, like all good things, may be carried so far that, as we guarantee better nutrition to the Fijians and turn them into competent functioning members of a world society, we may lose by inadvertence that earlier contribution which the uncivilized Fijian, and the uncivilized Arapaho and Andaman Islander and Zulu, had to make to the imagination of civilized man. There is great danger that we will actually neglect the very inventions to which we owe those processes of civilization which we are now sharing with the underdeveloped peoples of the world—the inventions by virtue of which our store of memories can be so different, so much richer than theirs. For, where the primitive was limited to what the wisest could learn and repeat or, at best, to some system of assigning different legends to different memories, we can preserve, as fresh as it was the day Cook sailed into Botany Bay, the wonder aroused in men of imagination when they saw other men so different from themselves. "Can these be men at all?" is as comprehensive a response to the strange as is our ethically and scientifically disciplined "There, by grace of Technical Assistance, go men who could be even as I."

The earliest theorists worked with this wonder, taking the records of travelers and missionaries, and in their armchair musings transmuted them into materials for speculative thought, for dreams of a golden age, a noble innocence, or a primal horde. And other men, hungry for the strange, fed avidly on *The Golden Bough* and *The Mystic Rose,* and the mystic participants of Lévy-Bruhl's French thinking neatly divided the world into parts—civilization (antiquity to modern Europe, especially France) and the prelogical world of the primitive.

When the field anthropologist went to live among primitive peoples and found them friendly as well as savage, busier with the details of everyday life than with odd exotic rites, there was a rebellion against the older emphasis. The savage was mystical, true, we found, but also practical and rational in many things. Initiation rites were all very well, but there was also such a biologically given phenomenon as puberty, which occurred among all peoples, whether it was celebrated by sub-incision on a helpless boy laid flat upon a living table of human flesh, or was marked by no ceremony at all. So "adolescence" became the category within which ethnological material was gathered; science gained, the democratic ethic gained. Yet in one of the most exhaustive modern textbooks on anthropology, there is only one page out of seven hundred devoted to "initiation" and in another contemporary textbook the word does not appear in the index at all.

Those of us who are fortunate enough to work initially for many years within a single growing discipline have a special responsibility to watch for such shifts in emphasis, to cry halt when some necessary reaction has gone too far, to hold ourselves accountable for the excesses of our own and succeeding generations. We took *The Golden Bough* off our reading lists; we forgot *The Mystic Rose.* We left them to the humanists, trained to allow for changes in period without loss of pleasure in the materials themselves. We review with lofty and wholly justified disapproval psychoanalytic books which revel, without the training of the humanists, in outworn views of primitive matriarchy or the importance of totemism.

We claim, with right, that scientists should use the most recent work of other contemporary scientists. Most of us, with less justification, are afraid to write English for fear that, no matter how solid our credentials and extensive our theoretical equipment, we may be regarded as unscientific by those who limit the word "science" to the task of testing hypotheses which someone else has developed. Meanwhile, a generation has grown up, properly nourished on modern monographs, scornful of the theoretical inadequacies of the earlier armchair anthropologists, innocent of the earlier literature, with a vague idea that if a native ever comes to life in the work of an anthropologist this is to be condemned as "impressionism" (not to be confused with the technical word for a school of modern painting!) or "popularizing." At the same time, a parallel generation of students in the humanities has been robbed of a rich heritage.

But I must hasten to add that this anthology is not a work of piety replete with evidences of repentance and the exaggerated protestations of the prodigal. I am not returning from eating husks. Under the wise tutelage of Ruth Benedict, I learned as a student to value the freshness of the early accounts of living primitive life—as told by explorer or by Jesuit priest. With her I worked happily to develop our understanding of cultures as configurations which made use of some human potentialities by disavowing others, configurations which were as satisfying as great works of art in their intensifications of some segment of the arc of human experience.

This anthology is, indeed, peculiarly indebted to Ruth Benedict's interest in the humanities—as well as the sciences—because it was out of Nicolas Calas' response to her work that he and I began to work together five years ago in a research project which she inaugurated and within which she found a place for many different gifts.

When Nicolas Calas suggested that we do an anthropological anthology, the suggestion did not find me ready and waiting to make atonement for the steadily developing myopia of the last twenty-five years. Nevertheless, as we talked of what might go into such an anthology, I realized that here was an opportunity to make a new start. It would be his eye and his ear—trained to the rediscovery of the textual inspiration of Hieronymus Bosch, newly disciplined by anthropological work on contemporary cultures to discriminate cultural patterns within different national versions of modern art (as he had done in his Metropolitan Museum lectures)—which would be actively involved. With me as a bibliographical resource, he could go directly to primary sources—to early explorers and to modern field workers, to the Jesuit Relations, to Sahagun—and choose from them what he found wonderful and strange, horrifying or beautiful.

English is a third language for Nicolas Calas, born a Greek, with later experience in Paris. He was neither reared on *Swiss Family Robinson,* oversuckled on an outworn dependence on *The Golden Bough,* nor taught to despise Frazer for the wrong reasons. Together, I realized, we might put together a book that would restore the sense of wonder earlier generations drew from accounts of primitive and exotic men. In it we might make a contribution to the growth of the disciplined human awareness that is the very breath of life for those new forms of civilization which must rise, not phoenix-wise from the ashes of the old, but like all living things, by reproduction through continuity of substance.

Differences among human beings are the very stuff on which human awareness feeds. These differences are striking enough to terrify the child, send adolescents off into timeless musings, baffle the most adjusted adult, and give life to the sententious repetitious aphorisms of the old. Even in the simplest human societies, contrasts between children of different ages, between the sexes, and between different constitutions and temperaments, have set men to wondering, to speculating, to elaborating. Is the newborn child quite human and should it be given a name? Should the rare infant born with teeth be allowed to live? Is not the sudden miracle which transforms the rangy little girl into a creature of curves and coquetry so magical that it is best to take precautions against having the creature about or even against letting her feed herself until she and those about her have assimilated the change? What is the difference between men to whom trees remain *trees,* no matter how thoroughly schooled they may be in the belief that at night trees walk about, and those other men for whom visions appear upon every empty plain? Throughout human history, human beings have nourished their imaginations on such contrasts, now gathering closely together in ritual recognition of experiences which seem most strange and precious, now turning in rage and revulsion to devour the living flesh of the enemy or the renegade, now piling human sacrifice upon human sacrifice to appease some god grown unappeasable as he fed first on their imaginations, then on their living bodies.

Cultures, the intricate, highly patterned systems of social inheritance through which each group of human beings attains and maintains the separate special version of the humanity of its members, are—from one point of view—human psychology writ large. The differences between the aristocrat and the peasant, the most hypersensitive esthete and the toughest-minded man of affairs, the brooding descendant of a thousand remembered ancestral deeds and the man to whom the past is nothing, the present everything—all the myriad differences which artist and writer find among the members of a complex society like our own can be found embodied in the whole ways of life of other peoples, of other times. And not only are they embodied in one human being, and therefore overdependent upon idiosyncrasies of physical appearance and other accidental qualities, but over and over in generations of men. Where the vision quest looms as the only way to acquire power (as it did among many American Indians), not only the visionary sees visions, but all men—even those with dull eyes and no spiritual gift—share, by virtue of their upbringing, in the willingness to fast until the eye sees and the ear hears something that may be felt to be a message from the supernatural. The contrasting patterns of different cultures, embodied in each gesture of their members, writ large because written so definitely, are also repeated in elaborate variations in every part of their lives, so that the onlooker to whom the design of a house means more than the sequence of a ceremony is rewarded equally with the spectator who finds meaning in the slow, trancelike unfolding of a rite grown beautiful through long precise use.

Shock and wonder at the differing ways of other peoples have been part of our human tradition since nomad tribes became willing to pause between flight to the fastnesses of the forest or fight so immediate that the practices of the enemy were only seen as they appeared in cicatrices on a dead body or the shape of a weapon held by a lifeless hand.

As men learned to tolerate the presence near them of others

different from themselves, their wits were sharpened by contrast; they came to admire the ways of their neighbors, or to fear them and shape their own customs as defenses against the alien and the strange. A new kind of objectivity, a new dimension of historical consciousness is born when men cease to call themselves simply "human beings," naming others as "eaters of snakes" or "dwellers farther inland," and instead apply to themselves names by which other men may speak of them. Slowly through history this process has developed—through the curiosity of the Greeks, to whom we owe our roots for the science of *ethnology,* the study of the barbarous, the non-Greek where, although observation flourished, ethnocentrism still reigned; through the proud expansiveness of Rome, ready to take over the barbarians and turn them into citizens of one world; through the ethnocentrism of the nineteenth century which saw "ourselves" as the end products of evolution—until we have acquired a capacity to see ourselves as having one culture among many. The young child makes a distinction between early use of his own name, through "me go," where the self as object and the self as subject are fused, to the distinction between the "me" which others respond to and the "I" that acts, until finally the "I" that is "me" and the other "I's" of those around "me" can all be conceptualized. In this manner, our ability to think about other men and their cultures has proceeded slowly and haltingly, with occasional flashes of sophistication and periodic returns to floundering in various morasses of ethnic self-centeredness.

Modern man's capacity to see his culture and that of his most savage contemporaries as both comparable and incomparable is still fleeting and evanescent. Whether we lose sight of one side of the picture and are ready to welcome the recent primitive into our legislative halls, but block completely on those potentialities of our own humanity which he—in his human sacrifices and magical precautions—so recently dramatized for us, or conversely, looking at the excesses of totalitarian states, shudder away from the "innate savagery of man" and despair of civilization, it is still a precarious balance. But tightrope walking is, after all, learned best by walking ropes.

So, in the present volume we have tried to place the recorded wonder and horror, joy and amazement of European and American commentators in a new framework. Like all proper anthologies, it is meant to stimulate the appetites of the reader and leave them actively unsatisfied—hungering and thirsting for more. It is neither inclusive nor comprehensive in any respect. We deeply hope that for each reader many selections will seem far too short, raise expectations which they fail to satisfy, leave the mind saturated with images which obstinately refuse to vacate the stage of the imagination.

No author has been included because of rank or status; no rite or usage has been chosen to round out any conventional set of categories. We have not confined our choices to works by anthropologists alone. Accounts by writers (Melville and Gide), by an artist (Maya Deren), and by missionaries and provincial governors have been tapped also. In the middle reaches of our planning we talked of many sets of categories, fear and hope, pity and horror, ecstasy and placidity, life and death. After our selections—chosen by Nicolas Calas, subject to a veto by me—were finally assembled, the present arrangement grew naturally against the larger original design in which it was planned to present first "The mythical past of anthropological theory," then the transition, represented by those who *used* the feeling for cultures as systematic wholes which grew out of the new field work, but who themselves worked creatively with other people's recorded work, followed by the major portion of the book which was to be—and is—devoted to first-hand observations. The arrangement of the materials may be attributed to the way in which those aspects of culture with which we have dealt are integral to man's nature as a mortal creature dependent for his sense of significance upon the elaborate rhythms of life and death.

MARGARET MEAD

New York, June, 1953

2. *The World as Stage*

In the world viewed as a stage, *Iphigenia in Aulis* is to anthropology what *Oedipus Rex* is to psychology: the dramatic presentation of a basic conflict. But, while in *Oedipus Rex* we are confronted with an emotional crisis which Freud discovered to be typical because it lays bare the complicated mechanism of our most hidden feelings, in *Iphigenia in Aulis* we are confronted with a borderline situation placed, as it were, between the world of ceremony and the world of tragedy.

From an economist's utilitarian point of view, Vilfredo Pareto was undoubtedly right to choose this episode of the sacrifice of Iphigenia as an example of foolish behavior, since the departure of the Greek fleet for Troy depended upon weather conditions and not upon the immolation of an innocent maiden. Likewise, the Danish mystic Kierkegaard was right to condemn Agamemnon's sacrifice of his daughter, for its horror could never be overcome by the comforting thought that a divine mystery had taken place, since, unlike Abraham, Agamemnon lacked faith in the God who gave him the painful commandment to immolate his child.

Fortunately, just as the criticisms of economists and moralists have not prevented those who love the theater from admiring Euripides' *Iphigenia in Aulis,* so the horror and disgust that the natives inspired in early missionaries and traders have not hindered anthropologists from discovering in sacrificial rites and initiation ceremonies aspects that are not merely expressions of sadistic impulses or the manifestations of a prelogical mentality.

Only by refraining from judging an unknown people by our own standards of value can we ever hope to comprehend them. The lasting merit of Rousseau's famous indictment of progress (written in 1749) in which he held progress responsible for all our vices, lies in the fact that he made it forever impossible for men of good will to dismiss the primitives as barbarians solely because they have not been able to enjoy the advantages progress has bestowed upon us.

The history of Herodotus, which taught the Greeks how humane and noble the barbarians could on occasion show themselves to be, awakens us to the fact that our progress is shockingly lopsided. We read of the gallantry with which Cambyses, the king of Persia, treated his defeated rival Psammenitus, a gallantry all the more impressive when we compare it to the way autocrats of our day deal with their enemies.

Yet, reading the *League of the Iroquois* a century after its first publication (1851), we smile at Morgan's attribution of all virtues to these Indians. How did they become so good when their ancestors had been famous for their cruelty? We have but to go through the volumes of the correspondence of the Jesuit Fathers written in the seventeenth century for evidence!

After scientists became aware that the difference between primitive peoples and civilized nations cannot be explained simply in terms of "progress," they introduced the concept of evolution. Following the example of Darwin, laws of evolution, of social evolution, were formulated so that the exact degree of economic, moral, legal and religious progress of primitive peoples might be exactly evaluated. However, great field anthropologists such as Boas, Malinowski, Lowie and Kroeber had no difficulty in providing a series of facts which the armchair anthropologist had not taken into account and which apparently contradict the theories of Engels, the French sociologists, or Freud. The field anthropologists failed to convince their opponents, and Marxist economists, French sociologists, and Freudian psychologists proved, to their own satisfaction at least, that it was possible to reinterpret the new anthropological data and make it fit their favorite theories.

As a result, this rather outdated controversy remained inconclusive but had the advantage of demonstrating that the term *evolution* when used in anthropology could be as misleading and as confusing as is the term *progress.* Both progress and evolution are achieved by *advancing* but, while progress implies advancing toward an *end in view,* evolution, in this frame of reference, suggests that one is *moving away from the point of departure.* We can view a runner either as running away from his starting point or as running toward a goal. What we are not accustomed to do is to view the runner without relating his activity to either the place he left behind him or to the place toward which he is moving. Yet, the Running Lamas of Tibet, described so vividly by David-Neel, will run for days and nights at a surprisingly rapid pace for no apparent purpose. Expressed in the above terms, the activity of these holy men looks foolish, but when we are told that, unlike *our* runners, they are not concerned with either arriving or leaving, we realize that we can compare their activity to ours on those occasions when we too are not interested in *arriving,* as it happens when we are playing and are disappointed when our game ends too soon. But we can go a step farther in this direction and point to situations in which people will do all they can to delay reaching an inevitable end. Such a situation Euripides must have had in mind when he wrote *Iphigenia in Aulis.* Agamemnon's attempt to save his daughter despite his awareness of the inefficacy of his efforts, when juxtaposed to the efforts of goal-oriented Marathon runners, must be comprehended as a desperate attempt to avoid an inevitable climax: the sacrifice. Conversely, all sacrifices, whether of men or beasts, can be seen as a theatrical presentation of the most fearful of all climaxes: death.

Had some of the authors who, from Bachofen to Freud, formulated laws of social evolution, made a distinction between climaxes and goals, they would have perceived that it is often less important for us to understand *what* progress has been accomplished in a given area than to realize *how* a situation was created in which the climax was delayed. Thus if, unlike Vilfredo Pareto, we regard the departure of the Greeks from Aulis as the climax reached in their relation to the families they were leaving behind, the moment of departure assumes the proportion of an event worthy of being accompanied by a ceremony so extraordinary that none of its participants would be likely to forget it. By being feasted, its passage into oblivion was indefinitely delayed. In other words, people of societies less complex than ours, be they the Greeks of the Homeric epoch or the Trobrianders of the time of Malinowski, are as able as we are to set and reach goals and yet have an entirely different idea of what farewell parties should be like.

The finest texts in anthropology were written by the specialists who were gifted with the artist's eye for the eventful and who, like the artist, show their sympathy for people involved in wonderful and strange situations. On the other hand, if Herodotus and Melville wrote pages that ought to be included in an anthropological anthology, it is because, when confronted with an exotic reality, they treated it with the same attention and care which they devoted to more familiar scenes and subjects.

The exotic is to space what the eventful is to time and, anthropologically speaking, what counts is the variety of ways in which basic themes have been treated in either space or time. In the variations a writer introduces in the elaboration of a basic plot, the modern anthropologist detects evidences of cultural differences. Thus, by a comparative study of T. S. Eliot's *Cocktail Party* and Plato's *Banquet* he is enabled to point out the particular circumstances required by an ancient Athenian and a contemporary Londoner or New Yorker to renounce the pleasures of the flesh. While the authors of tragedies impress us with the inevitability of an impending crisis, it is the anthropologist who can discern factors leading to the precipitation or delay of an inevitable climax.

A modern anthropologist could throw light on the tragedy of Finow, a Pacific Island king, by tracing the cultural background of the people of his island. As reported by Mariner, Finow, having had the temerity to alter the funeral rites for his daughter whom the gods, he felt, had not been gracious enough to save, fell dead during the performance of the unholy rites. Compared with Agamemnon, Finow's defiance seems foolish because, unlike the Greek king, he had not realized that the terror of sacrilege is more unbearable than the terror of death.

If kings act as heroes or villains, tragedians and anthropologists could be said to stand as witnesses between those who act and us, the spectators. Unfortunately this simple and satisfactory relationship is disturbed by the intrusion of would-be prophets who, by confusing seeing with doing, observing with imagining, adopt a slanted interpretation of events.

It is inevitable that in our evolution-minded era prophets of gloom should undertake to reinterpret the fall of man in anthropological terms. This series of prophets commenced with Rousseau, who detected everywhere signs of violation of the social contract free men had agreed to observe once upon a time. Rousseau's myth excited the imagination of later day apocalyptic writers, and Nietzsche dramatized the social contract by attributing violation of law to murder, Engels by attributing it to robbery.

If, as these seers claim, civilization is the outcome of a crime, the study of violence should take precedence over all other studies, and primitive society should be analyzed, as it is done by the French school of sociology, from the point of view of the ritual accompanying such a consecrated form of murder as sacrifice.

To the extent that the ingenious reconstruction of the origin of civilization proposed by the Nietzschean-minded Freudians, by Marxist-minded economists, and by legal-minded French sociologists are dramatizations of extraordinary moments in the life of primitive peoples, they mask the everyday reality that the anthropologist can confront and cannot afford to ignore. To the errors and weaknesses of men—serving as raw material for the plot of tragedies—he opposes the pattern that emerges when human behavior is studied from the point of view of interpersonal relations.

It is no coincidence that the theory of cultural patterns should have been so congenial to Edward Sapir, a scientist who studied primitive people from the aspect of language, because language is the basic form by means of which people gain an understanding of each other. Through verbal communication we come to realize that we must have something in common with our neighbors, which common thing Plato called idea and visualized as having form. Since the forms of speech and behavior that a group of people have in common are not used arbitrarily, we are able to study them in relation to their pattern.

In conclusion we might remark that as our appreciation of Plato's dialogues does not hinder our appreciation of the tragedies of Aeschylus or Euripides, so the fascination we experience when reading a beautiful description of an extraordinary event, such as Geoffrey Gorer's Dahomeyan bullfight, or Dorr's ride with Apaches, should not deter us from enjoying a beautiful description of the daily round as it is evoked by Margaret Mead in "A Day in Samoa" or by Herman Melville in "A Bathing Baby."

NICOLAS CALAS

New York, June, 1953

PRIMITIVE HERITAGE

PART 1

Anthropology in Antiquity

HERODOTUS (born circa 484 B.C.)

The Egyptians and Their Cats

Egypt, though it borders upon Libya, is not a region abounding in wild animals. The animals that do exist in the country, whether domesticated or otherwise, are all regarded as sacred. If I were to explain why they are consecrated to the several gods, I should be led to speak of religious matters, which I particularly shrink from mentioning; the points whereon I have touched slightly hitherto have all been introduced from sheer necessity. Their custom with respect to animals is as follows:—For every kind there are appointed certain guardians, some male, some female, whose business it is to look after them; and this honour is made to descend from father to son. The inhabitants of the various cities, when they have made a vow to any god, pay it to his animals in the way which I will now explain. At the time of making the vow they shave the head of the child, cutting off all the hair, or else half, or sometimes a third part, which they then weigh in a balance against a sum of

silver; and whatever sum the hair weighs is presented to the guardian of the animals, who thereupon cuts up some fish, and gives it to them for food—such being the stuff whereon they are fed. When a man has killed one of the sacred animals, if he did it with malice prepense, he is punished with death, if unwittingly, he has to pay such a fine as the priests choose to impose. When an ibis, however, or a hawk is killed, whether it was done by accident or on purpose, the man must needs die.

The number of domestic animals in Egypt is very great, and would be still greater were it not for what befalls the cats. As the females, when they have kittened, no longer seek the company of the males, these last, to obtain once more their companionship, practise a curious artifice. They seize the kittens, carry them off, and kill them, but do not eat them afterwards. Upon this the females, being deprived of their young, and longing to supply their place, seek the males once more, since they are particularly fond of their offspring. On every occasion of a fire in Egypt the strangest prodigy occurs with the cats. The inhabitants allow the fire to rage as it pleases, while they stand about at intervals and watch these animals, which, slipping by the men or else leaping over them, rush headlong into the flames. When this happens, the Egyptians are in deep affliction. If a cat dies in a private house by a natural death, all the inmates of the house shave their eyebrows; on the death of a dog they shave the head and the whole of the body.

The cats on their decease are taken to the city of Bubastis, where they are embalmed, after which they are buried in certain sacred repositories. The dogs are interred in the cities to which they belong, also in sacred burial-places. The same practice obtains with respect to the ichneumons; the hawks and shrew-mice, on the contrary, are conveyed to the city of Buto for burial, and the ibises to Hermopolis. The bears, which are scarce in Egypt, and the wolves, which are not much bigger than foxes, they bury wherever they happen to find them lying.

Cambyses and the Defeated King

Ten days after the fort had fallen, Cambyses resolved to try the spirit of Psammenitus, the Egyptian king, whose whole reign had been but six months. He therefore had him set in one of the suburbs, and many other Egyptians with him, and there subjected him to insult. First of all he sent his daughter out from the city, clothed in the garb of a slave, with a pitcher to draw water. Many virgins, the daughters of the chief nobles, accompanied her, wearing the same dress. When the damsels came opposite the place where their fathers sate, shedding tears and uttering cries of woe, the fathers, all but Psammenitus, wept and wailed in return, grieving to see their children in so sad a plight; but he, when he had looked and seen, bent his head towards the ground. In this way passed by the water-carriers. Next to them came Psammenitus' son, and two thousand Egyptians of the same age with him—all of them having ropes round their necks and bridles in their mouths—and they too passed by on their way to suffer death for the murder of the Mytilenæans who were destroyed, with their vessel, in Memphis. For so had the royal judges given their sentence—"for each Mytilenæan ten of the noblest Egyptians must forfeit life." King Psammenitus saw the train pass on, and knew his son was being led to death, but, while the other Egyptians who sate around him wept and were sorely troubled, he showed no further sign than when he saw his daughter. And now, when they too were gone, it chanced that one of his former boon-companions, a man advanced in years, who had been stripped of all that he had and was a beggar, came where Psammenitus, son of Amasis, and the rest of the Egyptians were, asking alms from the soldiers. At this sight the king burst into tears, and, weeping out aloud, called his friend by his name, and smote himself on the head. Now there were some who had been set to watch Psammenitus and see what he would do as each train went by; so these persons went and told Cambyses of his behaviour. Then he, astonished at what was done, sent a messenger to Psammenitus, and questioned him, saying, "Psammenitus, thy lord Cambyses asketh thee why, when thou sawest thy daughter brought to shame, and thy son on his way to death, thou didst neither utter cry nor shed tear, while to a beggar, who is, he hears, a stranger to thy race, thou gavest those marks of honour." To this question Psammenitus made answer, "O son of Cyrus, my own misfortunes were too great for tears; but the woe of my friend deserved them. When a man falls from splendour and plenty into beggary at the threshold of old age, one may well weep for him." When the messenger brought back this answer, Cambyses owned it was just; Crœsus, likewise, the Egyptians say, burst into tears—for he too had come into Egypt with Cambyses—and the Persians who were present wept. Even Cambyses himself was touched with pity, and he forthwith gave an order, that the son of Psammenitus should be spared from the number of those appointed to die, and Psammenitus himself brought from the suburb into his presence.

The messengers were too late to save the life of Psammenitus' son, who had been cut in pieces the first of all; but they took Psammenitus himself and brought him before the king. Cambyses allowed him to live with him, and gave him no more harsh treatment; nay, could he have kept from intermeddling with affairs, he might have recovered Egypt, and ruled it as governor. For the Persian wont is to treat the sons of kings with honour, and even to give their fathers' kingdoms to the children of such as revolt from them. There are many cases from which one may deduce that this is the Persian rule, and especially those of Pausiris and Thannyras. Thannyras was son of Inarus the Libyan, and was allowed to succeed his father, as was also Pausiris, son of Amyrtæus; yet certainly no two persons ever did the Persians more damage than Amyrtæus and Inarus. In this case Psammenitus plotted evil, and received his reward accordingly. He was discovered to be stirring up revolt in Egypt, wherefore Cambyses, when his guilt clearly appeared, compelled him to drink bull's blood, which presently caused his death. Such was the end of Psammenitus.

STRABO (born circa 63 B.C.)

Troglodytes

Now the Troglodytes live a nomadic life; and their several tribes are ruled by tyrants; and both wives and children are held in common except those of the tyrants; and the fine for anyone who corrupts the wife of a tyrant consists of a sheep. The women paint their eyelids carefully with stibi; and they wear shells for amulets round their necks. The Troglodytes go to war about pasturage, at first pushing their way through with their hands and then with stones, and also, when a wound is inflicted, with arrows and daggers; but the fighters are reconciled by the women, who advance into the midst of the combatants and ply them with entreaties. Their food consists of flesh and bones which are first chopped up together and wrapped in skins and then baked, or prepared in numerous other ways by the cooks (whom they call "unclean"), so that they not only eat the flesh, but also the bones and the skin; and they also use the blood mixed with milk. As for beverages, most of the people drink a brew of buckthorn, but the tyrants drink a mixture of honey and water, the honey being pressed out of some kind of flower. They have winter when the Etesian winds blow (for they have rains); but the rest of the time is summer. They always go lightly clad, wear skins, and carry clubs; and they not only mutilate their bodies, but some of them are also circumcised, like the Aegyptians. The Aethiopian Megabari have iron knobs on their clubs, and also use spears and shields made of rawhide, but the rest of the Aethiopians use the bow and arrow and lances. Before burying their dead, some of the Troglodytes bind the neck of the corpses to the legs with twigs of the buckthorn, and then immediately, with merriment and laughter, throw stones upon them until the body is hidden from sight; and then they place a ram's horn on the barrow and go away. They travel by night, first fastening bells to the male cattle, so as to drive away the wild beasts with the noise; and they also use torches and bows to repel the wild beasts; and, for the sake of their flocks, they also keep watch during the night, singing a kind of song near the fire.

TACITUS

German Tribes; Public and Private Life

They choose their kings by birth, their generals for merit. These kings have not unlimited or arbitrary power, and the generals do more by example than by authority. If they are energetic, if they are conspicuous, if they fight in the front, they lead because they are admired. But to reprimand, to imprison, even to flog, is permitted to the priests alone, and that not as a punishment, or at the general's bidding, but, as it were, by the mandate of the god whom they believe to inspire the warrior. They also carry with them into battle certain figures and images taken from their sacred groves. And what most stimulates their courage is, that their squadrons or battalions, instead of being formed by chance or by a fortuitous gathering, are composed of families and clans. Close by them, too, are those dearest to them, so that they hear the shrieks of women, the cries of infants. *They* are to every man the most sacred witnesses of his bravery—*they* are his most generous applauders. The soldier brings his wounds to mother and wife, who shrink not from counting or even demanding them and who administer both food and encouragement to the combatants.

Tradition says that armies already wavering and giving way have been rallied by women who, with earnest entreaties and bosoms laid bare, have vividly represented the horrors of captivity, which the Germans fear with such extreme dread on behalf of their women, that the strongest tie by which a state can be bound is the being required to give, among the number of hostages, maidens of noble birth. They even believe that the sex has a certain sanctity and prescience, and they do not despise their counsels, or make light of their answers. In Vespasian's days we saw Veleda, long regarded by many as a divinity. In former times, too, they venerated Aurinia, and many other women, but not with servile flatteries, or with sham deification.

In their councils an accusation may be preferred or a capital crime prosecuted. Penalties are distinguished according to the offence. Traitors and deserters are hanged on trees; the coward, the unwarlike, the man stained with abominable vices, is plunged into the mire of the morass, with a hurdle put over him. This distinction in punishment means that crime, they think, ought, in being punished, to be exposed, while infamy ought to be buried out of sight. Lighter offences, too, have penalties proportioned to them; he who is convicted, is fined in a certain number of horses or of cattle. Half of the fine is paid to the king or to the state, half to the person whose wrongs are avenged and to his relatives. In these same councils they also elect the chief magistrates, who administer law in the cantons and the towns. Each of these has a hundred associates chosen from the people, who support him with their advice and influence.

They transact no public or private business without being armed. It is not, however, usual for anyone to wear arms till the state has recognised his power to use them. Then in the presence of the council one of the chiefs, or the young man's father, or some kinsman, equips him with a shield and a spear. These arms are what the "toga" is with us, the first honour with which youth is invested. Up to this time he is regarded as a member of a household, afterwards as a member of the commonwealth. Very noble birth or great services rendered by the father secure for lads the rank of a chief; such lads attach themselves to men of mature strength and of long approved valour. It is no shame to be seen among a chief's followers. Even in his escort there are gradations of rank, dependent on the choice of the man to whom they are attached. These followers vie keenly with each other as to who shall rank first with his chief, the chiefs as to who shall have the most numerous and the bravest followers. It is an honour as well as a source of strength to be thus always surrounded by a large body of picked youths; it is an ornament in peace and a defence in war. And not only in his own tribe but also in the neighbouring states it is the renown and glory of a chief to be distinguished for the number and valour of his followers, for such a man is courted by embassies, is honoured with presents, and the very prestige of his name often settles a war.

When they go into battle, it is a disgrace for the chief to be surpassed in valour, a disgrace for his followers not to equal the valour of the chief. And it is an infamy and a reproach for life to have survived the chief, and returned from the field. To defend, to protect him, to ascribe one's own brave deeds to his renown, is the height of loyalty. The chief fights for victory; his vassals fight for their chief. If their native state sinks into the sloth of prolonged peace and repose, many of its noble youths voluntarily seek those tribes which are waging some war, both because inaction is odious to their race, and because they win renown more readily in the midst of peril, and cannot maintain a numerous following except by violence and war. Indeed, men look to the liberality of their chief for their war-horse and their blood-stained and victorious lance. Feasts and entertainments, which, though inelegant, are plentifully furnished, are their only pay. The means of this bounty come from war and rapine. Nor are they as easily persuaded to plough the earth and to wait for the year's produce as to challenge an enemy and earn the honour of wounds. Nay, they actually think it tame and stupid to acquire by the sweat of toil what they might win by their blood.

Whenever they are not fighting, they pass much of their time in the chase, and still more in idleness, giving themselves up to sleep and to feasting, the bravest and the most warlike doing nothing, and surrendering the management of the household, of the home, and of the land, to the women, the old men, and all the weakest members of the family. They themselves lie buried in sloth, a strange combination in their nature that the same men should be so fond of idleness, so averse to peace. It is the custom of the states to bestow by voluntary and individual contribution on the chiefs a present of cattle or of grain, which, while accepted as a compliment, supplies their wants. They are particularly delighted by gifts from neighbouring tribes, which are sent not only by individuals but also by the state, such as choice steeds, heavy armour, trappings, and neck-chains. We have now taught them to accept money also.

It is well known that the nations of Germany have no cities, and that they do not even tolerate closely contiguous dwellings. They live scattered and apart, just as a spring, a meadow, or a wood has attracted them. Their villages they do not arrange in our fashion, with the buildings connected and joined together, but every person surrounds his dwelling with an open space, either as a precaution against the disasters of fire, or because they do not know how to build. No use is made by them of stone or tile; they employ timber for all purposes, rude masses without ornament or attractiveness. Some parts of their buildings they stain more carefully with a clay so clear and bright that it resembles painting, or a coloured design. They are wont also to dig out subterranean caves, and pile on them great heaps of dung, as a shelter from winter and as a receptacle for the year's produce, for by such places they mitigate the rigour of the cold. And should an enemy approach, he lays waste the open country, while what is hidden and buried is either not known to exist, or else escapes him from the very fact that it has to be searched for.

They all wrap themselves in a cloak which is fastened with a clasp, or, if this is not forthcoming, with a thorn, leaving the rest of their persons bare. They pass whole days on the hearth by the fire. The wealthiest are distinguished by a dress which is not flowing, like that of the Sarmatæ and Parthi, but is tight, and exhibits each limb. They also wear the skins of wild beasts; the tribes on the Rhine and Danube in a careless fashion, those of the interior with more elegance, as not obtaining other clothing by commerce. These select certain animals, the hides of which they strip off and vary them with the spotted skins of beasts, the produce of the outer ocean, and of seas unknown to us. The women have the same dress as the men, except that they generally wrap themselves in linen garments, which they embroider with purple, and do not lengthen out the upper part of their clothing into sleeves. The upper and lower arm is thus bare, and the nearest part of the bosom is also exposed.

Their marriage code, however, is strict, and indeed no part of their manners is more praiseworthy. Almost alone among barbarians they are content with one wife, except a very few among them, and these not from sensuality, but because their noble birth procures for them many offers of alliance. The wife does not bring a dower to the husband, but the husband to the wife. The parents and relatives are present, and pass judgment on the marriage-gifts, gifts not meant to suit a woman's taste, nor such as a bride would deck herself with, but oxen, a caparisoned steed, a shield, a lance, and a sword. With these presents the wife is espoused, and she herself in her turn brings her husband a gift of arms. This they count their strongest bond of union, these their sacred mysteries, these their gods of marriage. Lest the woman should think herself to stand apart from aspirations after noble deeds and from the perils of war, she is reminded by the ceremony which inaugurates marriage that she is her husband's partner in toil and danger, destined to suffer and to dare with him alike both in peace and in war. The yoked oxen, the harnessed steed, the gift of arms, proclaim this fact. She must live and die with the feeling that she is receiving what she must hand down to her children neither tarnished nor depreciated, what future daughters-in-law may receive, and may be so passed on to her grand-children.

Thus with their virtue protected they live uncorrupted by the allurements of public shows or the stimulant of feastings. Clandestine correspondence is equally unknown to men and women. Very rare for so numerous a population is adultery, the punishment for which is prompt, and in the husband's power. Having cut off the hair of the adulteress and stripped her naked, he expels her from the house in the presence of her kinsfolk, and then flogs her through the whole village. The loss of chastity meets with no indulgence; neither beauty, youth, nor wealth will procure the culprit a husband. No one in Germany laughs at vice, nor do they call it the fashion to corrupt and to be corrupted. Still better is the condition of those states in which only maidens are given in marriage, and where the hopes and expectations of a bride are then finally terminated. They receive one husband, as having one body and one life, that they may have no thoughts beyond, no further-reaching desires, that they may love not so much the husband as the married state. To limit the number of their children or to destroy any of their subsequent offspring is accounted infamous, and good habits are here more effectual than good laws elsewhere.

PART 2

The Mythical Past

JEAN JACQUES ROUSSEAU

The First Societies

Man is born free; and everywhere he is in chains. One thinks himself the master of others, and still remains a greater slave than they. How did this change come about? I do not know. What can make it legitimate? That question I think I can answer.

If I took into account only force, and the effects derived from it, I should say: "As long as a people is compelled to obey, and obeys, it does well; as soon as it can shake off the yoke, and shakes it off, it does still better; for, regaining its liberty by the same right as took it away, either it is justified in resuming it, or there was no justification for those who took it away." But the social order is a sacred right which is the basis of all other rights. Nevertheless, this right does not come from nature, and must therefore be founded on conventions. Before coming to that, I have to prove what I have just asserted.

The most ancient of all societies, and the only one that is natural, is the family: and even so the children remain attached to the father only so long as they need him for their preservation. As soon as this need ceases, the natural bond is dissolved. The children, released from the obedience they owed to the father, and the father, released from the care he owed his children, return equally to independence. If they remain united, they continue so no longer naturally, but voluntarily; and the family itself is then maintained only by convention.

This common liberty results from the nature of man. His first law is to provide for his own preservation, his first cares are those which he owes to himself; and, as soon as he reaches years of discretion, he is the sole judge of the proper means of preserving himself, and consequently becomes his own master.

The family then may be called the first model of political societies: the ruler corresponds to the father, and the people to the children; and all, being born free and equal, alienate their liberty only for their own advantage. The whole difference is that, in the family, the love of the father for his children repays him for the care he takes of them, while, in the State, the pleasure of commanding takes the place of the love which the chief cannot have for the peoples under him.

FRIEDRICH ENGELS

The Gens, Its Simplicity

Once the gens is given as the social unit, we also see how the whole constitution of gentes, phratries, and tribes is almost necessarily bound to develop from this unit, because the development is natural. Gens, phratry, and tribe are all groups of different degrees of consanguinity, each self-contained and ordering its own affairs, but each supplementing the other. And the affairs which fall within their sphere comprise all the public affairs of barbarians of the lower stage. When we find a people with the gens as their social unit, we may therefore also look for an organization of the tribe similar to that here described; and when there are adequate sources, as in the case of the Greeks and the Romans, we shall not only find it, but we shall also be able to convince ourselves that where the sources fail us, comparison with the American social constitution helps us over the most difficult doubts and riddles.

And a wonderful constitution it is, this gentile constitution, in all its childlike simplicity! No soldiers, no gendarmes or police, no nobles, kings, regents, prefects, or judges, no prisons, no lawsuits—and everything takes its orderly course. All quarrels and disputes are settled by the whole of the community affected, by the gens or the tribe, or by the gentes among themselves; only as an extreme and exceptional measure is blood revenge threatened—and our capital punishment is nothing but blood revenge in a civilized form, with all the advantages and drawbacks of civilization. Although there were many more matters to be settled in common than today—the household is maintained by a number of families in common, and is communistic, the land belongs to the tribe, only the small gardens are allotted provisionally to the households—yet there is no need for even a trace of our complicated administrative apparatus with all its ramifications. The decisions are taken by those concerned, and in most cases everything has been already settled by the custom of centuries. There cannot be any poor or needy—the communal household and the gens know their responsibilities towards the old, the sick, and those disabled in war. All are equal and free—the women included. There is no place yet for slaves, nor, as a rule, for the subjugation of other tribes. When, about the year 1651, the Iroquois had conquered the Eries and the "Neutral Nation," they offered to accept them into the confederacy on equal terms; it was only after the defeated tribes had refused that they were driven from their territory. And what men and women such a society breeds is proved by the admiration inspired in all white people who have come into contact with unspoiled Indians, by the personal dignity, uprightness, strength of character, and courage of these barbarians.

We have seen examples of this courage quite recently in Africa. The Zulus a few years ago and the Nubians a few months ago—both of them tribes in which gentile institutions have not yet died out—did what no European army can do. Armed only with lances and spears, without firearms, under a hail of bullets from the breechloaders of the English infantry—acknowledged the best in the world at fighting in close order—they advanced right up to the bayonets and more than once threw the lines into disorder and even broke them, in spite of the enormous inequality of weapons and in spite of the fact that they have no military service and know nothing of drill. Their powers of endurance and performance are shown by the complaint of the English that a Kaffir travels farther and faster in twenty-four hours than a horse. His smallest muscle stands out hard and firm like whipcord, says an English painter.

That is what men and society were before the division into classes. And when we compare their position with that of the overwhelming majority of civilized men today, an enormous gulf separates the present-day proletarian and small peasant from the free member of the old gentile society.

FRIEDRICH NIETZSCHE

Blood and Cruelty As the Foundation of All Good Things

His conscience?—One apprehends at once that the idea "conscience," which is here seen in its supreme manifestation, supreme in fact to almost the point of strangeness, should already have behind it a long history and evolution. The ability to guarantee one's self with all due pride, and also at the same time to *say yes* to one's self—that is, as has been said, a ripe fruit, but also a *late* fruit:—How long must needs this fruit hang sour and bitter on the tree! And for an even longer period there was not a glimpse of such a fruit to be had—no one had taken it on himself to promise it, although everything on the tree was quite ready for it, and everything was maturing for that very consummation. "How is a memory to be made for the man-animal? How is an impression to be so deeply fixed upon this ephemeral understanding, half dense, and half silly, upon this incarnate forgetfulness, that it will be permanently present?" As one may imagine, this primeval problem was not solved by exactly gentle answers and gentle means; perhaps there is nothing more awful and more sinister in the early history of man than his *system of mnemonics*. "Something is burnt in so as to remain in his memory: only that which never stops *hurting* remains in his memory." This is an axiom of the oldest (unfortunately also the longest) psychology in the world. It might even be said that wherever solemnity, seriousness, mystery, and gloomy colours are now found in the life of the men and of nations of the world, there is some *survival* of that horror which was once the universal concomitant of all promises, pledges, and obligations. The past, the past with all its length, depth, and hardness, wafts to us its breath, and bubbles up in us again, when we become "serious." When man thinks it necessary to make for himself a memory, he never accomplishes it without blood, tortures, and sacrifice; the most dreadful sacrifices and forfeitures (among them the sacrifice of the first-born), the most loathsome mutilation (for instance, castration), the most cruel rituals of all the religious cults (for all religions are really at bottom systems of cruelty)—all these things originate from that instinct which found in pain its most potent mnemonic. In a certain sense the whole of asceticism is to be ascribed to this: certain ideas have got to be made inextinguishable, omnipresent, "fixed," with the object of hypnotising the whole nervous and intellectual system through these "fixed ideas"—and the ascetic methods and modes of life are the means of freeing those ideas from the competition of all other ideas so as to make them "unforgettable." The worse memory man had, the ghastlier the signs presented by his customs; the severity of the penal laws affords in particular a gauge of the extent of man's difficulty in conquering forgetfulness, and in keeping a few primal postulates of social intercourse ever present to the minds of those who were the slaves of every momentary emotion and every momentary desire. We Germans do certainly not regard ourselves as an especially cruel and hard-hearted nation, still less as an especially casual and happy-go-lucky one; but one has only to look at our old penal ordinances in order to realise what a lot of trouble it takes in the world to evolve a "nation of thinkers" (I mean: *the* European nation which exhibits at this very day the maximum of reliability, seriousness, bad taste, and positiveness, which has on the strength of these qualities a right to train every kind of European mandarin). These Germans employed terrible means to make for themselves a memory, to enable them to master their rooted plebeian instincts and the brutal crudity of those instincts: think of the old German punishments, for instance, stoning (as far back as the legend, the millstone falls on the head of the guilty man), breaking on the wheel (the most original invention and speciality of the German genius in the sphere of punishment), dart-throwing, tearing, or trampling by horses ("quartering"), boiling the criminal in oil or wine (still prevalent in the fourteenth and fifteenth centuries), the highly popular flaying ("slicing into strips"), cutting the flesh out of the breast; think also of the evil-doer being besmeared with honey, and then exposed to the flies in a blazing sun. It was by the help of such images and precedents that man eventually kept in his memory five or six "I will nots" with regard to which he had already given his *promise,* so as to be able to enjoy the advantages of society—and verily with the help of this kind of memory man eventually attained "reason"! Alas! reason, seriousness, mastery over the emotions, all these gloomy, dismal things which are called reflection, all these privileges and pageantries of humanity: how dear is the price that they have exacted! How much blood and cruelty is the foundation of all "good things"!

But how is it that that other melancholy object, the consciousness of sin, the whole "bad conscience," came into the world? And it is here that we turn back to our genealogists of morals. For the second time I say—or have I not said it yet?—that they are worth nothing. Just their own five-spans-long limited modern experience; no knowledge of the past, and no wish to know it; still less a historic instinct, a power of "second sight" (which is what is really required in this case)—and despite this to go in for the history of morals. It stands to reason that this must needs produce results which are removed from the truth by something more than a respectful distance.

Have these current genealogists of morals ever allowed themselves to have even the vaguest notion, for instance, that the cardinal moral idea of "ought" originates from the very material idea of "owe"? Or that punishment developed as a *retaliation* absolutely independently of any preliminary hypothesis of the freedom or determination of the will?—And this to such an extent, that a *high* degree of civilisation was always first necessary for the animal man to begin to make those much more primitive distinctions of "intentional," "negligent," "accidental," "responsible," and their contraries, and apply them in the assessing of punishment. That idea—"the wrong-doer deserves punishment *because* he might have acted otherwise," in spite of the fact that it is nowadays so cheap, obvious, natural, and inevitable, and that it has had to serve as an illustration of the way in which the sentiment of justice appeared on earth, is in point of fact an exceedingly late, and even refined form of human judgment and inference; the placing of this idea back at the beginning of the world is simply a clumsy violation of the principles of primitive psychology. Throughout the longest period of human history punishment was *never* based on the responsibility of the evil-doer for his action, and was consequently *not* based on the hypothesis that only the guilty should be punished;—on the contrary, punishment was inflicted in those days for the same reason that parents punish their children even nowadays, out of anger at an injury that they have suffered, an anger which vents itself mechanically on the author of the injury—but this anger is kept in bounds and modified through the idea that every injury has somewhere or other its *equivalent* price, and can really be paid off, even though it be by means of pain to the author. Whence is it that this ancient deep-rooted and now perhaps ineradicable idea has drawn its strength, this idea of an equivalency between injury and pain? I have already revealed its origin, in the contractual relationship between *creditor* and *ower,* that is as old as the existence of legal rights at all, and in its turn points back to the primary forms of purchase, sale, barter, and trade.

The realisation of these contractual relations excites, of course (as would be already expected from our previous observations), a great deal of suspicion and opposition towards the primitive society which made or sanctioned them. In this society promises will be made; in this society the object is to provide the promiser with a memory; in this society, so may we suspect, there will be full scope for hardness, cruelty, and pain: the "ower," in order to induce credit in his promise of repayment, in order to give a guarantee of the earnestness and sanctity of his promise, in order to drill into his own conscience the duty, the solemn duty, of repayment, will, by virtue of a contract with his creditor to meet the contingency of his not paying, pledge something that he still possesses, something that he still has in his power, for instance, his life or his wife, or his freedom or his body (or under certain religious conditions even his salvation, his soul's welfare, even his peace in the grave; so in Egypt, where the corpse of the ower found even in the grave no rest from the creditor—of course, from the Egyptian standpoint, this peace was a matter of particular importance). But especially has the creditor the power of inflicting on the body of the ower all kinds of pain and torture—the power, for instance, of cutting off from it an amount that appeared proportionate to the greatness of the debt;—this point of view resulted in the universal prevalence at an early date of precise schemes of valuation, frequently horrible in the minuteness and meticulosity of their application, *legally* sanctioned schemes of valuation for individual limbs and parts of the body. I consider it as already a progress, as a proof of a freer, less petty, and more *Roman* conception of law, when the Roman Code of the Twelve Tables decreed that it was immaterial how much or how little the creditors in such a contingency cut off, *"si plus minusve secuerunt, ne fraude esto."* Let us make the logic of the whole of this equalisation process clear; it is strange enough. The equivalence consists in this: instead of an advantage directly compensatory of his injury (that is, instead of an equalisation in money, lands, or some kind of chattel), the creditor is granted by way of repayment and compensation a certain *sensation of satisfaction*—the satisfaction of being able to vent, without any trouble, his power on one who is powerless, the delight *"de faire le mal pour le plaisir de le faire,"* the joy in sheer violence: and this joy will be relished in proportion to the lowness and humbleness of the creditor in the social scale, and is quite apt to have the effect of the most delicious dainty, and even seem the foretaste of a higher social position.

Thanks to the punishment of the "ower," the creditor participates in the rights of the masters. At last he too, for once in a way, attains the edifying consciousness of being able to despise and ill-treat a creature—as an "inferior"—or at any rate of *seeing* him being despised and ill-treated, in case the actual power of punishment, the administration of punishment, has already become transferred to the "authorities." The compensation consequently consists in a claim on cruelty and a right to draw thereon.

It is then in *this* sphere of the law of contract that we find the cradle of the whole moral world of the ideas of "guilt," "conscience," "duty," the "sacredness of duty,"—their commencement, like the commencement of all great things in the world, is thoroughly and continuously saturated with blood. And should we not add that this world has never really lost a certain savour of blood and torture (not even in old Kant the categorical imperative reeks of cruelty). It was in this sphere likewise that there first became formed that sinister and perhaps now indissoluble association of the ideas of "guilt" and "suffering." To put the question yet again, why can suffering be a compensation for "owing"?—Because the *infliction* of suffering produces the highest degree of happiness, because the injured party will get in exchange for his loss (including his vexation at his loss) an extraordinary counter-pleasure: the *infliction* of suffering—a real *feast,* something that, as I have said, was all the more appreciated the greater the paradox created by the rank and social status of the creditor. These observations are purely conjectural; for, apart from the painful nature of the task, it is hard to plumb such profound depths: the clumsy introduction of the idea of "revenge" as a connecting-link simply hides and obscures the view instead of rendering it clearer (revenge itself simply leads back again to the identical problem—"How can the infliction of suffering be a satisfaction?").

SIGMUND FREUD
The Totemic Feast

Let us now envisage the scene of such a totem meal and let us embellish it further with a few probable features which could not be adequately considered before. Thus we have the clan, which on a solemn occasion kills its totem in a cruel manner and eats it raw, blood, flesh, and bones. At the same time the members of the clan, disguised in imitation of the totem, mimic it in sound and movement as if they wanted to emphasize their common identity. There is also the conscious realization that an action is being carried out which is forbidden to each individual and which can only be justified through the participation of all, so that no one is allowed to exclude himself from the killing and the feast. After the act is accomplished the murdered animal is bewailed and lamented. The death lamentation is compulsive, being enforced by the fear of a threatening retribution, and its main purpose is, as Robertson Smith remarks on an analogous occasion, to exculpate oneself from responsibility for the slaying.[1]

But after this mourning there follows loud festival gaiety accompanied by the unchaining of every impulse and the permission of every gratification. Here we find an easy insight into the nature of the *holiday*.

A holiday is a permitted, or rather a prescribed excess, a solemn violation of a prohibition. People do not commit the excesses, which at all times have characterized holidays, as a result of an order to be in a holiday mood, but because in the very nature of a holiday there is excess; the holiday mood is brought about by the release of what is otherwise forbidden.

But what has mourning over the death of the totem animal to do with the introduction of this holiday spirit? If men are happy over the slaying of the totem, which is otherwise forbidden to them, why do they also mourn it?

We have heard that members of a clan become holy through the

[1] *Religion of the Semites,* Second Edition, 1907, p. 412.

consumption of the totem and thereby also strengthen their identification with it and with each other. The fact that they have absorbed the holy life with which the substance of the totem is charged may explain the holiday mood and everything that results from it.

Psychoanalysis has revealed to us that the totem animal is really a substitute for the father, and this really explains the contradiction that it is usually forbidden to kill the totem animal, that the killing of it results in a holiday and that the animal is killed and yet mourned. The ambivalent emotional attitude which today still marks the father complex in our children and so often continues into adult life also extended to the father substitute of the totem animal.

But if we associate the translation of the totem as given by psychoanalysis, with the totem feast and the Darwinian hypothesis about the primal state of human society, a deeper understanding becomes possible and a hypothesis is offered which may seem fantastic but which has the advantage of establishing an unexpected unity among a series of hitherto separated phenomena.

The Darwinian conception of the primal horde does not, of course, allow for the beginning of totemism. There is only a violent, jealous father who keeps all the females for himself and drives away the growing sons. This primal state of society has nowhere been observed. The most primitive organization we know, which today is still in force with certain tribes, is *associations of men* consisting of members with equal rights, subject to the restrictions of the totemic system, and founded on matriarchy, or descent through the mother. Can the one have resulted from the other, and how was this possible?

By basing our argument upon the celebration of the totem we are in a position to give an answer: One day the expelled brothers joined forces, slew and ate the father, and thus put an end to the father horde. Together they dared and accomplished what would have remained impossible for them singly. Perhaps some advance in culture, like the use of a new weapon, had given them the feeling of superiority. Of course these cannibalistic savages ate their victim. This violent primal father had surely been the envied and feared model for each of the brothers. Now they accomplished their identification with him by devouring him and each acquired a part of his strength. The totem feast, which is perhaps mankind's first celebration, would be the repetition and commemoration of this memorable, criminal act with which so many things began, social organization, moral restrictions and religion.[2]

In order to find these results acceptable, quite aside from our supposition, we need only assume that the group of brothers banded together were dominated by the same contradictory feelings towards the father which we can demonstrate as the content of ambivalence of the father complex in all our children and in neurotics. They hated the father who stood so powerfully in the way of their sexual demands and their desire for power, but they also loved and admired him. After they had satisfied their hate by his removal and had carried out their wish for identification with him, the suppressed

---

[2] The seemingly monstrous assumption that the tyrannical father was overcome and slain by a combination of the expelled sons has also been accepted by Atkinson as a direct result of the conditions of the Darwinian primal horde. "A youthful band of brothers living together in forced celibacy, or at most in polyandrous relation with some single female captive. A horde as yet weak in their impubescence they are, but they would, when strength was gained with time, inevitably wrench by combined attacks, renewed again and again, both wife and life from the paternal tyrant" (*Primal Law,* pp. 220–1). Atkinson, who spent his life in New Caledonia and had unusual opportunities to study the natives, also refers to the fact that the conditions of the primal horde which Darwin assumes can easily be observed among herds of wild cattle and horses and regularly lead to the killing of the father animal. He then assumes further that a disintegration of the horde took place after the removal of the father through embittered fighting among the victorious sons, which thus precluded the origin of a new organization of society; "An ever recurring violent succession to the solitary paternal tyrant by sons, whose parricidal hands were so soon again clenched in fratricidal strife" (p. 228). Atkinson, who did not have the suggestions of psychoanalysis at his command and did not know the studies of Robertson Smith, finds a less violent transition from the primal horde to the next social stage in which many men live together in peaceful accord. He attributes it to maternal love that at first only the youngest sons and later others too remain in the horde, who in return for this toleration acknowledge the sexual prerogative of the father by the restraint which they practise towards the mother and towards their sisters.

So much for the very remarkable theory of Atkinson, its essential correspondence with the theory here expounded, and its point of departure which makes it necessary to relinquish so much else.

I must ascribe the indefiniteness, the disregard of time interval, and the crowding of the material in the above exposition to a restraint which the nature of the subject demands. It would be just as meaningless to strive for exactness in this material as it would be unfair to demand certainty here.

tender impulses had to assert themselves.[3] This took place in the form of remorse, a sense of guilt was formed which coincided here with the remorse generally felt. The dead now became stronger than the living had been, even as we observe it today in the destinies of men. What the father's presence had formerly prevented they themselves now prohibited in the psychic situation of "subsequent obedience" which we know so well from psychoanalysis. They undid their deed by declaring that the killing of the father substitute, the totem, was not allowed, and renounced the fruits of their deed by denying themselves the liberated women. Thus they created two fundamental taboos of totemism out of the *sense of guilt of the son,* and for this very reason these had to correspond with the two repressed wishes of the Œdipus complex. Whoever disobeyed became guilty of the two only crimes which troubled primitive society.[4]

The two taboos of totemism with which the morality of man begins are psychologically not of equal value. One of them, the sparing of the totem animal, rests entirely upon emotional motives; the father had been removed and nothing in reality could make up for this. But the other, the incest prohibition, had, besides, a strong practical foundation. Sexual need does not unite men; it separates them. Though the brothers had joined forces in order to overcome the father, each was the other's rival among the women. Each one wanted to have them all to himself like the father, and in the fight of each against the other the new organization would have perished. For there was no longer any one stronger than all the rest who could have successfully assumed the rôle of the father. Thus there was nothing left for the brothers, if they wanted to live together, but to erect the incest prohibition—perhaps after many difficult experiences—through which they all equally renounced the women whom they desired, and on account of whom they had removed the father in the first place. Thus they saved the organization which

---

[3] This new emotional attitude must also have been responsible for the fact that the deed could not bring full satisfaction to any of the perpetrators. In a certain sense it had been in vain. For none of the sons could carry out his original wish of taking the place of the father. But failure is, as we know, much more favourable to moral reaction than success.

[4] "Murder and incest, or offences of like kind against the sacred law of blood are in primitive society the only crimes of which the community as such takes cognizance . . ." *Religion of the Semites,* p. 419.

had made them strong and which could be based upon the homosexual feelings and activities which probably manifested themselves among them during the time of their banishment. Perhaps this situation also formed the germ of the institution of the mother right discovered by Bachofen, which was then abrogated by the patriarchal family arrangement.

THEODOR REIK

The Jealous Father and Couvade

Let us attempt to represent the mental attitude of the primitive human being who has just become a father. One cannot conceive him having much fatherly tenderness. A strange being has come into his home and he feels no pleasure in supporting the little creature. On the contrary, he feels impelled to kill and devour the child. The deeper motive of this wish will become clearer later. For the present we need only refer to the fact that to-day the killing and eating of children is not unknown among certain peoples. These original wishes are not destroyed with the development of fatherly feelings, about which we have yet to speak, but are pushed back and finally repressed: they become unconscious, though none the less effective. The prohibition is constantly endangered by the urging of unconscious impulses and is forced to alter and extend its limits, because it is unwilling to grant instinctual gratification even through substitutive actions. Psycho-analysis can demonstrate the mental paths which lead from the wish to the building up of protective measures of this kind.

As already pointed out, only a small number of the mental determining factors of couvade customs are analysed in this work. Only a careful analysis of the puberty rites of primitive peoples will throw further important light on the male childbed.[1] The view

[1] The connection between the rites of couvade and of puberty become still closer when one thinks of the dieting, the ordeals and the symbolic castration of the novices. To the unconscious of the young father, the birth of his child is a disproof of the castration threats of his own father; it is

will there be reached that the displacement of the birth from the mother to the father has actually a real meaning besides the meaning we have already discussed; this real meaning has, of course, nothing to do with father- and mother-right. It corresponds to the phantasy of the father having given birth to the child, and is equivalent to a nullification of the child's birth from the mother. The affective basis of this phantasy lies in the unconscious incestuous fixation of the child on the mother which was created by the birth; and on this basis also rests the father's striving to detach this libido fixation from its object, and to transfer to himself the child's love. This nullification of incestuous attitude can have no more radical enforcement than by the denial of its first and most essential cause; it is not the mother who has given birth to the child, but the father; to him, therefore, the child's love must go. Here again we find it best to believe in what the rites represent, however senseless and stupid their external appearance may seem at first sight. If we consider that in the puberty rites a kind of rebirth of the boys from their father takes place, we have couvade represented as a temporarily displaced form of this phantasy charged with strong affects. We may compare this to the great rôle played by the father's unconscious fear of retaliation in couvade customs, and the particularly strict observance of the ritual at the birth of the first-born. Couvade and the puberty rites would, therefore, be the effects of the same unconscious attitude of feeling expressed in different forms, in which the ambivalency towards the son stands out with special prominence.

The scholars who affirm that couvade signifies a landmark in the development of mankind now seem to be justified. For it is, as it were, the boundary stone of a definite stage of civilisation, which marks the victory of the tender impulses for his wife and child on the part of the man. It shows us that the unconscious identification

---

before everything a triumph over his father, for he has reached the same state. Thus his reaction of anxiety (demon avoidance), and his homosexual and feminine identification with the woman who bears children becomes clear. Géza Róheim in a letter to me has reduced the rites of couvade to the theory of the anal child, in which the conception is orally (diet) represented. As a punishment for the unconscious tendency to kill the father (= the child) the man is himself impregnated and compelled to bear a child.

with his own father now begins to be a lasting one, and that his affection for him has so successfully suppressed the fear of retaliation that his concern about the new generation now becomes the central point in his emotional life as a parent. This signifies, however, a partial renunciation of the gratification of his impulses—a necessary condition in the advance to each higher stage of civilisation. At the same time it means that the father, in thus renouncing his own claims, regains the gratification he has lost in his new unity of feeling with his son.

If I may be permitted to conclude this study on a lighter note I may venture to sum it up by saying that among the half-civilised peoples who practise couvade lives a glimmer of that wisdom which, quoting freely from Wilhelm Busch, we may express thus: *"Vater sein ist nicht schwer, Vater werden dagegen sehr."* (It is not difficult to be a father; it is not easy to become one.)

PART 3

Theoretical Approaches

ERNEST CRAWLEY

The Undifferentiated Character of Primitive Society

The undifferentiated character of primitive culture, its reference of all departments of thought and practice to one psychological habit, the superstitious or religious, may be illustrated from higher stages. "The political and religious Governments of the Kaffir tribes are so intimately connected that the one cannot be overturned without the other; they must stand or fall together." [1] The great pagan civilisations show exactly the same homogeneity. The ideal society of early Christians was one where there should be no separation between Church and State, where public and private life and thought, politics and domestic affairs, individual and social morality, speculation and science, should all be subsumed under religion, and directed by the religious method. Such an ideal differs in degree only from the actual condition of primitive society; whatever term be used to describe this, it is homogeneous and monistic in practice and theory; one method is applied to its philosophy of nature and

[1] J. Maclean. *A Compendium of Kafir Laws and Customs* (1858), p. 107.

of man, its politics and public life, its sociology and human relations, domestic and social, its medical science and practice, its ethics and morality, its ordinary thought and action in everyday life, its behaviour and etiquette. Thus, as will also be shown by the way, there is a religious meaning inherent in the primitive conception and practice of all human relations, a meaning which is always ready to become actualised; and the same is true of all individual processes of sense and emotion and intellection and, in especial, of those functional processes that are most easily seen in their working and results. Not only "the Master knot of Human Fate," but all human actions and relations, all individual and social phenomena, have for primitive man, always potentially and often actually, a full religious content. So it is with that sub-division of human nature and human life caused by sex; all actions and relations, all individual and social phenomena conditioned by sex, are likewise filled with a religious meaning. Sexual relations and sexual processes, as all human relations and human processes, are religious to the primitive mind. The conception of danger, neither material nor spiritual, but both, which is the chief characteristic of early religious thought and practice, and which is due to the unscientific character of early speculation, is here intensified by the importance, physical and physiological, of the sexual life. As we proceed, this characteristic of sexual relations and sexual life will be made clear; it is seen in the phenomena of the individual life and of social relations, both in ordinary circumstances and, naturally intensified, in sexual crises. Thus, birth and baptism, confirmation and marriage, are attended by religious ceremonies. There is indeed a tendency amongst enquirers, due to the legal method of investigation, to ignore the religious character of the marriage ceremony; but it is only in later culture that marriage is a "civil act," and though in early Catholic times marriage was not necessarily performed by the Church, it was still in essence a religious rite, and had been so before Christianity, and was so in the earliest ages. One of the crudest modes of marriage known, that of the Arunta and other Central Australian tribes, is proved by a note of Messrs Spencer and Gillen to be a religious act,[1a] though to all appearance this would

[1a] Sir W. B. Spencer *and* F. J. Gillen, *The Native Tribes of Central Australia* (1899), p. 93.

seem impossible. As we shall see, even the ordinary intercourse of man with woman has for primitive man this religious meaning.

The primitive conception of danger, which leads to these precautions, religious or superstitious, so characteristic of early ritual, appears in two forms, the predication of evil influences and the imposition of taboos. Let us take a few preliminary instances, from ordinary life, and from sexual crises. In the Marquesas Islands the use of canoes is prohibited to the female sex by taboo: the breaking of the rule is punished with death. *Tapa*-making belongs exclusively to women, and it is taboo for men to touch it.[2] The Kaffirs will not from superstitious motives allow women to touch their cattle.[3] Amongst the Dakotas custom and superstition ordain that the wife must carefully keep away from all that belongs to her husband's sphere.[4] In New Zealand, to mention only one more of many similar cases, a man who has any important business in hand, either in peace or in war, is taboo and must keep away from the female sex.[5]

The fear of evil spirits shows itself from time to time during the long and wearisome marriage ceremonies of South Celebes, and methods are used to frustrate their evil intentions against the happiness of the young pair. There is also a fear that the soul of the bridegroom may fly away from sheer happiness.[6] In China, a new bride is apt to be attacked by evil spirits, causing her to be ill; hence the figure of "a great magician" (a Taoist priest), brandishing a sword, is painted on the sedan-chair which she uses on the wedding-day.[7] The sedan-chair in which a Manchu bride goes to the house of the bridegroom is "disinfected" with incense to drive

[2] H. Melville, *Narrative of a four months' residence among the natives of the Marquesas Islands* (1846), pp. 13, 245.

[3] E. Holub, "The Central South African Tribes," *Journal of the Anthropological Institute* (1881), x. 11; cf. H. L. Roth, "On the Origin of Agriculture," *J.A.I.* (1887), xvi. 119.

[4] H. R. Schoolcraft, *Historical and Statistical Information respecting . . . the Indian tribes of the United States* (1851–1860), iii. 230.

[5] E. Dieffenbach, *Travels in New Zealand* (1843), ii. 85–86.

[6] B. F. Matthes, *Bijdragen tot de Ethnologie van Zuid-Celebes* (1875), pp. 30, 33, 39; R. van Eck, "De Mangkasaren en Boegineezen," *De Indische Gids* (1881), III. ii. 1038.

[7] J. Doolittle, *Social Life of the Chinese* (1867), i. 95.

away evil spirits, and in it is placed a calendar containing the names of idols who control the spirits of evil.[8] The Druses "have a superstition that leads them to suppose that Gins or evil spirits are more than usually busy on the occasion of marriage," and may interfere with the happiness of the pair.[9] In English folklore "the malevolence of witchcraft seems to have taken the greatest pleasure in subtle assaults upon those just entering the married state." [10] In Russia all doors, windows, and even the chimney, are closed at a wedding, to prevent malicious witches flying in and hunting the bride and bridegroom.[11] The Chuvashes honour their wizards (*iemzyas*) and always invite them to weddings, for fear that an offended *iemzya* might destroy the bride and bridegroom.[12]

ROBERT RANULPH MARETT

The Individuality of the Primitive

There is a real danger lest the anthropologist should think that a scientific view of man is to be obtained by leaving out the human nature in him. This comes from the over-anxiety of evolutionary history to arrive at general principles. It is too ready to rule out the so-called "accident," forgetful of the fact that the whole theory of biological evolution may with some justice be described as "the happy accident theory." The man of high individuality, then, the exceptional man, the man of genius, be he man of thought, man of feeling, or man of action, is no accident that can be overlooked by history. On the contrary, he is in no small part the history-maker; and, as such, should be treated with due respect by the history-compiler. The "dry bones" of history, its statistical averages, and so on, are all very well in their way; but they correspond to the superficial truth that history repeats itself, rather than to the deeper truth that history is an evolution. Anthropology, then,

---

[8] J. H. S. Lockhart, "The Marriage Ceremonies of the Manchus," *Folk-Lore* (1890), i. 487.

[9] G. W. Chasseaud, *The Druses of the Lebanon* (1849), p. 168.

[10] J. Brand, *Popular Antiquities* (1849), iii. 305.

[11] W. R. S. Ralston, *The Songs of the Russian People* (1872), p. 381.

[12] V. M. Mikhailovskii, "Shamanism in Siberia," *J.A.I.* (1895), xxiv. 156.

should not disdain what might be termed the method of the historical novel. To study the plot without studying the characters will never make sense of the drama of human life.

It may seem a truism, but is perhaps worth recollecting at the start, that no man or woman lacks individuality altogether, even if it cannot be regarded in a particular case as a high individuality. No one is a mere item. That useful figment of the statistician has no real existence under the sun. We need to supplement the books of abstract theory with much sympathetic insight directed towards men and women in their concrete selfhood. Said a Vedda cave-dweller to Dr. Seligmann (it is the first instance I light on in the first book I happen to take up): "It is pleasant for us to feel the rain beating on our shoulders, and good to go out and dig yams, and come home wet, and see the fire burning in the cave, and sit round it." That sort of remark, to my mind, throws more light on the anthropology of cave-life than all the bones and stones that I have helped to dig out of our Mousterian caves in Jersey. As the stock phrase has it, it is, as far as it goes, a "human document." The individuality, in the sense of the intimate self-existence, of the speaker and his group—for, characteristically enough, he uses the first person plural—is disclosed sufficiently for our souls to get into touch. We are the nearer to appreciating human history from the inside.

LUCIEN LEVY-BRUHL

What the Natives Think of Pictures, Names and Dreams

It is a well-known fact that primitives, even members of communities which are already somewhat advanced, regard artificial likenesses, whether painted, carved, or sculptured, as real, as well as the individual they depict.

In North America, the Mandans believe that the portraits taken by Catlin are alive like their subjects, and that they rob these of part of their vitality. It is true that Catlin is inclined to draw a long bow, and his stories must be taken with a grain of salt. In this respect, however, the beliefs and sentiments he attributes to the Mandans are exactly what we find noted elsewhere in similar circumstances. "I know," says one man, "that this man put *many of our buffaloes in his book,* for I was with him, and we have had no buffaloes since to eat, it is true." [1]

"They pronounced me the greatest medicine-man in the world," writes Catlin, "for they said I had made *living beings*—they said they could see their chiefs alive in two places—those that I had made were a *little* alive—they could see their eyes move—could see them smile and laugh, and that if they could laugh, they could certainly speak, if they should try, and they must therefore have some life in them." [1] Therefore, most Indians refused him permission to take their likenesses. It would be parting with a portion of their own substance, and placing them at the mercy of anyone who might wish to possess the picture. They are afraid, too, of finding themselves faced by a portrait which, as a living thing, may exercise a harmful influence.

"We had placed," say the Jesuit missionaries, "images of St. Ignatius and St. Xavier upon our altar. They regarded them with amazement; they believed them to be living persons, and asked whether they were *ondaqui*" (plural form of *wakan,* supernatural beings): "in short, that which they recognize as superior to humanity. They inquired whether the tabernacle were their dwelling, and whether these *ondaqui* used the adornments which they saw around the altar." [2]

In Central Africa, too, "I have known natives refuse to enter a room where portraits were hanging on the walls, because of the *masoka* souls which were in them." [3] The same author tells the story of a chief who allowed himself to be photographed, and who, several months later, fell ill. In accordance with his request, the negative had been sent to England, and "his illness was attributed to some accident having befallen the photographic plate."

Thus the similitude can take the place of the model, and possess the same properties. In Loango, the followers of a certain eminent

[1] Catlin, *The North American Indians,* i. pp. 122–3 (Edinburgh, 1903).
[2] Ed. Thwaites, *Relations des Jésuites,* v. p. 256 (1633).
[3] Hetherwick, "Some Animistic Beliefs of the Yaos," *J.A.I.,* xxxii. pp. 89–90.

wonder-worker used to make a wooden image of their master, imbued it with "power," and gave it the name of the original. Possibly even they would ask their master to make his own substitute, so that after his death, as well as during his life, they could use it in performing their miracles.[4] On the Slave Coast, if one of twins happens to die, the mother ". . . to give the spirit of the deceased child something to enter without disturbing the survivor, carries about, with the latter, a little wooden figure, about seven or eight inches long, roughly fashioned in human shape, and of the sex of the dead child. Such figures are nude, as an infant would be, with beads around the waist." [5] With reference to the Bororo of Brazil we read "they begged Wilhelm most earnestly not to let the women see the drawings he had made of the bull-roarers; for the sight of the drawings would kill them as the real things would." [6] Many similar instances had already been collected by Tylor.[7]

Are these to be explained from a purely psychological point of view, as is so frequently the case, by the association of ideas? Must we say, with de Groot,[8] that it is impossible for them to distinguish a mere resemblance from identity, and admit that primitives suffer from the same illusion as the child who believes her doll to be alive? First of all, however, it is difficult to decide whether the child herself is quite sure of it. Perhaps her belief is part of the game and at the same time sincere, like the emotions of grown-up people at the theatre, shedding real tears about misfortunes which they nevertheless know to be but feigned. On the contrary, it is impossible to doubt that the primitives' beliefs which I have just mentioned *are* serious; their actions prove it. How then can a portrait be "materially and psychically" identified with its original? To my mind, it is not on account of a childish trust in analogy, nor from mental weakness and confusion; it is not due to a naïve generalization of the animist theory, either. It is because, in perceiving the similitude, as in looking at the original, the traditional collective representations imbue it with the same mystic elements.

---

[4] Dr. Pechuël-Loesche, *Die Loango-Expedition,* iii. 2, pp. 378–9 (1907).
[5] A. B. Ellis, *The Yoruba-speaking Peoples,* p. 80.
[6] K. von den Steinen, *Unter den Naturvölkern Zentralbräsiliens,* p. 386.
[7] *Primitive Culture,* ii, pp. 169 et seq.
[8] J. J. M. de Groot: *The Religious System of China,* ii. pp. 340–55.

If primitives view the pictured resemblance differently from ourselves, it is because they view the original otherwise also. In the latter we note its objective and actual characteristics, and those only: the shape, size, and proportions of the body; the colour of the eyes; the facial expression, and so forth; we find these reproduced in the picture, and there, too, we find these alone. But to the primitive, with his perceptions differently oriented, these objective features, if he apprehends them as we do, are neither the only ones nor the most important; most frequently, they are but the symbols or instruments of occult forces and mystic powers such as every being, especially a living being, can display. As a natural consequence, therefore, the image of such a being would also present the mingling of characteristics which we term objective and of mystic powers. It will live and prove beneficial or malevolent like the being it reproduces; it will be its surrogate. Accordingly we find that the image of an unknown—and consequently dreaded—object often inspires extraordinary dread. "I had," says Father Hennepin, "a pot about three feet high shaped like a lion, which we used for cooking our food in during the voyage. . . . The savages never ventured to touch it with their hands unless they had previously covered them with beaver skins. They imparted such terror of it to their wives that the latter had it fastened to the branches of a tree, for otherwise they would not have dared to sleep or even enter the hut if it were inside. We wished to make a present of it to some of the chiefs, but they would neither accept it nor make use of it, because they feared that it concealed some evil spirit which might have killed them."[9] We know that these Indians in the valley of the Mississippi had never before seen a white man, or a lion, or a cooking utensil. The likeness of an animal they did not know awakened in them the same mystic fears that its appearance among them would have done.

This identification which appears so strange to us must therefore occur naturally. It does not arise out of gross mental hallucination or childish confusion of ideas. As soon as we realize *how* primitives view entities, we see that they view reproductions of them in exactly the same way. If their perceptions of the originals ceased to be

[9] L. Hennepin, *Nouveau Voyage de l'Amérique Septentrionale,* pp. 366–7.

mystic, their images would also lose their mystic properties. They would no longer appear to be alive, but would be what they are to our minds—merely material reproductions.

In the second place, primitives regard their names as something concrete and real, and frequently sacred. Here are a few of the many proofs of it.

"The Indian regards his name, not as a mere label, but as a distinct part of his personality, just as much as are his eyes or his teeth, and believes that injury will result as surely from the malicious handling of his name as from a wound inflicted on any part of his physical organism. This belief was found among the various tribes from the Atlantic to the Pacific." [10] On the East African coast, "there is a real and material connection between a man and his name, and . . . by means of the name injury may be done to the man. . . . In consequence of this belief the name of the king . . . is always kept secret. . . . It appears strange that the birth-name only, and not an alias, should be believed capable of carrying some of the personality of the bearer elsewhere . . . but the native view seems to be that the alias does not really belong to the man." [11]

Accordingly all kinds of precautions become necessary. A man will avoid uttering his own name[12] and the names of others, while the names of the dead, above all, will never be pronounced; very frequently, too, even ordinary words in which the name of a dead person is implied will fall into desuetude. Alluding to a name is the same thing as laying hands on the very person or being that bears the name. It is making an attack upon him, outraging his individuality, or again, it is invoking his presence and forcing him to appear, a proceeding which may be fraught with very great danger. There are excellent reasons, therefore, for avoiding such a practice. "When they (the Santals) are hunting and see a leopard or a tiger they will always call the attention of their companions to the fact

[10] J. Mooney, "The Sacred Formulas of the Cherokees," *E. B. Rept.*, vii. p. 343.

[11] A. B. Ellis, *The Ewe-speaking Peoples*, pp. 98–9.

[12] Rivers, *The Todas*, p. 627.

by calling out 'a cat,' or some similar name." [13] With the Cherokees, too, "it is never said that a person has been bitten by a snake, but that he has been 'scratched by a brier.' In the same way, when an eagle has been shot for a ceremonial dance, it is announced that 'a snow-bird has been killed,' the purpose being to deceive the rattle-snake or eagle spirits which might be listening." [14] The Warramunga, instead of mentioning the snake *Wollunqua* by its name when speaking of it, call it *Urkulu nappaurima,* "because," say they, "if they were to call it too often by its right name, they would lose their control over it, and it would come out and eat them all up." [15]

At the beginning of a fresh epoch in his life,—at his initiation, for instance—an individual receives a new name, and it is the same when he is admitted to a secret society. A name is never a matter of indifference; it implies a whole series of relationships between the man who bears it and the source whence it is derived. "A name implies relationship, and consequently protection; favour and influence are claimed from the source of the name, whether this be the gens or the vision. A name, therefore, shows the affiliation of the individual; it grades him, so to speak." [16] In British Columbia, "names, apart from the staz or nickname, are never used as mere appellations to distinguish one person from another, as among ourselves, nor do they seem to have been used ordinarily as terms of address. They are primarily terms of relation or affiliation, with historic and mystic reference. They were reserved for special and ceremonial occasions. The ordinary terms of address among the Salish tribes, as among other primitive peoples, were those expressive of age." [17] With the Kwakiutl, "each clan has a certain limited number of names. Each individual has only one name at a time. The bearers of these names form the nobility of the tribe. When a man receives the totem of his father-in-law, he at the same time

---

[13] Bodding, "On Taboo Customs amongst the Santals," *Journal of the Asiatic Society of Bengal,* iii. p. 20 (1898).

[14] J. Mooney, *op. cit.,* p. 352.

[15] Spencer and Gillen, *The Northern Tribes of Central Australia,* p. 227.

[16] Dorsey, "Siouan Cults," *E. B. Rept.,* xi. p. 368.

[17] Hill Tout, "Ethnology of the Statlum of British Columbia," *J.A.I.,* xxxv. p. 152.

receives his name, while the father-in-law gives up the name, and takes what is called 'an old man's name,' which does not belong to the names constituting the nobility of the tribe." [18]

The mystic properties in the name are not separated from those in the beings they connote. To us the name of a person, an animal, a family, a town, has the purely external significance of a label which allows us to discern without any possibility of confusion who the person is, to what species the animal belongs, which family and which town it is. To the primitive, however, the designation of the being or object, which seems to us the sole function of the name, appears a mere accessory and of secondary importance: many observers expressly state that that is not the real function of the name. To make up for this, there are very important functions of which our names are deprived. The name expresses and makes real the relationship of the individual with his totemic group; with the ancestor of whom he is frequently a reincarnation; with the particular totem or guardian angel who has been revealed to him in a dream; with the invisible powers who protect the secret societies to which he belongs, etc. How does this arise? Evidently because beings and objects do not present themselves to the primitive's mind apart from the mystic properties which these relations involve. As a natural consequence, names derive their characteristics from the characteristics of these same beings and objects. The name is mystic, as the reproduction is mystic, because the perception of things, oriented differently from our own, through the collective representations, is mystic.

The primitive is, as we know, no less careful about his shadow than he is about his name or his counterfeit presentment. If he were to lose it he would consider himself hopelessly endangered. Should it come into the power of another, he has everything to dread. Folklore of all countries has made us familiar with facts of this kind; we shall cite but a few of them only. In the Fiji Islands, as in many places inhabited by people of a similar stage of development, it is a mortal insult to walk upon anybody else's shadow. In East Africa, murders are sometimes committed by means of a

[18] F. Boas, "The North-western Tribes of Canada," *Reports of the British Association,* p. 675 (1898).

knife or nail thrust through the shadow of a man; if the guilty person is caught in the act he is executed forthwith. Miss Kingsley, in reporting this fact, shows clearly to what extent the West African negroes dread the loss of their shadow. "It strikes one as strange," she writes, "to see men who have been walking, say, through forest or grass land, on a blazing hot morning quite happily, on arrival at a piece of clear ground or a village square, most carefully go round it, not across, and you will soon notice that they only do this at noontime, and learn that they fear losing their shadow. I asked some Bakwiri I once came across who were particularly careful in this matter, why they were not anxious about losing their shadows when night came down and they disappeared in the surrounding darkness, and was told that was all right, because at night all shadows lay down in the shadow of the Great God, and so got stronger. Had I not seen how strong and how long a shadow, be it of man or tree or of the great mountain itself, was in the early morning time?" [19]

Finally, the same considerations apply equally to another class of phenomena—dreams—which occupy an important place in the primitive mind. To primitives the dream is not, as it is to us, simply a manifestation of mental activity which occurs during sleep, a more or less orderly series of representations to which, when awake, the dreamer would give no credence, because they lack the conditions essential to objective validity. This last characteristic, though it does not escape the primitives, seems to interest them but slightly. On the other hand, the dream, to them, is of far greater significance than to us. It is first a percept as real as those of the waking state, but above all it is a provision of the future, a communication and intercourse with spirits, souls, divinities, a means of establishing a relation with their own special guardian angel, and even of discovering who this may be. Their confidence in the reality of that which the dreams make known to them is very profound. Tylor, Frazer, and the representatives of the English school of anthropology have brought together a vast number of facts which bear witness to this, collected by investigators of primitive peoples of the most diverse types. Shall I, too, quote some? In Australia "Some-

[19] Mary Kingsley, *West African Studies,* p. 176.

times a man dreams that someone has got some of his hair or a piece of his food, or of his 'possum rug, or indeed anything almost that he has used. If he dreams this several times he feels sure of it and calls his friends together, and tells them of his dreaming too much about 'that man,' who must have something belonging to him. . . . Sometimes natives only know about having their fat taken out by remembering something of it as in a dream." [20]

LUCIEN LEVY-BRUHL

The Primitive's Sense of Death

From among the many examples that occur to us, let us take one of the most familiar ones. In all uncivilized races everywhere, death requires to be explained by other than natural causes. It has frequently been remarked that when they see a man die, it would seem as if it might be the very first time such a thing had happened, and that they could never before have been witnesses of such an occurrence. "Is it possible," says the European to himself, "that these people do not *know* that everybody must die sooner or later?" But the primitive has never considered things in this light. In his eyes, the causes which inevitably bring about the death of a man in a certain (fairly definite) number of years—causes such as failure of the bodily organs, senile decay, diminution of functioning power—are not necessarily connected with death. Does he not see decrepit old men still alive? If, therefore, at a given moment death supervenes, it must be because a mystic force has come into play. Moreover, senile weakness itself, like any other malady, is not due to what we call natural causes; it, too, must be explained by the agency of a mystic force. In short, if the primitive pays no attention to the causes of death, it is because he *knows* already how death is brought about, and since he knows *why* it happens, *how* it occurs matters very little. Here we have a kind of *a priori* reasoning upon which experience has no hold.

Thus, to borrow examples from inferior races in parts where the influence of the white man had not yet been felt, in Australia

[20] Howitt, "On Australian Medicine-men," *J.A.I.*, xvi. I, pp. 29–30.

(in Victoria) "death is at all times by them attributed to human agency. When any black, whether old or young, dies, an enemy is supposed, during the night, to have made an incision in his side and removed his kidney fat. Even the most intelligent natives cannot be convinced that any death proceeds from natural causes." [1]

Neither the body of the sick man, nor his corpse after death, bears the slightest trace of the incision, but the Australian aborigine does not consider that any reason for doubting that it took place. What other proof of it than death itself is necessary? Would death have occurred if someone had not taken away the fat from the kidneys? Moreover, this belief does not involve any idea of a physiological rôle attributed to the fat; it is simply a question of a mystic act brought into operation by the mere presence of the organ which is its agent.

According to the notes furnished by Thomas Petrie, Dr. W. E. Roth says: "During the first years of European colonization, in the Brisbane district . . . nearly all aches, pains and diseases were ascribed to the quartz crystal in the possession of some medicine-man (*turrwan*). This crystal gave its owner supernatural powers. The spirit of the *turrwan* used to put the crystal into the victim, who could only be cured by getting a medicine-man to suck it out again; thus a medicine-man could make an individual sick even when he was miles away, and 'doom' him, so to speak." [2] "At Princess Charlotte Bay, all complaints of a serious nature, from malaria to syphilis, are ascribed to the action of a particular charm . . . formed of a pointed piece of human fibula stuck with wax on to a reed spear. It is believed that when the spear is thrown in the direction of the intended victim, the shaft remains in the hands of the thrower, while the bone splinter travels across the intervening space, becomes lodged in the victim's body—the wound immediately closing without leaving a scar—and so causes sickness or disease." [3]

Generally speaking, when a man dies, it is because he has been "doomed" by a sorcerer. "The predestined victim may depart as

---

[1] Hugh Jamieson: *Letters from Victorian Pioneers,* p. 247.

[2] Dr. W. E. Roth: "Superstition, Magic, and Medicine." *North Queensland Ethnology,* Bulletin 5, nr. 121, p. 30 (1907).

[3] Ibid., nr. 138.

usual on some hunting expedition . . . when he suddenly feels something at his leg or foot, and sees a snake just in the act of biting him. Strange to say, this particular kind of snake will now immediately disappear. . . . By this very process of invisibility the person bitten recognizes that some enemy has been pointing the *mangani* at him, and that through this form of it he is sure to die; nothing can possibly save him. He makes no effort to apply a remedy, loses heart, gives way, and lies down to die." [4]

Spencer and Gillen say, too: "All ailments of every kind, from the simplest to the most serious, are without exception attributed to the malign influence of an enemy in either human or spirit shape." [5] "Death by accident," says Howitt, "they can imagine, although the results of what we should call accident they mostly attribute to the effects of some evil magic. They are well acquainted with death by violence, but even in this they believe, as among the tribes about Maryborough (Queensland) that a warrior who happens to be speared in one of the ceremonial fights has lost his skill in warding off or evading a spear, through the evil magic of someone belonging to his own tribe. But I doubt if anywhere in Australia, the aborigines, in their pristine condition, conceived the possibility of death merely from disease. Such was certainly not the case with the Kurnai." [6] "If a man is killed in battle, or dies in consequence of a wound, he is supposed to have been 'charmed.' " [7] "Although the Narrinyeri are so often exposed to the bite of poisonous snakes, they have no remedy for an accident of this kind. Their superstition induces them to believe that it is the result of being bewitched." [8]

This attitude of mind is not peculiar to Australian tribes only. It is to be found occurring almost uniformly among uncivilized peoples who are widely removed from each other. That which does

---

[4] Ibid., nr. 147.

[5] Spencer and Gillen: *The Native Tribes of Central Australia,* p. 530 (1899).

[6] Rev. A. W. Howitt: *The Native Tribes of South-East Australia,* p. 357 (1904).

[7] A. Meyer: "Encounter Bay Tribe," in Woods' *The Native Races of South Australia,* p. 199 (1879).

[8] Rev. G. Taplin: *Manners, Customs, etc., of the South Australian Aborigines,* p. 49 (1879).

vary in their collective representations is the occult power to which they ascribe the disease or death which has supervened. Sometimes a wizard is the guilty person, sometimes it is the spirit of a dead man, sometimes powers which are more or less definite or individualized, ranging from the vaguest representation to the definite deification of a disease like smallpox. That which is similar, we might almost say identical, in these representations, is the preconnection between the illness and death on the one hand, and the invisible power on the other, which results in the comparative disregard of what we call natural causes, even when these are self-evident.

I shall give a few significant examples of this unanimity of idea. "Natives," says Dr. Chalmers, "never believe in being sick from anything but spiritual causes, and think that death, unless by murder, can take place from nothing but the wrath of the spirits. When there is sickness in a family, all the relatives begin to wonder what it means. The sick person getting no better, they conclude something must be done. A present is given; perhaps food is taken and placed on the sacred place, then removed and divided amongst friends. The invalid still being no better, a pig is taken on to the sacred place and there speared and presented to the spirits." [9] It is the same in (German) New Guinea. "According to the Kai, nobody dies a natural death." [10]

Among the Araucans, "all deaths save those caused by battle or combat, were supposed to be the effects of supernatural causes or sorcery. If a person died from the results of a violent accident it was supposed that the *huecuvus* or evil spirits had occasioned it, frightening the horse to make it throw its rider, loosening a stone so that it might fall and crush the unwary, temporarily blinding a person to cause him to fall over a precipice, or some other expedient equally fatal. In the case of death from disease, it was supposed that witchcraft had been practised and the victim poisoned." [11] Grubb says the same thing about the Chaco Indians. "Death is

---

[9] Rev. J. Chalmers: *Pioneering in New Guinea,* pp. 329–30 (1902).

[10] R. Neuhauss: *Deutsch Neu-Guinea,* iii. p. 140; cf. ibid., iii. pp. 466 et seq.

[11] R. E. Latcham: "Ethnology of the Auracanos," *Journal of the Anthropological Institute,* xxxix. p. 364.

invariably supposed by the Indian to result from the direct influence of the *kilyikhama* (spirits), either proceeding from their own desire to injure, or induced through the medium of a witch doctor." [12] Dobrizhoffer gives the same testimony as far as the Abipones are concerned.[13]

Similar beliefs, too, may be found to exist in nearly all the primitive peoples of the two Americas.

In South Africa we find the exact equivalent of what has been noted in Australia. "It is held to be possible for a man to give over a certain man, who has gone to hunt, to a buffalo, or elephant, or other animal. The wizard is believed to be able to 'charge' the animal to put the man to death! . . . And so when it is announced that a certain person has been killed in the hunting-field, some of his friends will remark: 'It is the work of enemies; he was given over to the wild beast.' " [14]

Bentley expresses the same idea in very definite fashion. "Sickness and death are considered by a Congo to be quite abnormal; they are in no way to be traced to natural causes, but always regarded as due to sorcery. Even such cases as death by drowning or in war, by a fall from a tree, or by some beast of prey or wild creature, or by lightning—these are all in a most obstinate and unreasoning manner attributed to the black art. Somebody has bewitched the sufferer, and he or she who has caused it is a witch." [15]

As far back as the seventeenth century Dapper had testified to the same beliefs in Loango. "These poor benighted creatures imagine that no accident ever happens to a man which is not caused by the *moquisies,* that is, his enemy's gods. For instance, if somebody falls into the water and is drowned, they will tell you that he has been bewitched; if he is devoured by a wolf or a tiger, it is because his enemy, by virtue of his magical powers, has been transformed into a wild beast; if he falls from a tree, if his house is burnt down, if the rainy season lasts longer than usual, it is all due to the

[12] W. B. Grubb: *An Unknown People in an Unknown Land,* p. 161 (1911).

[13] M. Dobrizhoffer: *An Account of the Abipones,* ii. pp. 83–4 (1822).

[14] J. Mackenzie: *Ten Years North of Orange River,* pp. 390–1 (1871).

[15] Rev. W. H. Bentley: *Pioneering on the Congo,* i. p. 263.

magic powers of some bad man's *moquisies*. It is only a waste of time to try and drive this foolish idea out of their heads; it is simply exposing oneself to their contempt and ridicule."[16]

EDWARD B. TYLOR

Animism

The first requisite in a systematic study of the religions of the lower races, is to lay down a rudimentary definition of religion. By requiring in this definition the belief in a supreme deity or of judgment after death, the adoration of idols or the practice of sacrifice, or other partially-diffused doctrines or rites, no doubt many tribes may be excluded from the category of religious. But such narrow definition has the fault of identifying religion rather with particular developments than with the deeper motive which underlies them. It seems best to fall back at once on this essential source, and simply to claim, as a minimum definition of Religion, the belief in Spiritual Beings. If this standard be applied to the descriptions of low races as to religion, the following results will appear. It cannot be positively asserted that every existing tribe recognizes the belief in spiritual beings, for the native condition of a considerable number is obscure in this respect, and from the rapid change or extinction they are undergoing, may ever remain so. It would be yet more unwarranted to set down every tribe mentioned in history, or known to us by the discovery of antiquarian relics, as necessarily having passed the defined minimum of religion. Greater still would be the unwisdom of declaring such a rudimentary belief natural or instinctive in all human tribes of all times; for no evidence justifies the opinion that man, known to be capable of so vast an intellectual development, cannot have emerged from a non-religious condition, previous to that religious condition in which he happens at present to come with sufficient clearness within our range of knowledge. It is desirable, however, to take our basis of enquiry in observation rather than from speculation. Here, so far as I can judge from the

[16] O. Dapper: *Description de l'Afrique,* p. 325 (1686).

immense mass of accessible evidence, we have to admit that the belief in spiritual beings appears among all low races with whom we have attained to thoroughly intimate acquaintance; whereas the assertion of absence of such belief must apply either to ancient tribes, or to more or less imperfectly described modern ones. The exact bearing of this state of things on the problem of the origin of religion may be thus briefly stated. Were it distinctly proved that non-religious savages exist or have existed, these might be at least plausibly claimed as representatives of the condition of Man before he arrived at the religious state of culture. It is not desirable, however, that this argument should be put forward, for the asserted existence of the non-religious tribes in question rests, as we have seen, on evidence often mistaken and never conclusive. The argument for the natural evolution of religious ideas among mankind is not invalidated by the rejection of an ally too weak at present to give effectual help. Non-religious tribes may not exist in our day, but the fact bears no more decisively on the development of religion, than the impossibility of finding a modern English village without scissors or books or lucifer-matches bears on the fact that there was a time when no such things existed in the land.

I propose here, under the name of Animism, to investigate the deep-lying doctrine of Spiritual Beings, which embodies the very essence of Spiritualistic as opposed to Materialistic philosophy. Animism is not a new technical term, though now seldom used.[1] From its special relation to the doctrine of the soul, it will be seen to have a peculiar appropriateness to the view here taken of the mode in which theological ideas have been developed among mankind. The word Spiritualism, though it may be, and sometimes is, used in a general sense, has this obvious defect to us, that it has become the designation of a particular modern sect, who indeed hold extreme spiritualistic views, but cannot be taken as typical

[1] The term has been especially used to denote the doctrine of Stahl, the promulgator also of the phlogiston-theory. The Animism of Stahl is a revival and development in modern scientific shape of the classic theory identifying vital principle and soul. See his "Theoria Medica Vera," Halle, 1737; and the critical dissertation on his views, Lemoine, "Le Vitalisme et l'Animisme de Stahl," Paris, 1864.

representatives of these views in the world at large. The sense of Spiritualism in its wider acceptation, the general belief in spiritual beings, is here given to Animism.

Animism characterizes tribes very low in the scale of humanity, and thence ascends, deeply modified in its transmission, but from first to last preserving an unbroken continuity, into the midst of high modern culture. Doctrines adverse to it, so largely held by individuals or schools, are usually due not to early lowness of civilization, but to later changes in the intellectual course, to divergence from, or rejection of, ancestral faiths; and such newer developments do not affect the present enquiry as to the fundamental religious condition of mankind. Animism is, in fact, the groundwork of the Philosophy of Religion, from that of savages up to that of civilized men. And although it may at first sight seem to afford but a bare and meagre definition of a minimum of religion, it will be found practically sufficient; for where the root is, the branches will generally be produced. It is habitually found that the theory of Animism divides into two great dogmas, forming parts of one consistent doctrine; first, concerning souls of individual creatures, capable of continued existence after the death or destruction of the body; second, concerning other spirits, upward to the rank of powerful deities. Spiritual beings are held to affect or control the events of the material world, and man's life here and hereafter; and it being considered that they hold intercourse with men, and receive pleasure or displeasure from human actions, the belief in their existence leads naturally, and it might almost be said inevitably, sooner or later to active reverence and propitiation. Thus Animism in its full development, includes the belief in souls and in a future state, in controlling deities and subordinate spirits, these doctrines practically resulting in some kind of active worship. One great element of religion, that moral element which among the higher nations forms its most vital part, is indeed little represented in the religion of the lower races. It is not that these races have no moral sense or no moral standard, for both are strongly marked among them, if not in formal precept, at least in that traditional consensus of society which we call public opinion, according to which certain actions are held to be good or bad, right or wrong. It is that the conjunction of ethics and Animistic philosophy, so intimate and powerful in the higher culture, seems scarcely yet to have begun in the lower. I propose here hardly to touch upon the purely moral aspects of religion, but rather to study the animism of the world so far as it constitutes, as unquestionably it does constitute, an ancient and world-wide philosophy, of which belief is the theory and worship is the practice. Endeavouring to shape the materials for an enquiry hitherto strangely undervalued and neglected, it will now be my task to bring as clearly as may be into view the fundamental animism of the lower races, and in some slight and broken outline to trace its course into higher regions of civilization. Here let me state once for all two principal conditions under which the present research is carried on. First, as to the religious doctrines and practices examined, these are treated as belonging to theological systems devised by human reason, without supernatural aid or revelation; in other words, as being developments of Natural Religion. Second, as to the connexion between similar ideas and rites in the religions of the savage and the civilized world. While dwelling at some length on doctrines and ceremonies of the lower races, and sometimes particularizing for special reasons the related doctrines and ceremonies of the higher nations, it has not seemed my proper task to work out in detail the problems thus suggested among the philosophies and creeds of Christendom. Such applications, extending farthest from the direct scope of a work on primitive culture, are briefly stated in general terms, or touched in slight allusion, or taken for granted without remark. Educated readers possess the information required to work out their general bearing on theology, while more technical discussion is left to philosophers and theologians specially occupied with such arguments.

The first branch of the subject to be considered is the doctrine of human and other Souls, an examination of which will occupy the rest of the present chapter. What the doctrine of the soul is among the lower races, may be explained in stating the animistic theory of its development. It seems as though thinking men, as yet at a low level of culture, were deeply impressed by two groups of biological problems. In the first place, what is it that makes the difference between a living body and a dead one; what causes waking, sleep.

trance, disease, death? In the second place, what are those human shapes which appear in dreams and visions? Looking at these two groups of phenomena, the ancient savage philosophers probably made their first step by the obvious inference that every man has two things belonging to him, namely, a life and a phantom. These two are evidently in close connexion with the body, the life as enabling it to feel and think and act, the phantom as being its image or second self; both, also, are perceived to be things separable from the body, the life as able to go away and leave it insensible or dead, the phantom as appearing to people at a distance from it. The second step would seem also easy for savages to make, seeing how extremely difficult civilized men have found it to unmake. It is merely to combine the life and the phantom. As both belong to the body, why should they not also belong to one another, and be manifestations of one and the same soul? Let them then be considered as united, and the result is that well-known conception which may be described as an apparitional-soul, a ghost-soul. This, at any rate, corresponds with the actual conception of the personal soul or spirit among the lower races, which may be defined as follows: It is a thin unsubstantial human image, in its nature a sort of vapour, film, or shadow; the cause of life and thought in the individual it animates; independently possessing the personal consciousness and volition of its corporeal owner, past or present; capable of leaving the body far behind, to flash swiftly from place to place; mostly impalpable and invisible, yet also manifesting physical power, and especially appearing to men waking or asleep as a phantasm separate from the body of which it bears the likeness; continuing to exist and appear to men after the death of that body; able to enter into, possess, and act in the bodies of other men, of animals, and even of things. Though this definition is by no means of universal application, it has sufficient generality to be taken as a standard, modified by more or less divergence among any particular people. Far from these world-wide opinions being arbitrary or conventional products, it is seldom even justifiable to consider their uniformity among distant races as proving communication of any sort. They are doctrines answering in the most forcible way to the plain evidence of men's senses, as interpreted by a fairly consistent and rational primitive philosophy. So well, indeed, does primitive animism account for the facts of nature, that it has held its place into the higher levels of education. Though classic and mediæval philosophy modified it much, and modern philosophy has handled it yet more unsparingly, it has so far retained the traces of its original character, that heirlooms of primitive ages may be claimed in the existing psychology of the civilized world. Out of the vast mass of evidence, collected among the most various and distant races of mankind, typical details may now be selected to display the earlier theory of the soul, the relation of the parts of this theory, and the manner in which these parts have been abandoned, modified, or kept up, along the course of culture.

To understand the popular conceptions of the human soul or spirit, it is instructive to notice the words which have been found suitable to express it. The ghost or phantasm seen by the dreamer or the visionary is an unsubstantial form, like a shadow or reflexion, and thus the familiar term of the *shade* comes in to express the soul. Thus the Tasmanian word for the shadow is also that for the spirit;[2] the Algonquins describe a man's soul as *otahchuk,* "his shadow";[3] the Quiché language uses *natub* for "shadow, soul";[4] the Arawak *ueja* means "shadow, soul, image";[5] the Abipones made the one word *loákal* serve for "shadow, soul, echo, image." [6] The Zulus not only use the word *tunzi* for "shadow, spirit, ghost," but they consider that at death the shadow of a man will in some way depart from the corpse, to become an ancestral spirit.[7] The Basutos not only call the spirit remaining after death the *seriti* or "shadow," but they think that if a man walks on the river bank, a crocodile may seize his shadow in the water and draw him in;[8] while in Old Calabar there is found the same identification of the spirit with the *ukpon* or "shadow," for a man to lose which is fatal.[9] There are

[2] Bonwick, "Tasmanians," p. 182.
[3] Tanner's "Narr." p. 291, Cree atchâk =.soul.
[4] Brasseur, "Langue Quichée," s.v.
[5] Martius, "Ethnog. Amer." vol. i. p. 705; vol. ii. p. 310.
[6] Dobrizhoffer, "Abipones," vol. ii. p. 194.
[7] Döhne, "Zulu Dic." s.v. "tunzi"; Callaway, "Rel. of Amazulu," pp. 91, 126; "Zulu Tales," vol. i. p. 342.
[8] Casalis, "Basutos," p. 245; Arbousset and Daumas, "Voyage," p. 12.
[9] Goldie, "Efik Dictionary," s.v.; see Kölle, "Afr. Native Lit." p. 324 (Kanuri). Also "Journ. Ind. Archip." vol. v. p. 713 (Australian).

thus found among the lower races not only the types of those familiar classic terms, the *skia* and *umbra,* but also what seems the fundamental thought of the stories of shadowless men still current in the folklore of Europe, and familiar to modern readers in Chamisso's tale of Peter Schlemihl. Thus the dead in Purgatory knew that Dante was alive when they saw that, unlike theirs, his figure cast a shadow on the ground.[10] Other attributes are taken into the notion of soul or spirit, with especial regard to its being the cause of life. Thus the Caribs, connecting the pulses with spiritual beings, and especially considering that in the heart dwells man's chief soul, destined to a future heavenly life, could reasonably use the one word *iouanni* for "soul, life, heart." [11] The Tongans supposed the soul to exist throughout the whole extension of the body, but particularly in the heart. On one occasion, the natives were declaring to a European that a man buried months ago was nevertheless still alive. "And one, endeavouring to make me understand what he meant, took hold of my hand, and squeezing it said, 'This will die, but the life that is within you will never die'; with his other hand pointing to my heart." [12] So the Basutos say of a dead man that his heart is gone out, and of one recovering from sickness that his heart is coming back.[13] This corresponds to the familiar Old World view of the heart as the prime mover in life, thought, and passion. The connexion of soul and blood, familiar to the Karens and Papuas, appears prominently in Jewish and Arabic philosophy.[14] To educated moderns the idea of the Macusi Indians of Guiana may seem quaint, that although the body will decay, "the man in our eyes" will not die, but wander about.[15] Yet the association of personal animation with the pupil of the eye is familiar to European folklore, which not unreasonably discerned a sign of bewitchment or approaching death in the disappearance of the image, pupil, or baby, from the dim eyeballs of the sick man.[16]

---

[10] Dante, "Div. Comm. Purgatorio," canto iii. Compare Grohmann, "Aberglauben aus Böhmen," p. 221. (See *ante,* p. 85.)

[11] Rochefort, pp. 429, 516; J. G. Müller, p. 207.

[12] Mariner, "Tonga Is." vol. ii. p. 135; S. S. Farmer, "Tonga," &c. p. 131.

[13] Casalis, l.c. See also Mariner, ibid.

[14] Bastian, "Psychologie," pp. 15–23.

[15] J. H. Bernau, "Brit. Guiana," p. 134.

[16] Grimm, "D. M." pp. 1028, 1133. Anglo-Saxon *man-lica.*

DOROTHY LEE

Being and Value in Primitive Society

The Trobrianders are concerned with being, and being alone. Change and becoming are foreign to their thinking. An object or event is grasped and evaluated in terms of itself alone, that is, irrespective of other beings. The Trobriander can describe being for the benefit of the ethnographer; otherwise, he usually refers to it by a word, one word only. All being, to be significant, must be Trobriand being, and therefore experienced at the appropriate time as a matter of course by the members of each Trobriand community; to describe it would be redundant. Being is never defined, in our sense of the word. Definition presents an object in terms of *what it is like* and *what it is unlike,* that is, in terms of its distinguishing characteristics. The Trobriander is interested only in *what it is.* And each event or being is grasped timelessly; in our terms, it contains its past, present, and future, but these distinctions are nonexistent for the Trobriander. There is, however, one sense in which being is not self-contained. To be, it must be part of an ordained pattern; this aspect will be elaborated below.

Being is discrete and self-contained; it has no attributes outside of itself. Its qualities are identical with it and without them it is not itself. It has no predicate; it is itself. To say a word representing an object or act is to imply the existence of this, and all the qualities it incorporates. If I were to go with a Trobriander to a garden where the taytu, a species of yam, had just been harvested, I would come back and tell you: "There are good taytu there; just the right degree of ripeness, large and perfectly shaped; not a blight to be seen, not one rotten spot; nicely rounded at the tips, with no spiky points; all first-run harvesting, no second gleanings." The Trobriander would come back and say "Taytu"; and he would have said all that I did and more. Even the phrase "There are taytu" would represent a tautology, since existence is implied in being, is, in fact an ingredient of being to the Trobriander. And all the attributes, even if he could find words for them at hand in his own language, would have been tautological, since the concept of taytu contains them all. In fact, if one of these were absent, the object would not have been a taytu. Such a tuber, if it is not at the proper harvesting ripeness, is not a taytu. If it is unripe, it is a bwanawa; if overripe, spent, it is not a spent taytu but something else, a yowana. If it is blighted it is a nukunokuna. If it has a rotten patch, it is a taboula; if misshapen, it is an usasu; if perfect in shape but small, it is a yagogu. If the tuber, whatever its shape or condition, is a post-harvest gleaning, it is an ulumadala. When the spent tuber, the yowana, sends its shoots underground, as we would put it, it is not a yowana with shoots, but a silisata. When new tubers have formed on these shoots, it is not a silisata but a gadena. An object can not change an attribute and retain its identity. Some range of growth or modification within being is probably allowed, otherwise speech would be impossible; but I doubt whether they are conscious of it. As soon as such change, if we may introduce one of our concepts here, is officially recognized, the object ceases to be itself.

As being is identical with the object, there is no word for *to be;* as being is changeless, there is no word meaning *to become*. Becoming involves temporality, but Trobriand being has no reference to time. With us, change in time is a value, and place in a developmental sequence is necessary for evaluation. We can not respond with approval or disapproval, unless we know that a thing is getting bigger or better or surer. If I am told that Robert Smith is an instructor at $3000, I can not respond to this adequately, unless I know that he is just out of graduate school, or that he used to be a professor at the age of forty, but now, at sixty, he has been demoted to this position. Our language is full of terms such as the one I have just used—demotion—giving us tools for the evaluation of being in terms of place in a climactic historical sequence. By dint of constant vigilance, we can refrain from using these terms; but we have no choice when it comes to placing events in time. Our language codifies reality in such a way as to predispose us to view events in terms of temporality. Even if I decide to use such expressions as "it be" or "it flow," I have achieved nothing, since you who hear me automatically make these acceptable to yourself by translating them into "it is" and "it flows," merely putting me down as uneducated. Whenever I make an assertion, I have to give it temporal limits, in reference to past, present, or future, or at any rate I have to imply temporality. Trobriand verbs are timeless, making no temporal distinctions. A Trobriander can, if he chooses, refer to an act as completed, but that, it seems to me, is an aspect of the act, not a temporal reference. History and mythical reality are not "the past" to the Trobriander. They are forever present, participating in all current being, giving meaning to all his activities and all existence. A Trobriander will speak of the garden which his mother's brother planted, or the one which the mythical Tudava planted, in exactly the same terms with which he will refer to the garden which he himself is planting now; and it will give him satisfaction to do so.

Being is evaluated discretely, in terms of itself alone, not in comparison with others. This, again, is foreign to our thinking, except perhaps in the sphere of art. To return to Robert Smith, if you tell me that he is an instructor at $3000 a year, I can respond to this with approbation, commiseration, etc., only if I know what the rank and pay of other men instructors are apt to be. To evaluate, I have to compare this being with other beings of its kind. To be good, being has to be as good as, if not better than. For the Trobriander, being is good only as itself.

Now our own language makes it easy, though not imperative, to compare beings at every turn. It provides us with a large number of comparatives, through morphology and vocabulary. Our speech is studded with terms such as better, bigger, inferior, average, compared to, normal, equal, in relation to, etc., showing that we constantly are passing judgment according to a comparative standard. The Trobriander has no such means, unless we accept his rarely used words "it-sames" and "it-differents" as comparative. The magic formulas given by Malinowski are full of similes, as only in this way can they be made comprehensible to his readers. But in Trobriand, these are all metaphors. Where Malinowski's translation reads, for example, "thy shoots are as quick as the eyes of the black ant," the Trobriand text reads, "no thine eye, thine eye black-ant."

When Malinowski says, "I am your senior" the Trobriand text reads, "old man I."

We can see this emphasis on *being* alone when we analyze the Trobriand sentence. Here we find that the words are presented discretely, without elements to show the relation of one word to the other. A verb contains its subject, a noun contains its "predicate" as well as its other attributes. The few words which Malinowski translated as adjectives are either nouns—a big-one, or verbs—it-goods. The language does not even express an object-to-object relationship, as ours does, for example, when it relates grammatical subject to the object which is acted upon. In English, we express this relationship through word order; when we say, for example, "Mary ate the pie," or, "John kicked Mary," we clearly distinguish the actor from the one acted upon, by order of precedence, and we can not avoid making the distinction. The Trobriander, on the other hand, merely expresses act and participants; "i-wo-ye tau" "it-beat-man" means either that the man is beating someone or that someone is beating the man. Such a phrase usually refers either to a known situation, which needs no elucidation, or is told within a context which makes its meaning clear. If, however, the Trobriander for some reason feels that he must specify, he can do so; but he does not do so as a matter of course, as we do, since his language does not predispose or constrain him to do so.

To be, an object must be true to itself, not in terms of its relationship with other beings. To be good, it must be the same always. Sameness is a value to the Trobrianders. Trobriand being never came into existence; it has always been, exactly as now, above ground in "historic" [1] times, below ground in mythical times. At some time the ancestress of each group emerged from a specific hole, bringing with her all the customs, skills, and beliefs of that group, their patterns of behavior, the details of their magic, their pedigreed yams. This "past" is immanent in all Trobriand being. Instead of description in terms of attributes, the Trobriander gives an account of historical or mythical past, presenting essence. In all his under-

---

[1] I use quotation marks for terms which we, from the point of view of our own culture, would apply; terms which would otherwise require cumbersome qualification whenever they appear.

takings, this "past" is present, giving to them validity and value. Wherever he goes, his surroundings have meaning for him; every waterhole, rock, or cleft is imbued with mythical significance. Myth and history, as intrinsic to being, enhance value. For example, the Trobrianders have certain important valuables which constitute the gifts in the *kula,* an endless circular series of ceremonial gift-givings which occupies, with the preparation involved, perhaps half the life of Trobriand men. These objects have value, but no "utility"; they are "ornaments" which can not be used to adorn the "owner"; and they can be possessed only a few months by each recipient. Giving-in-itself, that is, non-purposive giving, is good; through participation in this gift-giving pattern the kula valuables are good. Each valuable is named and its personal history known. In this lies much of its value; giver and recipient, and even the village of the "owner," get satisfaction out of the recounting of the specific kula acts of which the article was a part, going from named giver to named recipient. Chronology and historical sequence are irrelevant; the history is important not as development but as the ingredient of being.

The Trobriander has no word for history. When he wants to distinguish between different kinds of occasions, he will say, for example, "Molubabeba in-child-his," that is, "in the childhood of Molubabeba," not a previous phase of *this* time, but a different kind of time. For him, history is an unordered repository of anecdote; he is not interested in chronological sequence. For example, Malinowski recorded an account of a famine which was given with complete disregard to chronology; an effect which is achieved only deliberately by our sophisticated writers. If we rearrange the clusters of statements so that they represent for us a historical sequence, we have to give them in the following order: one, four, three, two, five.

For us, chronological sequence is of vital importance, largely because we are interested not so much in the event itself, but rather in its place within a *related* series of events; we look for its antecedents and its consequences. We are concerned with the causal or telic relationship between events or acts. To the Trobriander, events do not fall of themselves into a pattern of causal relationships, as they do for us. I am not here concerned with the question of whether causality is given, or is read into existence. Whichever may be the case, we in our culture automatically see and seek relationships, not essence, and express relationship mainly in terms of cause or purpose. The maddeningly persistent question of our young children is "why," because this is the question implicit in most of our ordinary statements and other behavior,[2] to be answered either in causal or telic terms, since cause and purpose are equally dynamic for us, and are identified in our use of "why." Esthetically, as well as practically, cause and purpose are both important to us; cause gives us a satisfying explanation and purpose ennobles or gives meaning to the act. We teach the importance of purposive action to infants, directly and indirectly by act and speech. We teach it in the schoolroom, in sports, in politics, in moral precept. The unreflective scientist takes causation for granted, the orthodox historian studies history to discover the causes for events. To the Trobriander, on the other hand, being or event remains discrete, sufficient unto itself, true and of value as itself, judged and motivated and understood in terms of itself alone. In the face of this apprehension of being, concepts such as causation and purpose appear irrelevant; I have introduced them here only because they are so basic to our thinking that we accept them as given in experience, and their presence is assumed by us in all cultures, as a matter of course. In the language of the Trobrianders, there are no terms such as because, so as to, cause, reason, effect, purpose, to this end, so that, why. This does not mean that the Trobrianders are incapable of explaining a sequence in terms of cause and effect, but rather that this relationship is of no significance. In the texts given by Malinowski *for* (pela) occurs occasionally, in such a context that it is possible to translate it as *because,* as Malinowski does, and it sounds natural that one should do so; and, once or twice, what-thing-for is used in such a position that we can take it to mean *for what purpose.* It is significant that "pela" is verbal, meaning *to jump,* not a connecting link but a leap to an other. I shall not go

[2] This does not mean that Trobriand parents are relieved from such questions; they are probably constantly asked "what." According to Margaret Mead this is what the Manus children are continually asking adults.

here into a discussion of the meaning of the doubtful "pela"; I do not think it is an expression of causality, but even if it is, it occurs extremely rarely and does not contradict the conclusion that, for the Trobriander, events do not automatically fall into the mold of causality or teleology. Malinowski's frequent "why" evoked from the Trobrianders either confused and self-contradictory answers, or the usual "It was ordained of old,"—not an explanation but a description of value, tautological but necessary for the ignorant ethnographer.

We ask here, how is influence or motivation or effect phrased among the Trobrianders? How is magical action understood, for example? The answer is, it is understood in exactly these terms, as action, not cause. The magician does not *cause* certain things to be; he *does* them. As the gardener with his material implements burns the brush, breaks the clods, etc., so the garden magician with his various formulas "awakens the sprout," "drives up the shoots overground," "throws the headgear of the taytu," "makes several branches," "pushes the taytu tubers into the soil," according to Trobriand account. This is not influence, nor the force of magic; rather it is "to magic." Malinowski, in presenting accounts of magic, uses purposive phraseology, since in this way only can his readers understand magic. But where he gives in translation: The okwala rite is made so that taytu might really grow, so that it might ripen, the Trobriand has actually said: okwala, it-grow truly, it-ripen; just a number of events. It so happens, in the example, that the sequence in the account corresponds to the actual order of fact; but quite often there is not even such correspondence. And in the acts themselves there is often not even the sequence into which we could at least read causality. For example, when the Trobriander wants to fell a tree he first exorcizes the tokway, the tree-dwelling spirit, reciting a spell which gets the tokway down. After that he gives the tokway some food. If the food was offered first, on the ground, or at least promised, we could see this as a causal inducement. Actually, the tokway has no alternative and no freedom of choice at all; he is brought down by the spell. The offering of the food itself is merely part of the established procedure, and is not causally related to the exorcism.

It follows that the Trobriander performs acts because of the activity itself, not for its effects; that he values objects because they are good, not good for; in fact, objects and activities that are good for, are of no value to him. Take, for example, his yams and his yam gardening. To Malinowski, who spent many months with them, dependent upon them socially as well as materially, gardening meant yam gardening, and food meant yams. It was only after he had occupied himself with his Trobriander material for about fifteen years and written several books on the subject. that he realized that taro was an ancient and substantial item of food, much easier to grow than yams, less demanding of care and good soil, perhaps almost as important as yams from the point of view of sheer material nourishment. But taro is only good for; it is only good for food, or, less than that, for stopping hunger; and it is grown for such use. Therefore it was of no value or importance to the Trobriander, and escaped Malinowski's notice. Yams, on the other hand, incorporate the social good. They are good in themselves, and participate daily in good situations, as free, non-utile gifts.

A man gardens yams with the expenditure of much care and effort, with physical and magical skills, putting in long, hot hours of work. He gardens as many plots as he is capable of—not as many as his neighbors, or as many as he "needs." About half of these he sets aside as the urigubu plots. These he harvests with pride, exhibiting beautiful heaps of taytu. Then he sends this harvest, by festively arrayed youths and maidens, not to his yam house, but to the hamlet of his sister's husband. In this man's garden the taytu are heaped again, and it is this man now who exhibits them with pride as the gift. Finally, his yam house is put in order, and magic is performed in it. Ideally, the magic makes the taytu rot uneaten in the yam house; it fills the owners with nausea at the thought of eating the taytu; it gives them, instead, an urge to go to the bush and eat what grows there. This keeps the taytu free of purpose; ideally, they are not food. Taytu are constantly being given and received as gifts, in a system of free giving without what we call ulterior motives; not for altruism, not in barter or exchange for. Most of the gift taytu are usually eaten eventually, but only incidentally. In the urigubu gardens of the man who grew them, have remained all the tubers which are not taytu; the ones which are misshapen, or unduly small or blighted in some way. These go to the gardener's not-good yam house. They are merely to be eaten, and we do not hear of them again. The taytu, however, have a very important place in the everyday, as well as the ceremonial, life of the people. Taytu are not, like the taro, good for. Taytu have value, not use; value lies in being, not in relationship.

The pariahs among the Trobrianders are the people who barter. There is one such unfortunate district of highly skilled manufacturers who have no adequate soil for the growing of taytu. They barter manufactured articles, spending their time in this not-good occupation, but more than that, they are lacking in the growing of taytu and in pure gift-giving, that is, in good. They are greatly despised by the agricultural villages. The coastal villages also can not grow many yams, and acquire more through what seems to us an exchange of fish for yams. However, this has been patterned along gift-giving lines, and escapes the purposiveness of barter. A man of a specific interior village will have a life-long gift-partner in a fishing village. Whenever he wants to, he arrives at the fishing village with some baskets of yams, and leaves them as a gift at a specific spot. This precipitates a pattern of events which ends in his returning home with a gift of fish. He can not go to *any* village with his taytu, or to *any* man within this village; the gift to anyone else would have no meaning, neither would it induce anyone else to go fishing. His taytu were not pay or inducement, but the opening step in a specific patterned procedure involving a specific individual.

Here another aspect of Trobriand being is involved. I have spoken of being as discrete, and apprehended as itself alone. I must now qualify this statement. Being has no independent existence. It is itself only as part of an established pattern. To members of our culture, being is defined by its attributes, relationships, and functions; temporally in terms of becoming, spatially in terms of its relationships. For the Trobrianders, being is defined by a fixed place in an established pattern. It is perhaps too much to ask my readers to believe that one element in a pattern can be and is perceived only in terms of its specific position within the pattern itself, and without reference to any other element; that in fact a pattern is conceived as something other than a system of relationships. Nevertheless, I believe such to be the case among the Trobrianders. Being is not seen in terms of its relationships to a plurality of elements in the pattern, but rather as a fixed point in a single, changeless whole. Only in this place can being be itself; only as it fills its place is it desired or valued. Being is good and true in terms of pattern. Gift-giving, for example, is good only within a patterned Trobriand situation. It is neither virtuous nor altruistic; both these terms involve meaningless relational concepts. In Trobriand gift-giving, the need of the recipient, or the effect upon him, is not involved. I doubt whether the Trobrianders could be persuaded to send yams to the starving Bikinians; and even if they did send yams, their act would not have value. The harvest gift to the sister's husband is not an act of altruism. The giver is concerned only with fulfilling his rôle, his place in a specific Trobriand pattern. If he gave taro to his sister's husband, the gift would not have been good; if he gave the yams to his own brother, his act would not have been good. What is good in this situation is the *urigubu.* To be good, this gift must be urigubu; to be true, that is, to be urigubu, it must be, (*a*) a gift of taytu; (*b*) from man to sister's husband; (*c*) at harvest time. Both the good and the true are defined by place in pattern. Taytu figure as gifts upon different occasions, between different individuals. In each case the gift is named and valued differently. When taytu are given to a friend at the launching of a canoe, they follow a different procedure, and are kabigodoya; when they are a harvest gift to a specialist, they are a karibudaboda. Taytu, then, are urigubu, kabigodoya, karibudaboda, according to their place in different patterns; and each gift derives different being, and different value in accordance to the pattern in which it has place. I should explain here that in each case the taytu remain taytu though they participate in different situations; it is the gift which is different according to its place in a different pattern.

This conception of being and value gave the early pearl traders much trouble. They found out soon that money or the things they offered were no inducement to work. They noticed, however, that the Trobrianders set great store by certain large blades made of stone. At first, they had these imitated carelessly, but found that the natives did not want them; then they had them made of slate in Europe, but these also were rejected by the Trobrianders. Finally they had the native stone quarried and sent to Parisian craftsmen; but these beautiful blades also were rejected. These things, of course, could not be valued, since they were not truly Trobriand, had not been made "as ordained of old"; but more than that, they could not be an inducement, and could have no meaning, since they were external to the pattern. When the Trobrianders were finally persuaded to dive for pay, it was only the natives of those villages which had always dived for oysters who were persuaded; those of the other coastal villages, where diving had not been ordained of old, would not dive. And the natives of the appropriate villages did so grudgingly. To the disgust of the pearl traders, they would leave their diving and go off fishing for the day, as soon as a number of baskets of yams made their appearance on the beach, even though the traders offered them twenty times as many yams. The natives would work for extraneous inducement as long as there was no good undertaking to indulge in; but when their gift-partners arrived with yams, they initiated a patterned situation which had meaning for the natives.

You will say, "But is not this an inducement or cause?" I think it is not. By themselves, the few baskets of yams on the beach are just a few baskets of yams. Offered by the trader they would have had no meaning. Brought from a different Trobriand village, they would have effected nothing; and when they come from the appropriate village, it is only the partners of the specific givers who go off fishing as a matter of course. Given from anyone to anyone, the taytu are of no value. I think the yams are not an inducement to action. The giving of them, however, starts a pattern; once the gift has taken place, the pattern becomes evident and the recipient is presented with a rôle which holds value for him; to get satisfaction from it, to be a good Trobriander, he must fill it. By us, the two acts, the receiving of the yams and the procuring of the fish, are seen in relationship; and this relationship is seen as dynamic; one act influences the other, or causes the other. To the Trobriander, what is dynamic is the validity and value derived from the pattern.

HENRY CLAY TRUMBULL
Blood Brotherhood

Travelers in the heart of Africa, also, report the covenant of "blood-brotherhood," or of "strong-friendship," as in vogue among various African tribes, although naturally retaining less of primitive sacredness there than among Semites. The rite is, in some cases, observed after the manner of the Syrians, by the contracting parties tasting each other's blood; while, in other cases, it is performed by the inter-transfusion of blood between the two.

Describing the ceremony, Livingstone says: [1] "It is accomplished thus: The hands of the parties are joined [in this case Pitsane and Sambanza were the parties engaged]. Small incisions are made on the clasped hands, on the pits of the stomach of each, and on the right cheeks and foreheads. A small quantity of blood is taken off from these points, in both parties, by means of a stalk of grass. The blood from one person is put into a pot of beer, and that of the second into another; each then drinks the other's blood, and they are supposed to become perpetual friends, or relations. During the drinking of the beer, some of the party continue beating the ground with short clubs, and utter sentences by way of ratifying the treaty. The men belonging to each [principal's party] then finish the beer. The principals in the performance of 'Kasendi' are henceforth considered blood-relations, and are bound to disclose to each other any impending evil. If Sekeletu [chief of Pitsane's tribe—the Makololo—] should resolve to attack the Balonda [Sambanza's—or, more properly, Manenko's—people], Pitsane would be under obligation to give Sambanza warning to escape; and so on the other side. [The ceremony concluded in this case] they now presented each other with the most valuable presents they had to bestow. Sambanza walked off with Pitsane's suit of green baize faced with red, which had been made in Loanda; and Pitsane, besides abundant supplies of food, obtained two shells [of as great value, in regions far from the sea, 'as the Lord Mayor's badge is in London,'] similar to that

[1] See Livingstone's *Travels and Res. in So. Africa,* p. 525.

[one, which] I had received from Shinte [the uncle of Manenko]." [2]

Of the binding force of this covenant, Livingstone says further: "On one occasion I became blood-relation to a young woman by accident. She had a large cartilaginous tumor between the bones of the forearm, which, as it gradually enlarged, so distended the muscles as to render her unable to work. She applied to me to excise it. I requested her to bring her husband, if he were willing to have the operation performed, and while removing the tumor, one of the small arteries squirted some blood into my eye. She remarked, when I was wiping the blood out of it, 'You were a friend before; now you are a blood-relation; and when you pass this way always send me word, that I may cook food for you.' " [3]

Of the influence of these inter-tribal blood-friendships, in Central Africa, Dr. Livingstone speaks most favorably. Their primitive character is made the more probable, in view of the fact that he first found them existing in a region where, in his opinion, the dress and household utensils of the people are identical with those which are represented on the monuments of ancient Egypt.[4] Although it is within our own generation that this mode of covenanting in the region referred to has been made familiar to us, the rite itself is of old, elsewhere if not, indeed, there; as other travelers following in the track of Livingstone have noted and reported.

Commander Cameron, who, while in charge of the Livingstone Search Expedition, was the first European traveler to cross the whole breadth of the African continent in its central latitudes, gives several illustrations of the observance of this rite. In June, 1874, to the westward of Lake Tanganyika, Syde, a guide of Cameron, entered into this covenant of blood with Pakwanya, a local chief.

"After a certain amount of palaver," says Cameron, "Syde and Pakwanya exchanged presents, much to the advantage of the former [for, in the East, the person of higher rank is supposed to give the more costly gifts in any such exchange]; more especially [in this case] as he [Syde] borrowed the beads of me and afterward forgot

[2] See Livingstone's *Travels and Res. in So. Africa,* pp. 324 f.
[3] *Ibid.,* p. 526.
[4] *Ibid.,* p. 213.

to repay me. Pakwanya then performed a tune on his harmonium, or whatever the instrument [which he had] might be called, and the business of fraternizing was proceeded with. Pakwanya's head man acted as his sponsor, and one of my askari assumed the like office for Syde.

"The first operation consisted of making an incision on each of their right wrists, just sufficient to draw blood; a little of which was scraped off and smeared on the other's cut; after which gunpowder was rubbed in [thereby securing a permanent token on the arm]. The concluding part of the ceremony was performed by Pakwanya's sponsor holding a sword resting on his shoulder, while he who acted [as sponsor] for Syde went through the motions of sharpening a knife upon it. Both sponsors meanwhile made a speech, calling down imprecations on Pakwanya and all his relations, past, present, and future, and prayed that their graves might be defiled by pigs if he broke the brotherhood in word, thought, or deed. The same form having been gone through with, [with] respect to Syde, the sponsors changing duties, the brother-making was complete." [5]

HENRI PIERRE EUGENE HUBERT and MARCEL MAUSS

Interpretation of the Sacrificial Ceremony

It is not sufficient that the sacrificer and the priest are sanctified in order that the sacrifice may begin. The latter cannot take place anywhere at any time, for all moments of the day or of the year are not equally propitious to sacrifices; there are some which are definitely excluded. In Assyria, for instance, the 7th, 14th, and 21st of the month were forbidden days. According to the nature and object of the ceremony, the hour of celebration differed. Now it had to be during the day, now in the evening or at night. The scene of the sacrifice itself must be sacred; taking place outside a sacred spot, the sacrifice is only a murder. When the sacrifice is made in a temple or in a spot already made sacred by a previous sacrifice, the preliminary consecrations are useless or at least very much

[5] Cameron's *Across Africa,* I., 333.

reduced. That is the case with Hebrew sacrifice as it is regulated by the ritual of the Pentateuch. It is celebrated in a unique temple, consecrated in advance, chosen by the divinity and made divine by his presence.

The Hindus had no temple. Every one could choose a place where he wanted to sacrifice; but this place had to be consecrated in advance by means of a certain number of rites, the most important of which consisted in the building of fires. One of these was lighted by friction so that it would be entirely new. Under these conditions, it had a magic virtue which dispersed evil spirits and demons. But it was more than a killer of demons, it was the god himself. According to certain old Biblical legends, the fire of the sacrifice was none other than the divinity himself who devoured the victim, or to speak more exactly, it was the sign of the consecration. Whatever divinity the sacrificial fire has is communicated to the place of sacrifice and consecrates it. This place is rectangular and fairly extensive and is called *Vihara.*

Within this space is another called *vedi,* whose sacred character is still more marked; it corresponds to the altar. The vedi thus holds a position more central than the fires which surround it. The outlines of the vedi are carefully drawn on the ground; for this purpose, they take a sword of magic wood and scratch the earth lightly, saying: "The wicked one is killed." All impurity is thus destroyed; the magic circle is drawn, the place is consecrated. Within the limits of the circle, the earth is dug up; the hole constitutes the altar. After a lustration, at once expiatory and purificatory, the bottom of the hole is covered with different kinds of turf. On this turf, the gods to whom the sacrifice is made sit down; from there, invisible but present, they take part in the ceremony.

One of the most important instruments used is the yupa, the stake to which the animal is going to be tied. It is not of mundane material, but the tree out of which it has been made had already of itself a divine nature which unctions and libations have further re-enforced. It holds an eminent position because to it will be tied the most important of the members who will take part in the ceremony, namely, the victim. The Brahmans also prescribe it as one of the points where all the religious forces which take part in the sacrifice converge and concentrate. Its slender stem refers to the way in which the gods mounted to Heaven; its upper part gives power over celestial things; its middle section, power over things of the air; its lower part, power over things of the earth. But at the same time it represents the sacrificer; it is the shape of the sacrificer which determines its dimensions. When one anoints it, one anoints the sacrificer, and when one strengthens it, it is the sacrificer who is strengthened. In it operates in a stronger manner than in the priest this fusion of the gods and of the sacrificer which will become more complete in the victim.

Everything is now in order. The actors are ready. The entrance of the victim is going to begin the play. One essential character of the sacrifice must be noted: its perfect continuity. From the beginning to the end it must continue without interruption and in the ritual order. All the operations must succeed each other without a gap and in their proper places. The forces which are in action escape from the sacrificer and the priest and react terribly against them, if they are not exactly directed in the prescribed way. This exterior continuity of rites is not enough. There must be a firm constancy in the state of mind in which the sacrificer, the priest and the victim find themselves concerning the gods, the victim, and the vow whose execution is demanded. In other words, the internal attitude must correspond to the external attitude.

The Victim

A series of circles are drawn inside the sacred space. On the exterior circle stands the sacrificer; then come successively the priest, the altar and the stake. Outside the circle, among the laity in whose interest the sacrifice takes place, religiosity is at a minimum. Thus the whole life of the sacrificial performance is centered around the altar and the victim, which is now ready to be brought on the scene.

Sometimes the victim, if an animal, was congenitally sacred; that is, the species to which it belonged was united to the divinity by special ties. These cases comprise those where the victims are totemic beings or former totems. But it is not logically necessary for sacred animals to have had this totemic character. The truth is, that in some way or other there is a definite relation between the god and his victim and the latter often arrives at the altar already sacred: hence no preliminary consecrating ceremony is necessary. But generally, appropriate rites were necessary to put it into the religious state which the part it was to play required. In certain cases where it had been designated a long time in advance, these ceremonies took place before it was led to the sacrifice. Often, also, it had nothing sacred about it at the moment. It was only expected to fulfil certain conditions which would make it fit to receive consecration. It had to be without fault, sickness, infirmity and have a certain color, age, sex, according to the effects desired to be produced. To raise it to the required degree of religiosity, it had to be submitted to a collection of ceremonies.

In certain countries, they dressed it up, painted it, bleached it, ornamented the horns, put a crown on the head, decorated it with ribbons, thus giving it a religious character. Sometimes even the costume was like that of the god who presided. This demi-consecration could be obtained in other ways. In Mexico and Rhodes, the victim was intoxicated. Intoxication was a sign that the divine spirit was taking possession of the victim.

The Hindu ritual enables us to follow the whole operation of consecration. After the victim is bathed, it is brought forward while different libations are poured upon it. Then the victim is addressed, laudatory adjectives being used while it is implored to be quiet. At the same time, the god of beasts is implored to give his consent to the taking of one of his flock as a victim. These precautions, propitiations, have a double purpose. First, they make the victim sacred by calling it excellent names and declaring it to be the property of the gods. They serve especially to induce the victim to allow itself to be sacrificed peaceably, not to avenge itself once dead on man. These usages do not mean, as has been said, that the sacrificed animal is always a former totemic animal. The explanation is nearer. There is in the victim a spirit which it is the object of the sacrifice to liberate. This spirit must be conciliated; otherwise, once freed, it would become dangerous.

The victim is now tied to the stake. At this moment, the *sacred* character which it is in process of acquiring is already such that the sacrificer can no longer touch it; even the attending priest hesitates to approach it. He has to be invited and encouraged by a special formula which a priest addresses to him. Nevertheless, to increase to the last limit this religious character which is already high, three series of rites are necessary. The animal is made to drink water, for water is divine; it is brushed underneath, on the back, everywhere. Then it is anointed with butter on the head, throat, two shoulders, croup and between both horns. These anointments correspond to those which were made with oil in the Hebrew sacrifice, to the cermony of *molasalsa* in Rome, to the grains which were thrown on the animal in Greece. Finally, after these lustrations and anointments there comes, in the vedi ritual a last ceremony which has for its purpose the enclosing of the victim itself in a last magic circle, smaller and more divine than the others. A priest takes a brand from the fire of the gods and carrying it in his hand circles the animal three times. In India they would thus walk around all victims, with or without fire; it was the god Agni who was surrounding the animal on all sides, making it sacred, isolating it.

But the victim must still maintain relations with man. The means employed to insure this communication is furnished in the religion which we are studying, through the principles of magic and religious sympathy. Sometimes there is direct representation; a father is represented by his son whom he is sacrificing. In general the sacrificer having undertaken to defray the expense of sacrifice, is, ipso facto, a representation. In other cases, this association of victim and sacrificer is realized by a material contact between the sacrificer (sometimes the priest) and the victim. This contact is obtained, in the Semitic ritual, by the imposition of hands or equivalent rites. As a result, the victim already representing the gods, is also found to represent the sacrificer. More than that, their personalities fuse. Even the identity is such, at least in the Hindu sacrifice, that from now on, its approaching death has a kind of reacting effect upon the sacrificer. Hence an ambiguous situation arises for the latter. He has to touch the animal in order to stay united with it; nevertheless, he is afraid to touch it, for he thereby exposes himself to death. The ritual solves the difficulty by a middle road. The sacrificer touches the victim only through the intermediary of the priest who himself in turn touches the victim only through the intermediary of an instrument.

The culminating point of the ceremony has now been reached. There remains only the supreme act. The victim is already sacred in the highest degree. But the spirit which is inside it, the divine principle it contains, is still attached to the body and remains as the last tie binding it to things profane. Death is going to disengage it. It is the solemn moment.

It is a crime that is about to begin, a kind of sacrilege. So while the victim is being led to the place of murder, certain libations and expiations are presented in the rituals. They ask forgiveness for the act, they weep for it as if it were a relative. They ask its pardon before striking it. They address the species to which it belongs as if it were a vast familiar clan whom they supplicate not to take revenge for the injury about to be committed on one of its members. Under the influence of the same ideas, it happened that the author of the murder was punished; they struck him or exiled him. In Athens, the priest at the sacrifice of the *Bouphonia* fled as he threw away his hatchet; all those who had taken part accused each other; finally they condemned the knife and threw it into the sea.

Also absolute quiet prevails immediately before death. In India the priests turn around; the sacrificer and the officiating priest turn around murmuring propitiatory verses. Nothing can be heard but the orders given in a clear voice by the priest to the sacrificateur. The latter then severs the cord which surrounds the throat of the animal; the victim is dead; the spirit has departed.

The rites of the murder were extremely varied. But each cult required that they be scrupulously observed. To change them was generally a black heresy punishable by excommunication and death. The fact is that by the murder, an ambiguous or blind force was leased, formidable because of the very fact that it was a force. It therefore had to be limited, directed and deified. Hence the rites. Generally the neck of the victim was cut. Slashing was an ancient rite which in Judea appeared only in cases of penal execution, and in Greece in certain feasts. Elsewhere the victim was smothered or hanged. Generally a prompt death was desired. If the cries of the animal were accounted bad omens, they tried to stifle them or conjure them away. Often they tried to regulate the flowing of the consecrated blood. They saw to it that it fell in a propitious spot or else that not a drop of it was scattered. Sometimes these precautions were indifferently taken. In Arcadia, Greece, the rite commanded that the victim be cut into pieces; interest might be taken in prolonging the agony. The slow as well as rapid death could diminish the responsibility of the sacrificateur. The rites were more simple when grain or cakes were sacrificed.

By this distinction, the essential act of the sacrifice was accomplished. The victim was separated definitely from the profane world; it was consecrated, sacrificed, and various languages applied the term sanctification to the act which put it in this state. But the phenomenon had also another aspect. If on the one hand the spirit had flown away, had gone completely behind the veil into the world of gods; on the other hand, the body of the animal remained visible and tangible; and it was also, by the act of consecration, filled with a sacred force which isolated it from the profane world. Its remains were surrounded with a religious aspect, and were now subject to a double series of operations. What was left of the animal was either allotted entirely to the sacred world, or to the profane world, or shared between the two.

ERNEST CRAWLEY

Eating in Privacy

We have now arrived at the prohibition against eating with certain persons, and the associated predilection for eating alone, as he prefers to be alone for the performance of other functions, from egoistic caution and fear of interruption. [We may begin with general rules and customs in this connection, pass on to special regulations in which the person with whom commensal relations are forbidden is specified, and of these bring together finally such as are connected with sexual taboo.

First, then, we have a few examples of the neurasthenic obsession, as we would now call it,[1] for eating alone.] The Karayas always eat

[1] See, F. Raymond *and* P. Janet, *Les obsessions et la psychasténie* (1903), ii. 386.

by themselves, with back turned.[2] Similarly amongst the Bakairi, who were "ashamed" when a European ate in their presence.[3] The Fijians consider it objectionable, just as we do, for several persons to drink out of the same vessel.[4] In some parts of Polynesia a man will never eat with another out of the same basket.[5] The Zafimanelos of Madagascar eat alone with locked doors.[6] [The Warua of Central Aırica put a cloth before their faces when drinking, and would not allow anyone to see them eating or drinking; in consequence every man and woman has a separate fire and does his or her own cooking.] [7] It is extremely unusual for Nubians and the Niam-Niam to take any meals in common.[8] Among the latter people, should they however drink together, they may be observed to wipe the rim of the cup before passing it on.[9] On the Loango coast, among numerous restrictions upon food, occurs a prohibition against eating in company with others.[10]

[Passing now to a series of cases in which the prohibition against commensal relations refers to a specific person, we have first a group in which that person is one superior (or inferior, according to the point of view) in rank to oneself.] The Maori gentleman eats in solitude.[11] In New Zealand a slave, therefore, may not eat with his master, nor even eat of the same food or cook at the same fire.[12] On one occasion a slave ate his chief's dinner by mistake; when told of what he had done, and when he realised that he had a tabooed person's "sacredness," [13] he was seized with convulsions and cramp in the stomach, and died at sundown.[14] In Tonga there are ranks

[2] K. von den Steinen, *Unter den Naturvölkern Zentralbrasiliens* (1894), p. 67.

[3] *Ibid.*, p. 66.

[4] C. Wilkes, *Narrative of the United States Exploring Expedition during the Years 1838–42* (1845), iii. 349.

[5] E. Dieffenbach, *Travels in New Zealand* (1843), ii. 43–44.

[6] *Antananarivo Annual*, ii. 219.

[7] —Cameron, "The Anthropology of Africa," *J.A.I.* (1877), vi. 173.

[8] G. Schweinfurth, *The Heart of Africa* (1873), i. 447.

[9] *Ibid.*, ii. 19.

[10] A. Bastian, *Die deutsche Expedition an die Loango-Küste* (1874–1875), i. 172.

[11] W. Yate, *An Account of New Zealand* (1835), p. 20.

[12] E. Shortland, *Traditions and Superstitions of the New Zealanders* (1854), p. 106.

[13] *Id.*, *Maori Religion and Mythology* (1832), p. 26.

[14] [F. E. Maning], *Old New Zealand* (1863), p. 114.

and orders that can neither eat nor drink together,[15] for here inferiors and superiors may not have commensal relations.[16] The Tuitonga may not eat in the presence of older members of his family.[17] If a native of Tonga has touched a superior chief or anything belonging to him, he may not feed himself with his own hands. Should he do so, he will infallibly swell up and die.[18] Still in Tonga, no one may see the king eat; therefore those present turn their backs upon him. Nor may one eat in his presence without averting the face.[19] Indeed, it is also forbidden to eat in the presence of a superior relation without turning the back.[20] In the Sandwich Islands no one could eat with the chief, who was "sacred." [21] In Fiji anyone who has touched a chief, living or dead, becomes taboo; he cannot handle food, but must be fed by others. Hence barbers are continually in this case.[22] The food of a Fijian chief may not be carried by boys who have not been tattooed, lest the meat be rendered "unclean," boys being "unclean" until then.[23] In Uripiv of the New Hebrides the males are divided into ten "castes" corresponding to age in life; promotion is marked by a change of name. The members of each "caste" mess together and may not eat with others. Unmarried mess-mates also sleep together.[24] Amongst the Alfoers of Celebes the priest who is responsible for the growth of the rice may not during his office eat or drink with anyone, nor drink out of another's cup.[25] It is forbidden in Wetar to eat or drink anything out of vessels used by the chiefs.[26]

[15] W. Mariner, *An Account of Natives of the Tonga Islands* (1817), ii. 234.

[16] J. S. C. Dumont d'Urville, *Voyage pittoresque autour du monde* (1834–1835), ii. 77.

[17] *Ibid.*, ii. 77.

[18] W. Mariner, *op. cit.*, i. 150; ii. 80.

[19] *Ibid.*, ii. 235.

[20] J. Cook, *A Voyage to the Pacific Ocean* (1784), i. 232.

[21] C. de Varigny, *Quatorze ans aux Iles Sandwich* (1874), p. 13.

[22] J. E. Erskine, *Journal of a Cruise among the Islands of the Western Pacific* (1853), p. 254.

[23] J. S. C. Dumont d'Urville, *op. cit.*, i. 166.

[24] B. T. Somerville, "Notes on some Islands of the New Hebrides," *J.A.I.* (1894), xxiii. 6–7.

[25] W. Hoezoo, "Over het doen overkomen van inlanders naar Nederland," *Nededeelingen van wege bet Nederlandsche Zendelinggenoetschap* (1867), xi. 126.

[26] J. G. F. Riedel, *De sluik-en kroesbarige rassen tusschen Selebes en Papua* (1886), p. 455.

In Cambodia people will not eat with a priest.[27] In Burma one is defiled by sitting or eating with the "impure" caste of Sandalas.[28] In Ceylon, under the Kandyan dynasty, a lady was degraded from her caste by a low-caste Rodiya transferring betel from his own mouth to hers; the degradation was considered indelible. There were two lower castes than the Rodiyas, who were so despised that no human being would touch rice cooked in their houses.[29] The ancient Brahmin who ate the food of "outcasts" became thereby an "outcast" himself.[30] In modern India still "eating together is one of the grand tests of identity of caste." [31] Members of different castes will not eat food cooked in the same vessel; if a person of another caste touches a cooking vessel, it must be thrown away.[32] Further, a Hindu must take precautions "to insulate himself, as it were, during his meal, lest he be contaminated by the touch of some undetected sinner who may be present.[33] On the other hand, the Santals hate the Hindus, and will not receive food from their hands.[34] The Pahrias regard themselves as superior to the Keriahs, with whom they may neither eat nor drink.[35] If anyone ate the Mikado's food, his mouth would swell up and death would ensue.[36] A carved and gilt wooden screen was always placed in front of Montezuma at his meals, that no one might see him while eating.[37]

The King of Susa at meals is concealed by a curtain from his guests.[38] In Ashanti a man of consequence never drinks before his inferiors without hiding his face from them. The belief is that an enemy can then "impose a spell on the faculties" of the man who

---

[27] É. Aymonier, "Note sur les coutumes et croyances superstitieuses des Cambodgiens," *Cochinchine française* (1887), vi. 170.

[28] J. S. C. Dumont d'Urville, *op. cit.,* i 173.

[29] Sir J. E. Tennent, *Ceylon* (1860), ii. 189.

[30] *The Laws of Manu,* xi. 176, 181; W. Ward, *A View of the History, Literature, and Religion of the Hindoos* (1817–1820), ii. 149.

[31] S. Mateer, *Native Life in Travancore* (1883), p. 331.

[32] W. Ward, *op. cit.,* ii. 317.

[33] H. T. Colebrooke, "The Religious Ceremonies of the Hindus," *Asiatick Researches* (1801), vii. 277.

[34] H. B. Rowney, *The Wild Tribes of India* (1882), p. 74.

[35] V. Ball, *Jungle Life in India* (1880), p. 89.

[36] J. S. C. Dumont d'Urville, *op. cit.,* i. 386.

[37] H. H. Bancroft, *The Native Races of the Pacific States of North America* (1875–1876), iii. 129.

[38] Sir W. C. Harnis, *The Highlands of Æthiopia* (1844), iii. 78.

is drinking.[39] In Dahomey it is death to see the king eat; if he drinks in public, a curtain is held up to conceal him.[40] Amongst the Niam-Niam the king takes his meals in private; no one may see the contents of his dish and everything that he leaves is carefully thrown into a pit set apart for the purpose. All that he handles is held as "sacred," and may not be touched; and a guest, though of higher rank, may not so much as light his pipe with embers from the king's fire.[41] The King of Congo eats and drinks in secret. If a dog should enter the house while the king is at table, it is killed. On one occasion the king's son, having accidentally seen his father drinking, was executed on the spot.[42] A crier proclaimed when the King of Cacongo was about to eat or drink, that the people might cover their faces or fall to the ground with down-turned eyes.[43] In Loango the king is sacred; from his birth he is forbidden to eat with anyone, and various foods are prohibited to him. He eats and drinks alone, in huts devoted to the purpose. The covered dishes containing his food are preceded by a crier, at whose proclamation all get out of the way and bolt their doors; for any person seeing the king eat is put to death. A privileged few may be present, but they are bound to conceal their faces, or the king places a robe over his head. All that leaves his table is at once buried.[44] The black Jews of Loango are so despised that no one will eat with them.[45] A Pongo chief never drinks in the presence of others without a screen to conceal him;[46] on the Pongo coast it is believed that no one is more liable to witchcraft than when eating, drinking or sleeping.[47] When the King of Canna was offered a glass of rum by Mr. Winwoode Reade, he hid his face and the glass under a Turkish

---

[39] T. E. Bowdich, *Mission from Cape Coast Castle to Ashanti* (1819), p. 438.

[40] J. L. Wilson, *Western Africa* (1856), p. 202; W. W. Reade, *Savage Africa* (1863), p. 53; Sir R. F. Burton, *A Mission to Gelele, King of Dahomey* (1864), i. 244.

[41] G. Schweinfurth, *op. cit.*, ii. 98.

[42] W. W. Reade, *op. cit.*, p. 359.

[43] A. Bastian, *Ein Besuch in San Salvador* (1859), p. 58.

[44] A. Bastian, *Die deutsche Expedition an die Loango-Küste* (1874–1875), i. 220, 262–263.

[45] *Ibid.*, i. 278.

[46] J. L. Wilson, *op. cit.*, p. 308.

[47] *Ibid.*, p. 310.

towel.[48] The King of the Monbuttu always takes his meals in private, and no one may see the contents of his dish.[49] The King of Abyssinia always dines alone.[50]

EDWARD SAPIR

The Unconscious Patterning of Behavior in Society

We may seem to be guilty of a paradox when we speak of the unconscious in reference to social activity. Doubtful as is the usefulness of this concept when we confine ourselves to the behavior of the individual, it may seem to be worse than doubtful when we leave the kinds of behavior that are strictly individual and deal with those more complex kinds of activity which, rightly or wrongly, are supposed to be carried on, not by individuals as such, but by the associations of human beings that constitute society. It may be argued that society has no more of an unconscious than it has hands or legs.

I propose to show, however, that the paradox is a real one only if the term "social behavior" is understood in the very literal sense of behavior referred to groups of human beings which act as such, regardless of the mentalities of the individuals which compose the groups. To such a mystical group alone can a mysterious "social unconsciousness" be ascribed. But as we are very far from believing that such groups really exist, we may be able to persuade ourselves that no more especial kind of unconsciousness need be imputed to social behavior than is needed to understand the behavior of the individual himself. We shall be on much safer ground if we take it for granted that all human behavior involves essentially the same types of mental functioning, as well conscious as unconscious, and that the term "social" is no more exclusive of the concept "unconscious" than is the term "individual," for the very simple reason that the terms "social" and "individual" are contrastive in only a

[48] W. W. Reade, *op. cit.*, p. 184.
[49] G. Schweinfurth, *op. cit.*, ii. 98.
[50] Sir W. C. Harris, *op. cit.*, iii. 171–172, 232.

limited sense. We will assume that any kind of psychology that explains the behavior of the individual also explains the behavior of society in so far as the psychological point of view is applicable to and sufficient for the study of social behavior. It is true that for certain purposes it is very useful to look away entirely from the individual and to think of socialized behavior as though it were carried on by certain larger entities which transcend the psychophysical organism. But this viewpoint implicitly demands the abandonment of the psychological approach to the explanation of human conduct in society.

It will be clear from what we have said that we do not find the essential difference between individual and social behavior to lie in the psychology of the behavior itself. Strictly speaking, each kind of behavior is individual, the difference in terminology being entirely due to a difference in the point of view. If our attention is focused on the actual, theoretically measurable behavior of a given individual at a given time and place, we call it "individual behavior," no matter what the physiological or psychological nature of that behavior may be. If, on the other hand, we prefer to eliminate certain aspects of such individual behavior from our consideration and to hold on only to those respects in which it corresponds to certain norms of conduct which have been developed by human beings in association with one another and which tend to perpetuate themselves by tradition, we speak of "social behavior." In other words, social behavior is merely the sum or, better, arrangement of such aspects of individual behavior as are referred to culture patterns that have their proper context, not in the spatial and temporal continuities of biological behavior, but in historical sequences that are imputed to actual behavior by a principle of selection.

We have thus defined the difference between individual and social behavior, not in terms of kind or essence, but in terms of organization. To say that the human being behaves individually at one moment and socially at another is as absurd as to declare that matter follows the laws of chemistry at a certain time and succumbs to the supposedly different laws of atomic physics at another, for matter is always obeying certain mechanical laws which are at one and the same time both physical and chemical according to the manner in which we choose to define its organization. In dealing with human beings, we simply find it more convenient for certain purposes to refer a given act to the psycho-physical organism itself. In other cases the interest happens to lie in continuities that go beyond the individual organism and its functioning, so that a bit of conduct that is objectively no more and no less individual than the first is interpreted in terms of the non-individual patterns that constitute social behavior or cultural behavior.

It would be a useful exercise to force ourselves to see any given human act from both of these points of view and to try to convince ourselves in this way that it is futile to classify human acts as such as having an inherently individual or social significance. It is true that there are a great many organismal functions that it is difficult to think of in social terms, but I think that even here the social point of view may often be applied with success. Few social students are interested, for instance, in the exact manner in which a given individual breathes. Yet it is not to be doubted that our breathing habits are largely conditioned by factors conventionally classified as social. There are polite and impolite ways of breathing. There are special attitudes which seem to characterize whole societies that undoubtedly condition the breathing habits of the individuals who make up these societies. Ordinarily the characteristic rhythm of breathing of a given individual is looked upon as a matter for strictly individual definition. But if, for one reason or another, the emphasis shifts to the consideration of a certain manner of breathing as due to good form or social tradition or some other principle that is usually given a social context, then the whole subject of breathing at once ceases to be a merely individual concern and takes on the appearance of a social pattern. Thus, the regularized breathing of the Hindu Yogi, the subdued breathing of those who are in the presence of a recently deceased companion laid away in a coffin and surrounded by all the ritual of funeral observances, the style of breathing which one learns from an operatic singer who gives lessons on the proper control of the voice, are, each and every one of them, capable of isolation as socialized modes of conduct that have a definite place in the history of human culture, though they are obviously not a whit less facts of individual behavior than the most casual and normal style of breathing, such as one rarely imagines to have other than purely individual implications. Strange as it may seem at first blush, there is no hard and fast line of division as to class of behavior between a given style of breathing, *provided that it be socially interpreted,* and a religious doctrine or a form of political administration. This is not to say that it may not be infinitely more useful to apply the social mode of analysis of human conduct to certain cases and the individual mode of analysis to others. But we do maintain that such differences of analysis are merely imposed by the nature of the interest of the observer and are not inherent in the phenomena themselves.

RUTH BENEDICT

Configurations of Culture

In the past twenty-five years the fact of prime importance in anthropology has without doubt been the accumulation of a few full-length portraits of primitive peoples. It is hard to think back to a time when as yet the chance of reconstructing even a passable picture of any primitive tribe was limited to two or three regions, each of them beset with difficulties. The best accounts that were available were not the outcome of any purposeful inquiry on the part of students of custom, but of the lucky chances that had brought together a good observer and a striking culture, the records of Sahagun, for instance, or Codrington in Melanesia.

The vast amount of available anthropological material was frankly anecdotal as in travelers' accounts, or schematically dissected and tabulated as in many ethnologists'. Under the circumstances general anthropological discussion of necessity had recourse, as in Tylor's day, to the comparative method, which is by definition anecdotal and schematic. It sought by collecting great series of observations detached from their context to build up "the" primitive mind, or "the" development of religion, or "the" history of marriage.

Out of the necessities of the same situation there flourished also the schools of strict diffusionists who made a virtue out of the limitations of materials at their disposal and operated solely with detached objects, never with their setting or function in the culture from which they came.

The growing dissatisfaction with these two dominant theoretical approaches of what we may well call the anecdotal period of ethnology has always been explicit in Boas' insistence upon exhaustive study of any primitive culture, and is today most clearly voiced by Malinowski. His vigor is directed against the diffusionist group rather than against the Frazers and the Westermarcks of the comparative method, but in his own work he insists always that anthropological theory must take into account not detached items but human cultures as organic and functioning wholes. He would have us realize that when a museum collection has been installed from the Niam-Niam or a monograph of like type has been published we still know in reality exactly nothing about them unless we know the way in which the arrangement of the house, the articles of dress, the rules of avoidance or of marriage, the ideas of the supernatural—how each object and culture trait, in other words, is employed in their native life. Malinowski, somewhat disappointingly, does not go on to the examination of these cultural wholes, but is content to conclude his argument with pointing out in each context that each trait functions in the total cultural complex, a conclusion which seems increasingly the beginning of inquiry rather than its peroration. For it is a position that leads directly to the necessity of investigating in what sort of a whole these traits are functioning, and what reference they bear to the total culture. In how far do the traits achieve an organic interrelation? Are the *Leitmotive* in the world by which they may be integrated many or few? These questions the functionalists do not ask.

Now the fact that becomes increasingly apparent as full-length accounts of primitive peoples come from the press is that these cultures, though they are so overwhelmingly made up of disparate elements fortuitously assembled from all directions by diffusion, are none the less over and over again in different tribes integrated according to very different and individual patterns. The order that is achieved is not merely the reflection of the fact that each trait has a pragmatic function that it performs—which is much like a great discovery in physiology that the normal eye sees and the normally muscled hand grasps, or, still more exactly, the discovery that nothing exists in human life that mankind has not espoused and rationalized. The order is due rather to the circumstance that in these societies a principle has been set up according to which the assembled cultural material is made over into consistent patterns in accordance with certain inner necessities that have developed within the group. These syntheses are of various sorts. For some of them we have convenient terminology and for some we have not. But they are in each case the more or less successful attainment of integrated behavior, an attainment that is all the more striking for the anthropologist because of his knowledge of the scattered and hybrid materials out of which the integration has been achieved.

The proposition that cultures must be studied from this point of view and that it is crucial in an understanding even of our own cultural history has been put forward by the German school headed by Wilhelm Dilthey and popularly represented in English-speaking countries by Oswald Spengler in his *Untergang des Abendlandes*.[1] For this philosophical school, history is the succession of culturally organized philosophies of life, and philosophy is the study of these great readings of life. For Dilthey himself the emphasis is only secondarily and as it were accidentally on the configuration of culture itself to express these varied readings of life. His primary emphasis is upon these great interpretations as expressing the variety of existence and is directed against the assumption that any one of them can be final. He argues vigorously that essential configurations in philosophy are incommensurable and that their fundamental categories cannot be resolved the one into the other.

Spengler, however, has elaborated the cultural aspect of the philosophy of his school. He has avoided their attempt to define and limit "the" types that may occur. For him the "destiny ideas" whatever they may be that evolve within a culture and give it individuality are what is dynamic and challenging in human life. These have differed profoundly one from another, and they condition their carriers so that certain beliefs and certain blindnesses are

[1] English translation: The Decline of the West. 2 vols. New York, 1929 and 1930.

inevitable to them. Each great culture has taken a certain direction not taken by another, it has developed beliefs and institutions until they are the expression of this fundamental orientation, and the full working out of this unique and highly individualized attitude toward life is what is significant in that cultural epoch. His study makes a confused impression owing to its discursiveness and the unresolved complexities of the civilizations with which he deals. From an anthropological point of view the fundamental criticism of his work is that it involves treating modern stratified civilization as if it had the essential homogeneity of a primitive culture. His picture, especially of the modern world-view which he calls the Faustian, is only one of the integrated pictures that could validly be drawn for modern man. It needs to be balanced by a picture of a Babbitt or a Roosevelt, for instance. Even at that, what with his rather mystic consideration of numbers, of architecture, of music, of painting, of will, space, and time, the definition of his types becomes confused, and the identification of his different Faustian "destiny ideas" in mathematics, finance, philosophy, and morals hard to make out.

The fundamental principle of the philosophy of Dilthey and his school has remained in its application to the civilization of western Europe stimulating and provocative rather than convincing. The difficulty, which Dilthey himself largely avoided by stressing primarily the dominant drives in philosophy instead of in cultures at large, in Spengler is very clear; historical data of western Europe are too complex and cultural stratification too thoroughgoing to yield itself in our present state of historical knowledge to the necessary analysis.

It is one of the philosophical justifications for the study of primitive peoples that ethnological data may make clear fundamental social facts that are otherwise confused and not open to demonstration. Of these none seem to me more important than this of fundamental and distinctive configurations in culture that so pattern existence and condition the emotional and cognitive reactions of its carriers that they become incommensurables, each specializing in certain selected types of behavior and each ruling out the behavior proper to its opposites.

I have recently examined from this point of view two types of cultures represented in the Southwest,[2] that of the Pueblo contrasted with those of the various surrounding peoples. I have called the *ethos* of the Pueblo Apollonian in Nietzsche's sense of the cultural pursuit of sobriety, of measure, of the distrust of excess and orgy. On the other hand Nietzsche's contrasted type, the Dionysian, is abundantly illustrated in all the surrounding cultures. It values excess as escape to an order of existence beyond that of the five senses, and finds its expression in the creation in culture of painful and dangerous experiences, and in the cultivation of emotional and psychic excesses, in drunkenness, in dreams, and in trance.

The situation in the Southwest gives an exceptionally good opportunity for the study of the extent to which contrasted psychological sets of this sort, once they have become institutionalized, can shape the resulting cultures. The Pueblo are a clearly marked-off civilization of very considerable known antiquity, islanded in the midst of highly divergent cultures. But this islanding of their culture cannot be set down as in Oceania to the facts of the physical environment. There are no mountain ranges, no impassable deserts, not even many miles that separate them from their neighbors. It is a cultural islanding achieved almost in the face of geographical conditions. The eastern Pueblo went regularly to the plains for the buffalo hunt, and the center of the Pima country is within a day's run on foot of Hopi and Zuñi. The fact therefore that they have a complex culture set off as strikingly as any in North America from that of their impinging neighbors makes the situation unmistakable. The resistance that has kept out of the Pueblo such traits as that of the guardian spirit and the vision, the shaman, the torture, the orgy, the cultural use of intoxicants, the ideas of mystic danger associated with sex, initiative of the individual and personal authority in social affairs, is a cultural resistance, not the result of an isolation due to physical facts of the environment.

The culture of the southwest Pueblo, as I have pointed out in the article referred to above, is a thoroughgoing, institutionalized elaboration of the theme of sobriety and restraint in behavior. This

---

[2] Psychological Types in the Cultures of the Southwest. ICA 23:572–581, 1928.

dominating theme has effectually prevented the development of those typical Dionysian situations which most North American tribes elaborate out of every phase of life, cultivating abandon and emotional excesses, and making birth, adolescence, menstruation, the dead, the taking of life, and any other life crises ambivalently charged occasions fraught with danger and with power. It has likewise refused such traits of surrounding cultures as self-torture, ceremonially used drugs, and the inspirational vision, along with all the authority that is usually derived from personal contact with the supernatural, i.e., shamanism. It hates disruptive impulses in the individual—I speak in an animistic shorthand, meaning that their cultural bias is opposed to and finally pares down to a minimum the potential human impulses to see visions and experiment in indulgences and work off its energy in excesses of the flesh.

Among these disruptive impulses the Pueblo *ethos* counts also the will to power. Just as surely as it has acted to obliterate self-torture it has acted to obliterate the human impulse toward the exercise of authority. Their ideal man avoids authority in the home or in public office. He has office at last thrust upon him, but even at that the culture has already taken away from the position he has to occupy anything that approaches personal authority in our sense; it remains a position of trust, a center of reference in planning the communal program, not much more.

Sanction for all acts comes always from the formal structure, not from the individual. He may not kill unless he has the power of the scalp or is planning to be initiated into it—that is, into the organized war society. He may not doctor because he knows how or acquires sanction from any personal encounter with the supernatural, but because he has bought his way up to the highest rank in the curing societies. Even if he is the chief priest he will not plant a prayer stick except at the institutionally prescribed seasons; if he does he will be regarded as practicing sorcery, as, according to the point of tales in which this situation occurs, he is indeed. The individual devotes himself therefore to the constituted forms of his society. He takes part in all cult activity, and according to his means will increase the number of masks possessed in Zuñi by having one made for himself—which involves feasting and considerable expense. He will undertake to sponsor the calendric kachina dances; he will entertain them at the great winter dance by building them a new house and assuming the expenses of his share of the ceremony. But he does all this with an anonymity that is hard to duplicate from other cultures. He does not undertake them as bids for personal prestige. Socially the good man never raises himself above his neighbor by displaying authority. He sets everyone at his ease, he "talks lots," he gives no occasion for offense. He is never violent, nor at the mercy of his emotions.

The whole interest of the culture is directed toward providing for every situation sets of rules and practices by means of which one gets by without resort to the violence and disruption that their culture distrusts. Even fertility practices, associated so universally in other cultures with excess and orgy, though they make them the leading motif of their religion,[3] are non-erotic rites based on analogies and sympathetic magic. I shall discuss later the thoroughness with which their rites of mourning are designed to this same end.

Such configurations of culture, built around certain selected human traits and working toward the obliteration of others are of first-rate importance in the understanding of culture. Traits objectively similar and genetically allied may be utilized in different configurations, it may be, without change in detail. The relevant facts are the emotional background against which the act takes place in the two cultures. It will illustrate this if we imagine the Pueblo snake dance in the setting of our own society. Among the western Pueblo, at least, repulsion is hardly felt for the snake. They have no physiological shudder at the touch of its body; in the ceremony, they are not flying in the face of a deep antipathy and horror. When we identify ourselves with them we are emotionally poles apart, though we put ourselves meticulously into the pattern of their behavior. For them, the poison of the rattlesnakes being removed, the whole procedure is upon the level of a dance with eagles or with kittens. It is a completely characteristic Apollonian dance expression, whereas with us, with our emotional reaction to the snake, the dance is not possible upon this level. Without chang-

[3] H. K. Haeberlin, The Idea of Fertilization in the Culture of the Pueblo Indians. AAA–M 3, no. 1, 1916.

ing an item of the outward behavior of the dance, its emotional significance and its functioning in the culture are reversed. And yet often enough, in ethnographic monographs, we are at a loss to know this emotional background even in traits where it becomes of first-rate importance, as for instance in the feeling directed toward the corpse. We need much more relevant data from the field in order to evaluate the emotional background.

The bereavement situation is characteristically handled in Dionysian and in Apollonian cultures according to their bias. Dionysian behavior for the bereaved has found several different channels of expression in the region we are discussing in North America. Among the western Plains it was a violent expression of loss and upheaval. Abandon took the form of self-mutilation, especially for women. They gashed their heads, their calves, they cut off fingers. Long lines of women marched through camp after the death of an important person, their legs bare and bleeding. The blood on their heads and legs they let cake and did not remove. When the body was taken out for burial everything in the lodge was thrown on the ground for any that were not relatives to possess themselves of it. The lodge was pulled down and given to another. Soon everything was gone and the widow had nothing left but the blanket about her. At the grave the man's favorite horses were killed and both men and women wailed for the dead. A wife or daughter might remain at the grave, wailing and refusing to eat, for twenty-four hours, until her relatives dragged her away. At intervals, even twenty years after a death had occurred, on passing the grave they cried for the dead.[4]

On the death of children especially, abandon of grief is described as being indulged. Suicide is often resorted to by one parent or the other. According to Denig, among the Assiniboine:

> should anyone offend the parent during this time his death would most certainly follow, as the man, being in profound sorrow, seeks something on which to wreak his revenge, and he soon after goes to war, to kill or be killed, either being immaterial to him in that state.[5]

---

[4] George Bird Grinnell, The Cheyenne Indians, 2:162. Yale University Press, 1923.

[5] Denig, The Assiniboine. BAE–R 46:573.

Such descriptions are characteristic of Plains mourning. They have in common fundamental social patternings of violent and uninhibited grief. This has nothing to do, of course, with the question of whether this is the emotion called up in all those who participate in the rites; the point at issue is only that in this region institutionalized behavior at this crisis is patterned upon free emotional indulgence.

In such a typical Apollonian culture as the pueblo of Isleta, on the other hand, Plains mourning is unthinkable. Isleta, like any other Apollonian society, provides itself with rules by which to outlaw violence and aggressive moods of any kind. Strong feeling is repulsive to it and even at death, which is the most stubbornly unescapable of the tragic occasions of life, their whole emphasis is to provide a routine for getting by with the least possible upheaval. In Isleta a priest who is known as the Black Corn Mother and who is a functionary of one of the four "Corn" divisions of the Pueblo, officiates at death. He is called immediately and prepares the corpse, brushing the hair and washing and painting the face with identification marks to indicate the social affiliation of the dead. After this the relatives come in, bringing each a candle to the dead, and the Corn Mother prays and sends the people away again. When they have gone he and his helpers "feed" the dead man ceremonially with the left hand—associated with ghosts—and make an altar in the room. Only once again during all this ritual tending of the dead are the relatives admitted, and that is when the priest has ready a small smudge from the combings of the dead man's hair. The bereaved breathe this in and will thereby cease to grieve over the dead person. The burial takes place the following day, but the family and relatives are ceremonially taboo for four days and remain in retreat in the house of the dead man, receiving certain ritual washings from the priest. The formalities that more nearly correspond to burial in other regions are performed over the burial of food for the deceased on the fourth day. They go outside the village for this, and after it is over, they break the pot in which water was carried, and the hairbrush that was used to prepare the body for burial, and on their return cut their trail with a deep incision with a flint knife. They listen and hear the dead man come, far off, to the place where they buried food for him. The house is filled with people awaiting their return, and the Black Corn Mother preaches to them, telling them this is the last time they need be afraid of the dead man's returning. The four days has been as four years to him and therefore those who remain will be the readier to forget. The relatives go to their houses but the housemates observe the ordinary taboos for ceremonial purity for eight days more, after which everything is over. The Black Corn Mother goes to the cacique and returns to him the power he received from him and must always receive from him for every death, but which he has this means of disposing of when he is not compelled to exercise it. It is a characteristic Apollonian touch, and very common in the Southwest.[6]

There is here no frank institutionalized indulgence in grief, no cutting off of fingers—not even of hair—nor gashing of bodies, no destruction of property, not even a show of its distribution. Instead of insistence upon prolonged mourning by the most closely bereaved, the emphasis is all upon immediate forgetting. The two pictures are of course familiar types of contrasted behavior, and they are here institutionalized for two contrasted cultures.

In the face of the evident opposition of these two institutionalized types of behavior it is at first sight somewhat bizarre to group them together over against another type in contrast to which they are at one. It is true nevertheless. In their different contexts, the Southwest and the Plains are alike in not capitalizing ideas of pollution and dread. This is not to say that fear of contamination or of the dangerous power of the dead are never to be detected in these regions; they are humanly potential attitudes and no culture is perhaps hermetically sealed against them. But the culture does not capitalize them. In contrast with the non-Pueblo Southwest, for instance, these two are alike in realistically directing their behavior toward the loss-situation instead of romantically elaborating the danger situation. In Isleta the clan head officiating at death does not have to be purified and the curse of contact with the dead lifted from him when the rites are over; he lays aside his official prerogatives as undertaker as he would his stole. He has not been polluted by his office. Nor is the smudge for the relatives designed to put

[6] Esther Schiff Goldfrank Isleta ms.

them beyond the pursuit of vengefulness of the dead, but rather to make them forget quickly.[7] They break his hairbrush, not the bones of his legs, because what they are symbolizing is the ending of this man's life, not precautions against his envy and vindictiveness. Similarly on the Plains[8] the giving away of property and the demeaning of one's self in personal appearance, which is so commonly a ruse for forestalling the jealousy of the deceased, is here a gesture of grief and associated with such other manifestations of oblivion of one's self and ordinary routine as going off mourning alone on the prairies, or starting off "to kill or be killed, either being immaterial to him" in his grief. They do not destroy the tipi and all the man's horses, for they are neither concerned with the contamination of the corpse nor with the malice of the ghost toward those who continue to enjoy them. On the contrary their one thought is to give them away. Neither do they capitalize that common theme for patterning a danger situation, the fear and hatred of the person who has used supernatural power to kill the deceased.

These themes however are the very basis of the mourning ceremony in surrounding regions. It is no uncommon thing to find that death rites are hardly directed at all toward the loss-situation but wholly preoccupied with contamination. The Navaho are by no means extreme examples. The Franciscan Fathers[9] tell us that in former times slaves were employed to prepare and carry the corpse and they were killed at the grave. Now members of the family must expose themselves to this defilement. Men and women strip themselves to a breechcloth for the duty and leave the hair flowing so that not even a hair string may be exposed. To the Navaho either type of behavior we have just been describing would be unthinkable. Only those who because of their close kinship cannot avoid the duty accompany the body. Four are necessary, one to lead the favorite horse which is to be killed on the grave of his master, two to carry the corpse, and one to warn any travelers along the way that they may turn aside and save themselves from defilement. To

[7] In Zuñi however certain scalp dance attitudes are explicitly associated with the widow and widower.

[8] In this entire discussion I exclude the Southern Sioux.

[9] An Ethnologic Dictionary of the Navajo Language, 454. St. Michael's, Arizona, 1910.

protect themselves the mourners keep strict silence. Meantime the hogan in which death occurred has been burnt to the ground. All the members of the family fast for four days and during this time a guard warns all comers off the trail between the hogan and the grave lest they incur danger.[10]

Besides the dominating fear of pollution, the Navaho have a strong fear also of the return of the ghost. If a woman fails in fasting or breaks silence, it will show the dead the way back and the ghost will harm the offender. This discomfort of the living before the dead is nearly universal, though it assumes very different proportions in different cultures.

On the other hand, the dreaded vengefulness of the ghost and his malice toward those who have been spared by death is not as popular in North America in the elaboration of the horror situation as it is in South America and in other parts of the world. It is a theme that for Crawley, for example, is fundamental in death practices, and it is striking that it should play so slight a role in North America. One of the clearest examples on this continent is from the Fox. The Central Algonkin have a strong belief in cruel antagonists which the dead must overcome along their route, and the custom of burying weapons with the body was in order that they might be armed against them. With the Winnebago, too,[11] war hatchets were buried with the dead so that they might kill animals they met along their way, and their relatives in this world be blessed in like fashion. But Jones records that among the Fox it was a frequent request of the dying that they might be provided in the grave with a war hatchet to protect themselves against Cracker of Skulls; but this the living would not do because the dead were feared and it was desirable that they be weaponless. Therefore they are helpless before Cracker of Skulls who scoops from each a fingerful of brain.[12]

The Mohave on the other hand made much of the fear and blame of the medicine-man who had supernaturally caused the death. A seer was employed to visit the land of the dead after a death. If the deceased was not there, it was known that the doctor who attended

---

[10] Gladys A. Reichard, Social Life of the Navajo Indians. CU–CA 7:142.
[11] Paul Radin, JAFL 22:312.
[12] Wm. Jones, ICA 15:266.

him was guilty of malpractice. "It is the nature of these doctors to kill people in this way just as it is the nature of hawks to kill little birds for a living," according to a Mohave in the 80's. A rich man remained rich in the other world and all those a medicine-man killed were under his chieftainship. He desired a large rich band. "I've killed only two. When I die I want to rule a bigger band than that." [13] When blame was attached to any medicine-man, anyone might take it upon himself to kill him.

The medicine-man openly avowed his complicity. He might hand a stick to a man and say, "I killed your father." Or he might come and tell a sick person, "Don't you know that it is I that am killing you? Must I grasp you and despatch you with my hands before you will try to kill me?" [14] The point is that this is supernatural killing. There has never been any intimation that it was the custom for a medicine-man to use poison or knife. It is a blame- and terror-situation open and declared, a situation more familiar in Africa than in North America.

It is well to contrast this Mohave attitude with the Pueblo witchcraft theories. In Zuñi the bereavement situation is not lost in a situation of sorcery and of vengeance taken upon sorcery; bereavement is handled as bereavement, however clearly the emphasis is upon putting it by as soon as possible. In spite of the great amount of anxiety about witches which is always present among the Pueblo, at an actual death little attention is paid to the possibility of their complicity. Only in an epidemic when death becomes a public menace is the witch theory ordinarily acted upon. And it is a community anxiety neurosis, not a Dionysian situation depending like the Mohave on the exercise of the shaman's will to supernatural power, and the ambivalent attitude of the group toward this power. I doubt whether anyone in Zuñi has any witch techniques which he actually practices; no one defies another over a dead or dying man. It is never the medicine-man who by virtue of his medicine powers is also the death bringer and embodies in his one person the characteristic Dionysian double aspects of power. Death is not dramatized

[13] John J. Bourke, JAFL 2:175, 1889.
[14] A. L. Kroeber, Handbook of the Indians of California. BAE–B 78:778.

as a duel between a shaman, thought of as a bird of prey and his victim. Even the existence of all the necessary ideas among the Pueblo—it is interesting that they are overwhelmingly European in their detail—does not lead to this Dionysian interpretation of death.

There are other themes upon which danger situations can be and have been built up around death in different cultures. The point we need for our discussion is that the Dionysian indulgence in emotion at death can be institutionalized around realistic grief at the loss of a member of the community, or around various constructs such as contamination, guilt, and the vengefulness of the dead. The contrast between cultures which indulge in danger constructs of this sort in every situation in life and those that do not is as striking as that between the Apollonian-Dionysian types.

The fullest collections of primitive material on the danger situation are of course the various works of Crawley. This was his outstanding subject throughout his work, and he interpreted it as a universal drive in human society. It is certainly one that is common in institutional behavior, but it is for all its wide distribution a particular configuration of culture, and contrasting configurations develop their contrasting behaviors.

There are of course aspects of culture, especially of material culture, which are independent of many of the aims and virtues a society may make for itself. I do not mean to imply that the fortunes of the sinew-backed bow will depend upon whether the culture is Dionysian or Apollonian. But the range of applicability of the point I am making is nevertheless greater than is generally supposed. Radin has for instance argued very cogently from Winnebago material for the great importance of individuality and individual initiative "among primitives." [15] Now the Plains and the Winnebago are among our great primitive examples, according to all observers, of high cultural evaluation of the individual. He is allowed institutionally guaranteed initiative in his life such as one cannot easily duplicate from other regions. One has only to compare it with the Pueblo to realize that Radin's point of very great personal

[15] Primitive Man as Philosopher, 32 ff.

initiative is a prime fact among the Winnebago and the western Plains, but not coextensive with primitive culture. It is an attitude to be studied independently in each area.

The same is also true of Malinowski's picture of the way in which the Trobrianders—and Melanesia generally, we may well add—have made reciprocity a basic behavior trait of their culture. He describes the reciprocal obligations of sea and land peoples, of chief and subjects, of the two sides of the house, of husband and wife and other selected reciprocating relatives, and he deduces from this that "tradition" is a weak word invoked by the anthropologist to cover our ignorance of what really holds "society" together, a function that is performed by reciprocity. But this organization of society here is of a definite type, highly uncharacteristic, say, of Siberia, and fundamental in any description of Melanesia. In what way it ties up with fundamental attitudes in that region is still to be defined.

Cultural configurations stand to the understanding of group behavior in the relation that personality types stand to the understanding of individual behavior. In the psychological field, behavior is no longer given the same interpretation, say, for the cycloid and the schizoid type. It is recognized that the organization of the total personality is crucial in the understanding or even in the mere description of individual behavior.[16] If this is true in individual psychology where individual differentiation must be limited always by the cultural forms and by the short span of a human lifetime, it is even more imperative in social psychology where the limitations of time and of conformity are transcended. The degree of integration that may be attained is of course incomparably greater than can ever be found in individual psychology. Cultures from this point of view are individual psychology thrown large upon the screen, given gigantic proportions and a long time span.

---

[16] See Clark Wissler, Science, 63:193–201, 1916.

PART 4

The Scene

CHARLES M. DOUGHTY

Last Night at Teyma

The Fejîr watered once more at Teyma; I saw the great cattle of our households driven in, and after the watering their burden camels were couched by the booths: for Mébsan and the rest would remove in the morning and return to the desert. Among the beasts I found my old nâga, and saw that she was badly galled on the chine; the wound might hardly be healed in fifteen or twenty days, but I must journey to-morrow. I brought nomad friends to look at her, who found that she had been ridden and mishandled, the marks of the saddle-tree cords yet appearing in the hairy hide. It could not be other than the fault of Zeyd's herdsman Îsa, a young man, whom I had befriended. So taking him by the beard before them all, I cursed "the father of this Yahûdy." The young man, strong and resolute, laid hands upon my shoulders and reviled me for a Nasrâny; but I said, "Sirrah, thou shouldst have kept her better," and held him fast by the beard. The tribesmen gathered about us kept silence, even his own family, all being my friends, and they had so good an opinion of my moving only in a just matter. Îsa seeing that his fault was blamed, must suffer this rebuke, so I plucked down the weled's comely head to his breast, and let him go. An effort of strength had been unbecoming, and folly it were to suffer any perturbation for a thing that is without remedy; I had passed over his fault, but I thought that to take it hardly was a necessary policy. Also the Arabs would have a man like the pomegranate, a bitter-sweet, mild and affectionate with his friends in security, but tempered with a just anger if the time call him to be a defender in his own or in his neighbour's cause. Îsa's father came bye and bye to my tent, and in a demiss voice the old hind acknowledged his son's error; "Yet, Khalîl, why didst thou lay upon me that reproach, when we have been thy friends, to name me before the people Yahûdy?" But as old Sâlih saw me smile he smiled again, and took the right hand which I held forth to him.

I found Zeyd, at evening, sitting upon one of the clay benches near the haddàj; he was waiting in the midst of the town, in hope that some acquaintance of the villagers coming by, before the sun's going down, might call him to supper. Returning after an hour I found Zeyd yet in the place, his almost black visage set betwixt the nomad patience of hunger and his lordly disdain of the Teyâmena. Zeyd might have seemed a prosperous man, if he had been liberal, to lay up friendship in heaven and in this world; but the shallow hand must bring forth leanness and faint willing of a man's neighbours again. I stayed to speak a word with Zeyd, and saw him draw at last his galliûn, the remedy of hunger: then he called a lad, who issued from the next dàr, to fetch a live coal, and the young villager obeyed him.

In the first hour of this night there fell upon us a tempest of wind and rain. The tall palms rocked, and bowing in all their length to the roaring gusts it seemed they would be rent by the roots. I found shelter with Méhsan in the house of Féjr our host; but the flat roof of stalks and rammed earth was soon drenched, and the unwonted wet streamed down inwardly by the walls. Méhsan spoke of my setting forth to-morrow with this Bishr, and, calling Féjr to witness, the timid friendly man sought to dissuade me, "also Zeyd, he said, had forsaken me, who should have commended me to them; it was likely I should see him no more."—"Should I wonder at that?—Zeyd has no heart," they answered both together: "Ay, billah, Zeyd has no heart," and repeated *ma láhu kalb,* He has no heart! Féjr was suffering an acute pain of "the stone," *el-hása,* a malady common in these parts, though the country is sand stone; yet sometimes it may be rather an inflammation, for they think it comes of their going unshod upon the burning soil. When the weather lulled, we went towards our wet tents to sleep out the last night at Teyma.

DAVID HERBERT LAWRENCE
The Australian Scene

That curious sombreness of Australia, the sense of oldness, with the forms all worn down low and blunt, squat. The squat-seeming earth. And then they ran at last into real country—rather rocky, dark old rocks, and sombre bush with its different pale-stemmed dull-leaved gum-trees standing graceful, and various heathy-looking undergrowth, and great spikey things like yuccas. As they turned south they saw tree-ferns standing on one knobbly leg, among the gums, and among the rocks ordinary ferns and small bushes spreading in glades and up sharp hill-slopes. It was virgin bush, and as if unvisited, lost, sombre, with plenty of space, yet spreading grey for miles and miles, in a hollow towards the west. Far in the west, the sky having suddenly cleared, they saw the magical range of the Blue Mountains. And all this hoary space of bush between. The strange, as it were *invisible* beauty of Australia, which is undeniably there, but which seems to lurk just beyond the range of our white vision. You feel you can't *see*—as if your eyes hadn't the vision in them to correspond with the outside landscape. For the landscape is so unimpressive, like a face with little or no features, a dark face. It is so aboriginal, out of our ken, and it hangs back so aloof. Somers always felt he looked at it through a cleft in the atmosphere; as one looks at one of the ugly-faced, distorted aborigines with his wonderful dark eyes that have such an incomprehensible ancient shine in them, across gulfs of unbridged centuries. And yet, when you don't have the feeling of ugliness or monotony, in landscape or in nigger, you get a sense of subtle, remote, *formless* beauty more poignant than anything ever experienced before.

ANDRE GIDE

The Beauty of the Congo Huts

I am astonished that the few rare travellers who have spoken of this country and of its villages and huts have only thought fit to mention their "strangeness." The Massas' hut, it is true, resembles no other; but it is not only strange; it is *beautiful;* and it is not its strangeness so much as its beauty that moves me. A beauty so perfect, so accomplished, that it seems natural. No ornament, no superfluity. The pure curve of its line, which is uninterrupted from base to summit, seems to have been arrived at mathematically, by an ineluctable necessity; one instinctively realizes how exactly the resistance of the materials must have been calculated. A little farther north or south and the clay would be too much mixed with sand to allow of this easy spring, terminating in the circular opening that alone gives light to the inside of the hut, in the manner of Agrippa's Pantheon. On the outside a number of regular flutings give life and accent to these geometrical forms and afford a foothold by which the summit of the hut (often twenty to twenty-five feet high) can be reached; they enable it to be built without the aid of scaffolding; this hut is made by hand like a vase; it is the work, not of a mason, but of a potter. Its colour is the very colour of the earth—a pinkish-grey clay, like the clay of which the walls of old Biskra are made. Birds' droppings often whiten the top part of the flutings and unexpectedly show up their relief.

Inside the hut the coolness of the air seems delicious, when one comes in from the scorching outside. Above the door, like some huge keyhole, is a kind of columbarium shelf, where vases and household objects are arranged. The walls are smooth, polished, varnished. Opposite the entrance is a kind of high drum made of earth, very prettily decorated with geometrical patterns in relief, painted white, red, and black. These drums are the rice bins. Their earthen lids are luted with clay, and are so smooth that they resemble the skin of a drum. Fishing tackle, cords, and tools hang from pegs; sometimes too a sheaf of assagais or a shield of plaited rush. Here, in the dim twilight of an Etruscan tomb, the family spend the hottest hours of the day; at night the cattle come in to join them—oxen, goats, and hens; each animal has its own allotted corner, and everything is in its proper place; everything is clean, exact, ordered. There is no communication with the outside as soon as the door is shut. One's home is one's castle.

These huts give shelter to their own fauna as well as to human beings and cattle; swallows with black and white tails have built their nests in the top of the rounded roof; bats flutter round the single ray of light, in which their wings look transparent; little lizards run along the walls, on which the mason-flies have built their nests like warts.

When a cow goes into one of these shell huts to pass the night, it has just room enough to get in by lowering its head. The door exactly fits the shape of the cow, which explains why it is wider at the height of the cow's body. The door-frame is in relief and very often decorated. At this place alone the wall is so thick that the embrasure forms what is almost a passage, like the opening of a conch. Certainly these curves, these angles, these splayings have been the same for centuries. Yes, these huts are really as beautiful as products of nature. If only some over-zealous administrator does not come in the name of hygiene, and order walls to be cut through and windows to be opened, and reduce the purity of these prime numbers to some sort of common divider!

These conic shells, which are of unequal height, are placed together in small groups. Their bases often touch, but do not impinge on each other; for their curve always starts from the ground, and the tangent circles which their plane would trace are perfect. The top of the passage which thus connects them forms a terrace halfway up their sides. Sometimes a round tower completes the ensemble and breaks the uniformity of its aspect. A very low wall goes from one hut to the other and throws, as it were, a circular girdle round all the buildings belonging to one community.

In front of some of these huts there is a floor of smooth beaten earth, where the Massas water their millet, which has got to sprout and ferment for the preparation of their "pipi" (a kind of beer). And this floor too, like everything else belonging to the Massas, is accurately laid out and perfectly shaped.

Besides the shells and round towers that serve as dwellings for the natives and their flocks, there are to be seen in the same enclosure other shells, considerably smaller; these have no flutings, but are sometimes decorated with vermicular markings and hatchings. These minor shells do not rest directly on the ground, but on a trellis-work of branches. They are granaries for storing millet, which has to be protected from rats, insects, and damp. A double belt of plaited grass enables the natives to reach the opening of the granary so as to draw upon its stores of grain.

Here and there near the dwellings we noted a sort of smooth, round, cup-shaped protuberance on the ground—a tomb.

On this first day the village was practically empty. The inhabitants were workings in the fields. We decided to go on to Pouss, where the porters who have been requisitioned to accompany us to Maroua are waiting for us.

SIEGFRIED FERDINAND NADEL

The Dead City of Bida

It seems characteristic that of the people of Sakpe, a backwood village in the centre of Bida Emirate, a large number have been to Bida, thirty miles away, but no one to Labozi, which is only ten miles away but lies in the opposite direction to Bida. There is only an apparent contradiction between this parochial outlook with respect to the community next door and this interest for the kingdom and its capital. It reflects the centripetal structure of the system of cultural "co-ordination" which we identified with the Nupe state. But let us examine first, under the aspect of community and common life, its capital, Bida.

Bida as it exists to-day is a comparatively young town. It was founded by the first Fulani Emir of Nupe about 1860. The old Beni village of Bida which stood on its site, a small village of four *efu*, forms to-day the "old city" of Bida, its innermost part, known as *ba nîn,* the Inside. At the time of the British occupation Bida is reported to have had a population of 60,000. Later it dropped rapidly: the enormous households of the feudal lords dissolved, slaves and private armies disappeared, and absentee landlords moved out into the country to live on their land. The old trade-route to the south which ran through Bida was diverted by the British, who suggested the shorter route from Zaria to Lokoja.[1] Trade began to avoid the defeated, impoverished capital. Some ten years ago Bida counted over 30,000 inhabitants; the last figure, for 1934, is 23,286. But the cosmopolitan character of the population still betrays its character of a metropolis: all tribal sections of Nupe are represented, and besides almost every tribe of Nigeria: Hausa, Yoruba, Yagba, Bunu, Kukuruku, Dakakari, Kamberi, Koro, Asaba, Gara, Tiv, and many more. The Nupe of Bida total over 20,000; of the strangers, Yoruba with nearly 600 and Hausa with 400–500 constitute the largest contingent in this medley of tribes and races.

And now the town itself. From a broken-off plateau that forms its northern edge, from the foot of two flat-topped hills, the town sweeps down into the plain. The town wall embracing the wide expanse of Bida runs over the edge of the plateau, climbs down into the plain, crosses two rivers and opens its gates upon four roads. This wall was estimated to measure twelve miles in circumference. To-day it has lost its former importance. It has broken down in many places and has been left unrepaired. A go-ahead Administrative Officer some two years ago had ordered all town gates to be pulled down—to make room for the increased motor traffic (which never came). Also, the town no longer fills the space within the wall, and many ruins and deserted places inside the wall betray the changes that have overtaken Bida and its people.

Four big roads lead through Bida, roughly in the shape of a cross, from east to west and north to south. The road from the Kaduna river enters Bida in the west, by the "Wuya gate," so named after the village on the banks of the Kaduna. Just outside the west gate is "New Bida"—a nucleus of New Bida—consisting to-day only of a few official buildings, among them the Emir of

[1] Dr. W. B. Baikie, R.N., *J. R. Geogr. Soc.*, 1867, p. 362.

Bida's newly built residence. We leave New Bida behind, with its brick buildings, its tin roofs, and glass windows, and enter the native town. In the town as it presents itself to the eyes of the visitor there are but few traces of modern influence. There are the modern roads, metalled, with stone parapets and bridges of concrete. But the houses which line the streets are still the same century-old Nupe houses: the big, naked wall enclosing the compound and, hidden behind it, the array of small thatched huts. As in the village, the compound wall opens upon the street in the *katamba,* the gateway or entrance-hall of the Nupe house. Its style and lay-out and the state it is in indicate better than anything else the status and position of the people who live there. There are the round gateways of the wealthy, some painted black, some in gay colours, with ornaments worked in relief into the clay, and the roomy gateways of the royal princes, with window recesses, and pillars and buttresses to support the high-gabled roof. Some *katamba* have raised platforms in front of the door, carefully levelled, and stained with the juice of the locust-bean which gives them the appearance of smooth asphalt. Others have coloured earthenware plates inlaid in the clay of the wall; others show, worked in relief, figures and emblems which took the builder's fancy or which are to indicate the owner's profession, such as the likeness of the wooden writing slate—the "trade-sign" of the learned Koran-teacher. And then there are the naked, sober *katamba* of the simple craftsman or farmer, and the dilapidated, neglected, and roofless entrance huts of the poor. *Katamba* follows *katamba,* house follows house, as we walk along the road. Side-streets branch off, winding between the compounds, a maze of small streets and paths, which are often just wide enough for a man on horseback to pass through. Here and there the walls recede and give room to an open square with a few trees, a little grass or a patch of cultivated ground, where goats and sheep graze, children play, and a few men, sitting in the shade, enjoy the hours of leisure.

We pass a blacksmiths' quarter, easily known by the open forges with their many doors and small triangular windows all round the walls. A little off the road live weavers and bead-makers. The road opens into a large square. To the right is a market, one of the three big day-markets of Bida, noisy and crowded with people who are buying and selling: foodstuffs, firewood, cloth, small pots. To the left, occupying one whole front of the square, is the residence of the Masaba dynasty. Two small bronze cannons formerly flanked the entrance-hall as symbol of the royal might. In the centre of the square stands a small throne hall; it used to be a pretty building, with painted and decorated pillars all round. But to-day, only a year since the death of the last *Etsu* from this house, it is already in a state of disrepair and neglect which symbolizes, more convincingly even than the disappearance of the bronze cannons, the passing of royal power. Houses of nobility and high office-holders occupy the other sides of the square. Walking on, past the long wall of the royal residence, we come to the street of the brass- and silversmiths. At all hours of the day their forges are busy, but not too busy to greet you with a little flourish of hammering on their anvils. Their women-folk are sitting outside the huts with baskets full of brass- and silverware in front of them, offering the products of the street to those who pass by.

It is a little over a mile from the west gate to the centre of Bida where the four main roads meet. Here stands another royal residence, the house of *Etsu* Usman Zaki—to-day almost in ruins. But the ruins, the enormous lay-out, the faded paintings and decorations, still speak of the ancient greatness. It is only ten years since the last ruler from this house, *Etsu* Bello, died. But ten years in this country, ten years with no royal household, no army of servants and slaves to take care of upkeep and repair, have sufficed to turn the king's palace into a desolate, half-deserted ruin in a corner of which the king's last descendants find ample room. Behind the house of Usman Zaki is the big town mosque where the Friday services are held, a building of red clay, with a tin roof perched on top, bare and singularly unattractive. In front, and all along the north wall of the royal residence, filling the wide open square, stretches the big "night-market"—the centre of Bida's pulsating life. It starts in the late afternoon, when peasants return from the farms, craftsmen stop work, and the women leave the houses, dressed for the occasion. Soon the large square is packed with people: men, women, children; townspeople and villagers, buyers and sellers, and those who come to the evening market to watch the crowds, meet friends, or to enjoy the excitement that goes with such public gatherings. The market is easy to survey. Every important commodity has its proper place. Horses and live stock, saddlery and fine coloured grass mats are sold behind the mosque; leather work, caps and straw hats, timber for roofing and coarse mats, in front of *Etsu* Usman's house. The butchers have a hut of their own, and so have the barbers, while traders and brokers who deal in cloth, gowns, ornaments, and swords occupy the long rows of booths which form the one rigid structure in this moving, seething multitude. Women are sitting in long rows all along the street, so close to each other that you can hardly move, selling food, native soap, kola-nuts, ornaments, silver bangles and glassware, beads and European cloth—anything that can be bought and sold in West Africa. Sometimes there are drummers, or a group of girls will sing and dance somewhere in the crowd; the "young men about town" walk up and down the street, shouting greetings to friends, and joking with girls. When it becomes dark the big trade ends; only the women continue their trade in the light of little clay lamps which they place in front of them—a truly enchanting illumination.

But then, in the dark of the night, the market changes its face: the respectable meeting-place of buyers and sellers becomes a market of Venus Pandemos. The women who remain so late are not dressed for work or trade: they wear their most beautiful dresses, light-coloured and embroidered cloth; they have bangles on their wrists and rings on their fingers; their eyes are painted with antimony, and their fingers and hands stained with henna. They never carry loads themselves—they always have a small girl with them to carry their baskets and bundles. They all sell kola-nuts—a man's article. They are always surrounded by men with whom they gossip and joke, and then, a whispered appointment, one of the men leaves, followed after a while by his companion for the night. One light after the other is extinguished. The market grows dark and quiet. After 9 o'clock the market-place and the streets are almost deserted.

But let us return to our daylight inspection of the town: we were standing at the crossing of the four main streets of Bida. Turn to the north, and you come to *lálemi,* the strangers' quarter of Bida, where Hausa and Yoruba are living in houses and huts built in their own tribal style and fashion. They are traders by profession, and shops and stalls line the long road to the north gate—shops in which you can buy everything at every hour of the day, from native food to a European wristwatch, from the powders and amulets of the Hausa medicine-man to brass buttons or bicycle spare parts offered for sale in a Yoruba man's shop. The road to the east bridges a stream and a stretch of marsh-land that runs across the town, with its fields of rice and sugar-cane; it runs past another quarter of brass-smiths, skirts the quarter of the *masagá,* the Bida glass-makers, and leaves the town by the Badeggi gate, so called after a village thirteen miles from Bida on the small rickety railway line (the oldest railway line in Nigeria) which links Baro on the Niger with Minna on the main line of the Nigerian Railway. The south road crosses another stream, with yellowish, dirty water in which children are bathing, grooms watering horses, and women washing their clothes and cleaning pots and pans. It runs on through a thickly populated part of the town, past a beautiful old mosque perched precariously on the edge of a deep trench; another day-market, and another royal residence. Another weavers' quarter, and another group of blacksmiths. Old Bida and New Bida mix for a while: still inside the town walls are Prison and Hospital; on the other side the Native Administration Workshops and the Middle School. And beyond this, the European Reservation, the Government Offices, and then open fields and farms.

This, then, is Bida. Like all large towns it is both more and less than one community. More, in that contacts, communications, and forms of intercourse stretch far beyond the town boundaries; and less, in that within the town walls of Bida there exists a vast number of different, almost independent, strata and "areas of common life." Some, perhaps the weakest and least tenacious, are defined by tribal origin. The social differentiation of rich and poor, of social status and political rank, create others—strata in which life is lived in different fashion, in which different values are valid and different patterns of behavior accepted as normal. But we have also observed the division of the town into three large districts, almost exact copies of each other, each with its day-market, its quarter of craftsmen, and its royal residence. The three districts are separated, geographically, by the two streams which run through Bida, and they are spoken of as three *ekpã,* "banks," and given the name of the royal house that stands on their ground. Here we deal with units of a different order: they represent political factions, organizations of partisanship and patronage, which cut across the other social, cultural, and tribal strata. They reflect specific political and economic interests, they are vested, ultimately, in that paramount political organization, the state. But that we shall understand more clearly as this description proceeds.

GEORGE GREY
Description of Australian Cave Paintings

Upon the rock which formed the left hand wall of this cave, and which partly faced you on entering, was a very singular painting, vividly coloured, representing four heads joined together. From the mild expression of the countenances, I imagined them to represent females, and they appeared to be drawn in such a manner, and in such a position, as to look up at the principal figure which I have before described; each had a very remarkable head-dress, coloured with a deep bright blue, and one had a necklace on. Both of the lower figures had a sort of dress, painted with red in the same manner as that of the principal figure, and one of them had a band round her waist. Each of the four faces was marked by a totally distinct expression of countenance, and although none of them had mouths, two, I thought, were otherwise rather good looking. The whole painting was executed on a white ground, and its dimensions were,—

	ft.	*in.*
Total length of painting	3	6¾
Breadth across two upper heads	2	6
Ditto across the two lower ones	3	1½

The next most remarkable drawing in the cave was an ellipse, three feet in length, and one foot ten inches in breadth: the outside line of this painting was of a deep blue colour, the body of the ellipse being of a bright yellow dotted over with red lines and spots, whilst across it ran two transverse lines of blue. The portion of the painting above described formed the ground, or main part of the picture, and upon this ground was painted a kangaroo in the act of feeding, two stone spear-heads, and two black balls; one of the spear-heads was flying to the kangaroo, and one away from it; so that the whole subject probably constituted a sort of charm by which the luck of an enquirer in killing game could be ascertained.

There was another rather humorous sketch, which represented a native in the act of carrying a kangaroo; the height of the man being three feet. The number of drawings in the cave could not altogether have been less than from fifty to sixty, but the majority of them consisted of men, kangaroos, &c.; the figures being carelessly and badly executed, and having evidently a very different origin to those which I have first described. Another very striking piece of art was exhibited in the little gloomy cavities situated at the back of the main cavern. In these instances some rock at the sides of the cavity had been selected, and the stamp of a hand and arm by some means transferred to it; this outline of the hand and arm was then painted black, and the rock about it white, so that on entering that part of the cave, it appeared as if a human hand and arm were projecting through a crevice admitting light.

The cave was twenty feet deep, and at the entrance seven feet high, and about forty feet wide. As before stated, the floor gradually approached the roof in the direction of the bottom of the cavern, and its width also contracted, so that at the extremity it was not broader than the slab of rock, which formed a natural seat. The principal painting in it was the figure of a man, ten feet six inches in length, clothed from the chin downwards in a red garment, which reached to the wrists and ankles; beyond this red dress the feet and hands protruded, and were badly executed.

The face and head of the figure were enveloped in a succession of circular bandages or rollers, or what appeared to be painted to represent such. These were coloured red, yellow, and white; and the eyes were the only features represented on the face. Upon the highest bandage or roller, a series of lines were painted in red, but although so regularly done as to indicate that they have some meaning, it was impossible to tell whether they were intended to depict written characters, or some ornament for the head. This figure was so drawn on the roof that its feet were just in front of the natural seat, whilst its head and face looked directly down on any one who stood in the entrance of the cave, but it was totally invisible from the outside. The painting was more injured by the damp and atmosphere, and had the appearance of being much more defaced, and ancient, than any of the others which we had seen.[1] There were two other paintings, one on each of the rocks which stood on either side of the natural seat; they were carefully executed, and yet had no apparent design in them; unless they were intended to represent some fabulous species of turtle; for the natives of Australia are generally fond of narrating tales of fabulous and extraordinary animals, such as gigantic snakes, &c.

One of the party who appeared much amused at these different paintings, walked straight up the cavern, gradually ascending the steps until he reached the slab at the end, and then taking his hat off with a solemn air, seated himself; to his own, and our surprise, his bare head just touched the roof of the cave, and on examining this part of it we found it fairly polished, and very greasy, from all appearance caused by the constant rubbing against it of the head of a person whilst seated on the rock. This and other circumstances led us to conjecture that the cave was frequented by some wise man or native doctor, who was resorted to by the inhabitants in cases of disease or witchcraft. We saw many footmarks about, and found other signs of the close presence of the natives, but they themselves remained invisible.

[1] This figure brings to mind the description of the Prophet Ezekiel:—"Men pourtrayed upon the wall, the images of the Chaldeans pourtrayed in vermilion, girded with girdles upon their loins, exceeding in dyed attire upon their heads, all of them princes to look to, after the manner of the Babylonians of Chaldea, the land of their nativity."—Chap. xxiii. 14, 15.

TOM HARRISSON

Bush Telegraph

When I arrived at Botowut, the news was out over the hills at once. It was sent in the nicest way news can be sent. A man stood in the centre of six upright slit-gongs, from two to eight feet high, and with a small log in each hand beat out in tones and times a perfect harmony describing me, my guide, my objective (counting people and talk-talk), calling in every village to see me, to examine my hair. At no time have I heard music so satisfactory and so absolutely in keeping with its environment. The sound runs over the echoing hills of my memory and down the green Pangkumu valley, from this vigorous little community perched in a tree-fern tangle of hills, whose dripping forests surround one like a sponge, in which it seems that no impression or use can ever be more than ephemeral. There were two club houses at Botowut. One was tabu for the group chief, an important person, impressively unpleasant. A peculiar female effigy indicated his tabu. The house in which I slept was swarming with hundreds of blue-bottle flies which zoomed and buzzed in the darkness, looking for native sores and dampness. Into the roof of the house were stuck the heads of dead men with clay-moulded skulls; these had, with their cobweb hair, a swarthy Red Indian sort of countenance. For an hour after sunset this desolate pocket of the mountains, deep in dew and mist, was made (if possible) more eerie and away from all that I had grown to be among, by the swinging of bull-roarers, the blowing of *nalawan* horns, noises from coconut shells filled with water on to which air is blown through a bamboo. A fine range of ghostly sound; part of the rites of youth seclusion.

BRONISLAW MALINOWSKI

Sailing on the Sea-Arm of Pilolu

Now at last the Kula expedition is properly set going. The canoes are started on a long stage, before them the sea-arm of Pilolu, stretching between the Trobriands and the d'Entrecasteaux. On the North, this portion of the sea is bounded by the Archipelago of the Trobriands, that is, by the islands of Vakuta, Boyowa and Kayleula, joining in the west on to the scattered belt of the Lousançay Islands. On the east, a long submerged reef runs from the southern end of Vakuta to the Amphletts, forming an extended barrier to sailing, but affording little protection from the eastern winds and seas. In the South, this barrier links on to the Amphletts, which together with the Northern coast of Fergusson and Goodenough, form the Southern shore of Pilolu. To the West, Pilolu opens up into the seas between the mainland of New Guinea and the Bismarck Archipelago. In fact, what the natives designate by the name of Pilolu is nothing else but the enormous basin of the Lousançay Lagoon, the largest coral atoll in the world. To the natives, the name of Pilolu is full of emotional associations, drawn from magic and myth; it is connected with the experiences of past generations, told by the old men round the village fires and with adventure personally lived through.

As the Kula adventurers speed along with filled sails, the shallow Lagoon of the Trobriands soon falls away behind; the dull green waters, sprinkled with patches of brown where seaweed grows high and rank, and lit up here and there with spots of bright emerald where a shallow bottom of clean sand shines through, give place to a deeper sea of strong green hue. The low strip of land, which surrounds the Trobriand Lagoon in a wide sweep, thins away and dissolves in the haze, and before them the southern mountains rise higher and higher. On a clear day, these are visible even from the Trobriands. The neat outlines of the Amphletts stand diminutive, yet firmer and more material, against the blue silhouettes of the higher mountains behind. These, like a far away cloud, are draped in wreaths of cumuli, almost always clinging to their summits. The nearest of them, Koyatabu—the mountain of the taboo—[1] on the North end of Fergusson Island, a slim, somewhat tilted pyramid, forms a most alluring beacon, guiding the mariners due South. To

[1] The word *tabu,* in the meaning of taboo—prohibition—is used in its verbal form in the language of the Trobriands, but not very often. The noun "prohibition," "sacred thing," is always *bomala,* used with suffixed personal pronouns.

the right of it, as we look towards the South-West, a broad, bulky mountain, the Koyabwaga'u—mountain of the sorcerers—marks the North-Western corner of Fergusson Island. The mountains on Goodenough Island are visible only in very clear weather, and then very faintly.

Within a day or two, these disembodied, misty forms are to assume what for the Trobrianders seems marvellous shape and enormous bulk. They are to surround the Kula traders with their solid walls of precipitous rock and green jungle, furrowed with deep ravines and streaked with racing water-courses. The Trobrianders will sail deep, shaded bays, resounding with the, to them unknown, voice of waterfalls; with the weird cries of strange birds which never visit the Trobriands, such as the laughing of the kookooburra (laughing jackass), and the melancholy call of the South Sea crow. The sea will change its colour once more, become pure blue, and beneath its transparent waters, a marvellous world of multi-coloured coral, fish and seaweed will unfold itself, a world which, through a strange geographical irony, the inhabitants of a coral island hardly ever can see at home, and must come to this volcanic region to discover.

In these surroundings, they will find also wonderful, heavy, compact stones of various colours and shapes, whereas at home the only stone is the insipid, white, dead coral. Here they can see, besides many types of granite and basalt and volcanic tuff, specimens of black obsidian, with its sharp edges and metallic ring, and sites full of red and yellow ochre. Besides big hills of volcanic ash, they will behold hot springs boiling up periodically. Of all these marvels the young Trobriander hears tales, and sees samples brought back to his country, and there is no doubt that it is for him a wonderful experience to find himself amongst them for the first time, and that afterwards he eagerly seizes every opportunity that offers to sail again to the Koya. Thus the landscape now before them is a sort of promised land, a country spoken of in almost legendary tone.

And indeed the scenery here, on the borderland of the two different worlds, is singularly impressive. Sailing away from the Trobriands on my last expedition, I had to spend two days, weatherbound, on a small sandbank covered with a few pandanus trees, about midway between the Trobriands and the Amphletts. A darkened sea lay to the North, big thunderclouds hanging over where I knew there was the large flat island of Boyowa—the Trobriands. To the South, against a clearer sky, were the abrupt forms of the mountains, scattered over half of the horizon. The scenery seemed saturated with myth and legendary tales, with the strange adventures, hopes and fears of generations of native sailors. On this sandbank they had often camped, when becalmed or threatened with bad weather. On such an island, the great mythical hero, Kasabwaybwayreta stopped, and was marooned by his companions, only to escape through the sky. Here again a mythical canoe once halted, in order to be re-caulked. As I sat there, looking towards the Southern mountains, so clearly visible, yet so inaccessible, I realised what must be the feelings of the Trobrianders, desirous to reach the Koya, to meet the strange people, and to *kula* with them, a desire made perhaps even more acute by a mixture of fear. For there, to the west of the Amphletts, they see the big bay of Gabu, where once the crews of a whole fleet of Trobriand canoes were killed and eaten by the inhabitants of unknown villages, in attempting to *kula* with them. And stories are also told of single canoes, drifted apart from the fleet and cast against the northern shore of Fergusson Island, of which all the crew perished at the hands of the cannibals. There are also legends of some inexperienced natives, who, visiting the neighbourhood of Deyde'i and arriving at the crystal water in the big stone basins there, plunged in, to meet a dreadful death in the almost boiling pool.

But though the legendary dangers on the distant shores may appall the native imagination, the perils of actual sailing are even more real. The sea over which they travel is seamed with reefs, studded with sandbanks and coral rocks awash. And though in fair weather these are not so dangerous to a canoe as to a European boat, yet they are bad enough. The main dangers of native sailing, however, lie in the helplessness of a canoe. As we have said before, it cannot sail close to the wind, and therefore cannot beat. If the wind comes round, the canoe has to turn and retrace its course. This is very unpleasant, but not necessarily dangerous. If, however, the wind drops, and the canoe just happens to be in one of the strong tides, which run anything between three and five knots, or if it becomes disabled, and makes leeway at right angles to its course, the situation becomes dangerous. To the West, there lies the open sea, and once far out there, the canoe would have slender chances of ever returning. To the East, there runs the reef, on which in heavy weather a native canoe would surely be smashed. In May, 1918, a Dobuan canoe, returning home a few days after the rest of the fleet, was caught by a strong South-Easterly wind, so strong that it had to give up its course, and make North-West to one of the Lousançay Islands. It had been given up as lost, when in August it came back with a chance blow of the North-Westerly wind. It had had, however, a narrow escape in making the small island. Had it been blown further West, it would never have reached land at all.

There exist other tales of lost canoes, and it is a wonder that accidents are not more frequent, considering the conditions under which they have to sail. Sailing has to be done, so to speak, on straight lines across the sea. Once they deviate from this course, all sorts of dangers crop up. Not only that, but they must sail between fixed points on the land. For, and this of course refers to the olden days, if they had to go ashore, anywhere but in the district of a friendly tribe, the perils which met them were almost as bad as those of reefs and sharks. If the sailors missed the friendly villages of the Amphletts and of Dobu, everywhere else they would meet with extermination. Even nowadays, though the danger of being killed would be smaller—perhaps not absolutely non-existent—yet the natives would feel very uncomfortable at the idea of landing in a strange district, fearing not only death by violence, but even more by evil magic. Thus, as the natives sail across Pilolu, only very small sectors of their horizon present a safe goal for their journey.

PART 5

Children

MATILDA STEVENSON

Childbirth Ceremonies of the Sia Pueblo

A typical labor case observed by the writer occurred at midnight, October 20, 1896. A child wife, not more than 15 years old, gave evidence of approaching parturition. She suffered from that time until 6 o'clock in the following evening, when she was delivered. Owing to the absence of her mother in Ojo Caliente, a farming district, the girl was confined in her mother-in-law's house. She wore only the camis, which leaves the arms exposed, and was covered with a heavy blanket. She lay most of the night on sheepskins spread on the floor near the south end of the room, pressing her feet during the pain against the ledge at the south wall of the room. She changed position from her side to her back and often lay face downward. The mother-in-law, who was a doctress, had no professional part in the treatment of her daughter-in-law, but took a seat on the floor beside the girl, offering no assistance. The two grandmothers of the girl were present and were much concerned over her suffering. The father, the father-in-law, and a paternal uncle were in an interior room. Their faces expressed anxiety, and they spoke in whispers. The husband of the girl, not expecting the birth of the child for several days, was absent at his farm in Ojo Caliente. The pains increased, and at 4 o'clock in the afternoon, two doctresses having been summoned, the kneading of the abdomen began. Each doctress took her turn, bestowing much strength and energy on the manipulation. With each pain the girl turned on her right side and caught the belt of the doctress before her, while the second doctress pressed hard upon the back, the girl pressing her feet against the ledge. The labor being prolonged, a doctress held the nostrils of the patient and blew into her mouth, occasionally releasing the pressure upon her nose for an instant. This heroic treatment appears cruel in the extreme, but it is supposed to force the child into the world. The girl wept continually. The sympathy expressed by the relatives and doctresses was enough to unnerve the sufferer. The juniper tea was frequently drunk and the girl occasionally stood over the urinal during the day, but did not leave her bed after 4 o'clock. Rupture of the membranes occurred an hour and a half before the birth of the child. Half an hour previous to delivery, one of the doctresses made an examination by inserting her hand. Apparently discouraged and alarmed, she notified the mother-in-law of her intention to call upon the officers of the Great Fire fraternity to come and sing their songs. This fraternity has four songs addressed to the Beast Gods for hastening delayed delivery. Should the child be born after the first song, the singing ceases, and so on. Should the child not be born soon after the fourth song, the heart of the patient is bad; the songs are not repeated, and the theurgists leave the house. Accordingly, the mother-in-law provided the doctress with a quarter of mutton and many yards of cotton and calico as an advance payment to the theurgists. For a long time the doctress was unsuccessful in her efforts to find the men, but she persisted in her search and finally returned with them just as the girl was being delivered of a male child. The four theurgists departed at once with the medicine of the Beast Gods and their rattles. As soon as the child's head was exposed, the girl was at once turned upon her back and most vigorously kneaded. Her drawn knees were held by two women and a doctress took her seat upon the ledge between the girl's knees and, pressing her hands to the sides of the infant's head, assisted the birth by slightly shaking the child as she pulled it to her.[1] Another doctress severed the umbilical cord with a steel knife, while the doctress holding the child pressed the cord close by the umbilicus until a cotton cord as thick as a lead pencil was procured and wrapped around it several times. In the meantime the abdomen of the young mother was manipulated until the placenta passed. It was held by the umbilical cord and hastily taken from under the blanket on the left side, dropped into a bowl, and carried from the house by the girl's maternal grandmother, who deposited it in the river with a prayer that the young mother might be blessed with many children. While this was happening the mother bit upon a white pebble, that the child's teeth might be strong and white. There seemed to be no evidence of life in the child for an hour after birth, still the doctresses and the paternal grandmother of the girl never ceased their efforts to produce respiration by pressing the nostrils, blowing into the mouth, manipulating the chest, and moving the arms, held outward and above the head. Warm clothes were kept around the body and over the head. There was great rejoicing when the faintest sign of life was discovered, but it was fully another hour before respiration was such as to give real hope of life for the child. The writer was surprised at the success of these patient efforts, as the case seemed to be a hopeless one. When no further anxiety was felt for the little one, the doctress called for piñon gum which had been boiled and, chewing it until it was white and pliable, mixed mutton grease with it, and then the paternal grandmother of the girl rubbed it on the stone floor until she produced a roll one-half inch in diameter and about 4 inches long. A blanket was now folded over the upturned feet and the extended legs of the doctress, who laid the child upon the blanket, its head resting against her feet. Opening the wrappings about the child, she raised the umbilical cord, which was about 2½ inches long and heavily wrapped with the cotton cord previously referred to, and encircled the umbilicus with the roll of piñon gum; then fluffing some carded wool and making an opening in the center, she drew the wrapped umbilical cord

---

[1] Though it is the aim of each doctress present at childbirth to bring the child into the world in order that if it be a boy, he will enter the ki'wi'sinĕ of her husband, there is no evidence of unfairness toward one another.

through, patting the wool over the piñon gum. This dressing, which was very clumsy, protruded more than an inch. The abdomen was covered with a bit of soiled cotton cloth, laid on warm, and the child's head was kept covered with a warm cloth. The paternal grandmother of the infant now dropped water upon its scrotum, and the doctress rubbed it over the parts, manipulating the penis until its form could be seen. The child's nose was frequently pinched, and the mouth and eyes were delicately manipulated. The latter when closed resembled the eyes of a frog, the lids protruding to a remarkable degree. The child's arms were now placed by its side and it was wrapped in a piece of cotton cloth and a tiny blanket, and these were held in place by strings of yucca over the shoulders, breast, and lower portion of the legs. The child was then laid upon a folded blanket. Meantime the young mother stood unassisted over the urinal, wrapped her belt around her to hold in place a heated stone, and took her seat on the ledge. Two women removed the sheepskin on which was a pool of the lochial discharge; this the maternal grandmother covered with sand, and the sand was then swept into a cloth and carried out. The girl then drank a cup of commercial tea without sugar,[2] which she enjoyed. After the young mother had taken this nourishment the father-in-law and mother-in-law brought a quantity of damp sand and deposited it upon the floor. One of the doctresses divided the sand into two portions, placed a hot stone slab under one portion and another slab on top of the sand, and worked the sand about the stones until it was thoroughly dry and heated, when she removed the stones and placed them with the other part of the sand, which was heated in the same manner. The second portion of sand was made into a circular mound, in which an elliptic depression was formed and made perfectly smooth. A circular depression to fit the child's head was made west of the ellipse, and a ridge of sand was raised between the two depressions to support the child's neck. Over the sand a heated cloth was laid. At this time much disappointment was felt that neither of the ears of corn which were brought by the mother-in-law was a ya'pota (perfect ear). One ear had three plumules, symboliz-

[2] There is great prejudice against the use of sugar at such times. The Zuñi doctors forbid the sweetening of tea or coffee.

ing fecundity; the other was a single ear. The latter[3] was held, pointing upward, back of the child's head by the mother-in-law, who also held the child. A basket of prayer meal was deposited at the head of the sand bed by the doctress who received the child into the world, and the latter offered a long prayer to A'wonawil'ona for long life and health to the child.[4] After the prayer the doctress raised the cotton cloth and sprinkled a line of meal from east to west over the sand bed, symbolic of the straight path the child must follow in order to receive the blessings of A'wonawil'ona and the Sun Father. The cloth was then returned to its place, the child was laid upon the bed, and the single ear of corn was placed at its left side. The maternal grandmother covered the child with a small blanket, which was a gift from herself. The doctress then struck the sides and ends in turn of a quaint little stool against the floor at the head of the bed, and placed it finally on its side at the head of the bed, with the seat next to the bed. An Apache basket tray was inverted over the child's head, one side resting on the edge of the stool, the other on the blanket covering, so as to raise from the face a cotton cloth which was thrown over the head. A small blanket was placed over the cotton covering. An occasional faint sound was to be heard from the infant, which caused genuine delight to the family and friends. The mother-in-law next proceeded to prepare the mother's bed with the second portion of sand, first heating the sand in the manner described. The ear of corn having three plumules was placed to the left of the bed, and when the young mother took her seat upon her bed, a bowl of mutton stew, a basket of mush boiled in corn husks, and a basket tray of wafer bread were deposited on the floor beside her. A number joined in the meal, none eating with more relish than the young mother, who sat up an hour and a half. During the meal the paternal grandfather of the infant came from the inner room. At this moment the child gave its first vigorous cry, which delighted all present, especially the grandfather. One hour after the birth of the child the mother's pulse was 80. At the first

---

[3] For a boy the single ear of corn, called the father, is used; a divided one, called the mother, is placed by a girl.

[4] The Zuñis believe that the span of life is marked out at birth. This belief, however, does not prevent their incessant prayers to A'wonawil'ona for health and a long life.

peep of the sun on the morning following the birth, the doctress who delivered the young mother, having been supplied with a vase of warm water, a gourd, and a basket of ashes, proceeded to bathe the infant. Dipping a gourd of water, she filled her mouth, and pouring the water from her mouth over the head of the child, washed its face and head, rubbing quite vigorously, after which ashes were rubbed over the face, a quantity adhering to the skin.[5] The infant's paternal grandmother now folded a blanket and laid it over the extended legs of the doctress, who placed the infant upon the blanket, its head against her upturned feet. The doctress sprinkled the breast of the infant with water, using her right hand, with a prayer for long life and health of the child; and, dipping her hand into the vase of water, she proceeded to bathe the child. After the bath the child's entire body was rubbed over with ashes. The cloth which had previously wrapped the infant was changed for another, which, however, was neither new nor clean. A blanket that had been previously warmed by the fire was afterward placed around the child. The young mother observed the bathing and wrapping of her infant with great interest. The infant was next laid upon a fresh sand bed prepared by the paternal grandmother, and the young mother walked to her bed and lay down, while a doctress bathed the lacerate perineum with warm root tea and afterward sprinkled the affected parts with a powder,[6] after which she manipulated the abdomen for thirty minutes. The young mother then sat upon the ledge by the fire while a fresh sand bed was prepared for her. After a time the child was placed to the breast, but it failed to get nourishment, though it made persistent effort. The hot juniper tea was drunk constantly after the confinement for the purpose of hastening the close of the lochial discharge, which ceased after the fourth day. On the second day, October 22, the pulse of the mother was 78. Though several efforts were made through the day to nourish the

[5] The Zuñis declare that in four days from the putting on of the ashes exfoliation occurs and a new skin appears. Ashes are used throughout the first year to render the face and other parts of the body depilous. With rare exceptions, these people are depilous, except on the scalp.

[6] In aggravated cases of laceration certain male theurgists are called in. In the case here mentioned the parts appeared to be entirely healed after the eighth day. The tea and powder were used only four days. The powder secured by the writer was not of sufficient quantity to admit an analysis.

child from the mother, the milk did not appear. On the 23d the pulse was 79. Mother and child were doing well. The lacerated perineum was much improved. The same treatment was continued. Though the feet and ankles were excessively swollen for days before parturition, they rapidly returned to their normal condition after the birth of the child. On the 24th the pulse was 79. Though the milk came, it appeared like pus, and the child refused it. The infant was so weak from lack of nourishment that the writer prepared condensed milk, upon which it was fed for some days, and its improvement was marked. On the 25th the pulse was 90. The infant was placed to the breast several times, but refused the milk. At the first light of day on the 26th, a line of meal, symbolic of the path of life, was sprinkled from the house to the point where the child was to observe for the first time the Sun Father. The doctress who had received the child when it came into the world, accompanied by the young mother and the paternal grandmother, carried the infant, with the ear of corn which had been by its side since its birth held close to its head. The doctress stooped and held the child to face east while she offered a prayer for the health and happiness, goodness of heart, and long life of the child. At sunrise the doctress dipped up several gourdfuls of water in which juniper had been steeped and emptied it into a bowl near the fireplace; then the paternal great-grandmother of the child pounded yucca root and handed it to the doctress, who made suds of it by beating it in the juniper water. As the bowl became filled with snowy froth, she took off the suds, putting them into a second bowl, and when this bowl was filled, the suds were warmed with hot juniper water. The paternal grandmother held the child until the doctress had removed her moccasins and was seated on a blanket spread on the floor. The physician held the infant, its head to the east, supporting it with the left hand. The great-grandmother and the paternal grandmother stood one on each side of the bowl. The doctress first dipped a handful of suds, and then the others took suds with their right hands. The young mother sat on the ledge near by, but took no part. The suds were held while the doctress offered a long prayer to A′wonawil′ona, the Sun Father, and the Earth Mother, that all blessings might come to the child. At the conclusion of the prayer the doctress placed the suds she held on the top of the child's head, and then the other two patted the suds on the head; and the head was then held over the bowl and thoroughly washed by the doctress. Great care was observed in bathing the eyes; they were smoothed over and over, and the nose was pinched many times. A blanket was folded and spread over the extended legs of the doctress, in the manner heretofore described, a wad being placed before the upturned feet where the child's head was to rest. The dressing was removed from the umbilicus, which was found entirely healed. The child was then bathed from a bowl containing only warm juniper water. The paternal grandmother was careful to warm the cloths in which the child was to be wrapped. Nothing was used to dry the child aside from the ashes which were rubbed over its entire body. The infant, still refusing its mother's milk, was fed with condensed milk from a spoon. It smacked its lips with satisfaction, much to the delight of the paternal grandfather and the others present. The child was then held by the grandmother, while the doctress worked up anew the yucca suds. The young mother's hair was loosed, and she bent her head over the bowl while the doctress, the mother-in-law, and the latter's mother and young niece dipped suds with their right hands and held them while the doctress prayed. After the prayer the doctress applied to the head the suds she held, and the others did the same, after which the doctress thoroughly washed the head and long hair. The young mother then took her seat while the doctress removed the remainder of her sand bed, which was carried in a blanket to the far end of the room and deposited in a heap. The doctress afterward placed by the sand heap the bowl of juniper water, in which the yucca suds had been deposited to bathe the infant, and proceeded to bathe the young mother, who was now at the other end of the room. The girl kept on her camis, which soon became thoroughly wet. The doctress poured water over her by the gourdful. The girl washed her own legs, standing while she did so. Twenty minutes were consumed in this bath, though the large room, except near the fire, was very cold. No cloth was used to dry the body. A soiled camis was slipped on her as she dropped the other, and, wrapping a heavy blanket around herself, the young mother walked over the cold stone floor in her bare feet, which were still swollen, and took her seat by the fire. Within twenty minutes after the bath the mother's pulse was 82. She seemed perfectly well and declared that she felt so. An excellent meal was served, but the grandfather was too absorbed to leave his work of attaching buckskin thongs and loops to the new cradle, which was a present from the paternal uncle Mauretio. On the cradle, just where the head of the infant should rest, was a perfectly round turquoise of excellent color. Inlaid below and close to the neck rest were three turquoises. When the cradle was completed, the child was strapped to it. In folding the wraps around the child care was observed first to bring around the piece of cotton from the right side of the child so as to prevent the arms from coming in contact with the body, the cloth passing under each arm. The other side of the cloth was then brought over both arms. The blanket was folded around and tied in two places. On the 27th the mother's pulse was 82. She was sitting up, dressed, and apparently perfectly well. The infant took the mother's milk for the first time. The pulse was the same on the 28th and 29th. The mother was up and sewing on the 29th, and the child took much notice and appeared brighter and more observing than any civilized child of the same age known to the writer.

WALTER E. ROTH

Precautions During Pregnancy in Guiana

Among the Pomeroon Arawaks, though the killing and eating of a snake during the woman's pregnancy is forbidden to both father and mother the husband is allowed to kill and eat any other animal. The cause assigned for the taboo of the snake is that the little infant might be similar, that is, able neither to talk nor to walk. Neither parent, however, when carrying a piece of cassava cake, may either turn it over in the hand, or curl it up at the sides; otherwise, the ears of the child, when born, will be found curled over. Any game hunted by dogs is strictly forbidden the pregnant woman of this tribe, just as it is at her menstruation; otherwise the dog would be spoiled for hunting purposes, permanently in the latter circumstances, temporarily in the former, the dog recovering its powers only when the baby was born. Hence, when a man brings home any animal that has been hunted by a dog, it is his wife's business to see that it is not partaken of by any woman in either of the states named.

As with the Caribs, so with the Arawaks and Warraus, it is practically the husband who is isolated, and does the "lying-in." Indeed, in these three tribes, the woman is isolated only during actual delivery, which takes place either out in the bush, in a separate shelter, or in a compartment specially partitioned off from the rest of the house. With the bath that she takes within a comparatively few hours after the interesting event has occurred, her isolation, and with it any dangerous influence of her recent condition, ceases.

The Broken Egg

Uraima once had in his possession a bird's egg, which he kept in a calabash; he took great care of it until it should hatch out. He met two girls on the road: they saw the egg and asked him to let them have it. "No!" he said, "I can not." They worried and even followed him, but he still refused. So they seized the egg, and in the course of the scuffle broke it. Uraima then spoke to the women as follows: "Since you have done this, trouble will follow you from now onward. Up to the present, the egg has belonged to man. For the future it will belong to woman and she will have to hatch it." It is only the female that lays eggs nowadays.

GEZA ROHEIM

Childhood Trauma in Australia

If we can show that a specific traumatic situation is bound to occur in the infancy of the average member of a primitive tribe we have found a new clue, perhaps the most important clue, to the development of national character. In discussing the sex *mores* of these people I mentioned the discovery of their peculiar sleeping customs. The mother lies on her son like the male on the female. This infantile trauma becomes repressed and gives rise to the myth of the *"alknarintja"* woman, the unattained goal of the boy's love, the phallic mother of mythology. This concept of the phallic mother is one of the deepest strata in the formation of the demon world. Nyiki related two anxiety dreams that he had had. In one of them he was frightened by an *erintja* and in one by a *ltana*. While relating these two dreams he is indulging in a kind of displaced onanism and playing with the sores on his leg. Then he gives another involuntary illustration of the latent content by drawing a snake in the sand. He talks about the ghost dream and said that his father died recently. His knowledge of the demons is derived from his mother. She told him that the *erintja* would come and fetch him if he did not behave himself. His illustration of the dream shows the *erintja* with the *tana* (trough) ready to fetch bad children. I ask him whether he has done anything bad and he answers, "Yes, I called my mother *'para takia'* (red penis)." Now it happens that Nyiki's mother was the very woman who first told me that she lies on her son (Nyiki is about ten years old) every night, so that we have cause and effect in one picture. Nyiki attributes the appearance of the cannibal demon to the fact that he called his mother a red penis and that is just what the demon is, a mother (child-carrier) with a penis, who lies on top of her son. The other children, both boys and girls, had similar dreams and phantasies. It is evident that the danger for the immature ego consists in a too great approximation to the primary wishes in a premature flooding of the organism with libido. Nyiki probably has an erection when lying under his mother, perhaps also an ejaculation without immission of the penis. A full gratification would not be tolerated by either parents and would also be made impossible by the shadow they have thrown into the scarcely formed infant; by the super-ego. Thus pleasure becomes a danger, the danger of being eaten (the passive rôle in coitus, castration, total annihilation) by the being with the huge genital. This very strong premature fixation is then dealt with in the demon-phobia, in the projected mother-image of the *alknarintja* women, and in certain character traits, to be discussed in connection with the subject of character-formation.

Attempting to summarize what we have found regarding the id of a Central Australian native we see that here too the Œdipus and castration complex forms the nucleus around which all other human strivings are crystallized. The essential differences are to be found not in the id at all but in the ego. In character development the straight line, i.e. sublimation, is predominant, while reaction formation of the anal type is absent. Repression goes only skin deep, there is no latency period and the phallic organization survives into adult age.

If we say that initiation is a dramatization of the formation of a super-ego, or if we call it a dramatization of repression, we are saying nearly the same thing. But perhaps it will be useful to envisage the events from this new angle. The boy has been living with the beloved mother and the father. His attitude towards the latter is ambivalent, as he represents for him restriction of his desires, although manifested only non-systematically in the form of occasional outbursts of temper. At the initiation ceremony the society of adults behaves like a powerful army which has been hitherto content with occasional threats against the rebellious forces, but now, seeing them growing in strength, decides to make a serious effort to quell the rebellion. A systematic effort is made to tell the boy what he may not do, i.e., an effort to reinforce the repressive forces at the time when puberty shows that his sexuality must now be taken seriously. An organized attempt is made to put repression into action at the most critical point by teaching the reincarnation doctrine. At the moment when the boys are about to become fathers, the old men jealously guarding their own privileges tell them that they can never become fathers because it is not they who make the children but the ancestors, the *churunga* in the sacred cave, the objects in the keeping of the old men. The elder generation is acting unconsciously, or rather it is dramatizing its own tension, and in this dramatization we get a clear picture of the process of repression. It begins by circumcision as a symbolic castration. The next phase is the blood ritual. Every day the initiators, "the fathers," pour the blood from their veins on the boy's body; he must always be covered with their blood. And from time to time he has to drink this blood which they have poured into a tree bark. The explanation they give for this ritual is that the boy should have a big body. It is the same thing as the consolation given by Kanakana to the boy after the circumcision, "Now you are like I am." By drinking the blood of the elders he becomes an elder himself; this is the process of identification. This leads to the crystallization of a new personality in the ego, the super-ego as materialized in the two *churungas* (body and penis) which he gets from the elders.

HERMAN MELVILLE

A Bathing Baby

One day, in company with Kory-Kory, I had repaired the stream for the purpose of bathing, when I observed a woman sitting upon a rock in the midst of the current, and watching with the liveliest interest the gambols of something, which at first I took to be an uncommonly large species of frog that was sporting in the water near her. Attracted by the novelty of the sight, I waded towards the spot where she sat, and could hardly credit the evidence of my senses when I beheld a little infant, the period of whose birth could not have extended back many days, paddling about as if it had just risen to the surface, after being hatched into existence at the bottom. Occasionally the delighted parent reached out her hands towards it, when the little thing, uttering a faint cry, and striking out its tiny limbs, would sidle for the rock, and the next moment be clasped to its mother's bosom. This was repeated again and again, the baby remaining in the stream about a minute at a time. Once or twice it made wry faces at swallowing a mouthful of water, and choked and spluttered as if on the point of strangling. At such times, however, the mother snatched it up, and by a process scarcely to be mentioned obliged it to eject the fluid. For several weeks afterwards I observed this woman bringing her child down to the stream regularly every day, in the cool of the morning and evening, and treating it to a bath. No wonder that the South Sea Islanders are so amphibious a race, when they are thus launched into the water as soon as they see the light. I am convinced that it is as natural for a human being to swim as it is for a duck. And yet in civilized communities how many able-bodied individuals die, like so many drowning kittens, from the occurrence of the most trivial accidents!

MARGARET MEAD

Early Influences that Mould the Arapesh Personality

How is the Arapesh baby moulded and shaped into the easy, gentle, receptive personality that is the Arapesh adult? What are the determinative factors in the early training of the child which assures that it will be placid and contented, unaggressive and non-initiatory, non-competitive and responsive, warm, docile, and trusting? It is true that in any simple and homogeneous society the children will as adults show the same general personality-traits that their parents have shown before them. But this is not a matter of simple imitation. A more delicate and precise relationship obtains between the way in which the child is fed, put to sleep, disciplined, taught self-control, petted, punished, and encouraged, and the final adult adjustment. Furthermore, the way in which men and women treat their children is one of the most significant things about the adult personality of any people, and one of the points at which contrasts between the sexes come out most sharply. We can only understand the Arapesh, and the warm and maternal temperament of both men and women, if we understand their childhood experience and the experience to which they in turn subject their children.

During its first months the child is never far from someone's arms. When the mother walks about she carries the baby suspended from her forehead in its special small net bag, or suspended under one breast in a bark-cloth sling. This latter method is the beach custom, the net-bag carrier belongs to the Plains, and the mountain women use both, depending in great part upon the health of the child. If the child is fretful and irritable, it is carried in the sling, where it can be given the comforting breast as swiftly as possible. A child's crying is a tragedy to be avoided at any cost, and this attitude is carried over into later life. The most trying period for the mother is when her child of three or so is too old to be comforted by the breast and too young and inarticulate to state clearly the reasons for its weeping. Children are held a great deal, often in a standing position so that they can push with their feet against the arms or legs of the person who holds them. As a result infants can stand, steadied by their two hands, before they can sit alone. Suckled whenever they cry, never left far distant from some woman who can give them the breast if necessary, sleeping usually in close contact with the mother's body, either hung in a thin net bag against her back, crooked in her arm, or curled on her lap as she sits cooking or plaiting, the child has a continuous warm sensation of security. It is only subjected to two shocks, and both of these have their reverberations in later personality development. After the first few weeks, during which it is bathed in a gingerly fashion with warmed water, the child is bathed under a jetting spout of cold water that is catapulted out upon it from a tipped bamboo water-carrier, a harsh, abrupt cold shock. Babies uniformly resent this treatment, and continue to hate the cold and the rain throughout their lives.[1] Also when an infant urinates or defecates, the person holding it will jerk it quickly to one side to prevent soiling his or her own person. This jerk interrupts the normal course of excretion and angers the child. In later life, the Arapesh have notably low sphincter-control, and regard its loss as the normal concomitant of any highly charged situation.

For the rest the little baby's life is a very warm and happy one. It is never left alone; comforting human skin and comforting human voices are always beside it. Both little boys and little girls are enthusiastic about babies—there is always someone to hold the child. When the mother goes to the garden to work, she takes a small boy or girl along to hold the baby, instead of laying the baby down on a piece of bark or hanging it up for the morning in its little net bag. If the little nurse is a boy, he will hold the child in his arms, if a girl, she will wear the baby-bag on her back.

---

[1] I do not suggest that the Arapesh dislike of the rain and the cold is entirely or even in major fashion caused by this practice, but it is interesting that the Tchambuli infants, who are bathed in the warm lake-water that hardly takes on a chill even after sunset, have none of the Arapesh dislike of the rain, and go about quite cheerfully in it all day long.

When the child begins to walk the quiet continuous rhythm of its life changes somewhat. It is now becoming a little heavy for the mother to carry about with her on long trips to the garden, and furthermore it can be expected to live without suckling for an hour or so. The mother leaves the child in the village with the father, or with some other relative, while she goes to the garden or for firewood. She returns often enough to a crying and disgruntled baby. Repentant, desirous of making restitution, she sits down and suckles the child for an hour. This rhythm, which begins as an hour's absence and an hour's compensatory suckling, develops into longer and longer periods, until by the time the child is three or so it is often being given a day's abstinence—supplemented, of course, by other food—followed by a day's nursing, in which the mother sits all day, holding the child on her lap, letting it suckle as it wishes, play about, suckle again, play with her breasts, gradually regain its sense of security. This is an experience that the mother enjoys as much as the child. From the time the little child is old enough to play with her breasts, the mother takes an active part in the suckling process. She holds her breast in her hand and gently vibrates the nipple inside the child's lips. She blows in the child's ear, or tickles its ears, or playfully slaps its genitals, or tickles its toes. The child in turn plays little tattoos on its mother's body and its own, plays with one breast while suckling the other, teases the breast with its hands, plays with its own genitals, laughs and coos and makes a long, easy game of the suckling. Thus the whole matter of nourishment is made into an occasion of high affectivity and becomes a means by which the child develops and maintains a sensitivity to caresses in every part of its body. It is no question of a completely clothed infant being given a cool hard bottle and firmly persuaded to drink its milk and get to sleep at once so that the mother's aching arms can stop holding the bottle. Instead, nursing is, for mother and child, one long delightful and highly charged game, in which the easy warm affectivity of a lifetime is set up.

Meanwhile, as the child grows older it learns to substitute new delights for its mother's breasts during her ever lengthening absences. It learns to play with its lips. This play it sees all about it among the older children, and the older children also play with the baby's lips and so set the first part of the pattern that fits in so well with the child's temporary loneliness and hunger. Interestingly enough, no Arapesh child ever sucks its thumb or sucks one finger continuously.[2] But it engages in every other conceivable type of lip-play. It flicks its upper lip with its thumb, with its first finger, with its second finger; it blows out its cheeks and pounds them; it bubbles its lips with the palm of its hand, with the back of its hand; it tickles the inside of its lower lip with its tongue; it licks its arms and its knees. A hundred different stylized ways of playing with the mouth are present in the play of the older children and gradually transmitted to the developing child.

This lip-play is the thread of behaviour which binds together the child's emotional life, which ties the happy security it felt in its yielding mother's arms to placid enjoyment of the long evenings by the fireside among its elders, and finally to a contented, unspecific sexual life. The Arapesh themselves regard playing with the lips as the symbol of childhood. Young boys and girls who tell legends that properly should only be told by grown-up people are warned to bubble their lips afterwards so that their hair will not become prematurely grey. And boys who have been initiated are told by the older men to cease playing with their lips; are they still children that they should do so? At the same time they are permitted to substitute betel-chewing and smoking, so that the lips, so long accustomed to constant stimulation, shall not be lonely. But the girls are permitted to bubble their lips until they have borne children, and we shall see how this fits in with the way in which the women's development is accounted slower than the men's.

While the small child lies on its mother's lap, warm and glowing from her attention, she builds up in it a trust of the world, a receptive and welcoming attitude towards food, towards dogs and pigs, towards persons. She holds a piece of taro in her hand, and as the child suckles the mother remarks in a soft singsong voice, "Good taro, good taro, would you eat, would you eat, would you eat, a little taro, a little taro, a little taro," and when the child releases the

---

[2] It is probable that thumb-sucking, absent among most primitive people, is a habit built up in the first few months of life, a period during which primitive children are almost always suckled whenever they cry.

breast for a moment, a bit of taro is slipped into its mouth. The dog or the little tame pig that thrusts an inquisitive nose under the mother's arm is held there, the child's skin and the dog's rubbed together, the mother gently rocking them both, and murmuring, "Good dog, good child, good dog, good, good, good." In the same way, all of the child's relatives are commended to its trust and the kinship words themselves are endowed with a happy content. Before the baby can be expected to understand what she says, the mother begins to murmur in its ear, pausing to blow softly between words: "This is your other mother (mother's sister), other mother, other mother. See your other mother. She is good. She brings you food. She smiles. She is good." So complete is this training that the words themselves come to carry so much reassurance that the child acts under their compulsion almost against the evidence of its senses. So when a two-year-old would run screaming from me, a stranger and of a strange colour, the mother could calm its fears by insisting that I was its mother's sister, or its father's sister, or its grandmother. The child who a moment before had been panting with terror would come and sit quietly in my lap, cuddling down in a safe world again.

No gradations of behaviour are forced upon the child except a very mild acknowledgment of difference in age. So a child will be bidden to run more swiftly on an errand for a grandfather than for a father; it will note the extra gentleness and sense of achievement and content with which its grandfather remarks: "I stay at home now and my grandchildren cluster about my house-ladder." The fact that it is second-born or third-born is quite often mentioned. "See, the second-born eats well, and the first-born sits and plays with its food," or, "The second-born goes now to work and the first-born sits quietly at home." Such remarks about its own position in the family and about the relative positions of its elders serve to stress the only point of differentiation to which the Arapesh pay much attention. For the rest, the child learns to trust and love and depend upon everyone whom it encounters. There is no one whom it does not call uncle, or brother, or cousin, or the comparable names for women. And because these terms are used with wide extensions and in complete disregard of generations, even the gradations of age implied in them are blurred. The child in arms is already accustomed to being chucked under the chin and called playfully "my little grandfather" or "my fat little uncle." Relationships are further blurred by the Arapesh casualness that permits a man to call the eldest of a group of brothers and sisters "uncle," the second "grandmother," and the third "son," depending upon the point of view from which he happens to be regarding his relationship at the moment. Or a man may call a woman "sister" and her husband "grandfather." In such a world, and a world where there is no special behaviour dictated between cousins or between brothers-in-law, where no one is shy of anyone else, and all relationships are tinged with mutual trust and affection, with assurance of gifts of food, co-operation, and a shared life, naturally the young child does not make any clear distinctions.

And although the distinction between the sexes is clear in terminology, it is blurred in behaviour. The child does not learn that only its father and mother may sleep unchaperoned in a house, while an aunt or a cousin would shy away from such close contact with a relative of opposite sex. The Arapesh know nothing about such restrictions. An Arapesh boy is taught by his parents: "When you travel, in any house where there is a mother's sister, or a father's sister, or a female cousin, or a niece, or a sister-in-law, or a daughter-in-law, or a niece-in-law, there you may sleep in safety." The opposite point, that people to whom sex-relations are forbidden had better not be left alone together, is a point so foreign to the Arapesh that it never enters their heads.

Neither little girls nor little boys wear any clothes until they are four or five; they are taught to accept their physiological differences without any shame or embarrassment. Excretion is not a matter about which privacy is insisted upon for small children; indeed the adults merely go casually to the edge of the village—their attitude is characterized by shyness but hardly by shame. Women sleep naked at night, and as has been said before, men at all times wear their G-strings carelessly, pushing them aside to scratch themselves. Little children are taught to observe the rules of cleanliness not through the invocation of shame, but merely through expressions of disgust. This is highly developed in them, so that four- and five-year-olds will shudder away from such new substances as mucilage or green mould on leather. The more usual association of excretion with a vivid consciousness of the genitalia, and consequently of sex-differences, is very slightly developed.

Small children are not required to behave differently to children of their own sex and those of opposite sex. Four-year-olds can roll and tumble on the floor together without anyone's worrying as to how much bodily contact results. Thus there develops in the children an easy, happy-go-lucky familiarity with the bodies of both sexes, a familiarity uncomplicated by shame, coupled with a premium upon warm, all-over physical contact.

As the child grows older, it is no longer confined so closely to the care of its own parents. Children are lent about. An aunt comes to visit and takes home the four-year-old for a week's stay, handing him on to some other relative for eventual return to his parents. This means that a child learns to think of the world as filled with parents, not merely a place in which all of his safety and happiness depend upon the continuance of his relationship to his own particular parents. It widens his circle of trust, without, however, overgeneralizing his affection. He does not see half a dozen mothers and half a dozen fathers all of the time, so that his own parents become blurred into a general parental picture. Instead, he sees his own parents most of all, and then other sets of parents, serially, in close intimacy, in the small compact family groups. The quick response of an Arapesh child to demonstrative affection is one of the ways in which this transfer from one household to another is effected. Half an hour's cuddling, and an Arapesh baby will follow one anywhere. Already trained to regard all the world as a safe place in which to wander, it follows happily the last member of the kind world who tickles its stomach, or scratches its always itching little back. Children wriggle about on the ground from one friendly adult to another, settling down beside anyone who pays definite attention to them.

There is no insistence at all upon children's growing up rapidly, or acquiring special skills or proficiencies, and there is a corresponding lack of techniques for training them physically. They are allowed to essay tasks far beyond their powers, to try to climb ladders and lose their nerve halfway up, to play with knives on which they will cut themselves if they are not constantly watched. There is one exception. Little girls are trained to carry; small bulky carrying-bags are placed on their heads while they are still so tiny that they themselves spend most of the time on the trail curled up in larger bags on their mothers' backs. They are permitted as a great favour to carry their parents' possessions, and learn to accept carrying as a proud badge of growing older. But with this one exception, the whole physical training of the children is informal. A baby tries to climb one of the notched logs that serve as house-ladders; overcome with fright, it screams. Someone immediately rushes forward to catch it. A child stumbles; it is picked up and cuddled. The result is that the child grows up with a sense of emotional security in the care of others, not in its own control over the environment. This is a cold, wet world, full of pitfalls, hidden roots in the path, stones over which small feet stumble. But there is always a kind hand, a gentle voice, to rescue one. Trust in those about one is all that is required. What one does one's self matters very little.

This whole attitude towards tools and the control of the body is reflected later in the casual and imperfect technical skills of the adults. The Arapesh have no well-defined techniques; even the knots with which they tie the parts of a house together are varied and made in different styles. When they measure a length, they almost always get it wrong, and far from correcting it, they adjust the rest of the structure to the one mistake. Their houses are carelessly and asymmetrically built. Their few handicrafts, mat-making, basket-making, arm-band and belt plaiting, are crude and imperfect. They constantly import beautifully made models and either degrade the design by crude copying, or give it up altogether. No discipline of hand and eye has ever been given them.

Painting is perhaps the art in which they do best. A large impressionistic style of painting on large pieces of bark makes it possible for the specially gifted man to create, almost without a tradition, occasional charming designs. But such a man's skill has little permanent effect upon the people's lack of belief in their own abilities, their continuing dependence upon the artistic work of other peoples because they believe themselves incapable. At best the children are schooled in enthusiasm, in quick happy delight when a bright colour or a new tune is presented to them. This attitude they catch from the adults, whose response to a coloured picture from an American magazine is not "What is it?" but always "Oh, how lovely!"

The continual moving about from one place to another has its reverberation in the children's lives. They are not accustomed to large enough groups to play group games; instead each child clings close to an adult or an older brother or sister. The long walks from one garden to another, or from garden-house to village, tire them out, and arrived at the end of the journey, while the mother cooks the supper and the father sits and gossips with the other men, the children sit about, bubbling their lips. Games are hardly ever played. Little children are only allowed to play with each other as long as they do not quarrel. The minute there is the slightest altercation the adult steps in. The aggressor—or both children if the other child resents the attack—is dragged off the scene of battle and held firmly. The angry child is allowed to kick and scream, to roll in the mud, to throw stones or firewood about on the ground, but he is not allowed to touch the other child. This habit of venting one's rage at others upon one's own surroundings persists into adult life. An angry man will spend an hour banging on a slit gong, or hacking with an ax at one of his own palm-trees.

The whole training of the little children is not to teach them to control emotion, but to see that its expression harms no one but themselves. In the case of girls, expression of anger is checked earlier. Their mothers make them pretty grass skirts that will be ruined by a tumble tantrum in the mud, and place on their heads net bags the contents of which it would be a pity to spill. As a result little girls control their fits of rage and crying much earlier than do little boys, who may roll and scream in the mud up to the age of fourteen or fifteen without any sense of shame. The sex-difference here is accentuated by two other points. When small boys are four or five they tend to transfer their major allegiance to their fathers; they follow them about, sleep in their arms at night, and are very dependent upon them. But a man can take a small child everywhere with him even less than a woman. So the small boy is more often deserted, rejected by the one upon whom he chiefly depends, and weeps in agony as his father starts off on a journey. As he grows a little older, his father will sometimes leave him, not to the care of his mother or his mother's co-wife whom the child also calls mother, but to older brothers, and here he feels even more deserted. The slightest teasing on the older boy's part, especially a refusal of food, will send him into fits of weeping, followed by a fit of rage. The old traumatic situation when his mother left him alone for hours at a time seems to be reinstated, and he seeks by his childish fit of rage to produce the old sequel, a devoted and repentant parent. And he does in part succeed, for all, including the teasing brothers, are aghast at his misery, and do their best to reassure the child. Little girls, however, join the work of the family earlier; they are more involved with the care of young children, and as they seldom become primarily attached to their fathers, they do not suffer this second weaning. It is notable that the three small girls who did have temper tantrums like the boys were all daughters of fathers who had no sons, and therefore treated the little girls as sons. The inevitable occasions would arrive when the father had to go away hunting or trading, or searching for the sorcerer who was charming a relative to death. Then the small girls tore off their grass skirts and rolled in the mud with as good a will as their brothers. But usually girls are not subjected to a second weaning procedure of this sort unless after they are grown their husbands die, when as widows they go through the traumatic experience of loss of parenthood again, with sometimes violent emotional disturbance. But this experience does not come to every woman, and comes to no girl until much later in life.

Furthermore, as it is considered appropriate for big men to simulate anger and defiance in their public speeches, to wield a spear, stamp their feet, and shout, the little boy has a model of violent expression before him that the little girl lacks, and he is too young to know that the behaviour of the big man is, at least in theory, always merely a theatrical performance.

These temper tantrums are almost always motivated by some insecurity or rejection point. A child is refused a request, is not permitted to accompany someone, is given a push or spoken to roughly by an older child, is rebuked, or, most important of all, is refused food. The trantrums that follow a refusal of food are the most numerous and the most interesting because the child is not to be placated by a subsequent offer of food. The refusal of the longed-for coconut or piece of sugar-cane has set off a whole train of response, far in excess of any power that the mere food has to stop it, and the child may weep for an hour, the helpless victim of a repeat situation in which the parent is equally powerless. These tantrums over rejection serve to channel anger as response to a hostile act on the part of another, and the definite training against aggressiveness towards other children completes this pattern.

The parental disapproval of fighting among children is always reinforced by rebukes couched in terms of relationship: "Would you, the younger brother, hit him who is first-born?" "Would you, his father's sister's son, hit your mother's brother's son?" "It is not right that two cousins should struggle with one another like little dogs." Children get no schooling in accepting harshness, in what we are accustomed to call good sportsmanship, that willingness to take it on the chin which is believed to be more consonant with the masculine temperament in our society. Arapesh small boys are as protected from aggression and struggle, from rude disciplinary measures on the part of older children and irritated parents, as is the most tenderly reared and fragile little daughter among ourselves. As a result, Arapesh boys never develop "good sportsmanship"; their feelings are intolerably wounded by a blow, or even a harsh word. The slightest gibe is taken as an expression of unfriendliness, and grown men will burst into tears at an unfair accusation.

They carry into adult life the fear of any rift between associates. The culture has a few external symbolic ways in which a genuine rift can be expressed, public signs of a disagreement that can be set up to handle the situation without actual personal clash between the individuals concerned. These are seldom used. It sometimes happens, however, that a man finally decides that his wife is incapable of feeding pigs. This is a very serious decision, for feeding pigs is one of woman's crowning glories in social achievement. The situation is further complicated by the fact that it is never, or hardly ever, her own or her husband's pigs that she feeds, but rather a pig belonging to one of her relatives, or to one of her husband's relatives. Its death through sickness, or straying, or capture by a hawk or a python, is a major tragedy, and one for which the husband feels it necessary to discipline her. He does this, in case several such tragic deaths occur and it is apparent to all that she is unfitted to raise pigs, by placing a sign outside her door. Through a piece of bark that has been the pig's feeding-trough he thrusts a spear on which he ties a piece of yam, a piece of taro, and so on. Through the corners of the bark he thrusts arrows. Then everyone will know how he feels about the matter, but he need not discuss the matter with his wife, and if she sulks, she sulks at a situation that has become impersonal and formal. So between relatives who are really angry at each other, the more enraged fastens a mnemonic knot of croton-leaf and hangs it up in his own doorway, which means that he will never eat with his annoying relatives again. To remove this formal sign of breach, a pig must be killed by the person who originally fastened the knot. So also a *buanyin* who finds the *buanyin* relationship intolerable may sever it by placing a carved wooden bowl, with a rim of twigs around it, on the *agehu,* thus declaring the relationship at an end. But all of these highly stylized methods of breaking off a relationship are rare; a man thinks a long time before taking such a drastic step and establishing a position that will be very uncomfortable to maintain and very expensive to withdraw from.

The fear and discomfort resulting from any expression of anger is further worked into the pattern of sorcery. An angry person may not hit another, he may not resort to any thorough-going abuse of another. But one may, in retaliation, take on for a moment the behaviour that is appropriate not to a relative and a member of the same locality, but to a Plainsman, a stranger and an enemy. Arapesh children grow up dividing the world into two great divisions: *relatives,* which division includes some three to four hundred people, all the members of their own locality, and those of villages in other localities which are connected with them or their relatives by marriage, and the long lines of the wives and children of their father's hereditary trade-friends; and *strangers* and *enemies,* usually formalized as *waribim,* Plainsmen, literally, "men from the river-lands." These Plainsmen play in the children's lives the dual rôle of the bogyman to be feared, and the enemy to be hated, mocked, outwitted, upon whom all the hostility that is disallowed in the group is actively displaced. Children hear the mutterings and cursing of their parents when the arrogant Plainsmen pass through; they hear death and misfortune laid to the sorcerers' doors. When they are only five or so they are cautioned: "Never leave any half-eaten food lying about in a place where there are strangers. If you break off a sugar-cane stem, be careful that no stranger sees you do it, or he will return and pick up the butt and use it to sorcerize you. If you eat an areca-nut be careful not to throw part of the kernel away in the husk. If you eat the durable tough yam, eat it all; do not leave a piece that a stranger may seize and use against you. When you sleep in a house where there are strangers, lie with your face up, that none of your saliva may drip on the bark, later to be carried away and hidden by the enemy. If anyone gives you an opossum-bone to gnaw, keep the bone until you can hide it somewhere when no one is looking." And a little boy is given a palm-leaf basket, a little girl a tiny net bag in which to carry about these food leavings so that they may not fall into the hands of the stranger. This constant cautioning about "dirt" makes everyone in Arapesh culture obsessive on the subject. By eating, by chewing areca-nut, by smoking, by sex-intercourse, one is constantly having to relinquish some portion of one's person that may fall into the hands of strangers, and falling there cause one to fall ill, or die. Fear of illness, of death, of misfortune, is dramatized in this insistence upon care about one's dirt. The child is led to believe that hostility, itself a feeling that exists only between strangers, normally, regularly expresses itself in the theft and secreting of a bit of dirt. This conception which links fear and anger with a definite behaviour-pattern is compulsive in the adult life of the Arapesh.

Suppose that a brother injures a man, or a cousin uses him hardly, not as a relative would normally act but becoming for the moment the "enemy," the "stranger." The injured man has no sense of gradation to fall back upon; he has not been reared to a small circle of very friendly close relatives and a slightly less friendly circle of less close relatives—to differential behaviour towards his brother and his brother-in-law. He knows only two categories of behaviour, that of a member of one's own wide and trusted group, and that of the enemy. The brother with whom he is angry enters for the moment the category of enemy, and he purloins his brother's dirt and gives it to the Plainsmen. Practically all of the dirt of mountain people that finds its way into the little caches of the Plains sorcerers is stolen not by these sorcerers, but by the mountain people themselves, by angry brothers and cousins and wives. This fact the mountain people know well enough. When they wish to locate which sorcerers' village probably holds the dirt of a sick man, they follow the line of hereditary trade-friends of the man to whom the sick man has most recently given cause for anger. But when a man dies, the death is not laid at the door of the man who stole the dirt. He is believed to have forgotten his anger long ago. It is attributed instead to the sorcerer, whose behaviour the angry man originally imitated, compulsively, during his rage at his friend.

So the lack of any intermediate expressions of annoyance and the existence of only two categories, complete friend or complete enemy, force the Arapesh to behave in a way that they themselves disown as invalid and intrusive, as the unexplained madness of a moment. And the lack of any kind of rough-and-tumble sport, any ordinary, lightly charged quarrelling among children, makes an Arapesh particularly vulnerable when he meets with the slightest expression of anger. Fear and panic result, and the compulsive theft of dirt is only too likely to follow. When a man relates such an act, he does it without affectation, as he might describe an involuntary movement of his eyes in the presence of a bright light: "He opposed me. He took sides against me. He helped the people who carried off my mother. He said she might remain married to that man. He did not help me. I was staying with him in the house of my mother's brother. He ate a piece of kangaroo-meat. He laid down the bone. He forgot it. He stood up and went outside the house. My eyes saw that no one was looking. My hand reached out and took the bone. I hid it quickly in my basket. The next day I met on the road a man from Dunigi whom I called 'grandfather.' I gave it to him. I just gave it to him. I gave him no ring with it." (If a piece of dirt is given to a sorcerer without a fee, it is understood that he will make no immediate moves, but will wait for a retaining-fee either from the man who originally gave him the dirt or from some more recently angered person; this latter fee is practically non-existent, but is invoked as an alibi.) Such an account as this is given in a low, emotionless voice, without either pride or remorse, without any admission of genuine complicity. The pattern learned in early childhood has simply asserted itself as a whole.

To return again to the play-training of the children: as children grow older and play games; they play none that encourage aggressiveness or competition.[3] There are no races, no games with two sides. Instead they play at being opossums or at being kangaroos, or one is a sleeping cassowary that the others startle. Many of the games are like the kindergarten games of very little children, singing games in which some simple pantomime like an imitation of sago-cutting accompanies the traditional words. And even these games are played very seldom. More often the times when children are together in large enough groups to make a game worth while are the occasions of a feast, there is dancing and adult ceremonial, and they find the rôle of spectatorship far more engrossing. This is a rôle to which their lip-bubbling has helped to reconcile them from earliest years. Also, as mere babies they danced on the shoulders of their mothers and aunts, all through the long night dances. In these dances, which celebrate the completion of some piece of work like a yam-harvest or a hunting-trip, the women prefer to dance with children on their shoulders, and so while the women sometimes dance and sometimes sit quietly smoking by the little fires, the little children are handed about from one dancing woman to another, and so dance the whole night through, bobbing up and down half-asleep on the swaying shoulders of the dancing women. Babies learn quite young to sleep astride the neck of an adult, supported by one hand grasped firmly by the adult's hand, adjusting themselves without waking to any movement that the adult makes.

[3] Football, played with a lime-fruit, is now being introduced by returned work-boys.

All of this early experience accustoms them to be part of the whole picture, to prefer to any active child-life of their own a passive part that is integrated with the life of the community.

In the life of children in groups there is one marked sex-difference that prevails throughout life. Little girls are mainly useful for carrying, weeding, gathering food, and carrying firewood. Whenever there is to be a harvest or a feast, all the small feminine relatives are requisitioned, and a whole bevy of little girls meet together to work hard for a day or so. This is practically the only time when they see each other, for on the actual occasions of the feasts they are even busier than on other working-occasions. After a day's carrying, with their small jaws shut tight and their foreheads glistening with sweat under the heavy loads, they are too tired even to gossip, and firm friends, aged eleven or twelve, fall asleep in each other's arms on the same bark bed, humming little tunes together. Crowds and work become closely associated in their minds, while easy conversation and freedom from too exacting labour are associated with the small group of close relatives, gathered about the evening fire in the "small hamlet," the residence village of the clan.

Boys have an exactly opposite experience. Their work lies not in groups but in accompanying a father or an elder brother on a hunting-expedition or into the bush to gather herbs or vines or to cut wood for house-building. One small boy and one or two older men is the pattern group for little boys' work. When there are no such expeditions on foot, then two or three or even more small boys may foregather to make toy bows and arrows and practise shooting at lizards or at targets made of bright orange fruit, to lay traps for rats, or to make rattles or pop-guns. Association with their own age-group is their most casual, happy time, and this may account for the greater restlessness of the men when they are long confined in a "small hamlet," their greater urge to be ever up and visiting their brothers and cousins. The men's greater desire to visit about is a constant cause of jesting reproach of the men by the women, and a man who is too fond of doing so will be nicknamed "Walk-about" or "Never-sit-down" by his wives. One of the forms that slight nervous instability takes among the Arapesh is an over-sensitivity to social situations; this may express itself either in the individual's becoming a hermit, and living in the heart of the bush, or in his eternally walking about from one festive occasion to another, unable to resist the sound of the most distant drums.

The training that children receive about property is one which encourages a respect for the property of others and a sense of easy security in the property of one's own family group, rather than any stronger sense of possessiveness. Children are rebuked if they injure the property of other people, and a gentle reiterative, "That is Balidu's, be careful of it. That is grandfather's, don't break it," will accompany a child's explorations on the premises of others. But the counter-remark, "That is not yours," which was the constant nagging comment of Manus mothers, is not made. The distinction between "mine" and "thine" is not the point emphasized, but rather the need to be careful of other people's things. The family possessions are treated very differently. The child is given anything it cries for, which often results in its breaking its mother's ear-rings or unstringing her necklace of bandicoot-teeth. The house in which a child lives is not a forbidden world filled with treasures that he is constantly being bidden to let alone, until they come to assume enormous importance in his eyes. If the parents have something that they feel the child will injure, they hide it securely away so that the child will never come to desire it. This whole attitude was vividly illustrated when I showed them a red balloon. It was the clearest and most beautiful piece of colour that the people had ever seen; the children screamed with excitement and even the adults held their breath with joy—for a moment. Then, "Better put it away," they said sadly. "You surely cannot have many such beautiful things, and the babies will cry for them."

As the child grows older, he is told that the carved wooden plate that is only used for feasts, or the bird-of-paradise headdress that his father wears when he dances, is his—the child's. But his parents continue to use these things. His father takes him into the bush and shows him clumps of young sago and, teaching him the names of the clumps, he explains that these also are his. "Own property" comes to mean things that belong to the future, something that is used by others now, or is not yet his own. When he grows up, he will similarly designate all of his belongings as his children's. In such a system no one becomes aggressively possessive about his own, and theft, locked doors, and the primitive equivalent of locks —black magic placed on property—are virtually unknown. The Arapesh possess a few protective garden charms of which they have so far lost the point that when they place them on their garden-fences, they believe that their own wives and children will also suffer from the effects of eating from their own gardens.

MELVILLE J. HERSKOVITS and
FRANCES S. HERSKOVITS

The Bush Negro Family

We were aroused early after our night of stories. The women were moving about, getting their morning meal before daybreak came to give them light for their harvesting. There was much they had to do. Late that afternoon they would be returning to their villages, for the next day was sacred to the Earth Mother, and no work could be done in the fields. Today, added to the round of harvesting were the preparations for the return to their village. The rice that had been cut during the week would have to be carried there for drying and winnowing, and yams and peanuts and beans were to be brought in.

Not far off, in the bush, the "baboons" were crying. We had been told how these howling monkeys lived in bands, and how they had an "old man" for leader. Their strange cries, ringing through the forest, sounded like despair made articulate. A terribly moving reiteration of four or five wailing notes went on and on, rising slowly in volume, until their cries blotted out all other sounds, and then, like a wave receding, diminishing until quiet reigned again. But when we had given up listening for its distant echo, there it was again, filling the darkness of the clearing with despair, until, at its very height, we heard the low, penetrating grunts of their "*G'aman* —Chief" and instantly all was still. They were done for the night. With daylight, they would go deeper into the bush.

Soon our men, too, began to stir, and, as we came out of our hammocks, Bayo and Angita entered the clearing. They were just now returning from the dance at Pa'aba.

"*A-yo, a baya hebi!*—Yes, they danced hard," Bayo told us. "Obia came strong."

With Angita was a man we had not seen before, holding a small child by the hand.

"This is Awingu, my brother-in-law," said Angita in explanation. "His eyes trouble him. I brought him to you for medicine."

After the exchange of courtesies demanded by the visit, we turned to the child.

"Is this your child, Awingu?" we asked.

His answer came promptly. "No, he is not my child. He is my wife's child. I made him."

Here was a fine distinction. He made him, but the child was not his.

Just then our cook came up with a small present for the child, but, since he would not take it from his hands or ours, Angita gave it to him.

"Thank you, father," he said to Angita.

Angita looked down affectionately at the youngster. "Two, three years more, Awingu, and he will be ready to go and live with his father at Gankwe. Do you remember your father at Gankwe? It was he who showed you how to make a gun from a reed. And you made it well. . . ."

There appeared, then, to be yet another father, for it was clear that Angita was not speaking of himself when he referred to the Gankwe father who had showed the child how to make a play gun.

All this, in itself, however confusing to a visitor, is by no means an unusual phenomenon. Different peoples have their own sanctions for establishing kinship and their own designations for relationships. In the city we had been told many tales of the manner of life of these Negroes of the bush. And the "matriarchate," as the custom of counting descent through the mother was termed, had often come up when these people were being discussed.

"Among them only the mothers count, because among savages, who can tell who the real father is? That is why a child calls many men 'father,' " we had heard variously explained and elaborated.

Yet here was a man who said without hesitation, "No, he is not my child. He is my wife's child. I made him." And the very next instant the child called Angita father, and Angita referred to still another man as the father who would in a few years take the child with him to live and train him for manhood.

Any number of questions came to our minds, but at daybreak a stranger coming to the planting ground of a village not his own is the least willing of talkers.

"This is not your child, Awingu," we took the occasion to remark when we were saying goodbye, "yet he seems to like you very much."

"Ma, tye! Ma Neng'e!—Mother of all Negroes! What would you have? I am his father!"

The man showed by his amused expression that this was a story to carry back to his village. Only the politeness due a stranger kept Awingu and Angita from laughing aloud at this strange question. But Awingu was a thoughtful fellow. "Tell me," he said, after a while, "in your white man's country, don't children care for their fathers?"

But there were not only multiple fathers, as the story told in the city ran. The matter was not disposed of so simply as that. In point of fact, each person seemed to have several mothers as well. Take the case of Angita himself, whose brother-in-law we met at dawn in the provision ground. Angita was first pointed out to us by Tita, who, behind her back, was called Mother Snake. It was at Gankwe when we came to see the dancing for the dead Zimbi.

"Look," she had said, as she indicated one of the principal dancers who wore seed rattles at his ankles. "This is Angita. He dances well. He is my son." And she had showed her pleasure at our appreciation of his excellent dancing.

The following day Angita came to our camp, bringing with him Kutai, a woman of about Tita's age. He left to go farther upstream for a time, but she remained with us and sat and talked with the others who were standing about, as they discussed the wood carvings we were in the act of buying.

"Have you seen Angita's carvings?" she asked us. "He is one of the best young carvers at Gankwe. When he is older, he will be one of the best on the Saramacca."

An old man standing by said drily, "Chicken says, 'You can lie about an egg, but you can't lie about a chicken.' "

"That's right," commented another. "We know Angita's carving. It is good, but . . ."

But Kutai would not be contradicted. She interrupted the speaker with a gesture. "I am his mother, and a mother knows her son. You can say what you like."

About the fifth day after we had started up the river for the country of the Granman, we came to a village where Angita stopped to supplement his food for the journey. When he returned, his arms were filled with the large cassava cakes. Behind him came a young girl with a bottle of palm oil, and some rice in an open calabash, and she was followed by the people of the village who came to see the Bakra. A woman of middle age, whom both the young girl and Angita resembled, took the rice from the girl and, wading into the shallow water, came up to our boat and gave it to us. "This is rice for you. I am Angita's mother. Angita is strong. You will walk well with him."

Later that day, when our boat found itself abreast of the dugout which Angita was poling, we lost no time in questioning him.

"Angita," we called, "is the woman who gave us the rice your mother?"

He nodded.

"But what of Tita, who said she was your mother, too?"

He was a quick-witted lad, and he saw at once what we had in mind. He said with a laugh, "You are asking about my true, true mother, the one who made me? It is not this one, and it is not Tita, who made me. It is Kutai."

"But who are the other two?"

"They are her sisters."

Yet the family life of the Bush Negro does not differ in any essential respect from that of any other group of individuals, who, related by close ties of blood, live their lives together. Men and women marry and beget children, and their children in turn marry and beget others. In reality, but for the fact that a man or a woman claimed more than one father and mother, and a great number of brothers and sisters, of uncles and aunts, there was little to indicate the existence of conventions of family life which differed radically from those we ourselves know.

None the less, there were differences, and, once we were permitted to see beneath the surface, a slight incident here, another hint there, threw into relief the life of these people, and their own attitudes toward their actual and spiritual relationships.

Let us take the instance of Misomba and his son. Misomba was a man of middle age, and the incident we tell occurred as we were sitting in his house in a village above the Mamadam. He was speaking of the wood he had cut and of his plans to take it to the city to sell. With him in the house were his wife and a young lad, perhaps fifteen or sixteen years old, and, besides ourselves, our paddler Kasanya, who was Misomba's wife's elder brother.

"I need someone to take the rafts down the river. There are none in my family who are free, and I need help. But Adyabu here," he said, indicating his son, "knows about taking down rafts, and it will be good for him to learn more of the river leading to the white man's city. I am glad you came, brother-in-law. Now I can ask you if he may go with me. Is it your wish that he go?"

Kasanya glanced at the boy, who showed by his manner his eagerness to accompany his father, and then at his sister. "How will it be with you, sister, if Adyabu goes? Do you want him to go with Misomba?"

"Yes," she replied. "Misomba will care for him. Let him go."

The three older people talked over the details of the trip down the river, until it was made clear to all that Adyabu would share whatever money his father might receive for the lumber.

"You will treat him well, brother-in-law," said Kasanya, with a smile, "for in a few years his girl will be ripe for marrying, and he will need money for a fine wedding."

That night we talked this over with Kasanya.

"Why must a man ask another if he may take his own son with

him on a journey? Is a man not to be trusted to take care of a boy he himself has made?"

"You do not understand, Bak'a. It is not that we don't trust Misomba," he replied. "He has lived with my sister for many years. She is his first wife, and my family have always liked him. When my sister's eldest daughter was asked in marriage by a man of this village, and our great family came together here to consider whether we should promise her to him or not, we asked Misomba to give us his advice. Misomba does not have a bold face. He did not speak until after much urging. To ask a man's advice about what does not concern his own family is a great honor. But we did this, and when he spoke, we found that what he said was good. So, you see, it is not that we do not trust Misomba."

We encouraged him to explain further.

"Adyabu is not his heir. He is the child of my sister and belongs to my family. I am the one to say what he is to do and what he is not to do, because I am the oldest living brother. Adyabu does not belong to Misomba's family. He is of my blood. When I die, he will inherit my possessions. When Misomba dies, his possessions will go to his own brothers and to his sisters' children. That is how we live here in the bush. That is how we do."

When a man marries, he either arranges to take his wife to live in his own village—his mother's village—or to stay in that of his wife. Whether he chooses the one village or the other, he has to build a house there for her, and this becomes her *wosu,* her household. If he wishes, he may build two houses, one in his own village, and one in the village of his wife. Kasanya's younger brother built two houses for his first wife. One was on the lower river, next to Kasanya's own house, and the other we would reach after two days' further travel up the river.

Yet the man, explained Kasanya, if the couple were living in the village of the wife, or the woman, if their house was in his village, was not entirely at home. In one's own village a person was a *gomi,* a child of the "ground." He belonged there. But when living in another's village, even though it was that of a husband or wife, one was a *wakama',* a stranger, and if a man of the village but uttered the word "wakama'" to such an individual, the outsider had to take up his belongings and leave at once. Were the stranger, in turn, to speak aloud the word "gomi," disaster would follow, for the earth spirits, having been disturbed, would be sure to take their toll.

The *wosu*—the household—is the unit of family life, whether, in its physical location, it is in one village or two villages. In it a woman lives with her husband, and here the children are reared. After the wosu comes the larger family unit, the *mbe,* composed of those who have come from the common womb of a more remote ancestress, while several of these larger or extended families form a clan.

"If a man has more than one wife," said Kasanya, "then he makes more than one house. A man never puts two wives in the same house. It would not be good. Each woman has her own house, where she lives with her children. It must be so. The children of the first wife belong to her family. The children of the second wife belong to the family of the second wife. A woman calls her husband's other wife by the name of kambosa. Do you know what kambosa means?" he asked, laughing. "*Kambosa*—the woman who makes trouble for me. So, you see, we people of the bush learned from our ancestors to give each wife her own house, where she might live with her own children."

But not alone the woman needed to have a house of her own. The man, too, built a house for himself. In it he stored his possessions. It was his sanctuary. No woman might enter it. On the carving of its door, a man lavished all his love of ornamentation, all his artistry.

"A man likes to have his own house for his possessions," explained Kasanya. "If he is a rich man, it is better that his wives do not know how much he has. You know what women are. They always ask for presents. But if a man is not rich, then it is better still that his wives do not know it. If they know, they will make life hard for him with nagging. They will talk of leaving him. And all the village will know, too."

In this house, then, which a man built for his wife, the children were reared. Sometimes, it is true, if the harvests were poor or the father had met with ill luck, the mother's brothers would come for the children, for children are the ones to carry on the line. It is through them that clan rank and material goods are inherited.

But if all went well with the father, then the attachments of the household were the closest, and they continued even after death. For the household was not entirely disrupted after the death of a parent. Unless the one who died had been a sorcerer, a leper, or a madman, the house where he lived was not torn down.

"When a man dies," Kasanya said, "the wife goes on living in the house, once it has been purified. If a woman dies, then the man keeps on living there."

"What of the children?" we asked. "What becomes of them?"

"If it is the man who is dead, then the woman takes her girl children to live with her, but her sons she sends away to live elsewhere. A man's spirit will not harm his daughters. He loves them. But his sons, he will kill. . . . When a woman dies, then it is the sons that the man will keep with him in the house, and the daughters must go away. The yorka of a woman will protect her sons, but she will destroy the daughters when she visits the place where she once lived."

DUDLEY KIDD
The Children's Meals

While in the case of adults the time of taking meals varies in different tribes, in the case of children there is no variation; this is due to the simple fact that children eat off and on all day long. But there are generally four fairly well-recognised meals for children. The men eat first by themselves and give what is left over to the women, who, however, do any cooking for the children or for themselves as occasion may require. In Gazaland a man eats with his wife, even out of the same dish, until the birth of the first child. He never eats with his wife after that. Young girls also eat off and on all day, for their value as wives turns on their fine physical condition. There are many parts of the meat that men do not eat, but the children are allowed to eat such portions. Small children are allowed to eat the head of the buck, but do so with their eyes tightly closed. There is thought to be danger of their eyes changing colour otherwise. The boys regard the lungs of the animal as their special portion. Very small children are allowed to hang round when the father is eating, but as soon as the boys get their second teeth they are supposed to leave the hut when they notice that their elders are about to eat. The parents are wonderfully kind to their small children, and go out of their way to please them. Thus the father frequently cuts small strips of meat from the ox that is offered to the ancestral spirits, and gets the big boys or girls to cook such portions for the little children. Again, a father before eating anything nice usually gives all the very small children a taste of his food. But should the children become a nuisance, as when there are very many of them in the kraal, or when there is but a small portion of some luxury, the father has his own way of getting rid of the children. Thus, as the food is about cooked, he tells the children to go and call some person living at a distance, whom he knows to be away from home. The children return after their vain journey to say the person is not at home. The parent then says, "What a pity; but our food is now all eaten so it does not matter." It takes many repetitions of this ruse to undeceive the children, who are very deficient in the critical faculty. If the above expedient fails, the parent plays on the imagination of the children in the following way. When the food is just about cooked, and the children are hanging round to get a taste, the father says, "Just go out into the veld and call *Nomgogwana* to come along quickly, for the food will not be cooked till he comes." This *Nomgogwana* is a fabulous monster whom it is most dangerous to trifle with. So the children run off to the veld calling out, *"Nomgogwana, Nomgogwana,* come along to the hut for there is nice food being cooked there." After waiting a short time in great excitement lest the food should be eaten before their return, the small children scamper home, and, bursting into the hut, say, "We called and called *Nomgogwana,* but he wouldn't answer at all!" Then one little chap, who notices the food is still cooking, suggests that it would be well to see whether the food is not cooked, for it is no use waiting any longer.

But the father says, "It is no use to see if the food is cooked, for you know it cannot be properly cooked till *Nomgogwana* comes; so run along and tell him to hurry up." This is probably sufficient, but should the children object, the father says in an off-hand manner, "Very well, sit where you are; the food will not cook, as you know, till *Nomgogwana* comes, and then when he *does* come he will be so angry at seeing the food uncooked that he will eat all the children he can find." So the children begin to be frightened, and as they are leaving the hut the father calls out to them, "Be sure you go far, far away into the veld, for otherwise *Nomgogwana* will not hear you: the reason why he did not hear you call before was that you did not go nearly far enough away; so be sure to go far away this time, lest you get eaten yourselves." With that the children scamper off, while the old people chuckle to themselves and eat their delicacies.

The Children's Evening Party

When a party is to be held, the parents have to consider very carefully which kraals should be invited. There are frequent feuds between certain families, and if the boys and girls from these rival kraals were to meet, quarrelling would be sure to follow; there would be bruised limbs, and probably broken heads, before the party broke up. It is therefore necessary to consider what kraals are on good terms with one another.

The Kafirs have no written language, and therefore invitations have to be sent out by word of mouth. As a rule the boys invite the boys, and the girls invite the girls. In the early morning, when the boys are driving out the cattle to pasturage, they arrange to meet the boys of another kraal, and the chief boy says, "Will the boys of your kraal come and play with us on such and such a night?"

"We shall be very glad indeed to come," replies the head-boy of the kraal invited, "but at what time shall we arrive?"

"Oh, come when you have finished milking the cows in the evening."

"We shall be very glad to come."

It is always understood that the invitation is addressed to all the boys of the kraal, for no one expects a separate invitation; only the very small children are kept at home and not allowed to go out to the party.

In similar fashion, when the girls go to fetch the water or wood for the day, they get into conversation with the girls of the kraals to be invited. When they have all filled their water-pots at the river, they sit down to chat, and the chief girl says, "We invite the girls of your kraal to a party at the Mabeleni (or whatever the name of their kraal may be) on such and such a night."

"We shall all be delighted to come; but tell us the hour at which you will expect us."

"Come at the time of the cooking of the evening meal."

The invited guests tell by the amount of time allowed for preparation how great a function to expect, and how to dress up. When the party is to be a great affair, the invitation is sent out a fortnight in advance; if only a few days' notice be given, every one knows that the party will be a small one. It takes about a fortnight for the boys and girls to prepare paint, bead-work, karosses, bangles and other ornaments for great occasions. At these great parties fully a hundred children may be present, and every one does his very best to look as smart as possible so as to attract attention.

For several days before a party, the children are very busy in the kraal; the girls bring out small grinding-stones very similar to those used by grown-up women for grinding corn; soft white stone is then broken into little pieces which are ground into a fine powder between the grinding-stones. This white powder is mixed with water, or fat, and smeared on the body. The children frequently paint their bodies in very fantastic ways, invariably making themselves look extremely ugly from the European point of view. There is much variety as to the colours used for painting, and as to the parts of the body painted. In Basutoland the girls are fond of red paint, while in Fingoland they prefer white. In these tribes the boys do not often paint themselves for parties; but in Zululand the boys frequently smear their head, trunk and legs with white paint, the girls only painting a white circle or band round their waists, sometimes adding a few touches of white on the cheeks.

The bigger children make extremely pretty bead-work, choosing very good combinations of colour. Bangles are made with grass, or with brass wire, and are worn round the ankle, calf, knee, waist, neck, elbow and wrist. Blankets are well rubbed with red clay, and often have their edges very prettily ornamented with bead-work. The skins of wild animals are worked up with grease until they are very soft and supple, and the tails of wild cats are made into ornaments for the loins. The children frequently tatoo themselves specially for these parties, using a pointed stick, which makes whitish marks in the skin; these marks only last for a few days. Thus the face and arms can be richly tatooed without leaving any permanent marks, as would be the case if they used hot embers. However, the girls sometimes make permanent marks on their skin; they cover a small portion of the arm with cow-dung, and then place glowing embers against the protected flesh. As soon as the heat reaches the skin small circular burns are made. When these burns heal, smooth circular patches of a lightish colour are left. The girls think such patches very beautiful.

On the day of the party the girls sometimes make garlands or coronets of leaves, very occasionally adding a few wild flowers to heighten the effect. The contrast of the bright green leaves against the dark burnt-sienna skin is very effective. The children have a special coating of grease given to their bodies so as to make them look smart and clean. It is striking how much improved in appearance are the boys after they have received a good rubbing with grease, for the scratches, which usually cover the body as a result of playing in the veld, are thus hidden.

The anxious mothers are also busy for days in advance of the party, telling the boys to be sure not to quarrel with other boys, lest it should be said they come from a quarrelsome kraal, and so the whole family should be disgraced publicly. They specially impress on the children not to eat too much; they tell them that if they show any signs of greediness the people will all say, "See, those children come from a kraal where there is famine." After that cutting sarcasm no one in the kraal could look the world in the face for many a day. But in spite of these days of coaching by anxious mothers, the children always eat too much, and the boys always quarrel and fight. As the children go off to the party the parents finally impress on the boys that they must not annoy the girls, nor forget to be very polite to the owners of the kraal who are giving the party.

The children are all very excited as they put the last touches on their toilette, which is very simple and strangely scant according to our ideas of what is decent. Europeans are inclined to call children *un*-dressed when they are thus decked out in bead-work. As the twilight dies and a rich afterglow of the deepest purple or violet suffuses the sky, there can be seen a string of little children streaming out of a hut on hands and knees—all silhouetted against a few low-lying clouds of orange colour—and hurrying over the veld in single file along the narrow Kafir footpath. At length this thin, wavy line of excited, talkative, chattering children arrives at the kraal, which is the focus of many other groups of children, dimly seen to be converging on it in the dusk.

On arriving at the kraal the guests have to salute the head-man of the place. If there should happen to be a chief present, the children walk up to him in single file, and as each child passes the chief, he or she has to stand still, shuffle the feet, point to the sky with the right hand, and say, "Bayete." If the greatest man present is only an ordinary head-man, the children shuffle their feet, and say, "Numzaan," rarely pointing with the hand to the sky. In some tribes it is not correct etiquette for guests to speak first on arriving at a kraal; it is expected that they should sit down in silence until the head-man first addresses them.

The greeting of the head-man of the kraal is one of the ways in which a Kafir shows respect and honour to him. But it has another very practical aspect. It is an excellent way of attracting attention, not so much to the head-man, as to one's self. It is as if the person were to say, "Take notice, all ye people; it is I who have arrived at the kraal." A Kafir loves to draw attention to himself and to obtain recognition; and of course he thinks a person cannot start too early in shuffling to the front in the race of life.

When the guests have saluted the great person, they next go and shake hands with his "great" wife, and after that they shake hands with the other women present and with the various guests, not a little kissing being indulged in between the women and the small children. When this process is over, the guests are told which huts are set apart for the evening, and, if the weather be cold, the children are ushered into one of the other huts, where the girls of the kraal usually hang up their blankets on a leather thong stretched between two poles. The guests pile their blankets on these leather ropes; they will not need their blankets again till the morning, for there are fires kept burning in every hut all night.

Since the party is to last till dawn, any children who may get unduly tired are free to go to one of the huts and enjoy a sleep whenever they like; when refreshed they can return to the party. If the party does not last the whole night, the children all sleep at the kraal of the person inviting them. Beds are quite unknown, for the people sleep in their blankets on grass mats, using blocks of wood for pillows. It is therefore a simple matter to find floor-space for a hundred visitors.

The Kafirs have no brightly lighted rooms with charming furniture and costly pictures; there are no soft carpets and draped curtains; nor are there any marble chimney-pieces. No carriages drive up to the door, and no liveried servants usher in the guests. The children creep in through a low doorway on their hands and knees, and find themselves in a large round hut with a fire burning in the centre of the floor. The smoke wanders round the blackened rafters and fills the hut, escaping as best it may through the dense thatch, which may be several feet thick. The walls of the hut are made of wattle and daub, and the floor consists of dried mud. Everything is of the colour of the earth, and at the back of the hut are to be seen some earthenware pots and calabashes. A tiny calf, or a few goats, may be tied up to one of the poles which support the roof, and a number of hens and dogs are sure to be found prowling round the hut, hunting for any small pieces of food they may chance to find.

When the visitors become accustomed to the smoke and darkness, they see some earth-coloured children putting the finishing strokes to their toilette, for there are no nurseries or nursery-maids. A number of gleaming eyes and glistening white teeth indicate these children.

As the guests arrive, one chubby little fellow about five years old is to be seen walking about with immense dignity; he looks as if he were weighed by vast State secrets which he is bursting to tell to some one. He is the eldest son of "the great wife," and so takes precedence over his many elder brothers. This little boy, who is called the "Bull of the Kraal," runs up to each party of guests as it arrives, singles out some big boy, and confides to him in a loud stage whisper, and with a most confidential air, some great mystery. It is impossible to translate the baby-talk of one language into the baby-talk of another, without making use of a very free translation.

"I say; do you know? Don't tell any one, but we have got twenty-free mouses all being cooked with their skins on; and we've firteen ickle birds which are to be eaten on the hill in the dark; they have all got their fevers and moufs and heads and tails on; so they will be ever so nice; but you won't tell any one, will you? it's a secret." This pantomime is acted over again at the arrival of each fresh batch of children. Since the little boy is to be a chief one day, and since every one is in a good humour at the beginning of a party, all the big boys patronise the little chap in a fatherly fashion. It is always well to keep in with the prospective chief.

The first great interest of the evening centres in the food. The big boys eat by themselves, and the small boys by themselves; the girls club together for their food. In ordinary daily life, as we have seen in a previous chapter, the men eat their food first by themselves, and give what is left over to the women and children. If there is not much meat, the men eat this by themselves, giving none to the women and children. But at a party, the children have the best of everything. The food may consist of the following: beef, mutton, goat and old hens; these are always boiled, unless small portions are cooked over the fire on little wooden skewers, or are placed on the embers. In addition to meat there is usually sour milk, pumpkins, fried locusts, Indian corn, and mice. But the favourite food is beef. Eggs are not eaten in most tribes, for it is sometimes thought that the eating of eggs causes the eyes to squint. A number of small birds, caught in traps, are sure to be found roasting over the fire. Such birds are cooked with their feathers on, and without receiving any cleaning. The little "Bull of the Kraal" has informed every one by this time of the fact!

The Kafirs have no "tea-things," but the children are very fond of making small toy clay plates and dishes, which they dry in the sun and afterwards bake in the fire. These are arranged on the floor for the small guests, for of course tables and chairs are unknown. Wooden spoons are supplied for these parties. In Basutoland the children imitate their elders and make, not small plates of earthenware, for Basutos do not use such things, but small grass mats and baskets to eat the food off. Small toy pots are also made to cook portions of food in.

Black girls are denied the supreme pleasure of white girls which consists in "pouring out" at a tea-party; but one privileged girl is allowed to "preside at the pot" (of the girls) which is the Kafir equivalent to pouring out the tea. A big boy presides at the boys' pot, unless the little "Bull of the Kraal" is very importunate. Most of the food is eaten out of the fingers because forks are unknown. Big boys, however, frequently have pocket-knives nowadays, and feel very proud in producing them at parties.

The small children get themselves into a dreadful mess during meal-time, for they are not bothered with bibs or napkins. They smear their faces and bodies with their food, and at the end of the meal the dogs come up and lick them clean.

Young men and women have a special dance which they engage in very smartly, using sticks to add to the gay effect. Let us try and picture the children dancing one of the Basutos dances in which the music is wild.

Imagine thirty boys in a row in the open air at night; they are clad in slender bead-work, or with the tails of wild animals tied in small bunches and suspended round their loins; the rest of the body is naked, except for bangles and ornaments. Opposite these boys are as many girls clad in blanket or skin petticoats of a scanty nature; frequently they are dressed only in very slight bead-work; round their arms, legs and waists are innumerable ornaments of brass or copper wire, or of bead-work. Every boy and girl holds a stick (or a bundle of sticks) in each hand. The dance begins with a low dull chant, to which all the dancers stamp the feet in time. Every now and then at certain turns in the chant, the rows move nearer to one another, and at other periods in the tune everybody lifts the right leg and left arm, bending the body into an awkward shape. The leg is poised in the air and suddenly thumped down on the ground. The music grows louder and faster, and the contortions of the limbs increase. Little children look on with interest as the tune grows wilder. Suddenly every one sings out, *"Seweliwelele, Seweliwelele,"* and at the sound of these words the contortions of swaying and stamping bodies grow more fierce, and each dancer moves round and round a little faster on his own small patch of ground. Soon the singing increases to a tremendous pace, and every one shouts *"Seweliwelele, Seweliwelele,"* till a wild frenzy of excitement seizes the dancers, who stamp and jump, and swing their bodies in the most bizarre way. Every one vies with every one else to be as fantastic as possible. The appearance of the dancers in the moonlight is most weird, for it is chiefly on moonlight nights that these open-air dances are held. The shouting, contorted, perspiring boys and girls, each intent on his or her own tune and contortions, make the most absurd grimaces as they chant their song. The admiring crowd of onlookers, young and old, applaud the various dancers and egg them on to wilder attempts. Suddenly the whole dance collapses abruptly in a torrent of sound; then dancers and audience chatter and jabber about the fun they have had. A boy, who thinks he has been doing wonders before the eyes of the girl whose love he wants to win, goes up to her boldly to make love, and is repelled by the biting saying of the girl, whose heart is fixed on another boy, "A cat and a mouse do not associate." The boy feels his ardour damped by this spiteful saying, and vows he will tame the girl later on. Dance after dance is held till every one seems tired, though it is surprising what an amount of dancing can be indulged in without tiring the people.

When it is about an hour or so past midnight the great event of the party—so far as the boys are concerned—takes place. For this the boys have been watching all the evening. The head-man tells the big boys—what they knew hours ago—that he has a sheep cooking for them in a large pot. The boys all fly off to the vessel, pull out the cooked sheep and tear it to pieces with their hands. Then they all rush off to some hill close by, where wood for fires has been collected before the party commenced; camp-fires are made, and the boys have a royal feast. It is at such times, when everything is in confusion in the kraal, that the boys pay out any grudges they owe to cantankerous women. The cats belonging to such women are stolen and carried off in the darkness, and are killed and cooked with their fur on. The unpopular aunt may complain next morning that she cannot for the life of her make out what has happened to her cat: it has vanished during the night; have any of the boys seen it? Though uncomfortably conscious of having eaten too much cat, and though they are feeling rather unwell from over-eating in general, the young culprits affect the utmost interest in the lost cat, and offer with unusual courtesy to go at once and hunt for it in the bush. Truly the Kafirs know how to pay out any person who makes himself or herself objectionable.

The cooked heart of the sheep is often impaled on a pointed stick, which is fixed in the ground. The biggest boy, whose hands are tied behind his back, tries to bite a mouthful out of the heart when it is fixed thus, and all the small boys are allowed to belabour him with sticks while he is trying to eat it. Then the next biggest boy has a bite under the same conditions, and as a result very little of the heart is left for the small ones. Lest the parents should think the tiny boys have received no share of the heart, the bigger boys smear the faces of the little ones with the half-cooked blood, and so the phrase, "You smear me with blood," comes to mean, "You accuse me falsely." The parents are supposed to imagine that since the faces of the small boys are bloodstained, they have had their due portion of the heart, though it is hard to believe the fathers forget the customs of their boyhood. The small boys dare not complain to their elders, or they would get unmercifully beaten for not having the sportsmanlike quality of refusing to tell tales.

The boys produce from their pockets the most marvellous things. Most boys carry under their arms a small bag which is suspended from the neck. This bag does duty for a pocket. It is proverbial what the pockets of an English boy can contain, but the Kafir boys have no cause to be ashamed of their performances in this direction. Here is a list of things found in the pockets of a few Kafir boys: string made from grass, mice, old pieces of food, bangles, dead birds, pins, needles for sewing frayed skins (these needles have no eyes), wooden spoons, snuff-boxes, edible roots, Indian hemp and a small horn to smoke it with, tobacco-pipes made from roots of trees, caterpillars, and, finally, lizards. A weird confusion of such articles is turned out beneath the silent stars, and all that is edible is cooked over the fire. Thus the sheep is supplemented with mice, rats, lizards, caterpillars, birds, edible roots, and other things of a similar nature.

When the mutton has vanished—all except the skin and the bare bones which have been gnawed clean, broken, and robbed of the marrow—the boys wax fat and "coxy." Every one seems to develop a fighting spirit. It needs but a few whiffs of the intoxicating smoke of Indian hemp to precipitate matters. Sides are soon formed, possibly one set of kraals fighting another set as in real life. The boys all pretend to be soldiers; there may be as many as twenty or thirty boys on each side. To prevent confusion in the dark, the boys of one side deck themselves with white paint. If there should be no men looking on, a war-dance is indulged in, the war-song being sung slowly and solemnly in subdued voices, for in all things the boys imitate their elders. The excitement grows as the song increases in volume and rhythm; before long the chant becomes boisterous and noisy, and when the spirit of the boys gets beyond control, the fighting commences in real earnest. Sticks are freely used, and many are the bruises received, and many are the scalps cut open. The natives say that in olden days boys were even killed in these midnight fights. There is such a strong sense of honour amongst the boys that they would scorn to "sneak" about their injuries, just as much as English boys at a public school would scorn to do so under similar circumstances. Wounds are patched up with a free coating of mud, and if any awkward questions should be asked next morning, the boys account for the suspicious-looking marks of mud, which rather accentuate than hide the wounds, by saying that they fell down hill in the dark, or got cut while playing games. The parents do not press their questions at such times, though they are shrewd enough to know what value to attach to the excuse.

Later on, swinging and dancing are indulged in on the hill-top, some suitable tree being selected for hanging the swing on. Games are played in the dark, and contests of skill are held. The boys do a good deal of betting over these contests in the darkness, and one may bet a hen, a goat, or some edible roots, when the comrade whom he idolises stands forth to fight a rival. If any one should misbehave himself, a court of imaginary chiefs is held to try the case. These boys' courts are often held in the veld by day, when the boys want to have some fun; but there is a peculiar charm in a court held at night. The ablest boy sits as chief, and the accused is brought before him; a full inquiry, with regular accusers and defenders, is instituted. But the decision of this play-court—like many of the more serious ones in after life—is fixed in advance. If the boy be popular, he is sure to be acquitted, but if he be not liked, he is certain to be found guilty. The boys thus pay out any one who makes himself disagreeable. The victim when found guilty is often tied to a stick, and another boy is told off to beat him; the blanket is, of course, removed for the operation, and the beating, which is given in real earnest, is usually taken in silence, for tears would but lead to a more severe thrashing for cowardice. But sometimes, in addition to corporal punishment, the little fellow is condemned to fag after the cattle all the next day, and is not allowed to eat any food in the veld, having to look on while the others enjoy themselves. If the weather should be cold—and children hate the winter, for they say the country is then desolate and devoid of edible berries—the boy may be made to go long distances to fetch wood for a fire in the veld, at which the others warm themselves, while the victim is made to sit far away from the fire, and is left to shiver in the cold.

Before returning to the huts at the first streak of dawn, the boys sit round the fire telling stories, all bragging of their prowess. At length a move is made to the huts, and an uproarious crowd of naked boys is seen sweeping down the hill with blankets waving from many an arm, for a race is being held, and blankets are carried on the arm so as not to impede the movement.

All the time the boys have been enjoying their midnight orgy on the hill, the girls have been occupied with quieter pursuits; some have been playing with clay dolls, and others have been gossipping about their sweethearts, while not a few have coaxed an old grandmother into a good temper, and have persuaded her to tell them some of the old nursery-tales, samples of which have been given in the preceding chapter. During the night some of the smaller children have been sleeping peacefully in another hut, having been worn out with excitement.

The return of the boys, who rush into the kraal like a hurricane, is the sign for the party to break up. Blankets are fetched out, and the tired children go to say good-bye to the head-man, shake hands with the women, and then emerge from the hut on hands and knees. There are many last words between the departing guests, and slowly a number of straggling rows of children file off along the various pathways to their respective homes. The children walk home with wavering, unsteady gait, for most of them are tired, and all of them are grumbling and cross. As the children reach home everything looks dreary in the false light of dawn; the old people are cross at being roused too early from their slumber, and resent the barking of the dogs and the sudden intrusion of the children. There arises a confused noise from the shouting out of angry orders to children and dogs; children are crying or simpering; the very cocks and hens are flying about the hut, for they have been disturbed from their roosts. Every one votes parties a nuisance; the girls wish they were boys to enjoy the midnight feast on the hill; the boys are aching in limb and bruised in body; the parents are suffering from the irritability that comes from a disturbed sleep. Yet with wonderful wisdom everybody will look forward to the next party with delight, not being one whit disillusioned by the memory of their experiences. It would be hard to recognise in these grumbling, weary, bedraggled boys and girls the eager and excited children who started off for the party but twelve hours previously with such gaiety and joy.

Secret Language of Children

Boys in Natal make a secret language by taking the leading syllable of a word to which they add "lande." They then skip the rest of the word, and pick out the leading syllable of the next word, and add "lande" to that. By this method boys converse very rapidly, and their talk is utterly unintelligible to the listener who has not practised this mode of forming a language. Sometimes the method is modified, especially when it is becoming a little too widely known, by adding some other syllable, or by cutting the word in two and adding a syllable to each half of the word. Fingo boys change the order of the syllables, placing the first half of the word last, and the last half of the word first; they thus completely mystify their parents, who cannot make out a word of what the boys are saying. A friend of mine was listening to a number of boys in Gazaland talking together, and at first thought they were talking gibberish; but after some time he discovered that they were talking a private language, which they made up thus. The language was Tshindao. The boys cut the words in half and inserted *Tshini, Tshino,* or *Tshina* between the two syllables. Thus the phrase "Ask for fire" is, in Tshindao, *"Kumbiro mwoto."* When the boys changed this into their slang language it became *"Kumbitshinoro mwotshinoto."* The effect is most puzzling when the words are spoken quickly. The boys practise their secret language when at work in the veld, and come to speak it as easily as their own normal language. And similarly the boys devise methods of talking about the cattle in a way that misleads their fathers. A boy who had lost the cattle while herding them, or who had let them stray into other people's gardens, might freely discuss such things with other boys before his father, by speaking as if it were some other boy who had been the defaulter, or as if it were a bangle or stick that had been lost. The other boys know instinctively that the herd-boy is referring to his own cattle, while he calls them the cattle of other people, or refers to them as bangles or sticks. When to all these ways of speaking in secret is added the fact that the normal woman's *hlonipa* language cannot be properly understood by a man when his own wife is using it to another woman, we see what a babel of languages exists in the Kafir kraal.

PART 6

Puberty

BALDWIN SPENCER and
FRANCES JONES GILLEN

Initiatory Ordeals

Another ceremony called the Quabara Anthinna of Arimurla was associated with a curious and rather complicated tradition. Anthinna is the opossum totem, and Arimurla is a place now called Winnecke's depot, by reason of its having been used as such during early days; it is in reality merely a gorge leading through the rocky ranges which form the eastern continuation of the Macdonnells. The ceremony refers to two Purula women of the opossum totem. They both originated at and never left Arimurla. Each of the performers had a curious T-shaped *Nurtunja* on his head. From the cross-bars of each there were suspended Churinga which had once belonged to the two women.

When the ceremony, which consisted of the usual swaying to and fro on the part of the performers, and of the running round and round of the other men, was concluded, we were told the following. In the Alcheringa a party of wild cat people who, unlike the other wild cat parties, consisted for the main part of Pulthara and Panunga, started from near Wilyunpa out to the east of Charlotte Waters. They journeyed on to the north, halting and forming *Oknanikilla* at various places. After a time they came close to Arimurla, but passed by without seeing the two Purula opossum women who were sitting down there. Going on they met a man who had come down from the salt water country far away to the north; he was of the same totem as themselves, but lived alone and was called *atnabitta,* a contemptuous name applied to a man who is given to interfering with women. Him they killed, and to the present day a stone in Paddy's creek at a spot called Achilpa Itulka represents the slain man. Having done this, they walked on, eating Hakea and driving mosquitoes before them, and, when they could not get water, drinking their own blood. At a place called Irri-miwurra they all died, but sprang up again as *Ulpmerka,* that is uncircumcised boys, and after that they went on eating plums. Reference to this will again be made when dealing with the question of the eating of the totem. In this, as in not a few of the traditions, we see that the eating of the totemic animal or plant seems to be a special feature, and one to which attention is particularly drawn.

After eight days had been spent in the performance of ceremonies, it was evident that an important change in the proceedings was about to take place. Under the direction of the leader of the Engwura the small gum boughs, which had hitherto decorated the top of the *Parra,* were removed, and the mound was left bare. All the young men were ordered away from the ground, and spent the greater part of the day in the bed of the river under the charge of the Alatunja of Alice Springs. Meanwhile, close by the *Parra,* a group of elder men who were already *Urliara* were assembled. All classes were represented, and the next five hours were spent in preparations for an important ceremony called the Quabara Unchichera of Imanda. At Imanda, which is known to white men as the Bad Crossing on the Hugh River, is an important Unchichera or frog totem centre, and during the Engwura a large number of ceremonies connected with this were enacted as the leader came from this locality, and, though not himself belonging to the frog totem, he had inherited a large number of ceremonies concerned with this and the wild cat totem from his father. He performed the ceremony himself. On his head was a large somewhat flat helmet made in the usual way, and completely covered with concentric circles of alternate pink and white down. These represented the roots of a special gum tree at Imanda. The whole of his back and chest as far down as the waist was a complete mass of white spots, each of which was encircled by white down; they were of various sizes, and indicated frogs of different ages; on the inner side of each thigh were white lines representing the legs of fully-grown frogs. On his head he wore a large frog Churinga, five feet in length, decorated with bands of down and tipped with a bunch of owl feathers. All around the base of this were arranged tufts of black eagle-hawk feathers, each fastened on to a stick, so that they radiated from the head-dress. About twenty strings, each of them two feet in length and made of opossum fur-string, had been covered with pink and white down, and ornamented at one end with tufts of the black and white tail tips of the rabbit-kangaroo. These were suspended all round from the head so as almost completely to hide the face, which was itself enveloped in a mass of down. The Churinga represented a celebrated tree at Imanda, and the pendant strings its small roots. When all was ready a shallow pit about a yard in diameter was scooped out in the sand, and in this the performer squatted with a short stick in his hands. Except for the presence of the latter, it was difficult to tell that the elaborate decoration concealed from view a man.

When he was seated in the pit, he sent out three old men who were *Urliara* across the river. Two of them carried small Churinga attached to the end of hair-string. The man who did not carry one went behind the spot where the young men were gathered together, while the other two went one to each side. Then the sound of the bull-roarer was heard, as the Churinga were whirled round and round, and, amidst much shouting and excitement, the young men were driven in a body across the river and up the opposite bank on to the Engwura ground. Running through the scrub which bordered the river, they suddenly came in sight of the performer, who was slightly swaying his body from side to side and digging the earth up with the stick in his hands. For a moment, when first he came in view, the young men halted and lifted up their hands as if in astonishment, and then driven up by the three *Urliara* men they ran up to and circled round and round the performer shouting *"wha! wha!"* at the tops of their voices. The old men stood to one side, and the two with the Churinga went round and round the young men as if to drive them in as close as possible. This went on for about three minutes, when one of the younger men, who was a Purula and the son of a dead man of the frog totem of Imanda, laid his hands on the shoulders of the performer, who then ceased moving, and the ceremony was over. After a short pause the decorated man got up, and first of all embraced the young man who had stopped him, and then went round and did the same to various old Bulthara and Panunga men, and touched with a piece of white down the navel of the old Purula man of the white bat totem, whose locality lay close to that with which the ceremony was associated.[1] Then he sat down and called the young Purula man up to assist him in removing the decorations.

After each ceremony the down is carefully removed from the body, though naturally a not inconsiderable portion adheres so firmly that it must be rubbed off, and so each performance means the loss of a certain amount. As soon also as ever a Churinga or a *Nurtunja* has once been used, the decorations are taken off. No *Nurtunja* is used more than once; even if two ceremonies follow close upon one another, each of them requiring one, a fresh one is made for each. The reason of this is that any particular *Nurtunja* represents and is symbolic of one particular object with which the ceremony is concerned, it may be a gum tree, a Hakea, an emu or a frog, and, when once that particular *Nurtunja* has been used in a ceremony, it is henceforth symbolic of one, and only one thing, though, so far as its appearance and structure are concerned, it may be precisely similar to a *Nurtunja* which means something totally different. Suppose, for example, that, as on the last occasion, a large Churinga or a *Nurtunja* represents a gum-tree, then in the mind of the native it becomes so closely associated with that object

---

[1] Imanda itself is the great centre of the frog totem; but occupying a strip along the southern bank of the Hugh River, close by, is a local centre of the Unchipera or small bat totem, while opposite to this on the north bank of the river is a centre of the Elkintera or large white bat totem.

that it could not possibly mean anything else; and if a precisely similar Churinga or *Nurtunja* were wanted an hour afterwards to represent, say an emu, then a new one must be made.

The reason for the showing of the performance just described, was that on the previous day the young Purula man already referred to had gone out into the bush and had brought in a present of game in the form of euro, as an offering to the older man who had charge of the Unchichera ceremonies of Imanda. This gift of food is called *chauarilia,* and when bringing it in he had told the old man that there was food waiting for him along the creek. This remark was perfectly understood as a request, though this must not be made in any more direct way, that he should be shown some ceremony connected with his dead father's totem. With this the third phase of the Engwura came to an end.

The fourth phase was a very well-marked one, as with it were ushered in the series of fire ordeals which are especially associated with the Engwura. The young men had already had by no means an easy time of it, but during the next fortnight they were supposed to be under still stricter discipline, and to have to submit themselves to considerable discomfort in order to prove themselves worthy of graduating as *Urliara.*

Just at sunrise the *Illpongwurra* were collected together close to the *Parra.* The leader of the Engwura had meanwhile appointed three elder men, who were already *Urliara,* to look after them during the day. About a dozen of the older men had provided themselves with small Churinga, and with a great amount of shouting, and amidst the strange weird roar and screech of the bull-roarers, no two of which sounded alike, the *Illpongwurra* were driven in a body away from the camp. Each man amongst them carried his shield, spear, and boomerang, for it was their duty now to go out into the bush all day hunting game for the benefit of the old men who stayed in camp performing ceremonies. The idea was to test still further the endurance of the young men and their obedience to their elders. Out in the bush they are not supposed to eat any of the game which they catch, but must bring it all in to the old men who may, or may not, give them a share of it when they return to camp. Whether this rule is rigidly adhered to on the part of the younger men may perhaps be doubted; the temptation offered by the sight of a fat little wallaby must be very strong to a full-grown young man who has not been having too much to eat for some three or four weeks past, and though old men go out in charge, it can be scarcely possible to keep a strict watch over all of the *Illpongwurra.*

Avoiding on this, the first morning of the new departure in the ceremonies, the women's camp, which lay out of sight of the Engwura ground on the other side of the river, the *Illpongwurra* were taken out through a defile amongst the ranges on the west side of the camp. As the day wore on it became evident that there was unusual excitement and stir in the women's camp. One of the older ones had been informed that the *Illpongwurra* would return in the evening, and that they must be ready to receive them. She had been through this part of the ceremony before, and knew what had to be done, but the great majority of the women required instructing. About five o'clock in the evening all the women and children gathered together on the flat stretch of ground on the east side of the river. The Panunga and Bulthara separated themselves from the Purula and Kumara. Each party collected grass and sticks with which to make a fire, the two being separated by a distance of about one hundred yards. A man was posted on the top of a hill overlooking the Engwura ground on the west, and just before sunset he gave the signal that the *Illpongwurra* were approaching. They stopped for a short time before coming into camp, at a spot at which they deposited the game secured, and where also they decorated themselves with fresh twigs and leaves of the Eremophila bush. These were placed under the head-bands, so that they drooped down over the forehead, under the arm-bands, and through the nasal septum. Then, forming a dense square, they came out from the defile amongst the ranges. Several of the *Urliara* who were carrying Churinga met them, some going to either side, and some going to the rear of the square. Then commenced the swinging of the bull-roarers. The women on the tip-toe of excitement lighted their fires, close to which were supplies of long grass stalks and dry boughs. The *Illpongwurra* were driven forwards into the bed of the river, pausing every now and then as if reluctant to come any further on. Climbing up the eastern bank, they halted about twenty yards from the first group of women, holding their shields and boughs of Eremophila over their heads, swaying to and fro and shouting loudly "*whrr! whrr!*" The Panunga and Bulthara women to whom they came first stood in a body behind their fire, each woman, with her arms bent at the elbow and the open hand with the palm uppermost, moved up and down on the wrist as if inviting the men to come on, while she called out *"kutta, kutta, kutta,"* keeping all the while one leg stiff, while she bent the other and gently swayed her body. This is a very characteristic attitude and movement of the women during the performance of certain ceremonies in which they take a part. After a final pause the *Illpongwurra* came close up to the women, the foremost amongst whom then seized the dry grass and boughs, and setting fire to them, threw them on to the heads of the men, who had to shield themselves, as best they could, with their boughs. The men with the bull-roarers were meanwhile running round the *Illpongwurra* and the women, whirling them as rapidly as possible; and after this had gone on for a short time, the *Illpongwúrra* suddenly turned and went to the second group of women, followed, as they did so, by those of the first, and here the same performance was again gone through. Suddenly once more the men wheeled round and, followed by both parties of women who were now throwing fire more vigorously than ever, they ran in a body towards the river. On the edge of the bank the women stopped, turned round and ran back, shouting as they did so, to their camp. The *Illpongwurra* crossed the river bed and then ran on to the Engwura ground where, sitting beside the *Parra,* was a man decorated for the performance of an Unjiamba ceremony. Still holding their shields, boomerangs, and boughs of Eremophila, they ran round and round him shouting *"wha! wha!"* Then came a moment's pause, after which all the men commenced to run round the *Parra* itself, halting in a body, when they came to the north end to shout *"wha! wha! whrr!"* more loudly than before. When this had been done several times they stopped, and then each man laid down his shield and boomerangs and placed his boughs of Eremophila so that they all formed a line on the east side of and parallel to the *Parra,* at a distance of two yards from this. When this was done the *Illpongwurra* came and first of all sat down in a row, so that they just touched the opposite side of the *Parra* to that on which the boughs were placed. In less than a minute's time they all lay down, in perfect silence, upon their backs, quite close to one another, with each man's head resting on the *Parra.*[2] All save one or two old men moved away, and these few stayed to watch the *Illpongwurra*. For some time not a sound was to be heard. None of them might speak or move without the consent of the old men in whose charge they were. By means of gesture language one or two of them asked for permission to go to the river and drink at a small soakage which had been made in the sand. In a short time they returned, and then it was after dark before they were allowed to rise. The sudden change from the wild dance round the performer and the *Parra,* accompanied by the loud shouting of the men whose bodies were half hidden by thick clouds of dust, which the strong light of the setting sun illuminated, was most striking.

About nine o'clock the men got up and began the usual singing, running sideways along by the *Parra,* shouting loudly as they did so. Shortly before midnight a curious ceremony was performed, which was associated with certain *Oruncha* men of Imanda. There were four performers, and the ceremony was divided into two parts. Three men were engaged in the first and more important scene. A long hole, just big enough to hold a man's body, but not deep enough to conceal it, was scooped out. In this, at full length, one of the men lay while a second knelt down over his legs and the third knelt at the head end. These two were supposed to be *Oruncha* men, engaged in baking the man in the earth oven, and each of them with two boomerangs imitated the action of basting him and of raking the embers up over his body, whilst he himself imitated admirably the hissing and spluttering noise of cooking meat. After a few minutes the three got up and joined the audience, and then out of the darkness—for the fire beside the *Parra* served only to light up the ceremonial ground—came a decorated man who was supposed to represent an Alcheringa man of the frog totem. He moved about

[2] They have to lie down so that the *Parra* is between them and the women's camp, and the latter must always lie to the east of the *Parra.*

from spot to spot, sniffing as if he detected the smell of cooking, but could not detect where it came from. After a minute or two he joined the audience and the performance stopped.

There was not much rest to be had that night; the *Illpongwurra* lay down again while the older men close to them kept up an incessant singing, and at two o'clock all were called up to witness the performance of a ceremony of the wild cat totem, in which three men took part, who were supposed to be performing an ordinary dancing festival or *altherta* in the Alcheringa. Just at daybreak another ceremony was ready, which was again connected with the frog totem of Imanda. It was performed by one of the oldest men present, the old white bat man, and he was decorated to represent a particular tree at Imanda, which suddenly appeared full-grown on the spot, where an Alcheringa man of the frog totem went into the ground; it became the *Nanja* tree of the spirit part of him which remained behind associated with his Churinga.

It was now getting daylight. The leader decided upon three *Urliara,* who were to accompany and take charge of the *Illpongwurra* during the day, and just after the sun rose they were once more driven out of the Engwura ground amidst the whirling of bull-roarers. The old men spent the day in camp preparing two or three ceremonies, but reserving a somewhat elaborate one for the benefit of the *Illpongwurra,* who were driven in at dusk by way of the women's camp, where the fire-throwing was repeated. Once more the ceremony of first sitting and then lying down by the *Parra* was enacted; in fact this was carried out every evening during the next two weeks.

At midnight the *Illpongwurra* were aroused to witness a ceremony of the white bat totem. Eleven men—the greatest number which we have seen taking part in any one of these sacred ceremonies—were decorated. Ten of them stood in a row facing and parallel to the *Parra,* and they were all connected together by a rope of human hair-string, which was decorated with pink and white down, and was passed through the hair waist-girdle of each man. Four of them had Churinga on their heads, and were supposed to represent special gum trees near to Imanda, the long rope being the roots of the trees; the other six were supposed to be bats resting in the trees.

The eleventh man was free from the rope and his decoration differed from that of the rest, who were ornamented with white pipe-clay and red and white down, while he had a long band of charcoal on each side of his body, outlined with red down. He began dancing up and down in front of the others, holding his body in a stooping position, and making all the while a shrill whistling noise, like that made by a small bat as it flies backwards and forwards. In his hands he carried twigs which he rubbed together. The ten men meanwhile moved in line, first to the right and then to the left, and with the other man dancing in front of them the whole formed a curious scene in the flickering light of the camp fire. At a signal from the leader of the Engwura two men went out from the audience, each carrying a long spear which was held behind the line of performers so as to touch the back of each man—the signal for them to stop. Each performer in turn touched with a piece of down first the stomach of the leader, and then that of the old white bat man to whom the ceremony belonged.

During the next day ceremonies were held as usual, but there was no fire-throwing. At sunrise on the following morning the *Illpongwurra* were driven out of camp to the sound of bull-roarers, by way of the women's camp, where they again had fire thrown over them, and in the evening the same ceremony was repeated when, just at sunset, they were brought in to camp over the ranges on the eastern side.

ROLAND B. DIXON

Shasta Puberty Ceremonies for Girls

Puberty ceremonies were held by the Shasta only for girls, and, so far as has been ascertained, the details of the ceremony appear to have been alike throughout the whole area occupied by the stock. According to the accounts, the ceremony begins at once, on the night after the girl attains puberty. She goes to her mother's menstrual hut or to a special hut built for her. Her face is painted with a number of vertical stripes in red, running from the forehead to the chin; and on her head she wears a feather head-dress consisting of a wide visor of bluejay-feathers, which shields the eyes completely, so that the wearer cannot look up, or see the sun or moon. In some cases there is a cap-like addition to the visor, so covering all the head, which tends to obviate evil dreams. In the menstrual hut the girl remains for a good part of the day, for ten days, and is always accompanied by her mother or an old woman (or more than one), who does everything for the girl, cutting up her food, washing her face, and combing her hair. She may not speak to any one, except her mother or female attendant, during this period of ten days, and only to her in a whisper. She must wear her moccasins all the while, and must use a large scratching-stick of bone for her head, and a smaller one for her eyelids. She must not come near a fire, nor look at one directly, during the whole period; nor may she look at people, or at the sun or moon. She must not get excited, nor hurry in doing anything. During the whole time, she is subjected to strict food-regulations, and may drink only water that has been warmed and into which a little clay has been stirred. She is allowed to sleep but very little, and that just before dawn. In sleeping, she must place her head in a mortar-basket across the small end of which a stick is placed. This is to keep evil spirits away from her head. The stick which is put across the opening is burned every morning by the girl's attendant, and a new one is prepared for the next night. All the time the girl remains in the hut, she must sit facing the east, and holding a deer-hoof rattle in her hand, which she shakes from time to time. Every day she must go up into the mountains and bring back several loads of wood, which are used for the fire for the evening dance. She must also bring a small quantity for every house in the village. She is accompanied on these excursions by two or three young girls, and, should she meet any one on the trail, they at once turn aside, and allow her to pass. Whatever she dreams of during this period, she confides to her mother, and all these dreams are bound to come true. Should she be so unfortunate as to dream of the death of any person in the village, or of a general conflagration, the only way the calamity can be averted is to burn the unfortunate girl alive. For this sacrifice, which, it is said, has several times been made, the girl is decked in all the finery the family possesses, and made to leap into the centre of a huge fire built by members of the family.

The first night of the period of ten days, during which all the above restrictions and regulations are in force, a dance is held. To this and the dances of the succeeding nights, many relatives and friends are invited; but all these do not arrive in time for the first dance. In this, the girl, painted as described, and dressed in her ordinary clothes (to which, however, deer-hoof rattles are attached), dances before all who are assembled. She wears the feather visor or cap, and carries deer-hoof rattles in her hands. The assembly at first consists mainly of women, although some men are always present. All the onlookers sit in rows, facing eastward, their backs to a large fire, lit to give light. Most of the men and women have rattles similar to that held by the girl. Some, however, have sticks with which they beat time on thin boards. The girl dances back and forth, east and west, always keeping her face to the east and her back to the fire. She herself does not sing, and when she grows tired, a man (or two men) dances with her, supporting part of her weight.

After this style of dancing has gone on for some time, a change occurs. In the succeeding form of dance, a large ring is made by the whole audience, on the east side of the fire, or two concentric rings, if the number is large. All hold hands, the girl and two or more helpers, however, standing in the middle of the ring, facing east, and dancing sideways from north to south; while the ring dances round them, first in one direction, and then in the other, singing the while.

By this time, it is probable that several parties of friends or relatives have arrived from neighboring villages. These may not, however, join in until certain ceremonies have first been gone through. A party, composed partly of men and partly of women, arriving near where the dance is going on, cut bunches of brush, and, holding their bows and arrows, advance slowly, crying out that they are coming, in order to warn the dancers of their approach. All are painted as if for a war-dance. As soon as the shout is heard, the dancers engaged in the "round dance" instantly stop, and the visitors approach in a long line, their backs to the fire, and the bunches of brush held over their faces, to conceal their identity. Then, holding the bunch of brush in both hands, the men point first to the right, and then to the left, and then all dance. This pointing and dancing alternate five times, while the girl herself comes out from the circle of dancers and runs back and forth in front of the line of visitors, keeping time with their song.

The pointing and dancing having alternated five times, the men throw away the brush, and, locking arms, dance sideways, this way and that, to a very lively song. At this juncture, the girls and women of the visiting-party, who thus far have remained out in the brush, run up, each seizing from behind the belt of a man, and dancing behind him, holding the belt in both hands. The girl herself at this stage stands at one side, still facing to the east. Five times the visiting men and women dance in line thus, the women holding the men by the belt; then all suddenly start, and run as fast as they can in a circle around the girl for whom the whole ceremony is held, and also around the whole dance-place, where all the other persons are standing or sitting. This being done, they at once fall into the circle of the "round dance" (interrupted by their arrival), and the latter dance then begins again as before, now with a larger number of dancers. The "round dance" is then continued till nearly dawn. This same ceremony is gone through with, in its entirety, with every new party of guests arriving. It sometimes happens that in the "round dance," the girl, or Wā′pxi, as she is called, leaves her place in the centre of the ring for a time, and joins in with those forming the circle, later returning to her place.

These two types of dances, the Ku′stirūma and the K!è′pxig, are kept up every night of the period of ten days during which the Wā′pxi has to remain in the hut, fasting, and gathering wood in the daytime, as above described. Toward the end of the period,—what with her fasting, her daily labor in carrying wood, and her long hours of dancing every night,—the Wā′pxi often gets so weak that she has to be supported almost constantly in the dance. On the tenth and last night she must remain in the centre of the ring of the K!è′pxig all the time, not leaving it at all. This night, the dance is kept up till dawn, when all stop for breakfast. This over, several different songs are sung and the dance is continued. As noon approaches, one or two of her men supporters now and then tap the feather visor which the Wā'pxi has worn all the time, and then lift it up a little, replacing it, however, at once. As time goes on, the visor is raised higher and higher, till finally it is taken entirely off and held over the head, only to be again put back. As noon comes still nearer, the visor is taken off and thrown into the air, and put back again, till, when it is just noon, the head-dress is removed, and thrown high into the air toward the east (outside the ring of the dancers), and is there caught by a man sent out for the purpose. Immediately the dance stops, and the girl and her mother go to the river, where they bathe, and put on new, clean clothes. While this takes place, the others sit down and rest. The girl now returns, dressed in her best, with all her ornaments, and all present then dance the war-dance; the girl dancing back and forth before the others, accompanied now by a young girl who as yet has not gone through the ceremony. The girl and her aid stand at opposite ends of the line, and dance then to the opposite end, and return, as described in speaking of the war-dance. When this dance is over, the girl's mother brings out a quantity of food in baskets, and all the guests partake, after which they return to their homes, and the ceremony is ended.

GUNNAR LANDTMAN

Initiation Ceremonies of the Kiwai Papuans

The *hóriómu* or *táera,* also known by other names, is one of the great secret ceremonies and comprehends a series of pantomimic dances and rites. It is connected with the cult of the dead, and, as usual, the men are the real performers. Masked and dressed up to impersonate the ghosts of departed people, the whole male population takes part in the ceremony, representing a large cast of different supernatural characters, each personage or group bearing a marked individuality of its own. The women, accompanied by the elder children, are the spectators, and by various devices they are induced to believe that they actually see their deceased friends and other ghosts, so on this account there is much wailing during part of the performance. Offerings of food to the dead are every day brought to the place by the women. One of the chief objects of the ceremony is to assist the people in the harpooning of dugong.

There is even a stage arrangement, and, in fact, the *hóriómu* ground in its main feature suggests a theatre. The curtain is represented by two long screens, about 2 m. high, with an opening in the centre where the ends overlap, so as to prevent the spectators from looking into the interior of the shrine. Within is the room of the spirits, partitioned off on one side by the screens and surrounded by the bush on the three remaining sides. The spirits appear in groups or singly through the aperture in the screens and dance on the open space outside, retiring into the shrine again after each performance. The *hóriómu* ground seems always to be chosen close to the beach, a short distance from the village, and the screens are put up parallel with the water-line. On one side of the dancing-ground, in front of the screens, is the place of the "orchestra," the musicians who accompany the dancers by beating their drums or else by pounding the ground with sticks, striking two shells together, or clapping their upper arms or knees with their hands. Occasionally the drummers sing also, whereas the dancers always remain silent so as not to be betrayed by their voices. Nearer to the beach is the place of the onlookers. Generally some fires are kept burning there, one for each of the five totem clans; they are used for cooking food. Inside the shrine there are five other fires exactly corresponding to the former; these are said to belong to the spirits. The arrangement with double fires is meant to delude the women, who might otherwise wonder where the ghosts cook their food. No firebrand must be taken outside from the shrine, for this would spell disaster to the people. Nor must anyone shoot off an arrow from inside the shrine, aiming at a bird or any other game; in fact, no bird or wallaby must be killed near the *hóriómu,* because it may be a ghost appearing in that shape.

The two screens, supported by posts stuck in the ground, consist of lattice-work of split bamboo, into which coconut leaflets are skilfully plaited. They are decorated with shells, feathers, masks, fringed leaves, etc., and the top ends of the posts, protruding over the rest of the screens, are capped with trumpet-shells. During the ceremony each totem clan keeps a number of harpoon-shafts (*wápo*) in the shrine, propped up against the screens; they are taken away at intervals to be used for harpooning expeditions. Some *súru* also (poles employed for building the harpooning platforms) are placed against the outer side of the screens and kept there in readiness for future use. At each end of the screens next to the bush there is an additional entrance occasionally used by the spirits during the rites. The two screens are a permanent erection, left intact during the interval between the ceremonies and put in order and redecorated each time they are needed. Thus the *hóriómu* shrine forms a sort of village sanctuary, sometimes used as an assembly-place, etc., in connection with other ceremonies also.

Within the shrine each of the five totem clans of the people occupies a distinct place of its own, exactly corresponding to those of the women's places on the beach.

The Initiation of the Grown Boys into the Secrets of the Hóriómu

After the *hóriómu* proper has begun, a couple of days are generally devoted for initiating the grown boys into the secrets of the ceremony. Some time previously the parents collect a great quantity of provisions to entertain the people who undertake to teach the boys.

The main features of these observances are the following. The young boy is first carried by some female relative on the mother's side to the beach, where he is thoroughly washed by his parents. This purports to "take away smell belong woman" from him, for up to that age he has, like all children, continuously associated with women. He is then rubbed with certain medicines calculated to make him a favourite with the girls, the principal ingredient being fringes of grass petticoats which the mother has secretly appropriated from a great number of girls (from her own and other villages), in particular from the front part of the petticoat. Another ingredient is sea-foam, which is the "laugh" of the sea: the boy shall not always be stern and bent on fighting, but also understand how to laugh, for the girls like that. Certain "medicine belong dugong and turtle" are added, and the whole is mixed with coconut oil in a bowl. A special fire is lighted for each boy with medicines burning in it, and the boy has to stand close to it so as to be enveloped in the smoke. A large heap of provisions is piled up beside the fire, probably representing the abundance of food he shall always have at his disposal.

After the boy has been taken back into the house, his mother lies down at the entrance on the verandah with her head resting on the threshold and her feet directed towards the ladder. The boy walks over her, treading with one foot on her abdomen. This step has a symbolic meaning: "what place boy he come from that time he born, he finish now along that place." At the ladder the boy is received by his *míduabéra* (maternal uncle), who carries him to the *hóriómu,* some medicine having first been placed on the shoulder where the boy sits. The mother, too, has kept some "medicine plants" on her body where the boy puts his foot, and these she afterwards secretly goes and strews over a place where the girls are sure to tread on them. This will cause the girls to fall in love with the boy.

On their way to the *hóriómu* the boys and their carriers are harassed by a number of masked spirits, who nearly frighten the youngsters out of their wits. The reason why the boys are carried during these observances is only explained by saying that the people "want make him grow quick."

All the new boys are then left for a while in the *hóriómu* shrine, the spirits withdrawing into the bush near by. While the *míduabéra* keeps the eyes of his ward covered with his hands, one group of spirits come and post themselves in a row in front of the boys, removing their masks and other head-gear. Suddenly some trumpet-shells and drums are sounded, and while all the men set up a roaring, *"huu-ooo!"* the boys are allowed to open their eyes and see that the spirits before them are men. In a similar way the other groups of spirits present themselves before the boys, some first dancing before them in their full attire and then uncovering their faces. The *míduabéra* teaches the boy everything he ought to know about the *hóriómu,* and many other things as well. Finally the boys too are painted and decorated, but during the whole ceremony they have to remain inside the shrine as long as the women are present.

The Mogúru or Life-giving Ceremony

The *mogúru* is the most secret, sacred and awe-inspiring ceremony of the Kiwai people. Shrouded in an atmosphere of mystery, it is never spoken of except among those initiated, and the mere mention of its name to women is a most serious offence. I had considerable difficulty in obtaining definite knowledge of the *mogúru*. Some of my informants only dared to come and tell about it late at night, first ascertaining by the aid of my lantern that no listener was hidden about my house. Then the man would sit quite close to me and whisper his statements into my ear, horrified at himself for betraying the secrets of his tribe. So disconcerted was my informant generally after the séance that he would avoid me for several days, and could only be induced to come back when his conscience had grown quieter and the temptation of the reward (or bribe) could again be felt. The more I was let into the various secrets of the people, the easier it was, however, to proceed. At last the resistance was wholly overcome, particularly when people found out that others were also telling me secrets.

The *mogúru* seems formerly to have been held every year, sometimes twice a year (on a smaller scale if the interval was a short one), in Kiwai with little regard to season, at Mawata generally during the north-west period. If some important event occurred in a village (for instance, the completion of a new long-house), the occasion was often celebrated by a *mogúru*. The ceremony always took place inside the gruesome and mysterious *dárinto* (men's house). It lasted quite a long time, sometimes up to two months.

The *mogúru* forms the one great exception to the strict rules of decorum and morality which on the whole are a very prominent characteristic of the people. The stupendous scenes which take place at the *mogúru,* forbidding as they are, do not primarily arise from sexual licentiousness, but must rather be considered as a mass-psychosis under the incitation of superstitious awe. In groups, one after another, the men betake themselves to the women's compartments, where soon a promiscuous intercourse is in progress. All jealousy, all marriage rules, otherwise so strongly emphasized, are laid aside, men exchange their wives, and any one may choose any partner he likes, avoiding only his closest blood relations. After the act the men empty the semen into the *báru,* and the women add in a similar way to the production of the potent medicine. Sometimes a separate coconut bowl (*núku*) seems to be used by the different couples, afterwards to be poured off into the *báru.* Everybody seems to be intent upon contributing as much as possible to the medicine, so that the *báru* should be filled up, and a great number of men, summoned from other villages, render assistance, their wives being among the other women.

Meanwhile the dancing and singing go on in the large room. Returning from the women's enclosures, the men pick up their drums again and join in the dance, afterwards renewing their visits to the women. The longer the orgies last, the looser becomes the general behaviour. The debauchery lasts till early morning, when everybody goes and swims, afterwards drying themselves at a fire and putting on their usual covering. The people then sleep most of the day. This part of the *mogúru* goes on several nights, in Waboda, so it is said, till some of the women show signs of pregnancy.

The Sexual Instruction of the Girls and Boys

The two gable ends of the *dárimo* (sometimes an ordinary communal long-house, *móto*) are partitioned off with mats, and into the one compartment are brought the girls to be taught, into the other the boys. There they are kept isolated for about a couple of weeks, each girl looked after by an *áramoróbo* (properly: *áramo órobo;* some near female relative) and each boy by an *áramo-dúbu* (male guardian). During this time they may only leave the building when occasionally carried outside by the *áramo* people. At night they are dressed up and brought to the central part of the house, where the girls and boys sit down on opposite sides of a group of older people, who sit in the middle; these also are painted and have their ornaments on. Some old man, who "savvy much," begins telling the girls and boys what they should know in various matters; the narrative is frequently interrupted by exclamations from the other elders, who confirm the truth of what is being said. Now and again the old people start a song, in which the youngsters are requested to join, as soon as they have learnt the words and tune. This instruction includes some of the more important folk-tales, as well as the customs and usages of the people in sexual and other matters. The young folk seem to be paired off, a little husband and his little wife, and these mock marriages appear in many cases to be intended for actual realization later on, although various circumstances may cause different unions to be concluded.

In former times it was particularly enjoined upon the young people to keep up the custom of lending wives to visitors. This custom is still prevalent in the eastern part of the estuary, and some traces of it may survive in certain parts of Kiwai island. It seems that one motive for this practice was to procure that important garden medicine, the male semen, that obtained from strangers being regarded as particularly powerful.

When the verbal instruction of the young folk is over, sometimes before, the older men in frequent cases have intercourse with the young girls, sometimes during the day, sometimes at night. Some of the girls shriek out and try to resist: "that's why they are taught." During the *máure mogúru* the girls are brought to the women's compartment in the *dárimo,* and there they are for a short time (one night, some of my informants said) abandoned with the rest to the men. The girls are generally married shortly after the *mogúru.*

The instruction just described seems, in fact, to apply much more to the girls than to the boys. A boy is not subjected to any actual practice in sexual matters during the *mogúru;* he is only taught "along mouth." Nor is he permitted to take part in the general intercourse accompanying the ceremonies before he is married, and then he brings his wife with him. He is not supposed to have connection with a girl until he has procured her from her people, but as a matter of fact all marriages are probably preceded by sexual intimacy.

Certain measures are taken in order to inspire the girls and boys with due respect and awe while they are staying in the *dárimo,* such as the following. A man, wearing the ordinary ornaments and gay-leaved branches and, in addition, a hideous mask, hides behind a partition of mats. After the young people have been told that the *sugúma* (or some other horrid being) has arrived, the mats are suddenly removed, and at the sight of the apparition they burst out shrieking. In another case they are taken into an enclosure of mats, after being warned that some strange being will shortly put in an appearance. While they are huddled together there, an old woman, fantastically attired, will begin to jump and dance about outside on all fours, making as much noise as she can and soon causing the boys and girls to be beside themselves with fright.

The *mogúru* is sometimes performed without the episode of the "teaching" of the girls and boys being included at all.

GREGORY BATESON

The Naven Ceremony in New Guinea

The Iatmul people live on the middle reaches of the Sepik River in the Mandated Territory of New Guinea. They are a fine, proud, head-hunting people who live in big villages with a population of between two hundred and a thousand individuals in each village. Their social organisation, kinship and religious systems are developed to an extreme of complexity. The community is subdivided into groups according to two independent systems with very little congruence between one system and the other. On the one hand there is a division into two totemic moieties which are further subdivided into phratries and clans; and on the other hand there is a division into two cross-cutting pairs of initiatory moieties which are subdivided into age grades. None of these groups are strictly exogamous. Membership of all the groups is determined by patrilineal descent.

In spite of this strong emphasis upon patriliny, the people pay a great deal of attention to kinship links through the mother or sister, and both the patrilineal and matrilineal links are preserved in a classificatory system through many generations. Thus the term *wau* (mother's brother) and *laua* (sister's child, m.s.) are used not only between one's own mother's brother and sister's children, but also in a classificatory way, so that the term *wau* includes such relatives as mother's mother's sister's son even though all three of the intervening women through whom the kinship is traced have married into different clans. It is with the relations between classificatory *waus*[1] and *laua*s that this book chiefly deals.

Occasions on which Naven are performed.

The ceremonies are called *naven* and are performed in celebration of the acts and achievements of the *laua* (sister's child). Whenever a *laua*—boy or girl, man or woman—performs some standard cultural act, and especially when the child performs this act for the first time in its life, the occasion may be celebrated by its *wau*. The possible occasions for the performance of *naven* are very numerous and very frequent. In the case of a boy the list of acts and achievements which may be celebrated in this way is a long one, and may conveniently be divided into five categories:

1. Major achievements which, though greeted with a more elaborate *naven* upon their first performance, are also received with some show of *naven* behaviour every time they occur. Of these the most important is homicide. The first time a boy kills an enemy or a foreigner or some bought victim is made the occasion for the most complete *naven*, involving the greatest number of relatives and the greatest variety of ritual incidents. Later in his life when the achievement is repeated, there will still be some *naven* performance on the part of the *wau*, but the majority of the ritual incidents will probably be omitted. Next to actual homicide, the most honoured acts are those which help others to successful killing. The man standing on the bow of a war canoe does not carry a spear-thrower but carries instead a very light paddle set in a long bamboo shaft; with this he wards off darts from the spear-throwers of the enemy. This man may be honoured with *naven* for any kills effected by members of his canoe. Another act contributory to killing which may be honoured is the enticing of foreigners into the village so that others may kill them. Far behind these in importance

[1] In the Iatmul language there is no suffix attached to substantives to indicate plurality. I have therefore used the English suffix, -s, for this purpose. In place of the Iatmul possessive suffix, *-na,* I have used the ordinary English -'s. Native words are in all cases italicised but the English suffixes remain in ordinary type.

come such achievements as the killing of a large crocodile, the killing of a wild pig, the spearing of a giant eel, etc.—achievements which are still sufficiently important whenever they are repeated to stimulate the *wau* at least to a ritual greeting and perhaps to the throwing of a cloud of lime at the *laua*.

2. Minor cultural acts which are celebrated only upon the first occasion of their achievement. Actually it would perhaps be correct to say that the first performance of *any* cultural act may be the excuse for a *naven*. An informant in Mindimbit village, however, gave me a long list, and I have added to it one or two other acts which I know may be celebrated with *naven*. This list, though of course it is not complete, is yet worth reproducing, because it illustrates the sort of act which may be noticed by the *wau*. It includes: killing any of the following animals—birds, fish, eel, tortoise, flying fox; planting any of the following plants—yams, tobacco, taro, coconut, areca, betel, sago, sugar-cane; spotting an opossum in the bush; felling a sago palm, opening it and beating sago; using a spear-thrower; using a throwing stick to kill a bird; using a stone axe (or nowadays a steel knife or axe); sharpening a fish spear; cutting a paddle; making a canoe; making a digging stick; making a spear-thrower; incising patterns on a lime gourd; plaiting an arm band; making a shell girdle; beating a hand drum; beating a slit-gong; blowing a trumpet; playing a flute; beating the secret slit-gongs called *wagan;* travelling to another village and returning; acquiring shell valuables; buying an axe, knife, mirror, etc.; buying areca nut; killing a pig and standing a feast.

3. Acts characteristic of *laua*. The relationship between *laua* and *wau* is marked by various forms of characteristic behaviour—acts which each performs in reference to the other. Such acts may be described as duties, services, or privileges, and it is not at all easy in any given case to decide which of these terms should be applied. In general, whenever the *laua* performs any conspicuous act which is characteristic of his position as *laua,* the *wau* will respond with some show of *naven* behaviour. These acts include such ceremonials as the exhibition of totemic ancestors of *wau*'s clan, dancing in masks which represent these ancestors and carving their images on the posts which are to stand in the section of the ceremonial house

which belongs to the *wau*'s clan. Several of the musical activities mentioned above—e.g. beating secret slit-gongs and playing flutes—may also fall within this category of services to the *wau*'s clan. A man may blow the flutes of his own clan and his musical accomplishment be greeted by *naven* upon the first occasion, but it is also his duty or privilege to blow the totemic flutes of his *wau*'s clan on certain special occasions; and this act, like other honouring of the *wau*'s totems, will be greeted with *naven* behaviour upon every occasion when it is repeated. Besides ritual duties and privileges, the *laua* will help his *wau* in such labours as house building; and in the formal debating in the ceremonial house, the *laua* will often speak on the side of his *wau*'s clan. All such acts will be hailed by the *wau* whenever they occur with gestures and exclamations reminiscent of *naven*.

4. Boasting in the presence of the *wau*. It is correct for a boy to boast in the presence of his *wau*, but the latter may resent this behaviour if it is carried to excess; and he will, in this event, make a gesture suggestive of turning his buttocks to his *laua*. I have never seen the complete gesture of rubbing the buttocks on the *laua*'s shin, the climax of the *naven*, carried out in reply to *laua*'s boasts; usually the threat is sufficient to curb the young man's tongue. But it is generally stated that, when exasperated, a *wau* may complete the gesture and, by so doing, involve the *laua* in a presentation of valuables to the *wau*. It is probable that this boasting in the presence of the *wau* should be classified with the other acts characteristic of the *laua*. But the case differs from the others in that the *naven* behaviour of the *wau* is carried out in anger or annoyance. In the other cases the *naven* behaviour is on the whole a method of complimenting or congratulating the *laua* upon his achievements.

5. Changes in social status. Such events in the boy's life as: the boring of his ears, the boring of his nasal septum, his initiation, his marriage, his becoming possessed by a shamanic spirit, may all be celebrated with *naven* when they occur. I feel some hesitation in applying the term *change of status* to these events, since the culture does not clearly emphasise the concepts of status and promotion. Even in the graded initiatory system, the event which the *wau* celebrates is not the promotion of the boy from one grade to the

next, but the completion of the ceremony of initiation which may take place years before the general shifting of age-grade membership. In any case it must be clearly understood that the *naven* ceremonies are in no sense *rites de passage*, although they may celebrate or emphasise the fact that such rites have been performed. The actual rites of initiation are performed by the elder age grade within a system of social groupings and moieties which is to a great extent independent of clans and totemism. The fact that the *rite de passage* has been performed is afterwards celebrated by the *wau* within the different social grouping which is organised on the basis of the family and totemic clans.

The other most important events in a man's life—his birth and his death—are neither of them celebrated by *naven*. In the case of birth, the *wau* will go to the child soon after it is born and present it with a coconut and a personal name which refers to the totemic ancestors of the *wau*'s clan. Though I have never seen this done, I believe that the *wau* might well exclaim: "*Lan men to!*" (husband thou indeed!) when the baby gripped his fingers. This exclamation, as we shall see later, is one of the characteristic details of *naven* behaviour. We shall see too that the giving of the special name is an act which demonstrates the existence of the *wau-laua* relationship; and that the coconut is the first in a long series of gift exchanges which will accompany *naven* and other ceremonies. In the case of death, there is again no *naven*, but the classificatory *wau* plays an important part in the mortuary ceremonies, and finally claims the dead man as in some special sense a member of the maternal clan, pulling the figure which represents him towards himself with a hook. In the land of the dead the ghost will henceforth live under the names which have been given to him by his *wau*.

The event of marriage may be celebrated not only by *wau*, but also, I believe, by *tawontu* (wife's brother). In one of the myths which I collected, there occurs a casual mention of the fact that a bride's own brother rubs his buttocks on the bridegroom's shin. I do not know of any other occasion which is celebrated in this way by *tawontu*.

There are more *naven* and more occasions for *naven* in the life of a boy or a man than in the life of a girl, but the achievements of a girl may also be occasions for *naven*. The list for a girl includes: catching fish with hook and line; collecting mayflies; washing sago; cooking sago pancakes; cooking sago paste; making a fish trap, a rain cape or a mosquito bag; and bearing a child. These events all fall into the category of cultural acts which are celebrated at their first accomplishment. Besides these there are two other events, initiation and dancing in the *tshugukepma* dances, both of which may be celebrated with *naven*. The initiation of girls is distinct from female puberty ceremonies and consists of scarification and the showing of flutes. It is a simplified version of the initiation of boys and is carried out by the men of the elder age grade. The ceremony is performed on only a very few women.

Description of the Ceremonies

The outstanding feature of the ceremonies is the dressing of men in women's clothes and of women in the clothes of men. The classificatory *wau* dresses himself in the most filthy of widow's weeds, and when so arrayed he is referred to as *"nyame"* ("mother"). They put on the most filthy old tousled skirts such as only the ugliest and most decrepit widows might wear, and like widows they were smeared with ashes. Considerable ingenuity went into this costuming, and all of it was directed towards creating an effect of utter decrepitude. On their heads they wore tattered old capes which were beginning to unravel and to fall to pieces with age and decay. Their bellies were bound with string like those of pregnant women. In their noses they wore, suspended in place of the little triangles of mother-of-pearl shell which women wear on festive occasions, large triangular lumps of old sago pancakes, the stale orts of a long past meal.

In this disgusting costume and with absolutely grave faces (their gravity was noted with special approbation by the bystanders), the two "mothers" hobbled about the village each using as a walking stick a short shafted paddle such as women use. Indeed, even with this support, they could hardly walk, so decrepit were they. The children of the village greeted these figures with screams of laughter and thronged around the two "mothers," following wherever they went and bursting into new shrieks whenever the "mothers," in their feebleness, stumbled and fell and, falling, demonstrated their femaleness by assuming on the ground grotesque attitudes with their legs widespread.

The "mothers" wandered about the village in this way looking for their "child" (the *laua*) and from time to time in high-pitched, cracked voices they enquired of the bystanders to learn where the young man had gone. "We have a fowl to give to the young man." Actually the *laua* during this performance had either left the village or hidden himself. As soon as he found out that his *wau*s were going to shame themselves in this way, he went away to avoid seeing the spectacle of their degraded behaviour.

If the *wau* can find the boy he will further demean himself by rubbing the cleft of his buttocks down the length of his *laua*'s leg, a sort of sexual salute which is said to have the effect of causing the *laua* to make haste to get valuables which he may present to his *wau* to "make him all right." [2] The *laua* should, nominally at least, fetch valuables according to the number of times that the *wau* repeats the gesture—one shell for each rubbing of the buttocks.

The *wau*'s gesture is called *mogul nggelak-ka*. In this phrase the word *mogul* means "anus," while *nggelak-ka* is a transitive verb which means "grooving," e.g., *ian nggelak-ka* means to dig a ditch. The suffix *-ka* is closely analogous to the English suffix, -ing, used to form present participles and verbal nouns.

This gesture of the *wau* I have only seen once. This was when a *wau* dashed into the midst of a dance and performed the gesture upon his *laua* who was celebrating the *wau*'s ancestors. The *wau* ran into the crowd, turned his back on the *laua* and rapidly lowered himself—almost fell—into a squatting position in such a way that as his legs bent under him his buttocks rubbed down the length of the *laua*'s leg.

But in the particular *naven* which I am describing, the two *wau*s did not find their *laua* and had to content themselves with wandering around the village in search of him. Finally they came to the big canoe which he had made—the achievement which they were cele-

---

[2] This is the pidgin English translation of an Iatmul phrase, *kunak-ket*. The suffix *-ket* is purposive; and the word *kunak* means to "make ready," "repair," or "propitiate."

brating. They then collapsed into the canoe and for a few moments lay in it apparently helpless and exhausted, with their legs wide apart in the attitudes which the children found so amusing. Gradually they recovered and picked up their paddles, and sitting in the canoe in the bow and stern (women sit to paddle a canoe, but men stand), they slowly took it for a short voyage on the lake. When they returned they came ashore and hobbled off. The performance was over and they went away and washed themselves and put on their ordinary garments. The fowl was finally given to the *laua* and it became his duty to make a return present of shell valuables to his *wau* at some later date. Return presents of this kind are ceremonially given, generally on occasions when some other dances are being performed. The shells are tied to a spear and so presented to the *wau*.

In more elaborate *naven,* especially those in which women play a part, there is a classificatory spreading of ritual behaviour not only to cause the classificatory relatives of the actual *laua* to perform *naven* for him, but also to cause persons not otherwise involved to adopt *naven* behaviour towards other individuals who may be identified in some way with the actual *laua*. For example, the characteristic *naven* behaviour of the elder brothers' wives is the beating of their husbands' younger brother when his achievements are being celebrated. Owing to the classificatory spreading of the *naven* not only does the boy who has worked sago get beaten by his elder brothers' wives, but also the boy's father's elder brothers' wives get up and beat the father. Further, men other than the performing *wau*s may take the opportunity to make presentations of food to their various *laua*s.

Some of this classificatory spreading occurred in the *naven* in Mindimbit which was celebrated for the children who had worked sago for the first time. In this ceremony only female relatives performed and their costume was in sharp contrast to that of the *wau*s described above. The *wau* dresses himself in the filthiest of female garments, but the majority of the women, when they put on the garments of men, wear the smartest of male attire. The female relatives who performed were sisters (*nyanggai*), fathers' sisters (*iau*), elder brothers' wives (*tshaishi*), mothers (*nyame*), and mothers' brothers' wives (*mbora*)—all these terms being used in a classificatory as well as in the narrow sense.

Of these relatives the sisters, fathers' sisters and elder brothers' wives dressed as men, borrowing the very best of feather headdresses and homicidal ornaments from their menfolk (husbands or brothers or fathers). Their faces were painted white with sulphur, as is the privilege of homicides, and in their hands they carried the decorated lime boxes used by men and serrated lime sticks with pendant tassels whose number is a tally of men killed by the owner. This costume was very becoming to the women and was admired by the men. In it the women were very proud of themselves. They walked about flaunting their feathers and grating their lime sticks in the boxes, producing the loud sound which men use to express anger, pride and assertiveness. Indeed so great was their pleasure in this particular detail of male behaviour that the husband of one of them, when I met him on the day following the performance, complained sorrowfully that his wife had worn away all the serrations on his lime stick so that it would no longer make a sound.

The mothers and mothers' brothers' wives wore different types of costume. The mother stripped off her skirt but did not put on any male ornaments, and the mothers' brothers' wives put on filthy widow's weeds, like those of the *wau,* described above.

The children's canoe came back from the sago swamps late in the morning and as soon as it was sighted from the banks of the river, word was shouted in to the village which lies back from the river on a little lake. The women assembled on the shores of the lake and when the canoe entered, they swam out to greet and splash the children, as is done when a canoe returns from a successful head-hunting raid. When the children had landed, the village appeared to go mad for awhile; fathers' sisters and elder brothers' wives dashing about searching respectively for their various brothers' children and husbands' younger brothers in order to beat them. The men who were expecting to be beaten did their best to avoid the ceremony by skulking in the ceremonial houses, but the women on these occasions have unusual licence (perhaps because they are in men's costume). Whenever a *iau* saw her *kanggat* (brother's child, w.s.) or a *tshaishi* saw her *tshuambo* (husband's younger brother) in one of the ceremonial houses, she dashed into the usually forbidden spot, stick in hand, and gave him several good blows; and, if he ran away, she chased him, beating him as he ran. On a similar occasion in Kankanamun, when the women were celebrating *naven* for a young man who had killed a pig and was standing a feast, they hesitated to enter a ceremonial house in which a debate was in progress. The men stopped the debate for their benefit and the whole crowd of them danced into the ceremonial house in a column. Arrived there, the column broke up and each woman went and beat her appropriate relatives.[3]

On the occasion in Mindimbit which I am describing, I did not see any activity of the mothers and sisters. The activity of the other women dressed as men continued off and on throughout the rest of the day. In the evening, the women had a small dance by themselves. It is the custom of the men to take off their public aprons after dark and the women accordingly stripped off the flying-fox-skin aprons, which they had borrowed from their husbands and brothers, and danced with their loins uncovered, still wearing their splendid feather headdresses and ornaments. There was no apparent embarrassment of the men at this exposure in their womenfolk—but the older men were rather shocked at this lack of embarrassment. The dance was held close to one of the smaller ceremonial houses and one of the old men remarked to me in scandalised tones that it was "shocking" to see the younger men crowding to this ceremonial house, where they had no business but a good view of the women's dance. It was the ceremonial house of a particular clan, but that evening it was full of young men, members of every clan in the village.

In the case of the *naven* in Mindimbit for the little girl who had caught a fish with hook and line, the performance was still more elaborate, not because the achievement was very important but per-

---

[3] To this account of the beatings, two points may be added which I did not observe at the time but of which I was later informed. It is said that the actual father of the hero would only be slightly beaten by his *tshaishi* but that the father's younger brother (*tshambwi-nyai'*) would be severely beaten. I was also told that on these occasions the *tshaishi* will exclaim "*tshuambo-ket wonggegio*"—(I will rape my young brother).

haps because the *wau*s were anxious to obtain shell valuables by presenting pigs to their *laua*s. From the accounts which I collected, it appears that in this *naven* both male and female relatives took part and eight pigs were killed. Besides the little girl who had caught a fish (a month or two before the ceremony), two other little girls were honoured, and the resulting *naven* spread to almost every individual in the village. One pig was even presented to a classificatory *laua* in the next village.

Four *wau*s were dressed as "mothers" and their skirts were tucked up so as to expose their genitals. Three of these *wau*s are described as carrying the little girls "on their heads"—presumably carrying girls in the position in which mothers habitually carry their children astride on the shoulder. The fourth *wau* was also dressed as a mother but wore no skirt. He was tied down on some sort of "bed" or stretcher, on which he was lifted and violently swung by a number of men who, while they rocked the stretcher, sang songs of the *wau*'s clan. The little girl who had caught the fish was placed on the belly of this *wau,* her father meanwhile standing by with an adze to which he had tied a mother-of-pearl crescent. This adze he gave into the little girl's hands and with it she cut the bonds which held her *wau* to the stretcher. She then gave the decorated adze to the *wau* and with it he raised himself to a sitting position on the stretcher, supporting himself by means of the adze. Similarly the fathers of the other little girls presented valuables to the girls' *wau*s and at the same time tossed the *wau*s' skirts. The *wau*s then resumed their normal male attire.

During the above performance a *mbora,* the wife of the *wau* who was tied to the stretcher, danced with her skirts tucked up to expose her genitals. She wore a string bag over her head and face, and carried a digging stick, holding it horizontally behind her shoulders with her hands raised to hold it on each side. At the conclusion of the dance she was presented with a mother-of-pearl crescent and three *Turbo* shells by the father of the little girl.

The whole of this ritual pantomime acted by the *wau* appears to me to be a representation of the birth of the little girl from the belly of her mother's brother, though none of my male informants (in Kankanamun where I made enquiries) had ever heard of the custom of tying the woman in labour on a stretcher. The dance of the *mbora* (mother's brother's wife), with her arms stretched back behind her head, also probably represents the position of a woman in labour.

It is not easy to judge how much of this mutual envy is developed between the sexes in Iatmul culture. Certainly the women take a very real pleasure in the adoption of male clothes and ways in the *naven,* and this factor—mild envy of the masculine ethos—may be regarded as an important motive in determining their transvesticism. But in the men, the corresponding envy cannot be detected. Outwardly, at least, they despise the womanly ethos, but it is not impossible that they have some unacknowledged envy of it. Their own ethos would not, in any case, permit them to acknowledge that there was anything to be said for the attitudes of the women and any envy which they may have they might well express in scorn of women—dressing in women's clothes for the purpose.[4]

Sex Ethos and Naven

The most important generalisation which can be drawn from the study of Iatmul ethos is that in this society each sex has its own *consistent* ethos which contrasts with that of the opposite sex. Among the men, whether they are sitting and talking in the ceremonial house, initiating a novice, or building a house—whatever the occasion—there is the same emphasis and value set upon pride, self-assertion, harshness and spectacular display. This emphasis

[4] I am here indebted to Dr Karin Stephen, who on the basis of her psycho-analytic experience in Europe suggested this possibility to me—that unconscious jealousy of the women's ethos may be one of the motives of the men's transvesticism.

I am very doubtful whether such a phrasing of the matter is permissible. I have endeavoured to use references to emotions only where such phrasing could be regarded as a rough, makeshift description of the *behaviour* of individuals, and I hesitate to launch into phrasings which would render my "behaviouristic" references to emotion ambiguous by implying that the behaviour may be the reverse of that primarily appropriate to the emotion.

I grant in general that theories of inversion, etc., are an attempt to express an important truth, but I suspect that the theories cannot be properly formulated or proven till we have techniques for analytical description of gestures, posture, etc., and can define the differences between inverted and direct behaviour.

leads again and again to over-emphasis; the tendency to histrionic behaviour continually diverts the harshness into irony, which in its turn degenerates into buffooning. But though the behaviour may vary, the underlying emotional pattern is uniform.

Among the women we have found a different and rather less consistent ethos. Their life is concerned primarily with the necessary routines of food-getting and child-rearing, and their attitudes are informed, not by pride, but rather by a sense of "reality." They are readily co-operative, and their emotional reactions are not jerky and spectacular, but easy and "natural." On special occasions, it seems, the women exhibit an ethos modelled upon that of the men, and it would appear from our consideration of Preferred Types that certain women are admired for what we may describe as Iatmul-masculine characteristics.

If we return at this point to the problems presented by the *naven* ceremonies, we see these problems in a new light. The elements of exaggeration in the *wau*'s behaviour appear, not as isolated oddities, but as patterns of behaviour which are normal and ordinary in Iatmul men. This answer may seem rather uninteresting but it involves a major generalisation about cultural behaviour, and in science every step is a demonstration of consistency within a given sphere of relevance. We might perhaps have studied this consistency more fully but the answer would still have been of the same type. To pursue the matter further we should be compelled to shift to some other scientific discipline, e.g. to the study of character formation.

In the case of the women, with a double emphasis running through their ethos, their *naven* behaviour can be completely classified as consistent either with their everyday ethos or with their special occasional pride. All the behaviour of the mother is patterned upon submission and negative self-feeling. Her action in lying naked with the other women while her son steps over them, and the cliché "that so small place out of which this big man came," are perfectly in keeping with the everyday ethos of Iatmul women, and constitute a very simple expression of her vicarious pride in her son. Thus the problem of the mother's behaviour, like that of the *wau*'s exaggerations, may now be referred to other scientific disciplines.

In the behaviour of the transvestite women, the father's sister and the elder brother's wife, we may see an expression of the occasional pride such as women exhibit on the rare occasions when they perform publicly with men as an audience.

Examination of Iatmul ethos has accounted for the tone of behaviour of the various relatives in *naven,* but there are many details which cannot be thus summarily dismissed. Consider the *wau:* his buffooning is normal, but that is no reason why he should dress as a woman in order to be a buffoon, and, as we have seen above, the structural premises within the culture, whereby the *wau* might regard himself as the *laua*'s wife, are still not a dynamic factor which would compel either the community or the *wau* to emphasise this aspect of the *wau-laua* relationship. We have still to find some component of the *naven* situation which shall act in a dynamic way to induce transvesticism.

I believe that we may find an answer to this problem if we examine the incidence of transvesticism in European society. In the *naven,* the phenomenon is not due to abnormal hormones nor yet to the psychological or cultural maladjustment of the transvestites; and therefore in looking for analogous phenomena in Europe we may ignore the aberrant cases and should examine rather the contexts in which some degree of transvesticism is culturally normal.

Let us consider the case of the fashionable horsewoman. Her breeches we may perhaps regard as a special adaptation, and she will say that her bowler hat is specially designed to protect her head from overhanging trees: but what of her coat, tailored on decidedly masculine lines? She wears feminine evening dress at the hunt ball, and her everyday behaviour is that of a culturally normal woman, so that we cannot explain her transvesticism by a reference to her glands or abnormal psychology.

The facts of the matter are clear: a culturally and physically normal woman wears, in order to ride a horse, a costume unusual for her sex and patterned on that of the opposite sex; and the conclusion from these facts is equally obvious: since the woman is normal, the unusual element must be introduced by the act of riding a horse. In one sense, of course, there is nothing exceptional in a woman's riding—women have ridden horses for hundreds of years in the history of our culture. But if we compare the activity of riding a horse with other activities which our culture has decreed suitable and proper for women, we see at once that horse-riding, which demands violent activity and gives a great sense of physical mastery,[5] contrasts sharply with the great majority of situations in a woman's life.

The ethos of women in our culture has been built up around certain types of situation and that of men around very different situations. The result is that women, placed by culture in a situation which is unusual for them but which is usual for men, have contrived a transvestite costume, and this costume has been accepted by the community as appropriate to these abnormal situations.

With this hint of the sort of situation in which transvesticism may be developed, we may return to Iatmul culture. First let us consider the contexts in which partial transvesticism occurs, namely, in the case of women who take part in spectacular ceremonies. Their position is very closely analogous to that of the horsewoman. The normal life of Iatmul women is quiet and unostentatious, while that of the men is noisy and ostentatious. When women take part in spectacular ceremonial they are doing something which is foreign to the norms of their own existence, but which is normal for men—and so we find them adopting for these special occasions bits of the culture of the men, holding themselves like men[6] and wearing ornaments which are normally only worn by men.

Looking at the *naven* ceremonies in the light of this theory we

---

[5] In Freudian phrasing the act of riding a horse might be regarded as sexually symbolic. The difference between the point of view which I advocate and that of the Freudians is essentially this: that I regard such sexual symbols as noses, flutes, *wagan*, etc., as symbolic of sex ethos, and I would even see in the sexual act one more context in which this ethos is expressed.

[6] In theatrical representations, humorous journalism and the like, there is a common belief that the postures, gestures, tones of the voice, etc., of the horsewoman are to some extent modelled on those of men, and we might see in this an analogy with the proud gestures of the transvestite and semi-transvestite Iatmul women. I am uncertain, however, to what extent these postures, etc., of the horsewoman occur in real life, and whether they are not perhaps imaginary.

can recognise in the *naven* situation conditions which might influence either sex towards transvesticism. The situation may be summed up by saying that a child has accomplished some notable feat and its relatives are to express, in a public manner, their joy in this event. This situation is one which is foreign to the normal settings of the life of either sex. The men by their unreal spectacular life are perfectly habituated to the "ordeal" of public performance. But they are not accustomed to the free expression of vicarious personal emotion. Anger and scorn they can express with a good deal of over-compensation, and joy and sorrow they can express when it is their own pride which is enhanced or abased; but to express joy in the achievements of another is outside the norms of their behaviour.

In the case of the women the position is reversed. Their co-operative life has made them capable of the easy expression of unselfish joy and sorrow, but it has not taught them to assume a public spectacular role.

Thus the *naven* situation contains two components, the element of public display and the element of vicarious personal emotion; and each sex, when it is placed by culture in this situation, is faced by one component which is easily acceptable, while the other component is embarrassing and smacks rather of situations normal to the life of the opposite sex. This embarrassment we may, I think, regard as a dynamic force which pushes the individual towards transvesticism—and to a transvesticism which the community has been able to accept and which in course of time has become a cultural norm.

Thus the contrasting ethos of the two sexes may be supposed to play and to have played in the past a very real part in the shaping of the *naven* ceremonies. It has provided the little push which has led the culture to follow its structural premises to the extremes which I have described. When the women take part in spectacular ceremonial other than *naven,* the structural premises which might justify complete transvesticism are lacking, and the women content themselves with wearing only a few masculine ornaments.

Lastly we may consider the adoption of widow's weeds by the *wau* and the wearing by the women of the best masculine ornaments obtainable. The former is no doubt a buffooning expression of the men's distaste for the women's ethos. We have seen that the context of mourning is one in which the differing ethos of the two sexes contrasts most strongly and most uncomfortably, and the wearing of a widow's weeds by the *wau* is clearly on all fours with the men's trick of caricaturing the dirging of the solitary widow as she paddles her canoe to her garden. In shaming himself he is, incidentally, expressing his contempt for the whole ethos of those who express grief so easily.

The women on the other hand have no discernible contempt for the proud male ethos. It is the ethos appropriate to spectacular display, and in the *naven* they adopt as much of that ethos as possible—and even exaggerate it, gaily scraping the lime sticks in their husbands' gourds till the serrations are quite worn away. Here it would seem that their joy in wearing masculine ornaments and carrying on in the swaggering ways of men has somewhat distracted them from the business in hand—that of celebrating the achievement of a small child. Apart from the one incident in which the women lie down naked while the hero steps over them, the *naven* behaviour of the women is actually as irrelevant as that of the men. Thus the presence of contrasting ethos in the two sexes has almost completely diverted the *naven* ceremonial from simple reference to its ostensible object.

Nevertheless, since *naven* behaviour is the conventional way in which a *wau* congratulates his *laua* upon any achievement, there is no doubt that this behaviour, distorted and irrelevant as it may seem to us, is yet understood by the *laua* as a form of congratulation.

VERRIER ELWIN

The Two-Sex Dormitories of the Muria

The Types of Ghotul

The dormitories fall into two clearly defined groups—one, of the semi-military "barracks" type, appears to aim at a strict segregation of the boys and is connected with war, hunting and magic; the other allows or even encourages them to have relations with the unmarried girls and possibly aims (though our knowledge is too fragmentary to assert this with confidence) at regulating the prenuptial interests of tribal youth. Both types of dormitory, like the Muria ghotul, fulfil important social and religious functions. Those of the first type are well summarized by Hutton Webster.

> The men's house is usually the largest building in a tribal settlement. It belongs in common to the villagers; it serves as council-chamber and town hall, as a guest-house for strangers, and as a sleeping resort of the men. Here the more precious belongings of the community, such as trophies taken in war or in the chase and religious emblems of various sorts, are preserved. Within its precincts, women and children, and men not fully initiated members of the tribe, seldom or never enter. When marriage does not follow immediately upon initiation into the tribe, the institution of the men's house becomes an effective restraint upon the sexual proclivities of the unmarried youth. It then serves as a club-house for the bachelors, whose residence within it may be regarded as a perpetuation of that formal seclusion of the lads from the women, which it is the purpose of the initiation ceremonies in the first place to accomplish.

Before proceeding further it is essential that we distinguish carefully between two different types of ghotul, for these are so sharply differentiated by rule and custom and the psychological conditions of each are so distinct that until this is done we can get no clear picture of the intimate relations between chelik and motiari.

The fundamental principle of the first type of dormitory, which is sometimes called the *jodidār*[1] or "yoking" ghotul, is that of fidelity to a single partner during the whole of the pre-marital period. Each chelik is paired off with a motiari; he is formally "married" to her; she may even take the feminine form of his title as her own. Divorce is allowed, though infidelity is punished.

In the second type of ghotul, which is probably a later development of the classic model, any kind of lasting attachment between chelik and motiari is forbidden. No one can say that such and such

---

[1] *A jodi* or *jori* is the word used for a life-long friend, yoke-fellow or husband and wife. A *jodi* is something definitely more than a temporary lover. It is the person yoked to whom one will pull the heavy plough of life. See V. Elwin and S. Hivale, *Folk-Songs of the Maikal Hills* (Bombay, 1944), pp. 240 f.

a motiari is *his* girl; if anyone sleeps with a particular girl for more than three days at a time, he is punished.

In all other matters, whether of discipline, routine, social duty or recreation, there is no difference between the two types of ghotul. We must, however, carefully distinguish them for their sexual customs and psychological conditions.

Although outwardly both types of ghotul are the same and often only the most careful investigation can distinguish them, the customs and atmosphere of the modern type are entirely distinct. Here everything is arranged to prevent long-drawn intense attachments, to eliminate jealousy and possessiveness, to deepen the sense of communal property and action. No chelik may regard a motiari as "his." There is no ghotul marriage, there are no ghotul partners. "Everyone belongs to everyone else" in the very spirit of *Brave New World.* A chelik and motiari may sleep together for three nights; after that they are warned; if they persist they are punished. If a boy shows any signs of possessiveness for a particular girl, if his face falls when he sees her making love to someone else, if he gets annoyed at her sleeping with another chelik, should he be offended if she refuses to massage him and goes to someone else, he is forcibly reminded by his fellows that she is not his wife, he has no *haq* or right over her, she is the *māl* or property of the whole ghotul, and if he looks like that he will be punished.

This type of ghotul is sometimes called the *mundi-badalna* because in it you change from girl to girl just as you change your rings from finger to finger.

How is it that this type of ghotul has so widely displaced the classical *jodidār* dormitory? Why is the process of change from one type to the other continuing today? There are many reasons.

In the Benur Pargana and at Koilibera I heard the phrase "so that they will not be ruined by love." This is certainly a genuine consideration. Too much love before marriage will mean too little after it. Sexual romance is not the best preparation for a life-long union. A strong and lasting attachment to a girl in the pre-nuptial period may lead to an elopement and an irregular marriage. Such a marriage disturbs the serenity of the home—which ultimately depends on the parents; it destroys the old alliances of families and prevents the repayment of ancient debts; it often turns out unsuccessful. In villages where several such elopements have occurred within a short time, the rules of the ghotul have been changed.

The modern rules are also intended as a contraceptive measure. The Muria believe that conception only occurs when the male and female remain together for a long period and enjoy an uninterrupted series of acts of coition with no divergence of interest. Both psychological and physical concentration in fidelity to a single partner is required for pregnancy.

A former Chalan of Golawand, for example, described how he consistently changed his ghotul partners and never made anyone pregnant; but two friends of his in the same ghotul slept every day with the same girls and impregnated them both. The Gaita at Koilibera said that a chelik could have congress three times a night and it would do no harm, but if he went to the same girl more than three days running he would fall ill and she might conceive.

The modern type of ghotul breaks up the coital sequence and is thus supposed to lessen the danger of conception. Statistics, however, show that this is not so. Among 2000 men, 80 made motiari pregnant during their ghotul period; of these 25 or 1 in 28·8 belonged to *jodidār* ghotul, and 55 or 1 in 23·2 to the modern type.

A more genuine reason for the prevalence of the newer rules is the Muria temperament which is fundamentally hostile to individualism, to exclusiveness, and to any kind of "possessiveness." The Muria believe that if everyone belongs to everyone else in the ghotul there will be no room for jealousy. I am not at the moment thinking whether this is true or not, but it is certainly what they think. "If we get jealous of each other," they said at Nayanar, "we exchange lovers." At Esalnar a chelik said, "We change partners because we want everyone to be happy; if one boy and one girl are always together as if they were man and wife, then some would be happier than others; the best boys and the best girls would be the property of individuals instead of being the property of the ghotul, and the rest would be miserable." When someone told the chelik at Kabonga that they were behaving like a lot of goats, they indignantly explained that "if a girl always sleeps with one boy, we feel that the unity of our life is being destroyed; in a ghotul all the girls should be the wives of all the boys." In Bhanpuri they used a similar phrase that "all the girls are the wives of the Kotwar," meaning that since the Kotwar is in charge of them and has the task of distributing them among the chelik, they must all be regarded as his wives in his capacity as a representative of the ghotul.

The result of this arrangement is—according to Muria theory—that everybody in the ghotul is in love with everybody else. "Boys and girls in a ghotul love each other as brothers love sisters, as parents love children, as husbands love their wives." It is remarkable that this general diffused love and affection among chelik and motiari should lead them to identify parental family and romantic love.

In Masora the boys gave as a reason for changing their partners the very human liking for change, "love's sweetest part, variety." One of them said, "You don't want to eat the same vegetable every day." The change of object undoubtedly stimulates the sexual instinct and makes ghotul life more exciting. But since the whole tendency of Muria society is towards stability, I doubt if the desire for variety has played a very important part in the development of the ghotul rules.

Another reason for the change of rules, given this time by the chelik of Sidhawand, was that if a chelik was always going about with the same motiari, the elders of the village would notice it and suspect that they had sexual relations. Yet at Chandabera, where there is a *jodidāṛ* ghotul, the Muria claimed that the boys and girls behaved with so much discretion that no one could ever guess how they were paired off. Here we come up against the strange convention that the elders of the village have no idea of what goes on in the ghotul, where they all spent their own childhood, but suppose it to be, as they said again at Sidhawand (where some had been to school), "a sort of Boy Scouts Club, whose members meet together for social service and for nothing else."

The extent of this convention should not be exaggerated. The elders are often equally prepared to make the most indecent comments on the sexual activities of the younger generation. But in the presence of outsiders at least, there is a general tendency to make a show of the decorum of village life.

Of this type of ghotul, Evelyn Wood has asked how its ideal can be achieved "without a sense of universal futility and frustration caused by such lavish dissipation of libidal power." The answer to this is, I think, that we must not overestimate the extent of ghotul promiscuity. There is no kind of orgy or licence; everything is strictly regulated and conducted with the utmost decorum. The average ghotul is small, with not more than twenty members. Of these twenty, several are bound to be closely related or of the same clan. In Palli, for example, which is a large ghotul, only three clans were represented, in Kajen only two. Moreover these boys and girls have grown up together from babyhood. When, therefore, we read that a chelik has to sleep with a new girl every three days, we are not to think of him as being able to pick and choose from an endless procession of new and exciting girls. He is going to spend his time in rotation among a little group of girls every one of whom he knows very well indeed. There is no doubt a certain dissipation of libidal energy, but I do not think that, except perhaps in the very large ghotul, it is excessive.

And further, a boy is not generally able to choose his partner at will. It is the Kotwar, in consultation with the Belosa, who decides how the chelik and motiari are to couple and when they are to change their partners. For example, at Kabonga the Kotwar himself told me, "I am the Raja of the motiari and every two or three days I rearrange them and tell the Belosa who is to sleep with whom." In Dongrigura, the Kotwar himself had the privilege of a permanent partner, and he and his "wife" made arrangements for the rest. There was the same custom in the neighbouring Palari. In Binjhli, it was the leading girls who made these arrangements.[2]

[2] With this we may compare the very interesting arrangements of the Masai *manyatia*-dormitory. When the warriors feel like it, which is "very, very often," they go in a group to stand outside the village and call to the girls. These approach and the warriors then say "Tasiukiu!" whereupon each girl selects one of the men; by her choice she binds herself to sleep with him that night. "It is a point of honour and etiquette that no girl so called upon to choose a man may refuse to do so, but she may make her choice from any of those men who were in the group that called to her." The Masai also

The rules differ from place to place. At Bakulwahi, where the girls slept in the ghotul only on Sundays, Wednesdays and Thursdays, and where there were in 1941 more chelik than motiari, the following procedure was adopted. Suppose there were thirty chelik and ten motiari, then on Sunday the motiari would comb the hair of all the chelik, but they would leave their combs in the hair of only ten as a sign that on that night those boys would have partners on their sleeping-mats. On Wednesday the girls would leave their combs in the hair of another ten; so also on Thursday. In this way every chelik was able to sleep with one of the motiari once a week. Should a girl not distribute her affections equally, she was punished, and should she leave her comb in the hair of the same boy two nights running she was heavily fined.

The typical Muria emphasis on equality is shown by an explanation given by the chelik of this ghotul when I raised the point that it was surely unusual that the number of girls could be divided so conveniently into the number of boys. If that were impossible, they pointed out, if for example there were twelve girls to the thirty boys, then twelve boys would sleep with twelve girls on Sunday and another twelve boys with the twelve girls on Wednesday. By Thursday only six boys would remain unpartnered for that week. On that night only six girls would leave their combs in the hair of these boys, and the other six girls and the other twenty-four boys would sleep alone. Any other arrangement would destroy the unity of the ghotul.

Ghotul Membership

In the first splendid ghotul, with its peacock roof and door of ogre's bones, Lingo gave the boys and girls names and duties. The oldest stories say that the first chelik were Mankor Singa, Jiha Guta Soma and Karata Guta Soma, and the first motiari Godakare Mode, Belosa and Kurumtuse Buke; the later tales give the girls' names as Belosa, Manjaro, Jalko and Dulosa. Lingo's own ghotul

---

have a system of selecting permanent lovers, though these can still sleep with other partners—but the permanent lovers can sleep together without formality whenever they desire.—L. S. B. Leakey, "Some Notes on the Masai of Kenya Colony," *JRAI*, Vol. LX, pp. 192 ff.

name was Manjhi. Since then every boy and girl, on becoming a full member of the dormitory, has received a title.

These titles are of great significance. Until they receive them, the children have no standing; they cannot get "ghotul-mates"; they are the servants and drudges of the others. But once they are named they enter into the full equality of the ghotul fellowship. They now almost forget their *mur podor* or home name, which must never be used in the ghotul or by the other children, and is indeed hardly ever used except at home, by parents and close relatives, or for some official purpose.

An ordinary name is often ugly or unkind, but the ghotul title has the tenderest and happiest associations, charged with romantic memories. For this reason it is never used by parents, who must pretend not to know it. A boy may sometimes tell his father his name but the girls never reveal it in the home. After marriage, a boy goes on using his title as indeed he continues for a time to exercise his old office; but a girl must never allow people to address her by a name which has so many memories of the free days of youth (though an old lover may, rarely, use it for that very reason), she should not call her husband by his old title, or refer in any way to hers in his presence. But I am told that when a group of old women who were once members of the same ghotul get together, they call each other by their ghotul names "to remind themselves of happiness." Close friends continue to address one another in this way all their lives.

For everybody treasures the memory of his title. When visiting the Jagdalpur in jail, I found the sulkiest Muria prisoners expand into beaming smiles when I addressed them by their old ghotul names.

As the children grow older, they are promoted from rank to rank in the ghotul hierarchy, and their titles are often changed. Sometimes, however, they are too attached to their original title to give it up. This may be one reason for the great diversity in the names of the leaders in different places. In different ghotul I have found the leader called variously Sirdar, Kotwar, Malik, Diwan, Jhoria, Malguzar, Silledar, Salya and Gaita, though elsewhere these titles may be given to quite junior boys. On the other hand, the majority of girls call their leader Belosa, though at Markabera she was Malko, in Binjhli Manjaro and in a group of three villages (Udanpur, Kapsi and Timnar) she was Suliyaro. There is no rule about this, and the children change their names as often as they retain them.

There is indeed no fixed list of titles with an order of precedence. In one village the Kotwar may be a subordinate; in the next he may be the leader. The Raja may rank below the Diwan, or the Tahsildar below the Constable. In the same way, though many of the titles carry duties with them, it is impossible to say that these duties will always be associated with the same titles. In Silati village, the Munshi has to see to the supply of wood, but in Taragaon it is the Tekedar who does this, while the Munshi has to "write" reports about absentees. In Haddigaon, it is the Budkher who collects the children and brings them to the ghotul; in the neighbouring Palli, it is the Sirdar.

The Sexual Act

> *Kosra ke kāte asan Muria ke lote. As is the reaping of millet, so is the intercourse of the Muria.*—MURIA PROVERB

In the ghotul there is no ceremony of sexual initiation, no formal rite of defloration, no permission (save in a few ghotul) is needed from the leaders for the first or any other intercourse. "Desire is not controlled by rules, nor is our copulation."

From their earliest days in the ghotul the little chelik and motiari play together until gradually, imperceptibly the vaginal entrance is enlarged and the hymen disappears without a tear. "We used to behave," said Nari, "exactly like little bulls and cows, sporting together till the bull could penetrate." "When you sleep with a girl night after night," said the Antar of Jamkot, "however small you may be, as long as flesh becomes wood, you try to beat her with it." And the Budhker of Kapsi described how he quarrelled with his parents and eloped with his still immature wife. "She was too young, and for a long time I only played with her and was quite happy with that till she was mature."

For it is not considered proper for the older boys to have congress with a motiari till she has passed the menarche. "Real happiness only comes when you are both mature. Of course the kids do it, but without the falling of water there's little pleasure. It is like eating a raw fruit. There is no sweetness in it. It is like rice without salt." This judgment comes from Kajen; another is from Kabonga. "To try to have a girl before she is mature is as hard as for a pig to dig up roots. Sometimes it manages it; it gets the root up and enjoys it. But it prefers its ordinary food." The Kotwar of Temrugaon said, "The first time I did it was with a little girl and it was very painful. She didn't like it either. One ought not to dig in the field of an immature girl, for one's *pulu* (digging-stick) may get damaged."

But after a girl's first menstruation, said Raunu of Jhakri, "everyone plans to be the first." Even now, however, the girl must not be forced or hurried; she must be wooed, persuaded, loved into yielding. Sometimes girls who are afraid of intercourse succeed in resisting the chelik for a long time. Often the first serious sexual experience of a girl is during a marriage, when everyone is excited and perhaps a little drunk, and no one asks questions or notices what is going on.

The ghotul leaders do not interfere unduly with the young children, but they see that they receive proper sexual training and instruction. "As a young bullock is broken to the plough, so a young boy is taught." The evidence for this sort of statement is best presented in actual "documents." Here is one from Kapsi.

> A big girl teaches a little boy by letting him fondle her breasts and hug her. Then she opens and spreads her legs and makes the little boy lie on her breasts. She shows him how to open her clothes and insert the little penis with his hand. The first time the boy doesn't know what to do and the juice comes out too soon. But the next day she says, "You only pressed me last night, nothing was done properly. I had no pleasure." The boy replies, "Today I'm really ready; now I know what to do."

In Munjmeta, the Melia recalled how he learnt to perform the sexual act from the very descriptions of the older boys. And in Markabera, the Diwan said,

I

A little boy doesn't need to be taught anything. Does a young crab have to be taught how to dig earth? But the elder boys generally tell them how to do it. When the little boys tell them their secrets and how they tried but failed, the older chelik show them the best way. The older girls do the same for the little girls. Sometimes older girls who get fond of little boys teach them themselves. But we learn everything by being in the ghotul. How can the little boys check themselves? Who doesn't feel a desire to eat when he sees people enjoying a feast in his presence?

Thus from a very early age the young chelik and motiari are trained in sexual technique, both by example and by actual instruction. A boy does not approach his marriage bed a virgin, but neither does he go to it a fool.

The immediate sexual approach and the technique of copulation practised by chelik and motiari are conditioned by the circumstances of ghotul life. Normal sexual congress should take place within the ghotul. It is believed that this precaution lessens the chances of conception (there is a "safe region" rather than a "safe period"); it protects boy and girl from the calamitous interference of magic; and it imposes a certain degree of restraint and discipline. Naturally there are many breaches of the rule; at marriages and festivals, on dancing expeditions and during everyday work in field and forest, chelik and motiari unite in intercourse—but this is regarded as irregular, not exactly condemned, but accepted as outside the routine.

This fact alone is sufficient to make the ghotul tradition almost unique. For here is a company of boys and girls, many of them close relatives, who perform the sexual act in public, often in a single room. For it is public, even though veiled by the mask of darkness and a convention that no one should watch his neighbour. In some of the bigger ghotul, of course, the boys and girls are able to thin out a little; they can scatter in the different huts; in the hot weather they can sleep out in the compound. But during a large part of the year chelik and motiari sleep together in one small smoky room. They do not care to leave the warmth and security of their cosy ghotul for the dangerous and inconvenient discomfort of field or jungle. So we find brothers performing the sexual act before their sisters, and elder brothers in the forbidden presence of their younger brothers' "wives." Sometimes they are so crowded together that they have great difficulty in achieving coitus without waking up their neighbours.

For this reason, because intercourse must be with all the secrecy possible, without display and without disturbance, the normal method of copulation inside the ghotul is not unlike the characteristic European method—the girl lies prone on her back, and the boy stretches himself upon her, forcing her legs apart and often raising them to place them round his thighs.

But when the lovers meet outside the ghotul, they are able to indulge more varied postures. At Jhakri the chelik knew of four—the girl prone on her back and the youth kneeling or squatting before her; both sitting and facing one another; the youth prone and fully extended above the girl who sometimes raises her legs and sometimes extends them; and both standing, the girl supported against a tree or wall. At Palari, a chelik said, "Usually we lie flat, but when a boy is very happy he sits above her."

A former Sirdar of Singarpuri described the difference between intercourse with a motiari in a crowded ghotul and with one's own wife in a private room. "To have a motiari is like living on borrowed money; you are always anxious, and afraid someone will notice what you're doing. But with your own wife at home, you can have her lying down, you can have her standing up, you can have her from the front, you can have her from behind. She is like a good crop which you can eat till you can eat no more."

JAMES R. MURIE

The Mischievous Society of Boys

An organization generally known as the mischievous society, but also as the circumcised, once existed among the Chauí.

Many years ago when the Chauí were alone, two young men were always running around during the night, playing bad tricks upon anyone they met. At this time the people wore no clothing, especially the boys. In the winter time the boys wore a bull calf hide, if they were well-to-do; but if they were poor they wore half a bull hide, their moccasins and leggings. They had neither shirt nor covering for their privates.

In a village of mud-lodges there happened to be one mud-lodge that was empty for all the people who lived in it had died. These two mischievous boys made their home in this lodge. People, especially the young men, were afraid to go near this lodge in the night for it was said that ghosts dwelt there. These two young men frightened people when they came near the lodge by making strange noises, whistling, and throwing mud at them.

In the daytime they watched the young men in the village and when they saw certain ones who seemed fearless they invited them to meet them in the empty mud-lodge. When they spoke of the mud-lodge, those who were cowards would refuse to go, but those who were brave accepted the invitation. These meetings were held in the winter time when the people lived in mud-lodges, for in the summer time they lived in tipis away from the village. When these young men met they would plan to send out young men to scare those who were prowling through the village during the night. The two leading boys appeared as if circumcised and invited to their meetings only those of similar appearance.

In their meetings in the deserted lodge they would do all sorts of mischievous and obscene things. When on a buffalo hunt in the winter time they would get together and make a grass lodge in which to hold their meetings. The boys in the village heard of their meetings and doings and many were anxious to join. When the people returned to their permanent village, the boys again held their meetings in their lodge. During the day the two leading young men would play with the boys of the village and whenever they observed one of circumcised appearance they would ask him to come to their meetings. Thus the society grew until they had many of the boys in the village. Every night they met in the lodge, each bringing a little dried buffalo meat and some parched corn, so that when their meeting was over they would have something to eat.

At last they became so numerous that one night in their meeting they talked of going on the warpath. (These boys never stole anything in the camp but kept others from stealing.) While they were discussing their war project, the boy who acted as a watcher announced that a young boy out there wanted to come to their meeting. The two leaders asked if he was of their kind, the answer was "no." Then the other boy was told to tell the boy to come to the lodge in the daytime.

The two leading boys now dismissed the others. When they were alone they began to plan for their altar. At last they agreed to have two long poles, about seven feet long and about one foot around. One end was to be forked, but the prongs trimmed off close, the whole shaped to serve as a phallus. When completed, both symbolic poles were blackened in the fire. After the altar had been arranged they considered how they could increase the membership and how young men wishing to join could be artificially circumcised. One of the eligible young men volunteered that his condition was due to accidental contact with the juice of the milkweed, causing a sore by which the foreskin was removed. This suggestion was adopted as part of future initiations.

The next day the two leaders entered the lodge each bearing a bunch of fresh milkweed. Here they sat down. Soon the other members came in. One of them was told to watch outside. When the candidate came to the lodge he was told to enter. When inside he was seized, thrown down upon the ground, and held while the two leaders applied the milkweed juice. He was then turned loose. He was told to sit among them and when tired to go home but that he must tell no one what had happened to him. This kind of work was carried on until there were many boys sick from the inflammation. People wondered why there were so many boys sick. The boys were not really sick but as they were naked in those days they did not want to go out and be seen in their condition.

Now the boys got the poles and prepared them as the two leaders wished. When completed they were placed at the altar in the lodge. They extended east and west, the head part toward the east. The leaders made clay pipes and baked them. The stems were of ash. During their meetings the leaders filled their pipes with native tobacco and offered smoke to the poles. Then they would send other young men out to frighten people who were prowling around in the night. When the boys returned to the lodge, before they told what they had done, they passed their hands over the poles and offered thanks for their help. Then they sat down between the poles and told their story. All would laugh.

Several years afterwards these boys had grown to be young men and began to talk about going upon the warpath in earnest. While they were planning one day an alarm was given: the enemy were coming to attack their village. The boys were all in their lodge. They were told to remain there until ordered to go out. Some wanted to run out for they wished to get their bows and arrows, but the two leaders would not let them go. The leaders took some grass from the lodge and burned it to make soot. They told the boys to do likewise. After they were all smeared with the soot, they were told to get their bows and arrows and join them. When the boys returned to the lodge with their bows and arrows, the two leading men took up the two black poles and ran to the battlefield. The line of men was extended clear along the battle front. Most of the men were massed at each end of the line. So these boys selected the center as their place. The two with the poles stood in the center, but the members scattered out. When the enemy attacked the boys, the leaders told their followers to shoot to kill. When one of the boys killed an enemy, one of the pole bearers would run forward and strike him with the pole and then return to his place. In this the two pole bearers alternated. Through the heroism of these boys the enemy was finally driven away and pursued by the mounted men.

The boys returned to their lodge for they were afoot and could not follow the enemy. When all the men had returned to the village, each one told what he had done in the battle. Some told of the strange-looking people in the center of the battle line and all wondered who they were, for all the lances known to the people were in the battle. The boys were careful and never spoke of their doings. Some men said that they saw one of the boys carrying an odd looking pole, but the people could not find out who the boys were.

Some time after the battle, when all the victory dances were over, the boys met in their lodge. When all the young boys were seated around the fireplace, the leader said, "Brothers, we are in our own lodge. I have something to say to you and if what I say is good, I want to know. You can all see how men go on the warpath for five or six months to return with many ponies and perhaps several scalps waving upon their poles. The people turn out to see them come in. The victorious party comes over the hills as if they were attacking the enemy. Chiefs and brave men go out to meet them. Women stand on the outskirts of the village giving their war cry. When the men are near the village we see their faces are smeared with charred grass, their lips white with clay. The black faces signify that they have traveled in the night and faced dangers; their white lips, that they were hungry for many days and finally came upon the enemy, conquered them, and captured their ponies. You have looked upon the leader who carried the sacred things upon his back. Chiefs and brave men honored him. I know all of you would like to be in his place. I know I would. Boys, we can do the same. We have been meeting here night after night. We now have two poles to lead us into the enemy's country. I have it in my heart to lead you. If we die at the hands of the enemy it will be well. Some of you boys are better off than the rest of us, for you have grandfathers and fathers who tell you that it is better to die at the hands of the enemy than to die of sickness in the village and be put under mother earth and have dirt rest upon you. Who of you are willing to go with me?"

Each boy said, "I will go with you." The leader was glad and said, "Brothers, when you go to your homes, let your sisters or grandmothers make you four pairs of moccasins and when they are completed let them fill them with parched corn or pemmican. Those of you who have neither sisters nor grandmothers go to your nearest of kin among the women and ask them for a piece of tanned buffalo hide, some sinew, and bring them to this lodge and make your own moccasins. Do not steal these things, but ask for them. We will make preparations for the next four days and on the fifth night we will start for the enemy's country."

Soon after this talk by their leader, the boys went to their homes. Most of them were orphans and it was hard to get anything from other people. The two leaders were orphans, they had no relatives or friends. They did not try to get anything from anybody. They sat in their lodge and made two small sticks to represent the two larger ones, so they could carry these sticks upon their backs. When the boys returned to the lodge the next day, some had more hide than they needed and some had several pairs of moccasins and they gave the leaders what they did not need.

The third night the boys met in their lodge, each brought his moccasins and other things he thought he might need. The leaders saw that each boy was provided with moccasins and provisions. Some of them had more and they willingly gave to others who had none. Now the leader said, "Brothers, you can hang up your bundles upon the walls and then go to your homes or to your friends and get you a knife, some arrows and a bow. Bring the things to the lodge at night and we will get ready to start. You may now go home."

At night the boys came into the lodge with things they needed. When all were in, the leader told each boy to take a bunch of grass and place it in his belt. When this was done he told them all to paint their faces with burnt grass. Then the leader said, "Brothers, we are seated here as warriors. We are about to go on the warpath. Tonight after all is quiet, we will go through the village. We will enter every lodge and sing our songs. When we stop singing them one of the boys must light the grass, then all must take their breech cloths off and dance in the light, naked. We will do this so that when we go on the warpath if we are not successful we will not return. In case the enemy attack us, we will fight until everyone is killed. As soon as we have marched through the village, all must come to this lodge for we are to start from here. If anyone returns to his lodge he cannot go with us. We will now march through the village."

The two leaders led the young men and as they entered the lodge, they stood in a circle around the fireplace and sang. When they stopped singing, one of the boys went to the fireplace where there were coals and lit the grass. The boys all took their coverings off and the women jeered at them. When the fire died out they went to another lodge. After they had visited every lodge they returned to their own. When all were seated, the leader told the boys that he was pleased for now the tribe knew that all the boys were circumcised.

The leader filled his pipe and offered four whiffs to the two large phallic poles and four whiffs to the two small ones which he was to take with him. As he offered smoke to the two large poles he said, "Fathers, we are about to go upon the warpath, we are to leave you in this lodge, but make us brave that we may conquer our enemy and make it easy for us to capture his ponies." Then he dumped the ashes at the ends of the poles. He wrapped the two small poles and the pipe in a coonskin, for he had dreamed that he was like a coon and had to get a coonskin to protect them. He tied the bundle on his back. Then he told the other leader to rise. Both stood at the altar. Then they told the other boys to take up their bundles and rise. They left the lodge and marched around the village by the north and west until they stood directly south of the village. Here they sang their songs, shouted, and ran towards the south. When they were some distance from the village, they squatted down and waited until daylight. The leader did not miss any of the boys and was glad. Now they marched on again.

One night the leader selected four boys to act as scouts. It was to be the duty of these boys to go out before daylight and see what was in the country. They were to report again before daylight. In the night they were also to look over the country and report to the leaders. One day the scouts came in and reported seeing fourteen or more tipis and many ponies. The leader now selected a thick timbered country. Here they cleared off the ground, made a fireplace, and built a big fire. The leader made an altar and placed the two sticks on it. He offered his smoke. Then it was time to have their mischievous doings which they kept up until dawn. The leader gave one of the sticks to the other leader and they started for the village. They stopped once and the leader selected seven boys to round up the ponies while the others attacked the village. Then they started. The seven men went to where the ponies were. The others surrounded the village. A shout went up, women and children ran out of the village, but the men were killed and scalped. The seven boys drove the ponies from the village. With scalps hung upon their belts the boys ran into tipis taking things that were of value. The enemy had run into the timber, but were now rallying so the boys ran to where the others were driving the ponies. Each boy caught a pony, mounted, and ran away. Two days and two nights, they journeyed north until they came to thick timbered country where they halted. When they jumped off their ponies, they were so sore they could hardly walk. Some of the young men were now sent out to get buffalo. When the meat was brought they all began to roast it for they were hungry. The boys with the scalps cut poles and hung the scalps upon them to dry. They all lay down and slept.

The next morning they were up at dawn and after eating some of the meat again took up their journey. So they kept on, only stopping at night until they were near the village. Then they decorated themselves with soot for they had no other paint. Now they got upon their ponies and rode to a high hill. Here they began to sing and yell until the village turned out and wondered who they were. Presently a messenger was sent out to meet them. When the messenger was near the leader shouted to him, "Tell the people the mischievous boys are coming with many ponies." The messenger went to the village and shouted, "The mischievous boys are coming with many ponies." The village turned out. The chief was among them. The leader gave one pony to the chief. The young men entered the village, their parents and friends meeting them.

Several times they went on the warpath and each time they were successful. As time went on some of the young men married and raised families. On a buffalo hunt these young men having fine horses were able to kill their own buffalo meat, so they were well provided for. Sometimes they feasted the poor in the village, then feasted the old people, and at last they feasted the chiefs. These young men killed buffalo and consecrated the meat, so now they became great men. In battle they were brave.

One of the leaders was riding near the place where they were to camp when they saw boys playing the javelin game. They rode up and looked on. The people were building their tipis. They called a young man and told him to go to the chief and tell him to place mats on the ground to have his ceremony. The chief, when notified, told the women to spread mats in a circle upon the ground. His soldier being there, the chief told him to call four other men. While the soldier was gone, the chief took the bustle, a spear, tomahawk, shield, and a war-bonnet and placed them on the mat. Then he brought out two water drums. As soon as the men came, two of them sat down by the drums, took up the drumsticks and began to sing. The chief himself was the first to take up the bustle and tied it around his waist. He now took up his bow and arrows; then he squatted down upon the ground; then he began to grunt, his head and shoulders shaking to keep time with the drumming. Finally, he arose and danced. When the singing ceased, the chief spoke in a loud voice, "I speak of a certain place I killed an eagle. I consecrated the eagle and that same year I killed an enemy, took his scalp, and consecrated the scalps to the gods in the heavens, and the gods received my smoke." Again he said, "I speak of a certain place I killed a wildcat and consecrated it and that same year I went upon the warpath and captured ponies. I was successful and when I returned to the village, I took one pony and gave it to the priest." Again he shouted, "I speak of a certain place. I killed a raccoon. I consecrated it to the gods in the heavens. That same year I went on the warpath and I captured many ponies. Upon my return to the village, I gave four horses to different men. To the men who want me to do this I have spoken. The gods in the heavens have heard me. They will make the path straight for you to do likewise." He then untied the bustle and threw it on the ground when the next man took and went through the same evolutions with it relating his deeds. Each man took up the bustle and told of his deeds.

Then the leading mischievous man came into the ring with two horses, eight robes, and two parfleches of meat. One parfleche was opened, the meat cut up and given to men, women, and children, who were looking on. The other parfleche was opened and the chiefs ate the meat. Then the presents were divided among the chiefs.

When the people returned to the village the mischievous men met in their lodge. The leader took up the poles, stood up and said, "Brothers, we all now have families, have attained places among our people and are respected. Our meetings must end. I now put these sticks into the fire. I ask that each of you join some of the societies and always be brave. My friend and I will join the brave lance people. You are all now released and we will not meet here again. This is all." They left the lodge and each went to his home.

ARTHUR BERNARD DEACON

Graded Associations and Secret Societies

The institution known as *Maki, Mangki,* or *Mwele* in the Central New Hebrides, and as *Sukwe* or *Hukwe* in the Northern, forms, or has formed in the past, the basis of a large part of the social, economic, and religious life of the inhabitants of these islands. Characteristically, the *Mangki* or *Sukwe* consists of a series of grades which are arranged in order of rank, from the lowest grade entered in childhood or early youth, to the highest grade, members of which hold the position almost equivalent to that of "chiefs." Typically, also, the men's house is divided into a number of compartments, corresponding to the number of grades in the society. The partitions between these compartments may consist only of logs laid across the floor, or some other conventional dividing line may be adopted. Within each is an oven or fireplace, at which members of the grade occupying that compartment cook their food. These fires are a fundamental feature of the institution, and each one is sacred, that is tabu to all but those who have purchased the right to use it. Originally no man might eat at the fire of a grade of which he was not a member. The "sanctity" of this fire is sometimes reflected in the grade name: thus in Mota one of the *Sukwe* ranks is called *Av-tapug, av* meaning "fire," and *tapug* tabu; and in South-West Bay, Malekula, there is a *Nimangki*[1] grade named *Naamb Tileo,* a compound of *naamb* "the fire," and *tileo* "sacred." In Ambrym and elsewhere the making of a new fire is a prominent feature in the ritual of rise in rank, but in Malekula this seems to

[1] Theoretically this name should be written *Mangki,* the *ni-* being but the definite article. It seems, however, that actually the word is never used by the natives except in the form *Nimangki,* and it has therefore been deemed advisable not to follow the example set by previous writers on the subject, but to adhere to that set by Deacon in his notes, and give it as *Nimangki* throughout. The form *Nimenggi,* which according to Layard n. 1 is that found at South-West Bay, is not recorded by Deacon, who spells the name of this society *Nimangki,* in all those parts of Malekula where it exists.—C. H. W.

have become of secondary importance. Here it is the erection of wooden or stone images which forms a constant character of the *Nimangki* ceremonies. One of these is cut for each candidate to membership (in the lower grades several men usually enter at the same time), kept for a while in the *amel,* and later brought out and set up in the dancing ground, where it remains until it has rotted away. Generally trees and shrubs of certain species and varieties play an important part in the ritual of entrance, and these, too, appear to be in some way sacred. Particularly noticeable in this connection are the cycas, the cordylines, and the crotons, the latter being classed generically in South Malekula as *naai limbu* "the holy tree." Sometimes grades take their names from these plants: thus in Mota there is one called *Mwele* (cycas), which probably corresponds to the *Nimweil* (the cycas) of South-West Bay. In Ambrym it is said that the cycas is the badge of "chieftainship."

In certain areas this graded association is not the only one of its kind; other "secret societies" co-exist with it. These are generally more secret in their nature, and in some instances there appears to be a definite connection between the two. In the Banks Islands, for instance, there are the *Sukwe* and the *Tamate* Societies; the former usually claimed as members the entire adult male population and had its house, the *ghamal,* in the village; the latter were more restricted in their membership and had their headquarters in private places in the bush. To attain high rank in the *Sukwe* it was necessary to have become a member of *Tamate Liwoa,* and conversely to become a member of any but the most inferior group of *Tamate* Societies it was first necessary to belong to the *Sukwe.*[2] In Malekula there exists as a parallel society to the more or less secular *Nimangki,* the secret and sacred *Nalawan.* Although these two are said not to be interdependent, there are, as will be shown later, certain indications which suggest that they are allied, and that the *Nalawan* may possibly be a variant of the *Tamate* of the northern islands. This becomes particularly apparent when we compare the ritual of *Tamate Liwoa* with that of *Nalawan Vinbamp* of Seniang district, of *Nalauen* of Lambumbu, and of the *Nimangki Tlel* or "Sacred *Nimangki*" of Lagalag.

[2] W. H. R. Rivers, 1914, vol. i, pp. 64, 87.

The principal public ceremonial of the *Nimangki* is that which takes place when a man makes a rise in rank. Entrance to a grade necessitates payments, often on a large scale, by the aspirant to those who are already members of it. These payments are made for certain rights and privileges, which are exercised by members of a grade and are "sold" by them to the candidate at the ceremony of his admission, and also for certain ornaments and structures which he assumes or uses during the ritual. The payments are made in pigs; thus one pig may be given for "making *Nimangki,*" that is for the privilege of admission to the new grade; and one pig each for such objects as the carved wooden images which are set up on the dancing ground; for the head-dress of these images; for the spear or hammer used in killing the pigs; for certain trees planted during the ceremonial; for stone circles sometimes placed around the images or trees; and for paints used in decorating the candidate or the image. Of all these pigs, the most important is that paid for "making *Nimangki.*" This is always the most valuable animal, and in general in Malekula, this is the only one of those paid which is killed during the rites.

Seniang

According to tradition, the *Nimangki* was instituted in Seniang by Nevinbumbaau, the ogress who is also associated with the *Nevinbur* ceremony, with the *Nalawan* and with the mythology, of the culture heroes called the *Ambat* brothers.[3] This society is by no means confined to this region of Malekula, but the bulk of information concerning it was acquired in Seniang. Here its religious aspect is much more evident than that of the Banks Islands' *Sukwe,* but it is nevertheless primarily a secular organization. It is composed of some thirty-two different grades, which are entered successively by men desirous of prestige among their fellows and possessed of sufficient wealth to satisfy this desire. Every grade has its individual

---

[3] Layard, however, records a myth which attributes the introduction of the *Nimangki* to a being called Atimis Malau, who is represented as coming out of the ground, peopling the village of Nemep, and introducing yams and pigs. This myth is curious, for Atimis Malau cannot be other than Temes Malau, who, as we shall see, is connected with the *Nalawan* society rather than with the *Nimangki.*

name, and a distinct title which is borne by its members, and which is, it seems, frequently used in daily life, superseding the man's own personal name. These grades are roughly grouped into two classes: the "high" and the "low" *Nimangki,* and a man's social standing is determined according as he is a member of one of the former or no. Authority is vested in the higher grades of the institution, and those who belong to such grades may be regarded as having in some sense the position of chiefs. This is sometimes expressed in the small incidents of daily life. Thus, should a man of high rank wish to make a present, as for instance a pudding, to one who is his *Nimangki* inferior, he will not give it directly but in a roundabout way, so that he may not be seen doing so. He will, perhaps, bury the pudding in the man's house, and then tell him to go and look for it there. Speaking of a member of *Tambap,* one of the high grades, a native said, expressing himself in pidgin: "He big man; he walk about by himself; we no go close up fire belong him; we no help him." Thus, among these people there is a definite aristocracy, though not an aristocracy of birth. There is no hard and fast line which marks off the "high" from the "low" grades; the distinction is indeed a loose one, but for all that it is one made and recognized by the natives themselves. It is perhaps most apparent in the type of effigy which is set up during the ritual of admission into a grade. A man entering one of the lower ranks erects an image of tree-fern, or of some other wood, but as he attains to a higher rank the image is of stone, varying in height from about 3 ft 6 in. to five feet, while for certain intermediate ranks the carved wooden post is enclosed in a circle of small monoliths. The use of stone in the *Nimangki* seems to be of significance, associated as it always is with the higher grades. It may be compared with the use in Espiritu Santo of stone tables or "altars" on which the pigs paid in purchasing the rise in rank are killed.[4] The images of the higher grades differ from those of the lower ones also in that they are regarded as being more "potent," as having the power to exercise a kind of negative protection over the grade at entrance to which they were set up. Thus they inflict sores, fits, and other illnesses or even death on men of lower grades who wilfully or acci-

[4] A. B. Deacon, 1929, p. 491.

dentally violate the distinctions between grades and treat the members, insignia, or image of a higher one, of which they are not members, with disrespectful familiarity.

Another distinction between high and low grades is shown by the place in the dancing ground where the images are erected. It will be remembered that every Malekulan village in the south-west is divided into two parts by a boundary called *naai seve,* on one side of which are the dwelling-houses, on the other the dancing ground with the *amel* at the far end. In passing from the *naai seve* towards the *amel* the space becomes increasingly *ileo* or sacred, the back of the *amel* being the most sacred place of all. In accordance with this we find that the images set up at entrance to the lower *Nimangki* grades are planted nearer to the *naai seve,* those of the higher grades nearer to the *amel,* while for the highest grade of all, *Neru Wenoung,* a stone carved with many faces and bodies is erected some distance behind the *amel,* in the wood at the back called *nimbimb lemwenei* ("the tangled undergrowth"). This stone is very *ileo,* and is supposed to be very potent; its spirit (*nimwinin*) may kill a man of any grade, other than a member of *Neru Wenoung,* who touches it or goes near to it.

The chief interest in the rites of the *Nimangki* centres around the giving and receiving of pigs. As we have seen, the male pigs are graded according to the degree of their tusk curvature. For every object which the candidate acquires one of these pigs must be paid, and others are also given by him to recompense certain participants in the ceremonies who perform special rôles. Further, male pigs of lesser worth are killed to provide refreshment for the guests. As a man ascends higher in the *Nimangki* the pigs which he gives must be of increasing value, and, since the number of objects which he buys also increases, the expense involved is often very considerable. In presenting a pig a definite ritual is performed. The animal is brought on to the dancing ground and the rope by which it is led is handed to one of the onlookers, often a close relative of the donor. This last then takes a conch in his hand and begins to dance round the gongs. The person who is to receive the pig, or more usually some one else whom he has delegated to act for him, then dances round the gongs also, in the opposite direction from that taken by the donor. Presently both men converge opposite the recipient. The animal is led up and the leading cord handed to the latter. This performance is a constant feature of all pig-presentations not only in the *Nimangki* but also in the *Nalawan,* and probably on other ceremonial occasions as well, and it may be referred to by the term, first suggested by Layard, "circling for pigs."

Yet although all pigs which change hands during *Nimangki* ceremonies are "circled" for in this way, the people of Seniang distinguish between two types of pig-presentation: *iomp* and *ihu.* The former may be translated "he throws," and is used when referring to the pig which the introducer gives to the candidate; the latter signifies "he pays" or "he presents" and is used in speaking of the pigs which the candidate gives for the various objects, regalia, and privileges which he uses or acquires during the performance of the ceremonies.

Nimbinben

In this grade, as in *Naamb Tileo,* a boy's introducer is his maternal uncle or maternal grandfather. This man makes three images of tree-fern wood, about the same size as that set up for the first grade. Each one is carved with a human face, but this is not painted nor is any body represented. The *temes* are apparently erected in the dancing ground, but on this occasion they are not enclosed in a *numbul.* The introducer then gives the candidate a pig which he kills and distributes among boys of his own age and status. At entrance to the grade a pig's tusk bracelet is given to the candidate and also an anklet or garter *nimbinben,* after which the grade is named. For these two objects as for the three *temes,* pigs are paid to the introducer, the father having given them to his son for this purpose. The new title which the candidate receives is Mwelipsal or Mwelipmbon, which, as before, is bestowed by the introducer while he and the candidate stand beside the three *temes.*

The ceremonies attendant upon entrance to the grades which follow upon *Naai Mbimbarap* (other than *Mbalmbal*) resemble each other in general outline. It is true that there are numerous variations of detail, and as we shall see the rites of *Nahavndal, Noulas, Mbat Ru,* and *Neliwis* have certain characters which set these four in a class apart. Nevertheless, since the *Nimangki* grade whose entrance ceremonies have been described most fully is *Nevelvel,* the eighteenth on Deacon's list, it will be well to give an account of these here, in order that the reader may become familiar with the general *Nimangki* procedure, the constant theme, as it were, upon which a number of variations are played.

Nevelvel

The man who is desirous of entering *Nimangki Nevelvel* goes to one who is already a member and, addressing him by his grade title, Muluwun, asks him to act as his introducer, saying: *"Muluwun nerirong nanraas nonggob"* ("Muluwun, I wish to set up a stone circle"). If the other is agreeable, he appoints a day when he will come to the candidate's village. When the time has arrived the introducer keeps his appointment, and he and the candidate go into the bush to seek out stones suitable for making the circle called *nonggob.* These are brought back and kept in the *amel,* and another day is fixed for setting them in place. When this day has come the introducer arrives once more in the candidate's village with certain of his mates, and together they dig a hole and set up the stones in a circle round it. For this grade the position of the hole is a little behind and to the left of the *amel.* A *malandr* bush, a plant characteristic of all the higher grades of the *Nimangki,* and for this reason called *malandr muluwun,* is torn up by the roots and planted in this hole, and just outside the stone circle a stake called *navan mbatia* is erected. At the foot of the *navan mbatia* a coco-nut leaf (*nerei nimetu*) is placed, leaning up against it. The men now go to the gongs and beat out the rhythms of all the *Nimangki* grades from *Naamb Tileo* up to and including *Nevelvel* in the order in which they are entered. When these are ended the candidate brings forward a number of his pigs and makes a pile of food comprising taro, "strong" yams (*nuwes*), yams, bananas, and other vegetables. This pile is for all the men of *Nevelvel* rank who are present; the pigs are to be paid for certain specific objects. One of the seniors is asked to perform the pig-giving ceremony. He takes the rope of each animal in turn and, speaking over each the prescribed formula, hands them over to the introducer. The first is given for "the opening of the door" (*resisewen*), the second for the *navan mbatia,* the third for the stone circle (*nonggob*), and the fourth for the *melandr* bush.[5] Immediately after the first pig has been paid, the coco-nut leaf at the foot of the *navan mbatia* is uprooted and cast away to symbolize the opening of the door of the *amel.* In the ceremonial of this degree the stone circle represents the *amel,* the *navan mbatia* represents the door of the *amel,* and the coco-nut frond at its foot is the fastening or lock of the door. Thus as soon as the candidate has paid the necessary pig for the "opening" of the door of the *nonggob,* the coco-nut frond fastening is thrown away and his right of entry thus acknowledged.

In Seniang, although the gongs are loosely spoken of as belonging to the village, each one is in fact individually owned, and the making of a new gong is accompanied by a ritual resembling that attending a rise in rank in the *Nimangki.* The man who wishes to make a new gong, and whom we may term the "buyer," approaches someone else who has already "bought" a gong, and says to him: "I desire you to make me a gong" (*"nerirong gunggur nimbwilei baram"*). If the latter is agreeable, he goes into the bush and selects an *umou* or a bread-fruit tree. Round this he digs a trench, and at the base of the trunk he kindles a fire. The flame eats away the wood until finally the tree crashes to the ground. It is left lying where it falls, and the gong-maker now proceeds to hollow out the trunk by means of a sharpened human bone. This appears to be the only implement used; it is certain that the difficult task is not hastened by burning or charring the wood. One end of the gong, that which will be uppermost when it is erected, is then carved in the semblance of a human face. When this is finished the "buyer"

---

[5] The formulæ run as follows: For the first pig, *"Muluwun nimbuas resisewen ran nonggob tinungk etangk";* for the second, *"Muluwun, nimbuas iveus in navan mbatia tinungk etangk";* for the third, *"Muluwun, nimbuas nimweil ivivul in nonggob tinungk etangk";* and for the fourth, *"Muluwun, nimbuas iveus in malandr tinungk etangk."* The *Muluwun* is the introducer; the *nimweil* referred to in the third formula is the candidate, this being the title which he holds in virtue of his membership of the grade *Nimweil,* which is pre-requisite for entrance to *Nevelvel.*

makes a payment of three pigs to the gong-maker, who is in the position of the "seller" in a *Nimangki* rite. One of these is for the piece of ground on which the tree stood—since the owner of this ground must be compensated; one is for the carving of the face on the gong; and the third is for a mask which the gong-maker constructs and which is to be placed on the gong during the ceremony of setting it up in the village. This mask is composed of a piece of bamboo, two or three internodes in length; the internode at one end is left intact, the other two are split longitudinally into several strips the ends of which are lashed at intervals to a hoop of cane or creeper, so that the whole looks like a skeleton cone. A length of the creeper called *nembrül* is now wound about the ribs of this cone from bottom to top, and over this a paste, made from moistened shredded *nembrül,* is plastered. On this foundation the maker paints a face in red, white, and black.

All preparations being ready, a day is appointed for setting up the gong. On this day it is dragged from its resting-place in the bush to the dancing ground of the village to which the "buyer" belongs. While this work is going forward, a number of men are gathered in the *amel* singing. The "buyer" then steps forth and pays a pig to the gong-maker (or "seller") for the dragging of the gong. The "seller" for his part hauls up one of his own pigs and gives it (*iomp*) to the "buyer," this being the "presentation pig" familiar in the *Nimangki* ceremonies. Now the gong is planted upright, the mask put over its head, and the "buyer" dances round it to the beat *naai neten mbwilei.* There now follows the typical *Nimangki* ritual of the dance of the trios, the beating of *ndelndelmas,* and the spearing of the presentation pig. When this is ended the "buyer" goes up to his new gong and, standing beside it, receives from the "seller" the honorific title *Telmbwir umou.* The ceremony is now over; the new gong is left standing with the others in the dancing ground, the mask is taken off it and hung up in the club-house.

PART 7

Marriage

ALFRED L. KROEBER

Arapaho Marriage

The following are statements by the Arapaho on the subject of marriage.

When a young man wants to marry, he sends a female relative to the tent of his desired father-in-law with several horses (from one to ten), which may be his own or his friends'. She ties the horses in front of the tent, enters, and proposes the marriage. The father has nothing to say, and refers the matter to his son. The son decides upon the proposal, unless he wishes to refer it to an uncle or other relative. The woman goes back and reports her success. If the proposal of marriage has been refused, she takes the horses back. If the suitor has been accepted, he waits until called, which is done as soon as the girl's mother and relatives have put up a new tent which is given her, and have got property together. This may be the same day or the same night that the proposal was made. The girl's brothers and father's brothers' sons all give horses and other presents. They bring the things inside the new tent, the horses in front of it. Then the girl's relatives notify the young man's father to come; sometimes they send the bride herself. Then the young man's relatives come over with him to the new tent, and enter it. His entering this tent signifies that he and the girl are married. He sits down at the head of the bed, which is on the left as one enters the tent (the entrance to Arapaho tents is always at the east; the owner's bed, along the southern side, with the head toward the west). The girl sits next to him at the foot of the bed, the other people all around the tent. The girl's father, or, if he is still young, an old man, stands before the door and cries out the names of those invited, calling to them to come and feast. Then they eat and smoke. Sometimes an old person that wants to, prays. Any one of the girl's male relatives makes a speech to her. He says to her that she is a woman now, and tells her to be true to her husband. The visitors leave whenever they please. The friends of the young man each take away as many horses as they gave (to the girl's relatives). Sometimes he gives his friends other presents besides. Now he is married. He pitches his tent by his father-in-law's. The young wife at first does not know how to cook, and goes to her mother's tent for food. The young man, however, does not enter this tent, because he and his mother-in-law may not look at or speak to each other.

Sometimes a young man and a girl run off without the knowledge of their parents. They remain some time in the tent of the young man's father or of some friend. Then his friends contribute horses and other property. The girl mounts a horse and leads the rest. Accompanied by her sister-in-law or mother-in-law, she brings the horses and other gifts to the tent of her parents. Then her parents are not angry any longer, and send her back with horses and presents of property, sometimes with a tent. They also give her food, with which a feast is held in the young man's tent. Then his friends take the horses and goods which he has received. Sometimes a young man, after taking a girl away, abandons her on the prairie.

Relatives know nothing about the courtship of a young man and a girl. This is kept secret by them until she is formally asked for by his relatives.

When a man wishes to run off with another's wife, the two make plans. They go off together a long distance. At first the husband, perhaps, does not know what has happened. When he becomes aware of it, he is angry. He may follow his wife; but he is not allowed to enter the tent where she and her lover are, because he might do them injury. If he finds them and speaks to them, they do not answer him, in order not to enrage him more, because they may not make any resistance to him. The lover tries to find the (ceremonial) grandfather of the husband. He gives him a pipe and two or three horses. The old man takes the pipe, the horses, and the wife to the husband. When the man sees his grandfather, he must do no violence nor may he become angry. The grandfather hands him the pipe. If he takes it, his wife is safe from harm. Sometimes he keeps her, sometimes he sends her back to her lover to keep. Often the husband cuts off the tip of her nose, slashes her cheek, or cuts her hair. Both men and women are jealous. A man will hit his wife for looking at a young man too much.

If a man treats his wife badly, her brothers may take her back to her father, tear his tent down, and take away his household property. Sometimes the man and woman live together again, sometimes she marries some one else. But the man still has a claim on her; and if another takes her, he must pay her first husband one or two horses to relinquish his claim.

Sometimes a husband, to show his love for his wife, gives away several horses to her relatives.

A wife's next younger sister, if of marriageable age, is sometimes given to her husband if his brother-in-law likes him. Sometimes the husband asks and pays for his wife's younger sister. This may be done several times if she has several sisters. If his wife has no sister, a cousin (also called "sister") is sometimes given to him. When a woman dies, her husband marries her sister. When a man dies, his brother sometimes marries his wife. He is expected to do so. Sometimes she marries another man.

In courting women, men cover themselves completely with a blanket except the eyes. Often they exchange blankets, so as not to be known. They wait on sand-hills, or similar places, until the women leave the camp for water or wood. Sometimes at night they turn the upper flaps of the tent, so that the smoke of the fire remains in the tent; when the woman goes outside to open the top of the tent, the man meets her. At night men catch women outdoors and hold them, trying to persuade them to yield to their wishes. (The Arapaho affirm this of the Cheyenne, but have the practice themselves.) Courting is much easier and more open now than formerly. In making advances to a woman, a man often begins by asking for a drink of the water she is carrying.

GEORGE BIRD GRINNELL

Cheyenne Marriage

A Cheyenne boy was expected to court a girl from one to five years. After he felt sure of her consent, he applied to her parents for theirs, sending either an old man—some friend or relation—or perhaps an old woman—his mother—to ask the girl in marriage. With the messenger he sent the number of horses that he could give. The messenger tied the horses in front of the father's lodge, and then went in and delivered the message, saying, "Such a young man [naming him] wishes your daughter [naming her] for his wife." The messenger did not wait for an answer, but at once went away.

Sometimes the father decided for himself whether or not he would consent to the marriage, but at other times he sent for his relatives to talk the matter over and to ask their advice before giving an answer. If this was unfavorable, the horses which the young man had sent were turned loose and driven back to his father's lodge; but if the marriage was acceptable, the girl's father sent her, and with her a number of horses, often greater than that sent by the young man, to the lodge of the young man's father.

The horses sent by the young man stood in front of the lodge of the prospective father-in-law until the question of the advisability of the marriage had been decided. Sometimes they stood there all day. Often not horses alone were sent, but any other presents that the suitor thought might be acceptable. Thus, if the girl had a young brother who was fond of going to war, the suitor might send a war-bonnet, or even his whole war outfit, bow, arrows, quiver, and his war clothes; or even a gun or a six-shooter.

The horses might not stand before the lodge of the girl's father more than one night; that is, twenty-four hours. They must be accepted or sent back within that time. Thus, there was no long engagement after the boy asked for the girl. The matter was soon decided, and the marriage often took place within twenty-four or forty-eight hours.

A young man who was courting a girl would often try to persuade her to run off with him and be married at once. She would not directly refuse, but would put him off, saying, "No, I cannot do it today; let us wait until some better opportunity occurs." If she had been given to a brother or a cousin to dispose of in marriage, she would be quite sure to reply to such a request, "No, I think too much of my brother—or cousin—to do that."

A girl might receive attention from ten or twelve young men; to be courted by five was very common. Sometimes an elopement actually took place, but in old times not often; usually a girl cared too much for her reputation to do a thing of that kind. Marriage without the consent of the parents and the conventional exchanging of gifts was thus very unusual, and when one took place, the father or brother might follow the couple and bring back the girl. More than once men have been killed on this account.

Sometimes it might happen that horses were sent, and the girl's hand was asked in marriage at a time when her brother was absent from the camp. He had a most important voice as to whether the marriage should or should not take place, and if he were absent, the horses might be returned to the sender, and the young man asked to send them again later. Usually, however, the suitor knew that the girl's brother was absent, and did not send to ask for her at such an inopportune time. He chose the most favorable occasion for getting a speedy and satisfactory answer.

In some cases parents gave a daughter over to a particular brother or cousin who was said to "own" the girl, that is, to have the charge or control of her disposal in marriage. When an offer of marriage was made for the girl in the absence of this young man, word was sent back that the person who had charge of the girl was absent. She could not be disposed of without his consent.

The young man who fell in love with a girl was likely to do everything he could to secure the favor of the one who controlled her marriage. If a suitor and the girl's brother were together on the war-path, the suitor might roast meat and bring it to the brother, or in various ways might try to make things easy for him. After a time he sent a friend to tell the brother that he loved his sister and wished to make her his wife.

The brother returned no answer, but when he reached home he told his mother of the kind things the young man had done for him and why he did them. The mother told this to the girl. If she was willing to accept the young man, she made no comment, but if unwilling, she said, "No, I do not wish to marry that young man"; and that ended the matter.

When the brother—or cousin—in charge of the girl made up his mind that the marriage might take place, he was likely to call into his lodge his brothers or cousins, or both, and tell them what was in contemplation. The matter was discussed. Some of those present might feel doubtful as to what should be done and might ask to have other relatives sent for to express their opinion. If the decision was favorable, the news was conveyed to the suitor, who called together his friends and told them that he was about to send presents to a certain lodge; that is, to the lodge of the brother or cousin who had charge of the young woman. His relatives and close friends contributed what they could afford. The horses were loaded, sent to the brother's lodge, and tied there.

Then the brother or cousin again sent for the friends and relatives with whom he had consulted about the marriage, and said to them, "There are the horses and other things." One by one they went out, and each took what he wished, it being understood that he was to return as much as he took. One perhaps led away a horse with its load. Another might say, "I do not think I can afford all this," and took from the pack a number of articles which he left on the ground. So all the presents were disposed of. A horse or two was always left for the young man who had control of the girl. Each man who took anything away would bring back something of about the same value—often of greater value—to be sent with the girl as a wedding gift. Property equal to or more than had been sent to the brother's lodge usually went with the girl. The girl did not set out for her new home on that day. She might go the next day or the day after that, but, at all events, within three or four days, and the time of her going was known.

Sometimes a girl who was fond of a man might learn that some other richer suitor was about to propose for her, and to send horses to her father. If she discovered this, she might anticipate the matter by running off with the man she loved. Perhaps then her parents might pretend anger with her, or really feel it, and when they learned of her act might send word to her not to return to their lodge, or might refuse to receive her if she came. In that case she went to the lodge of some near relative, an uncle, aunt, or favorite cousin, and was married from there. After a little while her parents again became friendly, and the old affectionate intercourse was renewed.

If a man whom she did not love sent horses for the girl, and she loved someone else, her parents would often try to make her marry the man who had offered himself; they talked to her, persuading and commanding her, and might induce her to accept the man against her will. They did not, however, beat or abuse her. In a case of this kind, the girl in her despair might go out and hang herself. Not a few cases of this kind have happened; for many girls were so obedient and so careful of appearances that they would not consider a suggestion to elope with their lover. Because her mother scolded her for meeting a young man of whom the mother did not approve, the sister of three women well known to me knotted a rope about a sagebrush root, on top of a high cutbank, put the noose about her neck, and swung herself over the bank. In very recent years one or two girls have hung or shot themselves for such reasons. At present, however, young people usually solve the problem by eloping; but in old times they did not do this, for an elopement was disgraceful, and was regarded as no marriage. But if, after it had taken place, the boy sent the customary gifts, this made the marriage valid, and the disgrace was wiped out.

Sometimes it might be understood beforehand with the girl's parents that she should run off with the young man. This was informal and unusual, but where a girl loved one man, and her brothers and cousins favored another, while the parents sympathized with the girl, they might encourage her to marry the man of her choice, merely to avoid trouble in the family. In such a case the girl might go off with the young man to his father's lodge.

The next morning the young man's parents were likely to dress the girl finely, put her on a horse, and send her, with other horses and many good presents, back to her father's lodge. When she reached her former home, her father and mother sent for her brothers, cousins, and all her kinsfolk. They came to the lodge, and the men divided the horses among them, while the other presents, dresses, blankets, and so on, were distributed among the women relatives. Then the girl's mother cooked food for a feast, and her father gave away horses to anyone whom he might select, to show that he was pleased with the match. Late in the day, when they were ready to return to the lodge of the young man's father, the girl's male relations would bring horses to take back with her, and the women would bring presents of all sorts, sometimes even lodges. Besides the horses which they brought, young men used to bring many arrows. All these things they took back to the lodge of the young man's father, and they were divided among his kinsfolk.

During the four, five, or six years over which in old times a young man's courtship extended, he seldom or never made direct presents to the girl, but often made gifts to her father. If he returned successful from a war trip, he might drive four, five, six, or eight horses to her father's lodge, and leave them there. While a girl's lover—who was regularly courting her—was absent on a war journey, she might ornament a pair of moccasins, and perhaps a pair of leggings and a robe, with quills, and when he returned might present them to him, with a horse. This was an evidence of affection and appreciation. She, however, very seldom received a gift from him, unless perhaps a brass ring, or some trifling, inexpensive trinket. If he wished to make a present to her, and so to testify to his affection for her, he made it to her father. The marriage ceremony began when the young man sent his mother, or some other person, to the lodge with horses, to ask for the girl's hand.

To send as marriage gifts for a girl horses just taken from the enemy was the highest compliment that could be paid to the girl and to her family. Sometimes a young man very much devoted to a girl and eager to make a good impression on her family, went on the war-path, took horses and sent them as a present for the girl.

After it had been determined to return a favorable answer, the horses presented by the young man were at once given to the near and dear relatives of the girl. One might go to a favorite brother, another to an uncle who was very fond of her, perhaps another to a favorite first cousin. Each of these relatives was likely then to catch his best horse and send it to her father's lodge, to go with the horses that were to be sent to the young man. Besides the horses, they usually sent other good presents. It was generally known beforehand that the marriage was likely to take place, and some preparations for it had been made.

The girl was now put on one of the best horses, which was led by a woman not related to her, and her mother followed behind, leading a number of the horses, all of which wore ropes or bridles. The other horses were all led by women. Before they reached the lodge of the young man's father, some of his relatives came out, carrying a fine blanket, which was spread on the ground; the girl was lifted from the horse and set in the middle of the blanket, and the young men, taking it by the corners and edges, carried her into the lodge. Sometimes, instead of carrying her in the blanket, the horse which she rode was led close to the lodge door; the women ran out from the lodge; the girl dismounted, put her arms about her mother-in-law's neck, from behind; other women took hold of her ankles, and lifted her feet from the ground, and she was thus carried into the lodge without stepping across the threshold. This was all done in silence.

When the girl set out she was dressed in fine new clothing, but after she had been taken into her mother-in-law's lodge, the sisters or cousins of her husband took her to the back of the lodge, removed the clothing that she wore, and dressed her in new clothing they had made, combing and rebraiding her hair, painting her face, and hanging about her various ornaments as gifts.

The husband's mother had of course prepared food, and when the young people had seated themselves side by side, she offered it to them. That prepared for the girl was cut into small pieces by the mother-in-law, so that the girl need make no effort in eating.

After the marriage had taken place, the girl's mother began to make up her wedding outfit, and in this work the mother-in-law also took part. The girl's mother usually provided the lodge and most of its furniture, such as beds, back-rests, cooking and eating utensils. Many of the other things, however, were furnished by the uncles, aunts, and other relatives of both the young people. When all these things had been prepared and were ready, the mother of the girl would pitch the lodge—usually somewhere near her own—and would furnish it with all the articles that had been contributed; and then would go to her daughter and say: "Daughter, there is your lodge; it is your home; go and live in it."

Sometimes the lodge was made in advance, and the day before the couple were married was pitched in the circle, near the home of the father of the young man or woman. If near the lodge of the wife's father, it was set a little back of that lodge, in order that the young man might not see his mother-in-law too often.

R. F. FORTUNE

Betrothal by Mother-in-Law

We have already seen that convention compels a boy who has arrived at puberty to leave his parents' house for sleeping, while the daughter of the house of equivalent age is allowed to remain. The houseless boys usually sleep in the house of a divorced man who is temporarily without a wife, or, more frequently, roam in the night until they find a girl each who will grant them sex intercourse and houseroom for sleeping. No one builds a house except for marriage, the houses for food-storage excepted. The boys prefer to sleep with a different girl every night in order to avoid permanent entanglement. If a boy sleeps many times in succession with the same girl her parents will marry the pair out of hand by enforcing public recognition and public economic exchanges between the boy's kindred and themselves. Faithfulness between the pair is then considered necessary. If, however, a boy sleeps with very many different girls he avoids marriage, and his affairs he keeps private with no public recognition whatever. He must leave the girl's house before dawn to avoid being seen by the adult members of her village.

If he oversleeps and is caught publicly in the place of his sleeping he has to marry the girl. The boys are careful to avoid entanglement usually until they are at least eighteen or more. Then one by one they become weary of the rigorous regime of late roving nights and early morning risings; they fall into a deeper attachment with one preferred girl, and become afraid that a rival will marry her to their complete estrangement from her. So they deliberately oversleep one morning. The mother of the girl gets up before the young pair and steps out on to the house platform. There she sits calmly blocking up the exit with her body. The young man rises. If even now he has an impulse to flee he cannot. He respects the girl's mother too much to ask her to stand aside. The villagers see an unusual event has occurred. They gather curious to see what youth will emerge. They send word to neighbouring villages and people from the environs gather. Everyone circles around and stares. Into this glare of curious publicity the youth and the girl descend at last from the house and sit side by side on a mat on the ground. The spectators remain and do nothing but stare for half an hour or so. This staring ceremony makes the engagement. It is aggressive publicity directed towards a relationship which was before as aggressively private. For no youth or maiden would speak of a mere sex relationship to any one whatever—except to perhaps one child confidant and helper. Before betrothal privacy is as aggressively sustained as at betrothal privacy is aggressively and staringly outraged. Finally, the starers disperse. The girl's mother, now formally the youth's mother-in-law, places a digging-stick into the youth's hand and says, "Go, make a garden," or if it is not yet the new garden season she gives him other seasonal work.

The youths do not sleep with the girls of their own village, terminologically their sisters. Their general relationship to the people of the villages where they do sleep with the girls, is peculiar. We have seen how Those-resulting-from-marriage are rifted apart from their spouses at their spouses' death, and how the *susu* steps in to deal with intimate mourning and the disposal of the corpse, to enforce an onerous and unpleasant kind of mourning upon the surviving widow or widower for a year (sometimes it is for two years), and finally how the *susu* leads the widow or widower away from their village never to be allowed to show face in it again at peril of death from the *susu* owners of the village. There is much more than ceremonial dictation in this matter. More often than not the rift will be reinforced by a wall of sullen suspicion on the one hand and resentment of suspicion on the other. The Owners of the Village suspect the village kin of the surviving spouse, widow, or widower as the case may be, of treacherous secret murder, by forces that leave no trace, done against their dead kinsman. Over this wall of private suspicion public gift exchanges between the rifted places will follow when next harvest home sets a wide round of mourning ceremonial in operation between all the villages. The observer of such exchanges will see no friendly intermingling of the parties concerned, but a distance set and strictly maintained, distance in sitting arrangements and reserve or even hostility in manner. It is unlike ceremonial hostility as commonly found. There are no social forms of hostility, only very real private feeling of the type that cannot be discussed in public. Moreover, the kin of the widow or widower pay to release their kinsman from mourning durance. They do not obtain a fair gift of equal value in exchange. But when later the survivor dies the balance in gift exchange will be redressed by the kin of the earlier dying party to the marriage reversing the arrangement. There will, however, be no one of their number to mourn the survivor at his (or her) death as he (or she) mourned his (or her) predecessor in death. The forces of murder that are suspected between the villages are sorcery and witchcraft.

One marries into a village of enemies, witches, and sorcerers, some of whom are known to have killed or to be the children of those known to have killed members of one's own village. The night divides the villages—apart from love-making, a hundred yards is as far as a thousand or ten thousand for all practical purposes. Even roaming for love-making should be done while the night is still young. In the dark spaces between the villages the agents of death roam—the death-dealing spirits of the women and men of all other villages, witches and sorcerers all. This village parochiality, cut off from all other villages by the great fear of the terrors of the night, a child grows up in. It is never forgotten. Later, in sentiment, the land of the village of birth and upbringing is felt as own land with a completeness of feeling probably deeper than that of our own landed families. In Dobu it is two villages by residence—but marriage with the father's village occurs very rarely. The feeling of strangeness in the village of marriage remains unaltered.

The boys who go out for love-making then, go out with great boldness into a night filled with terrors. They are usually supported by a good conscience in that they have not given offence to the adults of other villages, a fact not so true of their parents. Nevertheless, they go into dangerous territory, for it is well known that in matters of sorcery and witchcraft native vengeance may visit the sins of the fathers, mothers, and mothers' brothers upon the children down the generations.

The terrors of the night are very real in Dobu. Bloodcurdling shrieking breaks the silence of the night or the small hours of the morning fairly often in the villages, and more often than not the inmates of the terrified house are sick, listless, and stay at home next day.

In imagination, then, we can to some extent reconstruct the feelings of the youth caught definitely and finally in a strange village. Probably like Kinosi, my house boy, he remembers vividly a scare of his childhood when he went to stay a while with relatives afield. Iyem, Kinosi's younger brother, was better developed physically than Kinosi, despite his comparative youth. But Kinosi while yet a small child went to visit a strange place. The woman of the house he stayed in was a powerful witch. She swallowed Kinosi whole and passed him out whole through her anus. Kinosi's growth suffered thereafter, and his younger brother grew better than he. Strange places are places where nightmare is reality.

Accordingly the youth feels respect and fear for the powerful old witch, his mother-in-law, as she sits blocking the exit of her house where he has lain with her daughter. Under the staring ordeal of the strangers, many of them sorcerers and witches far feared, he feels respect and no little awe. They are Owners here and he a stranger, one of Those-resulting-from-marriage, hereafter in this place. When his mother-in-law gives him the digging-stick he goes off most obediently to dig a garden. So the economic system lays firmer hold of a boy than ever it did before. Now he is responsible to his relatives-in-law as well as to his own kin and his work is doubled at a stroke.

He begins at once to avoid the personal names of the owners in the girl's village. He cannot eat or drink in the sight of any one of the owners until he is finally married. Before this takes place he must satisfy his future mother-in-law and father-in-law that he has a good garden, and he must work with them in their gardens. He continues to sleep with his betrothed regularly at night, but during the day he avoids her village unless he is specifically asked to enter it with gifts for his betrothed's kin.

Early in the morning he goes from her village with her father and mother to garden. The three work; then about ten o'clock her mother cooks a little food in the garden and the elders, husband and wife, eat together. The unfortunate future son-in-law cannot eat or drink in the presence of his future parents-in-law. He goes on working, hungry and tired. Let the anthropologist speak to a parent-in-law while the affair is still at this stage, and the old man guffaws most merrily at the miserable predicament of his future son-in-law. He is so very hungry—guffaw—but he cannot eat—guffaw—he digs and digs and digs most earnestly and strongly—guffaw. To the Dobuan father-in-law it is a most humorous and highly appreciated situation. But the young man gets away about noon, hungry, hot, and weary, and escapes to his own village to satisfy his needs.

When he is not working for his parents-in-law to be, the youth is working with his own kin to accumulate the food and gifts that must be exchanged between the villages against the marriage. Then when, after a year's betrothal or longer all is prepared, the marriage takes place. The groom's relatives take a gift of ornamental valuables, arm rings of white shell and necklaces of red shell, to the bride's relatives. The bride's mother receives the gift and distributes it to her kin. She and her female relatives then go to the groom's village and formally sweep it throughout. At the same time they take a big gift of uncooked food, and after they have swept the village and given away most of this uncooked food, they cook some of the food which they retained for the purpose in the groom's village, give it to the groom's kin and receive a smaller gift of cooked food from the groom's kin.

Next day the groom's kin carry a big gift of uncooked food to the bride's village, give it to the bride's kin, cook a small part of it in the bride's village and give it to the bride's kin, and receive a smaller gift of cooked food from the bride's kin.

The bride's mother formally puts some food of her cooking into the groom's mouth. Bride and bridegroom sleep in the house of the groom's parents for the first time. Next day the groom's mother prepares food and formally puts some of it in the bride's mouth. The pair are now married. Marriage is merely economic exchanges between groom's kin and bride's kin, and the groom eating food in the presence of his mother-in-law in her village for the first time, and the bride eating food in the presence of her mother-in-law in her mother-in-law's village for the first time.

During the betrothal period the youth often gave gifts of betel nut to his parents-in-law to be, but nothing further except gardening service.

Incest

I heard of one case of son-mother incest outside my range of true knowledge. It is regarded as contamination, as father-daughter incest, or child and father's sister incest is not so seriously regarded. But greatest of all crimes, outrage of all outrages against the social system, is adultery between a man and his mother's brother's wife or a man and his sister's son's wife. Son-mother incest, after the father's death, is not interfered with actively. It is a private sin, not a public attack on the social system. Blood brother interfering with blood brother's wife, or blood brother-blood sister incest I did not hear of. But I heard of two cases of trouble between sister's son and mother's brother over their wives. Here the *susu,* bulwark of Dobuan life, is rent, with difference in generation to make the matter worse. The mother's brother is guardian of the sister's son, his heir and ward. I heard of one such trouble in each group I was in—one historical case in Tewara Island, one more recent case in my Eduagaura locality of Dobu Island.

In Tewara a man committed adultery with his own sister's son's wife. His sister's son heard of it. He sought out his own mother's brother and drove a spear through his body killing him on the spot. The killer's mother sought out her village brothers and committed her own son to their vengeance urging them to take his blood for their and her brother's blood. His mother's village brothers so encouraged by their sister, his mother, pursued him through the island and into the sea at the straits of Gadimotu. There they hurled spears at the young man as he fled seawards until a spear thrown underwater caught him near the ankle. He collapsed and was killed. His mother went into mourning for her brother and her son. Then months after when the canoes were beached on the small island of Gabuwana many miles from home, the young true brothers of the hounded and slain young man slew the slayer who had thrown the spear which found its mark in their brother's ankle. They roasted the corpse and ate it. Other members of the party which pursued the boy trying to kill him took no vengeance on the boy's brothers for killing their brother's killer.

CHARLES HOSE

A Marriage in Borneo

Courting is sensible and easy. When the youth begins to feel strongly the attraction of the other sex, he finds opportunities of paying visits, with a few companions, in friendly houses. It is then said in his own house that he has gone "to seek tobacco," a phrase which is well understood to mean that he has gone to seek female companionship. A youth of average presentability will usually succeed, if not in "walking out" with a girl, at least in "sitting in" with her; and he is usually not much over twenty years of age when he becomes accepted as the future husband of a girl some years his junior.

The initiative is taken in nearly all cases by the young man. He begins by paying attention somewhat furtively to a "fancy-girl." He will often be found passing the evening in her company in her parents' room. There he displays his skill on the *keluri,* or sings the favourite love-song of his people. If the girl looks with favour on his advances and wishes him to stay, she gives him a cigarette tied in a peculiar manner, winding the strip which ties its sheath of dried banana leaf close to the narrow mouthpiece. On all other occasions this strip is wound about the middle of the cigarette.

Thus encouraged, the young man repeats his visits. If his suit makes progress he may hope that the fair one will draw out the hairs of his eyebrows and lashes with a pair of brass tweezers while he reclines on his back with his head in her lap.

When the courtship has advanced to this stage, the girl may attract her suitor to the room by playing on the mouth-harp: on this she speaks to him what is presumably the language of the heart. The youth thus encouraged may presume to remain beside his sweetheart till early morning, or when the rest of the house have retired, to return to her side.

At this stage it becomes necessary to secure that public recognition which constitutes a formal betrothal. The prospective husband charges some elderly friend of either sex, in many cases his father or mother, to inform the chief of his desire.

If the chief and parents favour the match, the young man presents a brass gong or a valuable bead to the girl's family as pledge of his sincerity. If for any reason beyond his control the match is broken off, this is returned to him.

The actual wedding usually takes place after the harvest. If, however, the omens are regarded as evil, the wedding is postponed for a year. Such omens are hardly ever disregarded, even if the girl is far advanced in pregnancy. The wife incurs no odium, but is treated as if she were a married woman, and her child is regarded as legitimate.

When the appointed time draws near, the "best man" is sent to open negotiations with the bride's family. He carries with him a number of presents, varying according to the position of the bridegroom's parents. For some time each side fences about, neither pretending to know the reason for the visit, until finally the legate comes to the point and asks on behalf of his friend a definite date at which he may marry the daughter.

If the parents accept the proposal (which is not always the case), the best man hands to them five sets each of sixteen beads, the beads of each set being of uniform shape and colour, namely, (1) small yellow beads; (2) black beads; (3) a set known as *habarani,* which may not be worn by the bride before the naming of her first child; (4) light blue beads; (5) dark blue beads. Each of these sets of beads is held to ensure to the bride some moral benefit. The date of the marriage is fixed with regard to the phases of the moon, the time of the new moon being considered the most favourable. Tally is kept by both parties of the date agreed upon. On two long strips of rattan an equal number of knots is tied. Each party keeps one of these tallies (often it is carried tied below the knee) and cuts off one knot each morning, until none are left.

On the actual day the parties on both sides invite their friends and relatives, who crowd the gallery of the bride's house. Early in the morning the bridegroom arrives with his best man and a party of young friends in full war-dress; they land from a boat even though they have come but a few yards by water. They march up to the house, some of them carrying large brass gongs; ascending the ladder, they lay the gongs along the gallery from the head of the ladder towards the door of the bride's room at intervals of about eighteen inches. It is understood that these gongs become the property of the bride and her parents. Others of the bridegroom's band bring other articles of value, which they offer to the family, under the fiction that the bridegroom, being a sort of invader, must pay for admission. A mock conference between the two parties now takes place; which having failed, a sham fight takes place: the men of the defending party make a sortie from the room fully armed, and repel the attackers with every show of violence.

At last the bridegroom and his supporters are admitted to the room, and they rush in, only to find, perhaps, that the bride has slipped away through the small door which generally gives access to a neighbouring room. The impatient suitor cannot discover where she is, and so he and his men resignedly sit down in the room and accept cigarettes. Presently the bride relents and returns to her parents' room accompanied by a number of her girl friends. The bridegroom has now changed his tactics, and affects to take no notice of her entry. Meanwhile the inevitable pig decked in skeins of beads has been laid in the gallery, together with a few gifts for the *dayong* who is to "read" its liver. Here the final steps of the bargaining are conducted by the friends of the bridegroom. (It is impossible to say in each case how far this bargaining is genuine and how far pre-arranged.) More gongs are added to the row upon the floor, until the row extends to the door of the bride's room. The pig is then slaughtered and its liver examined; if it proves unpropitious, other pigs are killed, until one whose liver permits of favourable interpretation is found. A series of unsatisfactory livers would lead to the postponement of the marriage.

The *dayong* now sprinkles pig's blood and water from a gong upon all the assembly, invoking the blessing of the gods upon the young couple, asking for them long life and many children. Then the bride and bridegroom walk up and down the row of gongs eight times, stepping only upon the metal. In some cases the bridegroom descends to his boat at the landing-stage during these processions, as if to prove that he is free to come and go as he pleases, and that he is under no obligation. In this degenerate age this act terminates the ceremony, except for feasting and speech-making. But in the old days the bride descended with the groom and his party to his boat, and was then carried off at full speed, pursued by several boat-loads of her family. The fleeing party would then check the pursuit by throwing out on to the bank every article of value still remaining among them; each article in turn would be snapped up by the pursuers, who then, having thus extorted the highest possible price from the bridegroom, would make a truce, and welcome back the Prodigal Children.

After the marriage the bridegroom usually becomes a member of the room of his father-in-law and remains there for some years before carrying off his wife once more to his own house. During this time he works in the fields of his father-in-law, and generally helps in the support of the household, showing due deference towards his wife's parents. If the bride is the only child of a chief her husband may remain permanently in her home and succeed her father as chief. But in most cases the young couple, before the end of the third year of marriage, migrate to the husband's house. This move takes place generally on the occasion of the building of a new Long

House, or on the death of the husband's father, either of which events affords him the opportunity of becoming the head of a room and of a family.

ALFRED REGINALD RADCLIFFE-BROWN

Marriage Classes: Diagrammed

There are many different forms of social organization in Australia, but it will appear, I think, that they can all be regarded as different varieties of a single general type. The easiest way to give a descriptive account is therefore to describe the general type first and then go on to describe, and as far as possible classify, the different varieties. That is the procedure that will be followed here.

The basic elements of social structure in Australia are (1) the family, *i.e.*, the group formed by a man and his wife and their children, and (2) the horde, a small group owning and occupying a definite territory or hunting ground. Together with these there is, of course, a grouping for social purposes on the basis of sex and age. It is on the basis of the family and the horde that the somewhat complex kinship organizations of Australia are built.

It is not easy to give a precise and accurate account of the local organization of Australia. In the first place there are many difficulties in the way of a study of the local organization amongst the natives themselves, which can only be overcome with unlimited patience and ample time, and the use of a strict method of enquiry such as that afforded by the collection of genealogies.

The important local group throughout Australia is what will here be spoken of as the *horde*. The horde is a small group of persons owning a certain area of territory, the boundaries of which are known, and possessing in common proprietary rights over the land and its products—mineral, vegetable and animal. It is the primary land-owning or land-holding group. Membership of a horde is determined in the first place by descent, children belonging to the horde of their father. There is normally, in the tribes about which we have adequate information, no provision by which a man could leave his own horde and be "adopted" or "naturalized" in another. Therefore, as a normal thing, male members enter the horde by birth and remain in it till death. In many regions the horde is exogamous. But even where there is not a strict rule against marriage within the horde, the great majority of marriages are outside the horde. The woman, at marriage, leaves her horde and joins that of her husband.

The horde, therefore, as an existing group at any moment, consists of (1) male members of all ages whose fathers and fathers' fathers belonged to the horde, (2) unmarried girls who are the sisters or daughters or son's daughters of the male members, (3) married women, all of whom, in some regions, and most of whom, in others, belonged originally to other hordes, and have become attached to the horde by marriage.

It may be added that normally throughout Australia each horde is independent and autonomous, managing its own affairs and acting as a unit in its relations with other hordes.

Throughout Australia hordes are grouped into larger local or territorial units, which will be spoken of as *tribes*. The primary mark of a tribe is that it consists of persons speaking one language, or dialects of one language. Its unity is primarily linguistic. The name of the tribe and the name of its language are normally the same. So that the easiest way to ascertain to what tribe an individual belongs is usually to ask him what language he speaks. In addition to this unity that comes from a common language there is also a unity of custom throughout the tribe.

It is often difficult, however, to say whether a particular recognized local group is a tribe, or a subdivision of a tribe, or whether another group is a tribe or a larger unit consisting of a number of related tribes. Thus within what might be regarded as a large tribe there may be differences of dialect (and differences of custom) in different parts, so that it is divided into *sub-tribes*. Again, adjoining tribes frequently resemble one another in language and custom. It is therefore sometimes difficult to decide whether we are dealing with a tribe subdivided into sub-tribes or with a group of related tribes.

So far as Australia is concerned, therefore, we have to define a tribe as a body of persons having a certain homogeneity of language and custom sufficient to permit them to be recognized as a group, and to demarcate them as distinct from other and neighbouring groups.

A tribe is commonly spoken of as possessing a certain territory, and is regarded as a land-holding group. So far as Australia is concerned, this is not quite accurate. It is true that each tribe may be regarded as occupying a territory, but this is only because it consists of a certain number of hordes, each of which has its territory. The territory of the tribe is the total of the territories of its component hordes. Moreover, in some instances at least, the boundary between one tribe and another may be indeterminate. Thus in western Australia a horde lying on the boundary of the Ngaluma and Kariera tribes was declared to me to be "half Ngaluma, half Kariera," *i.e.*, belonging properly to neither of the two tribes. Similar instances of hordes which occupy an indeterminate position between two adjoining tribes of similar language and custom occur elsewhere in Australia.

A tribe is also sometimes spoken of as a body of kindred. It will be shown later that the kinship organization of Australia spreads over the tribal boundaries. A man may have as many kin in another tribe or in other tribes as he has in his own. It is therefore impossible to define the tribe in terms of kinship.

The Australian tribe has usually, if not always, no political unity. There is no central authority for the tribe as a whole, nor does the tribe act as a unit in warfare. The political unit, if it can be properly called such, and normally the war-making unit, is the horde. A number of hordes may unite together in warfare, but they fight as independent allies.

We see, therefore, that the tribe in Australia consists essentially of a number of neighbouring hordes, which are united by the possession of a common language and common customs. The group is often an indeterminate one because it is difficult to say exactly where one language ends and another begins.

Most of the tribes of Australia have some sort of division into two, four, or eight parts, which, since they were supposed to regulate marriage, have been called "marriage classes." This name is for several reasons unsuitable. In sociology it is convenient to reserve the term "class" as a technical term for social groups marked off from one another by differences of rank or occupation. It will be shown that it is somewhat misleading to call the divisions marriage divisions or exogamic divisions. Further, the four divisions of such a tribe as the Mara are of quite a different character and constitution from the four divisions of the Kamilaroi or the Kariera, yet both are commonly spoken of as classes. I shall therefore avoid the term "class," and shall attempt to substitute a more systematic terminology.

Where there are two divisions I shall speak of *moieties*. In both western and eastern Australia there are tribes that have a division into matrilineal moieties. Thus in the neighbourhood of Perth the tribe was divided into two parts called Manitjmat and Wardangmat after the crow (*wardang*) and the white cockatoo (*manitj*). A man of one division (moiety) had to take his wife from the other. The children belonged to the moiety of the mother. Other tribes had a division into patrilineal moieties. Thus in Central Victoria the natives were divided into moieties named after the eaglehawk and the crow. A man of the eaglehawk moiety might only marry a crow woman, and the children would be eaglehawk like the father.

A large number of tribes have a division into four parts, which will be spoken of throughout this essay as *sections*.[1] Thus in the Kariera tribe the four sections are named Banaka, Burung, Karimera and Palyeri. A man of one section may only marry a woman of one other particular section. Thus a Banaka man may only marry a Burung woman. The children belong to a section different from that of either the father or the mother. The children of a Banaka man and a Burung woman are Palyeri, and they in their turn may only marry with Karimera. It is convenient to represent the system of marriage and descent by means of a diagram.

Banaka = Burung
Karimera = Palyeri

The sign = connects the two sections that intermarry; the arrow sign connects the section of a mother with that of her child. Substituting letters for the specific names we have as the general scheme for the four section system—

1 3
A = B
C4 = D 2

Reading off the rules from this diagram[2] we have—

[1] The term has been criticized, but I have failed to find a better.
[2] In this and similar tables the capital letters stand for males and the lower case letters for females.

A	marries	b,	children	are	D	and	d
B	"	a,	"	"	C	"	c
C	"	d,	"	"	B	"	b
D	"	c,	"	"	A	"	a

I propose to speak of the two sections that intermarry as forming a *pair*. The two pairs are therefore AB, CD. The sections that contain father and child I shall speak of as a *couple*. The two couples are therefore AD and BC. If a man belongs to one section his children belong to the other section of his own couple. The children of Banaka men are always Palyeri.

It will be readily seen that this system of four sections involves a division of the society into two matrilineal moieties and also a cross division into two patrilineal moieties. Thus in the diagram the sections A and D (Banaka and Palyeri) constitute one patrilineal moiety, and B and C (Burung and Karimera) the other. While A and C constitute one matrilineal moiety and B and D the other. In many of the tribes of eastern Australia there are names for the matrilineal moieties in addition to the names for the sections. It is important to remember that the moieties exist in every section system whether they are named or not.

A still more complex system is that in which the tribe has eight subdivisions. These will be called *subsections*, since they can be shown to be subdivisions of the sections of the four-section system. The following diagram shows the rules of marriage and descent in the system of eight subsections:

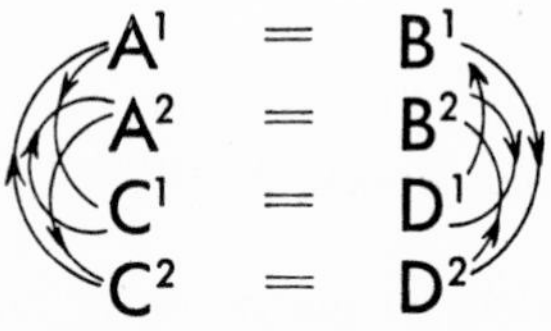

$$A^1 = B^1$$
$$A^2 = B^2$$
$$C^1 = D^1$$
$$C^2 = D^2$$

The sign = connects two intermarrying subsections. I shall speak of two such together as an *intermarrying pair* or simply a *pair*. The lines at the side connect the subsection of a woman with that of her child, the arrow indicating the direction in which the line is to be followed. Thus, reading the diagram we have

A^1	marries	b^1	and the children are	D^2	and	d^2
A^2	"	b^2	" " "	D^2	"	d^1
B^1	"	a^1	" " "	C^1	"	c^1
B^2	"	a^2	" " "	C^2	"	c^2
C^1	"	d^1	" " "	B^1	"	b^1
C^2	"	d^2	" " "	B^2	"	b^2
D^1	"	c^1	" " "	A^2	"	a^2
D^2	"	c^2	" " "	A^1	"	a^1

I shall speak of the subsection of a father and the subsection of his child as together forming a *couple* of subsections. Thus the couples are A^1 D^3, A^2 D^1, B^1 C^2, B^2 C^3. If a man belongs to one subsection his child belongs to the other subsection of the same couple.

It will also be convenient to use the term *cycle* to denote the four subsections that constitute a matrilineal moiety. A^1 C^1 A^2 C^2 form one cycle. Thus if a woman is a^1 her daughter is c^1, her daughter's daughter is a^2, her daughter's daughter's daughter is c^2, and her daughter's daughter's daughter's daughter is a^1 like herself. The two cycles are

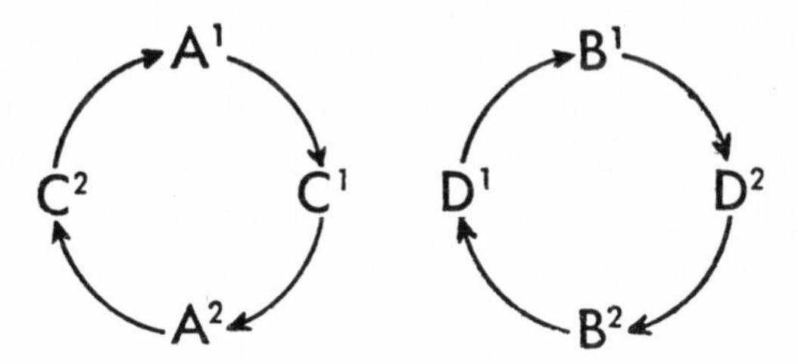

This system of eight subsections extends over a large area, including the greater part of the Northern Territory and part of western Australia.

There are a few tribes in the region of the Gulf of Carpentaria which really have a system of subsections, but instead of having names for the eight subsections have only names for four divisions, each of which consists of a patrilineal couple of subsections. The subsections exist but are not named. If we consider the diagram of the subsection system we have one division P corresponding to A^1

and D^2 together, Q including A^2 and D^1, R including B^1 and C^1, and S including B^2 and C^2. The rules of marriage and descent can be presented in diagrammatic form as follows:

$$\begin{array}{ccc} P^a & = & R^b \\ Q^a & = & S^b \\ R^c & = & Q^d \\ S^c & = & P^d \end{array}$$

An example of this system is that of the Mara tribe, where the four divisions are named Murungun, Mumbali, Purdal and Kuial. Arranged in the form of the diagram—

Murungun α	=	Purdal β
Mumbali α	=	Kuial β
Purdal γ	=	Mumbali δ
Kuial γ	=	Murungun δ

Murungun and Mumbali together form a patrilineal moiety named Muluri, and Purdal and Kuial constitute the other moiety named Umbana. Since each of these named couples of subsections forms a half of a moiety it will be convenient to refer to them as *semi-moieties.*

That the eight subsections really exist in this system, although they are not named, can be demonstrated by examining the arrangement of marriage. Murungun men may marry either Purdal or Kuial women. Their sons divide into two groups, Murungun α who are the children of Kuial mothers, and Murungun δ who are the children of Purdal mothers. The marriage rule is that a man may not marry a woman of the same semi-moiety as his mother. Those of the first group, Murungun α, sons of Kuial women, may only marry Purdal, and those of the second group, Murungun δ, may only marry Kuial. It can be shown that in this way each of the four semi-moieties consists of two groups which are exactly equivalent to the subsections of other tribes. Spencer and Gillen have demonstrated this also, by showing the relations with respect to kinship and marriage between the tribes with the Mara system and those with eight named sub-sections.

What at first sight seems a quite anomalous system is found in western Australia, in the neighbourhood of Southern Cross. Here there are two divisions, named Birangumat and Djuamat, with a rule that a man may only marry a woman of his own division, and the children must belong to the other division. This is really a modification of the system of four sections. The sections exist but are not named. Each of the named divisions is equivalent to one intermarrying pair of sections. The system may therefore be represented thus:

↑(A) Birangumat	=	(B) Birangumat↰	
↳(C) Djuamat	=	(D) Djuamat ↙	

There are a few scattered areas in Australia in which there are no divisions of the kinds described above.

With reference to these named divisions we can therefore classify Australian tribes into seven groups:

1. With two matrilineal exogamous moieties.
2. With two patrilineal moieties.
3. With four sections—
   (*a*) with named matrilineal moieties.
   (*b*) " " patrilineal "
   (*c*) without named moieties.
4. With eight subsections.
5. With four named patrilineal semi-moieties.

PART 8

Art, Thought and Sport

PAUL RADIN

A Non-Religious Individual

The Coercion of the World

It is one of the salient traits of so-called primitive man, we have just seen, that he allows a full and appreciative expression to his sensations. He is pre-eminently a man of practical common sense just as is the average peasant. Now this does not merely mean manual dexterity or an exclusive interest in the purely material side of life. It has much deeper implications. This tough-mindedness leads to a recognition of all types of realities, realities which primitive man sees in all their directness and ruggedness, stripped of all that false and sentimental haze so universal among civilized peoples. We cannot dwell upon this point now but will return to it later. Here we desire merely to point out that primitive man is endowed with an overpowering sense of reality and possesses a manner of facing this reality, which to a western European implies an almost complete lack of sensitiveness. And this is true of even the more avowedly intellectual among them, such as the medicine-men and the leaders of the ceremonies. It is true that the facts of everyday life, in every primitive community, are clothed in a magical and ritualistic dress, yet it is not unfair to say that it is not the average native who is beguiled into an erroneous interpretation of this dress but the ethnologist.

To illustrate what I mean I shall give an example that came under my own observation. An American Indian, pursued by the enemy, took refuge in a cave where he could easily defend himself against direct attack but where escape was apparently completely cut off. This particular individual was not religious. He had during his lifetime had so little interest in getting into the proper *rapport* with the deities of his tribe that he knew the conventional methods of addressing them but little else. In his dilemma, with death staring him in the face, he mechanically offers tobacco to the spirits. That much he knew. But he did not know what to say nor whom to address. So he prayed—if we are inclined to call this a prayer—"To you, O spirits, whoever you are, wherever you are, here is tobacco. May I be saved!" Through an almost miraculous piece of good luck the enemy fled and he was saved. "By the will of God," a devout Christian would have ejaculated; in Indian phraseology, "The spirits have heard me." Here, if anywhere, we might have expected an almost mystical feeling of heavenly intervention and a well-nigh complete obliteration of the mere workaday world. Yet nothing of the kind occurred to this very hard-minded individual. He sought to explain nothing. I can picture him saying to himself in his humorous way—for he was the professional humorist in the tribe—"Let the medicine-men explain; they like such things. All I know is that I was pursued by the enemy; I took refuge in a cave; my attackers withdrew and here I am." The ritualistic paraphernalia were all there but they did not obscure his vision of the nature of a true fact.

This man was of course an unusual specimen of the tough-minded species. So much will have to be granted unhesitatingly. Yet this intense realism, this refusal to be deluded by the traditional phraseology employed, is a salient feature of most primitive communities. That there are many individuals who take the phraseology more seriously we know. The medicine-man, the thinker, the poet, these insist upon a less matter-of-fact explanation and clearly enjoy the wrappings. Did they not in fact devise these explanations and are they not continually elaborating them? But in spite of the inner necessity that prompts them to prefer a supermundane formula they, too, are deeply rooted in the workaday-world conception of reality.

FRANK HAMILTON CUSHING

Zuñi Breadstuff

Watching one day a white-headed Zuñi grandmother who was stirring vigorously some yellow batter with a bundle of splints, I asked her what she was making. "Hoe-cakes," she answered, only she called it *mu'-we*.

"How do you make them?" I inquired.

"Sa-k'o, o'-lut-si-na ta k'ia'-kok-shi, hi-ni-na hâ i'-ya si'; tem kwi'l-ip-nan, hâ ko-la ma-we ta i'-sha-nan wo-lu, shél-an-an ul-üp, he'-po-k'on wo'-tap, te'-na-lap, u-li'-hap,—tchim i'-to-na-k'ia, a'ya-naie'!"—replied the old woman.

This is as hard as Zuñi milling; but I will try to grind it into English.

"Meal, soft corn-flour and good water, equally I mix; then stirring, red-pepper, salt, and suet, I put in, into husks I roll this, into an oven all place shutting the hole; time passed, I take them out. Now then, for eating they are ready!"

Do not imagine the old woman knew no other way of making corn-food. As prolific of resources as the Chinese are with their rice, not more so are they than are the ancient Zuñis with their corn.

Indeed so important to the Zuñi is his corn, that it plays an all-essential part, not only in his daily but also in his industrial, religious, and mythologic life, and even in the tales with which he amuses the children about the fireside in winter-time.

That this may be better understood among those controlled by a culture totally at variance with that of the Zuñis; that the many observances, ceremonials, and formulæ connected with corn, its growth, treatment, and preparation for food, hereinafter to be described, may not seem meaningless, it is necessary that an outline of the Zuñi mythology connected with corn, and that some, at least, of the philosophy and folk-lore which have grown out of this mythology, be recorded.

Thus, by following me in the pursuit of a useful purpose, I anticipate that my readers will find some part of the interest and pleasure which fell to my lot when, on long winter nights, I listened, in the light of piñon-fires on Zuñi hearthstones, to the recitals which first gave me knowledge of these strange beliefs and things.

Thus listening, I once heard a Zuñi priest say:

"Five things alone are necessary to the sustenance and comfort of the 'dark ones' [Indians] among the children of earth:

"The sun, who is the Father of all.

"The earth, who is the Mother of men.

"The water, who is the Grandfather.

"The fire, who is the Grandmother.

"Our brothers and sisters the Corn, and seeds of growing things."

This Indian philosopher explained himself somewhat after the following fashion:

"Who among men and the creatures could live without the Sun Father? for his light brings day, warms and gladdens the Earth Mother with rain which flows forth in the water we drink and that causes the flesh of the Earth Mother to yield abundantly seeds, while these,—are they not cooked by the brand of fire which warms us in winter?"

That he reasoned well, may be the better understood if we follow for a while the teachings which instructed his logic. These relate that:

First, there was sublime darkness, which vanished not until came the "Ancient Father of the Sun," revealing universal waters. These were, save him, all that were.

The Sun Father thought to change the face of the waters and cause life to replace their desolation.

He rubbed the surface of his flesh, thus drawing forth *yep'na*.

The *yep'na* he rolled into two balls. From his high and "ancient place among the spaces" (*Te'-thlä-shi-na-kwin*) he cast forth one of these balls and it fell upon the surface of the waters. There, as a drop of deer suet on hot broth, so this ball melted and spread far and wide like scum over the great waters, ever growing, until it sank into them.

Then the Sun Father cast forth the other ball, and it fell, spreading out and growing even larger than had the first, and dispelling so much of the waters that it rested upon the first. In time, the first became a great being—our Mother, the Earth; and the second became another great being—our Father, the Sky. Thus was divided the universal fluid into the "embracing waters of the World" below, and the "embracing waters of the Sky" above. Behold! this is why the Sky Father is blue as the ocean which is the home of the Earth Mother, blue even his flesh, as seem the far-away mountains, though they be the flesh of the Earth Mother.

Now, while the Sky Father and the Earth Mother were together, the Earth Mother conceived in her ample wombs—which were the four great underworlds or caves—the first of men and creatures. Then the two entered into council that they might provide for the birth of their children.

"How shall it be?" said the one to the other. "How, when born forth, shall our children subsist, and who shall guide them?"

"Behold!" said the Sky Father. He spread his hand high and abroad with the hollow palm downward. Yellow grains like corn he stuck into all the lines and wrinkles of his palm and fingers. "Thus," said he, "shall I, as it were, hold my hand ever above thee and thy children, and the yellow grains shall represent so many shining points which shall guide and light these, our children, when the Sun Father is not nigh."

Gaze on the sky at night-time! Is it not the palm of the Great Father, and are the stars not in many lines of his hand yet to be seen?

"Ah yes!" said the Earth Mother, "yet my tiny children may not wander over my lap and bosom without guidance, even in the light of the Sun Father, therefore, behold!"

She took a great terraced bowl into which she poured water; upon the water she spat, and, whipping it rapidly with her fingers, it was soon beaten into foam as froths the soap-weed, and the foam rose high up around the rim of the bowl. The Earth Mother blew the foam. Flake after flake broke off, and bursting, cast spray downward into the bowl.

"See," said she, "this bowl is, as it were, the world, the rim its farthest limits, and the foam-bounden terraces round about, my features, which they shall call mountains whereby they shall name countries and be guided from place to place, and whence white clouds shall rise, float away, and, bursting, shed spray, that my children may drink of the water of life, and from my substance add unto the flesh of their being. Thou hast said thou wilt watch over them when the Sun Father is absent, but thou art the cold being; I am the warm. Therefore, at night, when thou watchest, my children shall nestle in my bosom and find there warmth, strength, and length of life from one daylight to another."

Is not the bowl the emblem of the Earth, our mother? For from it we draw both food and drink, as a babe draws nourishment from the breast of its mother, and round, as is the rim of a bowl, so is the horizon, terraced with mountains, whence rise the clouds. Is not woman the warm, man the cold being? For while woman sits shivering as she cooks by the fire in the house-room, man goes forth little heeding the storms of winter, to hunt the feed and gather pine-fagots.

Yet, alas! men and the creatures remained bounden in the lowermost womb of the Earth Mother, for she and the Sky Father feared to deliver them as a mother fears for the fate of her first offspring.

Then the Ancient Sun pitied the children of Earth. That they might speedily see his light, he cast a glance upon a foam-cap floating abroad on the great waters. Forthwith the foam-cap became instilled with life, and bore twin children, brothers one to the other, older and younger, for one was born before the other. To these he gave the *k'ia-al-lan,* or "water-shield," that on it they might fly over the waters as the clouds, from which it was spun and woven, float over the ocean; that they might blind with its mists the sight of the enemy, as the clouds darken the earth with rain-drops. He gave them for their bow, the rainbow, that with it they might clear men's trails of enemies, as the rainbow clears away the storm-shadows;

and for their arrows gave he them the thunderbolts, that they might rive open the mountains, as the lightning cleaves asunder the pine trees, and then he sent them abroad to deliver, guide, and protect the children of Earth and the Sky Father. With their bow they lifted from his embraces the Sky Father from the bosom of the Earth Mother, "for," said they, "if he remain near, his cold will cause men to be stunted and stooped with shivering and to grovel in the earth," as stunted trees in the mountains delve under the snow to hide from the cold of the Sky Father. With their thunderbolts they broke open the mountain which gave entrance to the cave-wombs of the Earth Mother, and upon their water-shields they descended into the lowermost of the caves, where dwelt the children of Earth—men and all creatures.

Alas! It was dark as had been the world before the coming of the Sun, and the brothers found men the beings sadly bewailing their lot. When one moved it was but to jostle another, whose complaints wearied the ears of yet others; hence the brothers called a council of the priest-chiefs,—even ere the coming forth of men such lived,—and they made a ladder of tall canes which they placed against the roof of the cavern. Up this rushed the children of Earth. Some, climbing out before of their own wills, found deliverance from the caves above and, wandering away, became the ancestors of nations unknown to us; but our fathers followed in the footsteps of the older and younger brothers. Does not the cane grow jointed today, showing thus the notches which men traversed to daylight?

In the second cave all was still dark, but like starlight through cloud rifts, through the cleft above showed the twilight. After a time the people murmured again, until the two delivered them into the third world where they found light like that of early dawn. Again they grew discontented, again were guided upward, this time into the open light of the Sun—which was the light of this world. But some remained behind, not escaping until afterward; and these were the fathers of the western nations whom our ancients knew not.

Then indeed for a time the people complained bitterly, for it was then that they first saw the light of the Sun Father, which, in its brilliancy, smote them so that they fell grasping their eyeballs and moaning. But when they became used to the light they looked around in joy and wonderment; yet they saw that the earth seemed but small, for everywhere rolled about the great misty waters.

The two brothers spread open the limbs of the Earth Mother and cleft the western mountains with their shafts of lightning, and the waters flowed down and away from the bosom of the Earth Mother, cutting great cañons and valleys which remain to this day. Thus was widened the land, yet the earth remained damp. Then they guided the people eastward.

Already before men came forth from the lower worlds with the priest-chiefs, there were many gods and strange beings. The gods gave to the priests many treasures and instructions, but the people knew not yet the meaning of either. Thus were first taught our ancients incantations, rituals, and sacred talks (prayer), each band of them according to its usefulness. These bands were, the "Priesthood" (*Shi'-wa-na-kwe*), the "Hunter-band" (*Sa'-ni-a-k'ia-kwe*), the "Knife-band" (*A'tchi-a-k'ia-kwe* or Warrior), and the *Ne'-we-kwe,* or Band of Wise Medicine Men. The leaders of each band thus came to have wonderful knowledge and power—even as that of the gods! They summoned a great council of their children—for they were called the "Fathers of the People"—and asked them to choose such things as they would have for special ownership or use. Some chose the macaw, the eagle, or the turkey; others chose the deer, bear, or coyote; others the seeds of earth, or *a'-tâ-a,* the spring vine, tobacco, and the plants of medicine, the yellow-wood and many other things. Thus it came about that they and their brothers and sisters and their children, even unto the present day, were named after the things they chose in the days when all was new, and thus was divided our nation into many clans (*a'-no-ti-we*) of brothers and sisters who may not marry one another but from one to the other. To some of the elders of these bands and clans was given some thing which should be, above all other things, precious. For instance, the clans of the Bear and Crane were given the *mu'-et-ton-ne,* or medicine seed of hail and snow. For does not the bear go into his den, and appears not the crane when come the storms of hail and snow?

When more than one clan possessed one of these magic medicines, they formed a secret society, like the first four, for its keeping and use. Thus the Bear and Crane peoples became the "Holders of the Wand"—who bring the snow of winter and are potent to cure the diseases which come with them. In time they let into their secret council others, whom they had cured, that the precious secrets of their band might not be wasted. Thus it was that one after another were formed the rest of our medicine bands, who were and are called the finishers of men's trails, because, despite disease and evil, they guard and lengthen our lives; but in the "days of the new" there were only four bands.

RUTH L. BUNZEL

Psychology of the Pueblo Potter

One of the most important factors in determining the character of Zuni decorative style is the strict limitation of the number of designs admissible on any vessel. It is quite clear in the minds of all artists that the number of designs is fixed, and that the patterns selected must be enlarged or reduced to a size suitable for the particular surface to be decorated. Along with this goes a very marked aversion to overcrowding. This is so very characteristic, that I shall quote a few comments of informants:

> I do not like to have the whole jar covered with paint. If I use large designs, I leave large spaces between, so that it won't look dirty.
>
> There should be a good deal of white showing. If you put on too many small designs, the jar is too black and that is not nice. I do not use too much black because it makes the jar dirty looking.
>
> If there is room, I sometimes use four big designs on a large jar. If the jar is very large, I use larger designs. I never use more than four. . . . I like a lot of white showing.

All the potters had very decided number preferences, and on these they were pretty well agreed. Expressed preferences were as follows: for simple designs, four was considered best, three also is very good, six is permissible, five is not good, and more than six is very bad; for composite designs, a two part arrangement is to be preferred to three part, more than three should not be used. An examination of pottery, however, shows that actual numerical preferences are not the ones expressed. In simple arangements anything from three to nine may be used, the number depending in a large measure on the particular pattern selected. The arrangement of composite designs also shows certain peculiarities in the use of number. Where vertical panels are used, a two-part division is almost invariable, but where medallions are used instead, examples seem to be fairly evenly distributed between two and three part divisions.

In the decoration of bowls a balanced design of two or four units is exceedingly common, but three part arrangements are by no means unknown. In fact, there seems to be the requisite number for certain designs, particularly the large spiral designs which are so common in the decoration of bowls.

I find this discrepancy between expressed preference and actual usage exceedingly interesting in view of other phases of Zuni life. The importance of the number four in custom and belief is very marked. Furthermore, the literary pattern is always four, and, in a very large measure, the ceremonial pattern. It is therefore perfectly fitting and logical that Zuni artists in talking of their painting should always express a preference for the number four. But apparently at the moment of execution a purely esthetic factor intervenes in the feeling for decorative form, and substitutes the number three for the expected four.

The Personal Element in Design

We are now ready to return to our potter, whom we left some time back, holding in her hands the carefully molded and polished vessel, ready to receive its painted decoration. What will she do with this gleaming white or yellow or black surface? What is in her mind as she turns the vessel over in her hands, studying its proportions with reference to the style of decoration traditional in her group? Up to this point she has been guided wholly by sense and intuition. Her appreciation of form and surface is non-intellectual and non-analytical. But the manipulation of design involves something more. "Anyone can make a good shape, but you have to use your head in putting on the design," as the pueblo potter naively remarks. This same comment has been heard from many women in many different villages and is their recognition of mental processes of different orders. The relative importance of rational and non-rational functions in the creation of these artistic products will become clearer in the following pages. Whether the potter actually constructs her designs intelligently, or merely rationalizes about them, the tendency to analyze is always present. She can always give an *ex post facto* explanation of design, but never of form.

THE PLANNING OF DESIGNS The frame of mind in which the artists approach the problem of decorating a pot may best be described in their own words:

While I am making a jar, I think all the time I am working with the clay about what kind of design I am going to paint on it. When I am ready, I just sit and think what I shall paint. I do not look at anything but just think what I shall draw and then when the pot is dry, I draw it. . . . I think about designs all the time. . . . I always know just how it will look before I start to paint. (Zuni.)

I always know the whole design before I start to paint. (Zuni.)

When I have finished with the shape, my thoughts are always on the design that I shall put on. Generally I have the whole design in my head before I begin to paint. (Laguna.)

All the time when I am not working, I am thinking about what designs I shall make, and when I start to paint, I have it all in my mind. (Hopi.)

I think about designs when I am working and I have the whole design in my head before I start to paint. (Hopi.)

Whenever I am ready to paint, I just close my eyes and see the design, and then I paint it. (Hopi.)

I could continue to quote statements of this kind. However, I think this is sufficient to show that the whole scheme of decoration is most carefully planned and is fixed in the mind of the artist before she begins on any part of her design. Only one informant did not "see just how it will look" before starting to paint, although several admitted that their achievements often fell short of their original plan. Of course we must not take too literally the statements of the artists that they never deviate from the chosen plan. We need only examine pottery to see numerous examples of asymmetries, cases where the original plan is not fully carried out. This is particularly true in the case of fillers which are not always used consistently throughout the vessel,—sometimes because irregular spacing makes this impossible, but frequently for no apparent reason save the artist's carelessness in carrying out her plan. Sometimes designs of this character are differently painted on the same jar, red hatching being used in one place and black in another, although the intention was unmistakably to make them alike. Nevertheless, in spite of these accidental deviations, there can be no question that as a rule the pottery is painted in accordance with a carefully considered plan, which has been worked out in detail in the mind of the artist before the first stroke appears on the jar.

THE SOURCES OF DESIGN The seriousness of these potters goes deeper than concern with the technical excellence of their products. We shall discuss elsewhere the religious associations which attach themselves to pottery designs. But aside from this, the importance which they attach to the purely esthetic aspects of pottery design is greater than is ordinarily assumed. Most of these women display the same symptoms which are common to creative artists among more sophisticated people. They all speak of sleepless nights spent in thinking of designs for the pot to be decorated in the morning, of dreams of new patterns which on waking they try and often fail to recapture, and above all, the constant preoccupation with decorative problems even while they are engaged in other kinds of work. The following quotations from a number of different women all illustrate this earnestness. That this is not a pose assumed before a foreigner and a prospective buyer is indicated in a remark made by an expert Zuni potter to me,—the potter being a very matter-of-fact person who was not blessed with the artistic temperament. She laughed heartily at the idea of dreaming about designs. "I never dream about designs. I know some women dream about them, but only the women who don't know how to paint dream about it. I always know just what I want to paint, and so I don't dream about it, and I don't worry about it."

Regarding the sources of design women speak as follows:

I am always thinking about designs, even when I am doing other things, and whenever I close my eyes, I see designs in front of me. I often dream of designs, and whenever I am ready to paint, I close my eyes and then the designs just come to me. I paint them as I see them. (Hopi.)

One night I dreamed and saw lots of large jars and they all had designs on them. I looked at them and got the designs in my head and next morning I painted them. I often dream about designs, and if I can remember them, I paint them. (Hopi.)

I think about designs all the time. Sometimes when I have to paint a pot, I can't think what design to put on it. Then I go to bed thinking about it all the time. Then when I go to sleep, I dream about designs. I can't always remember them in the morning, but if I do, then I paint that on the pot. (Zuni.)

While I am making a jar, I think all the time I am working with the clay about what kind of design I am going to paint on it. When I am ready to paint, I just sit and think what I shall paint. (Zuni.)

I get all my ideas from my thoughts. I think of my thoughts as a person who tells me what to do. I dream about designs too. Sometimes before I go to bed, I am thinking about how I shall paint the next piece, and then I dream about it. I remember the designs well enough to paint in the morning. That is why my designs are better than those of other women. Some people do not think that pottery is anything, but it means a great deal to me. It is something sacred. I try to paint all my thoughts on my pottery. (Laguna.)

I never copy other women's designs. I use all the old Laguna designs. . . . I used to watch my aunt while she made pottery because she was such a good potter. That is how I learned to paint. (Laguna.)

I make up all my designs and never copy. I learned this design from my mother. I learned most of my designs from my mother. (Laguna.)

I never use other women's designs, and they never use mine. . . . I always have lots of designs in my head and never mix them. (Hopi.)

I like all kinds of designs. My jars are all different. I don't make the same design twice. Sometimes I make two or three alike, but not often. I don't like to do that. (Acoma.)

I like best to make new designs. I never copy other women's designs. Sometimes I see a design I like on a jar and if I want to make it, I ask the woman to give it to me. It would not be right to use another woman's design without asking. (Zuni.)

This is a new design. I learned the different parts of it from my mother, but they are put together in a new way. I always make new designs. I never copy the designs of other women. It is not right to do that. You must think out all your designs yourself. Only those who do not know copy. (Zuni.)

I go down to the ancient village and pick up pieces of pottery and try to put them together and get the line of the design. I never use other women's designs and they never use mine. . . . When I am not working, I think about what designs I will make and when I start to paint, I have it all in my mind. (Hopi.)

Nampeyo is my mother's sister, and she teaches me designs. When I find a piece of old pottery, I save it and get the design in my mind. Once I dreamed and saw lots of large jars and they had designs on them. I looked at them and got the designs in my mind and in the morning I remembered them and painted them. I often dream about designs and sometimes I remember them, and then I always use them. . . . I always use different designs. (Hopi.)

I save all the pieces of old pottery and try to work out the whole design from these scraps. Sometimes I use one of the old designs around the rim of a jar and make the rest of the design out of my head. I think about designs when I am not working and have the whole design in my head before I start to paint. Once I made a jar that I dreamed about. (Hopi.)

When I am ready to paint, I think how I am going to paint. I pick out pieces from the old village where I have my peach trees and try to get the line of the design and think how it went. I put the pieces together and pick out the best. That is how I learned to paint, from copying the old designs. When I first started to paint, I always used the designs from the old pottery, but now I sometimes make up new designs of my own. I always think about pottery even when I am doing other things. When I dream about designs, I paint them the next day. Whenever I close my eyes, I see the designs right in front of me. When I dream about designs, they are always new designs. When I am ready to paint, I just close my eyes and see the design and then I paint it. The designs just come to me, and I paint them as I see them. Every woman paints differently. (Hopi.)

It is apparent from these few extracts that not only does a great deal of thought go into the creation of these objects, but also there seems to be a definite attempt to make them a vehicle for personal experience. To say, "We paint our thoughts," is common in the villages where designs are clothed with symbolic meaning. But even where symbolism plays no role in decoration, as, for instance, among the Acoma and the Hopi, there is nevertheless a strong feeling that each pot is an individual and a significant creation. The condemnation of copying the designs of other women is unanimous. All women denied copying from other potters, and most of them disclaimed repetition of their own designs. Even at Zuni where the inventive faculty is at a low ebb and where choice of design is narrowly circumscribed by prevailing taste, in spite of all this, each pot is approached as a new creation, the decoration of which is evolved only after much thought and inner communings. However much theory and practice may be at variance, there can be no doubt concerning the theory. And strangely enough, it is at Zuni where the ideal is stated with the deepest conviction that it is most frequently violated. This discrepancy between theory and practice in the invention of designs might be paralleled in our own and other civilizations.

The psychological implications of this very simple and rather amusing condition are profound and far-reaching, and rather disconcerting in the light they throw upon the workings of the human mind. There are other factors besides sterility of imagination involved. A woman in all sincerity reproduces a familiar type of ornament, believing it to be something derived from her own consciousness. The decorative content and treatment are long since familiar to the ethnologist; he can analyze the whole pattern into definite well known motives which regularly appear together, and the details of arrangement are those already noted for these motives. An analysis of the material with the potter is illuminating. She is puzzled and somewhat chagrined to have it pointed out that she has used three designs on the jar, although she has frequently expressed a decided preference for four designs. She can offer but one explanation: "We always use three when we make this design." They always *do* use three in this particular design, but of this fact, so striking to the ethnologist, she has never before thought. She is also much interested to have pointed out to her that the particular rim design chosen is invariably used with this body design and one other of similar character, but is never used in association with the very different deer and sunflower design. "Yes, that is right. We always do it that way, but I never thought about it before." As a matter of fact, however much she may rationalize, she has probably never thought about the design, its structure, or its elements, at all. She has experienced it unanalytically as a configuration, just as she has experienced the forms of her vessels. The design is a constellation of which the essential part is a relationship. The various elements may later be abstracted, as words may be isolated from the sentences of a naive speaker, who for many years has been correctly speaking his native tongue, though innocent of the simplest rules of grammar. In art, as in language, it is not difficult to bring into consciousness these unexpressed feelings for formal relationships.

One important point that is implicit, rather than explicitly expressed in the statements of the women, is the importance of the visual image in the creation of design. Only one woman speaks of shutting her eyes and seeing designs, but it seems safe to infer that all the women who speak of seeing "just how it will look" have a perceptual rather than an intellectual approach to the artistic problem. At Zuni, where principles of design are clearly recognized and where, furthermore, religious ideas are associated with designs, we might expect to find a strengthening of the intellectual point of view at the expense of the more purely esthetic, but so far as our information goes, this does not seem to be the case. Here as elsewhere, sensation and intuition play a larger role than intellect in the creation of design. The very inarticulateness of the artists on all general problems of expression favors a conclusion which cannot be documented.

Symbolism

We are justified in using the word symbol only where the association between the design and the object or idea suggested is fixed and recognized. Zuni designs, with their shifting meanings are neither tribal nor individual symbols.

The patterns on meal bowls are, in a sense, symbolic. They are realistic or conventionalized but always recognizable representations of certain supernatural beings that figure in mythology and belief in association with springs and standing water. Their use on ceremonial pottery is explained by natives as a kind of compulsive magic. "These are all creatures who frequent springs. If we paint them on our bowls, our bowls will always be full of water like the springs." It is indirect magic, since they are never used on the bowls or jars that are actually used for drawing or storing water. They are employed only on bowls used to hold the sacred cornmeal that is sprinkled as part of every prayer. The use of particular designs on these bowls is part of the rain ritual.

There is, however, one symbol in Zuni art, the "road." This is the line which divides the neck from the body of jars. It is called *onane,* road, the usual Zuni term for the span of life. It is identified not with the life of a being inhabiting the pot, as Cushing claims, but with the life of the potter. For this reason, it is always left unjoined. "When I finish it, I shall finish my road," i.e. end my life. This is a true symbol, the only one in Zuni art. Meal bowl patterns are magical representations.

There is at Zuni one other design which might be regarded as a symbol, namely the pattern used on the outer rims of bowls. This has been variously interpreted as feathers and prayer-sticks, and the explanation which I heard once is that women paint it on their bowls when they have a prayer, because they do not make prayer-sticks. The designation "feather" is not confined to this design; "prayer-stick," however, is. It is interesting to note that this is one design whose usage is fixed. It is used only on the outside of bowls and its use there is, at the present time, almost obligatory.

In spite of this absence of fixed symbolism, we cannot overlook the tendency at Zuni to invariably associate decorative designs with ideas of a religious character. This is not a personal peculiarity of one woman, but is a general pattern of Zuni thought. At the request of my informant, I did not show the design sketches to other women for their identifications, but whenever I asked the significance of a particular design, I received explanations of a similar character.

Two general types of associations predominate: those concerning the weather, and those concerning the ceremonies for controlling the weather. An overwhelming number of designs suggest clouds of different kinds,—rain, snow, wind, lightning, flowers "because they come out after the rain." Almost all the rest suggest ceremonial paraphernalia, especially the regalia of the masked dancers who figure in the great rain bringing ceremonies. These are the two most important facts in Zuni life. Indeed, it is artificial to make any distinction between them. In Zuni ideology the clouds and the masked dancers are one. The interpretations are, therefore, all of one piece. It is an example of the extraordinary pervasiveness of ceremonialism in Zuni life and thought. It is the integrating principle with which all things that make any bid for attention must be related.

The strength of this tendency, coupled with the inconsistency of specific associations, has been interpreted as the last stage in a decaying system of symbolism. It is claimed that these designs were once symbolic and that the knowledge of their significance persists, although the precise meanings have been lost. I cannot see any evidence whatever that this is taking place. There is a definite tendency to associate design, the fluidity of which we have already observed, with the dominating concerns of life. Under the combined influence of the stagnation of art, and the increasing despotism of ritual—two developments which we can observe at Zuni at the present time—this loose association may in time crystallize into fixed symbolism. It may, of course, be the other way round, that it is the increasing fixation of symbolism that causes stagnation. The evidence from other pueblos where design is more fluid, all pointing towards the distinctly secondary nature of interpretations, does not favor this conclusion. But either way, symbolism and rigidity go hand in hand, and Zuni art is not less, but more symbolic today than it was seventy-five years ago.

TOM HARRISSON

The Hebridean as Artist

The impulse to art form is tradition, via ritual (and religion). The object of art form is the satisfaction of function or of ritual; and the intensification of life beyond mere necessity into beauty, fury or ecstasy. It plays its part in a whole cycle of pre-birth to after-death, in sacrifice and resurrection especially—into this pattern all things fall. Creative art is very rare; tradition dominates this part of life as it dominates all parts. In any tribe the war-clubs, for example, are of only two or three types. One of the commonest has four knobs at the end, always and only four knobs; not three knobs or five knobs. No man would consider the making of other than four.

The method of art is exact imitation through training, with tabus that must be respected during the period of art-work. Intangible things co-operate in every effort of making, from human conception to canoe building. A man does not carve a bird figure; he partakes in the carving. In every incident of life, except marriage, some art form is concerned.

The art of dancing is, in their own view, their highest. By now that should be clear to the reader. The Na-leng dances include dramatic performances and improvised pantomime, sometimes exceedingly funny. Dancing is not done independent of ritual. Music is used almost exclusively with dancing, not as a thing in itself. There are ten sorts of musical instruments, notably the slit-gong, pan-pipe, nose flute and musical bow. Flute music has (for me) a simple fairy charm; gong music depends on volume, rhythm, and incessant clamouring for physical action. Gong rhythms are so complicated that no white seems able to learn or transcribe them. Song is similarly intricate, forceful. The musical system is on a high descant, pentatonic principle with modal variations and undivided semitones. I have never heard music with more social content or physiological effect.

Songs are a form of story-telling. Words are a native art with an intricate circular pattern. The lay-out and content in the thousand myths which every child learns (often word perfect, and one story may last hours) are a whole library. While every incident in daily life can form a story. Any native may tell you, for a couple of hours, about how Taveta tried to steal Karai's woman. He will describe exactly how the missionary came, he picked up a piece of orange peel, just here, he held it in two fingers, these fingers, so, talking, there, and he said the following words. . . . And his right foot was against the far side of the root, just out of sunlight, the left foot was wearing a groove as deep as a thumb nail, he seemed to be nervous; some hairs, grey ones, were over his ears, etc., etc., on and on, incredible observation and detail—yet so well done that it does not get boring, the hearers are held in a web of spun words.

Conversational wit and repartee are rare. The essence of good

Hebridean talk is monologue. A conversation or council is a series of uninterrupted monologues—a good arrangement. The natives easily learn to write after white impact. They regard it as a curious and useless performance. They say: "Cannot a man remember and speak?" They will also point out: "Missionaries say they brought writing to here. They brought a new sort with more marks to be made to have meanings. But there is a writing belong black man." They call, in particular, simple angular marks on the lips of Santo pottery "writing." Also the extraordinarily elaborate continuous-line sand-drawings. The angular patterns on clothing mats are, in a way, writing. Each type of system of lines tells a story; represents a grade, a privilege, a payment and legend. So do the angular patterns of bead armlets. On such objects, woven or strung by the women, patterns are always angular. There is no loom in most islands; the mechanical difficulties thus exclude curvilinear or representative designs, for work which is slow and intricate anyway. Garments and ornaments are not made without designs, nor is pottery. There is no potter's wheel; pottery is moulded flat at Wus, built up in layers on a cross-section of bamboo at Prespea a few miles away.[1]

Curvilinear design is rare in most parts. An acute angle of about 40 degrees predominates. Houses and lay-outs are angular. The people are angular-minded. But on Erromango, in the south, the houses and many things are circular, as in much of Polynesia. Spirals derived from frigate-birds' beaks have become a dominant art form in north Melanesia, as also New Zealand. In the New Hebrides a sacred banner, in north Malekula, has such a spiral, and some are found among petroglyphs on the rocks of Aneityum; also some spirals in tattoo, which is absent in most tribes and is only well developed on Omba, where some women are tattooed all over.

Monoliths, dolmens, stone walls and traps, stone piles and forts

[1] Pot-making seems to have died out a considerable time ago in many areas. Wherever the jungle is cleared, pottery will be found in fragments all over the place. In many parts there is no native name for pottery; it is called *nesaucepan!* Possibly scanty clay supplies may have been exhausted or dried out. The tabus on pot-makers in Santo, where it is women's work, are very elaborate. They include long periods of seclusion indoors, peculiar diet, periods when urination is forbidden. If any tabu is broken all the pots will break.

are widespread in the islands. The more vigorous heathen tribes keep up complicated stone-works to this day. Stone may be dressed and faced, arranged often in decimal systems which may record happenings, generations, etc. Stone-work is frequently associated with ten petromorphic culture heroes, fratricidal brothers, who by treachery caused the youngest to be caught by a giant clam on the reef.

The devil Lesevsev is often in the form of a stone, which blocks the way to the after-life and seeks to devour those who come, unless they have killed enough pigs to satisfy. Stones are vital in magic—which is really a whole art of its own. The most important rites of south Malekula centre round phallic stones, like the stone called the penis of Ambat.

Stone is employed usually in the more important rites. The dark different Sakaus of north-east Santo do not use stone. They concentrate on fine gardening, with bright coloured flowers and leaf crotons. The people of Santo in general are excellent gardeners. They make stone terraces and irrigate large areas, divert streams through ditches and pipes, scatter vivid coloured plants through the vegetable greenness of taro. Flowers and colours are needed by all men and some women.

There are local fashions or traditions in colour—as in all things, the chief men are its arbiters. The colour vocabulary is limited; it must be remembered that the tribes who live away from the sea live in a world that is overwhelmingly green with grey skies. Six colours are commonly made: yellow, red, purple, blue, white and black, from vegetable concoctions and certain stones. Purple and white are the most frequent, red the most sacred. Colours are not mixed to make shadings. Some interesting effects are got by bleaching in sunlight and firelight. Faces are often painted blue. There are especial face-patterns for different occasions, grand body-patterns in colour for dances.

Flowers and feathers co-operate in ornamentation. Flowers are put in the hair, coloured leaves in the belt. Some birds' feathers may be worn at any time, others only on ritual occasions or by high-ranked men. Magnificent headdresses of fowl, parrot, swift and dove feathers occur in the central group, and feathered belts from honey-eater and shearwater. There is nothing so elaborate as the *Kura* feather-cloaks of Polynesia, which seem to resemble rather closely some from ancient Peru. It is probable that the feather cult was developing in the New Hebrides when the white man arrived, as were bird conceptions in general, especially those of a bird-of-prey with associated representative and curvilinear, as well as angular, art forms.

Tools are of the simplest. These unscientists have not sought better ones. For centuries that was their success, in slow growth from firm roots. Stone implements imposed their simplicity upon the things made. The Hebridean seldom greatly elaborates material objects; he reserves that for ideas, for dances and drawings in the sand which are his dramatised labyrinth, in some sense the same as the Labyrinth of Crete. He complicates inwards.

BRONISLAW MALINOWSKI

Launching a Canoe

Soon after the painting and adorning of the canoe, a date is fixed for the ceremonial launching and trial run, the *tasasoria* festivities, as they are called. Word is passed to the chiefs and headmen of the neighbouring villages. Those of them who own canoes and who belong to the same Kula community have always to come with their canoes and take part in a sort of regatta held on the occasion. As the new canoe is always constructed in connection with a Kula expedition, and as the other canoes of the same Kula community have to be either done up or replaced, it is the rule that on the *tasasoria* day a whole fleet of brand new or renovated canoes assemble on the beach, all resplendent in fresh colours and decoration of cowrie shells and bleached pandanus streamers.

The launching itself is inaugurated with a rite of the *mwasila* (Kula magic), called *Kaytalula wadola waga* ("staining red of the mouth of the canoe"). After the natives have taken off the plaited coco-nut leaves with which the canoe is protected against the sun, the *toliwaga* chants a spell over some red ochre, and stains both bow and stern of the canoe. A special cowrie shell, attached to the prow-board (*tabuyo*) is stained at each end. After that the canoe is launched, the villagers pushing it into the water over pieces of wood transversely placed which act as slips. This is done amidst shouts and ululations, such as are made on all occasions when some piece of work has to be done in a festive and ceremonial manner, when, for instance, the harvest is brought in and given ceremonially by a man to his brother-in-law, or when a gift of yams or taro is laid down before a fisherman's house by an inland gardener, or the return gift of fish is made.

Thus the canoe is finally launched after the long series of mingled work and ceremony, technical effort and magical rite.

After the launching is done, there takes place a feast, or, more correctly, a distribution of food (*sagali*) under observation of all sorts of formalities and ritual. Such a distribution is always made when the *toliwaga* has not built the canoe himself, and when he therefore has to repay the cutter of the canoe and his helpers. It also takes place whenever the canoe of a big chief is launched, in order to celebrate the occasion, to show off his wealth and generosity, and to give food to the many people who have been summoned to assist in the construction.

After the *sagali* (ceremonial distribution of food) is over, as a rule, in the afternoon, the new canoe is rigged, the mast is put up, the sail attached, and this and all the other boats make a trial run. It is not a competitive race in the strict sense of the word. The chief's canoe, which indeed would as a rule be best and fastest, in any case always wins the race. If it did not sail fastest, the others would probably keep back. The trial run is rather a display of the new canoe, side by side with the others.

In order to give one concrete illustration of the ceremonial connected with canoe building and launching, it may be well to relate an actual event. I shall therefore describe the *tasasoria,* seen on the beach of Kaulukuba, in February, 1916, when the new canoe of Kasana'i was launched. Eight canoes took part in the trial run, that is, all the canoes of Kiriwina, which forms what I have called the "Kula community," the social group who make their Kula expeditions in a body, and who have the same limits within which they carry on their exchange of valuables.

The great event which was the cause of the building and renovating of the canoes, was a Kula expedition planned by To'ulawa and his Kula community. They were to go to the East, to Kitava, to Iwa or Gawa, perhaps even to Muruwa (Woodlark Island), though with this island the natives do not carry on the Kula directly. As is usual in such cases, months before the approximate date of sailing, plans and forecasts were made, stories of previous voyages were recounted, old men dwelt on their own reminiscences and reported what they had been told by their elders of the days when iron was unknown and everyone had to sail to the East in order to get the green stone quarried in Suloga on Woodlark Island. And so, as it always happens when future events are talked over round village fires, imagination outran all bounds of probability; and the hopes and anticipations grew bigger and bigger. In the end, everyone really believed his party would go at least to the Easternmost Marshall Bennetts (Gawa), whereas, as events turned out, they did not sail beyond Kitava.

For this occasion a new canoe had to be constructed in Kasana'i, and this was done by Ibena himself, the chief of that village, a man of rank equal to the highest chief (his kinsman, in fact) but of smaller power. Ibena is a skilled builder as well as a fair carver, and there is no class of magic in which he does not profess to be versed. The canoe was built, under his guidance; he carved the boards himself, he also performed the magic, and he was, of course, the *toliwaga*.

In Omarakana, the canoe had to be slightly altered in construction; it had to be re-lashed and re-painted. To do this To'uluwa, the chief, had summoned a master builder and carver from the island of Kitava, the same one who a couple of years before, had built this canoe. Also a new sail had to be made for the Omarakana boat, as the old one was too small. The ceremony of *tasasoria* (launching and regatta) ought by rights to have been held on the beach of Kasana'i, but as its sister village, Omarakana, is so much more important, it took place on Kaulukuba, the sea-shore of the latter.

As the date approached, the whole district was alive with preparations, since the coastal villages had to put their canoes in order, while in the inland communities, new festive dresses and food had to be made ready. The food was not to be eaten, but to be offered to the chief for his *sagali* (ceremonial distribution). Only in Omarakana, the women had to cook for a big festive repast to be eaten on return from the *tasasoria.* In the Trobriands it is always a sign that a festive event is pending when all the women go in the evening to the bush to collect plenty of firewood. Next morning, this will be used for the *kumkumuli,* the baking of food in the ground, which is one of the forms of cooking used on festive occasions. On the evening of the *tasasoria* ceremony, people in Omarakana and Kasana'i were also busy with the numerous other preparations, running to the shore and back, filling baskets with yams for the *sagali,* getting ready their festive dress and decorations for the morrow. Festive dress means, for a woman, a new grass skirt, resplendent in fresh red, white and purple, and for the man a newly bleached, snow-white pubic leaf, made of the stalk of an areca palm leaf.

Early in the morning of the appointed day, the food was packed into baskets of plaited leaf, the personal apparel on top of it, all covered as usual with folded mats and conveyed to the beach. The women carried on their heads the large baskets, shaped like big inverted bells, the men shouldered a stick with two bag-shaped baskets at each end. Other men had to carry the oars, paddles, rigging and sail, as these paraphernalia are always kept in the village. From one of the villages, one of the large, prismatic receptacles for food made of sticks was carried by several men right over the *raybwag* (coral ridge) to be offered to the chief of Omarakana as a share in the *sagali.* The whole village was astir, and on its outskirts, through the surrounding groves, parties from inland could be seen making their way rapidly to the shore. I left the village with a party of notables at about eight o'clock in the morning. After leaving the grove of fruit and palm trees which grows especially densely around the village of Omarakana, we entered between the two walls of green, the usual monotonous Trobriand road, which passes through the low scrub. Soon, emerging on a garden space, we could see, beyond a gentle declivity, the rising slope of the *raybwag,* a mixture of rank vegetation with monumental boulders of grey coral standing out here and there. Through this, the path led on, following in an intricate course between small precipices and towering outcrops, passing huge, ancient ficus trees, spreading around them their many trunks and aerial roots. At the top of the ridge, all of a sudden the blue sea shone through the foliage, and the roar of waves breaking on the reef struck our ears. Soon we found ourselves among the crowd assembled on the beach, near to the big boat-shed of Omarakana.

By about nine o'clock, everybody was ready on the beach. It was fully exposed to the Eastern sun, but this was not yet sufficiently high to drop its light right from above, and thus to produce that deadly effect of tropical mid-day, where the shadows instead of modelling out the details, blur every vertical surface and make everything dull and formless. The beach appeared bright and gaudy, and the lively brown bodies looked well against the background of green foliage and white sand. The natives were anointed with coco-nut oil, and decorated with flowers and facial paint. Large red hibiscus blossoms were stuck into their hair, and wreaths of the white, wonderfully scented *butia* flowers crowned the dense black mops. There was a good display of ebony carvings, sticks and lime spoons. There were decorated lime pots, and such objects of personal adornment as belts of red shell discs or of small cowrie shells, nose sticks (very rarely used nowadays), and other articles so well known to everybody from ethnological collections in museums, and usually called "ceremonial," though, as said above the description "objects of parade" would be much more in agreement with the correct meaning of the words.

Such popular festivities as the one just being described are the occasions on which these objects of parade, some of which astonish us by their artistic perfection, appear in native life. Before I had opportunities to see savage art in actual display, in its proper, "living" setting, there seemed to me always to exist some incongruity between the artistic finish of such objects and the general crudity of savage life, a crudity marked precisely on the æsthetic side. One imagines greasy, dirty, naked bodies, moppy hair full of vermin, and other realistic features which make up one's idea of the "savage," and in some respects reality bears out imagination. As a matter of fact though, the incongruity does not exist when once one has seen native art actually displayed in its own setting. A festive mob of natives, with the wonderful golden-brown colour of their skins brought out by washing and anointing and set off by the gaudy white, red and black of facial paint, feathers and ornaments, with their exquisitely carved and polished ebony objects, with their finely worked lime pots, has a distinct elegance of its own, without striking one as grotesque or incongruous in any · æsthetic detail. There is an evident harmony between their festive mood, the display of colours and forms, and the manner in which they put on and bear their ornaments.

Those who have come from a distance, and who would spoil their decorations by the long march, wash with water and anoint themselves with coco-nut grease immediately before arriving at the scene of festivities. As a rule the best paint is put on later on, when the climax of the proceedings approaches. On this occasion, after the preliminaries (distribution of food, arrival of other canoes) were over, and when the races were just going to be started, the aristocracy of Omarakana—the wives and children of To'uluwa, his relatives and himself—withdrew behind the shelters, near the boat shed, and proceeded to put on the red, white and black of full facial paint. They crushed young betel-nut, mixed it with lime, and put it on with the pestles of betel mortars; then some of the aromatic black resin (*sayaku*) and white lime were applied. As the habit of mirrors is not quite well established yet in the Trobriands, the painting was done by one person on the face of another, and great care and patience were displayed on both sides.

The numerous crowd spent the day without taking much refreshment—a feature strongly differentiating Kiriwinian festivities from our ideal of an entertainment or picnic. No cooking was done, and only a few bananas were eaten here and there, and green coco-nuts were drunk and eaten. But even these refreshments were consumed with great frugality.

As always on such occasions, the people collected together in sets, the visitors from each village forming a group apart. The local natives kept to their own boat houses, those of Omarakana and Kurokaiwa having their natural centres on the beach of Kaulukuba.

The other visitors similarly kept together in their position on the beach, according to their local distribution; thus, men from the Northern villages would keep to the Northern section of the beach, those from the South would stick to that point of the compass, so that villages which were neighbours in reality would also be side by side on the shore. There was no mingling in the crowd, and individuals would not walk about from one group to another. The aristocrats, out of personal dignity, humble folk because of a modesty imposed by custom, would keep in their places. To'uluwa sat practically during the whole performance, on the platform erected for this purpose, except when he went over to his boat, to trim it for the race.

The boat shed of Omarakana, round which the chief, his family and the other villagers were grouped, was the centre of all the proceedings. Under one of the palms, a fairly high platform was put up to accommodate To'uluwa. In a row in front of the sheds and shelters, there stood the prismatic food receptacles (*pwata'i*). They had been erected by the inhabitants of Omarakana and Kasana'i, on the previous day, and partially filled with yams. The rest had to be supplied by people from the other villages, on the day of the boat races. As the natives came to the beach on that day, village after village, they brought their contribution, and before settling down on their particular spot on the shore, they paid a visit to the chief and offered him their tributes. These would be put into one of the *pwata'i*. Not all the villages contributed their share, but the majority did, though some of them brought only a few baskets. One of the villages brought one complete *pwata'i*, filled with yams, and offered the whole to the chief.

In the meantime, the eight canoes arrived, including that of Kasana'i, which had been ceremonially launched that morning with the accompanying magical rite, on its own beach about half a mile away. The canoe of Omarakana had also been launched on this morning, and the same rite performed over it. It ought to have been done by To'uluwa, the chief. As he, however, is quite incapable of remembering magical spells—in fact, he never does any of the magic which his rank and office impose on him—the rite was performed on this occasion by one of his kinsmen. This is a typical case of a rule very stringently formulated by all informants when you ask about it, yet in reality often observed with laxity. If you inquire directly, everyone will tell you that this rite, as all others of the *mwasila* (Kula magic) has to be done by the *toliwaga*. But every time when he ought to perform it, To'uluwa will find some excuse, and delegate it to another.

When all the canoes were present, as well as all the important villages, at about eleven o'clock a.m., there took place the *sagali* (ceremonial distribution). The food was given to people from various villages, especially such as took part in the races, or had assisted in the building of the new canoe. So we see that food contributed by all the villages before the *sagali* was simply redistributed among them, a considerable quantity having been added first by the chief; and this indeed is the usual procedure at a *sagali*. In this case, of course, the lion's share was taken by the Kitavans who helped at the building.

After the *sagali* was over, the canoes were all brought up to one spot, and the natives began to prepare them for the race. The masts were stepped, the fastenings trimmed, the sails made ready. After that the canoes all put off and gathered about half a mile off the shore, beyond the fringing reef; and at a sign given by some one on one of them, they all started. As said before, such a run is not a race properly speaking, in which the canoes would start scrupulously at the same minute, have the same distance to cover, and which would clearly show which is the fastest. In this case, it was merely, as always, a review of the boats sailing along as well as they were able, a review in which they all began to move, more or less at the same time, went in the same direction, and covered practically the same distance.

As to the time table of the events, the *sagali* was over before mid-day. There was a pause; and then, at about one p.m., the natives began rigging the canoes. Then all hands had a spell, and not before three p.m. were the races started. The whole affair was over by about four o'clock, and half an hour later, the boats from the other villages started to sail home, the people on the shore dispersed, so that by sunset, that is, about six o'clock, the beach was almost deserted.

Such was the *tasasoria* ceremony which I saw in February, 1916. It was a fine sight from the spectacular point of view. A superficial onlooker could have hardly perceived any sign of white man's influence or interference. I was the only white man present, and besides myself only some two or three native missionary teachers were dressed in white cotton. Amongst the rest of us there could be seen sparsely a coloured rag, tied round as a neckerchief or head-dress. But otherwise there was only a swarm of naked brown bodies, shining with coco-nut oil, adorned in new festive dress, with here and there the three-coloured grass skirt of a woman.

WILLIAM MARINER

Rat Shooting

A party of chiefs and others having resolved to go rat-shooting, their attendants are ordered to roast some cocoa-nut, which being done, and the chiefs having informed them what road they mean to take, these attendants proceed along the appointed road, chewing the roasted nut very finely as they go, and spitting, or rather blowing, a little of it at a time out of their mouths with considerable force. In doing this, great care is taken not to scatter the particles far from each other; for if they were widely distributed, the rat would not be tempted to stop and pick them up; and if the pieces were too large, he would run away with one piece, instead of stopping to eat his fill. The bait is thus distributed, at moderate distances, on each side of the road, and the men proceed till they arrive at the place appointed for them to stop at. If in their way they come to any cross roads, they stick a reed in the ground in the middle of such cross roads, as a *tábоо* or mark of prohibition for any one to come that way, and disturb the rats while the chiefs are shooting; and this no one will do. Even were a considerable chief to approach, on seeing the *tábоо* he would stop at a distance, and sit down on the ground, out of respect or politeness to his fellow-chiefs, and wait patiently till the shooting party has gone by. A petty chief, or one of the lower orders, would not dare to infringe upon this *tábоо* at the risk of his life. The distributors of the bait being arrived at the place appointed for them to stop at, sit down to prepare cava, having previously given the orders of their chiefs to the owners of the neighbouring plantations to send a supply of refreshments, such as pork, yams, fowls, and ripe plantains.

The company of chiefs having divided themselves into two parties, set out about ten minutes after the *boóhi* (the distributors of bait), and follow each other closely in a row along the middle of the road, armed with bows and arrows. It must be noticed, however, that the two parties are mixed; the greatest chief, in general, proceeding first, behind him one of the opposite party, then one of the same party with the first, and behind him again one of the other party, and so on alternately. The rules of the game are these: no one may shoot a rat that is in advance of him, except he who happens to be first in the row (for their situations change, as will directly be seen); but any one may shoot a rat that is either abreast of him or behind him. As soon as a man has shot, whether he hits the rat or not, he changes his situation with the man behind him, so that it may happen that the last man, if he has not shot so often as the others, may come to be first, and *vice versa* the first come to be last; and for the same reason, two or three, or more, of the same party, may come to be immediately behind one another. Whichever party kills ten rats first, wins the game. If there be plenty of rats, they generally play three or four games. As soon as they arrive at any cross roads they pull up the reeds placed as a *táboo,* that passengers coming afterwards may not be interrupted in their progress. When they have arrived at the place where the *boóhi* are waiting, they sit down and partake of what is prepared for them; afterwards, if they are disposed to pursue their diversion, they send the *boóhi* on to prepare another portion of the road. The length of road prepared at a time is generally about a quarter of a mile. If, during the game, any one of either party sees a fair shot at a bird, he may take aim at it; if he kills it, it counts the same as a rat; but whether he hits it or not, if he venture a shot, he changes place with the one behind him. Every now and then they stop and make a peculiar noise with the lips, like the squeaking of a rat, which frequently brings them out of the bushes, and they sit upright on their haunches, as if in the attitude of listening. If a rat is alarmed by their approach, and is running away, one or more cry out *too!* (stop!) with a sudden percussion of the tongue,—a term used, we may suppose, on account of the sharp and sudden tone with which it may be pronounced. This has generally the effect of making the rat stop, when he sits up, and appears too much frightened to attempt his escape. When he is in the act of running away, the squeaking noise with the lips, instead of stopping him, would cause him to run faster. They frequently also use another sound, similar to what *we* use when we wish to answer in the affirmative without opening the lips, consisting in a sort of humming noise, sounding through the nostrils, but more loud, short, and sudden. The arrows used on these occasions are nearly six feet long (the war-arrows being about three feet), made of reed, headed with iron-wood. They are not feathered, and their great length is requisite, that they may go straight enough to hit a small object; besides which, it is advantageous in taking an aim through a thick bush. Each individual in the party has only two arrows; for, as soon as he has discharged one from his bow, it is immediately brought to him by one of the attendants who follow the party. The bows also are rather longer than those used in war, being about six feet, the war-bows being about four feet and a half; nor are they so strong, lest the difficulty of bending them should occasion a slight trembling of the hand, which would render the aim less certain.

GEORGE CATLIN
A Choktaw Ball Game

Of fifteen thousand, are another tribe, removed from the Northern parts of Alabama, and Mississippi, within the few years past, and now occupying a large and rich tract of country, South of the Arkansas and the Canadian rivers; adjoining to the country of the Creeks and the Cherokees, equally civilized, and living much in the same manner.

In this tribe I painted the portrait of their famous and excellent chief, *Mo-sho-la-tub-bee* (he who puts out and kills), who has since died of the small-pox. In the same plate will also be seen, the portrait of a distinguished and very gentlemanly man, who has been well-educated, and who gave me much curious and valuable information, of the history and traditions of his tribe. The name of this man is *Ha-tchoo-tuck-nee* (the snapping turtle), familiarly called by the whites *"Peter Pinchlin."*

These people seem, even in their troubles, to be happy; and have, like all the other remnants of tribes, preserved with great tenacity their different games, which it would seem they are everlastingly practicing for want of other occupations or amusements in life. Whilst I was staying at the Choctaw agency in the midst of their nation, it seemed to be a sort of season of amusements, a kind of holiday; when the whole tribe almost, were assembled around the establishment, and from day to day we were entertained with some games or feats that were exceedingly amusing: horse-racing, dancing, wrestling, foot-racing, and ball-playing, were amongst the most exciting; and of all the catalogue, the most beautiful, was decidedly that of ball-playing. This wonderful game, which is the favorite one amongst all the tribes, and with these Southern tribes played exactly the same, can never be appreciated by those who are not happy enough to see it.

It is no uncommon occurrence for six or eight hundred or a thousand of these young men, to engage in a game of ball, with five or six times that number of spectators, of men, women and children, surrounding the ground, and looking on. And I pronounce such a scene, with its hundreds of Nature's most beautiful models, denuded, and painted of various colours, running and leaping into the air, in all the most extravagant and varied forms, in the desperate struggles for the ball, a school for the painter or sculptor, equal to any of those which ever inspired the hand of the artist in the Olympian games or the Roman forum.

I have made it an uniform rule, whilst in the Indian country, to attend every ball-play I could hear of, if I could do it by riding a distance of twenty or thirty miles; and my usual custom has been on such occasions, to straddle the back of my horse, and look on to the best advantage. In this way I have sat, and oftentimes reclined, and almost dropped from my horse's back, with irresistible laughter at the succession of droll tricks, and kicks and scuffles which ensue, in the almost superhuman struggles for the ball. These plays generally commence at nine o'clock, or near it, in the morning; and I have more than once balanced myself on my pony, from that time till near sundown, without more than one minute of intermission at a time, before the game has been decided.

It is impossible for pen and ink alone, or brushes, or even with their combined efforts, to give more than a *caricature* of such a scene; but such as I have been able to do, I have put upon the canvas. I will convey as correct an account as I can, and leave the reader to imagine the rest; or look to *other books* for what I may have omitted.

While at the Choctaw agency it was announced, that there was to be a great play on a certain day, within a few miles, on which occasion I attended, and made three sketches, and also the following entry in my note-book, which I literally copy out:

Monday afternoon at three o'clock, I rode out with Lieutenants S. and M., to a very pretty prairie, about six miles distant, to the ball-play-ground of the Choctaws, where we found several thousand Indians encamped. There were two points of timber about half a mile apart, in which the two parties for the play, with their respective families and friends, were encamped; and lying between them, the prairie on which the game was to be played. My companions and myself, although we had been apprised, that to see the whole of a ball-play, we must remain on the ground all the night previous, had brought nothing to sleep upon, resolving to keep our eyes open, and see what transpired through the night. During the afternoon, we loitered about amongst the different tents and shantees of the two encampments, and afterwards, at sundown, witnessed the ceremony of measuring out the ground, and erecting the "byes" or goals which were to guide the play. Each party had their goal made with two upright posts, about 25 feet high and six feet apart, set firm in the ground, with a pole across at the top. These goals were about forty or fifty rods apart; and at a point just half way between, was another small stake, driven down, where the ball was to be thrown up at the firing of a gun, to be struggled for by the players. All this preparation was made by some old men, who were, it seems, selected to be the judges of the play, who drew a line from one bye to the other; to which directly came from the woods, on both sides, a great concourse of women and old men, boys and girls, and dogs and horses, where bets were to be made on the play. The betting was all done across this line, and seemed to be chiefly left to the women, who seemed to have martialled out a little of everything that their houses and their fields possessed. Goods and chattels—knives—dresses—blankets—pots and kettles—dogs and horses, and guns; and all were placed in the possession of *stake-holders,* who sat by them, and watched them on the ground all night, preparatory to the play.

The sticks with which this tribe play, are bent into an oblong hoop at the end, with a sort of slight web of small thongs tied across, to prevent the ball from passing through. The players hold one of these in each hand, and by leaping into the air, they catch the ball between the two nettings and throw it, without being allowed to strike it, or catch it in their hands.

The mode in which these sticks are constructed and used, will be seen in the portrait of *Tullock-ckish-ko* (he who drinks the juice of the stone), the most distinguished ball-player of the Choktaw nation, represented in his ball-play dress, with his ball-sticks in his hands. In every ball-play of these people, it is a rule of the play, that no man shall wear moccasins on his feet, or any other dress than his breech-cloth around his waist, with a beautiful bead belt, and a "tail," made of white horsehair or quills, and a *"mane"* on the neck, of horsehair dyed of various colours.

This game had been arranged and "made up," three or four months before the parties met to play it, and in the following manner:—The two champions who led the two parties, and had the alternate choosing of the players through the whole tribe, sent runners, with the ball-sticks most fantastically ornamented with ribbons and red paint, to be touched by each one of the chosen players; who thereby agreed to be on the spot at the appointed time and ready for the play. The ground having been all prepared and preliminaries of the game all settled, and the bettings all made, and goods all "staked," night came on without the appearance of any players on the ground. But soon after dark, a procession of lighted flambeaux was seen coming from each encampment, to the ground where the players assembled around their respective byes; and at the beat of the drums and chaunts of the women, each party of players commenced the "ball-play dance." Each party danced for a quarter of an hour around their respective byes, in their ball-play dress; rattling their ball-sticks together in the most violent manner, and all singing as loud as they could raise their voices; whilst the women of each party, who had their goods at stake, formed into two rows on the line between the two parties of players, and danced also, in an uniform step, and all their voices joined in chaunts to the Great Spirit; in which they were soliciting his favour in deciding the game to their advantage; and also encouraging the players to exert every power they possessed, in the struggle that was to ensue. In the mean time, four old *medicine-men,* who were to have the starting of the ball, and who were to be judges of the play, were seated at the point where the ball was to be started; and busily smoking to the Great Spirit for their success in judging rightly, and impartially, between the parties in so important an affair.

This dance was one of the most picturesque scenes imaginable, and was repeated at intervals of every half hour during the night, and exactly in the same manner; so that the players were certainly awake all the night, and arranged in their appropriate dress, prepared for the play which was to commence at nine o'clock the next morning. In the morning, at the hour, the two parties and all their friends, were drawn out and over the ground; when at length the game commenced, by the judges throwing up the ball at the firing of a gun; when an instant struggle ensued between the players, who were some six or seven hundred in numbers, and were mutually endeavouring to catch the ball in their sticks, and throw it home and between their respective stakes; which, whenever successfully done, counts one for the game. In this game every player was dressed alike, that is, *divested* of all dress, except the girdle and the tail, which I have before described; and in these desperate struggles for the ball, when it is *up* (where hundreds are running together and leaping, actually over each other's heads, and darting between their adversaries' legs, tripping and throwing, and foiling each other in every possible manner, and every voice raised to the highest key, in shrill yelps and barks)! there are rapid successions of feats, and of incidents, that astonish and amuse far beyond the conception of any one who has not had the singular good luck to witness them. In these struggles, every mode is used that can be devised, to oppose the progress of the foremost, who is likely to get the ball; and these obstructions often meet desperate individual resistance, which terminates in a violent scuffle, and sometimes in fisticuffs; when their sticks are dropped, and the parties are unmolested, whilst they are settling it between themselves; unless it be by a general *stampedo,* to which they are subject who are down, if the ball happens to pass in their direction. Every weapon, by a rule of all ball-plays, is laid by in their respective encampments, and no man allowed to go for one; so that the sudden broils that take place on the ground, are presumed to be as suddenly settled without any probability of much personal injury; and no one is allowed to interfere in any way with the contentious individuals.

There are times, when the ball gets to the ground, and such a confused mass rushing together around it, and knocking their sticks together, without the possibility of any one getting or seeing it, for the dust that they raise, that the spectator loses his strength, and everything else but his senses; when the condensed mass of ball-sticks, and shins, and bloody noses, is carried around the different parts of the ground, for a quarter of an hour at a time, without any one of the mass being able to see the ball; and which they are often thus scuffling for, several minutes after it has been thrown off, and played over another part of the ground.

For each time that the ball was passed between the stakes of either party, one was counted for their game, and a halt of about one minute; when it was again started by the judges of the play, and a similar struggle ensued; and so on until the successful party arrived to 100, which was the limit of the game, and accomplished at an hour's sun, when they took the stakes; and then, by a previous agreement, produced a number of jugs of whiskey, which gave all a wholesome drink, and sent them all off merry and in good humour, but not drunk.

After this exciting day, the concourse was assembled in the vicinity of the agency house, where we had a great variety of dances and other amusements; the most of which I have described on former occasions. One, however, was new to me, and I must say a few words of it: this was the *Eagle Dance,* a very pretty scene, which is got up by their young men, in honour of that bird, for which they seem to have a religious regard. This picturesque dance was given by twelve or sixteen men, whose bodies were chiefly naked and painted white, with white clay, and each one holding in his hand the tail of the eagle, while his head was also decorated with an eagle's quill. Spears were stuck in the ground, around which the dance was performed by four men at a time, who had simultaneously, at the beat of the drum, jumped up from the ground where they had all sat in rows of four, one row immediately behind the other, and ready to take the place of the first four when they left the ground fatigued, which they did by hopping or jumping around behind the rest, and taking their seats, ready to come up again in their turn, after each of the other sets had been through the same forms.

In this dance, the steps or rather jumps, were different from anything I had ever witnessed before, as the dancers were squat down, with their bodies almost to the ground, in a severe and most difficult posture.

HENRI JUNOD

Sermons by Natives Converted to Christianity

So far, the training of Natives has been mostly in religious subjects, and I beg to give my readers some examples of their mode of comparison which I noted while hearing evangelists preaching, examples which strongly bear the impress of Bantu character. Sometimes the imagination is so subtle that it becomes almost incoherent. For them it is enough if the point which the two things compared have in common, that which grammarians call the "tertium comparationis," is almost infinitesimal.

For instance a Tembe Christian exhorting his hearers to fight against evil, says:

Let us, in this fight, take the shield which has been made from the skin of this ox slaughtered for our sake, Jesus Christ.

A moment of reflection is required to find the logical tie which unites all these images. The Bantu shield being made of ox-hide, the scriptural image of the slaughtered lamb had to be transformed into that of an ox, for the sake of comparison!

Another evangelist, whose discourses were specially interesting because he was a master in this art, one day spoke for more than half an hour on the text "Charity which is the bond of perfectness." In Thonga, bond, string, or rope is expressed by the same word (ngoti). So he showed how a string could be compared to charity by a great number of images, of which I remember at least the two following ones:

This rope, charity, is the rope which attaches the donkey to the trunk of a tree. In the evening you tie up the donkey. It can graze the whole night all round the tree without any fear of being lost. So when we remain in connection with our Saviour, who is the tree, then we are happy and protected against any danger.

He evidently remembered the words of Christ: I am the vine. And he added:

Charity is the string, the string which ties up a parcel. You have plenty of precious things in your parcel . . . But if you possess no string to tie up all these things, they will be lost on the way, one after the other, and you will reach the end of your journey (or of your life) having kept none of your spiritual advantages, etc.

Hear how Simeon Gana tried to explain what conscience is:

Conscience resembles two companions who have made an arrangement to plunder, with impunity, another man's field of sweet potatoes. One of them climbs a tree, the other takes the hoe and digs up the potatoes. As soon as the owner of the field appears, the one on the tree whistles and the other promptly runs away, so that he is never caught. But one day, the climber ran a thorn in his foot and he was obliged to sit down and extract it, as he could not climb to his post of observation in that condition. In the meantime his companion was stealing the potatoes in perfect assurance, thinking his companion was on watch. The owner arrived on the scene and caught him. Now you clearly see that conscience is the man who climbed on the tree. As long as he was doing his duty, success attended their plan. As soon as he does not work, man falls into disgrace. So let our conscience always be awake and warning us!

Another comparison bearing on a similar subject:

The words of God are powerful and they stir up the heart. They are like intestinal worms (manyokwana) which for a long time remain quiet in the body. But one fine night they awake and man cries from pain, and says: "I am ill!" For years the man used to mock the word of God, but that day he has felt its power!

I add this one which occurred to the imagination of one of my pupils:

We, preachers of the Gospel, are messengers of mourning. We have been sent to inform people of the great mourning of Jesus-Christ by which He saved the world. Let us not resemble that messenger who had to go to another country to deliver his errand. On the way he passed a village where people were drinking beer. He heard the songs, looked at the dance, entered and did not deliver his message. Such would we be, if distracted by worldly amusements, we were to neglect our sacred duty of preaching the cross.

G. T. EMMONS

A Native Account of the Meeting with La Perouse

Lituya Bay is a deep, narrow inlet penetrating the American mainland just beyond that point where the broken, rocky part of the north Pacific coast gives place to the broad, sandy shore of the Gulf of Alaska. Originally the bed of a great glacier it has long since been taken possession of by the sea, that floods and ebbs through its restricted entrance with a force that makes it the most justly dreaded harbor on the Pacific coast. At its head it branches into two arms, at right angles to the original course, which receive much ice from a number of active glaciers. The narrow mouth is still further contracted by half submerged ledges and sand pits that extend from either shore, and the constant warfare of the ocean waves and tidal currents have formed a bar, over which the rollers break with terrific force, and, except in fair weather, at slack water, the passage is fraught with extreme peril. Within, the calm is almost supernatural, the mirror-like surface of the water, protected by steep, high shores, is unaffected by winds from any quarter, and reflects with the truth of reality the translucent ice tints of the floating bergs as they are carried hither and thither by each reçurring tide. These peculiar conditions in times past attracted the sea otter in great numbers, and, notwithstanding the dangerous waters, this has always been a favorite hunting ground of the natives from Chatham Straits to Dry Bay.

Lituya is a compound word in the Tlingit language meaning "the lake within the point," and the place is so called from the almost enclosed water within the extended spit. On the maps of the eighteenth and nineteenth centuries it appears variously as Port Française, Altona, Alituya, Ltooa, as well as Lituya.

Like primitive peoples elsewhere the Tlingit endowed all nature with spirit life, and so accounted for the many mysteries that compassed them about. In their imagination, the glacier was the child of the mountains, born in regions of eternal snow, and, when its arch-enemy the sun looks down to destroy it, the parents tear the rocks from their sides and scatter them over the surface for protection; in the scintillating aurora they saw the warrior spirits at play in the highest heaven; and when nature was at its best the spirit of the tree and the rock came forth as the shadow and slept upon the calm waters. And so the legend of Lituya tells of a monster of the deep who dwells in the ocean caverns near the entrance. He is known as Kah Lituya, "the Man of Lituya." He resents any approach to his domain, and all of those whom he destroys become his slaves, and take the form of bears, and from their watch towers on the lofty mountains of the Mt Fairweather range they herald the approach of canoes, and with their master they grasp the surface water and shake it as if it were a sheet, causing the tidal waves to rise and engulf the unwary.

It can be seen how this phenomenon appealed to the Tlingit, as of all deaths that by drowning was alone dreaded. The end might come in any other way and he met it unflinchingly, with perfect resignation. But his crude belief in a future life of comfort and warmth required that the body be cremated, while, if lost in the water, its spirit must ever remain in subjection to some evil power.

This legend of Lituya is illustrated by a carved wooden pipe, of splendid proportions, which was obtained in 1888 from the chief of the Tuck-tane-ton family of the Hoon-ah Kow, who claimed this bay as his hereditary sea-otter hunting ground. It was used only upon occasions of particular ceremony—when the clan assembled to honor the dead, or to deliberate upon some important question of policy. At one end is shown a frog-like figure with eyes of haliotis shell, which represents the Spirit of Lituya, at the other end the bear slave sitting up on his haunches. Between them they hold the entrance of the bay, and the two brass-covered ridges are the tidal waves they have raised, underneath which, cut out of brass, is a canoe with two occupants, that has been engulfed.

In 1786 La Perouse, the French navigator, in his exploration of the Northwest Coast to the southward of Bering Bay, when abreast of the Fairweather Mountains, descried an opening in the shore which his boats entered and reported as an available anchorage. The following day he stood in for the entrance, which he had hardly gained, when the wind hauled ahead, and, notwithstanding he shivered his sails and threw all aback, he was carried in by the irresistible force of the flood, and narrowly escaped shipwreck. He remained here twenty-six days making observations, surveying, and trading with the natives. He gave to the bay the name of Port des Françaises and his minute description of the country and its inhabitants forms one of the most pleasing and exact records that has come down to us from any of the early narrators. But his visit was made most memorable by the loss of two of his boats and their crews of twenty-one officers and men, in their attempted reconnaissance of the mouth of the bay.

In 1886, one hundred years after this event, Cowee, the principal chief of the Auk qwan of the Tlingit people, living at Sintakaheenee, on Gastineaux Channel, told me the story of the first meeting of his ancestors with the white man, in Lituya Bay, where two boats of the strangers were upset and many of them were drowned. This narrative had been handed down by word of mouth for a century. These people possess no records nor had the chief, who spoke no word of our tongue, ever heard of La Perouse from outside sources; so we can here authenticate by an exact date a most interesting piece of native history in detail, the truth of which is substantiated by the fact that La Perouse was the only one of the early navigators to visit this locality in a large ship and by the attending loss of life in the destruction of his two boats.

Before the coming of the white man, when the natives had no iron, the Chilkat and Hoon-ah made long canoe trips each summer to Yakutat, to trade with the Thlar-har-yeek for copper, which was fashioned into knives, spears, ornaments, and tinneh[1] and which again were exchanged with the more southern tribes for cedar canoes, chests, food boxes, and dishes.

One spring a large party of Thluke-nah-hut-tees from the great village of Kook-noo-ow on Icy Straits, started north, under the leadership of three chiefs—Chart-ah-sixh, Lth-kah-teech, and Yan-yoosh-tick.

In entering Lituya, four canoes were swallowed by the waves and Chart-ah-sixh was drowned. The survivors made camp and mourned for their lost companions. While these ceremonies were being enacted, two ships came into the bay. The people did not know what they were, but believed them to be great black birds with far reaching white wings, and, as their bird creator, Yehlh, often assumed the form of a raven, they thought that in this guise he had returned to earth, so in their fright they fled to the forest and hid. Finding after a while that no harm came to them, they crept to the shore and, gathering leaves of the skunk cabbage, they rolled them into rude telescopes and looked through them, for to see Yehlh with the naked eye was to be turned to stone.

As the sails came in and the sailors climbed the rigging and ran out on the yards, in their imagination they saw but the great birds folding their wings and flocks of small black messengers rising from their bodies and flying about. These latter they believed to be crows, and again in fear they sought the shelter of the woods.

One family of warriors, bolder than the rest, put on their heavy coats of hide, the wooden collar and fighting head-dress, and, armed with the copper knife, spear, and bow, launched a war canoe. But

[1] The well-known "coppers" or shield-like pieces that might be considered as money, and which had a fixed value in accordance with their size.

scarcely had they cleared the beach when a cloud of smoke rose from the strange apparition followed by a voice of thunder, which so demoralized them that the canoe was overturned and the occupants scrambled to the shore as best they could.

Now one nearly blind old warrior gathered the people together, and said, that his life was far behind him and for the common good he would see if Yehlh would turn his children to stone, so he told his slaves to prepare his canoe, and, putting on a robe of the sea otter, he embarked and paddled seaward. But as he approached the ships the slaves lost heart and would turn back, and all deserted him save two, who finally placed him alongside. He climbed on board, but being hardly able to distinguish objects, the many black forms moving about still appeared as crows, and the cooked rice that they set before him to eat looked like worms, and he feared to touch it. He exchanged his coat of fur for a tin pan and with presents of food he returned to the shore. When he landed the people crowded about surprised to see him alive, and they touched him and smelled of him to see if it were really he, but they could not be pursuaded to eat the strange food that he had brought to them.

After much thought the old man was convinced that it was not Yehlh that he had gone to and that the black figures must be people, so the natives, profiting by his experience, visited the ships and exchanged their furs for many strange articles.

It was at this time that two boats were lost at the mouth of the bay and many of the white men were drowned.

PART 9

The Daily Round

FREDERICK EDWARD MANING

Complimentary Robbery among the Maori

There were in the old times two great institutions, which reigned with iron rod in Maori land—the *Tapu* and the *Muru*. Pakehas who knew no better, called the *muru* simply "robbery," because the word *muru,* in its common signification, means to plunder. But I speak of the regular legalized and established system of plundering as penalty for offences, which in a rough way resembled our law by which a man is obliged to pay "damages." Great abuses had, however, crept into this system—so great, indeed, as to render the retention of any sort of moveable property almost an impossibility, and to, in a great measure, discourage the inclination to labour for its acquisition. These great inconveniences were, however, met, or in some degree softened, by an expedient of a peculiarly Maori nature, which I shall by-and-by explain. The offences for which people were plundered were sometimes of a nature which, to a *mere* pakeha, would seem curious. A man's child fell in the fire and was almost burnt to death. The father was immediately plundered to an extent that almost left him without the means of subsistence: fishing nets, canoes, pigs, provisions—all went. His canoe upset, and he and all his family narrowly escaped drowning—some were, perhaps, drowned. He was immediately robbed, and well pummelled with a club into the bargain, if he was not good at the science of self-defence—the club part of the ceremony being always fairly administered one against one, and after fair warning given to defend himself. He might be clearing some land for potatoes, burning off the fern, and the fire spreads farther than he intended, and gets into a *wahi tapu* or burial-ground. No matter whether any one has been buried in it or no for the last hundred years, he is tremendously robbed. In fact, for ten thousand different causes a man might be robbed; and I can really imagine a case in which a man for scratching his own head might be legally robbed. Now, as the enforcers of this law were also the parties who received the damages, as well as the judges of the amount, which in many cases (such as that of the burnt child) would be everything they could by any means lay hands on, it is easy to perceive that under such a system personal property was an evanescent sort of thing altogether. These executions or distraints were never resisted; indeed, in many cases, as I shall explain by-and-by, it would have been felt as a slight, and even an insult, *not* to be robbed; the sacking of a man's establishment being often taken as a high compliment, especially if his head was broken into the bargain; and to resist the execution would not only have been looked upon as mean and disgraceful in the highest degree, *but it would have debarred the contemptible individual from the privilege of robbing his neighbours,* which was the compensating expedient I have alluded to. All this may seem a waste of words to my pakeha Maori readers, to whom these things have become such matters of course as to be no longer remarkable; but I have remembered that there are so many new people in the country who don't understand the beauty of being knocked down and robbed, that I shall say a few more words on the subject.

The tract of country inhabited by a single tribe might be say from forty to a hundred miles square, and the different villages of the different sections of the tribe would be scattered over this area at different distances from each other. We will, by way of illustrating the working of the *muru* system, take the case of the burnt child. Soon after the accident it would be heard of in the neighbouring villages; the family of the mother are probably the inhabitants of one of them; they have, according to the law of *muru,* the first and greatest right to clean out the afflicted father—a child being considered to belong to the family of the mother more than to that of the father—in fact it is their child, who the father has the rearing of. The child was moreover a promising lump of a boy, the makings of a future warrior, and consequently very valuable to the whole tribe in general, but to the mother's family in particular. "A pretty thing to let him get spoiled." Then he is a boy of good family, a *rangatira* by birth, and it would never do to let the thing pass without making a noise about it. That would be an insult to the dignity of the families of both father and mother. Decidedly, besides being robbed, the father must be assaulted with the spear. True, he is a famous spearman, and for his own credit must "hurt" some one or another if attacked. But this is of no consequence; a flesh wound more or less deep is to be counted on; and then think of the plunder! It is against the law of *muru* that any one should be killed, and first blood ends the duel. Then the natural affection of all the child's relations is great. They are all in a great state of excitement, and trying to remember how many canoes, and pigs, and other valuable articles, the father has got: for this must be a clean sweep. A strong party is now mustered, headed probably by the brother of the mother of the child. He is a stout chap, and carries a long tough spear. A messenger is sent to the father, to say that the *taua muru* is coming, and may be expected tomorrow, or the next day. He asks, "Is it a great *taua?*" "Yes; it is a very great *taua* indeed." The victim smiles, he feels highly complimented, he *is* then a man of consequence. His child is also of great consideration; he is thought worthy of a large force being sent to rob him! Now he sets all in motion to prepare a huge feast for the friendly robbers his relations. He may as well be liberal, for his provisions are sure to go, whether or no. Pigs are killed and baked whole, potatoes are piled up in great heaps, all is made ready, he takes out his best spear, and keeps it always ready in his hand. At last the *taua* appears on a hill half a mile off; then the whole fighting men of the section of the tribe of which he is an important member, collect at his back, all armed with spear and club, to show that they could resist if they would—a thing, however, not to be thought of under the circumstances. On comes the *taua*. The mother begins to cry in proper form; the tribe shout the call of welcome to the approaching robbers; and then with a grand rush, all armed, and looking as if they intended to exterminate all before them, the *kai muru* appear on the scene. They dance the war dance, which the villagers answer with another. Then the chief's brother-in-law advances, spear in hand, with the most alarming gestures. "Stand up! —stand up! I will kill you this day," is his cry. The defendant is not slow to answer the challenge. A most exciting, and what to a new pakeha would appear a most desperately dangerous, fencing bout with spears instantly commences. The attack and defence are in the highest degree scientific; the spear shafts keep up a continuous rattle; the thrust, and parry, and stroke with the spear shaft follow each other with almost incredible rapidity, and are too rapid to be followed by an unpractised eye. At last the brother-in-law is slightly touched; blood also drops from our chief's thigh. The fight instantly ceases; leaning on their spears, probably a little badinage takes place between them, and then the brother-in-law roars out *"murua! murua! murua!"* Then the new arrivals commence a regular sack, and the two principals sit down quietly with a few others for a friendly chat, in which the child's name is never mentioned, or the inquiry as to whether he is dead or alive even made. The case I have just described would, however, be one of more than ordinary importance; slighter "accidents and offences" would be atoned for by a milder form of operation. But the general effect was to keep personal property circulating from hand to hand pretty briskly, or indeed to convert it into public property; for no man could say who would be the owner of his canoe or blanket in a month's time. Indeed, in that space of time, I once saw a nice coat, which a native had got from the captain of a trading schooner, and which was an article much coveted in those days, pass through the hands, and over the backs, of six different owners, and return, considerably the worse for wear, to the original purchaser; and all these transfers had been made by legal process of *muru*. I have been often myself paid the compliment of being robbed for little accidents occurring in my family, and have several times also, from a feeling of politeness, robbed my Maori friends, though I can't say I was a great gainer by these transactions. I think the greatest haul I ever made was about half a bag of shot, which I thought a famous joke, seeing that I had sold it the day before to the owner for full value. A month after this I was disturbed early in the morning by a voice shouting, "Get up!—get up! I will kill you this day. You have roasted my grandfather. Get up!—*stand* up!" I, of course, guessed that I had committed some heinous though involuntary offence, and the "stand up" hinted the immediate probable consequences; so out I turned, spear in hand, and who should I see, armed with a bayonet on the end of a long pole, but my friend the erstwhile owner of the bag of shot. He came at me with pretended fury, made some smart bangs and thrusts, which I parried, and then explained to me that I had "cooked his grandfather"; and that if I did not come down handsome in the way of damages, deeply as he might regret the necessity, his own credit, and the law of *muru,* compelled him either to sack my house or die in the attempt. I was glad enough to prevent either event, by paying him two whole bags of shot, two blankets, divers fish-hooks, and certain figs of tobacco, which he demanded. I found that I had really and truly committed a most horrid crime. I had on a journey made my fire at the foot of a tree, in the top of which the bones of my friend's grandfather had once been deposited, but from which they had been removed ten years before; the tree caught fire and had burnt down: and I, therefore, by a convenient sort of figure of speech, had "roasted his grandfather," and had to pay the penalty accordingly.

It did not require much financial ability on my part, after a few experiences of this nature, to perceive that I had better avail myself of my privileges as a pakeha, and have nothing further to do with the law of *muru*—a determination I have kept to strictly. If ever I have unwittingly injured any of my neighbours, I have always made what I considered just compensation, and resisted the *muru* altogether; and I will say this for my friends, that when any of them have done an accidental piece of mischief, they have, in most cases without being asked, offered to pay for it.

HERMAN MELVILLE
A Typical Day

Nothing can be more uniform and undiversified than the life of the Typees; one tranquil day of ease and happiness follows another in quiet succession; and with these unsophisticated savages the history of a day is the history of a life. I will, therefore, as briefly as I can, describe one of our days in the valley.

To begin with the morning. We were not very early risers—the sun would be shooting his golden spikes above the Happar mountain, ere I threw aside my tappa robe, and girding my long tunic about my waist, sallied out with Fayaway and Kory-Kory and the rest of the household, and bent my steps towards the stream. Here we found congregated all those who dwelt in our section of the valley; and here we bathed with them. The fresh morning air and the cool flowing waters put both soul and body in a glow, and after a half-hour employed in this recreation, we sauntered back to the house—Tinor and Marheyo gathering dry sticks by the way for firewood; some of the young men laying the coco-nut trees under contribution as they passed beneath them; while Kory-Kory played his outlandish pranks for my particular diversion, and Fayaway and I, not arm in arm to be sure, but sometimes hand in hand, strolled along, with feelings of perfect charity for all the world, and especial good-will towards each other.

Our morning meal was soon prepared. The islanders are somewhat abstemious at this repast; reserving the more powerful efforts of their appetite to a later period of the day. For my own part, with the assistance of my valet, who, as I have before stated, always officiated as spoon on these occasions, I ate sparingly from one of Tinor's trenchers of poee-poee; which was devoted exclusively for my own use, being mixed with the milky meat of ripe coco-nut. A section of a roasted breadfruit, a small cake of "amar," or a mess of "kokoo," two or three bananas, or a mawmee apple; an annuee, or some other agreeable and nutritious fruit served from day to day to diversify the meal, which was finished by tossing off the liquid contents of a young coco-nut or two.

While partaking of this simple repast, the inmates of Marheyo's house, after the style of the indolent Romans, reclined in sociable groups upon the divan of mats, and digestion was promoted by cheerful conversation.

After the morning meal was concluded, pipes were lighted; and among them my own especial pipe, a present from the noble Mehevi. The islanders, who only smoke a whiff or two at a time, and at long intervals, and who keep their pipes going from hand to hand continually, regarded my systematic smoking of four or five pipefuls of tobacco in succession as something quite wonderful. When two or three pipes had circulated freely, the company gradually broke up. Marheyo went to the little hut he was for ever building. Tinor began to inspect her rolls of tappa, or employed her busy fingers in plaiting grass-mats. The girls anointed themselves with their fragrant oils, dressed their hair, or looked over their curious finery, and compared together their ivory trinkets, fashioned out of boars' tusks or whales' teeth. The young men and warriors produced their spears, paddles, canoe-gear, battle-clubs, and war-conchs, and occupied themselves in carving all sorts of figures upon them with pointed bits of shell or flint, and adorning them, especially the war-conchs, with tassels of braided bark and tufts of human hair. Some, immediately after eating, threw themselves once more upon the inviting mats, and resumed the employment of the previous night, sleeping as soundly as if they had not closed their eyes for a week. Others sallied out into the groves, for the purpose of gathering fruit or fibers of bark and leaves; the last two being in constant requisition, and applied to a hundred uses. A few, perhaps, among the girls, would slip into the woods after flowers, or repair to the stream with small calabashes and coco-nut shells, in order to polish them by friction with a smooth stone in the water. In truth these innocent people seemed to be at no loss for something to occupy their time; and it would be no light task to enumerate all their employments, or rather pleasures.

My own mornings I spent in a variety of ways. Sometimes I

rambled about from house to house, sure of receiving a cordial welcome wherever I went; or from grove to grove, and from one shady place to another, in company with Kory-Kory and Fayaway, and a rabble rout of merry young idlers. Sometimes I was too indolent for exercise, and accepting one of the many invitations I was continually receiving, stretched myself out on the mats of some hospitable dwelling, and occupied myself pleasantly either in watching the proceedings of those around me or taking part in them myself. Whenever I chose to do the latter, the delight of the islanders was boundless; and there was always a throng of competitors for the honor of instructing me in any particular craft. I soon became quite an accomplished hand at making tappa—could braid a grass sling as well as the best of them—and once, with my knife, carved the handle of a javelin so exquisitely, that I have no doubt, to this day, Karnoonoo, its owner, preserves it as a surprising specimen of my skill. As noon approached, all those who had wandered forth from our habitation began to return; and when mid-day was fairly come scarcely a sound was to be heard in the valley: a deep sleep fell upon all. The luxurious siesta was hardly ever omitted, except by old Marheyo, who was so eccentric a character, that he seemed to be governed by no fixed principles whatever; but, acting just according to the humor of the moment, slept, ate, or tinkered away at his little hut, without regard to the proprieties of time or place. Frequently he might have been seen taking a nap in the sun at noonday, or a bath in the stream at midnight. Once I beheld him perched eighty feet from the ground, in the tuft of a coco-nut tree, smoking; and often I saw him standing up to the waist in water, engaged in plucking out the stray hairs of his beard, using a piece of mussel-shell for tweezers.

The noontide slumber lasted generally an hour and a half; very often longer; and after the sleepers had arisen from their mats they again had recourse to their pipes, and then made preparations for the most important meal of the day.

I, however, like those gentlemen of leisure who breakfast at home and dine at their club, almost invariably, during my intervals of health, enjoyed the afternoon repast with the bachelor chiefs of the Ti, who were always rejoiced to see me, and lavishly spread before me all the good things which their larder afforded. Mehevi generally produced among other dainties a baked pig, an article which I have every reason to suppose was provided for my sole gratification.

The Ti was a right jovial place. It did my heart, as well as my body, good to visit it. Secure from female intrusion, there was no restraint upon the hilarity of the warriors, who, like the gentlemen of Europe after the cloth is drawn and the ladies retire, freely indulged their mirth.

After spending a considerable portion of the afternoon at the Ti, I usually found myself, as the cool of the evening came on, either sailing on the little lake with Fayaway, or bathing in the waters of the stream with a number of the savages, who, at this hour, always repaired thither. As the shadows of night approached, Marheyo's household were once more assembled under his roof: tapers were lit, long and curious chants were raised, interminable stories were told (for which one present was little the wiser), and all sorts of social festivities served to while away the time.

The young girls very often danced by moonlight in front of their dwellings. There are a great variety of these dances, in which, however, I never saw the men take part. They all consist of active, romping, mischievous evolutions, in which every limb is brought into requisition. Indeed, the Marquesan girls dance all over, as it were; not only do their feet dance, but their arms, hands, fingers, aye, their very eyes, seem to dance in their heads. In good sooth, they so sway their floating forms, arch their necks, toss aloft their naked arms, and glide, and swim, and whirl, that it was almost too much for a quiet, sober-minded, modest young man like myself.

The damsels wear nothing but flowers and their compendious gala tunics; and when they plume themselves for the dance, they look like a band of olive-colored Sylphides on the point of taking wing. In an instant, two of them, taller than their companions, were standing, side by side, in the middle of a ring, formed by the clasped hands of the rest. This movement was made in perfect silence.

Presently the two girls join hands overhead, and, crying out, "Ahloo! ahloo!" wave them to and fro. Upon which, the ring begins to circle slowly; the dancers moving sideways, with their arms a little drooping. Soon they quicken their pace; and, at last, fly round and round: bosoms heaving, hair streaming, flowers dropping, and every sparkling eye circling in what seemed a line of light.

Meanwhile, the pair within are passing and repassing each other incessantly. Inclining sideways, so that their long hair falls far over, they glide this way and that, one foot continually in the air, and their fingers thrown forth, and twirling in the moonbeams.

"Ahloo! ahloo!" again cry the dance queens; and, coming together in the middle of the ring, they once more lift up the arch, and stand motionless.

"Ahloo! ahloo!" Every link of the circle is broken; and the girls, deeply breathing, stand perfectly still. They pant hard and fast, a moment or two; and then, just as the deep flush is dying away from their faces, slowly recede, all round; thus enlarging the ring.

Again the two leaders wave their hands, when the rest pause, and now, far apart, stand in the still moonlight, like a circle of fairies. Presently, raising a strange chant, they softly sway themselves, gradually quickening the movement, until, at length, for a few passionate moments, with throbbing bosoms and glowing cheeks, they abandon themselves to all the spirit of the dance, apparently lost to everything around. But soon subsiding again into the same languid measure, as before, they become motionless; and then, reeling forward on all sides, their eyes swimming in their heads, join in one wild chorus, and sink into each other's arms.

Unless some particular festivity was going forward, the inmates of Marheyo's house retired to their mats rather early in the evening; but not for the night, since, after slumbering lightly for a while, they rose again, relit their tapers, partook of the third and last meal of the day, at which poee-poee alone was eaten, and then, after inhaling a narcotic whiff from a pipe of tobacco, disposed themselves for the great business of night, sleep. With the Marquesans it might almost be styled the great business of life, for they pass a large portion of their time in the arms of Somnus. The native strength of their constitutions is no way shown more emphatically than in the quantity of sleep they can endure. To many of them, indeed, life is little else than an often interrupted and luxurious nap.

LEWIS H. MORGAN
Iroquois Hospitality

One of the most attractive features of Indian society was the spirit of hospitality by which it was pervaded. Perhaps no people ever carried this principle to the same degree of universality, as did the Iroquois. Their houses were not only open to each other, at all hours of the day and of the night, but also to the wayfarer and the stranger. Such entertainment as their means afforded was freely spread before him, with words of kindness and of welcome. Not unfrequently one of these houses contained from ten to twenty families, all bound together by the nearer ties of relationship, and constituting in effect one family. They carried the principle of "living in common" to its full extent. Whatever was taken in the chase, or raised in the fields, or gathered in its natural state by any member of the united families, enured to the benefit of all, for their stores of every description were common. They had regular hours for cooking through the whole establishment, and whatever was prepared was free to all. The Indian had no regular meal after the morning repast, but he allayed his appetite whenever the occasion offered. As they used no tables in ancient times, they took their food separately, and whenever it could be done with the least trouble, the males first, and the females afterwards. The care of the appetite was left entirely with the women, as the Indian never asked for food. Whenever the husband returned, at any hour of the day, it was the duty and the custom of the wife to set food before him. If a neighbor or a stranger entered her dwelling, a dish of hominy, or whatever else she had prepared, was immediately placed before him, with an invitation to partake. It made no difference at what hour of the day, or how numerous the calls, this courtesy was extended to every comer, and was the first act of attention bestowed. This custom was universal, in fact one of the laws of their social system; and a neglect on the part of the wife to observe it, was regarded both as a breach of hospitality, and as a personal affront. A neighbor, or a stranger, calling from house to house, through an Indian village, would be thus entertained at every dwelling he entered. If the appetite of the guest had thus been fully satisfied, he was yet bound in courtesy to taste of the dish presented, and to return the customary acknowledgment, *Hi-ne-ä'-weh,* "I thank you"; an omission to do either being esteemed a violation of the usages of life. A stranger would be thus entertained without charge, as long as he was pleased to remain; and a relation was entitled to a home among any of his kindred, while he was disposed to claim it. Under the operation of such a simple and universal law of hospitality, hunger and destitution were entirely unknown among them. This method of dealing with the human appetite strikes the mind as novel; but it was founded upon a principle of brotherhood, and of social intercourse, not much unlike the common table of the Spartans. The abounding supplies of corn yielded, with light cultivation, by their fruitful fields, and the simple fare of the Indian, rendered the prevailing hospitality an inconsiderable burden. It rested chiefly upon the industry, and therefore upon the natural kindness of the Indian woman; who, by the cultivation of the maize, and their other plants, and the gathering of the wild fruits, provided the principal part of their subsistence, for the warrior despised the toil of husbandry, and held all labor beneath him. But it was in exact accordance with the unparalleled generosity of the Indian character. He would surrender his dinner to feed the hungry, vacate his bed to refresh the weary, and give up his apparel to clothe the naked. No test of friendship was too severe, no sacrifice to repay a favor too great, no fidelity to an engagement too inflexible for the Indian character. With an innate knowledge of the freedom and the dignity of man, he has exhibited the noblest virtues of the heart, and the kindest deeds of humanity in those sylvan retreats, which we are wont to look back upon as vacant and frightful solitudes.[1]

---

[1] Canassatego, a distinguished Onondaga chief, who flourished about the middle of the last century, thus cuttingly contrasted the hospitality of the Iroquois with that of the whites, in a conversation with Conrad Weiser, an Indian interpreter. "You know our practice. If a white man, in travelling through our country, enters one of our cabins, we all treat him as I do you. We dry him if he is wet, we warm him if he is cold, and give him meat and drink that he may allay his hunger and thirst."

ALEXANDER HENRY
Business Methods of the Piegans

The Slaves, indeed, all the Meadow tribes which I have seen, are much given to gusts of passion; a mere trifle irritates them and makes a great commotion, which a stranger would suppose must result in bloodshed. But the matter is soon adjusted, and their passion as quickly subsides. They are fickle and changeable; no confidence can be placed in them; the most trifling circumstance will change their minds. In smoking there is more ceremony among the Piegans than I observed in any other tribe. Some of them will not smoke while there is an old pair of shoes hanging up in the tent; some of them must rest the pipe upon a piece of meat; others upon a buffalo's tongue. Some will smoke only their own pipe, which they themselves must light; others, again, must have somebody to light it for them, and then it must be lighted by flame only; no live coal must touch it, nor must the coal be blown into a blaze. No person must pass between the lighted pipe and the fire, particularly when in a tent. The first whiff from the pipe is blown toward the earth, while the stem is pointed up; the second whiff is blown up, and the stem is pointed down, or sometimes to the rising sun; the midday and setting sun may also receive their share of attention. Those ceremonies being over, the pipe is handed around, as usual. I once observed a fellow who would not smoke in our houses, but having been given a bit of tobacco, he took his own pipe, went out of doors, and made a hole in the ground in which to rest the bowl while he smoked. Such proceedings are tedious and often troublesome to us in our business when a large band comes in, as the whole performance is slow and serious. They are superstitious to the utmost in various other things; some must have a person to cut their meat into small pieces ready to eat; others always eat and drink out of one particular bowl or dish, which they carry for that purpose; some never taste wild fowl or fish; some never eat particular kinds of flesh, or allow their victuals to be cooked in a kettle used for such viands. Every movement of the Slaves is a parade. When coming in to trade, young men are sent on ahead to inform us of their approach and demand a bit of tobacco for each principal man or head of a family. Six inches of our twist tobacco is commonly sent, neatly done up in paper, to which is tied a small piece of vermilion, both being considered tokens of friendship. The young men are treated to a glass of liquor, four inches of tobacco, and a small paper of vermilion, with which they immediately return to their friends. The tobacco is delivered, and a smoking-match takes place, while the messengers relate the news of the place, and give an account of their reception. This ceremony being concluded, they move on their journey in one long string. On the day of their arrival the men assemble at a convenient spot in sight of the fort, where they make a fire and smoke; during which time the women and children come to the fort and erect their tents near the stockades. Observing that business to be nearly completed, the men rise and move toward the fort in Indian file, the principal chief taking the lead, the others falling in according to rank or precedence, derived from the number of scalps taken in war. The master of the place is always expected to go out and shake hands with them at a short distance from the gates, and the further he goes to meet them, the greater the compliment. This ceremony over, he walks at their head, and thus conducts them to the Indian hall. There he desires the principal chief to take the seat of honor, in the most conspicuous place; the others sit according to rank around the room on benches provided for that purpose. The pipe is then lighted and presented to the chief, who, having performed the usual ceremonies, takes a few whiffs and passes it to the next person on the right, always in rotation, with the course of the sun. All having taken a few whiffs of the trader's pipe, the principal chief produces his own, which he fills and presents to the trader, who must take a few whiffs before it is sent around. The compliment is greater if the chief presents the pipe to the trader to light. If the Indians are numerous their own pipes are then demanded, filled by us, and presented to them, each one lighting according to his own particular notions of ceremony; but we must always have people to hand them fire, as their consequential impertinence does not permit them to rise for that purpose. The more pipes there are in circulation at once, the greater is the compliment. After the first round we give them each half a gill of Indian liquor, beginning always with the principal chief, who is about as ceremonious in taking a drink as he is in smoking. He dips his finger into the liquor and lets a few drops fall to the ground; then a few drops are offered above; but he drinks the rest without further delay. Each chief has some particular ceremony to perform before tasting the first glass, but after that he gets drunk as fast as possible. Smoking continues till the room is filled with smoke, and in half an hour another glass is served, and soon after that we present each man with a one-quart keg of Indian liquor; a dram then finishes the business, and all are ordered to retire to their tents to enjoy their liquor. Should the party exceed 15 or 20 heads of families, we give them their quantum in one large keg; this they prefer, as one gallon in a large keg looks bigger to them than double that quantity in several small kegs. Such is the common method of receiving them when no person of distinction bears a flag. In this case the flag-bearer walks ahead, though he may not be the principal man; precedence being allowed him, on such occasions, out of respect for the flag. The trader meets them as before, receives the flag, and carries in into the house, where the ceremonies already described are performed. The principal chief frequently advances, leading a horse by a line, which he delivers to the trader after shaking hands. This is considered as a present, and sometimes the horse has a small parcel of furs or skins on his back to enhance the value of the gift. The owner often wears a handsomely painted robe, which he takes off his own back to cover the trader. His dressed fox-skin cap may be added, and this he must be allowed to adjust upon the trader's head. His ceremonies being over, if there be any other individuals inclined to make a present, they rise up and cover the trader with their robes, and if they have a fox-skin worth presenting, it is adjusted on the top of the first one. Thus, when a large party arrives, the trader often finds himself covered with eight or ten heavy robes, and wears on his head as many fox-skins. All this he must endure, and sit with a serious countenance until the principal smoking ceremonies are over, when he is at liberty to order the robes and skins into the storehouse. It is always expected, however, that these presents will be paid for, even to double their value.

After the Indians have retired to their tents and drunk up all their liquor, if they are inclined to purchase any more, they bring some bits of meat, tongues, or other trash, which we must buy with liquor, which Piegans will not consent to pay for in skins or furs. The drinking-match continues all day and until about midnight, when they all fall asleep, and next morning finds them sober; for a drinking-match among the Slaves seldom lasts over night. The next day, when they trade, we pay them for their previous presents. But if what we offer for the horse does not answer the owner's expectations, he demands the horse, and it must be delivered up to him. Altercation is useless, for he gets sullen, and walks away with his horse. But a present of skins and furs is never demanded to be returned; whatever is offered for it being accepted. If a flag has been brought in, it is returned to the owner on his departure, tied up with a few yards of gartering, to which is attached a foot of tobacco. They seldom remain longer than one day at our forts. The women are all sent off first, while the men remain to smoke with the trader, and put him out of all patience by begging. The women being all gone, each man gets four or five balls and powder, about four inches of tobacco, and a dram; but they never set off till they have so pestered us for different articles that we are heartily tired of our customers. While drinking at our houses almost every man is provided with a rattle, to keep chorus with his rude singing. These rattles are made of raw hide, sewed and stretched in the shape of a calabash, and stuffed with sand until they are dry, when they are emptied and small pebbles put into them. The Piegans are noisy when drinking, but not insolent. Singing and bellowing seem to be their pleasure, while the men and women all drink together.

MARGARET MEAD

A Day in Samoa

The life of the day begins at dawn, or if the moon has shown until daylight, the shouts of the young men may be heard before dawn from the hillside. Uneasy in the night, populous with ghosts, they shout lustily to one another as they hasten with their work. As the dawn begins to fall among the soft brown roofs and the slender palm trees stand out against a colourless, gleaming sea, lovers slip home from trysts beneath the palm trees or in the shadow of beached canoes, that the light may find each sleeper in his appointed place. Cocks crow, negligently, and a shrill-voiced bird cries from the breadfruit trees. The insistent roar of the reef seems muted to an undertone for the sounds of a waking village. Babies cry, a few short wails before sleepy mothers give them the breast. Restless little children roll out of their sheets and wander drowsily down to the beach to freshen their faces in the sea. Boys, bent upon an early fishing, start collecting their tackle and go to rouse their more laggard companions. Fires are lit, here and there, the white smoke hardly visible against the paleness of the dawn. The whole village, sheeted and frowsy, stirs, rubs its eyes, and stumbles towards the beach. "Talofa!" "Talofa!" "Will the journey start to-day?" "Is it bonito fishing your lordship is going?" Girls stop to giggle over some young ne'er-do-well who escaped during the night from an angry father's pursuit and to venture a shrewd guess that the daughter knew more about his presence than she told. The boy who is taunted by another, who has succeeded him in his sweetheart's favour, grapples with his rival, his foot slipping in the wet sand. From the other end of the village comes a long drawn-out, piercing wail. A messenger has just brought word of the death of some relative in another village. Half-clad, unhurried women, with babies at their breasts, or astride their hips, pause in their tale of Losa's outraged departure from her father's house to the greater kindness in the home of her uncle, to wonder who is dead. Poor relatives whisper their requests to rich relatives, men make plans to set a fish trap together, a woman begs a bit of yellow dye from a kinswoman, and through the village sounds the rhythmic tattoo which calls the young men together. They gather from all parts of the village, digging sticks in hand, ready to start inland to the plantation. The older men set off upon their more lonely occupations, and each household, reassembled under its peaked roof, settles down to the routine of the morning. Little children, too hungry to wait for the late breakfast, beg lumps of cold taro which they munch greedily. Women carry piles of washing to the sea or to the spring at the far end of the village, or set off inland after weaving materials. The older girls go fishing on the reef, or perhaps set themselves to weaving a new set of Venetian blinds.

In the houses, where the pebbly floors have been swept bare with a stiff long-handled broom, the women great with child and the nursing mothers, sit and gossip with one another. Old men sit apart, unceasingly twisting palm husk on their bare thighs and muttering old tales under their breath. The carpenters begin work on the new house, while the owner bustles about trying to keep them in a good humour. Families who will cook to-day are hard at work; the taro, yams and bananas have already been brought from inland; the children are scuttling back and forth, fetching sea water, or leaves to stuff the pig. As the sun rises higher in the sky, the shadows deepen under the thatched roofs, the sand is burning to the touch, the hibiscus flowers wilt on the hedges, and little children bid the smaller ones, "Come out of the sun." Those whose excursions have been short return to the village, the women with strings of crimson jelly fish, or baskets of shell fish, the men with cocoanuts, carried in baskets slung on a shoulder pole. The women and children eat their breakfasts, just hot from the oven, if this is cook day, and the young men work swiftly in the mid-day heat, preparing the noon feast for their elders.

It is high noon. The sand burns the feet of the little children, who leave their palm leaf balls and their pin-wheels of frangipani blossoms to wither in the sun, as they creep into the shade of the houses. The women who must go abroad carry great banana leaves as sunshades or wind wet cloths about their heads. Lowering a few blinds against the slanting sun, all who are left in the village wrap their heads in sheets and go to sleep. Only a few adventurous children may slip away for a swim in the shadow of a high rock, some industrious woman continue with her weaving, or a close little group of women bend anxiously over a woman in labour. The village is dazzling and dead; any sound seems oddly loud and out of place. Words have to cut through the solid heat slowly. And then the sun gradually sinks over the sea.

A second time, the sleeping people stir, roused perhaps by the cry of "a boat," resounding through the village. The fishermen beach their canoes, weary and spent from the heat, in spite of the slaked lime on their heads, with which they have sought to cool their brains and redden their hair. The brightly coloured fishes are spread out on the floor, or piled in front of the houses until the women pour water over them to free them from taboo. Regretfully, the young fishermen separate out the "Taboo fish," which must be sent to the chief, or proudly they pack the little palm leaf baskets with offerings of fish to take to their sweethearts. Men come home from the bush, grimy and heavy laden, shouting as they come, greeted in a sonorous rising cadence by those who have remained at home. They gather in the guest house for their evening kava drinking. The soft clapping of hands, the high-pitched intoning of the talking chief who serves the kava echoes through the village. Girls gather flowers to weave into necklaces; children, lusty from their naps and bound to no particular task, play circular games in the half shade of the late afternoon. Finally the sun sets, in a flame which stretches from the mountain behind to the horizon on the sea, the last bather comes up from the beach, children straggle home, dark little figures etched against the sky; lights shine in the houses, and each household gathers for its evening meal. The suitor humbly presents his offering, the children have been summoned from their noisy play, perhaps there is an honoured guest who must be served first, after the soft, barbaric singing of Christian hymns and the brief and graceful evening prayer. In front of a house at the end of the village, a father cries out the birth of a son. In some family circles a face is missing, in others little runaways have found a haven! Again quiet settles upon the village, as first the head of the household, then the women and children, and last of all the patient boys, eat their supper.

After supper the old people and the little children are bundled off to bed. If the young people have guests the front of the house is yielded to them. For day is the time for the councils of old men and the labours of youth, and night is the time for lighter things. Two kinsmen, or a chief and his councillor, sit and gossip over the day's events or make plans for the morrow. Outside a crier goes through the village announcing that the communal breadfruit pit will be opened in the morning, or that the village will make a great fish trap. If it is moonlight, groups of young men, women by twos and threes, wander through the village, and crowds of children hunt for land crabs or chase each other among the breadfruit trees. Half the village may go fishing by torchlight and the curving reef will gleam with wavering lights and echo with shouts of triumph or disappointment, teasing words or smothered cries of outraged modesty. Or a group of youths may dance for the pleasure of some visiting maiden. Many of those who have retired to sleep, drawn by the merry music, will wrap their sheets about them and set out to find the dancing. A white-clad, ghostly throng will gather in a circle about the gaily lit house, a circle from which every now and then a few will detach themselves and wander away among the trees. Sometimes sleep will not descend upon the village until long past midnight; then at last there is only the mellow thunder of the reef and the whisper of lovers, as the village rests until dawn.

ERIK H. ERIKSON

The Yurok Salmon Fisherman

For comparison and counterpoint, let us turn from the melancholy "warriors without weapons" to a tribe of fishermen and acorn gatherers on the Pacific coast: the Yurok.[1]

The Sioux and the Yurok seem to be diametrically opposite in the basic configurations of existence. The Sioux roamed the plains and cultivated spatial concepts of centrifugal mobility; their horizons were the roaming herds of buffalo and the shifting enemy bands. The Yurok lived in a narrow, mountainous, densely forested river valley and along the coast of its outlet into the Pacific. Moreover, they limited themselves within the arbitrary borders of a circumscribed world.[2] They considered a disk of about 150 miles in diameter, cut in half by the course of their Klamath River, to include all there was to this world. They ignored the rest and ostracized as "crazy" or "of ignoble birth" anyone who showed a

---

[1] A. L. Kroeber, "The Yurok," in *Handbook of the Indians of California*, Bureau of American Ethnology, Bulletin 78, 1925.

[2] T. T. Waterman, *Yurok Geography*, University of California Press, 1920.

marked tendency to venture into territories beyond. They prayed to their horizons, which they thought contained the supernatural "homes" from which generous spirits sent the stuff of life to them: the (actually non-existent) lake upriver whence the Klamath flows; the land across the ocean which is the salmon's home; the region of the sky which sends the deer; and the place up the coast where the shell money comes from. There was no centrifugal east and west, south and north. There was an "upstream" and a "downstream," a "toward the river," and an "away from the river," and then, at the borders of the world (i.e., where the next tribes live), an elliptical "in back and around": as centripetal a world as could be designed.

Within this restricted radius of existence, extreme localization took place. An old Yurok asked me to drive him to his ancestors' home. When we arrived, he proudly pointed to a hardly noticeable pit in the ground which, to judge from its appearance, may or may not have been the site of a dugout and said: "This is where I come from." Such pits retain the family name forever. In fact, Yurok localities exist by name only in so far as human history or mythology has dignified them. These myths do not mention mountain peaks or the gigantic redwoods which impress white travelers so much; yet the Yurok will point to certain insignificant-looking rocks and trees as being the "origin" of the most far-reaching events. The acquisition and retention of possessions is and was what the Yurok thinks about, talks about, and prays for. Every person, every relationship, and every act can be exactly valued and becomes the object of pride or ceaseless bickering. The Yurok had money before they ever saw a white man. They used a currency of shells of different sizes which they carried in oblong purses. These shells were traded from inland tribes; the Yurok, of course, never "strayed" near the places on the northern coast where they could have found these shells in inflationary numbers.

This little, well-defined Yurok world, cut in two by the Klamath, has, as it were, its "mouth open" toward the ocean and the yearly mysterious appearance of tremendous numbers of powerful salmon which enter the estuary of the Klamath, climb its turbulent rapids, and disappear upriver, where they spawn and die. Some months later their diminutive progeny descend the river and disappear out in the ocean, in order that two years later, as mature salmon, they may return to their birthplace to fulfill their life cycles.

The Yurok speak of "clean" living, not of "strong" living, as do the Sioux. Purity consists of continuous avoidance of impure contacts and contaminations, and of constant purification from possible contaminations. Having had intercourse with a woman, or having slept in the same house with women, the fisherman must pass the "test" of the sweat house. He enters through the normal-sized door; normal meaning an oval hole through which even a fat person could enter. However, the man can leave the sweat house only through a very small opening which will permit only a man moderate in his eating habits and supple with the perspiration caused by the sacred fire to slip through. He is required to conclude the purification by swimming in the river. The conscientious fisherman passes this test every morning.

This is only one example of a series of performances which express a world image in which the various channels of nature and anatomy must be kept apart. For that which flows in one channel of life is said to abhor contaminating contact with the objects of other channels. Salmon and the river dislike it if anything is eaten on a boat. Urine must not enter the river. Deer will stay away from the snare if deer meat has been brought in contact with water. Salmon demands that women on their trip up or down river keep special observances, for they may be menstruating.

Only once a year, during the salmon run, are these avoidances set aside. At that time, following complicated ceremonies, a strong dam is built which obstructs the ascent of the salmon and permits the Yurok to catch a rich winter supply. The dam building is "the largest mechanical enterprise undertaken by the Yurok, or, for that matter, by any California Indians, and the most communal attempt" (Kroeber). After ten days of collective fishing, orgies of ridicule and of sexual freedom take place along the sides of the river, reminiscent of the ancient pagan spring ceremonials in Europe, and of Sioux license before the Sun Dance.

The supreme ceremony of the fish dam is thus the counterpart of the Sioux's Sun Dance; it begins with a grandiose mass dramatization of the creation of the world, and it contains pageants which repeat the progress of Yurok ethos from centrifugal license to the circumscribed centripetality which finally became its law and its reassurance of continued supply from the Supernatural Providers.

To these ceremonials we shall return when we can relate them to Yurok babyhood. What has been said will be sufficient to indicate that in size and structure the Yurok world was very different from—if not in almost systematic opposition to—that of the Sioux.

And what different people they are, even today! After having seen the apathetic erstwhile masters of the prairie, it was almost a relief, albeit a relief paired with shock, on arrival at a then nearly inaccessible all-Yurok village, to be treated as a member of an unwelcome white minority and to be told to go and room with the pigs—"they are the white man's dog."

There are several all-Yurok villages along the lower Klamath, the largest representing a late integration, in the Gold Rush days, of a number of very old villages. Situated on a sunny clearing, it is accessible only by motorboat from the coast, or over foggy, hazardous roads. When I undertook to spend a few weeks there in order to collect and check my data concerning Yurok childhood, I met immediately with the "resistive and suspicious temperament" which the Yurok as a group are supposed to have. Luckily I had met and had worked with some Yurok individuals living near the estuary of the Klamath; and Kroeber had prepared me for what in reality are folkways of stinginess, suspicion, and anger. I could therefore refrain from holding their behavior against them—or, indeed, from being discouraged by it. So I settled down in an abandoned camp by the river and waited to find out what might in this case be specifically the matter. It appeared that, at the coast, I had visited and had eaten meals with deadly enemies of an influential upriver family. The feud dated back to the eighties of the last century. Furthermore, it seemed that this isolated community was unable to accept my declaration of scientific intention. Instead, they suspected me of being an agent come to investigate such matters as the property feuds brought about by the discussion of the Howard-Wheeler Act. According to ancient maps, existing only in people's minds, Yurok territory is a jigsaw puzzle of community land, land with common ownership, and individual family property. Opposition to the Howard-Wheeler Act, which forbids the Indians to sell their land except to one another, had taken the form of disputing what the single Yurok could claim and sell if and when the act should be repealed, and one of my suspected secret missions apparently was that of trying under false pretenses to delineate property rights which the officials had been unable to establish. In addition, the fatal illness of a young Shaker and the visit of high Shaker clergy from the north had precipitated religious issues. Noisy praying and dancing filled the night air. Shakerism was opposed at the time not only by the government doctor, with whom I had been seen downriver, and by the few survivors of the ancient craft of Yurok medicine, but also by a newly arrived missionary. He was a Seventh-Day Adventist, the only other white man in the community, who by greeting me kindly, although with undisguised disapproval of the cigarette in my hand, compromised me further in the eyes of the natives. It took days of solitary waiting before I could discuss their suspicions with some of the Indians, and before I found informants who further clarified the outlines of traditional Yurok childhood. Once he knows you are a friend, however, the individual Yurok loses his prescribed suspicion and becomes a dignified informant.

The unsubdued and overtly cynical attitude of most Yurok toward the white man must, I think, be attributed to the fact that the inner distance between Yurok and whites is not as great as that between whites and Sioux. There was much in the centripetal A B C of Yurok life that did not have to be relearned when the whites came. The Yurok lived in solid frame houses which were half sunk in the ground. The present frame houses are next to pits in the ground which once contained the subterranean dwellings of ancestors. Unlike the Sioux, who suddenly lost the focus of his economic and spiritual life with the disappearance of the buffalo, the Yurok still sees and catches, eats and talks salmon. When the Yurok man today steers a raft of logs, or the Yurok woman grows vegetables, their occupations are not far removed from the original manufacture of dugouts (a one-time export industry), the gathering of acorns, and the planting of tobacco. Above all, the Yurok has been concerned all his life with property. He knows how to discuss a matter in dollars and cents, and he does so with deep ritual conviction. The Yurok need not abandon this "primitive" tendency in the money-minded white world. His grievances against the United States thus find other than the inarticulate, smoldering expression of the prairie man's passive resistance.

On the Fourth of July, when "the mourners of the year" were paid off, I was permitted to take part in this ceremony. On this occasion I had the opportunity to see many children assembled to watch a night's dance, the climax of which was not expected until dawn. They were vigorous and yet graceful, even-tempered, and well-behaved throughout the long night.

EDWARD EVANS EVANS-PRITCHARD
The Character of the Nuer

That every Nuer considers himself as good as his neighbour is evident in his every movement. They strut about like lords of the earth, which, indeed, they consider themselves to be. There is no master and no servant in their society, but only equals who regard themselves as God's noblest creation. Their respect for one another contrasts with their contempt for all other peoples. Among themselves even the suspicion of an order riles a man and he either does not carry it out or he carries it out in a casual and dilatory manner that is more insulting than a refusal. When a Nuer wants his fellows to do something he asks it as a favour to a kinsman, saying, "Son of my mother, do so-and-so," or he includes himself in the command and says: "Let us depart," "Let the people return home," and so forth. In his daily relations with his fellows a man shows respect to his elders, to his "fathers," and to certain persons of ritual status, within the circuit of its reference, so long as they do not infringe on his independence, but he will not submit to any authority which clashes with his own interests and he does not consider himself bound to obey any one. I was once discussing the Shilluk with a Nuer who had visited their country, and he remarked, "They have one big chief, but we have not. This chief can send for a man and demand a cow or he can cut a man's throat. Whoever saw a Nuer do such a thing? What Nuer ever came when some one sent for him or paid any one a cow?"

I found Nuer pride an increasing source of amazement. It is as remarkable as their constant aloofness and reticence. I have already described how Nuer would interrupt my inquiries. I mention here three incidents typical of the cavalier way in which they treated me. On one occasion I asked the way to a certain place and was deliberately deceived. I returned in chagrin to camp and asked the people why they had told me the wrong way. One of them replied, "You are a foreigner, why should we tell you the right way? Even if a Nuer who was a stranger asked us the way we should say to him, 'You continue straight along that path,' but we would not tell him that the path forked. Why should we tell him? But you are now a member of our camp and you are kind to our children, so we will tell you the right way in future."

On one occasion some men gave me information about their lineages. Next day these same men paid me a visit and one of them asked me, "What we told you yesterday, did you believe it?" When I replied that I had believed it they roared with laughter and called to others to come and share the joke. Then one of them said, "Listen, what we told you yesterday was all nonsense. Now we will tell you correctly." I could relate many such stories.

The Nuer have been rightly described as dour, and they are often gruff and curt to one another and especially to strangers. But if they are approached without a suggestion of superiority they do not decline friendship, and in misfortune and sickness they show themselves kind and gentle. At such moments they permit themselves to show sympathy which their pride stifles at other times, for even when Nuer approve of one they cannot bear that one shall see it and are the more truculent to hide their friendliness. Never are they truckling or sycophantic. When a Nuer wants a gift he asks for it straight out, and if you refuse it he remains in good humour. Their only test of character is whether one can stand up for oneself. One rises in Nuer estimation the more one lives their kind of life and accepts their values.

If you wish to live among the Nuer you must do so on their

terms, which means that you must treat them as a kind of kinsmen and they will then treat you as a kind of kinsman. Rights, privileges, and obligations are determined by kinship. Either a man is a kinsman, actually or by fiction, or he is a person to whom you have no reciprocal obligations and whom you treat as a potential enemy. Every one in a man's village and district counts in one way or another as a kinsman, if only by linguistic assimilation, so that, except for an occasional homeless and despised wanderer, a Nuer only associates with people whose behaviour to him is on a kinship pattern.

Kinsmen must assist one another, and if one has a surplus of a good thing he must share it with his neighbours. Consequently no Nuer ever has a surplus. But the European has a surplus and if his possessions are of any use to the Nuer he ought, in their opinion, to share them with the people among whom he is living. Travellers have often remarked that the Nuer have plagued them for gifts. They beg from one another with equal persistence. No Nuer is expected to part with his cattle or household property and, except in special circumstances, these would not be asked for. But were a man to possess several spears or hoes or other such objects he would inevitably lose them. Deng, a Government chief and a man of standing, told me, as I was leaving his village on the Pibor River, that he was grateful for the fishing spears I had distributed among his kinsmen, but added that they would not be able to keep them when his relatives at Fadoi came to spend next dry season on the Pibor.

The only way of keeping tobacco among the Nuer is to deny that one possesses it and to keep it well hidden. When I gave Deng a big lump of Anuak tobacco he managed to place a small piece of it in his pipe, but he had at once to distribute the rest of it. When I used to give tobacco to youths at Yakwac they generally took a small piece for immediate use as snuff and asked me to hide the rest, so that they could come and get a bit when they wanted it without any one knowing that they possessed it. I had hiding-places all over my tent. No Nuer can resist the pleadings of his kinsman for tobacco. Age-fellows do not even ask for snuff or tobacco, but, if they find it in a man's byre, they just take it. My own system was to give away at the first opportunity anything I possessed which Nuer might covet and to rest in poverty and peace. Arab merchants are driven almost crazy by Nuer demands for gifts, but they generally speak Nuer well and have considerable knowledge of Nuer habits and so are able to hold their own. Nevertheless I have often observed that they make gifts where no return is to be expected.

Nuer are most tenacious of their rights and possessions. They take easily but give with difficulty. This selfishness arises from their education and from the nature of kinship obligations. A child soon learns that to maintain his equality with his peers he must stand up for himself against any encroachment on his person and property. This means that he must always be prepared to fight, and his willingness and ability to do so are the only protection of his integrity as a free and independent person against the avarice and bullying of his kinsmen. They protect him against outsiders, but he must resist their demands on himself. The demands made on a man in the name of kinship are incessant and imperious and he resists them to the utmost.

PART 10

Ceremony and Economics

FRANZ BOAS

The Potlatch

Before proceeding any further it will be necessary to describe the method of acquiring rank. This is done by means of the potlatch, or the distribution of property. This custom has been described often, but it has been thoroughly misunderstood by most observers. The underlying principle is that of the interest-bearing investment of property.

The child when born is given the name of the place where it is born. This name it keeps until about a year old. Then his father, mother, or some other relative, gives a paddle or a mat to each member of the clan and the child receives his second name. When the boy is about 10 or 12 years old, he obtains his third name. In order to obtain it, he must distribute a number of small presents, such as shirts or single blankets, among his own clan or tribe. When the youth thus starts out in life, he is liberally assisted by his elders, particularly by the nobility of the tribe.

I must say here that the unit of value is the single blanket, nowa-days a cheap white woolen blanket, which is valued at 50 cents. The double blanket is valued at three single blankets. These blankets form the means of exchange of the Indians, and everything is paid for in blankets or in objects the value of which is measured by blankets. When a native has to pay debts and has not a sufficient number of blankets, he borrows them from his friends and has to pay the following rates of interest:

For a period of a few months, for 5 borrowed blankets 6 must be returned (Lē′k·ō); for a period of six months, for 5 borrowed blankets 7 must be returned; for a period of twelve months or longer, for 5 borrowed blankets 10 must be returned.

When a person has a poor credit, he may pawn his name for a year. Then the name must not be used during that period, and for 30 blankets which he has borrowed he must pay 100 in order to redeem his name. This is called q'ā′q'oaxō (selling a slave).

The rate of interest of the Lē′k·ō varies somewhat around 25 per cent, according to the kindness of the loaner and the credit of the borrower. For a very short time blankets may be loaned without interest. This is designated by the same term.

When the boy is about to take his third name, he will borrow blankets from the other members of the tribe, who all assist him. He must repay them after a year, or later, with 100 per cent interest. Thus he may have gathered 100 blankets. In June, the time set for this act, the boy will distribute these blankets among his own tribe, giving proportionately to every member of the tribe, but a few more to the chief. This is called Lā′X'uit. When after this time any member of the tribe distributes blankets, the boy receives treble the amount he has given. The people make it a point to repay him inside of a month. Thus he owns 300 blankets, of which, however, he must repay 200 after the lapse of a year. He loans the blankets out among his friends, and thus at the close of the year he may possess about 400 blankets.

The next June he pays his debts (qoana′) in a festival, at which all the clans from whom he borrowed blankets are present. The festival is generally held on the street or in an open place near the village. Up to this time he is not allowed to take part in feasts. But now he may distribute property in order to obtain a potlatch name. This is also called Lā'X'uit.

At this time the father gives up his seat (Lā'Xoē) in favor of his son. After the boy has paid his debts, the chief calls all the older members of the tribe to a council, in which it is resolved that the boy is to receive his father's seat. The chief sends his speaker to call the boy, and his clan go out in company with the speaker. The young man—for henceforth he will be counted among the men—dresses with a black headband and paints long vertical stripes, one on each side of his face, running down from the outer corners of the eyes. The stripes represent tears. He gives a number of blankets to his friends, who carry them into the house where the council is being held. The speaker enters first and announces his arrival. The young man follows, and after him enter his friends, carrying blankets. He remains standing in front of the fire, and the chief announces to him that he is to take his father's seat. Then the boy distributes his blankets among the other clans and sells some for food, with which a feast is prepared. His father gives up his seat and takes his place among the old men. The blankets given away at this feast are repaid with 100 per cent interest. In this manner the young man continues to loan and to distribute blankets, and thus is able, with due circumspection and foresight, to amass a fortune. Sometimes it happens that the successor to a man's name already has a name of his own. In all such cases (also when the name is acquired by inheritance) the successor gives up his name and his property to his own successor.

Possession of wealth is considered honorable, and it is the endeavor of each Indian to acquire a fortune. But it is not as much the possession of wealth as the ability to give great festivals which makes wealth a desirable object to the Indian. As the boy acquires his second name and man's estate by means of a distribution of property, which in course of time will revert to him with interest, the man's name acquires greater weight in the councils of the tribe and greater renown among the whole people, as he is able to distribute more and more property at each subsequent festival. Therefore boys and men are vying with each other in the arrangement of great distributions of property. Boys of different clans are pitted against each other by their elders, and each is exhorted to do his utmost to outdo his rival. And as the boys strive against each other, so do the chiefs and the whole clans, and the one object of the Indian is to outdo his rival. Formerly feats of bravery counted as well as distributions of property, but nowadays, as the Indians say, "rivals fight with property only." The clans are thus perpetually pitted against each other according to their rank. The Kwakiutl tribes are counted as the highest in rank. In intertribal rivalry they do not strive against each other, but the

> Guē′tEla against the Ma′malēleqala.
> Q'ō′moyuc against the Qœ̄′xsōt′ēnôx.
> Q'ō′mk·ūtis against the NE′mqîc or Laō′koatx.
> Wā′las Kwakiutl against the Lau′itsîs or Ts'ā′mas.

I referred several times to the distribution of blankets. The recipient in such a distribution is not at liberty to refuse the gift, although according to what I have said it is nothing but an interest-bearing loan that must be refunded at some future time with 100 per cent interest. This festival is called p'a′sa, literally, flattening something (for instance, a basket). This means that by the amount of property given the name of the rival is flattened.

There is still another method of rising in the social scale, namely, by showing one's self superior to the rival. This may be done by inviting the rival and his clan or tribe to a festival and giving him a considerable number of blankets. He is compelled to accept these, but is not allowed to do so until after he has placed an equal number of blankets on top of the pile offered to him. This is called dāpEntg·ala and the blankets placed on top of the first pile are called dā′pEnō. Then he receives the whole pile and becomes debtor to that amount, i.e., he must repay the gift with 100 per cent interest.

A similar proceeding takes place when a canoe is given to a rival. The latter, when the gift is offered to him, must put blankets to the amount of half the value of the canoe on to it. This is called dā′g·ōt, taking hold of the bow of the canoe. These blankets are kept by the first owner of the canoe. Later on, the recipient of the canoe must return another canoe, together with an adequate number of blankets, as an "anchor line" for the canoe. This giving of a canoe is called sā′k·a.

Still more complicated is the purchase or the gift, however one chooses to term it, of a "copper." All along the North Pacific Coast, from Yakutat to Comox, curiously shaped copper plates are in use, which in olden times were made of native copper, which is found in Alaska and probably also on Nass River, but which nowadays are worked out of imported copper. The front of the copper is covered with black lead, in which a face, representing the crest animal of the owner, is graven. These coppers have the same function which bank notes of high denominations have with us. The actual value of the piece of copper is small, but it is made to represent a large number of blankets and can always be sold for blankets. The value is not arbitrarily set, but depends upon the amount of property given away in the festival at which the copper is sold. On the whole, the oftener a copper is sold the higher its value, as every new buyer tries to invest more blankets in it. Therefore the purchase of a copper also brings distinction, because it proves that the buyer is able to bring together a vast amount of property.

It was described above how a boy is introduced into the distributions of property going on among the tribe. It remains to state how he acquires his first copper. When the young man has acquired a certain number of blankets, one of his older friends invites him to take a share in the purchase of one of the cheaper coppers, which may have a value of, say, 500 blankets. The boy contributes 200 blankets as his share and the other man purchases it, announcing the young man as his partner in the transaction. The copper is delivered to the young man, who becomes a debtor to his partner for the amount of blankets contributed by the latter. He announces at once that he will sell the copper the following year, but that he is willing to deliver the copper on the spot. With these words he lays it down before the tribe. One of the chiefs of a rival tribe takes the copper and pays as a first installment 100 blankets. Then the boy promises a distribution of blankets for the following year and loans out the 100 blankets which he has received. The next year he calls in his outstanding debts and invites all the neighboring tribes to a feast, to which his own tribe contributes food and fuel. In the course of the festival he pays the chief who took his copper 200 blankets, being the value of the 100 blankets received the previous year, together with 100 per cent interest. Then the purchaser pays the sum of 750 blankets for the copper, including boxes and belt. Of this amount 700 are distributed on the following day in the prescribed fashion among the neighboring tribes. Now the young man proceeds to loan out his blankets until within a few years he is able to repay the share of his partner who first helped him to buy the copper. When the time has come for this transaction, his partner pays him double the amount of what he (the partner) has contributed, and the young man returns to him double of this amount.

The rivalry between chiefs and clans finds its strongest expression in the destruction of property. A chief will burn blankets, a canoe, or break a copper, thus indicating his disregard of the amount of property destroyed and showing that his mind is stronger, his power greater, than that of his rival. If the latter is not able to destroy an equal amount of property without much delay, his name is "broken." He is vanquished by his rival and his influence with his tribe is lost, while the name of the other chief gains correspondingly in renown.

Feasts may also be counted as destruction of property, because the food given can not be returned except by giving another feast. The most expensive sort of feast is the one at which enormous quantities of fish oil (made of the oulachon) are consumed and burnt, the so-called "grease feast." Therefore it also raises the name of the person who can afford to give it, and the neglect to speedily return it entails a severe loss of prestige. Still more feared is the breaking of a valuable copper. A chief may break his copper and give the broken parts to his rival. If the latter wants to keep his prestige, he must break a copper of equal or higher value, and then return both his own broken copper and the fragments which he has received to his rival. The latter may then pay for the copper which he has thus received. The chief to whom the fragments of the first copper are given may, however, also break his copper and throw both into the sea. The Indians consider that by this act the attacked rival has shown himself superior to his aggressor, because the latter may have expected to receive the broken copper of his rival in return so that an actual loss would have been prevented.

In by far the greater number of cases where coppers are broken the copper is preserved. The owner breaks or cuts off one part after the other until finally only the T-shaped ridge remains. This is valued at two-thirds of the total value of the copper and is the last part to be given away. The rival to whom the piece that has been broken off is given, breaks off a similar piece, and returns both to the owner. Thus a copper may be broken up in contests with different rivals. Finally, somebody succeeds in buying up all the broken fragments, which are riveted together, and the copper has attained an increased value. Since the broken copper indicates the fact that the owner has destroyed property, the Indians pride themselves upon their possession.

The rivalry between chiefs, when carried so far that coppers are destroyed and that grease feasts are given in order to destroy the prestige of the rival, often develop into open enmity. When a person gives a grease feast, a great fire is lighted in the center of the house. The flames leap up to the roof and the guests are almost scorched by the heat. Still the etiquette demands that they do not stir, else the host's fire has conquered them. Even when the roof begins to burn and the fire attacks the rafters, they must appear unconcerned. The host alone has the right to send a man up to the roof to put out the fire. While the feast is in progress the host sings a scathing song ridiculing his rival and praising his own clan, the feats of his forefathers and his own. Then the grease is filled in large spoons and passed to the rival chief first. If a person thinks he has given a greater grease feast than that offered by the host, he refuses the spoon. Then he runs out of the house (g·ē′qEmx'it=chief rises against his face) to fetch his copper "to squelch with it the fire." The host proceeds at once to tie a copper to each of his house posts. If he should not do so, the person who refused the spoon would on returning strike the posts with the copper, which is considered equal to striking the chief's face. Then the man who went to fetch his copper breaks it and gives it to the host. This is called "squelching the host's fire." The host retaliates as described above.

The following songs show the manner in which rivals scathe each other.

First NEqa'pEnk·Em (=ten fathom face) let his clan sing the following song at a feast which he gave:

1. Our great famous chief is known even outside of our world, oh! he is the highest chief of all. [Then he sang:] The chiefs of all the tribes are my servants, the chiefs of all the tribes are my speakers. They are pieces of copper which I have broken.

[The people:] Do not let our chief rise too high. Do not let him destroy too much property, else we shall be made like broken pieces of copper by the great breaker of coppers, the great splitter of coppers, the great chief who throws coppers into the water, the great one who can not be surpassed by anybody, the one surmounting all the chiefs. Long ago you went and burnt all the tribes to ashes. You went and defeated the chief of all the tribes; you made his people run away and look for their relatives whom you had slain. You went and the fame of your power was heard among the northern tribes. You went and gave blankets to everybody, chief of all tribes.

2. Do not let us stand in front of him, of whom we are always hearing, even at the outermost limits of this world. Do not let us steal from our chief, tribes! else he will become enraged and will tie our hands. He will hang us, the chief of the tribes.

[Neqa'pEnk·Em sings:] Do not mind my greatness. My tribe alone is as great as four tribes. I am standing on our fortress; I am standing on top of the chiefs of the tribes. I am Copper Face, Great Mountain, Supporter, Obstacle; my tribes are my servants.

At another feast he let his people sing:

1. Do not look around, tribes! do not look around, else we might see something that will hurt us in the great house of this really great chief.

2. "Do not look around, tribes! do not look around, else we might see something formidable in the great house of this really great chief. His house has the Ts'o'noqoa.[1] Therefore we are benumbed and can not move. The house of our double chief,[2] of the really great chief, is taking our lives and our breath."

3. "Do not make any noise, tribes! do not make any noise, else we shall precipitate a landslide of wealth from our chief, the overhanging mountain."

4. [Neqa'pEnk·Em sings:] "I am the one from whom comes down and from whom is untied the red cedar bark[3] for the chiefs of the

[1] A fabulous monster.
[2] The war chief and potlatch chief.
[3] The emblem of the winter ceremonial.

tribes. Do not grumble, tribes! do not grumble in the house of the great double chief, who makes that all are afraid to die at his hands, over whose body is sprinkled the blood of all those who tried to eat in the house of the double chief,[4] of the really great chief. Only one thing enrages me, when people eat slowly and a little only of the food given by the great double chief."

While these songs are merely a praise of the deeds of the singer, the following reply by He′nak·alaso, the rival of NEqa′pEnk·Em is bitter to the extreme. In it the singer ridicules him for not yet having returned a grease feast.

1. I thought another one was causing the smoky weather. I am the only one on earth—the only one in the world who makes thick smoke rise from the beginning of the year to the end, for the invited tribes.[5]

2. What will my rival say again—that "spider woman"; what will he pretend to do next? The words of that "spider woman" do not go a straight way. Will he not brag that he is going to give away canoes, that he is going to break coppers, that he is going to give a grease feast? Such will be the words of the "spider woman," and therefore your face is dry and moldy, you who are standing in front of the stomachs of the chiefs.

3. Nothing will satisfy you; but sometimes I treated you so roughly that you begged for mercy. Do you know what you will be like? You will be like an old dog, and you will spread your legs before me when I get excited. You did so when I broke the great coppers "Cloud" and "Making Ashamed," my great property and the great coppers, "Chief" and "Killer Whale," and the one named "Point of Island" and "The Feared One" and "Beaver." This I throw into your face, you whom I always tried to vanquish; whom I have maltreated; who does not dare to stand erect when I am eating; the chief whom even every weak man tries to vanquish.

4. Now my feast! Go to him, the poor one who wants to be fed from the son of the chief whose own name is "Full of Smoke" and "Greatest Smoke." Never mind; give him plenty to eat, make him drink until he will be qualmish and vomits. My feast steps over the fire right up to the chief.[6]

In order to make the effect of the song still stronger, an effigy of the rival chief is sometimes placed near the fire. He is lean, and

[4] This refers to the fact that he killed a chief of the Awi′k·′enôx in a feast.

[5] Namely, by the fire of the grease feast.

[6] The first grease feast went as far as the center of the house. As NEqa′pEnk—Em did not return it, the second one stepped forward across the fire right up to him.

is represented in an attitude as though begging that the fire be not made any hotter, as it is already scorching him.

Property may not only be destroyed for the purpose of damaging the prestige of the rival, but also for the sole purpose of gaining distinction. This is done mainly at the time when houses are built, when totem poles are erected, or when a son has been initiated by the spirit presiding over the secret society of his clan. It seems that in olden times slaves were sometimes killed and buried under the house posts or under totem posts. Later on, instead of being killed, they were given away as presents. Whenever this was done, the inverted figure of a man, or an inverted head, was placed on the pole. In other cases coppers were buried under the posts, or given away. This custom still continues, and in all such cases coppers are shown on the post, often in such a way that they are being held or bitten by the totem animals. At the time of the initiation of a member of the clan slaves were also killed or coppers were destroyed, as will be described in greater detail later on. The property thus destroyed is called the o'mayu, the price paid for the house, the post, or for the initiation.

The distribution or destruction of property is not always made solely for the purpose of gaining prestige for one's self, but it is just as often made for the benefit of the successor to the name. In all such cases the latter stands during the festival next to the host, or, as the Indian terms it, in front of him, and the chief states that the property is distributed or destroyed for the one "standing in front of him," which is therefore the term used for the chief's eldest son, or, in a more general sense, for the heir presumptive.

CLARK WISSLER

Ceremonial Bundles

Introduction

The ceremonials described in this paper are those to which we have given the name medicine bundles. By the Blackfoot, they are designated as *saam,* which we have translated as medicine, a word now used in anthropological literature to express a similar concept.

These medicine bundles are associated with the rituals to which they are, after all, entirely secondary. As every bundle and its ritual is conceived of as owned by a single person, we have limited this paper to the study of rituals of individual ownership. These do not constitute the entire ceremonial culture of the Blackfoot for they maintain societies and associations similar in number and character to those found among their neighbors. In most of these, however, the fundamental conceptions of the bundle scheme prevail, from which it follows that a proper understanding of this subject will suffice for the comprehension of the chief characteristics in this aspect of Blackfoot culture. Because of this and the somewhat unique conceptions involved, we have felt justified in assigning a distinct paper to bundles and their rituals, reserving the data on collective ceremonies for a future publication.

The data were gathered at various times since 1903, partly by the writer and partly by Mr. D. C. Duvall, the latter checking over with different informants all the earlier notes. Notwithstanding the rather extended series of investigations, we cannot claim completeness in any case, but have, we believe, illustrated the chief characteristics of each important type of bundle. It was our original plan to collect all the different rituals in the various groups but this was interrupted by Mr. Duvall's untimely death whence it seems best to publish our results as they stand. Had we been able to present the fifty or more rituals for the tipi bundles and the some twenty-odd for the pipes as contemplated, a satisfactory insight into the genesis of these rituals would doubtless have resulted. In lieu of this completeness of data, we have accepted statements from informants as to similarities and relationships between rituals when confirmed by objective or analytic evidence. In the following paper we have given, according to our judgment, all the more important concrete data collected through the Duvall manuscripts reporting in full the statements of various informants and his own observations contain much further detail.

Medicine Experiences

As an introduction to this phase of Blackfoot culture we present a number of personal narratives recounting medicine experiences.

That these seven men actually experienced these happenings in their subjective aspects is, of course, impossible of proof; but all of them seemed to lead lives of integrity and sincerity and to bear reputations of honesty except the third, who was held in some distrust but recognized as a medicineman of more than ordinary powers. We, ourselves, detected in his narratives certain evidences of plagiarism, but the value of the data does not depend upon the actuality of the events narrated. We are certain that these narratives are typical accounts of the kinds of experiences a Blackfoot of some importance is assumed to have passed through. Even the most commonplace Indian is accustomed to explain any special aptitude he is credited with by similar narratives, though often of the crudest sort. We are not sure that such of these narratives as do recount real experiences (dreams or visions) are complete, for the discussion of this aspect of a Blackfoot's inner life is a delicate matter admitting of no cross-questioning. As stated elsewhere, it is a social breach to ask a direct question about any such experiences. In the case of several narratives, the man felt called upon to pray to the power concerned for permission to speak frankly of the relation between himself and it, explaining that he was about to do this for my enlightenment, etc. No doubt some of this was for effect, a feature present in most acts of a medicineman, but on the other hand, this was usually so mumbled that its import alone could be detected. If we were put to it for an opinion we would say that we believed narrators A and D absolutely sincere, while the others may have incorporated some experiences of other men legitimately transferred to them, which, as we shall see later, gave them the right to feel that they had the same experience. The following narratives are offered, therefore, as types of assumed personal experiences.

We have used the term medicineman to signify a man skilled in the handling of bundles and conducting their ceremonies. There is nothing to distinguish him from other men, for most men own some kind of a bundle however small, and thus stand in gradual gradation. We accepted the Blackfoot designations: i.e., those called medicinemen by them are so termed by us; but they themselves recognize the vagueness of the conception and the gradation. A doctor, on the other hand, is one who treats disease by virtue of powers obtained through dreams or visions and in no other manner. Thus, while doctors may be great and small, they are nevertheless doctors by virtue of this experience. A medicineman may have owned all rituals and stand preëminent in ceremonial skill and yet not be a doctor. By material wealth one may take high rank as a medicineman, as we shall see later; but all this will not suffice to make him a doctor. By transfer, a kind of purchase, a medicineman may acquire the visions and supernormal experiences of others; but a doctor must himself have the experiences and further, such experiences as confer on him power to treat the sick. Medicinemen may have experiences of their own in which powers are conferred, but unless these give them definite control over disease they are not doctors. Obviously, a medicineman may also be a doctor and the reverse. This paper, however, is concerned almost exclusively with the medicineman, his bundle and its ritual.

Once I dreamed that I saw an old woman facing the sun. Her hair was white with age. She had her back towards me and at her side stood an old man wearing a headdress like mine. I had in my hand a fan of feathers and the old woman requested me to give the fan to her. This I promised to do. Then the old woman said, "Look at me, my son, see how fine I look." Then I looked at her and could see her face through her head. Her face was painted with a black circle and a dot on the nose. Then the old man sang four songs. You will remember that in the sun dance I painted the faces of women with black circles and dots. This is why I did it.

One time I had a dream in which a man came to me and said, "My son, what are you doing here?" I explained to him that I was sleeping out in the hope that I might get some kind of power. "Well," said the man, "here is a weasel skin, and you will be able to cure many people with it." This man also gave me a squirrel tail and with these things I cure disorders of the bowels. The way I do this is to tie the squirrel tail on the man's belt, allowing him to wear it four nights.

Now another time I had a dream in which a man appeared to me and said, "I give you my body. You must carve its image in wood and carry it with you. Whenever anyone has a hemorrhage put the image on his body and the hemorrhage will stop." With this I have cured wounds, disorders of the bowels and hemorrhage.

ORIGINS OF RITUALS By this time the reader has become aware that a dream is the origin of all these medicines and that the object is after all but an objective part of a ritual. Hence, it seems best to discuss at some length certain aspects of this phase of culture together with certain beliefs and conceptions pertaining thereto, because the complex rituals in the succeeding sections of this paper will thereby be better understood. The great importance still attached to dreams seems to be but a surviving remnant of what once absorbed almost the entire attention of the leading men, for we read in the journal of Henry that, "If a Piegan dreams something particular, on awakening, he instantly rouses his wife, makes a speech about his dream, and begins to sing, accompanied by this woman, and sometimes all his wives join in chorus. If he dreams of having drunk liquor, he gets up, relates the circumstances, sings for a long time with his women, and then, if not too far from the fort, comes in to have his dream accomplished. During my short stay here I have frequently been awakened by such speeches and songs in the dead of the night."[1]

There are many reasons why such dream experiences as we have considered are desirable to every Blackfoot man, and for that matter, women also, though the women take a far less active part in such activities. Consequently, such dreams are sought. Several individuals have told us in apparent good faith that they never had a dream that could be considered as in any way belonging to this class; one or two of them had sought the experience without success. The usual procedure where such experiences are sought is to go out to some lonely place and fast night and day until the dream comes. A youth is likely to be directed by a man of medicine ex-

---

[1] Henry and Thompson, *New Light on the Early History of the Great Northwest*, N. Y., p. 732.

perience and to be made the object of preliminary ceremonies to propitiate the dream, but he makes the journey alone. While at the chosen place the seeker of dreams or visions is expected to beseech all the things of the sky, earth, and water, to take pity on him. This call is a mournful wail almost like a song, the words being composed at will. The only object used is a filled pipe offered to all the beings addressed and kept in readiness for the manifestation of the dream person previously discussed. It is said that the majority of young men fail in this ordeal as an unreasonable fear usually comes down upon them the first night, causing them to abandon their post. Even old experienced men often find the trial more than they can bear. Men of medicine experience seldom resort to these tortures, as dreams of a satisfactory character are said to come to them in normal sleep. At present, the majority of men seems content to secure their charms and other medicines from those who do have dreams or from the large stock of such available for transfer. On the other hand, every man of consequence is supposed to have one experience in which he acquired a supernatural helper and received a song. Of this, he never speaks definitely, except to an intimate friend to whom he will say, "When I am about to die, you are to paint me and sing this song. Then I may recover." This song is thus secret and never used except in the face of death. We were told by one man that in such an experience as gave a man one of these songs or rituals, the being manifest in the vision announces that he will give his body to the recipient and cause a small object to pass into the body of the recipient, which passes out again at death.

Medicine Bundles

By medicine bundle we mean any object or objects, kept in wrappings when not in use, guarded by the owner according to definite rules and associated with a ritual containing one or more songs. To the Blackfoot this is a definite term denoting an array of such associations, ranging from the simplest war charm to the huge complex beaver bundle. Single or individual ownership is the rule and though the tribe may in a sense have an interest in any large bundle, and relatives may have a property, or investment, relation to it, the fact remains that all the associations treated in this paper are considered by the Blackfoot as examples of rituals of individual ownership.

WEASEL-TAIL SUITS A special decoration of weasel tails for men's shirts and leggings is regarded as a medicine bundle, those suits being transferred and cared for according to a definite ritual. The entire body of the purchaser is painted yellow and a red band marked across the eyes and mouth. A smudge of sweetgrass is made and the suit passed through the smoke. The purchaser puts it on. Then he dances with the seller on three bunches of sage grass, to the northeast, the southeast and the southwest of the fire, moving around to the south and dancing the fourth time at the starting point. This practically ends the ceremony. From four to seven songs may be sung at this time. Formerly, these suits were worn to war and the songs belong to the war group. Drums are used in the ceremony.

According to one informant these suits were primarily for war and though formerly always transferred in accordance with the ritual are now given and sold quite freely. Yet, occasionally, the ceremony is carried out even at the present day.

Headdresses

War-bonnets are spoken of as *saam,* medicine in the Indian sense. Of these, there were two general types, those with horns and those with feathers. The latter are of the familiar Plains type, a row of erect tail feathers around the head with strips of weasel fur hanging down. Those without tails are called "straight-up bonnets" and those with tails "straight-up bonnets with boss ribs." The feathers are tipped and the construction otherwise like that employed among the Dakota and elsewhere. The "horn bonnets" have no tail feathers, but bear a pair of horns and weasel fur fringes. Some of the horns are shaved thin and a specimen in the collection has horns cut from rawhide. One peculiar type has a single horn projecting from the front. The two distinct general types are shown in Piegan drawings.

When a war-bonnet is to be transferred a sweat house is made and the bonnet in its rawhide bag placed on top of it. The hole in this sweat house is round and the dirt taken out of it is placed outside of the house on the west side. Lighter colored dirt is spread around the hole and towards the door. All the songs sung in this sweat house are bull society songs. The ashes from the pipe which is smoked are emptied on the southeast, southwest, northwest, and northeast side of the sweat house and the remainder are put in the bottom of the hole.

Four groups of four songs each are sung, between each of which the door is opened. At the fourth opening of the door curtain, the sweat house ceremony ends. Sweetgrass is used for the smudge in the sweat house.

When the men enter the tipi of the owner of the war-bonnet, he sits down on the right side near the rear, while the purchaser sits on the left side opposite him. The bonnet, still in its leather case, is tied to one of the lodge poles at the rear, over head. The smudge place is circular, about a foot and a half across; the grass is cleared away and lighter dirt spread over the smudge place and a row of buffalo dungs and sage placed on the west side.

While the bonnet owner holds up some sweetgrass to make the smudge, he sings: "Above is powerful. The ground is powerful." Then he places the grass on the live coal and the bonnet, in its leather case, is taken down and placed on a blanket near the smudge place. Then as they sing another song the owner holds the purchaser's hand, and placing it on the bonnet, unties the cords and slowly pulls out the bonnet, stopping four times, while doing so. He sings, "Buffalo I take," and takes the bonnet out of its case. As the bonnet is still in its calico wrappings, another song is sung as follows: "Buffalo I have taken." As he removes the cloth from it, he shakes the bonnet, and the men all cheer the purchaser. In this ceremony four drums are used. Taking a cup of water and some white dirt, he sings the painting song: "The ground is our medicine." He takes some of the white dirt, dips his fingers into the cup of water, sings, "The water is my medicine," and then rubs the paint in his hands, scratches a cross on his painted hand and stamps this three times across his forehead. During the next song he paints the purchaser's face yellow with a red streak across the eyes and then the white cross spots across his forehead which are to represent the dirt on buffalo when they have been rolling in the mud. The wife of the purchaser is painted in the same way as her husband.

The two men and their wives wear buffalo robes with the hair side out, and white cross spots of paint stamped here and there on the robes. In the next song the owner goes through the motions of dancing, holding the bonnet in his hand. He bellows in imitation of a buffalo bull. He holds the bonnet in front of him, to his forehead, each side of his head, at the back of his head, puts it on and bellows, going through motions of hooking. He sings: "Man, I want to hook," and takes off the bonnet. As he goes through running motions with his hands, he sings: "The ground is our medicine." This refers to the buffalo running on the earth. Another song, and he passes the bonnet four times to the smudge place, holds it against the purchaser's left shoulder, his right shoulder, his back, his breast, and then places it on his head. All those in the tipi shout and cheer the purchaser. The two men then make movements as if hooking at each other.

Now the bonnet is given to the wives of the two men who go through the same performances with it as the men. When the women have completed their part in the ceremony, the purchaser puts on the bonnet, and he and the owner rise. Four bunches of sage grass are placed about a foot apart on the north of the fireplace. The purchaser's right foot is passed toward the smudge four times and then placed on the first bunch of sage grass. Then he walks on all four bunches of sage grass. The two men dance in place on the north of the fireplace, all the spectators shouting and cheering them. They then dance successively in the same manner at the east, south, and west of the fireplace and take their places, thus ending the transfer of the war-bonnet.

When the bonnet is not in use it is kept in a cylindrical leather case and hung on a tripod and kept out on the west side of the tipi. A smudge is made for it three times every day. There are many songs for the war-bonnet, mostly war songs.

Some of the taboos connected with the war-bonnet are as follows: A buffalo head must never be broken in the tipi, nor may any part of the head be thrown into the fire. The owner of the bonnet must not allow anyone to pass in front of him while in the tipi. Should anyone do so he would become blind.

It is said that a bonnet was transferred to Big-brave, an informant, who paid a horse for it. Not long after he received it, he wore the bonnet in a battle and through its power escaped many bullets and arrows and was unharmed.

An important point is the general belief that all these types of headdresses were once exclusively the regalia of members of the bull society. The songs used are said to be from the ritual of that organization. It is said that when the society ceased to exist the regalia was still transferred from person to person, the ritual and songs of the society being used. Thus, in a way, the ritual of the order is still in existence. We collected some phonographic records of the songs:—

That above, Man, he hears me.
It is sun.
That below, he hears me.
I want to sit there.

My medicine (bonnet), it is powerful.
Buffalo, he says, on the ground I am looking around for a place to sit.
It is powerful.
It is powerful, where he sits.

The first is the smudge song and a buffalo is supposed to be singing. In the second, the headdress is held up as if it were a buffalo's head, moved about in keeping with the song and then put down.

SHIELDS While shields had some practical value, no doubt, they were nevertheless medicine objects and treated as bundles. Their rituals were composed of songs and certain definite manipulations. The decorations were symbolic and offered a means of classification, first, in that one type had such designs upon the shield itself while others bore them upon a buckskin cover. The belief seems to be that those with a design cover were acquired from other tribes, chiefly the Crow, while those painted directly upon the rawhide were the older and original type acquired before the introduction of horses. Naturally, there is no direct evidence on these points. Of those regarded as Blackfoot in origin the designs represent either the buffalo, the sun, the moon, or stars. There were, perhaps, exceptions to this, but they have not so far come to notice. Feathers and parts of animals were sometimes fastened to appropriate parts of the design.

As with all medicines, shield rituals must be formally transferred. In general, a smudge is made with sweetgrass, the shield passed through the smoke four times, and placed upon a blanket at the rear of the tipi. There the purchaser is painted; usually a yellow ground over the face and hands, which is streaked by drawing the finger tips downward, and a red transverse band across the mouth and the eyes. Special songs are sung at this time and four drums used. The seller then takes up the shield and pretends to be dodging about to avoid blows, as in a fight. The purchaser then steps into the looped carrying strap and draws it up to his neck, the shield hanging on his back, the conventional way of carrying it. The purchaser and seller then dance while the others sing, shout and make all the noise they can. In the dance, they proceed around in the tipi to the right, pausing and dancing at four points: on the south, on each side of the door, and on the north. As a rule, sweat houses are not used. The purchase price is a horse, with blankets, etc.

THE MEDICINE-PIPE Among the more important medicines of the Blackfoot are the sacred pipe bundles. Something more than seventeen of these are distributed among the several reservations and while there are some differences, as will be noted later, the greater number are of one type and may be assumed to have had a common origin. We refer to what may be considered the thunder's pipe, or the ritual handed down by the thunder, a Blood version of which may be found in our collection of myths.

The outer wrapping for these bundles should be the hairy skin of a black bear and next to this a scraped elk hide. Around the middle of the bundle is a broad strip of elkskin. The contents are made up into two bundles which we shall designate as primary and secondary. The former is a long slender poke made of red flannel, both ends open. It contains the decorated stem, or the pipe proper, and a head band of white buffalo skin, with the hair, and an eagle feather to tie on the owner's head. The bundle should always hang so that the mouthpiece of the stem points to the north (in the ceremony, toward the east) and as a guide to this the ends of the poke are tied with different colored cords. The secondary bundle contains a smaller pipestem,[2] an owl, two loons, two white swans, two cranes, a muskrat skin, an otterskin, a rattle, a skin of a fawn, a whistle, and sometimes the skin of a prairie dog. These are wrapped in pieces of gaily colored calico. Tobacco is put into the bird skins. The rattle is kept in a poke of prairie dog skin. Naturally, the contents of this secondary bundle differ somewhat for the various pipes.

When Bear-skin was about twenty years old he purchased a horn bonnet and paid a horse for it. Next he bought a shield, paying a horse, kept it five years, then he bought the Never-sits-down-shield. Some Blood Indians stole the last from its tripod one evening. Next he bought a disc of brass used as a headdress and war medicine for which he gave a horse. Four years afterward he sold it and bought a horse bonnet for which he also paid a horse. Five years later his father died with whose body he placed the horse bonnet. Next he purchased an otter painted-tipi and later a weasel-tail suit. Next he bought a hair-lock suit at whose transfer the sun-offering songs were rendered. Some time after this, his brother-in-law, then upon his death bed, gave him a medicine-pipe but he did not go through the transferring ceremony whence the pipe was sold to Three-bears. Then Bear-skin bought the striped painted-tipi which was the last thing he owned. Bear-skin is now about seventy-five years old and says that when a man has once bought many different medicine bundles he is spoken of as a wealthy man although he may in reality be very poor.

When we say that it is one's religious duty to own bundles we have in mind several obligations. For one thing all bundles should

[2] The pipe bowls are not kept in the bundle and the medicine stem is rarely smoked. About the only time it is so used is when the bundle is opened at the sun dance and brought into the enclosure. There it must be lighted with flint and steel by a person who has captured a medicine-pipe from the enemy.

be properly cared for. Though owned by an individual, others are not free to stand idly by and see him shirk the requirements of the ritual. Hence, it follows that competent owners should always be found. As one man or even a few men cannot afford to own all the bundles many must come forward to bear part of the burden. On the other hand, the feeling is that a man owes something to himself. We suppose that in all religions there are definite compensations; anyhow a Blackfoot expects long life, health, and happiness to follow the ownership and proper care of bundles. Thus it becomes a part of his duty to take out insurance, as it were. Even the ex-owner of a bundle is believed to participate forever, though to a less degree, in this insurance against the wrath of the supernatural.

On the social side a man is judged wealthy and resourceful if many important bundles have passed through his hands. It was formerly a custom to call all the married men together for a formal smoke when each in turn announced the bundles he had owned and the amount of property sacrificed. Those having a long list were cheered while those having a short one were ridiculed. There is also something like the recognition of intellectual attainments in the respect accorded those who learn many rituals and show skill in conducting the ceremonies. Thus, it will be said, that A must be well informed and wise because he owned many bundles. Even though one may fall a victim to utter poverty, he may still, if the ex-owner of many bundles, be spoken of as wealthy and powerful.

If A transfers a bundle to B, the latter must give the former presents of horses or other property. There seems to be no fixed price, but B is expected to give as much as A dispensed when he himself secured the bundle. A announces before the people that he gave so many horses, blankets, etc., whence B can ill afford to give less; in fact, it is expected that he give more.[3] Thus, the tendency

---

[3] New-breast, an informant, says that when a bundle owner is about to sell his bundle he calls on a man to transfer it and usually makes arrangements with him to try to procure as much as he can for it. During the ceremony, the transferrer prompts the purchaser as to what he must pay for each song or object in the bundle, the owner keeping silent as to the fees. While the transfer is going on the purchaser is frequently cheered to distract his attention and thus lead him to pay larger fees. As the transferrer is paid for his work by the bundle owner he usually tries to induce the purchaser to buy the bundle, telling him that he can sell it some day. Some, of course,

would be to increase the expense, a supposition confirmed by our informants for, whereas for example, medicine-pipes formerly required but two or three horses, they now often go to thirty head. This tendency toward increased valuation seems not to be considered by the Blackfoot, but they do regard a bundle as a good investment because of its absolute indestructible nature and its ready convertibility. As stated elsewhere, the bundle may be lost or destroyed without seriously damaging the owner, since he owns the ritual which is immaterial. Further, most bundles can be forced upon another against his will. For example, a pipe owner wishing to convert his bundle into property selects a well-to-do man and forces the transfer, thus making sure of full return on his investment. However, it is not always possible to realize in full for when a man makes a vow to secure a bundle, the owner has no recourse but to accept whatever the transferrer is able to give. Even at other times, the transferee may defy ridicule and give something less than the transferrer received. Again, the bundle may fall into disrepute and be taken for a small return. All these are, however, exceptions. While with us young men are exhorted to open a savings account, among the Blackfoot they are advised to become owners of medicine bundles. Even after transferring a bundle to another, one may be called upon to officiate in its ceremony for which he receives fees, which is an additional source of profit. Since bundles are frequently transferred such returns are almost as sure as annuities. Should a bundle owner die with it in his possession, it will be cared for by some ex-owner and eventually transferred by him to a new owner, the family, or heirs, of the deceased receiving the property given, less a fee for the administrator. Thus, it is clear that the system of bundle ownership and transfer has a recognized economic function, remotely similar to the potlatch, though we see no basis for assuming an historical relation.

The relatives of a bundle purchaser may coöperate in supplying horses and other property. It often happens that a man purchasing

---

gain through the transaction, while others lose. For instance, one man may buy a bundle for six horses, and sell it for ten, while the second purchaser may sell it for only five horses. The idea all through the transfer is to get as much in fees as possible. Although a man may not get as much for a bundle as he paid for it, he cannot take it back.

a bundle is himself poor and able to offer but a single horse. In such cases it is customary for a herald to ride about the camp making a public announcement that so-and-so is about to purchase a bundle and that it is incumbent upon his relatives to bring in horses and other property so that he may make proper return. So far as we could learn, such coöperation was usual, since only a few wealthy head men were able to purchase large and important bundles without such help. Individuals who thus contributed, had no property rights in the bundle nor privileges of any kind, except that when the bundle was again transferred, they expected to receive an equal return for what they contributed.

The following is a typical announcement of a transfer, translated from a text on the transfer of an otter painted-tipi: "Married-men, old-men, and women, take heed! He invites you; he is to receive a medicine; Tail-feathers-coming-over-the-hill is his name. That there yellow painted-tipi you see, is the place. Come to help him out with many things, this here man that is to receive the medicine. Chief Heavy-runner, gather things together. You Fat-roasters (a band) get together all things needed for this transfer, for this is also your chief that is to receive medicine."

Another interesting point is that the transferrer and transferee are often spoken of as father and son. Thus, if A buys a bundle from B, and C leads the transfer ceremony, B is the father, A, the son, and C is called the transferrer. The bundle owner and his wife are always the father and mother, while the purchaser and his wife are always the son and daughter. Even in the case of a bundle owner himself transferring the bundle, he is still the father, though this is seldom the case as a third person must always be called on to lead the transfer.

Should one of the men be single, he must secure a female relative to take the woman's part and in consequence she would be identified with the bundle so long as he owned it. Weasel-tail suits, hair-lock suits, shields and many small bundles do not require a woman, but with these exceptions the owner's wife has a definite place and function. Thus, a transfer ceremony requires at least six persons: the owner and his wife, the prospective owner and his wife, and the conductor of the transfer ceremony and wife. A man is not supposed to transfer his own bundle. The relation of father and son, mother and daughter, reminds one of the adoption feature of the Dakota hunka. On the other hand, the Dakota make this adoption the primary phase of the ceremony, whereas among the Blackfoot, it is an empty form. Among the Omaha, Pawnee, and perhaps other tribes, bundles change hands at the death of their owner and usually pass by inheritance to the nearest of kin. Now, the hereditary feature is wanting among the Blackfoot. It is true that among them a son may receive the bundle of a deceased father but only after the proper transfer ceremony has been performed. The chances are, however, that it will go to a stranger. Any way the universal tendency to transfer all bundles to anyone whatsoever, even though alien, is conclusive evidence of the non-hereditary character of Blackfoot bundle ownership. Finally, we seem to have the transfer conception displacing the usual hereditary form of bundle transmission.

Conventionalized Dandyism. When Bad-old-man, an informant, was young, it was customary for all wealthy young single men to be well dressed. They were waited on a great deal. They usually wore the most expensive clothing, blankets, weasel-tail suits, war-bonnets, and horn bonnets. They were also the owners of shields, the medicine lance, the black-covered pipe, and other similar medicine objects. These were usually purchased as a means to show their wealth. The horses they rode were decorated with bells; their saddle blankets were of panther skin; and their bridles much ornamented. On their bridles was tied a stick with pendant feathers and the horse bonnets were used. These things were not used all the time but whenever a dance was given or the camps moved. Therefore a wealthy young single man was always distinguishable from others.

In the tipi their beds were always placed on the guest side near the rear. When camp was to be broken, these men usually went a short distance away and sat on a butte or hill while the parents took down the tipi, performed other duties, saddled the young man's horse and led it up to where he sat. They ride a short distance to one side of the rest of the people. When they reach camp, they wait until all is ready, when they are asked to come down to their tipis.

They usually carry whips with two lashes, a bone or horn handle, and a beaded wristlet, while some carry an ornamented war club.

These young men used to paint their lips with the white paint after meals to make people believe that they were not great eaters. They of course do not always turn out the greatest war chiefs, for it has often happened that poor young men have gone on the war-path, captured horses, bought fine clothes, and medicine bundles and become leaders among the people.

This is of some interest since in the older literature of the Missouri Area we find occasional mention of these dandies but no where any such clear account as the above.

HERBERT C. DORR

A Ride with the Apaches on a Visit to the Zuñis

[*The following sketch has been prepared from the unpublished Narrative of José Mendivil, who was a captive of the Apaches, and became by adoption one of the tribe, remaining with them seven years.*]

The Apaches are in the habit of making, about once a year, a grand visit to the Zuñi Indians, for the purpose of trade and talk; to hear and tell stories; occasionally, to get wives, or see a sweetheart secretly. This visit to the Zuñis is an event in the Apache calendar—like a journey to some renowned city or great natural wonder—and for it they make much preparation. Their horses are fattened in advance until their coats are glossy and sleek, and they are trained daily, like racers for the racetrack, with the utmost care. Each Indian strives to make the greatest impression on his Zuñi friends, by the quality of his horse, his fleetness and strength, the splendor of his trappings, and the magnificence of his rider, as well as by the value and beauty of the presents he carries with him.

The trappings of a single horse sometimes have the value of hundreds of dollars. If they can obtain them, by theft or purchase, they have the richest Mexican saddles embossed with silver, and sometimes even set with gems, their bridles of the finest wrought leather, resplendent with silver ornaments, and all the adornments which the Mexican, in his luxurious taste, lavishes upon a favorite horse.

A half-dozen horses are sometimes killed in the training, before one is found of sufficient bottom and fleetness to satisfy the fastidious savage. The horse is shod with rawhide, and many extra pairs of shoes are carried along, lest the hoofs of the favorite should become tender before the home-journey. The Indian himself dresses in the best style that his circumstances will permit. He wears the garments of any nation, or of any class of Mexicans or Americans that he may have recently robbed and murdered on the highways of travel. The Mexican garb, with pants open at the sides and garnished with silver bells, pleases him the best; but, if all else fail, a red or gray shirt taken from a murdered soldier will do, in addition to his national costume of paint and the *thchlacah* (waistcloth, worn around the loins), which constitutes their only raiment in warm weather.

Every body in the encampment manifests the greatest interest in the intended expedition. Nothing else is talked about. They no longer speak of the *gente* (the generic term applied to all civilized people, their hereditary enemies); no one goes out to see whether there is a distant cloud of dust—the sign of an immigrant train; all interest is lost in deer, antelopes, wild turkeys, or bears: they talk of Zuñis only—of what presents they shall take, what articles of barter, what presents they probably will get in return, etc. A list of the articles desired is talked over until it is impossible to forget it. An Apache, however, never forgets what his wife, or sister, or sweetheart, and especially his mother, tells him to do. He first remembers and obeys the latter.

There is no duty more binding on the Apache warrior, or more willingly performed, than that of pleasing and providing for his mother. The longest life does not release him from the duty of obedience and respect to her. For her all else must give place; she takes the precedence of all other relations; her wants are paramount to those of self, or wife, or child. If she commands it, even an enemy is spared for the time, though when she is out of sight vengeance again takes its course. These bloody and remorseless savages possess singular virtues, in contrast with their extreme cruelties.

At length, the long-looked-for morning of departure arrives. The day has hardly dawned before the encampment is all awake, and out of its lodges. Old and young, women and children, are standing around, and all talking. The children are playing all sorts of pranks, to catch the last glance of the departing braves: they run foot-races, play leap-frog, stand on their heads. All is mirth and hilarity. All prophesy success and a speedy return. They supply themselves with an abundance of the choicest provisions, such as dried meats, wheaten bread, and sweet-cakes made of flour and sugar. The wheat is of their own raising, as they often grow large crops in various places remote from their dwellings; and it is ground into flour by their women, in the same mode used by the Mexicans. They carry, on this journey, no water or beverage, but only gourd-cups to drink from; also, no one accompanies them a part of the way and then comes back, as in their hunting and marauding expeditions. They take extra horses for presents to their Zuñi friends, and others for barter. They also take with them presents and goods for exchange: Mexican saddles and bridles, finely wrought *lomillos* (*lomillo* is the crouper-cloth or bear-skin attached to the saddle behind), *lariatas* of excellent make, and splendid *serapes Saltilleros* —a kind of blanket, in which are interwoven gold and silver threads, so fine and soft that one can be put in the coat-pocket. These *serapes* are made in the city of Saltillo, Mexico, and bought or stolen by the Apaches in their forays.

They also take with them fine swords and curiously wrought javelins and daggers, which have been stolen from Mexico, or stripped from travelers. In short, all curious or remarkable things, for which they have no use themselves, they carry to their æsthetic friends, the Zuñis, who have boundless tastes for articles of luxury and ornamentation. Finally, having applied the last touches of paint to their faces, until they are so masked that their friends will hardly recognize them, the journey begins; first at a gallop, amid shouts and cheers, and, after they are out of sight, slackening to a slow pace, and making the pilgrimage in an easy, leisurely manner, resting at every spot where there is good grass for their horses.

The distance from the place occupied by the Apaches to the Zuñi villages is about three hundred miles, over a country diversified with mountains, low hills, broad valleys, and some desert spots. One comes suddenly upon an island of trees, in the midst of a plain or valley verdant with waving grass. Again, a narrow belt of cottonwood and willows, winding along for miles, indicates the place of a water-course, which, however, contains running water only during the rainy months of the year. A tuft of green willows and rushes, intermingled with flowering grasses, marks the site of a spring low down on the mountain side. Around these verdant places the painted savages gather, and while one runs to the nearest eminence to keep a lookout against a surprise from some lurking foe, the others tether their horses in the grass, and then throw themselves on the ground for a moment's sleep. The more restless young men practice shooting arrows at small game, or engage in a game of cards with a well-worn pack, saved from the sack of an immigrant's baggage, or purchased in the town of Chihuahua. In this manner the five or six days' journey is passed. When within a few miles of the Zuñi villages, a final halt is made. The horses are fed and rubbed; the gallants paint themselves anew; packs are seen to; presents are talked over and arranged in the most attractive manner. Now comes the full-dress charge of this barbaric cavalcade. Their long, plaited hair streaming in the wind as they gallop in full career toward the entrance to the Zuñi towns; their plumes and gay-colored *serapes,* jingling spurs, and the gaudy trappings of their glistening steeds, with the crowds of Zuñis running to meet them, and shouting their welcome after an absence of a year; the lofty mountains of the Sierra Madre in the near distance; the quaint, immemorial architecture of the Zuñi buildings, and their strange occupants—sole remnant of the ancient races who lived in the golden age of centuries past—all unite in making a panorama, which for natural, scenic splendor is rarely surpassed.

The Apaches now dismount, and mingle with their hereditary friends—friends with whom, for a thousand years, they have never broken faith; and who, in their turn, through the ages have been friendly with the Apaches. Their language being the same, differing only in accent, intonation, and cadence, they understand each other without difficulty. The Zuñi, or Apache, language is very flexible and *suave,* and may at some time have been the court language of the ancient races. It is often as expressive of fine shades of distinction as even the Greek itself. It preserves—in the *adyta* of its wonderful radicals—the traditional duality of the human race: its dual, as well as singular and plural, forms of speech.

Groups of Apaches and Zuñis may now be seen in different places in front of the houses, and in the public places under the trees. Meat is brought, and bread with wild fruits is spread in profusion before the hungry guests. The children gather round to see the painted strangers, and the beautiful horses, with their gaudy trappings. After the eating, which is always in the morning (that being the time the Apaches select for entering the Zuñi city), the packs are opened and presents distributed with grave solemnity to the principal men of the city; for the Zuñis have high and low, rich and poor. They have judges and justices of the peace, as well as a sort of high-court of appeal, in which all questions of equity are settled; they have also policemen and officers like our constables, to arrest offenders and bring them before the judges. To these men of influence presents are given, without any definite expectation of an equivalent. If the Zuñis give presents in return, it is well; if not, the Apaches are equally well satisfied. If the Zuñi presents are more or less in value, it is all the same: no questions are asked, no remarks made either to their friends or to each other.

Next comes the trading. This is carried on with much spirit, and with mutual concessions. When it is over, both parties are satisfied: they never accuse each other of cheating or attempting to cheat, and there is no manifestation of anger on either side. It is not uncommon for them to decide a question of value by a wager. The Apache and the Zuñi agree that the one who can run and jump a longer distance at a single leap, shall have the price he has asked. In such wagers the Apache is almost always the winner, owing to his greater agility from long training, as well as from the difference in modes of life.

It sometimes happens that an Apache becomes stricken with one of the Zuñi beauties. In that case, if the woman is unmarried, unengaged, and willing to marry him, the arrangement of details with the Zuñi chiefs is not impossible. The Apache names the number of horses, or the amount and kind of other goods, he will give for the damsel; and, if the patriarchs are willing, she returns with her husband. If it should afterward happen that she is treated cruelly, or that he neglects her, then by the terms of the contract she is free, and may return unmolested to the home of her ancestors, who receive her back with tenderness and love. It is, however, very rare that a woman ever leaves her Apache husband. Even Mexican female prisoners, who have become wives and mothers, would not accept of liberty, were it offered to them. José Mendivil, who narrates these things, says that he has seen many of them refuse to escape when it was perfectly easy. He has known them, while in the neighborhood of Mexican towns, when all the Indians were away hunting, to refuse to walk into the towns and ask protection, preferring the life of a savage to the affection and affluence of the homes of their girlhood.

When at length the trading, feasting, and perhaps love-making are ended; when the sports and story-telling are finished, then the Indians begin to prepare for their return to their mountain fastnesses. In an instant, all is haste and enthusiasm. Like children, hurrying and talking of their return, they immediately forget every thing but their families waiting for them hundreds of miles away. Slowly and cautiously they had made the outward journey, so as not to weary their horses, in order that they might be fresh and fleet, to excite the admiration of the Zuñis. But now, even the horses seem to know that they are expected to go like the wind on the return career. The Apaches being mounted, a score or more of young Zuñis, on their fleetest horses, escort their friends out of the great gate of their walled town, and also many miles on their homeward way. Not unfrequently horses are exchanged, in token of friendship, in the last moments of parting; but the generous Zuñi will never exchange unless he is quite certain his horse has more speed and bottom than the other, lest his friend should fall behind in that terrible homeward race.

This race soon begins in earnest. There is no more quarter for horse or rider; the three hundred miles must be made in two days and nights. On dash the cavalcade, each far from the other, the wild horses snuffing the clear air of the mountains; on—on—swifter and swifter, increasing their speed constantly. The ruins of Aztec cities and fields seem to fly past like clouds driven by the blast. There are deserts of sand and salt, along the green margin of which these demon-steeds sweep with the clatter and noise of a thousand charging horses. The lips of the Apache are firm-set; his limbs almost encircle his horse; he leans forward nearly to his neck; his hair streams out, like a sheet of darkness, above his painted, swelling shoulders. The eyes of rider and horse are like fire, and their mouths dry as ashes; but no water is allowed to wet their lips until more than a hundred miles have been passed over at this terrible speed. Herds of antelopes see the demon-chase, snuff the air, turn to run, wheel and gaze again, while the whole band of savages have passed like meteors out of sight down some precipitous wall of rocks. In a moment their tossing manes and streaming masses of black braids are seen waving, still at a gallop, as they mount up the opposite cliffs and along the crest of the mountain summit, that seems a dark line drawn against the morning sky. A yell and a wild shout, and down they go into the depths of the forest, whose dim paths only they and the wild beasts have ever known. Streams are passed like dry land, even while the horse and rider are famishing with thirst: they dare not stop and taste, lest their terrible energy for one moment should diminish. On—on—thunder these weird wanderers, looking not to right nor to left, but ever onward, toward the turrets and domes of those distant mountains, in whose shaded vales their swarthy wives and kindred are watching for their return.

And now the savages take a few hours of sleep while their horses are grazing; again they mount, and for a few leagues ride slowly; then is heard a yell and a scream that echo among the hills, and away they dash in full career. The pebbles and stones fly behind them, the plains sweep round them as the horizon around a flying train, and the mountains echo with their screams. Their horses are spotted with foam, like waves in a storm; their nostrils are wide and red as blood: if they should halt now, they could never start again. One more hill, and one more plain, and the curling smoke of their lodge-fires will be seen against the distant sky. But what is that thick cloud of dust coming directly toward them? Higher and higher it rises: now the line of horsemen can be seen, rising and falling like a far-off bark on the waves; nearer the coming horsemen speed, but the home-bound Apaches stop not, nor turn to right or left: they ride, as if to the charge, right into the faces of the approaching band. They had seen and recognized each other long ago; their keen vision discerned the riders as friends when first they rose, a faint black line, on the horizon. They, too, are Apaches from the camp, mounted on fresh horses, and come to meet their friends for fifty miles, well knowing their reckless speed, and that their horses will drop dead if not exchanged at the end of the race. All cast themselves from their panting steeds, as if by word of command; and sooner than it can be told, horses are exchanged, the tired ones released from their loads and driven at speed in advance, while on they go toward the distant smoke in the aisles of the hills. At last appear the well-known paths; and now old men, women, and children are seen grouped among the lodges of the tribe. The braves dash wildly in, and leaping to the ground, stretch themselves upon the sward. Their horses are unladen by willing hands, meat is brought to the famishing men, and water is offered. Then the whole story of the journey is told. They boast their own superiority over the Zuñis in all athletic games, in the speed of their horses, and the utility of their women for getting food and cultivating the fields. This pleases their women, and, if no husband has returned with a Zuñi wife, all are happy.

The presents—of inestimable value to the Indians—are distributed as impartially as possible. Soon may be seen Apache women clad in the shell trinkets and the gaudy sashes of the Zuñis. Savages walk proudly folded in the splendidly colored blankets of the friendly dwellers in the walled towns, although but Indians like themselves. Thus a day or two is passed, and then all return to the usual routine of hunting, eating, starving, feasting, stealing, and passing life away in savage indifference.

BRONISLAW MALINOWSKI
The Kula

The Kula is a form of exchange, of extensive, inter-tribal character; it is carried on by communities inhabiting a wide ring of islands, which form a closed circuit. This circuit joins a number of islands to the North and East of the East end of New Guinea. Along this route, articles of two kinds, and these two kinds only, are constantly travelling in opposite directions. In the direction of the hands of a clock, moves constantly one of these kinds—long necklaces of red shell, called *soulava.* In the opposite direction moves the other kind—bracelets of white shell called *mwali.* Each of these articles, as it travels in its own direction on the closed circuit, meets on its way articles of the other class, and is constantly being exchanged for them. Every movement of the Kula articles, every detail of the transactions is fixed and regulated by a set of traditional rules and conventions, and some acts of the Kula are accompanied by an elaborate magical ritual and public ceremonies.

On every island and in every village, a more or less limited number of men take part in the Kula—that is to say, receive the goods, hold them for a short time, and then pass them on. Therefore every man who is in the Kula, periodically though not regularly, receives one or several *mwali* (arm-shells), or a *soulava* (necklace of red shell discs), and then has to hand it on to one of his partners, from whom he receives the opposite commodity in exchange. Thus no man ever keeps any of the articles for any length of time in his possession. . . .

The Kula is not a surreptitious and precarious form of exchange. It is, quite on the contrary, rooted in myth, backed by traditional law, and surrounded with magical rites. All its main transactions are public and ceremonial, and carried out according to definite rules. It is not done on the spur of the moment, but happens periodically, at dates settled in advance, and it is carried on along definite trade routes, which must lead to fixed trysting places. Sociologically, though transacted between tribes differing in language, culture, and probably even in race, it is based on a fixed and permanent status, on a partnership which binds into couples some thousands of individuals. This partnership is a lifelong relationship, it implies various mutual duties and privileges, and constitutes a type of inter-tribal relationship on an enormous scale. As to the economic mechanism of the transactions, this is based on a specific form of credit, which implies a high degree of mutual trust and commercial honour —and this refers also to the subsidiary, minor trade, which accompanies the Kula proper. Finally, the Kula is not done under stress of any need, since its main aim is to exchange articles which are of no practical use.

From the concise definition of Kula given at the beginning of this chapter, we see that in its final essence, divested of all trappings and accessories, it is a very simple affair, which at first sight might even appear tame and unromantic. After all, it only consists of an exchange, interminably repeated, of two articles intended for ornamentation, but not even used for that to any extent. Yet this simple action—this passing from hand to hand of two meaningless and quite useless objects—has somehow succeeded in becoming the foundation of a big inter-tribal institution, in being associated with ever so many other activities. Myth, magic and tradition have built up around it definite ritual and ceremonial forms, have given it a halo of romance and value in the minds of the natives, have indeed created a passion in their hearts for this simple exchange.

The definition of the Kula must now be amplified, and we must describe one after the other its fundamental characteristics and main rules, so that it may be clearly grasped by what mechanism the mere exchange of two articles results in an institution so vast, complex, and deeply rooted.

First of all, a few words must be said about the two principal objects of exchange, the arm-shells (*mwali*) and the necklaces (*soulava*). The arm-shells are obtained by breaking off the top and the narrow end of a big, cone-shaped shell (*Conus millepunctatus*), and then polishing up the remaining ring. These bracelets are highly coveted by all the Papuo-Melanesians of New Guinea, and they spread even into the pure Papuan district of the Gulf, where the men have put them on on purpose to be photographed.

The use of the small discs of red spondylus shell, out of which the *soulava* are made, is also of a very wide diffusion. There is a manufacturing centre of them in one of the villages in Port Moresby, and also in several places in Eastern New Guinea, notably in Rossell Island, and in the Trobriands. I have said *"use"* on purpose here, because these small beads, each of them a flat, round disc with a hole in the centre, coloured anything from muddy brown to carmine red, are employed in various ways for ornamentation. They are most generally used as part of earrings, made of rings of turtle shell, which are attached to the ear lobe, and from which hang a cluster of the shell discs. These earrings are very much worn, and, especially among the Massim, you see them on the ears of every second man or woman, while others are satisfied with turtle shell alone, unornamented with the shell discs. Another everyday ornament, frequently met with and worn, especially by young girls and boys, consists of a short necklace, just encircling the neck, made of the red spondylus discs, with one or more cowrie shell pendants. These shell discs can be, and often are, used in the make-up of the various classes of the more elaborate ornaments, worn on festive occasions only. Here, however, we are more especially concerned with the very long necklaces, measuring from two to five metres, made of spondylus discs, of which there are two main varieties, one, much the finer, with a big shell pendant, the other made of bigger discs, and with a few cowrie shells or black banana seeds in the centre.

The arm-shells on the one hand, and the long spondylus shell strings on the other, the two main Kula articles, are primarily ornaments. As such, they are used with the most elaborate dancing dress only, and on very festive occasions such as big ceremonial dances, great feasts, and big gatherings, where several villages are represented. Never could they be used as everyday ornaments, nor on occasions of minor importance, such as a small dance in the village, a harvest gathering, a love-making expedition, when facial painting, floral decoration and smaller though not quite everyday ornaments are worn. But even though usable and sometimes used, this is not the main function of these articles. Thus, a chief may have several shell strings in his possession, and a few arm-shells. Supposing that a big dance is held in his or in a neighbouring village, he will not put on his ornaments himself if he goes to assist at it, unless he intends to dance and decorate himself, but any of his relatives, his children or his friends and even vassals, can have the use of them for the asking. If you go to a feast or a dance where there are a number of men wearing such ornaments, and ask any one of them at random to whom it belongs, the chances are that more than half of them will answer that they themselves are not the owners, but that they had the articles lent to them. These objects are not owned in order to be used; the privilege of decorating oneself with them is not the real aim of possession.

Indeed—and this is more significant—by far the greater number of the arm-shells, easily ninety per cent., are of too small a size to be worn even by young boys and girls. A few are so big and valuable that they would not be worn at all, except once in a decade by a very important man on a very festive day. Though all the shell strings can be worn, some of them are again considered too valuable, and are cumbersome for frequent use, and would be worn on very exceptional occasions only.

This negative description leaves us with the questions: why, then, are these objects valued, what purpose do they serve? The full answer to this question will emerge, but an approximate idea must be given at once. As it is always better to approach the unknown through the known, let us consider for a moment whether among ourselves we have not some types of objects which play a similar rôle and which are used and possessed in the same manner. When, after a six years' absence in the South Seas and Australia, I returned to Europe and did my first bit of sight-seeing in Edinburgh Castle, I was shown the Crown jewels. The keeper told many stories of how they were worn by this or that king or queen on such and such occasion, of how some of them had been taken over to London, to the great and just indignation of the whole Scottish nation, how they were restored, and how now everyone can be pleased, since they are safe under lock and key, and no one can touch them. As I was looking at them and thinking how ugly, useless, ungainly, even tawdry they were, I had the feeling that something similar had been told to me of late, and that I had seen many other objects of this sort, which made a similar impression on me.

And then arose before me the vision of a native village on coral soil, and a small, rickety platform temporarily erected under a pandanus thatch, surrounded by a number of brown, naked men, and one of them showing me long, thin red strings, and big, white, worn-out objects, clumsy to sight and greasy to touch. With reverence he also would name them, and tell their history, and by whom and when they were worn, and how they changed hands, and how their temporary possession was a great sign of the importance and glory of the village. The analogy between the European and the Trobriand *vaygu'a* (valuables) must be delimited with more precision. The Crown jewels, in fact, any heirlooms too valuable and too cumbersome to be worn, represent the same type as *vaygu'a* in that they are merely possessed for the sake of possession itself, and the ownership of them with the ensuing renown is the main source of their value. Also both heirlooms and *vaygu'a* are cherished because of the historical sentiment which surrounds them. However ugly, useless, and—according to current standards—valueless an object may be, if it has figured in historical scenes and passed through the hands of historic persons, and is therefore an unfailing vehicle of important sentimental associations, it cannot but be precious to us. This historic sentimentalism, which indeed has a large share in our general interest in studies of past events, exists also in the South Seas. Every really good Kula article has its individual name, round each there is a sort of history and romance in the traditions of the natives. Crown jewels or heirlooms are insignia of rank and symbols of wealth respectively, and in olden days with us, and in New Guinea up till a few years ago, both rank and wealth went together. The main point of difference is that the Kula goods are only in possession for a time, whereas the European treasure must be permanently owned in order to have full value.

The *vaygu'a*—the Kula valuables—in one of their aspects are overgrown objects of use. They are also, however, *ceremonial* objects in the narrow and correct sense of the word.

It must be kept in mind that here we are trying to obtain a clear and vivid idea of what the Kula valuables are to the natives, and not to give a detailed and circumstantial description of them, nor to define them with precision. The comparison with the European heirlooms or Crown jewels was given in order to show that this type of ownership is not entirely a fantastic South Sea custom, untranslatable into our ideas. For—and this is a point I want to stress—the comparison I have made is not based on purely external, superficial similarity. The psychological and sociological forces at work are the same, it is really the same mental attitude which makes us value our heirlooms, and makes the natives in New Guinea value their *vaygu'a.*

The exchange of these two classes of *vaygu'a,* of the arm-shells and the necklaces, constitutes the main act of the Kula. This exchange is not done freely, right and left, as opportunity offers, and where the whim leads. It is subject indeed to strict limitations and regulations. One of these refers to the sociology of the exchange, and entails that Kula transactions can be done only between partners. A man who is in the Kula—for not everyone within its district is entitled to carry it on—has only a limited number of people with whom he does it. This partnership is entered upon in a definite manner, under fulfilment of certain formalities, and it constitutes a life-long relationship. The number of partners a man has varies with his rank and importance. A commoner in the Trobriands would have a few partners only, whereas a chief would number hundreds of them. There is no special social mechanism to limit the partnership of some people and extend that of the others, but a man would naturally know to what number of partners he was entitled by his rank and position. And there would be always the example of his immediate ancestors to guide him. In other tribes, where the distinction of rank is not so pronounced, an old man of standing, or a headman of a hamlet or village would also have hundreds of Kula associates, whereas a man of minor importance would have but few.

Two Kula partners have to *kula* with one another, and exchange other gifts incidentally; they behave as friends, and have a number of mutual duties and obligations, which vary with the distance between their villages and with their reciprocal status. An average man has a few partners near by, as a rule his relations-in-law or his friends, and with these partners, he is generally on very friendly terms. The Kula partnership is one of the special bonds which unite two men into one of the standing relations of mutual exchange of gifts and services so characteristic of these natives. Again, the average man will have one or two chiefs in his or in the neighbouring districts with whom he *kulas*. In such a case, he would be bound to assist and serve them in various ways, and to offer them the pick of his *vaygu'a* when he gets a fresh supply. On the other hand he would expect them to be specially liberal to him.

The overseas partner is, on the other hand, a host, patron and ally in a land of danger and insecurity. Nowadays, though the feeling of danger still persists, and natives never feel safe and comfortable in a strange district, this danger is rather felt as a magical one, and it is more the fear of foreign sorcery that besets them. In olden days, more tangible dangers were apprehended, and the partner was the main guarantee of safety. He also provides with food, gives presents, and his house, though never used to sleep in, is the place in which to foregather while in the village. Thus the Kula partnership provides every man within its ring with a few friends near at hand, and with some friendly allies in the far-away, dangerous, foreign districts. These are the only people with whom he can *kula*, but, of course, amongst all his partners, he is free to choose to which one he will offer which object.

Let us now try to cast a broad glance at the cumulative effects of the rules of partnership. We see that all around the ring of Kula there is a network of relationships, and that naturally the whole forms one interwoven fabric. Men living at hundreds of miles' sailing distance from one another are bound together by direct or intermediate partnership, exchange with each other, know of each other, and on certain occasions meet in a large inter-tribal gathering. Objects given by one, in time reach some very distant indirect partner or other, and not only Kula objects, but various articles of domestic use and minor gifts. It is easy to see that in the long run, not only objects of material culture, but also customs, songs, art motives and general cultural influences travel along the Kula route. It is a vast, inter-tribal net of relationships, a big institution, consisting of thousands of men, all bound together by one common passion for Kula exchange, and secondarily, by many minor ties and interests.

Returning again to the personal aspect of the Kula, let us take a concrete example, that of *an average man* who lives, let us assume, in the village of Sinaketa, an important Kula centre in the Southern Trobriands. He has a few partners, near and far, but they again fall into categories, those who give him arm-shells, and those who give him necklaces. For it is naturally an invariable rule of the Kula that arm-shells and necklaces are never received from the same man, since they must travel in different directions. If one partner gives the arm-shells, and I return to him a necklace, all future operations have to be of the same type. More than that, the nature of the operation between me, the man of Sinaketa, and my partner, is determined by our relative positions with regard to the points of the compass. Thus I, in Sinaketa, would receive from the North and East only arm-shells; from the South and West, necklaces are given to me. If I have a near partner next door to me, if his abode is North or East of mine, he will always be giving me arm-shells and receiving necklaces from me. If, at a later time he were to shift his residence within the village, the old relationship would obtain, but if he became a member of another village community on the other side of me the relationship would be reversed. The partners in villages to the North of Sinaketa, in the district of Luba, Kulumata, or Kiriwina all supply me with arm-shells. These I hand over to my partners in the South, and receive from them necklaces. The South in this case means the southern districts of Boyowa, as well as the Amphletts and Dobu.

Thus every man has to obey definite rules as to the geographical direction of his transactions. At any point in the Kula ring, if we imagine him turned towards the centre of the circle, he receives the arm-shells with his left hand, and the necklaces with his right, and then hands them both on. In other words, he constantly passes the arm-shells from left to right, and the necklaces from right to left.

Applying this rule of personal conduct to the whole Kula ring, we can see at once what the aggregate result is. The sum total of exchanges will not result in an aimless shifting of the two classes of article, in a fortuitous come and go of the arm-shells and necklaces. Two continuous streams will constantly flow on, the one of necklaces following the hands of a clock, and the other, composed of the arm-shells, in the opposite direction. We see thus that it is quite correct to speak of the *circular* exchange of the Kula, of a ring or circuit of moving articles. On this ring, all the villages are placed in a definitely fixed position with regard to one another, so that one is always on either the arm-shell or on the necklace side of the other.

Now we pass to another rule of the Kula, of the greatest importance. As just explained "the arm-shells and shell strings always travel in their own respective directions on the ring, and they are never, under any circumstances, traded back in the wrong direction. Also, they never stop. It seems almost incredible at first, but it is the fact, nevertheless, that no one ever keeps any of the Kula valuables for any length of time. Indeed, in the whole of the Trobriands there are perhaps only one or two specially fine arm-shells and shell-necklaces permanently owned as heirlooms, and these are set apart as a special class, and are once and for all out of the Kula. 'Ownership,' therefore, in Kula, is quite a special economic relation. A man who is in the Kula never keeps any article for longer than, say, a year or two. Even this exposes him to the reproach of being niggardly, and certain districts have the bad reputation of being 'slow' and 'hard' in the Kula. On the other hand, each man has an enormous number of articles passing through his hands during his life time, of which he enjoys a temporary possession, and which he keeps in trust for a time. This possession hardly ever makes him use the articles, and he remains under the obligation soon again to hand them on to one of his partners. But the temporary ownership allows him to draw a great deal of renown, to exhibit his article, to tell how he obtained it, and to plan to whom he is going to give it. And all this forms one of the favourite subjects of tribal conversation and gossip, in which the feats and the glory in Kula of chiefs or commoners are constantly discussed and re-discussed."[1] Thus every article moves in one direction only, never comes back, never permanently stops, and takes as a rule some two to ten years to make the round.

This feature of the Kula is perhaps its most remarkable one, since it creates a new type of ownership, and places the two Kula articles in a class of their own. Here we can return to the comparison drawn between the *vaygu'a* (Kiriwinian valuables) and the European heirlooms. This comparison broke down on one point: in the European objects of this class, permanent ownership, lasting association with the hereditary dignity or rank or with a family, is one of its main features. In this the Kula articles differ from heirlooms, but resemble another type of valued object, that is, trophies, gauges of superiority, sporting cups, objects which are kept for a time only by the winning party, whether a group or an individual. Though held only in trust, only for a period, though never used in any utilitarian way, yet the holders get from them a special type of pleasure by the mere fact of owning them, of being entitled to them. Here again, it is not only a superficial, external resemblance, but very much the same mental attitude, favoured by similar social arrangements. The resemblance goes so far that in the Kula there exists also the element of pride in merit, an element which forms the main ingredient in the pleasure felt by a man or group holding a trophy. Success in Kula is ascribed to special, personal power, due mainly to magic, and men are very proud of it. Again, the whole community glories in a specially fine Kula trophy, obtained by one of its members.

All the rules so far enumerated—looking at them from the individual point of view—limit the social range and the direction of the transactions as well as the duration of ownership of the articles. Looking at them from the point of view of their integral effect, they shape the general outline of the Kula, give it the character of the

[1] This and the following quotations are from the Author's preliminary article on the Kula in *Man*, July, 1920. Article number 51, p. 100.

double-closed circuit. Now a few words must be said about the nature of each individual transaction, in so far as its *commercial technicalities* are concerned. Here very definite rules also obtain.

The main principle underlying the regulations of actual exchange is that the Kula consists in the bestowing of a ceremonial gift, which has to be repaid by an equivalent counter-gift after a lapse of time, be it a few hours or even minutes, though sometimes as much as a year or more may elapse between payments.[2] But it can never be exchanged from hand to hand, with the equivalence between the two objects discussed, bargained about and computed. The decorum of the Kula transaction is strictly kept, and highly valued. The natives sharply distinguish it from barter, which they practise extensively, of which they have a clear idea, and for which they have a settled term—in Kiriwinian: *gimwali*. Often, when criticising an incorrect, too hasty, or indecorous procedure of Kula, they will say: "He conducts his Kula as if it were *gimwali*."

The second very important principle is that the equivalence of the counter-gift is left to the giver, and it cannot be enforced by any kind of coercion. A partner who has received a Kula gift is expected to give back fair and full value, that is, to give as good an arm-shell as the necklace he receives, or vice versa. Again, a very fine article must be replaced by one of equivalent value, and not by several minor ones, though intermediate gifts may be given to mark time before the real repayment takes place.

If the article given as counter-gift is not equivalent, the recipient will be disappointed and angry, but he has no direct means of redress, no means of coercing his partner, or of putting an end to the whole transaction. What then are the forces at work which keep the partners to the terms of the bargain? Here we come up against a very important feature of the native's mental attitude towards wealth and value. The great misconception of attributing to the savage a pure economic nature, might lead us to reason incorrectly

---

[2] In order not to be guilty of inconsistency in using loosely the word "ceremonial" I shall define it briefly. I shall call an action ceremonial, if it is (1) public; (2) carried on under observance of definite formalities; (3) if it has sociological, religious, or magical import, and carries with it obligations.

thus: "The passion of acquiring, the loathing to lose or give away, is the fundamental and most primitive element in man's attitude to wealth. In primitive man, this primitive characteristic will appear in its simplest and purest form. *Grab and never let go* will be the guiding principle of his life." [3] The fundamental error in this reasoning is that it assumes that "primitive man," as represented by the present-day savage, lives, at least in economic matters, untrammelled by conventions and social restrictions. Quite the reverse is the case. Although, like every human being, the Kula native loves to possess and therefore desires to acquire and dreads to lose, the social code of rules, with regard to give and take, by far overrides his natural acquisitive tendency.

This social code, such as we find it among the natives of the Kula is, however, far from weakening the natural desirability of possession; on the contrary, it lays down that to possess is to be great, and that wealth is the indispensable appanage of social rank and attribute of personal virtue. But the important point is that with them to possess is to give—and here the natives differ from us notably. A man who owns a thing is naturally expected to share it, to distribute it, to be its trustee and dispenser. And the higher the rank the greater the obligation. A chief will naturally be expected to give food to any stranger, visitor, even loiterer from another end of the village. He will be expected to share any of the betel-nut or tobacco he has about him. So that a man of rank will have to hide away any surplus of these articles which he wants to preserve for his further use. In the Eastern end of New Guinea a type of large basket, with three layers, manufactured in the Trobriands, was specially popular among people of consequence, because one could hide away one's small treasures in the lower compartments. Thus the main symptom of being powerful is to be wealthy, and of wealth is to be generous. Meanness, indeed, is the most despised vice, and the only thing about which the natives have strong moral views, while generosity is the essence of goodness.

---

[3] This is not a fanciful construction of what an erroneous opinion might be, for I could give actual examples proving that such opinions have been set forth, but as I am not giving here a criticism of existing theories of Primitive Economics, I do not want to overload this chapter with quotations.

This moral injunction and ensuing habit of generosity, superficially observed and misinterpreted, is responsible for another widespread misconception, that of the *primitive communism of savages.* This, quite as much as the diametrically opposed figment of the acquisitive and ruthlessly tenacious native, is definitely erroneous.

Thus the fundamental principle of the natives' moral code in this matter makes a man do his fair share in Kula transaction and the more important he is, the more will he desire to shine by his generosity. *Noblesse oblige* is in reality the social norm regulating their conduct. This does not mean that people are always satisfied, and that there are no squabbles about the transactions, no resentments and even feuds. It is obvious that, however much a man may want to give a good equivalent for the object received, he may not be able to do so. And then, as there is always a keen competition to be the most generous giver, a man who has received less than he gave will not keep his grievance to himself, but will brag about his own generosity and compare it to his partner's meanness; the other resents it, and the quarrel is ready to break out. But it is very important to realise that there is no actual haggling, no tendency to do a man out of his share. The giver is quite as keen as the receiver that the gift should be generous, though for different reasons. Then, of course, there is the important consideration that a man who is fair and generous in the Kula will attract a larger stream to himself than a mean one.

The two main principles, namely, first that the Kula is a gift repaid after an interval of time by a counter-gift, and not a bartering; and second, that the equivalent rests with the giver, and cannot be enforced, nor can there be any haggling or going back on the exchange—these underlie all the transactions. A concrete outline of how they are carried on, will give a sufficient preliminary idea.

"Let us suppose that I, a Sinaketa man, am in possession of a pair of big arm-shells. An overseas expedition from Dobu in the d'Entrecasteaux Archipelago, arrives at my village. Blowing a conch shell, I take my arm-shell pair and I offer it to my overseas partner, with some such words as 'This is a *vaga* (opening gift)—in due time, thou returnest to me a big *soulava* (necklace) for it!' Next year, when I visit my partner's village, he either is in possession of an equivalent necklace, and this he gives to me as *yotile* (return gift), or he has not a necklace good enough to repay my last gift. In this case he will give me a small necklace—avowedly not equivalent to my gift—and he will give it to me as *basi* (intermediary gift). This means that the main gift has to be repaid on a future occasion, and the *basi* is given in token of good faith—but it, in turn, must be repaid by me in the meantime by a gift of small arm-shells. The final gift, which will be given to me to clinch the whole transaction, would then be called *kudu* (clinching gift) in contrast to *basi*."

Although haggling and bargaining are completely ruled out of the Kula, there are customary and regulated ways of bidding for a piece of *vaygu'a* known to be in the possession of one's partner. This is done by the offer of what we shall call solicitary gifts, of which there are several types. "If I, an inhabitant of Sinaketa, happen to be in possession of a pair of arm-shells more than usually good, the fame of it spreads, for it must be remembered that each one of the first-class arm-shells and necklaces has a personal name and a history of its own, and as they circulate around the big ring of the Kula, they are all well known, and their appearance in a given district always creates a sensation. Now, all my partners—whether from overseas or from within the district—compete for the favour of receiving this particular article of mine, and those who are specially keen try to obtain it by giving me *pokala* (offerings) and *kaributu* (solicitary gifts). The former (*pokala*) consist as a rule of pigs, especially fine bananas, and yams or taro; the latter (*kaributu*) are of greater value: the valuable, large axe-blades (called *beku*), or lime spoons of whale bone are given." The further complication in the repayment of these solicitary gifts and a few more technicalities and technical expressions connected herewith will be given later on.

ARTHUR BERNARD DEACON

Pig-Giving at Funerals

The giving and receiving of pigs is a marked characteristic of Malekulan funerals. In the account of the rites following upon the death of Apwil Naandu, four occasions were recorded on which pigs were presented. The first of these was after the bier on which the corpse was lying had been placed on the *nsai vor* in the dancing ground. The pigs then distributed were those which had belonged to the deceased. They were given by his son to certain of the dead man's relatives, including his classificatory brothers and sisters' sons. In this way the majority of a man's property (which consists mainly of pigs) is dissipated after his death. The second pig-presentation took place on the fifth day after the death; it was, more accurately, a series of presentations. First the grandson of the deceased brought two of his grandfather's pigs which were killed by two men of high *Nalawan* rank selected from among the visitors. Then five small pigs were given to the five men of high *Nalawan* rank who had thrown the coco-nuts at the amel, gongs, etc., and handed over to their friends. These pigs were then killed, and portions of the flesh presented to one man of *Nalawan* rank in every village represented at the funeral. To these men also, vegetable food was given to go with the pork. Thirdly, all members of the *Nimangki* grades to which the deceased had belonged received pieces of pig, this transaction being performed without any ceremony.

The third recorded occasion of pig-giving was the ceremony for the conclusion of mourning, when each mourner brought a small pig which he presented to the dead man's son who in return gave a pig of equal value.

The final gift of pigs was that by which the widow dissociated herself from her husband's community by paying to his son a portion of the bride-price which had been given for her.

Other notes on the disposal of the dead in Seniang mention still further exchanges of pigs and food.

Rather curiously the account of Apwil Naandu's funeral omits all mention of what is really the most important pig-presentation of all. The funeral rites may be said to depend essentially upon the killing and giving of one pig; if this pig is not killed the ceremonial connected with the dead man's *Nalawan* and *Nimangki* grades cannot go forward. The animal, which must have belonged to the dead man, is brought up to the gongs. His greatest friend then steps forward with a spear[1] and seizes hold of the rope to which the pig is tied, as though for the moment he were about to kill it. At once, however, he turns to the crowd, looking quickly among it, towards the man who is considered the second-best friend of the deceased. This man then steps out; the first hands him the spear and rope, and moves back away from the proceedings. In the same manner this second man is relieved of the spear and pig by another, the third-best friend of the dead man; the third by a fourth, and so on, along a long line of "diminishing friendship," each man emphasizing his close bond with the deceased by refusing to kill the pig. As the more distant friends are called upon, each successive one comes forward in a more off-hand manner and takes the spear and rope with a greater appearance of reluctance (*sic*), and the ceremonial halts and pauses as men are waited for. At last there appears a man who was not a friend of the deceased and who, therefore, is going to accept the pig. He takes the spear and rope and with the assistance of others in like position with himself he kills the animal. Bananas and yams are then given to him and later he takes both pork and vegetables home to his village, where they are eaten. Should there be more pigs to be disposed of in this way, the same procedure is gone through for each one of them.

The meaning of this ceremony can only be interpreted in the light of the Malekulan conception of friendship. Two men who habitually eat together, sharing a common meal, come to feel that they are united by a very intense bond, by something that may be described almost as love. (Even between those who eat together at such communal meals, as, for instance, that of a *Nimangki* grade, something of the same sentiment is present, but it is less intense.)

---

[1] According to Layard's informant a wooden pig-killer is used on this occasion.

If two men are thus closely bound together, and one of them dies, then the surviving friend is overwhelmed with uncontrollable grief; he is filled with a sense of the hopelessness and futility of all things. *Nin rimrimien nin nirong merevenien imbou len ei gen nimwirien wut imes* ("The meditation of the sorrow is great within him for his friend that is dead"). *Nin rimrimien nimwirien imes et imbou len, inrimrim hur in en nimorot ar resvages malas ve binggen* ("The thinking that his friend is dead is great within him, he meditates on him, and men do not speak unto him as yet"). One expression of this grief and desolation is a repugnance for any acts which are intimately associated with the memory of the intense bond of affection which united him to the deceased. In particular he is loth to eat anything belonging to or in any way connected with his dead friend. Seeing a pig which had belonged to the latter, the survivor thinks: "If he were alive it is we who would eat this pig together; but he is dead now, let those who are his enemies feast on it." One native expressed the attitude by saying that when he looked at the pig he thought "it was the dead man." On the same principle, if a man has two friends who are not friends of each other, then after his death these two men will avoid giving each other any gift in memory of the deceased. Such a gift would rouse anger and anguish in the recipient's bosom, and he might and, indeed, frequently would, shoot the giver, because of the anger which he felt towards him on account of the gift. This general principle acts most intensely where food belonging to the dead man is concerned. Thus the clansmen of the deceased would not, in general, make gifts of yams and other vegetables to his great friends in other clans. Were they to do so, they would be liable to be shot at or poisoned by the other. This comes out very clearly in the annual ceremony of the *Neerew Rahulemp,* when yams are presented in memory of those who have died to some person belonging to a village with which the deceased had not been friendly. If two men who were friends were also friends of a third who was dead, and one of them made the other a gift of a yam or pig in the name of the dead man, the other would sit down and weep bitterly, saying: "Why have you done this? If you were not my friend I would not let it pass, I would shoot you; but you are my friend. Why have you done this?"

The ceremonial connected with the acceptance of the pig, described above, has, when witnessed, all the appearance of spontaneity. Nevertheless, the whole succession, from the greatest friend to the first non-friend of the deceased, is known or at least prepared beforehand. The general method appears to be as follows. The greatest friend of the dead man, who is generally his son, the master of the ceremonies (though sometimes there is a little dispute about the matter), asks the man whom he deems to be the next greatest friend to find some one to eat the dead man's pig. This next best friend does the same to another man, and so the request is passed on. At first each man merely asks his successor formally whether he will take the pig, but after a time the last man commissioned asks his successor genuinely whether he will eat the animal. The man may answer: "No; I am a friend of A's," or he may feel that he is a sufficiently distant friend and say, "All right, I will." If he answers thus, then he seeks out three or four other men, who are also non-friends of the deceased, and asks them to help him eat the pig. It appears that the greatest friend, that is the first of the series, will generally decide how many men are to be asked. If he decides that there shall be ten men, then it is the ninth who must really find someone who will accept the pig. Even the choice of this non-friend is not quite arbitrary, for it seems to be the practice to select as recipient a man belonging to a clan from which you yourself have received such a pig on the death of one of its members.

A further presentation of pigs, which is not a recognized or necessary part of the funeral ceremonies, may take place on the death of any person. It is said that supposing a man of Ndawu were to die in his home village, some man, either a close relative belonging to another clan, or a great friend, might grieve exceedingly and express his grief by coming to Ndawu and presenting the dead man's son with a pig. In return the latter would give him a pig of small value. It may be, however, that this friend or relative is not only sorry at the death, but angry with the people of Ndawu for having allowed his friend to die. Then, when he assumes the ashes of mourning he will take an oath that he will not look upon the face of a man of Ndawu. This estrangement may last for a little while, but in the end the men of Ndawu will consider among themselves, saying: "That man may die soon and we shall not have seen each other; it is good that this avoidance cease." Then, one of them, for instance, the son of the deceased, will take a pig and give it to the man, *neles mbwisnen* ("to see his mourning"), that is to have the permission to see him again. On this occasion the pig given is a well-grown one, as the man is not only sorry but angry. On the other hand, if a man were to die away from home, in a village to which he does not belong and occupied by men of another clan, his son may be very angry with the people of that village for having permitted his father to die. He will then intimate to them that unless they give him a pig he will seek out an opportunity of shooting one of them. Should they agree to give him what he asks he will go to the said village, taking with him an animal having the same degree of tusk-curvature as that which is promised him. This he presents to the men of that village as a contribution towards the pigs which are to be killed and distributed to *Nalawan* representatives of the villages present at the death-feast. At the same time he takes the pig which is being given to him to assuage his anger. Thus neither the son nor the men of the village in which the death took place lose anything, but the indignation which the former felt at the death of his father is satisfied, and, in addition, he gets the credit of having contributed a pig to the funeral ceremonies.

PART 11

Religious Experience

HENRY CALLAWAY

The Initiation of a Diviner

The condition of a man who is about to be an inyanga[1] is this: At first he is apparently robust; but in process of time he begins to be delicate, not having any real disease, but being very delicate. He begins to be particular about food, and abstains from some kinds, and requests his friends not to give him that food, because it makes him ill. He habitually avoids certain kinds of food, choosing what he likes, and he does not eat much of that; and he is continually complaining of pains in different parts of his body. And he tells them that he has dreamt that he was being carried away by a river. He dreams of many things, and his body is muddled [2] and he be-

[1] A diviner.

[2] *Dungeka.—Ukudunga* is to stir up mud in water, so as to make the water turbid, or muddy; and is hence applied by metaphor to confusion or muddling of mind by trouble,—disturbance of a family or a village by contention and quarrelling, and, as above, to general derangement of the body from disease. (Compare Muddle, *Wedgwood's Dictionary of English Etymology*.) From this word we have the compounds *Idungamvzî,* a stirrer up of strife in a village, or Village-muddler; and *Idungandhlu,* a stirrer up of strife in a house, or House-muddler.

comes a house of dreams.[3] And he dreams constantly of many things, and on awaking says to his friends, "My body is muddled to-day; I dreamt many men were killing me; I escaped I know not how. And on waking one part of my body felt different from other parts; it was no longer alike all over." At last the man is very ill, and they go to the diviners to enquire.

The diviners do not at once see that he is about to have a soft head.[4] It is difficult for them to see the truth; they continually talk nonsense, and make false statements, until all the man's cattle are devoured at their command, they saying that the spirit of his people demands cattle, that it may eat food.

So the people readily assent to the diviners' word, thinking that they know. At length all the man's property is expended, he being still ill; and they no longer know what to do, for he has no more cattle, and his friends help him in such things as he needs.

At length an inyanga comes and says that all the others are wrong. He says, "I know that you come here to me because you have been unable to do any thing for the man, and have no longer the heart to believe that any inyanga can help you. But, my friends, I see that my friends, the other izinyanga, have gone astray. They have not eaten impepo.[5] They were not initiated in a proper way. Why have they been mistaken, when the disease is evident? For my part, I tell you the izinyanga have troubled you. The disease does not require to be treated with blood.[6] As for the man, I see nothing else but that he is possessed by the Itongo.[7] There is nothing else. He is

---

[3] *A house of dreams,* meaning that he dreams constantly; that dreams take up their abode with him. Many dreams are supposed to be caused or sent by the Amatongo, but not all.

[4] *A soft head,* that is, impressible. Diviners are said to have *soft* heads.

[5] *Impepo* is of two kinds—white and black.

The *black* is first used as an emetic to remove all badness and causes of dimness from the system.

The *white* is burnt as incense when sacrificing to the Amatongo; izinyanga use it as an emetic to prevent the return of dimness of the inner sight after the use of the black impepo; they also eat it; and place it under their heads at night, that they may have clear, truthful dreams. They believe that by the use of this medicine they are enabled to divine with accuracy. Hence to have "eaten impepo" means to be a trustworthy diviner.

[6] *Treated with blood,* that is, of sacrifices.

[7] *Umhlaba,* i.e., the Itongo.

possessed by an Itongo. Your people[8] move in him. They are divided into two parties; some say, 'No, we do not wish that our child should be injured. We do not wish it.' It is for that reason and no other that he does not get well. If you bar the way against the Itongo, you will be killing him. For he will not be an inyanga; neither will he ever be a man again; he will be what he is now. If he is not ill, he will be delicate, and become a fool, and be unable to understand any thing. I tell you you will kill him by using medicines. Just leave him alone, and look to the end to which the disease points. Do you not see that on the day he has not taken medicine, he just takes a mouthful of food?[9] Do not give him any more medicines. He will not die of the sickness, for he will have what is good[10] given to him."

So the man may be ill two years without getting better; perhaps even longer than that. He may leave the house for a few days, and the people begin to think he will get well. But no, he is confined to the house again. This continues until his hair falls off. And his body is dry and scurfy; and he does not like to anoint himself. People wonder at the progress of the disease. But his head begins to give signs of what is about to happen. He shows that he is about to be a diviner by yawning again and again, and by sneezing again and again. And men say, "No! Truly it seems as though this man was about to be possessed by a spirit." This is also apparent from his being very fond of snuff; not allowing any long time to pass without taking some. And people begin to see that he has had what is good given to him.

After that he is ill; he has slight convulsions, and has water poured on him, and they cease for a time. He habitually sheds tears, at first slight, and at last he weeps aloud, and in the middle of the night, when the people are asleep, he is heard making a noise, and wakes the people by singing; he has composed a song, and men and women awake and go to sing in concert with him.

---

[8] *Your people move in him,* that is, the Amatongo. Or, he is possessed by your people.

[9] When he takes medicines, he eats nothing, and is worse than usual. When he leaves off medicines he is better, and takes a little food.

[10] *What is good,* viz., the power to divine.

In this state of things they daily expect his death,[11] he is now but skin and bones, and they think that to-morrow's sun will not leave him alive. The people wonder when they hear him singing, and they strike their hands in concert. They then begin to take courage, saying, "Yes; now we see that it is the head."[12]

Therefore whilst he is undergoing this initiation the people of the village are troubled by want of sleep; for a man who is beginning to be an inyanga causes great trouble, for he does not sleep, but works constantly with his brain; his sleep is merely by snatches, and he wakes up singing many songs; and people who are near quit their villages by night when they hear him singing aloud, and go to sing in concert. Perhaps he sings till the morning, no one having slept. The people of the village smite their hands in concert till they are sore. And then he leaps about the house like a frog; and the house becomes too small for him, and he goes out, leaping and singing, and shaking like a reed in the water, and dripping with perspiration.

At that time many cattle are eaten. The people encourage his becoming an inyanga; they employ means for making the Itongo white, that it may make his divination very clear. At length another ancient inyanga of celebrity is pointed out to him.[13] At night whilst asleep he is commanded by the Itongo, who says to him, "Go to So-and-so; go to him, and he will churn for you emetic-ubulawo, that you may be an inyanga altogether." Then he is quiet for a few days, having gone to the inyanga to have ubulawo churned for him; and he comes back quite another man, being now cleansed and an inyanga indeed.

And if he is to have familiar spirits, there is continually a voice saying to him, "You will not speak with the people; they will be told by us every thing they come to enquire about." And he continually tells the people his dreams, saying, "There are people[14] who tell me at night that they will speak for themselves to those

---

[11] Lit., It is now seen by the morning, viz., that he is still alive. They retire to rest doubtful whether they shall find him still living at daybreak.

[12] Lit., We see the head, viz., that it is affected in that way which is followed by the power to divine.

[13] That is, by the Itongo in a dream.

[14] *People,* viz., the dead, the Amatongo.

who come to enquire." At last all this turns out to be true; when he has begun to divine, at length his power entirely ceases, and he hears the spirits who speak by whistlings[15] speaking to him, and he answers them as he would answer a man; and he causes them to speak by asking them questions; if he does not understand what they say, they make him understand every thing they see. The familiar spirits do not begin by explaining omens which occur among the people; they begin by speaking with him whose familiars they are, and making him acquainted with what is about to happen, and then he divines for the people.

This then is what I know of familiar spirits and diviners.

If the relatives of the man who has been made ill by the Itongo do not wish him to become a diviner, they call a great doctor to treat him, to lay the spirit, that he may not divine. But although the man no longer divines, he is not well; he continues to be always out of health. This is what I know. But although he no longer divines, as regards wisdom he is like a diviner. For instance, there was Undayeni. His friends did not wish him to become a diviner; they said, "No; we do not wish so fine and powerful a man to become a mere thing which stays at home, and does no work, but only divines." So they laid the spirit. But there still remained in him signs which caused the people to say, "If that man had been a diviner, he would have been a very great man, a first-class diviner."

As to the familiar spirits, it is not one only that speaks; they are very many; and their voices are not alike; one has his voice, and another his; and the voice of the man into whom they enter is different from theirs. He too enquires of them as other people do; and he too seeks divination of them. If they do not speak, he does not know what they will say; he cannot tell those who come for divination what they will be told. No. It is his place to take what those who come to enquire bring, and nothing more. And the man and the familiar spirits ask questions of each other and converse.

When those who come to seek divination salute him, he replies, "O, you have come when I am alone. The spirits departed yesterday. I do not know where they are gone." So the people wait. When

---

[15] The supposed voice of the familiar spirits is always in a shrill, whistling tone; hence they are called *imilozi.*

they come they are heard saluting them, saying, "Good day." They reply, "Good day to you, masters." And the man who lives with them also asks them saying, "Are you coming?" They say they are. It is therefore difficult to understand that it is a deception, when we hear many voices speaking with the man who has familiar spirits, and him too speaking with them.

R. F. FORTUNE

How to Become a Sorcerer

I give below the statements of an important conversation which I had with my mentor, Christopher,[1] after four and a half months of his company. We went to a solitary place—a bare rock slab on the edge of a great cliff, on a day when the New Guinea mainland showed up clearly in the distance. Christopher chanted the names of the spells for making the charmer invisible. I took out my note book, and wrote four names. The fifth I forgot, and I could not get it out of him again.

I asked for details—*Akasaoleole* or *Duntna Moligogona,* which he had sung over rapidly and had come out intending to give me, was to make a man invisible for stealing purposes. I could use it in Sydney and take what I liked from the shops without fear of detection. He had stolen often with it and never been caught—cooked pig and what not.

Then *Sineboganbaura?*—That was to make a man invisible from the flying witches in time of shipwreck.

Then *Mokakasi?*—That was to enable a man to strike and kill a woman with her children in the garden (remaining invisible the while as in the stealing aid). The sorcerer's charm.

And *Sekaikaiawana?*—Like *Mokakasi.*

Here I took down *Akasaoleole* and had it interpreted from the magical language into the normal language of every day speech.

Then we talked idly—and I said:

"*Mokakasi?*—I will write that down."

He gave it me somewhat reluctantly, looking at me strangely.

[1] A pseudonym.

Then after, before I had time to ask for its interpretation, he said: "My friend, I lied; it is not a *logau*—but a *yauboda*." He got up, strung a creeper across the path charmed in spitting on to it—showed me how a woman or a man or child coming along the track would breast it or take it in the stomach and push it to the side—crawled into a bush near by, concealed himself—how he would wait till the person passed by.

He came out, took the creeper in hand, charming briefly as he did so. Then he told me how he would smoke it all day on the smoking shelf and at night crumble it in his hand and burn it on a firestick. He illustrated how meanwhile he would feign sickness, lying contorted and groaning horribly. He said he would eat nothing that day or night—if he did his stomach would get cold—it was necessary that his body should be hot—in the morning the man would be dead, the mourners would come wailing and find him washed, bathed all over, anointed with oil, his face painted and all in best array—so he would eat. But all day and night his closest relatives would think him dying.

He told me how it could be done to a child, or to a pregnant woman, how the child would die within her and how she would die from it.

Then I went over the charm in detail—

crab
inside your earth cave
your throat clogs up
(as the crab clogs up his hole)
your body fat congeals
your foot crouches bends
your seat of the voice rots
your heel gives under you standing
your seat of urine secretion clogs up
your tongue hangs out with spue vomiting
your intestines flow out your anus.

All this in the esoteric language where *lakua,* crab, becomes *mokakasi,* for example.

Then he took the creeper and repeated the formula again for unloosing it after the victim's body had been seen to brush it aside—

your throat (i.e. mind) I roll up
your heart I crumble up
I crumble up striking dead
your throat (seat of mind) I roll up

rolling the creeper compact in his hand. Again he illustrated the smoking of it, the feigned illness and groaning on his part, the burning of the rolled up creeper at night.

I waited silent a while. He said: "Two men I killed so." "For what reason?" I asked.

He told me how his father-in-law, a noted and feared sorcerer, had given him the charm, how a certain man had acted in a vain and proud manner. "He had said: 'That—he does not know *mokakasi*. His father-in-law has not given it him.' So I said: 'Very well —you slight me in proud fashion—later I will kill you.' He beached his canoe at Muria. I twined the *dutu* creeper on the track—charmed it and hid. He brushed it aside—I saw it. I lay feigning sickness all day and night—I did not do so in the village—I remained in the bush. I did not eat. He fell sick. Next morning he was dead."

"And the other man?" I asked.

"That was overseas exchange. He (naming the man) got from my debtor the necklace which my debtor should have given me in return for an armshell I had given him before. I did in like manner to him. Next day he was dead."

"You gave them the poison," I said, using the term for the sorcerer's poisoning tactics.

"That," he said, "is different, another method."

"You combined the methods?" I said.

"No," he said, "the poison is given without magic. That was a child I killed."

"Why?" I said.

"My father told me of the poison, it is *budobudo,* plenty of it grows by the sea. The day after to-morrow we shall go and I shall instruct you in it. *I wanted to try it out.* We draw the sap from it. I took a coco-nut, drank from it, squeezed the sap into it, the remainder, and closed it up. Next day I gave it to the child, saying:

"I have drunk of it, you may drink." She fell ill at mid-day. In the night she died."

"She was of X—— village."

"No, her village is grass and weeds."

"L——," I said, naming his father's village.

"Yes," he said, "my classificatory cross-cousin, father's village sister's daughter. My father poisoned her mother with the *budobudo*. I poisoned the orphan later."

"What was the trouble?" I said.

"She bewitched my father, he felt weak—he killed her and his body grew strong again."

"You chew *mwadi* (ginger)?" he asked.

"No," I said. "Not generally. I have chewed it."

"It sharpens the charm," he said, "we spit with it."

"You combine the charm and the *budobudo,*" I said.

"No," he replied. "If we like we do. It is not necessary. The *budobudo* was different—that was a child. The charm was different —that was two men—in one moon one man; two moons later, the second." (Later) "The Boyowans use *soki*. Here we who know this secret, use *budobudo*."

Christopher gave me some plant food to eat when he returned to the village. Fresh from his revelations I hesitated just one second before eating, although the food came from his wife's pot. He noticed it, for his eyes bulged with a queer expression. He was wondering, as I was, how far we really trusted each other.

The fear of being poisoned dominates native life. Food or tobacco is not accepted except within a small circle. The woman of the house when cooking does not leave the pot and go away for as long as a half minute even. The antithesis "The Boyowans (Trobriands) use *soki;* here we who know the secret use *budobudo*" was merely an expression of the moment. For at a later time Christopher told me that he had caught a *soki* fish, and had it now concealed in a private hiding place in the bush. It is a globe fish with a gall which contains a swift and fatal poison. Despite the fear of accepting food or drink, poisoned, from false friends, mistakes are sometimes made.

WILLIAM MARINER
Consultation of the Oracle

Pangaimotoo is not more than three quarters of a mile distant from the island of Tonga, separated from it only by a long narrow reef. As soon as they landed, they sat down to eat, not having taken any refreshment since morning, with the exception of some of the men, whose stomachs not being the most delicate, had partaken of some yams and plantains which were found roasting along with the bodies of the dead in the general conflagration at Nioocalofa.

They remained here several days, during which time several canoes were sent to an uninhabited part of Tonga for the purpose of procuring reeds to rebuild the fortress of Nioocalofa; which step was taken by the admonition of the gods, consulted on the occasion through the medium of the priests: and as the invocation of the gods, and inspiration of the priests, are circumstances that will often occur in the course of this work, it will be well to take the present opportunity of describing them.

The night previous to the consultation of the oracle, the chief orders his cooks to kill and prepare a hog, and to procure a basket of yams, and two bunches of ripe plantains. These things being got ready, the next morning they are carried to the place where the priest is, who is sometimes previously apprised of the circumstance, at other times not. The chiefs and matabooles then clothe themselves in mats, and repair thither. If it be at a house, the priest seats himself just within the eaves;[1] if at a distance, on any convenient spot of ground, and the matabooles range themselves on either hand, so as to form a circle, or rather an ellipsis, leaving a considerable space vacant opposite the priest. In this space, at the bottom of the circle, sits the man who prepares the cava, the root being previously chewed by the cooks, attendants, and others, who sit behind him. Behind these again sit the chiefs indiscriminately

[1] Their houses are built somewhat in form of a shed, open all round, and the eaves coming within about four feet of the ground.

among the people, conceiving that such modest demeanour must be acceptable to the gods.

As soon as they are all seated, the priest is considered as inspired, the god being supposed to exist within him from that moment. He remains for a considerable time in silence, with his hands clasped before him, his eyes cast down, and motionless. During this time the victuals are being shared out, and the cava preparing, and the matabooles begin to consult him. Sometimes he answers them, at other times not; in either case he remains as formerly. Frequently he will not utter a word till the repast is finished, and the cava too. When he speaks, he generally begins in a low and very altered tone of voice, which gradually rises to nearly its natural pitch, though sometimes a little above it. All that he says is supposed to be the declaration of the god, and he accordingly speaks in the first person as if he were the god. All this is done generally without any apparent inward emotion or outward agitation; but on some occasions his countenance becomes fierce, and, as it were, inflamed, and his whole frame agitated with inward feeling. He is seized with an universal trembling; the perspiration breaks out on his forehead, and his lips, turning black, are convulsed; at length, tears start in floods from his eyes, his breast heaves with great emotion, and his utterance is choked. These symptoms gradually subside. Before this paroxysm comes on, and after it is over, he often eats as much as four hungry men, under other circumstances, could devour. The fit being now gone off, he remains for some time calm, then takes up a club that is placed by him for the purpose, turns it over and regards it attentively; he then looks up earnestly, now to the right, now to the left, and so on, for several times. At length he suddenly raises the club, and, after a moment's pause, strikes the ground, or the adjacent part of the house, with considerable force. Immediately the god leaves him, and he rises up and retires to the back of the ring among the people. If the company now wish for any more cava, Finow, or the greatest chief present, goes and sits at the head of the ring.

It might be supposed that this violent agitation on the part of the priest is merely an assumed appearance for the purpose of popular deception; but Mr Mariner has no reason at all to think so. There can be little doubt but that the priest, on such occasions, often summons into action the deepest feelings of devotion of which he is susceptible, and by a voluntary act disposes his mind, as much as possible, to be powerfully affected; till at length, what began by volition proceeds by involuntary effort, and the whole mind and body become subjected to the overruling emotion. But there is nothing new in all this. Ancient times, as well as modern, afford numerous instances of this nature; and savage nations, as well as civilized, display ample testimony that false religions, and false notions of religion, act upon some minds with such extraordinary impulses, that they are mistaken for divine inspirations.

It happens in the Tonga Islands, that persons, who are not priests, are often visited by the gods, particularly females, but who are never affected in the manner above described. They are generally low-spirited and thoughtful, as if some heavy misfortune had befallen them. As the symptom increases, they generally shed a profusion of tears; and sometimes swoon away for a few minutes. The height of the paroxysm generally lasts from a quarter to half an hour. These are also called fits of inspiration, and are firmly believed to be visitations from some god who accuses the party of neglect of religious duty, not by an apparent audible warning, but by an inward compunction of conscience. But these things are also common enough in all parts of the world, at home as well as abroad. Some of the natives are such adepts at this sort of mysterious conversation with the divinities, that they can bring on a fit of inspiration whenever they feel their mind at all so disposed. Mr Mariner, indeed, did once witness a rare instance of a man who was disappointed in this particular. Finding himself, as he thought, about to be inspired, some cava was brought to him, (as is usual on such occasions), but, in a little while, he was obliged to acknowledge that the god would not visit; at which all present were greatly surprised, and the cava was taken away again.

These imaginations, however, have sometimes produced very serious consequences. To give an instance. On one occasion a certain chief, a very handsome young man, became inspired, but did not yet know by whom. On a sudden he felt himself exceedingly low-spirited, and shortly afterwards swooned away. When recovered from this, still finding himself very ill, he was taken to the house of a priest,[2] who told the sick chief that it was a woman, mentioning her name, who had died two years before, and was now in Bolotoo,[3] that had inspired him; that she was deeply in love with him, and wished him to die, (which event was to happen in a few days)., that she might have him near her. The chief replied, that he had seen the figure of a female two or three successive nights in his sleep, and had begun to suspect he was inspired by her, though he could not tell who she was. He died two days afterwards. Mr Mariner visited him three or four times, at the house of the priest, and heard the latter foretell his death, and to what he ascribed it.

Now that we are upon this subject, it may not be amiss to mention Finow's son, who at this period of our history was at the Navigator's islands, and used to be inspired by the spirit of Toogoo Ahoo, the late king of Tonga, who, it may be recollected, was assassinated by Finow and Toohó Nuha. When this young chief returned to Hapai, Mr Mariner, who was upon a footing of great friendship with him, one day asked him how he felt himself when the spirit of Toogoo Ahoo visited him; he replied, that he could not well describe his feelings; but the best he could say of it was, that he felt himself all over in a glow of heat, and quite restless and uncomfortable, and did not feel his own personal identity as it were, but seemed to have a mind different from his own natural mind, his thoughts wandering upon strange and unusual subjects, although perfectly sensible of surrounding objects. He next asked him how he knew it was the spirit of Toogoo Ahoo? his answer was, "There's a fool! how can I tell you *how* I knew it; I felt and knew it was so by a kind of consciousness; my *mind* told me that it was Toogoo Ahoo." Finow used occasionally to be inspired by the ghost of Moomooi, a former king of Tonga.

---

[2] It is customary to take sick persons to the house of a priest, that the will of the gods may be known. The priest becomes immediately inspired, and remains almost constantly in that state while the sick person is with him. If he does not get better in two or three days, he is taken to another priest, &c.

[3] Bolotoo is the name they give to their paradise, and is supposed to be an island to the north-westward. The souls of deceased nobles become gods of the second rank in Bolotoo.

ROBERT HENRY CODRINGTON
Mana

The Melanesian mind is entirely possessed by the belief in a supernatural power or influence, called almost universally *mana*.[1] This is what works to effect everything which is beyond the ordinary power of men, outside the common processes of nature; it is present in the atmosphere of life, attaches itself to persons and to things, and is manifested by results which can only be ascribed to its operation. When one has got it he can use it and direct it, but its force may break forth at some new point; the presence of it is ascertained by proof. A man comes by chance upon a stone which takes his fancy; its shape is singular, it is like something, it is certainly not a common stone, there must be *mana* in it. So he argues with himself, and he puts it to the proof; he lays it at the root of a tree to the fruit of which it has a certain resemblance, or he buries it in the ground when he plants his garden; an abundant crop on the tree or in the garden shows that he is right, the stone is *mana*,[2] has that power

[1] Professor Max Müller, in his Hibbert Lectures of 1878, did me the honour of quoting the following words from a letter. "The religion of the Melanesians consists, as far as belief goes, in the persuasion that there is a supernatural power about belonging to the region of the unseen; and, as far as practice goes, in the use of means of getting this power turned to their own benefit. The notion of a Supreme Being is altogether foreign to them, or indeed of any being occupying a very elevated place in their world . . . There is a belief in a force altogether distinct from physical power, which acts in all kinds of ways for good and evil, and which it is of the greatest advantage to possess or control. This is Mana. The word is common I believe to the whole Pacific, and people have tried very hard to describe what it is in different regions. I think I know what our people mean by it, and that meaning seems to me to cover all that I hear about it elsewhere. It is a power or influence, not physical, and in a way supernatural; but it shews itself in physical force, or in any kind of power or excellence which a man possesses. This Mana is not fixed in anything, and can be conveyed in almost anything; but spirits, whether disembodied souls or supernatural beings, have it and can impart it; and it essentially belongs to personal beings to originate it, though it may act through the medium of water, or a stone, or a bone. All Melanesian religion consists, in fact, in getting this Mana for one's self, or getting it used for one's benefit—all religion, that is, as far as religious practices go, prayers and sacrifices.

[2] The word *mana* is both a noun substantive and a verb; a transitive form of the verb, *manag, manahi, manangi,* means to impart *mana,* or to influence with it. An object in which *mana* resides, and a spirit which naturally has *mana,* is said to be *mana,* with the use of the verb; a man has *mana,* but cannot properly be said to be *mana.*

in it. Having that power it is a vehicle to convey *mana* to other stones. In the same way certain forms of words, generally in the form of a song, have power for certain purposes; a charm of words is called a *mana*. But this power, though itself impersonal, is always connected with some person who directs it; all spirits have it, ghosts generally, some men. If a stone is found to have a supernatural power, it is because a spirit has associated itself with it; a dead man's bone has with it *mana,* because the ghost is with the bone; a man may have so close a connexion with a spirit or ghost that he has *mana* in himself also, and can so direct it as to effect what he desires; a charm is powerful because the name of a spirit or ghost expressed in the form of words brings into it the power which the ghost or spirit exercises through it. Thus all conspicuous success is a proof that a man has *mana;* his influence depends on the impression made on the people's mind that he has it; he becomes a chief by virtue of it. Hence a man's power, though political or social in its character, is his *mana;* the word is naturally used in accordance with the native conception of the character of all power and influence as supernatural. If a man has been successful in fighting, it has not been his natural strength of arm, quickness of eye, or readiness of resource that has won success; he has certainly got the *mana* of a spirit or of some deceased warrior to empower him, conveyed in an amulet of a stone round his neck, or a tuft of leaves in his belt, in a tooth hung upon a finger of his bow hand, or in the form of words with which he brings supernatural assistance to his side. If a man's pigs multiply, and his gardens are productive, it is not because he is industrious and looks after his property, but because of the stones full of *mana* for pigs and yams that he possesses. Of course a yam naturally grows when planted, that is well known, but it will not be very large unless *mana* comes into play; a canoe will not be swift unless *mana* be brought to bear upon it, a net will not catch many fish, nor an arrow inflict a mortal wound.

The Melanesians believe in the existence of beings personal, intelligent, full of *mana,* with a certain bodily form which is visible but not fleshly like the bodies of men. These they think to be more or less actively concerned in the affairs of men, and they invoke and otherwise approach them. These may be called spirits; but it is most important to distinguish between spirits who are beings of an order higher than mankind, and the disembodied spirits of men, which have become in the vulgar sense of the word ghosts. From the neglect of this distinction great confusion and misunderstanding arises; and it is much to be desired that missionaries at any rate would carefully observe the distinction. Any personal object of worship among natives in all parts of the world is taken by the European observer to be a spirit or a god, or a devil; but among Melanesians at any rate it is very common to invoke departed relatives and friends, and to use religious rites addressed to them. A man therefore who is approaching with some rite his dead father, whose spirit he believes to be existing and pleased with his pious action, is thought to be worshipping a false god or deceiving spirit, and very probably is told that the being he worships does not exist. The perplexed native hears with one ear that there is no such thing as that departed spirit of a man which he venerates as a ghost but his instructor takes to be a god, and with the other that the soul never dies, and that his own spiritual interests are paramount and eternal. They themselves make a clear distinction between the existing, conscious, powerful, disembodied spirits of the dead, and other spiritual beings that never have been men at all. It is true that the two orders of beings get confused in native language and thought, but their confusion begins at one end and the confusion of their visitors at another; they think so much and constantly of ghosts that they speak of beings who were never men as ghosts; Europeans take the spirits of the lately dead for gods; less educated Europeans call them roundly devils. All Melanesians, as far as my acquaintance with them extends, believe in the existence both of spirits that never were men, and of ghosts which are the disembodied souls of men deceased: to preserve as far as possible this distinction, the supernatural beings that were never in a human body are here called *spirits,* men's spirits that have left the body are called *ghosts*.

WALDEMAR BOGORAS

First Symptoms of a Shamanistic Calling

The shamanistic call begins to manifest itself at an early age, in many cases during the critical period of transition from childhood to youth. It is also the period of rapid and intense growth; and it is well known that many persons of both sexes manifest during this time increased sensitiveness, and that the mind often becomes unbalanced. It is easy to understand that this critical period of human life, which is always full of unexpected changes and developments, is peculiarly adapted to the first implanting of shamanistic inspiration.

Nervous and highly excitable temperaments are most susceptible to the shamanistic call. The shamans among the Chukchee with whom I conversed were as a rule extremely excitable, almost hysterical, and not a few of them were half crazy. Their cunning in the use of deceit in their art closely resembled the cunning of a lunatic.

The Chukchee say that young persons destined to receive shamanistic inspiration may be recognized at a very early age, even in their teens, by the gaze, which, during a conversation, is not turned to the listener, but is fixed on something beyond him. In connection with this, they say that the eyes of a shaman have a look different from that of other people, and they explain it by the assertion that the eyes of the shaman are very bright, which, by the way, gives them the ability to see "spirits" even in the dark. It is certainly a fact that the expression of a shaman is peculiar,—a combination of cunning and shyness; and by this it is often possible to pick him out from among many others.

The Chukchee are well aware of the extreme nervousness of their shamans, and express it by the word nıñı'rkılqin ("he is bashful"). By this word they mean to convey the idea that the shaman is highly sensitive even to the slightest change of the psychic atmosphere surrounding him during his exercises. For instance, the Chukchee shaman is diffident in acting before strangers, especially shortly after his initiation. A shaman of great power will refuse to show his skill when among strangers, and will yield only after much solicitation: even then, as a rule, he will not show all of his power. He is shy of strange people, of a house to which he is unaccustomed, of "alien" drums and charms which are hidden in their bags, and of "spirits" that hover around. The least doubt or sneer makes him break off the performance and retire.

The shamanistic "spirits" are likewise described as "fleeting," meaning that they want to flee before every unusual face or voice. When too many strange visitors come to the shaman, the "spirits" are shy of appearing, and, even when they do come, they are all the time anxious to slip away. Once when I induced a shaman to practise at my house, his "spirits" (of a ventriloquistic kind) for a long time refused to come. When at last they did come, they were heard walking around the house outside and knocking on its walls, as if still undecided whether to enter. When they entered, they kept near to the corners, carefully avoiding too close proximity to those present.

"Ke′let belong to the wilderness," say the shamans, "just as much as any wild animal. This is the reason that they are so fleeting." Ke′let of the animal kind have this shyness to an extreme degree. When coming at the call of the shaman, they sniff and snort, and finally, after some short exercise on the drum, flee back to the freedom of the wilderness. All this, of course, is brought about by ventriloquism. Even the ke′let of diseases, especially those who cannot harm man much,—as, for instance, rheum or cold,—are described as very "fleeting." Thus, in one tale, the rheum, before mustering sufficient courage to enter a human habitation, makes several attempts, and each time goes back overcome by its shyness. When caught on the spot, it manifests the utmost fear, and in abject terms begs for freedom.

The Chukchee generally are highly susceptible to any physical or psychical impressions of a kind to which they are unused; as, for instance, to unfamiliar odors. This is especially the case in regard to diseases; and the saying, "The Chukchee people are 'soft to die' " (nuthiwi′qin), is frequently heard among them. Thus, though they are able to endure excessive hardships, they succumb quickly to any contagious disease brought from civilized countries. This sensitiveness is shared by other native tribes of northeastern Siberia, and even by the Russian creoles, who are just as susceptible to psychic influences of an unusual character; for instance, to warning received in dreams or from strange people, to threats on the part of shamans or high officials, etc. During the last epidemic of measles, a creole in Gishiga lived but one night after having been told by an official, who meant no harm, that in a dream he had seen him die. There have been several instances of suicide among the cossacks and Russianized natives as the result of reproof on the part of officials. In other cases, native guides of Lamut or Yukaghir origin, travelling with parties of Russian officials on exploring expeditions, have, on losing their way in the uninhabited country, run away from fear and despair, and every trace of them thereafter has been lost. Suicides are also frequent among the Chukchee.

It seems to me that Mr. Jochelson has in mind the same high degree of susceptibility when he calls attention to the fact that the young men of the Yukaghir were said in ancient times to be exceedingly bashful, so much so that they would die when a sudden affront was given them, even by their own relatives.[1] The shamans possess this nervous sensitiveness in a still higher degree than other people. This finds expression in the proverb that shamans are even more "soft to die" than ordinary people.

While speaking of this subject, let me add, that the slightest lack of harmony between the acts of the shamans and the mysterious call of their "spirits" brings their life to an end. This is expressed by the Chukchee when they say that "spirits" are very bad-tempered, and punish with immediate death the slightest disobedience of the shaman, and that this is particularly so when the shaman is slow to carry out those orders which are intended to single him out from other people.

On the other hand, apart from the displeasure of his ke'let, a shaman is said to be "resistant to death" and especially "difficult to kill," even when vanquished by enemies. Thus, in a description of a murder which took place in the Anui country in the nineties of

[1] See Jochelson, Yukaghir Materials, Introduction, pp. VI, XIII.

the last century, the native, whose words were written down verbatim, says,—

"With an incantation of theirs they made him sleep. While he was sleeping, they attacked him from both sides. One cut his throat; the other stabbed him in the direction of the heart, the source of life and death. Nevertheless he jumped up. But he had no arms. They were also "knowing people"; and thus they induced him, likewise by incantations, to leave the camp unarmed. If he had had only a small knife, perhaps he would have been able to overpower them. Now, though he (being a shaman) stood up, with what could he fight them, except with his teeth and nails? Thus they stabbed him; but his wounds immediately healed and he was as before. For a very long time they could not kill him. At last they fell upon him from both sides, and, throwing him down, scooped out his eyes, pierced the eyeballs with a knife and flung them far away. Then they cut his body here and there; also the heart they tore away and cut to pieces. All these pieces they buried in the ground in separate places, because they were afraid to bury them together, lest he should revive." [2]

Another account of similar kind says,—

"She [the murderer] came to her neighbor, a woman, who was busy with her fireboard, trying to make a fire. She stabbed her from behind. But the girl continued to work on the fire, because she was a shaman-girl, a woman able to stab herself (in shamanistic performance). Therefore she could not kill her, but only severed the tendons of her arms and legs." [3]

A third account, referring to the small-pox epidemic of 1884 in the country of the western Kolyma, says,—

"Then A′mčê began to think about his son-in-law, because his daughter left him ill in the vacant camp. A′mčê said, 'Let us go and visit him.' He said, 'He is one able to resist death, he is a shaman.' " [4]

The shamanistic call manifests itself in various ways. Sometimes it is an inner voice, which bids the person enter into intercourse with the "spirits." If the person is dilatory in obeying, the calling "spirit" soon appears in some outward, visible shape, and communicates the call in a more explicit way. For instance, Aiñanwa′t says that at one time, after a severe illness, when his soul was ripe

---

[2] See Bogoras, Chukchee Materials, p. 19.
[3] Ibid., p. 32.
[4] Ibid., p. 40.

for inspiration, he saw several "spirits," but did not give much heed to the fulfilment of their orders. Then a "spirit" came to him. He was gaunt, and black of color, and said that he was the "spirit" of reindeer-scab. Aiñanwa't felt himself very much drawn toward that "spirit," and wanted him to stay and become his constant companion. The "spirit" hesitated at first, and then refused to stay. He said, however, "I may consent, if your desire for my company is strong enough,—if you wish me enough to take the drum, to handle it for three days and three nights, and to become a shaman." Aiñanwa't, in his turn, refused, and the "spirit" immediately vanished.[5]

The shamanistic call is also manifested by various omens, such as meeting a certain animal, finding a stone or a shell of peculiar form, etc. Each of these omens has in itself nothing extraordinary, but derives its significance from its mystical recognizance in the mind of the person to whose notice it is brought. This process resembles the finding of amulets; and, indeed, the stone found, or the animal met, becomes the protector and the assistant "spirit" of the person in question.

Young people, as a rule, are exceedly reluctant to obey the call, especially if it involves the adoption of some characteristic device in clothing or in the mode of life. They refuse to take the drum and to call the "spirits," leave the amulets in the field, from very fear,[6] etc.

The parents of young persons "doomed to inspiration" act differently, according to temperament and family conditions. Sometimes they protest against the call coming to their child, and try to induce it to reject the "spirits" and to keep to the ordinary life. This happens mostly in the case of only children, because of the danger pertaining to the shamanistic call, especially in the beginning. The protest of the parents is, however, of no avail, because the rejection of the "spirits" is much more dangerous even than the acceptance of their call. A young man thwarted in his call to in-

[5] Ibid., p. 385.

[6] Compare also the story in Krasheninnikoff, in which it is told that a Koryak found an important amulet on the bank of the river, but left it there from sheer fright. He became very ill, and his illness was ascribed to the anger of the amulet. After a considerable lapse of time he came back to look for the amulet, and at last carried it away with him.

spiration will either sicken and shortly die, or else the "spirits" will induce him to renounce his home and go far away, where he may follow his vocation without hindrance.

On the other hand, it is entirely permissible to abandon shamanistic performances at a more mature age, after several years of practice; and the anger of the "spirits" is not incurred by it. I met several persons who asserted that formerly they had been great shamans, but that now they had given up most of their exercises. As reason for this, they gave illness, age, or simply a decrease of their shamanistic power, which in the course of time manifested itself. One said that because of illness he felt as if his arms and legs were frozen, and that thereafter they did not thaw, so that he was unable to "shake himself" well upon the drum. Another said that he and his "spirits" became tired of each other. Most of the cases, probably, were simply the result of recovery from the nervous condition which had made the persons in question fit subjects for the inspiration. While the shaman is in possession of the inspiration, he must practise, and cannot hide his power. Otherwise it will manifest itself in the form of bloody sweat or in a fit of violent madness similar to epilepsy.

Training of the Shaman

There are parents who wish their child to answer the call. This happens especially in families rich in children, with large herds, and with several tents of their own. Such a family is not inclined to feel anxious about a possible loss of one of its members. On the contrary, they are desirous of having a shaman of their own,—made to order, so to speak,—a special solicitor before the "spirits," and a caretaker in all extraordinary casualties of life.

A shaman by the name of Tei'ñet, in the country near the Wolverene River, told me that, when the call came to him and he did not want to obey, his father gave him the drum and induced him to begin the exercise. After that, he continued to feel "bashful" for several years. On days of ceremonials he even fled from the camp and hid himself, lest his relatives should find him out and bring him back to camp, to show to the assembled people his newly acquired and growing skill.

For men, the preparatory stage of shamanistic inspiration is in most cases very painful, and extends over a long time. The call comes in an abrupt and obscure manner, leaving the young novice in much uncertainty regarding it. He feels "bashful" and frightened; he doubts his own disposition and strength, as has been the case with all seers, from Moses down. Half unconsciously and half against his own will, his whole soul undergoes a strange and painful transformation. This period may last months, and sometimes even years. The young novice, the "newly inspired," loses all interest in the ordinary affairs of life. He ceases to work, eats but little and without relishing the food, ceases to talk to people, and does not even answer their questions. The greater part of his time he spends in sleep.

Some keep to the inner room and go out but rarely. Others wander about in the wilderness, under the pretext of hunting or of keeping watch over the herd, but often without taking along any arms or the lasso of the herdsman. A wanderer like this, however, must be closely watched, otherwise he might lie down on the open tundra and sleep for three or four days, incurring the danger, in winter, of being buried in drifting snow. When coming to himself after such a long sleep, he imagines that he has been out for only a few hours, and generally is not conscious of having slept in the wilderness at all. The accounts of such prolonged sleep are, of course, greatly exaggerated.

The Chukchee, however, sometimes, in case of sickness, fall into a heavy and protracted slumber, which may last many days, with only the necessary interruptions for physical needs, and which may, perhaps, end in death, though this is by no means assured. For instance, two years before my coming to the Anadyr, one Rıke'whi, a Chukchee living at Mariinsky Post, and his wife, both had an attack of grippe, which ravages the country at short intervals. The woman died. The man slept it out for more than two months. During this time he took but little food, mostly dried fish, and very rarely could he have a hot meal prepared for him by sympathetic women among his neighbors. All this was corroborated by the Russian cossacks living at Mariinsky Post, in close proximity to the natives.

The before-mentioned Aiñanwa't also told me that in 1884 he lost his whole family by small-pox, but slept it out himself for two weeks, during which time he conversed with "spirits." It is also believed that the "spirits" communicate with novices during their slumbers, and gradually assert their power over their minds and their whole persons.

The process of gathering inspiration is so painful to young shamans, because of their mental struggle against the call, that they are sometimes said to sweat blood on the forehead and the temples. Afterwards every preparation of a shaman for a performance is considered a sort of repetition of the initiative process: hence it is said that the Chukchee shamans during that time are easily susceptible to hemorrhage and even to bloody sweat. I myself witnessed two cases of bleeding from the nose among Chukchee shamans before their performances. As regards the bloody sweat, I knew of only one case, and even in that I was suspicious that the shaman in question, having an attack of nose-bleed, had happily thought to smear his temples with blood in order to increase our respect for his shamanistic powers. At least, he kept repeating that he was not like the modern shamans, but that he was the equal of the ancient "genuine" shamans, who sweated blood from the strain of their inspiration. He was, however, a typical specimen of a Chukchee shaman,—a very unsteady, excitable nature; and after all, I am not quite sure that he tricked us with his bloody sweat.

The preparatory period is compared by the Chukchee to a long, severe illness; and the acquirement of inspiration, to a recovery. There are cases of young persons who, having suffered for years from lingering illness (usually of a nervous character), at last feel a call to take to shamanistic practice, and by this means overcome the disease. Of course it is difficult to draw the line of demarcation, and all these cases finally come under one and the same class. The preparatory period of inspiration is designated by the Chukchee by a special term, meaning "he gathers shamanistic power" (the verb tewitɪ'ñɪrkɪn and its derivatives). With weaker shamans and with women, the preparatory period is less painful, and the call to inspiration comes mainly in dreams.

To people of more mature age the shamanistic call may come

during some great misfortune, dangerous and protracted illness, sudden loss of family or property, etc. Then the person, having no other resource, turns to the "spirits," and claims their assistance. It is generally considered that in such cases a favorable issue is possible only with the aid of the "spirits": therefore a man who has withstood some extraordinary trial of his life is considered as having within himself the possibilities of a shaman, and he often feels bound to enter into closer relations with the "spirits," lest he incur their displeasure at his negligence and lack of gratitude.

The single means used by the Chukchee shamans, novice or experienced, for communication with "spirits," is the beating of the drum and singing. As said before, the usual family drum is employed with a drum-stick of whalebone, while a wooden drum-stick is used chiefly in ceremonials. Some drums have two whalebone drum-sticks, of which the extra one is supposed to be intended for the use of "spirits," when they approach and want to "shake themselves"; that is, to beat the drum.

The beating of the drum, notwithstanding its seeming simplicity, requires some skill, and the novice must spend considerable time before he can acquire the desired degree of perfection. This has reference especially to the power of endurance of the performer. The same may be said of the singing. The manifestations continue for several hours, during all which time the shaman exercises the most violent activity without scarcely a pause. After the performance he must not show any signs of fatigue, because his is supposed to be sustained by the "spirits"; and, moreover, the greater part of the exercise is asserted to be the work of the "spirits" themselves, either while entering his body, or while outside his body. The degree of endurance required for all this, and the ability to pass quickly from the highest excitement to a state of normal quietude, can, of course, be acquired only by long practice. Indeed, all the shamans I conversed with said that they had to spend a year, or even two years, before sufficient strength of hand, and freedom of voice, were given to them by the "spirits." Some asserted that during all this preparatory time they kept closely to the inner room, taking up the drum several times a day, and beating it as long as their strength would allow.

The only other means of training for inspiration, of which I am aware, is abstention from all fat and rich foods, as well as great moderation in eating. The same strictness is observed ever afterwards in the preparation for each individual performance, in which the shaman tries to abstain wholly from food.

Various tricks performed by the Chukchee shamans, including ventriloquism, have to be learned in the preparatory stage. However, I could obtain no detailed information on this point, since the shamans, of course, asserted that the tricks were done by "spirits," and denied having any hand whatever in proceedings of such a character.

In some cases, evidently, the old men have taught the younger generation, who are said to have received their power from them. The transfer is final, and cannot be revoked. The man who gives a part of his power to another man loses correspondingly, and can hardly recover the loss afterwards. To transfer his power, the older shaman must blow on the eyes or into the mouth of the recipient, or he may stab himself with a knife, with the blade of which, still reeking with his "source of life," he will immediately pierce the body of the recipient. These methods are also supposed to be used by shamans in the treatment of their patients.

ALEXANDRA DAVID-NEEL
Running Lamas

Under the collective term of *lung-gom* Tibetans include a large number of practices which combine mental concentration with various breathing gymnastics and aim at different results either spiritual or physical.

If we accept the belief current among the Lamaists we ought to find the key to thaumaturgy in that curious training. Keen investigations do not, however, lead to extraordinary enthusiasm for the result obtained by those who have practised it, seeking to acquire occult powers. Nevertheless, it would also be an error to deny that some genuine phenomena are produced by the adepts of *lung-gom.*

Though the effects ascribed to *lung-gom* training vary considerably, the term *lung-gom* is especially used for a kind of training which is said to develop uncommon nimbleness and especially enables its adepts to take extraordinarily long tramps with amazing rapidity.

Belief in such a training and its efficacy has existed for many years in Tibet, and men who travelled with supernormal rapidity are mentioned in many traditions.

We read in Milarespa's biography that at the house of the lama who taught him black magic there lived a *trapa* who was fleeter than a horse. Milarespa boasts of similar powers and says that he once crossed in a few days, a distance which, before his training, had taken him more than a month. He ascribes his gift to the clever control of "internal air."

However, it should be explained that the feat expected from the *lung-gom-pa* is one of wonderful endurance rather than of momentary extreme fleetness. In this case, the performance does not consist in racing at full speed over a short distance as is done in our sporting matches, but of tramping at a rapid pace and without stopping during several successive days and nights.

Beside having gathered information about the methods used in training *lung-gom-pas,* I have been lucky enough to catch a glimpse of three adepts. In this I was extremely fortunate as, though a rather large number of monks endeavour to practise some kind of *lung-gom* exercises, there is no doubt that very few acquire the desired result, and in fact true *lung-gom-pas* must be very rare.

I met the first *lung-gom-pa* in the Chang thang[1] of Northern Tibet.

Towards the end of the afternoon, Yongden, our servants and I were riding leisurely across a wide tableland, when I noticed, far away in front of us, a moving black spot which my field-glasses showed to be a man. I felt astonished. Meetings are not frequent in

[1] An immense wild grassy region at a high level, inhabited only by a few tribes of nomad herdsmen living in tents. Literally, *chang thang* means "northern plain," but this term is used to designate any large track of wild land, similar to the solitudes of Northern Tibet.

that region, for the last ten days we had not seen a human being. Moreover, men on foot and alone do not, as a rule, wander in these immense solitudes. Who could the strange traveller be?

One of my servants suggested that he might belong to a trader's caravan which had been attacked by robbers and disbanded. Perhaps, having fled for life at night or otherwise escaped, he was now lost in the desert. That seemed possible. If such was really the case, I would take the lone man with us to some cowherd's encampment or wherever he might wish to go if not far out of our route.

But as I continued to observe him through the glasses, I noticed that the man proceeded at an unusual gait and, especially, with an extraordinary swiftness. Though, with the naked eyes, my men could hardly see anything but a black speck moving over the grassy ground, they too were not long in remarking the quickness of its advance. I handed them the glasses and one of them, having observed the traveller for a while, muttered:

"Lama lung-gom-pa chig da." [2] (It looks like a lama *lung-gom-pa.*)

These words *"lama lung-gom-pa"* at once awakened my interest. I had heard a great deal about the feats performed by such men and was acquainted with the theory of the training. I had, even, a certain experience of the practice, but I had never seen an adept of *lung-gom* actually accomplishing one of these prodigious tramps which are so much talked about in Tibet. Was I to be lucky enough to witness such a sight?

The man continued to advance towards us and his curious speed became more and more evident. What was to be done if he really was a *lung-gom-pa?* I wanted to observe him at close quarters, I also wished to have a talk with him, to put him some questions, to photograph him. . . . I wanted many things. But at the very first words I said about it, the man who had recognized him as a lama *lung-gom-pa* exclaimed:

"Your Reverence will not stop the lama, nor speak to him. This would certainly kill him. These lamas when travelling must not break their meditation. The god who is in them escapes if they cease

[2] Written: *blama rlung sgom pa chig hdrah.* (It is like a lama *lung-gom-pa.*)

to repeat the *ngags,* and when thus leaving them before the proper time, he shakes them so hard that they die."

Put in that way, the warning seemed to express pure superstition. Nevertheless it was not to be altogether disregarded. From what I knew of the "technique" of the phenomena, the man walked in a kind of trance. Consequently, a sudden awakening, though I doubt if it could cause death, would certainly painfully disturb the nerves of the runner. To what extent that shock would harm him I could not guess and I did not want to make the lama the object of a more or less cruel experiment. Other reasons also forbade me to gratify my curiosity. Tibetans had accepted me as a lady-lama, they knew that I was a professed Buddhist and could not guess the difference existing between my philosophic conception of the Buddha's doctrine and lamaist Buddhism. Common Tibetan folk completely ignore the fact that the term Buddhism includes a number of sects and views. Sc, in order to enjoy the confidence, respect and intimacy which my religious garb brought me, I was compelled to behave in close accordance with Tibetan customs, especially with religious ones. This was a serious hindrance, and often deprived my observations of a great part of their scientific interest, but it was the unavoidable price I had to pay for being admitted on ground still much more jealously guarded than the material territory of Tibet. This time, again, I had to repress my desire for full investigation and remain satisfied with the sight of the uncommon traveller.

By that time he had nearly reached us; I could clearly see his perfectly calm impassive face and wide-open eyes with their gaze fixed on some invisible far-distant object situated somewhere high up in space. The man did not run. He seemed to lift himself from the ground, proceeding by leaps. It looked as if he had been endowed with the elasticity of a ball and rebounded each time his feet touched the ground. His steps had the regularity of a pendulum. He wore the usual monastic robe and toga, both rather ragged. His left hand gripped a fold of the toga and was half hidden under the cloth. The right held a *phurba* (magic dagger). His right arm moved slightly at each step as if leaning on a stick, just as though the *phurba,* whose pointed extremity was far above the ground, had touched it and were actually a support.

My servants dismounted and bowed their heads to the ground as the lama passed before us, but he went his way apparently unaware of our presence.

I thought I had done enough to comply with local customs by suppressing my desire to stop the traveller. I already began to vaguely regret it and thought that at any rate I would see some more of the affair. I ordered the servants to remount their beasts at once and follow the lama. He had already covered a good distance; but without trying to overtake him, we did not let that distance increase and, with the glasses as well as with our naked eyes, my son and I looked continually at the *lung-gom-pa.*

It was no longer possible to distinguish his face, but we could still see the amazing regularity of his springy steps. We followed him for about two miles and then he left the track, climbed a steep slope and disappeared in the mountain range that edged the steppe. Riders could not follow that way and our observations came to an end. We could only turn back and continue our journey.

I wondered if the lama had, or had not, noticed that we were following him. Of course, though we were a good distance behind him, anyone in a normal state would have been aware of the presence of a troop of six riders. But, as I said, the traveller seemed to be in a trance and I could not therefore tell whether he was only pretending not to have seen us and climbed the hill to escape our inquisitive looks, or if he really did not know that he was being followed, and merely went in that direction because it was his way.

On the morning of the fourth day after we had met the *lung-gom-pa,* we reached the territory called Thebgyai, where there are a number of scattered *dokpas*[3] encampments. I did not fail to relate to the herdsmen how we had approached a lama *lung-gom-pa* as we joined the track that led to their pasture ground. Now some of the men had seen the traveller when gathering their cattle together at sunset the day before we had met him ourselves. From that information I made a rough reckoning. Taking into account the ap-

[3] *Dokpas,* literally "men of the solitudes," herdsmen.

proximate number of hours we had actually travelled each day at the usual speed of our beasts—leaving out the time spent camping and resting—I came to the conclusion that in order to reach the place where we met him, the man, after he had passed near the *dokpas,* must have tramped the whole night and next day, without stopping, at about the same speed as he was going when we saw him.

To walk for twenty-four hours consecutively cannot be considered as a record by the hillmen of Tibet who are wonderful walkers. Lama Yongden and I, during our journey from China to Lhasa, have sometimes tramped for fully nineteen hours, without stopping or refreshing ourselves in any way. One of these marches included the crossing of the high Deo pass, knee deep in the snow. However, our slow pace could not in any way be compared to that of the leaping *lung-gom-pa,* who seemed as if carried on wings.

JAMES MOONEY

An Indian Messiah

There are hours long departed which memory brings
Like blossoms of Eden to twine round the heart.

Moore.

The wise men tell us that the world is growing happier—that we live longer than did our fathers, have more of comfort and less of toil, fewer wars and discords, and higher hopes and aspirations. So say the wise men; but deep in our own hearts we know they are wrong. For were not we, too, born in Arcadia, and have we not—each one of us—in that May of life when the world was young, started out lightly and airily along the path that led through green meadows to the blue mountains on the distant horizon, beyond which lay the great world we were to conquer? And though others dropped behind, have we not gone on through morning brightness and noonday heat, with eyes always steadily forward, until the fresh grass began to be parched and withered, and the way grew hard and stony, and the blue mountains resolved into gray rocks and thorny cliffs? And when at last we reached the toilsome summits, we found the glory that had lured us onward was only the sunset glow that fades into darkness while we look, and leaves us at the very goal to sink down, tired in body and sick at heart, with strength and courage gone, to close our eyes and dream again, not of the fame and fortune that were to be ours, but only of the old-time happiness that we have left so far behind.

As with men, so is it with nations. The lost paradise is the world's dreamland of youth. What tribe or people has not had its golden age, before Pandora's box was loosed, when women were nymphs and dryads and men were gods and heroes? And when the race lies crushed and groaning beneath an alien yoke, how natural is the dream of a redeemer, an Arthur, who shall return from exile or awake from some long sleep to drive out the usurper and win back for his people what they have lost. The hope becomes a faith and the faith becomes the creed of priests and prophets, until the hero is a god and the dream a religion, looking to some great miracle of nature for its culmination and accomplishment. The doctrines of the Hindu avatar, the Hebrew Messiah, the Christian millennium, and the Hesûnanin of the Indian Ghost dance are essentially the same, and have their origin in a hope and longing common to all humanity.

Probably every Indian tribe, north and south, had its early hero god, the great doer or teacher of all first things, from the Iuskeha and Manabozho of the rude Iroquoian and Algonquian to the Quetzalcoatl, the Bochica, and the Viracocha of the more cultivated Aztecs, Muyscas, and Quichuas of the milder southland. Among the roving tribes of the north this hero is hardly more than an expert magician, frequently degraded to the level of a common trickster, who, after ridding the world of giants and monsters, and teaching his people a few simple arts, retires to the upper world to rest and smoke until some urgent necessity again requires his presence below. Under softer southern skies the myth takes more poetic form and the hero becomes a person of dignified presence, a father and teacher of his children, a very Christ, worthy of all love and reverence, who gathers together the wandering nomads and leads them to their destined country, where he instructs them in agriculture, house building, and the art of government, regulates authority, and inculcates peaceful modes of life. "Under him, the earth teemed with fruits and flowers without the pains of culture. An ear of Indian corn was as much as a single man could carry. The cotton, as it grew, took of its own accord the rich dyes of human art. The air was filled with intoxicating perfumes and the sweet melody of birds. In short, these were the halcyon days, which find a place in the mythic systems of so many nations in the Old World. It was the golden age of Anahuac." When at last his work is well accomplished, he bids farewell to his sorrowing subjects, whom he consoles with the sacred promise that he will one day return and resume his kingdom, steps into his magic boat by the seashore, and sails away out of their sight to the distant land of sunrise.

The great revolt of the Pueblo Indians in August, 1680, was one of the first determined efforts made by the natives on the northern continent to throw off the yoke of a foreign oppressor. The Pueblo tribes along the Rio Grande and farther to the west, a gentle, peaceful race, had early welcomed the coming of the Spaniards, with their soldiers and priests, as friends who would protect them against the wild marauding tribes about them and teach them the mysteries of a greater "medicine" than belonged to their own kachinas. The hope soon faded into bitter disappointment. The soldiers, while rough and overbearing toward their brown-skin allies, were yet unable to protect them from the inroads of their enemies. The priests prohibited their dances and simple amusements, yet all their ringing of bells and chanting of hymns availed not to bring more rain on the crops or to turn aside the vengeful Apache. "What have we gained by all this?" said the Pueblos one to another; "not peace and not happiness, for these new rulers will not protect us from our enemies, and take from us all the enjoyments we once knew."

The pear was ripe. Popé, a medicine-man of the Tewa, had come back from a pilgrimage to the far north, where he claimed to have visited the magic lagoon of Shipapu, whence his people traced their origin and to which the souls of their dead returned after leaving this life. By these ancestral spirits he had been endowed with occult powers and commanded to go back and rouse the Pueblos to concerted effort for deliverance from the foreign yoke of the strangers.

Wonderful beings were these spirit messengers. Swift as light and impalpable as thought, they passed under the earth from the magic lake to the secret subterranean chamber of the oracle and stood before him as shapes of fire, and spoke, telling him to prepare the strings of yucca knots and send them with the message to all the Pueblos far and near, so that in every village, the chiefs might untie one knot from the string each day, and know when they came to the last knot that then was the time to strike.

From the Pecos, across the Rio Grande to Zuñi and the far-distant Hopi mesas, every Pueblo village accepted the yucca string and began secret preparation for the rising. The time chosen was the new moon of August, 1680, but, through a partial discovery of the plot, the explosion was precipitated on the 10th. So sudden and complete was the surprise that many Spaniards in the Pueblo country, priests, soldiers, and civilians, were killed, and the survivors, after holding out for a time under Governor Otermin at Santa Fé, fled to El Paso, and in October there remained not a single Spaniard in all New Mexico.

Wovoka the Messiah

> When the sun died, I went up to heaven and saw God and all the people who had died a long time ago. God told me to come back and tell my people they must be good and love one another, and not fight, or steal, or lie. He gave me this dance to give to my people.—*Wóvoka.*

When Tävibo, the prophet of Mason valley, died, about 1870, he left a son named Wovoka, "The Cutter," about 14 years of age. The prophetic claims and teachings of the father, the reverence with which he was regarded by the people, and the mysterious ceremonies which were doubtless of frequent performance in the little tulé wikiup at home must have made early and deep impression on the mind of the boy, who seems to have been by nature of a solitary and contemplative disposition, one of those born to see visions and hear still voices.

The physical environment was favorable to the development of such a character. His native valley, from which he has never wandered, is a narrow strip of level sage prairie some 30 miles in length, walled in by the giant sierras, their sides torn and gashed by volcanic convulsions and dark with gloomy forests of pine, their towering summits white with everlasting snows, and roofed over by a cloudless sky whose blue infinitude the mind instinctively seeks to penetrate to far-off worlds beyond. Away to the south the view is closed in by the sacred mountain of the Paiute, where their Father gave them the first fire and taught them their few simple arts before leaving for his home in the upper regions of the Sun-land. Like the valley of Rasselas, it seems set apart from the great world to be the home of a dreamer.

The greater portion of Nevada is an arid desert of rugged mountains and alkali plains, the little available land being confined to narrow mountain valleys and the borders of a few large lakes. These tracts are occupied by scattered ranchmen engaged in stock raising, and as the white population is sparse, Indian labor is largely utilized, the Paiute being very good workers. The causes which in other parts of the country have conspired to sweep the Indian from the path of the white man seem inoperative here, where the aboriginal proprietors are regarded rather as peons under the protection of the dominant race, and are allowed to set up their small camps of tulé lodges in convenient out-of-the-way places, where they spend the autumn and winter in hunting, fishing, and gathering seeds and piñon nuts, working at fair wages on ranches through spring and summer. In this way young Wovoka became attached to the family of a ranchman in Mason valley, named David Wilson, who took an interest in him and bestowed on him the name of Jack Wilson, by which he is commonly known among the whites. From his association with this family he gained some knowledge of English, together with a confused idea of the white man's theology. On growing up he married, and still continued to work for Mr Wilson, earning a reputation for industry and reliability, but attracting no special notice until nearly 30 years of age, when he announced the revelation that has made him famous among the tribes of the west.

Following are the various forms of his name which I have noticed: Wo'voka, or Wü'voka, which I have provisionally rendered "Cutter," derived from a verb signifying "to cut"; Wevokar, Wopokahte, Kwohitsauq, Cowejo, Koit-tsow, Kvit-Tsow, Quoitze Ow, Jack Wilson, Jackson Wilson, Jack Winson, John Johnson. He has also been confounded with Bannock Jim, a Mormon Bannock of Fort Hall reservation, Idaho, and with Johnson Sides, a Paiute living near Reno, Nevada, and bitterly opposed to Wovoka. His father's name, Tävibo, has been given also as Waughzeewaughber. It is not quite certain that the Paiute prophet of 1870 was the father of Wovoka. This is stated to have been the case by one of Captain Lee's informants and by Lieutenant Phister. Wovoka himself says that his father did not preach, but was a "dreamer" with supernatural powers. Certain it is that a similar doctrine was taught by an Indian living in the same valley in Wovoka's boyhood. Possibly the discrepancy might be explained by an unwillingness on the part of the messiah to share his spiritual honors.

In proportion as Wovoka and his doctrines have become subjects of widespread curiosity, so have they become subjects of ignorant misrepresentation and deliberate falsification. Different writers have made him a Paiute, a half-blood, and a Mormon white man. Numberless stories have been told of the origin and character of his mission and the day predicted for its final accomplishment. The most mischievous and persistent of these stories has been that which represents him as preaching a bloody campaign against the whites, whereas his doctrine is one of peace, and he himself is a mild tempered member of a weak and unwarlike tribe. His own good name has been filched from him and he has been made to appear under a dozen different cognomens, including that of his bitterest enemy, Johnson Sides. He has been denounced as an impostor, ridiculed as a lunatic, and laughed at as a pretended Christ, while by the Indians he is revered as a direct messenger from the Other World, and among many of the remote tribes he is believed to be omniscient, to speak all languages, and to be invisible to a white man. We shall give his own story as told by himself, with such additional information as seems to come from authentic sources.

Notwithstanding all that had been said and written by newspaper correspondents about the messiah, not one of them had undertaken to find the man himself and to learn from his own lips what he really taught. It is almost equally certain that none of them had even seen a Ghost dance at close quarters—certainly none of them understood its meaning. The messiah was regarded almost as a myth, something intangible, to be talked about but not to be seen. The first reliable information as to his personality was communicated by the scout, Arthur Chapman, who, under instructions from the War Department, visited the Paiute country in December, 1890, and spent four days at Walker lake and Mason valley, and in the course of an interview with Wovoka obtained from him a detailed statement similar in all essentials to that which I obtained later on.

After having spent seven months in the field, investigating the new religion among the prairie tribes, particularly the Arapaho, and after having examined all the documents bearing on the subject in the files of the Indian Office and War Department, the author left Washington in November, 1891, to find and talk with the messiah and to gather additional material concerning the Ghost dance. At last a shout from our driver brought us all together. He declared that he had heard sounds in front, and after listening a few minutes in painful suspense we saw a shower of sparks go up into the darkness and knew that we had struck the camp. Going back to the wagon, we got in and drove straight across to the spot, where we found three or four little wikiups, in one of which we were told the messiah was awaiting our arrival.

On entering through the low doorway we found ourselves in a circular lodge made of bundles of tulé rushes laid over a framework of poles, after the fashion of the thatched roofs of Europe, and very similar to the grass lodges of the Wichita. The lodge was only about 10 feet in diameter and about 8 feet in height, with sloping sides, and was almost entirely open above, like a cone with the top cut off, as in this part of the country rain or snow is of rare occurrence. As already remarked, the deep snow at the time was something unusual. In the center, built directly on the ground, was a blazing fire of sagebrush, upon which fresh stalks were thrown from time to time, sending up a shower of sparks into the open air. It was by this means that we had been guided to the camp. Sitting or lying around the fire were half a dozen Paiute, including the messiah and his family, consisting of his young wife, a boy about 4 years of age, of whom he seemed very fond, and an infant. It was plain that he was a kind husband and father, which was in keeping with his reputation among the whites for industry and reliability. The only articles in the nature of furniture were a few grass woven bowls and baskets of various sizes and patterns. There were no Indian beds or seats of the kind found in every prairie tipi, no rawhide boxes, no toilet pouches, not even a hole dug in the ground for the fire. Although all wore white men's dress, there were no pots, pans, or other articles of civilized manufacture, now used by even the most primitive prairie tribes, for, strangely enough, although these Paiute are practically farm laborers and tenants of the whites all around them, and earn good wages, they seem to covet nothing of the white man's, but spend their money for dress, small trinkets, and ammunition for hunting, and continue to subsist on seeds, piñon nuts, and small game, lying down at night on the dusty ground in their cramped wikiups, destitute of even the most ordinary conveniences in use among other tribes. It is a curious instance of a people accepting the inevitable while yet resisting innovation.

Wovoka received us cordially and then inquired more particularly as to my purpose in seeking an interview. His uncle entered into a detailed explanation, which stretched out to a preposterous length, owing to a peculiar conversational method of the Paiute. Each statement by the older man was repeated at its close, word for word and sentence by sentence, by the other, with the same monotonous inflection. This done, the first speaker signified by a grunt of approval that it had been correctly repeated, and then proceeded with the next statement, which was duly repeated in like manner. The first time I had heard two old men conversing together in this fashion on the reservation I had supposed they were reciting some sort of Indian litany, and it required several such experiences and some degree of patience to become used to it.

At last he signified that he understood and was satisfied, and then in answer to my questions gave an account of himself and his doctrine, a great part of the interpretation being by Dyer, with whom he seemed to be on intimate terms. He said he was about 35 years of age, fixing the date from a noted battle between the Paiute and the whites near Pyramid lake, in 1860, at which time he said he was about the size of his little boy, who appeared to be of about 4 years. His father, Tävibo, "White Man," was not a preacher, but was a *capita* (from the Spanish *capitan*) or petty chief, and was a dreamer and invulnerable. His own proper name from boyhood was Wovoka or Wüvoka, "The Cutter," but a few years ago he had assumed the name of his paternal grandfather, Kwohitsauq, or "Big Rumbling Belly." After the death of his father he had been taken into the family of a white farmer, David Wilson, who had given him the name of Jack Wilson, by which he is commonly known among the whites. He thus has three distinct names, Wovoka, Kwohitsauq, and Jack Wilson. He stated positively that he was a full-blood, a statement borne out by his appearance. The impression that he is a half-blood may have arisen from the fact that his father's name was "White Man" and that he has a white man's name. His followers, both in his own and in all other tribes, commonly refer to him as "our father." He has never been away from Mason valley and speaks only his own Paiute language, with some little knowledge of English. He is not acquainted with the sign language, which is hardly known west of the mountains.

When about 20 years of age, he married, and continued to work for Mr Wilson. He had given the dance to his people about four years before, but had received his great revelation about two years previously. On this occasion "the sun died" (was eclipsed) and he fell asleep in the daytime and was taken up to the other world. Here he saw God, with all the people who had died long ago engaged in their oldtime sports and occupations, all happy and forever young. It was a pleasant land and full of game. After showing him all, God told him he must go back and tell his people they must be good and love one another, have no quarreling, and live in peace with the whites; that they must work, and not lie or steal; that they must put away all the old practices that savored of war; that if they faithfully obeyed his instructions they would at last be reunited with their friends in this other world, where there would be no more death or sickness or old age. He was then given the dance which he was commanded to bring back to his people. By performing this dance at intervals, for five consecutive days each time, they would secure this happiness to themselves and hasten the event. Finally

God gave him control over the elements so that he could make it rain or snow or be dry at will, and appointed him his deputy to take charge of affairs in the west, while "Governor Harrison" would attend to matters in the east, and he, God, would look after the world above. He then returned to earth and began to preach as he was directed, convincing the people by exercising the wonderful powers that had been given him.

In 1890 Josephus, a Paiute informant, thus described to the scout Chapman the occasion of Wovoka's first inspiration: "About three years ago Jack Wilson took his family and went into the mountains to cut wood for Mr Dave Wilson. One day while at work he heard a great noise which appeared to be above him on the mountain. He laid down his ax and started to go in the direction of the noise, when he fell down dead, and God came and took him to heaven." Afterward on one or two other occasions "God came and took him to heaven again." Wovoka also told Chapman that he had then been preaching to the Indians about three years. In our conversation he said nothing about a mysterious noise, and stated that it was about two years since he had visited heaven and received his great revelation, but that it was about four years since he had first taught the dance to his people. The fact that he has different revelations from time to time would account for the discrepancy of statement.

He disclaimed all responsibility for the ghost shirt which formed so important a part of the dance costume among the Sioux; said that there were no trances in the dance as performed among his people—a statement confirmed by eye-witnesses among the neighboring ranchmen—and earnestly repudiated any idea of hostility toward the whites, asserting that his religion was one of universal peace. When questioned directly, he said he believed it was better for the Indians to follow the white man's road and to adopt the habits of civilization. If appearances are in evidence he is sincere in this, for he was dressed in a good suit of white man's clothing, and works regularly on a ranch, although living in a wikiup. While he repudiated almost everything for which he had been held responsible in the east, he asserted positively that he had been to the spirit world and had been given a revelation and message from God himself, with full control over the elements. From his uncle I learned that Wovoka has five songs for making it rain, the first of which brings on a mist or cloud, the second a snowfall, the third a shower, and the fourth a hard rain or storm, while when he sings the fifth song the weather again becomes clear.

I knew that he was holding something in reserve, as no Indian would unbosom himself on religious matters to a white man with whom he had not had a long and intimate acquaintance. Especially was this true in view of the warlike turn affairs had taken across the mountains. Consequently I accepted his statements with several grains of salt, but on the whole he seemed to be honest in his belief and his supernatural claims, although, like others of the priestly function, he occasionally resorts to cheap trickery to keep up the impression as to his miraculous powers. From some of the reports he is evidently an expert sleight-of-hand performer. He makes no claim to be Christ, the Son of God, as has been so often asserted in print. He does claim to be a prophet who has received a divine revelation. I could not help feeling that he was sincere in his repudiation of a number of the wonderful things attributed to him, for the reason that he insisted so strongly on other things fully as trying to the faith of a white man. He made no argument and advanced no proofs, but said simply that he had been with God, as though the statement no more admitted of controversy than the proposition that 2 and 2 are 4. From Mr J. O. Gregory, formerly employed at the agency, and well acquainted with the prophet, I learned that Wovoka had once requested him to draw up and forward to the President a statement of his supernatural claims, with a proposition that if he could receive a small regular stipend he would take up his residence on the reservation and agree to keep Nevada people informed of all the latest news from heaven and to furnish rain whenever wanted. The letter was never forwarded.

From a neighboring ranchman, who knew Wovoka well and sometimes employed him in the working season, I obtained a statement which seems to explain the whole matter. It appears that a short time before the prophet began to preach he was stricken down by a severe fever, during which illness the ranchman frequently visited and ministered to him. While he was still sick there occurred an eclipse of the sun, a phenomenon which always excites great alarm among primitive peoples.

The Doctrine of the Ghost Dance

You must not fight. Do no harm to anyone. Do right always.—*Wovoka.*

The great underlying principle of the Ghost dance doctrine is that the time will come when the whole Indian race, living and dead, will be reunited upon a regenerated earth, to live a life of aboriginal happiness, forever free from death, disease, and misery. On this foundation each tribe has built a structure from its own mythology, and each apostle and believer has filled in the details according to his own mental capacity or ideas of happiness, with such additions as come to him from the trance. Some changes, also, have undoubtedly resulted from the transmission of the doctrine through the imperfect medium of the sign language. The differences of interpretation are precisely such as we find in Christianity, with its hundreds of sects and innumerable shades of individual opinion. The white race, being alien and secondary and hardly real, has no part in this scheme of aboriginal regeneration, and will be left behind with the other things of earth that have served their temporary purpose, or else will cease entirely to exist.

All this is to be brought about by an overruling spiritual power that needs no assistance from human creatures; and though certain medicine-men were disposed to anticipate the Indian millennium by preaching resistance to the further encroachments of the whites, such teachings form no part of the true doctrine, and it was only where chronic dissatisfaction was aggravated by recent grievances, as among the Sioux, that the movement assumed a hostile expression. On the contrary, all believers were exhorted to make themselves worthy of the predicted happiness by discarding all things warlike and practicing honesty, peace, and good will, not only among themselves, but also toward the whites, so long as they were together. Some apostles have even thought that all race distinctions are to be obliterated, and that the whites are to participate with the Indians in the coming felicity; but it seems unquestionable that this is equally contrary to the doctrine as originally preached.

Different dates have been assigned at various times for the fulfillment of the prophecy. Whatever the year, it has generally been held, for very natural reasons, that the regeneration of the earth and the renewal of all life would occur in the early spring. In some cases July, and particularly the 4th of July, was the expected time.

PART 12

Extreme Changes in the Body Image and in Interpersonal Relations

WALDEMAR BOGORAS

The Invert as Shaman

A separate branch of Chukchee shamanism, dealing with the perversion of sexual sense, has acquired a somewhat peculiar form. The sexual organs play a part in various branches of Chukchee shamanism. Especially do the malignant spells acquire additional force through the performing of certain prescriptions regarding the organs of sex, male and female. Thus, a "mischievous shaman," when he desires to make an especially powerful incantation, must strip himself naked and go out of his house at night, while the moon is shining. Then he must call to the moon and make an incantation, saying, "O moon! I show you my private parts. Take compassion on my angry thoughts. I have no secrets from you. Help me on such and such a man!" Saying this, the shaman tries to weep in order to win the compassion of the moon. He also makes peculiar movements with his mouth, as if catching something, and drawing it inward. This symbolizes his desire to catch and eat up the victim.

Incantations of this kind are often mentioned by the Chukchee. Scratching-Woman confessed having used them once against a foe of his, who shortly afterward became dangerously ill.

I was also told that some shamans arrange, every year or every other year, a special thanksgiving performance, to take place on the day of some yearly ceremonial of their family. In this performance they appear naked, and pronounce an incantation with the mention of the genital parts, which is addressed to their assistant "spirits."

The branch of shamanism, however, of which I am about to speak, is of a more special character, and refers to that shamanistic transformation of men and women in which they undergo a change of sex in part, or even completely. This is called "soft man being"; "soft man" meaning a man transformed into a being of a softer sex. A man who has changed his sex is also called "similar to a woman" and a woman in similar condition, "similar to a man." Transformation of the first kind is much the more frequent; indeed, I had no opportunity of seeing personally an instance of the second kind, and my information is gathered only from hearsay.

Transformation takes place by the command of the ke'let, usually at that critical age of early youth when shamanistic inspiration first manifests itself. It is, however, much dreaded by the youthful adepts; and in most of those cases in which I spoke of the young shamans preferring death to obedience to the call of the "spirits," there was connected with the call a reference to change of sex. There are, however, various degrees of transformation of this kind.

In the first stage, the person subjected to it personates the woman only in the manner of braiding and arranging the hair of the head. This usage is widespread among the Chukchee, and is adopted not only by shamans at the command of the "spirits," but also by sick persons at the bidding of shamans. In the latter case the aim is to change the appearance of the patient so as to make him unrecognizable by the "spirits."

The second stage is marked by the adoption of female dress,

which is also practised either for shamanistic or for medico-magical purposes. It does not imply complete change of sex. For instance, Kɪ′mɪqäi, who claimed for himself shamanistic powers, wore woman's clothes, which he assumed in his early youth. He was afflicted with a strange illness, which caused him to sleep in his inner room day after day, almost without interruption. At length a ke′lᴇ appeared to him in his sleep and ordered him to put on woman's dress, which he did accordingly. Notwithstanding this, Kɪ′mɪqäi had a wife and four children, one of which was still nursing when I saw him. The cheeks of Kɪ′mɪqäi were also covered with a stubby black beard, and there could be no misunderstanding about the sex to which he really belonged.

A young man, by name Čaivu′urgɪn, a native of Indian Point, was told by a shaman to put on a woman's dress in order to relieve him from a chronic disease to which he had been subjected from childhood.

The instances of such practices, however, are by no means frequent, since the adoption of the dress, although the most conspicuous feature of the transformation, does not confer the extraordinary power which is considered to be the rightful appurtenance of the change.

The third stage of transformation is more complete. A young man who is undergoing it leaves off all pursuits and manners of his sex, and takes up those of a woman. He throws away the rifle and the lance, the lasso of the reindeer herdsman, and the harpoon of the seal-hunter, and takes to the needle and the skin-scraper. He learns the use of these quickly, because the "spirits" are helping him all the time. Even his pronunciation changes from the male to the female mode. At the same time his body alters, if not in its outward appearance, at least in its faculties and forces. He loses masculine strength, fleetness of foot in the race, endurance in wrestling, and acquires instead the helplessness of a woman. Even his psychical character changes. The transformed person loses his brute courage and fighting spirit, and becomes shy of strangers, even fond of small-talk and of nursing small children. Generally speaking, he becomes a woman with the appearance of a man.

Of course it is difficult to find out how far auto-suggestion is responsible for the change in a person transformed in such a manner, and which of these changes are merely assumed by him in order to make an impression on the public mind.

The most important of the transformations is, however, the change of sex. The "soft man" begins to feel like a woman. He seeks to win the good graces of men, and succeeds easily with the aid of "spirits." Thus he has all the young men he could wish for striving to obtain his favor. From these he chooses his lover, and after a time takes a husband. The marriage is performed with the usual rites, and I must say that it forms a quite solid union, which often lasts till the death of one of the parties. The couple live much in the same way as do other people. The man tends his herd and goes hunting and fishing, while the "wife" takes care of the house, performing all domestic pursuits and work. They cohabit in a perverse way, *modo Socratis,* in which the transformed wife always plays the passive rôle. In this, again, some of the "soft men" are said to lose altogether the man's desire and in the end to even acquire the organs of a woman; while others are said to have mistresses of their own in secret and to produce children by them.

The transformed men, however, keep their former masculine names. All of the "soft men" I met, or of whom I knew, had men's names. One only was called "Woman's-Dress-Amo'ɛlên," the latter part being a male name. In contrast to this, some of the ordinary people even are given women's names by shamans, either at the time of their birth, or later on.

The state of a transformed man is so peculiar that it attracts much gossip and jests on the part of the neighbors. Such jests are of course interchanged only in whispers, because the people are extremely afraid of the transformed, much more so than of ordinary shamans.

GEORGE DEVEREUX

Mohave Homosexuality

The Mohave recognize only two definite types of homosexuals. Male transvestites, taking the rôle of the woman in sexual intercourse, are known as alyha·. Female homosexuals, assuming the rôle of the male, are known as hwame·.[1] Their partners are not considered homosexuals, and from the evidence of our case-histories appear to have been invariably persons of bisexual tendencies, who did not go through any formal initiation and were not designated by any special name.

Ceremony of Initiation

We possess three accounts of the ceremony in question. The general patterns of all accounts are similar, but the differences are by no means negligible. It is suggested tentatively that Mohave ritualism is extremely loose, and that in the case of a comparatively rarely performed semi-private ceremony considerable variations were likely to occur. Furthermore the time element must be taken into consideration. The ceremony in question has not been performed for several decades. It has been thought best to quote all available versions.

The following account has been published by Kroeber.[2]

> Four men who have dreamed about the ceremony are sent for, and spend the night in the house, twisting cords and gathering shredded bark for the skirt the prospective *alyha* will thereafter wear. The youth himself lies, with two women sitting by him. As they twist the cords, the men sing:
>
> *ihatnya vudhi* . . . . roll it this way.
> *ihatnya va'ama* . . . . roll it that way.
>
> When the petticoat nears completion:
>
> *istum* . . . . I hold it.
> *icham* . . . . I place it.
> *hilyuvik* . . . . it is done.
> *havirk* . . . . it is finished.
> *ka'avek* . . . . hear!
> *kidhauk* . . . . listen!
>
> These songs the singers dreamed when they were with the god Mastamho, and during the night they tell and sing of how they saw him ordering the first performance of this ceremony.

[1] Kroeber, A. L. Handbook of the Indians of California. *Bureau of American Ethnology,* Bulletin No. 78, p. 748, 1925.
[2] Kroeber, A. L. *Op. cit.,* pp. 748–749.

In the morning the two women lift the youth and take him outdoors. One of the singers puts on the skirt and dances to the river in four steps, the youth following and imitating. Then all bathe. Thereupon the two women give the youth the front and back pieces of his new dress and paint his face white. After four days he is painted again and then is an *alyha*. Such persons speak, laugh, smile, sit, and act like women. They are lucky at gambling, say the Mohave, but die young. It is significant that a variety of venereal sickness which they treat is also called *alyha*.

Sometimes, but more rarely, a girl took on man's estate, among both Yuma and Mohave, and was then known as *hwami*, and might marry women. There was no ceremony to mark her new status.

The next two accounts were obtained by the present writer.

The first was obtained from an old woman of about eighty, who was not herself a hwame·. She stated that she had heard of this ceremony from a woman who in her youth used to be on friendly terms with an alyha·. "She always thought that this alyha· was really a woman, until the transvestite lifted something one day and as the fibers of the bark-skirt parted his penis became visible. My friend was aghast when she noticed that her *girl-friend* had a penis and testes. This transvestite told her about the ceremony, and she told me about it." (It is to be suspected that the "astonishment" was a mere flower of speech, in view of the fact that sex and transvestites are regularly discussed.)

"The ceremony was held on a flat stretch of land. The crowd foregathered on both sides of the terrain. On one side were the women with the skirt and on the other the boy with the singer. The singer sang and the boy danced. When this part of the ceremony was over, the singer explained to the boy every part of the feminine wearing apparel. Since not all women know how to make a dress, the singer had chosen beforehand some capable woman to make the initiate's dress. The alyha· was then taken to the river where he bathed. He kept his old name. He did not assume the gentile name which is borne by the females in every lineage. I don't know whether or not they held ceremonies for the hwame·. I knew a hwame· once. She was dressed like a woman but she was married to other women. I have never seen the ceremony myself. They don't hold it any more."

This informant also stated that the hwame· did not change their name for a name of the male type, which is obviously a mistake, as is apparent from the name of the hwame· Sahaykwisa (contraction of masahay: childless girl or woman; and matwisa·: soul or shadow, i.e. girl's shadow, which is a typically male name).

It is true however that no male transvestite adopted a gentile name. Tampering with gentile affiliations and with the quasi-sanctity of the perpetuation of the lineages and of the tribe, by dragging it into the humoristically viewed homosexual cluster, would have been repulsive to the Mohave.

In ancient times the hwame· wore male garments.

The next account was obtained from a "normal" male shaman, an unusually well informed and willing informant. He derived most of his knowledge on this subject from a long friendship with the late Kuwal, who had married several alyha·.

"The boys who became alyha· were initiated fairly early. They did not have their noses pierced, because they did not go through the male puberty ritual." (This would place the transvestite initiation as early as the tenth or eleventh year of age.) A subsidiary informant also claimed that if a man was found to have submitted to rectal intercourse he was compelled to undergo the initiation, but this statement has been unanimously discredited. (Curiously enough, it was said that some women became hwame· after having borne a child.)

"When the child was about ten years old his relatives would begin discussing his strange ways. Some of them disliked it, but the more intelligent began envisaging an initiation ceremony. They prepared in secret the female wearing apparel. There was no singing, lest the boy should discover what was going on. Then they asked a singer to perform the ceremony on a certain day. They did not want the boy to know of it ahead of time. The ceremony was meant to take him by surprise. It was considered both an initiation and an ultimate test of his true inclinations. If he submitted to it he was considered a genuine homosexual. Word was sent to various settlements, inviting people to attend the ceremony. They wanted them to see it and become accustomed to seeing the boy in a woman's dress." (Such "accustoming" feasts were also held when someone lost an eye.) "The time and place were set by mutual accord of the boy's family and relatives. There was no feasting, only a gathering which was held early in the morning. If the boy acted in the expected fashion during the ceremony he was considered an initiated homosexual, if not, the gathering scattered, much to the relief of the boy's family."

"The singer drew a circle in the centre of the track with a pointed stick. The boy was led by two women, usually his mother and maternal grandmother, since women have more to do with children than the males, into the centre of the circle. If the boy showed willingness to remain standing in the circle, exposed to the public eye, it was almost certain that he would go through with the ceremony. The singer, hidden behind the crowd, began singing the songs. As soon as the sound reached the boy he began to dance as women do. Gradually the singer approached the dancer. The dance-steps do not change, except insofar as the boy plays a pantomime in accordance with the text of the songs. Were the boy unwilling to become a homosexual officially, he would refuse to dance. As it is, the song goes right to his heart and he will dance with much intensity. He cannot help it. After the fourth song he is proclaimed a homosexual. The same women who led him into the circle, accompanied by other women, take him down to the Colorado River. After a bath he receives his skirt. He is then led back to the dance-ground, dressed as a woman and the crowd scatters. The same ceremony is enacted for the hwame· who then dons the breech-clout."

As may be seen from the three versions presented they are complementary rather than divergent, except for minor details.

The effects of the ceremony were permanent. Just how far the chance of making a display of himself in front of a crowd of adults may have swayed a boy with some bisexual tendencies, is not easy to decide.

The initiated transvestites then assumed a name befitting a person of the opposite sex. They resented afterwards being called by their former names. The Mohave change their names fairly often and resent being called by their discarded names. "They get tired of their old names." A curious feature of Mohave name-giving may be mentioned here. Persons often assume names which are a slur on or a reference to the opposite sex, or an uncomplimentary remark upon certain habits of other persons. A certain man is known by the name of hiθpan utce· (vagina charcoal) and a woman called herself hama utce· (testicle charcoal) in retaliation.

It is emphatically stated by the Mohave that the ceremony did not operate the change in the initiate's personal habits. It was merely a test and a public acknowledgment of the shift from one sex to the other. I pointed out elsewhere that the Mohave believe that at creation and during the early periods of the mythical era there existed sexually undifferentiated stages. Thus it was not too great an effort for them to believe in the reality of such a shift.

GEORGE BIRD GRINNELL

The Society of Contraries

Among the Cheyennes there were certain men known as *Hōhnŭhk'e,* a word which conveys the idea of doing precisely the reverse of what is said. They were called Contraries. There was no band or guild of these: they were merely individuals bound by certain beliefs. They were, however, braves of much importance, and were often intrusted with serious duties—even with leadership—in battle. For this reason it may be proper to speak of them in this place. There were usually two or three Contraries in the tribe. On occasions there may have been four, but this is regarded as doubtful.

These Contraries acted by opposites. If they wished to signify assent, they said "No." If one requested a Contrary to go away, he came nearer. If asked to ride, he walked. If he called out to his woman, "Do not bring any more wood, we have plenty," she knew that the wood in the lodge was exhausted and that more should be brought.

A man became a Contrary because he feared the Thunder. He carried a peculiar lance which was the especial property of the Thunder, and a Contrary had no fear of being struck by lightning.

My old friend, Brave Wolf, for many years a Contrary, became one through fear. For years, whenever a heavy thunderstorm was approaching, he always believed he saw, standing on the clouds, a man holding a Contrary lance in his raised left hand. This vision caused him to fear the Thunder—the lightning—and as from time to time it appeared to him more and more frequently, his fears grew stronger, so that, as he said, his fear of thunder became so great that he was foolish. At length, in a dream, the man that he had seen in the clouds told him that if he carried one of these bow-lances, he need no longer fear the Thunder. When the man told him this, he determined to have one.

Brave Wolf asked a Contrary in the tribe to give him his lance, and the Contrary did so. For it Brave Wolf paid eight horses and much other property, and from that time felt no fear of the Thunder. The spiritual power of this lance was very great; it was one of the most potent medicines of the tribe, handed down from long ago. A man who possessed one of these lances, and did what he ought to do, need not fear the Thunder; yet if he failed to treat the weapon reverently, the lightning might kill him.

Brave Wolf carried this lance for about ten years (1866 to 1876). While carrying it he was always painted red, and wore leggings, moccasins, and a blanket made of old lodge-skins. When he lay down, he had no bed to rest on. The Contrary might not even sit on a bed. If he entered a lodge, the host or hostess at once moved things out of the way and the Contrary sat on the naked floor of the lodge. When he rose to go, the Contrary passed white sage over the ground to purify it, for he always carried with him a bundle of the plant for use in the ceremony of purification.

The Contraries were not chiefs, they were merely braves. They bore the usual weapons carried by warriors, but besides, each carried one of these lances—*Hōhnŭhkawo',* Contrary bow—shaped like a bow strung with two strings, but with a lance-head on one end,[1] and adorned with various mysterious symbols. The lance was about five feet in length, and near one end was tied the stuffed skin of a bird (*maivĭsh,* an oriole), in the South. In the North the Louisiana tanager, which has some red on the head instead of merely

[1] Compare Morice, Western Denés, Trans., Canadian Inst., vol. IV, p. 60, March, 1894.

yellow or orange, was used for this purpose. The name came from the North. The red painting of the person and clothing of the thunder-bow bearer is said to have been in imitation of the color of this bird, which represents, they say, the body of the man who carries the thunder-bow. At each end of the lance, tied on with a white string of bear intestine, was a bunch of the feathers of owls, hawks, and eagles. When not in use, the lance was wrapped in a piece of tanned buffalo-hide. Its owner wore a cap or fillet of owl-feathers, and to the heel of each moccasin was attached the beard of a buffalo-bull. The braids of his hair were wrapped with strips of dressed buffalo-hide, each strip split at the end so as to make two little tags, something like those at the heel of a moccasin. A whistle of ash wood hung about the neck by a string of dressed buffalo-hide. It was five or six inches long and as thick as a man's finger.

Lashed to the lance outside of the buffalo-hide wrapper was a short, forked stick, sharpened at the butt, painted red, and with two prongs of unequal length. When the lance was unwrapped for use in a fight, or for other purpose, the sharpened end of the forked stick was thrust in the ground, and the lance was rested on it, the point up, so that the point should not touch the ground. When the Contrary took up his lance to go into the fight, he might hand this stick to any young man to carry. It was supposed to give the young man good luck in battle, because it was one of the belongings of a great medicine. When the lance was first taken out of the wrapper, sweet grass was burned over a coal and the lance held over the smoke, and as this was done it was lightly shaken four times.

Only the Contrary himself might handle the lance; not even his wife might touch it. Occasionally, if a Contrary was obliged to leave his lance, to do something, he might give it to a man to hold, but after the Contrary had taken it back, a ceremony of purification must be performed on the one who had held it.

If in a fight the bearer of the thunder-lance was shot, or if his horse was shot, so that he was out of the fight, he might hand his lance to any man, to be used in the fight in counting coup. If he did this, the user must be purified after carrying the weapon. These bow-lances were sometimes called thunder-bows, because they had the power to influence the thunder—that is, the lightning. Anyone who was careless about the possessions of a Contrary, or showed lack of respect for him, was likely to be killed by lightning.

In the camp, the Contrary lance was usually hung, by day, upon a pole which stood in the ground behind the lodge, and when the sun set, the pole was brought close to the back of the lodge and was leaned up against it. If, by any chance, the lance touched anyone, the person so touched must be rubbed off with a brush of white sage; or if in riding a horse, the lance touched it—as it was quite sure to do—the horse, before being turned loose, must be wiped off with white sage and prayed over. If children playing about the camp knocked against the lance, or against the pole on which it hung, or if a horse did the same, the lightning was likely to kill them, unless they were thus purified.

In the lodge of a Contrary, no one slept at the back of the lodge; at night or in stormy weather this place was reserved for the thunder-bow. No one, not even the Contrary himself, might pass between the bow and the fire; only the pipe could pass there. No dogs were allowed in this lodge—the Contrary might not own dogs.

When going into a fight, the Contrary carried his thunder-bow in the hollow of his left arm. So long as he held the lance in the left hand, he might advance and retreat, fighting like anyone else, but if he shifted his lance to his right hand, and blew his whistle, then he might not turn back, but must rush upon the enemy, no matter how many guns were being shot at him; he was obliged to press on until he reached the enemy. When he passed the lance to his right hand, blew his whistle, and cried like a burrowing owl as he rushed toward his enemy, these various acts were thought to cause the bows of the enemy to break, if they were armed with bows, or, if they carried guns, they would cause them to miss fire. The thunder-bow was used to touch the enemy in counting coup; it was not a fighting weapon.

When transferred from left hand to right, the lance was not passed in front of the body, that is, before the face, but behind it, over the back of the neck. The point of the lance might not be turned toward the ground, except when the owner passed it from left hand to right behind his back; then he threw the point down slantwise toward the ground.

When a charge was made, the Contrary must be off to one side by himself. If he rode behind or before anyone, it would bring bad luck to that person—perhaps his horse might break down. In the same way, on the march, the Contrary might not follow the trail made by the others, but must travel off to one side.

As no one might step in the tracks of a Contrary, nor he in those of anyone else, lest that person should become footsore and lame, so it was the duty of the Contrary to step in the tracks of enemies, in order that they might become exhausted and be overtaken. If an enemy stole horses from the tribe, it was part of the duty of the Contrary to pierce the tracks of the stolen horses with the points of his lance, for the same reason.

In the old days when the Cheyennes traveled chiefly on foot, if a man became exhausted by running or marching, the possessor of a thunder-bow might put sprigs of white sage in the moccasins of the person to renew his strength. Scouts who were about to be sent out often went to the bearer of the thunder-bow and asked him so to treat their moccasins that they might not become tired out on their journey.

Contraries have sometimes been killed in battle. Bear Foot was killed by the Crows, on the Little Big Horn River. His people hung his lance up in a big tree near where he fell. No one would have dared to take it away.

It was proper for the Contraries to repair and renew their lances at the time the medicine arrows were renewed. When this was done there must be no noise whatsoever. The old men who went into the lodge to see the thunder-bows renewed, did not wear good clothing; their garments were old and worn, and the men were painted red. While they were in the lodge, it was not permitted to scratch the head with the fingers; a little pointed stick must be used for the purpose.

The roots and herbs used by the bearer of the thunder-bow are said to have been peculiar to this office and quite different from all other medicines used by priests or doctors in the tribe.

In late years the point of the Contrary lance was made from the bottom of a frying-pan. It was notched or slightly barbed, just above where it entered the wood. Black Bear, *Mōhkstămō'ăhts,* long ago dead, was a noted maker of such lancepoints.

In the old times the men who carried thunder-bows were usually single men, or, at least, men who at the time had no wives. The case is cited of Gray Head, who in 1865 had a thunder-bow made for him, and because he had been married the occurrence created a scandal, and his power was not highly regarded. In later years married men had these thunder-bows made for them, but they were not considered real thunder-bows, and the power of the owners was not very highly esteemed.

When a man felt that he must become a Contrary, he tried to take over the position from someone who held it. For this he was obliged to pay a large price—horses, arms, clothing, and robes. Though carrying with it much hardship and many responsibilities, the office was one of great power and importance.

Anyone who might dream of the thunder-bow, or of the thunder, might ask a Contrary for his lance, the symbol of his power. Until someone did this, the Contrary could not escape from his office. It had come to him as an order, and if no one asked for the thunder-bow, the Contrary was obliged to keep it. Thus a man might be a Contrary for a long time. Men have carried these lances so long that they felt they could no longer endure the responsibility, and having made a rawhide sack, they have put the lances away for a time.

A Contrary might not associate on terms of equality or familiarity with the rest of the camp. He might not joke, nor have a good time, but was obliged always to be alone and apart. People might visit his lodge, but they were expected to do so with dignity and decorum, moving slowly, and not remaining long. The Contrary's lodge, and most of his possessions, were painted red. He ate and drank from a special dish, made from the horn of a mountain sheep, which no one else might use, or even touch. After the owner had used it, the dish was wiped out with sage, and was put away.

Thus the ownership of a thunder-bow involved not a little hardship. The care, responsibility, and loneliness which went with it were not pleasant. A Contrary might be in a crowd only during a fight, when all were charging. In the camp he was always alone—often on a distant hill by himself. If there were two Contraries in the camp, they might be together, but no one else might associate with them, and a single one led a lonely life. No one became a Contrary by choice; but from the warning which came to him there was no escape.

ALEXANDRA DAVID-NEEL
Displacing the Soul

Another exercise which, however, seems to be seldom practiced, consists in "displacing one's consciousness in one's own body." It is explained as follows.

We feel our consciousness in our "heart." Our arms seem to us to be "annexes" to our body, and our feet seem to be a distant part of our person. In fact, arms, feet and other parts of the body are looked at as if they were *objects* for a *subject* dwelling elsewhere.

Now the student will endeavour to make the "consciousness" leave its habitual abode and transfer it, for instance, to his hand, then he must feel himself to have the shape of five fingers and a palm, situated at the extremity of a long attachment (the arm) which joins on to a big moving structure, the body.

That is to say, he must experience the sensation that we might have if, instead of having the eyes and the brain in the head, we had them in the hand and then the hand was able to examine the head and the body, reversing the normal process which is to look downwards in order to see the hands or the body.

What can be the aim of such strange exercises? The most frequent answer given to my questions will probably seem unsatisfactory by many inquirers, yet it is probably quite correct.

Some lamas have told me that the aim of these practices can hardly be explained, because those who have not felt their effects could not understand the explanations.

One attains, by the means of these strange drills, psychic states entirely different from those habitual to us. They cause us to pass beyond the fictitious limits which we assign to the *self*. The result being that we grow to realize that the *self* is compound, impermanent; and that the self, *as self,* does not exist.

One of these lamas seized upon a remark I had made as an argument in support of his theory.

When he spoke of the heart as the seat of thought and mind, I had said that Westerners would rather place thoughts and mind in the brain.

"You see," immediately replied my interlocutor, "that one may feel and recognize the mind in different places. Since these Philings[1] experience the sensation of thinking in their *head,* and I experience it in my *heart,* one may believe that it is quite possible to feel it in the *foot.* But all these are only deceitful sensations, with no shadow of reality. The mind is neither *in the heart* nor *in the head,* nor somewhere outside of the body, apart, separated, alien to it. It is to help one realize this fact that these apparently strange practices have been devised."

Here again we meet with the "clearing" process. All these exercises aim at destroying habitual notions accepted by routine and without personal investigation. The object is to make one understand that other ideas can be put in their place. It is hoped that the disciple will conclude that there cannot be any absolute truth in ideas derived from sensations which can be discarded while others, even contradictory to them, take their place.

Kindred theories are professed by the followers of the Chinese Ts'an sect. They express them in enigmatical sentences such as:

"Lo, a cloud of dust is rising from the ocean and the roaring of the waves is heard over the land."

"I walk on foot, and yet on the back of an ox I am riding."

"When I pass over the bridge, lo! the water floweth not, but the bridge floweth."

"Empty handed I go, and behold! the spade's handle is in my hand."

And so on.

The doctrine of the Ts'an sect has been defined by one of its followers as "the art of perceiving the polar star in the Austral

---

[1] Foreigners.

hemisphere." This paradoxical saying resembles that of the lama who said to me: "One must discover the white in the black and the black in the white."

Bringing a Corpse to Life

The Corpse Who Dances

Another mysterious rite is called *rolang* (the corpse who stands up). Traditions and ancient chronicles relate that, before the introduction of Buddhism into Tibet, it was practised by the Bönpo shamans during the funeral ceremony. However, the brief movement made by a dead body in such circumstances cannot be compared with what happens in the course of the horrible and grotesque *tête-à-tête*, that Tibetan occultists depict.

There exist several kinds of *rolang*. These must not be mistaken for the *trong jug*[2] rite which causes the "spirit" of another being to pass into a corpse and apparently resuscitate it, though the corpse is not animated by its original occupant.

One of these lugubrious *rolang* was described to me as follows by a *ngagspa* who said he had practised it himself.

The celebrant is shut up alone with a corpse in a dark room. To animate the body, he lies on it, mouth to mouth, and while holding it in his arms, he must continually repeat mentally the same magic formula,[3] excluding all other thoughts.

After a certain time the corpse begins to move. It stands up and tries to escape; the sorcerer, firmly clinging to it, prevents it from freeing itself. Now the body struggles more fiercely. It leaps and bounds to extraordinary heights, dragging with it the man who must hold on, keeping his lips upon the mouth of the monster, and continue mentally repeating the magic words.

At last the tongue of the corpse protrudes from its mouth. The critical moment has arrived. The sorcerer seizes the tongue with his teeth and bites it off. The corpse at once collapses.

Failure in controlling the body after having awaked it, means certain death for the sorcerer.

---

[2] Written *grong hjug.*
[3] This differs according to the masters.

The tongue carefully dried becomes a powerful magic weapon which is treasured by the triumphant *ngagspa.*

The Tibetan who gave me these details described most vividly the gradual awakening of the corpse: the first conscious look which brightened its glazed eyes and its feeble movements slowly growing in strength until he became unable to prevent the agitation of the jumping monster and needed all his strength to hold it. He described his sensations when he could feel the tongue issuing from the mouth of the corpse and touching his own lips, and realized that the terrible moment had come when, if he failed to conquer it, the horrible being would kill him.

Had that fantasic struggle not been purely subjective? Had it not taken place during one of these trances which are frequently experienced by Tibetan *naljorpas,* which they also voluntarily cultivate? I doubted and asked to see *"the tongue."* The sorcerer showed me a desiccated blackish object which might have been "a tongue," but it was not sufficient to prove the origin of the hideous relic.

Be that as it may, numbers of Tibetans believe that the *rolang* rite really takes place.

Besides corpses being revived by special rites, Tibetans believe also that any corpse is liable to rise suddenly and harm the living. It is for this reason that dead bodies are continually watched by some one who recites the liturgic words which prevent that sham resurrection.

A *trapa* from Sepogön in the vicinity of the Salween told me the following story.

While still a boy novice, he had accompanied three lamas of his monastery to a house where a man had died. There the lamas were to perform the daily rite for the dead till the day appointed to carry the corpse to the cemetery. At night they had retired to sleep in a corner of the large room where the body was kept, tied up in a seated posture with many scarves and swathed in clothes.

"The charge of reciting the magic formulas had been entrusted to me. In the middle of the night I was overcome with the continuous wearisome repetition and may have dozed a few minutes. A small noise awaked me! a black cat passed by the corpse and went out of the room. Then I heard a kind of cracking noise like tearing cloth, and to my horror, I saw the dead body moving and freeing himself from his bands. Mad with fright, I ran out of the house, but before I had escaped from the room I saw the ghost stretching out one hand and creeping upon the sleeping men.

"In the morning the three men were found dead; the corpse had returned to his place but the scarves were torn and the clothes lay on the floor around him."

Tibetans have great faith in such stories.

The touch of the *rolang* is mortal and the mischievous ghost does not fail to lay his hand on all who are within his reach: only the lamas who perform the rites of the dead are said to know magic words and gestures which avert that danger, by controlling the corpse and causing it to sit back if it attempts to move.

We are also told of *rolangs* which escape from the house where they have revived and roam about the country. Again, others are said to disappear without leaving any trace.

One could fill numbers of books with the stories one hears about *rolangs* among the good people of Tibet.

ALEXANDER HENRY
Self-Mutilation

The greater part of the men—Big Bellies, Mandanes, and Saulteurs [Souliers]—have lost a joint of several fingers, particularly of the left hand, and it is not uncommon to see only the two fore-fingers and thumbs entire. Amputation is performed for the loss of a near relation, and likewise during the days of penance, on which they display their fortitude and courage in the following manner: When a young man has attained the age of 20 years, he generally, in the depth of winter, performs his penance by setting out entirely naked and alone, with only two or three pairs of shoes, the iron barb of an arrow, and no means of making a fire. In this condition he repairs to a certain high hill, a day's journey from the village. On this hill he must remain as many days as his strength will permit, during which time he neither eats, drinks, nor sleeps, but passes the time in dancing, bawling, howling, and lamenting. Here also he amputates a finger with the iron barb brought for that purpose. Some have been known to be absent seven days in the severest weather. This may appear incredible, but I have it from several eye-witnesses of such pilgrimages, and do not doubt it. After several days—more or fewer—the penitent makes his appearance, coming at full speed, and as there is continually somebody upon the huts, information is instantly given of his return. He is met by a particular friend, who has kept account of the number of days he has been absent, and for every day has been prepared a bull's head, to which has been fastened 1½ fathoms of cord. The other end of this is affixed to an incision in the penitent's back or shoulders, by pinching up a fold of skin and flesh, through which is thrust the barb of an arrow; as many days as he has been absent, so many must be the incisions, and the number of heads must also tally with them. He must then walk around the village, howling and bawling, with all those bulls' heads trailing on the ground; in some places, where the ground is rough, the poor fellow must pull and tug hard to get through, as the horns continually catch in uneven spots, and often fall into some of the empty corn pits, where they would hold until the skin gave way or the cord broke, were they not attended to by some children who make it their business to disengage the horns. So many days as he has been absent, so many times must he walk round the village, never ceasing to utter lamentations. Some have been known to fall senseless during this painful ordeal; but even then they only allow themselves a few moments to recover, and proceed again. Having finished the necessary rounds, he is disengaged from the bulls' heads by his friend, with a long harangue, applauding his courage and fortitude; he may then retire to his hut and take care of his wounds, as he is in a shocking condition. Some never recover, and others languish for months before they get well.

They have another custom of putting their courage and contempt of pain to task by tormenting their flesh in a most atrocious manner. This is done by pinching up a fold of the skin and flesh an inch broad, under which they pass the iron barb of an arrow; they raise stripes in this manner from the back of the hand to the shoulder, and thence to the breast, there joining three or four separate circles of incisions made in the same manner on the lower part of the breast. Some content themselves by raising stripes of different lengths upon their arms and thighs, and forming crescentic cuts on the breast in a very regular manner, one within another; some with the horns upward, others downward, according to fancy.

Most of the women have their faces tattooed in a very savage manner, lines a quarter of an inch broad passing from the nose to the ear, and down each side of the mouth and chin to the throat. This disfigures them very much; otherwise, some would have tolerably good faces.

MARTIN DOBRIZHOFFER
Abolishing Words

The Abiponian language is involved in new difficulties by a ridiculous custom which the savages have of continually abolishing words common to the whole nation, and substituting new ones in their stead. Funeral rites are the origin of this custom. The Abipones do not like that any thing should remain to remind them of the dead. Hence appellative words bearing any affinity with the names of the deceased are presently abolished. During the first years that I spent amongst the Abipones, it was usual to say *Hegmalkam kahamátek?* When will there be a slaughtering of oxen? On account of the death of some Abipon, the word *kahamátek* was interdicted, and, in its stead, they were all commanded, by the voice of a cryer, to say, *Hegmalkam négerkatà?* The word *nihirenak,* a tiger, was exchanged for *apañigehak; peúe,* a crocodile, for *kaeprhak,* and *Kaáma,* Spaniards, for *Rikil,* because these words bore some resemblance to the names of Abipones lately deceased. Hence it is that our vocabularies are so full of blots, occasioned by our having such frequent occasion to obliterate interdicted words, and insert new ones. Add to this another thing which increases the difficulty of learning the language of the Abipones. Persons promoted to the rank of nobles are called *Hëcheri,* and *Neleřeycatè,* and are distinguished from the common people even by their language. They generally use the same words, but so transformed by the interposition, or addition of other letters, that they appear to belong to a different language. The names of men belonging to this class, end in *In;* those of the women, who also partake of these honours, in *En.* These syllables you must add even to substantives and verbs in talking with them. The sentence, This horse belongs to Captain Debayakaikin, would be rendered by an Abipon, speaking the vulgar tongue, in this manner: *Eneha ahëpegak Debayakaikin lela.* But in the language of the Hëcheri you must say, *Debayakaikin lilin.* They salute a plebeian with *Là nauichi?* Art thou come? to which he replies *Là ñauè,* I am come. If a noble person is addressed, he must be saluted in these words: *Là náuirin,* Art thou come? and he, with much importance, and pompous modulation of his voice, will reply, *Là ñauerinkie,* I am come. Moreover, they have some words peculiar to themselves, by which they supersede those in general use. Thus, the common people call a mother, *Latè,* the nobles, *Lichiá.* The former call a son *Laétar̂at,* the latter *Illalèk,* not to mention other instances. Both in the explanation of religion, and in common conversation, we chose to use the vulgar tongue, because it was understood by all.

I have said that there are three kinds of Abipones, the *Riikahes,* the *Nakaikétergehes,* and the *Yaaukanigas.* All of them, however, speak the same language; all understand each other, and are understood. Yet each of these classes has some words peculiar to itself. The Riikahes *ayte* means many, and *apatáye* is derived from *napàta,* a mat, which they use to cover their tents with; and so great is the multitude of gnats in the lands of the Abipones that the inhabitants seem not only covered but oppressed by them. To drink with the Riikahes is expressed by *neèt,* with the Nakaikétergehes by *nañàm.* The latter call a head *Lapañik,* the former *Lemar̂at.* The Yaaukanigas, in the use of words, sometimes imitate one, sometimes the other; but in a few they differ from both. The rest call the moon *Grauèk,* but they, by antonomasia, name it *Eergr̂aik,* a star. The rainbow is called by the rest, *Oáhetà,* but by the Yaaukanigas, *Apich.* But this variety creates neither difficulty nor wonder. The Teutonic language is used by many nations, but how greatly does it differ in different provinces, not only in dialect but also in words! How different is Tuscan from the languages spoken at Milan, Savoy, and Venice! How different is Castilian from the languages of Arragon, Andalusia, Navarre, and Valencia!

EDWARD SAPIR

Abnormal Types of Speech in Nootka

An interesting linguistic and cultural problem is the use in speech of various devices implying something in regard to the status, sex, age, or other characteristics of the speaker, person addressed, or person spoken of, without any direct statement as to such characteristics. When we say "big dog make bow-wow" instead of "the dog barks," it is a fair inference that we are talking to a baby, not to a serious-minded man of experience. Further, when we hear one use "thee" where most would say "you," we suspect that we are listening to an orthodox Quaker. In neither of these cases is there an explicit reference to a baby as person addressed or to a Quaker as person speaking. Such implications are common in all languages and are most often effected by means of the use of special words or specific locutions. Thus, in Nootka there are special words used in speaking of obscene matters to or in the presence of women; a number of "baby-words" also exist. Generally it is the speaker or person addressed that is thus signalized, but it is quite possible, though less frequent, to thus imply something also in regard to the third person. A more specialized type of these person-implications is comprised by all cases in which the reference is brought about not by the use of special words or locutions, that is, by lexical, stylistic, or syntactic means, but by the employment of special grammatical elements, consonant or vocalic changes, or addition of meaningless sounds, that is, by morphologic or phonetic means.

To enumerate all the possible types of person-implication expressed in language, from the point of view of resulting classifications of human beings, would lead one far afield. Two types, however, seem to stand out most prominently—those referring to sex-discrimination and to rank-discrimination. Several languages make a distinction between words or forms used by males and such as are restricted to females. Such a distinction, for instance, is made by certain Eskimo dialects, in which, at least in earlier times, according to Boas,[1] final *p, t, k,* and *q* were pronounced by the women as the corresponding nasals *m, n, ŋ,* and *ɲ*. In Yana, an isolated linguistic stock of northern California, the forms used by the women, whether in speaking to one another or to males, differ from the fuller forms used by the latter in the unvoicing of final vowels; final *-na* (*-hi* in Southern Yana), a common noun ending, is replaced by aspiration in the speech of the women, who further lengthen final vowels to express the interrogative, while the males suffix an element *-n*. Most languages that make such sex distinctions differentiate the sexes as speakers. In Yana, however, a further discriminating factor is the sex of the person spoken to, in so far as the men in speaking to the women use the forms characteristic of the latter.

More widespread in language seems to be a discrimination of forms according to the rank or social status of the person speaking, addressed, or spoken of. Here belong the etiquette forms characteristic of several East Asiatic and Indonesian languages, by which the social grading of the speakers as inferiors or superiors in reference to one another is clearly reflected in their speech. An analogous American instance is the use in Nahuatl of reverential forms to imply respect to the person addressed or spoken of. These are morphologically nothing but indirectives or causatives in *-lia, -tia,* or *-ltia* with reflexive pronominal prefixes; "he sleeps" is thus more politely expressed as "he causes himself to sleep." Here belongs also the use in so many European languages (French, German, Russian, and others) of second or third person plurals, instead of the more logical second person singulars, in speaking to people with whom one is not on the most intimate terms. This usage has its parallel in Yana, where brothers and sisters address each other in the plural;[2] other Californian examples of a similar nature have been given by Goddard[3] and Kroeber.[4]

---

[1] Franz Boas, *Handbook of American Indian Languages,* Bureau of American Ethnology, Bulletin 40, pt. 1 (Washington, G. P. O., 1911), p. 79.

[2] Sapir, *Yana Texts,* Univ. Calif. Publ. Am. Arch. and Ethn., 9 (1910): 95, n. 139: 101, p. 150.

[3] Goddard, *Kato Texts,* ibid., 5 (1909): 142, fn. 185.

[4] Kroeber, *The Languages of the Coast of California North of San Francisco,* ibid., 9 (1911): 321 (Pomo).

These preliminary remarks are intended merely to indicate the general class of linguistic phenomena to which belong the more specialized Nootka examples to be given presently. At the same time they will serve to render these latter less glaringly bizarre by providing them with parallels of a more general character. The data here presented were chiefly obtained in November, 1910, in the course of ethnologic and linguistic research for the Geological Survey of Canada among the Nootka Indians of Alberni canal, Vancouver island; the informant was Dan Watts, the young chief of the *Hōpâtc!as'at*ʜ[a] tribe. Further data on this subject were obtained in the winter of 1913–14 from Alex Thomas, a young Indian of the *Ts!icâ'at*ʜ[a] tribe of the same region.

It is possible and often customary in Nootka to imply in speech some physical characteristic of the person addressed or spoken of, partly by means of suffixed elements, partly by means of "consonantal play." Consonantal play consists either in altering certain consonants of a word, in this case sibilants, to other consonants that are phonetically related to them, or in inserting meaningless consonants or consonant clusters in the body of the word. The physical classes indicated by these methods are children, unusually fat or heavy people, unusually short adults, those suffering from some defect of the eye, hunchbacks, those that are lame, left-handed persons, and circumcised males.

In speaking to or about a child it is customary to add the regular diminutive suffix *-'is* to verb or other forms, even though the word so affected connotes nothing intrinsically diminutive; affection may also be denoted by it. The *-'is* comes before temporal, modal, and pronominal suffixes. Thus, the normal *qwístci'* "do so!" (*qwis-* "to do thus"; *-tci'* second person singular imperative, "go and . . !") is changed to *qwís'istci'* "do so, little one!" when speaking to a child. Similarly, *qwísma'* "he does so" (*-ma'* third person present indicative) is charged to *qwís'isma'* when one is speaking about a child. In speaking about oneself or others when addressing a child, it does not seem to be customary to use the diminutive suffix except to show affection at the same time. Thus, the word *wałcíʟa*ʜ "I am going home" (*wał-* "to return home"; *-ciʟ-* inceptive; *-a*ʜ "I") may be changed to *wałciʟ'įsa*ʜ "I am going home, little one" when addressed to a child for whom one wants to show love, but this form would not be used in speaking to a child that is a stranger. As might be expected, diminutive verbal and other forms occur in lullabies, in some of which the child is represented as speaking about itself. Thus, in a lullaby supposed to be sung by a whale mother to its child, occur the words *'OHª'ésọkᵉ 'émiti'* ("my) little name is" (*'OHª-* "to be"; *-'is-* diminutive; *-ọkᵉ* "of, belonging to"; *'.émịti'* "name"). Some people were said by Dan to have the habit of using the diminutive suffix in order to belittle others, as though the persons addressed or referred to were of no more importance than children as compared to themselves. If a chief does this to too great an extent, he is set down as haughty.

In talking to or about fat people or people of unusual size, the suffixed element *-aq'* is used in a manner analogous to the diminutive *-'is*. Thus, the normal *hínt'ciLwe'inᵗ* "he comes, it is said" (*hin-* "empty" verb stem "to be, do"; *-t'-*, shortened form of *-inᵗ* "to come"; *-ciL-* inceptive; *-we'inᵗ* quotative) becomes *hínt'ciLaq'we'inᵗ; 'ọtsátcịLma'* "he goes to it" (*'ọ-* "empty" noun stem meaning "something"; *-tsa-* "to start for, go to"; *-tcịL-* inceptive, used after vowels; *-ma'* third person present indicative) becomes *'ọtsatcịLá-q'ma'*. Other examples are: *ha'ọ́kwaq'ma'* "he, clumsy one, eats"; (*ha'w-* "to eat"; *-okw-* intransitive verbal suffix); and *ha'ọkwá-qit'Hak'* "did you eat, fatty?" (*-it'* tense suffix denoting past time; *-Ha-* interrogative; *-k'* second person singular).

People who are abnormally small are spoken of in forms with the diminutive suffix; moreover, in such cases, all sibilant consonants (*s, ts, ts!; c, tc, tc!*) become palatalized *c-* sounds (*ś, tś, tś!* compare, for *ś*, Polish *ś* and Sanskrit *ç;* for *tś*, compare Polish *ć*), which sound accoustically midway between *s-* and *c-* sounds; the diminutive *-'is* itself becomes *-'iś*. Thus, *hínt'ciLwe'inᵗ* "he comes, they say" is changed to *hínt'śiL'iśwe'inᵗ* "he, little man, comes, they say." These *ś-* forms are also used to refer to small birds, such as sparrows and wrens. Sometimes a meaningless *ś* is added to the word, as in *wikáHªś tóHauk'* from *wikáHª tóHauk'* "I am not afraid" (*wik-* verb stem "to be not"; *-āHª* first person singular present indicative; *tōH-* verb stem "to be afraid"; *-uk'*, diphthongized to *-auk'* because of preceding *a- timbred* H, intransitive suffix). We shall meet this consonantal change again further on in another connexion.

Quite analogously to dwarfs, are addressed or spoken of those suffering from some defect of the eye. Under this category are included cross-eyed people, those who squint, and such as have one eye run out, but not the blind. Here again the diminutive suffix is used, with the added feature that all *s*- sounds and *c*- sounds are converted into the corresponding voiceless lateral stops or spirants (*s* and *c* become *ł*; *ts* and *tc* become ʟ; *ts!* and *tc!* become ʟ*!*); the diminutive *-'is* itself becomes *-'ił*. This style of speech is termed ʟ*!a*ʟ*!átck!in*ʿ "to talk in sore-eyed fashion" (cf. ʟ*!a*ʟ*!âtck'suł* "one-eyed person"). Thus, *qwísma*ʿ "he does so" is changed to *qwíł'iłma*ʿ. Similarly, *tc!ịtcị*ʟ*ma*ʿ "he cuts" (*tc!ị*- "to cut"; *-tcị*ʟ- inceptive; *-ma*ʿ third person present indicative) becomes ʟ*!ị*ʟ*ị*ʟ*'iłma*ʿ. A full-grown Indian named Sammy (or *Sê'mi* as pronounced in Nootka), who is cross-eyed, is referred to as *łê'mí'ił* "little cross-eyed Sammy." Another Indian of the same tribe, *Tô'mic,* who has only one good eye, is, in parallel fashion, referred to as *Tô'mił'ił* "little one-eyed Tô'mic." It should be remarked that such people, particularly when adult, are apt to become offended if addressed in this fashion, and that one would not use such forms in their presence unless with the express purpose of showing contempt or of teasing. As will be seen again later on, ʟ*!a*ʟ*!átck!in*ʿ forms are used also in referring to the deer[5] and mink. Thus, the mythological Mink, *tc!âstimits'mit*ʿ "Mink-son," is generally referred to as ʟ*!âłtimi*ʟ*'mit*ʿ.

Hunchbacks (*k!wápị*ʿ) are also addressed or spoken of in forms provided with the diminutive suffix, a further peculiarity in these being the change of ordinary *s*- sounds and *c*- sounds to peculiar thickish *c*- sounds, pronounced with the lower jaw held in front of the upper; the diminutive *-'is* appears as *-'iç*. We may represent these *c*- sounds by *ç*. In this hunchback talk *qwísma*ʿ becomes *qwíç'içma*ʿ. Other examples are: *yâtçuk*ʷ*'içma*ʿ "he is walking" (*yāts,*- "to walk"; *-uk*ʿ- intransitive verb suffix); *tçlôtçk*ʷ *mini*ʜ*ᵃ'içma*ʿ "all of them are" (*tc!ōtck*ʿ- "to be all"; *'mini*ʜ*ᵃ*- plural); and *tç!áx̣çị*ʟ*'içma*ʿ "he spears" (*ts!ax̣*- "to spear"; *-cị*ʟ- inceptive).

[5] Deer is associated with sore eyes also in other Indian mythologies. An Ojibwa example may be found in P. Radin, *Some Myths and Tales of the Ojibwa of Southeastern Ontario,* Geological Survey of Canada, Memoir 48 (No. 2, Anthropological Series), p. 3 (episode *d*).

Here again these distinctive forms are generally avoided when in the presence of humpbacked people, for fear of giving offence. However, a humpbacked child who is well known to the speaker would hardly take offence and would be addressed as described. Or, if an old humpbacked woman is good-natured, *c̣-* forms may well be used when she is about, as though to show that she is happy and not easily ruffled. Here the notions of contempt and affection commingle.

In speaking of lame people the diminutive suffix is again used, this time in its normal form. Besides this, the meaningless element *Lc* or *Lci* is inserted in the body of the word somewhere before the diminutive suffix, its exact position apparently depending on the whim of the speaker. Thus, *hinínI'aLma'* "he comes now" (*hin-* "empty" verb stem; *-inI-* "to come"; *-'aL-* determinative suffix marking point of time, "now"; *-ma'* third person present indicative) becomes *hinínILcị'its!aLma'* (diminutive *-'is* and *-'aL* regularly combine to form *-'its!aL*) or *hiLcnínI'ịts!aLma'* "the lame chap is coming." Similarly, the verb *tc!ịtcị'aLma'* "he cuts now" (inceptive *-tcịL* and *-'aL* combine into *-tcị'aL*) is changed to *tc!itcịLc'ịts!aLma'* when a lame person is spoken of. The word *t!a'nẹ́'is'i'* "the child" (*t!a'na-* "child, son, daughter"; *-'is* diminutive suffix, *i* causing preceding *a* to become umlauted to *ẹ́*; *-'i'* nominalizing element, about equivalent to our definite article) becomes *t!aLcnẹ́'is'i'* "the young lame fellow," which may be used in speaking to children.

In speaking of or to left-handed people the diminutive suffix is used in its normal form, besides which the meaningless element *tc*H^a is inserted after the first syllable of the word. Thus, *yā́ł'aLma'* "there now he is" (*yāł-* "to be there"; *-'aL* and *-ma'* as above) becomes *yā́łtc*H^a*'its!aLma'* (*-'is* and *-'aL* combine to form *-'its!aL*) "there now he is, poor little left-handed chap!" Similarly, from *sukwí'aLma'* "now he takes it" (*su-* verb stem "to take"; *-kwiL* inceptive suffix, changed to *-kwi-* before *-'aL*) is formed *sútc*H^a*-kwiL'its!aLma'*. The diminutive suffix may also be omitted. Examples are: *hitc*H^a*nín*^{i} from *hinín*^{i} "to come"; and *t!itc*H^a*tciLa*H from *t!itciLa*H "I throw it down" (*t!i-* "to throw"; *-tciL* inceptive suffix; *-a*H first person singular indicative). Such a form as the last might be appropriately used in speaking to a left-handed person that one is well acquainted with and who will not take offence at being thus twitted. It is customary, particularly for jokers, to use these left-hand forms also in talking about bears, who are supposed to be left-handed.[6]

In speaking of or to circumcised males, forms known as *'i'ict'k!in'* "to make *ct'*- sounds" are used. In these the meaningless element *ct'* is inserted after the first syllable of the word. One of the *Ts!i-cá'at*Hᵃ Indians, named *T!ō̓x̣mis* "Slaying-while-moving-from-beach-to-beach," is often humorously referred to as *T!ōctx̣mis* because of his having been born circumcised. Other examples of this class of forms are: *hict'nín*ɪ*ma'* from *hinín*ɪ*ma'* "he comes"; and *háct''ọk'ᵘ* from *há'ọkᵘ* "to eat."

Similar phonetic changes are made in forms used to refer to one or two classes of individuals characterized by some mental quality. Thus, greedy people are addressed or referred to in forms having a meaningless *tcx* inserted after the first syllable of the word. Thus, from *'o*Hᵃ*sáma*H "I hunger for it" (*'o*- "empty" stem which may be rendered by "something" or "so and so"; -Hᵃ*sā*- verbifying suffix "to desire to eat"; -*ma*H first person singular present indicative, used after vowels) is formed *'utcx*H*sáma*H. Similarly, *hiní-n*ɪ*'a*L*ma'* "now he comes" becomes *hitcxnín*ɪ*'a*L*ma'* "now he comes, greedy fellow that he is." These *tcx*- forms are also used to refer to ravens, regularly to the mythological Raven, a character noted for his gluttony.

Cowards may be satirized by "making one's voice small" in referring to or addressing them, in other words by speaking in a thin piping voice that suggests timidity.

It is interesting to notice that in several of the above usages, the notions of mere smallness, of contempt, and of affection are found side by side, and doubtless the precise nuance of feeling expressed depends much on the relations subsisting between the speaker and the person addressed or spoken of. What is meant in the spirit of pitying affection for a poor lame or humpbacked child or for a good-natured squinting old grandpa, might be intended to convey

---

[6] According to Dr. Paul Radin, the Winnebago also consider the bear to be left-handed. In the bear clan feast of these Indians the guests eat with a spoon in their left hand.

contempt when addressed to a young man and would be promptly resented as an insult. It is significant that the various types of abnormal forms of speech that we have reviewed are used with little or no reserve when speaking of the persons referred to or when addressing children, but are, on the whole, avoided when within ear-shot of adults so referred to. It seems further significant that the traits satirized are chiefly such as are inherent in a person, not merely acquired in the accidental course of events, whereby he is set apart by nature as falling short in some respect of the normal type of individual and is to that extent stamped as inferior. This may explain why blindness, which is more often acquired rather late in life than congenital, is not made the subject of speech-mockery. Added to this may be the feeling that blindness is too grave an affliction to be treated light-heartedly, an explanation which gains weight when the well-known sensitiveness of the Indian is considered.

S. M. SHIROKOGOROFF

Speaking to Tigers but Not to Bears

The observations of the life of the tiger and bear have brought the Tungus to the idea that these animals may in some respects be treated in the same manner as man. The Tungus recognize that these animals would not attack the man if he does not want to harm them. So in order to make the tiger understand that the hunter does not intend to interfere with the tiger's hunting, the man must leave his rifle, putting it on the ground, and address the tiger with a speech in which he states that he will not interfere with the tiger's interest in the region, that he only visits it on his way to his own hunting region etc. The tiger is supposed to understand not word by word because the tiger cannot speak, but by a special method of penetrating into the sense of the speech.

The facts of speaking to the tiger are known from other regions too. So, for instance, V. K. Arseniev relates about it and under similar circumstances in his records (of "Darsu" etc.). Here it ought to be pointed out that the speaking to the animals is observed amongst almost all peoples of the earth. However, the purpose and ideas are not the same. If one takes all formally similar cases together, then one may confound the facts of different origin and function. I will not now go into the details which may take us very far, but it must be pointed out that the same Tungus do speak sometimes to themselves (psychologically this is the case of monologing), they do speak to the implements although they do not believe in the existence of soul or mentality in the implements and the latter have no special spirits. Yet, the Tungus would speak to an inanimate placing for the spirit (which may be especially made, or may be a tree or a rock), but he will speak to the spirit and not to the placing for the spirit. These are different cases of "speaking." However, in the case of speaking to the tiger he actually speaks to the animal with the intention of being understood. The ethnographers very often, if not usually, take for granted that the "primitive" people believe that the animals understand human speech as men do. It is not so, at least in reference to the Tungus in the case of their speaking to the tigers. According to the Tungus, the animal does not understand word by word, but it grasps man's speech in the sense of the man's behaviour. In fact when meeting a tiger without any intention of fighting it, the Tungus *must speak something and with a certain sincerity* in order to be trusted by the tiger. Naturally in a similar case he would remember what he had heard from the experienced hunters and he would repeat more or less exactly the sense of the speech heard by him. Under certain circumstances it may take the form of pure convention and even degenerate into a "magic" trick. Thus, one cannot take this case as evidence of the fact that the Tungus believe in the tiger's ability to understand human speech in general. The other facts mentioned above and to which we shall return, have entirely different meaning and function in the Tungus complex. I think that all similar facts must be carefully analysed before being used for generalization like that of a recent writer on this question who trusting himself to the scientific reliability of Sir J. Frazer inferred "the primitive man attributes to the animals the understanding of human language" which he needs for developing his own variation of Sir J. Frazer's theory of taboo. I do not deny the possibility of such an attribution amongst some ethnical groups and in certain conditions, e.g., as a special theory or as a magic method etc. but I cannot agree that this is a typical "primitive" character. Indeed, it is a late and secondary inference, perhaps a new adaptation of badly understood cultural elements borrowed from the original inventors.

If the tiger is not "stupid" he will leave the man alone and the man does not longer need to think about the tiger,—the tiger will not attack him. The Tungus believe that the tiger is not friendly to the man, but the tiger does not dare to fight man for the latter is well armed. Yet, the fact is that the Tungus when behaving unfriendly towards the tiger may be attacked by the tiger,—what happens rather often with inexperienced hunters. Owing to this the man must demonstrate before the tiger his peaceful intention as shown. The Tungus believe,—and it seems to be a matter of observation,—that the tiger recognizes his *Right on a Certain Territory* which cannot be harmlessly visited by the man, or large bears as well as other adult tigers. The tiger would not attack the man or large bear outside of his own territory and he will not attack the man or bear on his own territory if they do not show hostility. The tigers, bears and many other animals, according to the Tungus, know perfectly well the meaning of the fact when the man is armed with a gun, or with a spear. The same recognition of territorial right is supposed to exist amongst the large bears. The Tungus of Manchuria are inclined to see the idea of property amongst the small bears too, when they put their marks on the tree (by biting them) located at the radius of 25 or so metres from the den. They do the same with the entrance to the den if it is located in a hole of a tree. So the Tungus find the bears when they want to hunt them. A recent biting is recognized by the freshness of the bite which becomes gray after the period of summer rain. Other bears do not disturb the bear which already hibernates. However, if marks are put on the trees for indicating the region occupied by the bear, a fight between the two bears is possible. Again, as I have pointed out, this is used as a method of finding animals. The Tungus also recognize such a distinction of ownership of territory and they would not go into war with their neighbours,—the tigers and bears,—unless they are forced to take away the territory occupied by them. In the Tungus mind it is a war. According to the Tungus, such a war is very dangerous because the bears or tigers may destroy the family of the hunter and his domesticated animals during his absence, while he cannot stay all the time watching his family and household. The ownership of territory and non-attacking policy, are recorded in different parts of the world—e.g., in Africa, Canada, also in the Maritime Gov.—so they seem to be a fact. The complexity of relations between the man, tiger and bear is thus only a particular case of local adaptation of these animals, in the midst of which the Tungus does not underestimate and probably does not overestimate his own power of control of the territory and thus he remains a realist. The methods of arranging relations with these animals are gradually worked out, and they are effective as an empiric solution of the problem. Yet, when a Tungus speaks to the tiger, he leaves his gun down etc. and does not believe the tiger to be a being endowed with supernatural power. He hopes to be understood but if he fails he has to fight.

It is different with the bear which cannot understand speech. However, if the Tungus is not armed—which is usual with the women and they are not afraid to go alone—the bear would not attack him. Yet the bear may be frightened by something unusual and may lose his ordinary way of acting. So, for instance, a Tungus (Nerčinsk) meets a female bear with a young cub, and since he knows that the female is dangerous and he has no cartridge in his gun, he takes his gun in both hands and begins to beat a tree with it and to cry with a harsh voice. The female bear is surprised at his attitude and retires, while according to her usual behaviour she would attack. Therefore the Tungus say that the bear is not as intelligent as the tiger which cannot be surprised by such a simple trick. The bear cannot be killed at once unless it is hit in the heart. Practically it is almost impossible to do this unless the bear stands upon its hind legs and leaves the chest exposed. The bear as a matter of fact does this when it approaches the man for attacking him with its paw. But some of them rise up too late for enabling the hunter to shoot, so the hunter has to do something unusual to make it stand up at a certain distance. Sometimes the Tungus begins to dance and cry which produces the necessary effect on the bear. The intelligence of the bear is seen by the Tungus in occurrences which happen from time to time with some Tungus, when they are attacked by the bears. After a successful attack when the man is down the bear considers first by smelling and carefully looking whether the man is alive or not. If it believes that the man is dead it will bury the man supposedly killed, under a pile of the trunks of trees, of shrubs, leaves and earth; then it will again return and verify whether the man is there or not and at last it will leave the place. Naturally the man under such circumstances must do his best not to show he is alive.

The intelligence of the bear and tiger is seen in their ability to know those people who were touched by them. Here the theories and observation of facts and inferences cannot be surely distinguished so I will confine myself to the statement of facts. The Tungus of Manchuria assert that these animals, especially the bear, as a rule attack the people who were once attacked by them. On my question how these animals know it, I received a definite reply: —by their smelling. The things which have been touched by them are also recognized in the same way. The term used by the Tungus of Manchuria is *gálegda,* and the act of touching *galenk'i* [they may be found in other dialects as derived from the stem·*ŋale*]. The stem is *gale* (*ŋale*)—to fear, to be frightened. In reference to the man they say *s'i gálegda boje b'is'in'i,*—i.e. "you *galegda* man are"; and the hunting rule is: *gálegda ǰakava osin gada,*—the *gálegda* things one does not take (with on going to hunt).[1] In its further extension the idea of *gálegda* resulted in the hunters' avoidance of persons touched by bear. Yet, as a rule (amongst the Birarčen), the things touched once by the bear must be buried with the man who was touched by the bear. Yet the Tungus avoid touching the trees bitten by bears. The hunter who did not succeed in killing the animal and who was touched by it, is recommended not to hunt these animals any more, for he is not fearless, he is *gálegda.* Perhaps in this case the chief reason is that the hunter possesses no special ability for hunting these dangerous animals, or even perhaps

[1] The term *gálegda* has still greater use, namely, it may be referred to the localities and things touched by certain spirits. It must not be, however, inferred that in this term and behaviour of bears and tigers as described, there is some thing connected with the "religious" conceptions.

he becomes unable to do it owing to his previous unfortunate experience.

When the bear attacks the hunter and if it succeeds in taking possession of the spear or gun, it immediately breaks the arms. This fact is also considered as an indication of a special intelligence of the bear. In such a case when the Tungus are informed of the bear's attack they go well armed and with the dogs immediately to meet the animal's aggressors. This attitude could be compared with the custom of vendetta, but I do not want to insist upon it. In the same way the Tungus recognize the intelligence of the bear in the fact that bears store food in the earth and carry it from one place to another until it is finished. However, they say that the bears are not good to their young for which they do not leave food (meat). So that some Tungus call bears "dirty," "bad-natured" animals, for the bear finishes all its food alone, and it is often found overburdened with the food, and asleep, at just the place where the food is stored. Similar facts incline some Tungus to the idea that the bear is not very intelligent but the other facts convince them that the bear is not a bad hearted animal, and under certain conditions can be trusted, e.g., the bear very often collects berries at a short distance from the women also gathering berries. Thus according to the Tungus the bear is intelligent enough to understand the real danger for himself. The Tungus know that the bear is fearful when surprised which may result in spontaneous excretion of feces which makes the animal very weak. They know the peculiar character of the bear when it hibernates. It may be stated that the Tungus know all the steps in the life of this animal which they recognize as possessing certain rights of life and territory, which they consider as a more or less intelligent being, possessing a soul as man does, possessing certain peculiarities of character. Naturally when the Tungus needs to have a bear skin and meat, he would not hesitate to kill it, but if he does not need them he would not do it, for according to the Tungus idea of hunting—as it is a professional point of view—there is no need to kill an animal if one does not need the meat or skin. The abstaining from killing the bear is based upon this practical consideration and lack of experience of hunting this powerful and intelligent animal.

The behaviour of this animal shows to the Tungus that the bear has a soul, which will leave the body after the bear's death and as any other soul it may harm the man if he was wrong. Hence there are complex customs connected with the managing of the bear's soul. This complex is increased with the other elements borrowed from various groups. If we add to this the aesthetic side of performance and its justification, then we will have the complex of ceremonial eating of the bear, its funeral in the form of exposing the bones (as the Tungus did with man's bones), cutting off the furred skin on the legs, prohibition to the women to sit on the bear's skin and at last prohibition to the women to eat bear's meat, some dancing and singing, which formerly followed the human funeral perhaps. The partial abstaining from eating the bear's meat in the conditions of Transbaikalia and Manchuria is not of great economic consequence for the bear is rather rare and cannot become an essential component of the daily food.

PART 13

Feasts and Sacrifices

BERNARDINO DE SAHÁGUN (1495–1590)

Confession to a Mexican God

Now we come to Tlaculteutl, the goddess of carnal matters, who had three different names. First, Tlaculteutl, which means goddess of carnality. The second name was Ixcuina; they called her thus because they said there were four sisters; the first born or oldest was Tiacapan; the second was the youngest and they called her Teicu, the third was the middle one, called Tlaco; the fourth was the youngest of all Xucotzin. All these four sisters were the goddesses of carnality; in these names all women are included who are fit for the carnal act. The third name of the goddess is Tlaclqüani, which means eater of filthy things. This signifies that, according to their sayings, all such carnal men and women confessed their sins to these goddesses, no matter how uncouth and filthy they might have been, and they were forgiven. It is also said that this goddess or these goddesses had the power to produce lust; that they could provoke carnal intercourse and favored illicit love affairs, and that after such sins had been committed, they also held the power of pardoning and cleansing them of the sin, forgiving them if they confessed them to their Sátrapas (priests), who were the soothsayers who kept the books of divination and of the fate of the newly born, of witchcraft and prognostication as well as of ancient traditions, which were transmitted from mouth to mouth from the ancients down to them.

When a penitent was ready for confession, he would at once go in search of one of these priests or divines to whom they were wont to confess, saying to him: "Sir, I want to go to god almighty, who is the protector of all (this god almighty is called Yoallichccatlostees-tezcatlipoca) for I wanted to speak in secret of my sins." Hearing this, the Sátrapa would answer: "Be very welcome, my son, for what you say you wish to do is for your salvation and advantage." After saying this he would at once consult his book of divination which was called Tonalamatl, in order to find out by this book what day would be the most opportune for such a deed. As soon as he had found the propitious day, he would say: "Come on such and such a day, for on that day the sign is favorable to do this successfully." When the appointed day had come for the penitent to return he would buy a new mat (petate), white incense which they call copalli, and wood for the fire, over which the copalli was to be burned. If the penitent was a prominent man or invested with some official dignity, the priest would go to his house to confess him (or by chance the penitent man even being a prominent person might choose to go to the house of the priest). Upon arrival (wherever it might be), the place where the new mat was to be spread was very well swept and the confessor seated himself on the mat; the fire was lighted and he, the Sátrapa, threw the incense into it, and addressed himself to the fire, saying to it: "I wish to inform you, oh, lord, who are the father and the mother of all the gods and who are the most ancient god, that there has come today one of your vassals, this your servant, who comes here weeping in deep sorrow; he comes with great suffering; by all this it is clear that he has erred, that he stumbled and met with and found some of the obscenity of sin even with serious crime worthy of death, and he is very sad about it and downcast. Our very merciful lord who are our protector and supporter, accept the penitence and listen to the anguish of your servant and vassal." This prayer finished, the priest then turned to the penitent and spoke to him as follows: "Son, you have come into the presence of god, the helper and supporter of all; you came to tell him your inward shame and rottenness, to disclose unto him the secrets of your heart; be careful not to lead a riotous life nor to throw yourself headlong into it, nor get lost by lying in the presence of our lord. Rid yourself and throw out all your shame and disgrace in the presence of our lord, whose name is Yoallichectla, that is to say, Tezcatlipoca. It is a fact that you are before him (in his presence), although you are not worthy to see him; and even if he doesn't speak to you, because he is invisible and not palpable, mind how you come before him, with what kind of a heart; do not fear to declare your secrets in his presence, tell him your life, tell your (good) deeds in the same way you confessed your excesses and offenses, pour out your evil deeds in his presence, tell them all sorrowfully to our lord god, who is the protector of all, and who holds his arms open and is ready to embrace you and to carry you. See to it that you do not omit anything out of shame or cowardice!" When the penitent had heard all this, he took the oath to tell the truth,—in their own way of taking an oath, which is touching the earth with the hand and licking off whatever had stuck to it. He then threw copal into the fire, which was another way of taking an oath. Then he seated himself opposite the priest and, considering him (in this instance), as god's representative, he began his confession, saying: "Oh, lord, who accepts and helps everyone, listen to my baseness and rottenness. In your presence I disclose myself. I throw out all my shameful acts as many as I have committed, for, to be sure, none of the wickedness I am guilty of is hidden from you, because all things are apparent and clear to you." After this he at once began to tell his sins in the order he had committed them, with entire calm and distinctness, like a person who recites a poem or legend, very slowly and well enunciated, or, like one who goes on a very straight road without deviating to one side or the other. After having thus confessed everything he had done, the priest spoke to him and said, "My son, you have spoken before our lord god, telling him of all your wicked acts; now also in his name I shall tell you what you are obliged to do. When the goddesses called Civapipilti come down to earth, or when the feast to the goddesses of carnality whose name is Yxtuiname, is celebrated, you are to fast for four days, punishing your stomach and your mouth, and on the very day of the feast of Yxtuiname, in the morning or at daybreak, you are to make the proper penitence as suits your sins, and that is to pass through your tongue from one side to the other some twigs of what they call teucalcacatl or tlacotl, and if you should wish to do more than that, pass them through the ears, one or the other. This you do as penitence and atonement for your sins; it is not to be as a merit, but as a penitence for your evil deeds. You are to pierce first your tongue in the middle with a maguey thorn and through that same hole you will pass the twigs, passing each one in front of your face and, as you pull them out of the tongue, throw them behind you toward your back. If you should wish to unite (tie) all of them, you may attach one to the other, be there four hundred or eight hundred, in short, just as many as you wish to pass through your tongue; doing this, all the wickedness and filth you committed will be forgiven you." If the penitent has not committed neither very many nor serious sins, the priest to whom he confesses tells him, "My son, you are too fast; tire your stomach by hunger and your mouth by thirst, eating only once a day at noon and repeating this for four days," or he might tell some penitent to go and offer papers at the accustomed places and make images and to cover these images—as many and fashioned as his devotion would command,—with these papers and go through the devotional ceremony of singing and dancing, as is customary in their presence." Or he might say: "You offended god by getting drunk, so you must appease the god of wine, called Totochti, and when you go to comply with your penance you are to go at night, naked with only a paper in front and one at the back to cover your privy parts; when you are ready to return after your prayers are offered, you are to throw the papers that had covered your front and back at the feet of the gods that are there."

Once his confession made and after having received the penance he was to make, the penitent would go home and try never again to incur the same sins he had just confessed, because it was said that if these same sins were repeated then there was no more absolution.

Confessions of great sins, such as adultery, were only made by old men, and this for the simple reason to escape worldly punishment meted out for such sins; to escape from being condemned to death, which was either having their head crushed or ground to powder between two stones. It must be said that the priests who heard confessions were utterly discreet, never disclosing what they had learned in confession; this was because they considered that it was not they personally who had heard these confessions, but their god, who was the only one before whom sin was revealed, hence it was not supposed that any human heard them, nor had they been told to human ears, only to god (in his representative). It is well known that even after Christianity had been implanted, they (those Indians) insisted on confessing the most serious and nefarious sins, such as homicide, adultery, etc., and that by carrying out the penitence (penance) imposed in expiation as in times past, the courts of justice also would pardon them. Even now, if one of them kills or commits adultery, he will come to our homes or monasteries and without saying a word about their evil deeds, simply say that they want to do penance. They will work in the orchard, they will sweep the house, or do anything else they are ordered; after a few days they will go to confession, and after that will tell about their crimes, and give the reason why they came to do penance. After confession they ask a statement signed by the confessor with the intention to show it to those in power, be it the governor or the mayors, and thus let them know that they have done penance and have gone to confession, therefore justice has no case against them. Hardly any of the friars (monks) nor of the civil authorities understand this, mainly because they do not know anything about that ancient custom mentioned above, but rather think that the Indians ask for the certificate to show compliance with religious duties (to show that they have confessed that year). We are well aware of this condition on account of the great experience we acquired among them. It is said that the old men confessed their great (serious) sins of the flesh from which fact we may deduce that they probably had greatly sinned in their youth but did not confess until they were old, but that they could continue sinning while young, for it was their belief that once confessed they could not sin again. From the above we may safely deduce that those Indians of New Spain considered it their obligation to go to confession at least once in their lifetime, and that they did this even long before they had any knowledge of the Christian faith.

Aztec Human Sacrifice

This festival was held under the signs of the fifth month, which they called Toxcatl. In this month they celebrated a paschal festival in honor of the principal god called Tezcatlipoca, or by another name Tlilacaoan, or Yautl, and by still other names Telpuchtli or Tlamatzincatl. At this festival they killed (sacrificed) a youth of great elegance of carriage (great fitness or perfect health and proportion) whom they had maintained for a whole year in constant delight. They said he was (represented) the image of Tezcatlipoca. Once this youth was dead, they immediately put another one in his place, whom they petted and spoiled for another year, and so on, always replacing the one they sacrificed, and they had a great number of them in readiness from which to choose the successor to the one they killed at the festival. They selected for this purpose the best looking men among their captives and kept them in the Calpixques; they took great pains to choose the most intelligent and best suited there might be, without the least physical defect. The youth chosen for the coming year was carefully trained to play the flute very well, to gather and bring in the "smoke-sticks" (cañas de humo) and the flowers, as is the custom among chieftains and courtiers; they also taught him how to swallow smoke and smell the perfume of flowers, walking about as do the nobles and people of the court. Even while these young men were still under the care of the Calpixques and prior to the announcement of their ultimate destiny, they were carefully instructed by these same Calpixques in good manners in speech and behavior, in the correct way to bow to those they met on the street, and all other good habits. The one appointed for the sacrifice at the next festival of this god was greatly venerated by all those who met him, and they kissed the earth in his honour and worshipped him. If, due to the good treatment (good food) he grew stout, they would make him drink salt-water to keep slender.

The young man thus chosen to die at the next feast went through the streets playing the flute, carrying flowers, and smoke-sticks. He was free to be out day and night wherever he chose to go in town; he was always attended by eight pages, dressed like those of the palace, and he himself was given elegant and precious clothing by his master, for henceforth he was considered as a god himself. His whole body and face were anointed; his head was adorned with white chicken-feathers pasted on with resin; his hair was allowed to grow to reach the waist. After he was all dressed they adorned him with a wreath of flowers called izquixuchitl, and a long garland of the same was fastened on both shoulders and hung down to the armpit on both sides. In the ears he carried gold ornaments like ear-rings (pendants). Around the neck he wore a string of precious stones with a large pendant of a beautiful white stone hanging down to the chest. They put around his neck also a long helmet beaver, made of sea-shells; on the back he wore an ornament shaped like a bag, of the size of one square span (eight inches) made of white linen with its tassels and fringe. On the arms above and below the elbow he wore gold rings (armlets), and around the wrists strings of precious stones, which they call macuextli, which covered almost the entire forearm. He was covered with a very rich looking blanket fashioned like a net, with a very fancy fringe around the edges. Close to his body he wore a very odd piece of cloth which they used to cover the lower part of their bodies, called maxtlatl; the lower part of this maxtlatl had a very elaborate border about a span in width, and this border hung down in front as far as the knees. On the legs he wore golden rattles (or jingles), which sounded at every step. His feet were clad in elaborately painted sandals, which they called ocelunacace. Thus the youth was clothed for the first part of the year. Twenty days before the feast these clothes were changed; they washed the dye off his skin, and they married him to four maidens, with whom he lived for these last twenty days of his life. They now cut his hair in the style worn by war-captains, tying it like a tassel on top of the head with a very elaborate fringe and adorned that hair-bundle with two tassels with their buttons, made of feathers, gold and techomitl very oddly made, and which they called aztaxelli.

The four girls they gave him as wives and who had likewise been reared with special care for that purpose were given names of four goddesses; one bore the name of Xochiquetzatl, another the one of Xiionen, the third was called Atlatonan, and the fourth Vixtocioatl. Five days before the sacrifice they worshipped the young man as one of their gods. The lord remained alone in his house while all those of the court followed his example and solemn banquets and dances were held in very elaborate costumes. On the first day they feasted the youth in the district (of the city) called Tecanman; on the second day in the place where they kept the image of Tezcatlipoca; the third on the little hillock; the fourth at what is called Tepetzinco, which is in the lagune called ilquioa, antlalpia, antlalcuya, micontlalpia, itoci; on the fourth day on another hillock, also in the lagune, and called Tepepulco. After this fourth day they placed him in a canoe in which the king was wont to navigate, and which was covered by an awning; with him went his four wives, consoling him. Leaving Tepepulco they navigated towards a place called Tlapizaoaian, which is near the plain of Ixtapalapan, and extends toward Chalco, where rises the little hillock of Acaquilpan or Olcoaltepec. At this place his wives and all the other people left him, returning to the city, and he remained only with the eight pages who had been his followers for the entire year. They took him to a small and poorly decorated temple which stood near the highway (road) outside the city at a distance of almost a league from it. As they reached the foot of the Cú, the young man mounted the steps by himself, and on the first one he broke one of the flutes he had played on during that past year of prosperity; on the second one another, and so successively until he had broken them all, and thus reached the top. There he was awaited by the Sátrapas or priests who were to kill him, and these now grabbed him and threw him onto the stone-block and, holding him by feet, hands and head, thrown on his back, the priest who had the stone knife with a mighty thrust buried it in the victim's breast and, after drawing it out, thrust one hand into the opening and tore out the heart, which he at once offered to the sun. In this manner they killed all those who were offered to Tezcatlipoca, but instead of throwing the bodies down the steps after the sacrifice as they did on other occasions, this young man was carried down these steps by four men into the court, where they cut off his head, which they stuck onto a pole called Tzompantli. Thus ended the life of this unfortunate youth who for an entire year had been petted and honored by everybody. They said that this (sacrifice) signified that those who had possessed riches and pleasures in their lifetime would thus end in poverty and sorrow.

For this feast they also used to make the image of Vitzilopuchtli in dough, called Azoalli, of the size of a man down to the waist and that, in order to place this image in the Cú, which they called Vitznaoac, they would erect a stand the wood of which was carved to resemble snakes, their heads tied on the four sides of the pedestal, head against head, so that on all four sides there were tails and heads. For arms they inserted two sticks of mizguitl, and then inflated the dough in such a way that it resembled the bust of a man. They made this bust in the house (oratory) where the image of Vitzilopuchtli was always kept. After finishing the bust they adorned it with the vestments of the god; a jacket made of embroidered cloth of "besos de hombres" (whatever that may be), they covered the image with a very transparent blanket of "nequen" (probably henequen), and they crowned him with a crown shaped like a basket, very closely fitting to the head and widening at the top where it was elaborated with a plume; over a paper in the center rose a mask also made of feathers, and at the top of the mask a flint knife was inserted like the cross-iron of an anchor (ancon) dipped in blood to the middle of it (one half of it dipped in blood). Another blanket made entirely of elaborate feather-work was thrown over the bust. In the center of this feather-blanket was a round plaque (medallion) of hammered gold. At the bottom were ornaments made of tzoalli in the shape of kisses[1] close to the foot of the image, and these were covered also by the first mantle on which similar kisses had been elaborated, as well as limbs of a cut-up human body. The mantle or blanket thus adorned was called Tlaquaquallo.

They made still another ornament to honor this god, and which

[1] Besos. In Spain these "besos" are a sort of pastry very much like our "meringues," of white of egg and shaped like lips.

consisted of an enormous piece of paper, twenty fathoms (six feet each) long by one in width, and one finger thick. This paper was carried by a number of strong young men in front of the image, holding it on either side. In order to prevent this paper from tearing they mounted it on shafts or darts which they call teumitl, and these shafts or darts were adorned with feathers close to the arrow-head, in the center and at the end. These darts were so arranged that one crossed the width of the paper above, another underneath, so that in order to carry this large paper one youth would hold the two lower ends of the shafts together, another one the points, thus pressing the paper tightly held between them. When this was done, the image (bust of Azoalli) on its pedestal (platform) was raised onto the shoulders of a number of captains and warriors who, grouped on either side, carried it like a litter with the long paper always in front. Thus they proceeded in a procession, singing the songs to the god and dancing before him a solemn dance. Arriving at the foot of the temple steps, they tied ropes to the pedestal or platform in order to mount it up the stairway, and they did this very carefully so as not to tip the statue to either side. Those who carried the large paper again mounted ahead of the statue, and to prevent tearing it, those who climbed first at once began rolling the paper up with great care, pulling out the arrow shafts as they proceeded, and handing them to the one whose duty it was to gather them in a big bunch. As soon as the statue had reached the top they placed it where it belonged on its throne or chair, and they laid in front of the platform the roll of paper securely tied, to prevent its unrolling. Then all but the Sátrapas (priests) left the Cú, and the latter were on duty guarding the idols. This ceremony being over at about sunset, tamales and other kinds of food were placed in front of the image as offerings. The next morning at dawn everyone made this offering of food to the image of Vitzilopuchtli, which he had in his own house, and all of them went to the Cú to offer the blood of quails to the image they had installed there on the previous day. The chieftain or lord came first, pulling off the heads of four quails, which latter he then offered to the image, then followed the priests with their sacrifices, and after them the people. After pulling off their heads they threw the beheaded birds at the feet of the idol, where they fluttered until death felled them. They then were gathered by the shield-bearers and warriors of the king, who had them peeled, roasted and salted, dividing them then among themselves. A certain amount, however, belonged first to the king or lord, to the chiefs, to the priests, and only what was left was of the shield-bearers. They all brought their braziers; a fire was built in the Cú and live coal was produced, for the burning of incense, for they all brought their "copalli" (copal-incense) and their own earthen incense-burners, which look like cups with holes, very ornate, and which they called tlemaitl; they also brought copal (incense) of all kinds, and proceeded with the ceremonies of the service of that god (according to rules). At a certain stage of the ceremonial the priests took live coal from the fire, put it into their incense-burners, and incensed the image of Vitzilopuchtli, which they had brought to the Cú shortly before. This ceremony was not only performed in the Cú, but also in all the homes by the owners who on that occasion incensed all the statues of the different gods they happened to have. After the incensing they threw the live coal left in the incensories into a round hearth of about two spans in height made of clay, which was in the center of the patio, and which they called tlexictli.

At this festival all the young girls painted (beautified) their faces, adorned their arms and legs with red feathers, and carried certain papers flatly stuck (fastened) on sticks which they called tetelvitl; these papers were painted with ink (dye). If they happened to be daughters of chieftains or wealthy people, they wore instead of the paper very thin blankets called "canaoc." The blankets were also painted in black in the shape (or form) of commas, vertically. These papers or clothes on their sticks they carried in their hands on high (like banners), and walked in procession with the other people to honor their god. These girls also danced, holding their paper (or cloth) banners in both hands, around the hearth, upon which stood two shield-bearers with faces dyed with ink, who carried on their back something that looked like cages made of candlewood, around the edges of which small paper flags were stuck. They carried them, not in the fashion (way) men carry their long bundles of firewood, fastened by a strap about the forehead, but in women's way, tied over the breast. These two men, on top of the hearth guided the dance of the women surrounding it, dancing in woman-fashion. At the same time the priests of the temple danced with their companions and these two groups, the men and the women, danced or rather hopped a dance called Toxcachocholoa, which means jumping or dancing on the festival of Toxcatl. The priests wore around their foreheads a sort of paper disk shirred in the shape of roses. All the priests had their heads adorned with white chicken-feathers; their faces and lips were bedaubed with honey after they had been painted black, as they always did, and the honey shone on that dark background. As was their custom, they wore undergarments of paper called amasmaxtli; in their hands they carried sceptres of palm leaves, at the top of which was a flower of black feathers; this sceptre was called cuitlacuchtli, after the knot or ball it had at the lower end. The part of the sceptre they held in hand was wrapped in paper painted with black stripes or lines, and when they danced they bent right down to the soil in a certain figure of the dance, resting on the sceptre. Those who furnished the music for dancing were stationed within the house called calpulco, so that dancers and musicians could not see each other; the latter were seated; in their midst was the kettle-drum, and all played jingles and all the other instruments used by them for dancing. All the employees (people of the palace), even the warriors, old and young, danced in other (separate) parts of the courtyard, holding each other by the hand, and winding in and out (wriggling) in snake-fashion, very similar to the popular dances the people of Castilla la Vieja, men and women, dance today. Among these warriors one could also see maidens dancing, very well painted, and their arms and legs adorned with red feathers. On the head they wore small hoods which, instead of flowers, were made of roasted corn (popcorn) which they call momochitl, of which each grain looks like a (very) white flower. These little hoods were very much like the flower-hoods the country girls of Castilla wear in the month of May. They also wore strings of this same popcorn hanging from both shoulders to the armpits. They call this sort of dance tlanaoa, which means embraced; "quinaoain Vitzilopuchtli," to embrace Vitzilopuchtli. All this was done with great circumspection and modesty, and if anyone looked or spoke dishonourably, he was at once punished, for there were people (men) stationed nearby to watch over them. These dances lasted until nightfall.

While after having given him a year of luxury they killed the youth who was supposed to be the image of Tlitacaoan, at the beginning of this festival, they had already begun to educate, together with him, another young man whom they called Yxteucali, by another name Tlacabepan, or also Teicauhtzin. They always were together, although this latter one was not worshipped like the former, nor was he so highly esteemed. As soon as the above-mentioned festival was over with its rejoicing and its ceremonies, they killed Tlacabepan, the image of Vitzilopuchtli, and for this purpose adorned him with papers all painted with black wheels (or circles). On his head they put a mitre of eagle-feathers with many tufts on the top, and in the center of which was a flint-knife, stuck upright, one half of it tinted with blood and adorned with red feathers. On his back he wore an ornament, one span square, made of very thin cloth, and which they call icuechin, tied by means of cotton strings around the breast and over the cuechin there was a small bag called patoxin. On one of his arms there was an ornament made of the skin of a wild animal, shaped like a maniple such as (in the Catholic church) is used for saying mass. They called this maniple imatacox. His legs were adorned with golden jingles such as are worn by dancers. Thus attired, he danced during the festival and he guided (or led) the plebeian dances, at the head of the dancers. This youth of his own free will and at his own time, delivered himself into the hands of those who were to kill him. The priests who took care of these young men and watched over them until they were to be sacrificed were called Tlatlacaanalti, and they were the ones who cut the respective victim's breast and extracted the heart, later beheading him and sticking the head on a pole in the Tzompantli close to that of the first youth, above-mentioned. On that same day the priests inflicted wounds, with a flint knife, on boys and girls, on the breast, the stomach, on the muscles of the arms or on the wrist. It appears that these wounds were meant to represent marks of the demon with which he marked his sheep, and those who even today practice this are suspected of practicing idolatry if these marks are made after baptism, but of old, children were thus marked every year.

HERMAN MELVILLE
The Taboo Groves

From the verdant surfaces of the large stones that lay scattered about, the natives were now sliding off into the water, diving and ducking beneath the surface in all directions—the young girls springing buoyantly into the air, and revealing their naked forms to the waist, with their long tresses dancing about their shoulders, their eyes sparkling like drops of dew in the sun, and their gay laughter pealing forth at every frolicsome incident.

On the afternoon of the day that I took my first bath in the valley, we received another visit from Mehevi. The noble savage seemed to be in the same pleasant mood, and was quite as cordial in his manner as before. After remaining about an hour, he rose from the mats, and motioning to leave the house, invited Toby and myself to accompany him. I pointed to my leg; but Mehevi in his turn pointed to Kory-Kory, and removed that objection; so, mounting upon the faithful fellow's shoulders again—like the old man of the sea astride of Sindbad—I followed after the chief.

The nature of the route we now pursued struck me more forcibly than anything I had yet seen, as illustrating the indolent disposition of the islanders. The path was obviously the most beaten one in the valley, several others leading from either side into it, and perhaps for successive generations it had formed the principal avenue of the place. And yet, until I grew more familiar with its impediments, it seemed as difficult to travel as the recesses of a wilderness. Part of it swept round an abrupt rise of ground, the surface of which was broken by frequent inequalities, and thickly strewn with projecting masses of rocks, whose summits were often hidden from view by the drooping foliage of the luxuriant vegetation. Sometimes directly over, sometimes evading these obstacles with a wide circuit, the path wound along—one moment climbing over a sudden eminence smooth with continued wear, then descending on the other side into a steep glen, and crossing the flinty channel of a brook. Here it pursued the depths of a glade, occasionally obliging you to stoop beneath vast horizontal branches; and now you stepped over huge trunks and boughs that lay rotting across the track.

Such was the grand thoroughfare of Typee. After proceeding a little distance along it—Kory-Kory panting and blowing with the weight of his burden—I dismounted from his back, and grasping the long spear of Mehevi in my hand, assisted my steps over the numerous obstacles of the road; preferring this mode of advance to one which, from the difficulties of the way, was equally painful to myself and my wearied servitor.

Our journey was soon at an end; for, scaling a sudden height, we came abruptly upon the place of our destination. I wish that it were possible to sketch in words this spot as vividly as I recollect it.

Here were situated the Taboo groves of the valley—the scene of many a prolonged feast, of many a horrid rite. Beneath the dark shadows of the consecrated breadfruit-trees there reigned a solemn twilight—a cathedral-like gloom. The frightful genius of pagan worship seemed to brood in silence over the place, breathing its spell upon every object around. Here and there, in the depths of these awful shades, half screened from sight by masses of overhanging foliage, rose the idolatrous altars of the savages, built of enormous blocks of black and polished stone, placed one upon another, without cement, to the height of twelve or fifteen feet, and surmounted by a rustic open temple, enclosed with a low picket of canes, within which might be seen, in various stages of decay, offerings of breadfruit and coco-nuts, and the putrefying relics of some recent sacrifice.

In the midst of the wood was the hallowed "Hoolah-Hoolah" ground—set apart for the celebration of the fantastic religious ritual of these people—comprising an extensive oblong "pi-pi," terminating at either end in a lofty terraced altar, guarded by ranks of hideous wooden idols, and with the two remaining sides flanked by ranges of bamboo sheds, opening towards the interior of the quadrangle thus formed. Vast trees, standing in the middle of this space, and throwing over it an umbrageous shade, had their massive trunks built round with slight stages, elevated a few feet above the ground, and railed in with canes, forming so many rustic pulpits, from which the priests harangued their devotees.

This holiest of spots was defended from profanation by the strictest edicts of the all-pervading "taboo," which condemned to instant death the sacrilegious female who should enter or touch its sacred precincts, or even so much as press with her feet the ground made holy by the shadows that it cast.

Access was had to the enclosure through an embowered entrance on one side, facing a number of towering coco-nut trees, planted at intervals along a level area of a hundred yards. At the further extremity of this space was to be seen a building of considerable size, reserved for the habitation of the priests and religious attendants of the groves.

In its vicinity was another remarkable edifice, built as usual upon the summit of a pi-pi, and at least two hundred feet in length, though not more than twenty in breadth. The whole front of this latter structure was completely open, and from one end to the other ran a narrow verandah, fenced in on the edge of the pi-pi with a picket of canes. Its interior presented the appearance of an immense lounging-place, the entire floor being strewn with successive layers of mats, lying between parallel trunks of coco-nut trees, selected for the purpose from the straightest and most symmetrical the vale afforded.

To this building, denominated in the language of the natives the "Ti," Mehevi now conducted us. Thus far we had been accompanied by a troop of the natives of both sexes; but as soon as we approached its vicinity, the females gradually separated themselves from the crowd, and standing aloof, permitted us to pass on. The merciless prohibitions of the taboo extended likewise to this edifice, and were enforced by the same dreadful penalty that secured the hoolah-hoolah ground from the imaginary pollution of a woman's presence.

On entering the house, I was surprised to see six muskets ranged against the bamboo on one side, from the barrels of which depended as many small canvas pouches, partly filled with powder. Disposed about these muskets, like the cutlasses that decorate the bulkhead of a man-of-war's cabin, were a great variety of rude spears and paddles, javelins, and war-clubs. This then, said I to Toby, must be the armory of the tribe.

As we advanced further along the building, we were struck with the aspect of four or five hideous old wretches, on whose decrepit forms time and tattooing seemed to have obliterated every trace of humanity. Owing to the continued operation of this latter process, which only terminates among the warriors of the island after all the figures stretched upon their limbs in youth have been blended together—an effect, however, produced only in cases of extreme longevity—the bodies of these men were of a uniform dull green color—the hue which the tattooing gradually assumes as the individual advances in age. Their skin had a frightful scaly appearance, which, united with its singular color, made their limbs not a little resemble dusty specimens of verd-antique. Their flesh, in parts, hung upon them in huge folds, like the overlapping pleats on the flank of a rhinoceros. Their heads were completely bald, whilst their faces were puckered into a thousand wrinkles, and they presented no vestige of a beard. But the most remarkable peculiarity about them was the appearance of their feet; the toes, like the radiating lines of the mariner's compass, pointed to every quarter of the horizon. This was doubtless attributable to the fact, that during nearly a hundred years of existence, the said toes never had been subjected to any artificial confinement, and in their old age, being averse to close neighborhood, bid one another keep open order.

These repulsive-looking creatures appeared to have lost the use of their lower limbs altogether; sitting upon the floor cross-legged in a state of torpor. They never heeded us in the least, scarcely looking conscious of our presence, while Mehevi seated us upon the mats, and Kory-Kory gave utterance to some unintelligible gibberish.

In a few moments a boy entered with a wooden trencher of poee-poee; and in regaling myself with its contents I was obliged again to submit to the officious intervention of my indefatigable servitor. Various other dishes followed, the chief manifesting the most hospitable importunity in pressing us to partake, and to remove all bashfulness on our part, set us no despicable example in his own person.

The repast concluded, a pipe was lighted, which passed from mouth to mouth, and yielding to its soporific influence, the quiet of the place, and the deepening shadows of approaching night, my companion and I sank into a kind of drowsy repose, while the chief and Kory-Kory seemed to be slumbering beside us.

SAMUEL CROWELL

The Dog Sacrifice of the Senecas

On the second day of February, 1830, I witnessed an interesting, and to me, a novel religious ceremony of the Seneca tribe of Indians, then occupying that portion of territory now comprising a part of the counties of Seneca, and Sandusky, Ohio, familiarly known to the inhabitants of this region, as the Seneca reservation.

Shortly after our arrival at the house of this chief, Mr. D. retired; not so with our friendly host and myself—while sitting near a clean, brick hearth, before a cheerful fire, Hard Hickory unbosomed himself to me unreservedly. Mr. D. was asleep and the chief and I were the only persons then awake in the house.

Hard Hickory told me, among other things, that it was owing chiefly to him, that this feast was now celebrated; that it was in part to appease the anger of the *Good Spirit,* in consequence of a dream he lately had; and as an explanation he gave me the following narration:

"He dreamed he was fleeing from an enemy, it was, he supposed, something supernatural; perhaps, an evil spirit; that, after it had pursued him a long time, and for a great distance, and every effort to escape from it seemed impossible as it was just at his heels, and he almost exhausted; at this perilous juncture, he saw a large water, towards which he made with all his remaining strength, and at the very instant when he expected each bound to be his last, he beheld, to his joy, a canoe near the shore; this appeared as his last hope; breathless and faint, he threw himself into it, and, of its own accord, quick as an arrow from the bow, it shot from the shore leaving his pursuer on the beach!"

While relating this circumstance to me, which he did with earnestness, trepidation and alarm, strongly expressed in his countenance, he took from his bosom something neatly and very carefully enclosed in several distinct folds of buckskin. This he began to unroll, laying each piece by itself, and on opening the last, there was enclosed therein, a canoe in miniature! On handing it to me to look at, he remarked, that no other person save himself and me, had ever seen it, and that, as a memento, he would wear it, as "long as he lived." It was a piece of light wood, resembling cork, about six inches long, and, as intended, so it was, a perfect model of a canoe.

This chief, being now in a communicative mood, I took the liberty to inquire of him "when they intended to burn their dogs?" for I began to fear I should miss the express object which I came to witness. After giving me to understand that "the red men did not care about the pale faces being present at, nor, if they chose, joining in the dance, but burning their dogs was another thing—this was offering sacrifice to, and worshiping the Great Spirit; and while engaged in their devotions they objected to the presence and interference of the whites; yet, as I had never been present, and coming as the friend of Mr. Dickinson, who was a good man, he would tell me they would burn their dogs soon to-morrow morning." The night being now far advanced, he pointed to the bed and told me to sleep there; but that he must go to the council house, to the dance, for his people would not like it, if he would stay away, and wishing me good night, he withdrew.

Anxiety to witness the burnt offering almost deprived me of sleep. Mr. D. and I, therefore, rose early and proceeded directly to the council house, and though we supposed we were early, the Indians were already in advance of us. The first object which arrested our attention, was a pair of the canine species, one of each gender suspended on a *cross!* one on either side thereof. These animals had been recently *strangled—not a bone was broken* nor could a distorted hair be seen? They were of a beautiful cream color, except a few dark spots on one, naturally, while the same spots had been put on the other, artificially, by the devotees. The Indians are very partial in the selection of dogs entirely white, for this occasion; and for which they will give almost any price.

Now for part of the decorations to which I have already alluded, and a description of one will suffice for both, for they were *par similes*. A scarlet ribbon was tastefully tied just above the nose; and near the eyes another; next round the neck was a white ribbon, to which was attached something bulbous, concealed in another white ribbon; this was placed directly under the right ear, and I suppose it was intended as an amulet or charm. Then ribbons were bound round the forelegs, at the knees, and near the feet—these were red and white alternately. Round the body was a profuse decoration—then the hind legs were decorated as the fore ones. Thus were the victims prepared and thus ornamented for the burnt offering.

While minutely making this examination, I was almost unconscious of the collection of a large number of the Indians who were there assembled to offer their sacrifices.

Adjacent to the cross, was a large fire built on a few logs; and though the snow was several inches deep, they had prepared a sufficient quantity of combustible material, removed the snow from the logs, and placed thereon their fire.

It was a clear, beautiful morning, and just as the first rays of the sun were seen in the tops of the towering forest, and its reflections from the snowy surface, the Indians simultaneously formed a semicircle enclosing the cross, each flank resting on the aforesaid pile of logs. Good Hunter who officiated as high priest, now appeared, and approached the cross; arrayed in his pontifical robes, he looked quite respectable. The Indians being all assembled—I say Indians (for there was not a squaw present during all this ceremony—I saw two or three pass outside of the semi-circle, but they moved as if desirous of being unobserved), at a private signal given by Good Hunter, two young chiefs sprang up at the cross, and each taking off one of the victims, brought it down, and presented it on his arms to Good Hunter, who, receiving it with great reverence, in like manner advanced to the fire, and with a very grave and solemn air, laid it thereon—and this he did with the other—but to which, whether male or female, he gave the preference, I did not learn. This done, he retired to the cross.

In a devout manner, he now commenced an oration. The tone of his voice was audible and somewhat chanting. At every pause in his discourse, he took from a white cloth he held in his left hand, a portion of dried, odoriferous herbs, which he threw on the fire; this was intended as incense. In the meanwhile his auditory, their eyes on the ground, with grave aspect, and in solemn silence, stood motionless, listening attentively, to every word he uttered. Thus he proceeded until the victims were entirely consumed, and the incense exhausted, when he concluded his service; their oblation now made, and the wrath of the Great Spirit, as they believed, appeased, they again assembled in the council house, for the purpose of performing a part in their festival, different from any I yet had witnessed. Each Indian as he entered, seated himself on the floor, thus forming a large circle; when one of the old chiefs rose, and with that native dignity which some Indians possess in a great degree, recounted his exploits as a warrior; told in how many fights he had been the victor; the number of scalps he had taken from his enemies; and what, at the head of his braves, he yet intended to do at the Rocky mountains; accompanying his narration with energy, warmth, and strong gesticulations; when he ended, he received the unanimous applause of the assembled tribe.

This meed of praise was awarded to the chief by three times three articulations, which were properly neither nasal, oral, nor guttural, but rather abdominal. Indeed I am as unable to describe this kind of utterance, as I am, the step in the dance. I have seen some whites attempt to imitate the step, and heard them affect the groan or grunt, but it was a mere aping thereof. Thus many others in the circle, old and young, rose in order, and *proforma,* delivered themselves of a speech. Among those was Good Hunter; but he

> "Had laid his robes away,
> His mitre and his vest."

His remarks were not filled with such bombast as some others; but brief, modest, and appropriate; in fine, they were such as became a priest of one of the lost ten tribes of Israel!

After all had spoken who wished to speak, the floor was cleared, and the dance renewed, in which Indian and squaw united, with their wonted hilarity and zeal.

Just as this dance ended, an Indian boy ran to me, and with fear strongly depicted in his countenance, caught me by the arm, and drew me to the door, pointing with his other hand towards something he wished me to observe. I looked in that direction, and saw the appearance of an Indian running at full speed to the council house; in an instant he was in the house, and literally in the fire, which he took in his hands, and threw coals of fire and hot ashes in various directions, through the house, and apparently all over himself! At his entrance, the young Indians, much alarmed, had all fled to the further end of the house, where they remained crowded, in great dread of this personification of the evil spirit! After diverting himself with the fire a few moments, at the expense of the young ones, to their no small joy he disappeared. This was an Indian disguised with an hideous false face, having horns on his head, and his hands and feet protected from the effects of the fire. And though not a professed fire king, he certainly performed his part to admiration.

During the continuance of this festival, the hospitality of the Senecas was unbounded. In the council house, and at the residence of Tall Chief, were a number of large fat bucks, and fat hogs hanging up, and neatly dressed. Bread also, of both corn and wheat in great abundance. Large kettles of soup ready prepared, in which maple sugar, profusely added, made a prominent ingredient, thus forming a very agreeable saccharine coalescence, and what contributed still more to heighten the zest—it was all *impune* (scot free). All were invited, and all were made welcome; indeed a refusal to partake of their bounty, was deemed disrespectful, if not unfriendly.

In the afternoon I left them enjoying themselves to the fullest extent: and so far as I could perceive, their pleasure was without alloy. They were eating and drinking (on this occasion, no ardent spirits were permitted), dancing and rejoicing—caring not, and, probably, thinking not of to-morrow.

GEOFFREY GORER

Dahomeyan Sacrifice of the Bull

The dance of the Legba is always performed first, to avert evil spirits; for the same reason the legba dancer always prances in front of the other performers, waving his olisbos in the air. The most general dance is the gobahun, which is danced in pairs, very quick with vehement arm movements and sudden twists. Both men and women dance this; for both the principal item of dress is a full skirt reaching a little below the knees, in various materials but chiefly white; when the dancers turn suddenly it spreads out wide like a ballet skirt. The most dramatic of the thunder dances is the adahoun; it is danced by a very few young men naked to the waist except for a necklace of big red and blue beads, and wearing a short very full skirt about nine inches long, like a tiny tutu, tight-fitting velvet drawers reaching to the knee and a scarf knotted under the skirt so that its ends fall down like a tail. They dance with one or occasionally two sossyabi, holding it in the mouth or the left hand. Their dance is completely wild, for they represent the destructive element of thunder; with the sossyabi in their teeth—no mean feat for it is very heavy—they rush in every direction with their hands held out and their head jerking backwards and forwards; they are completely bacchic and frenzied, and their big-pupilled eyes are fixed on infinity. They destroy whatever comes under their hand—plants, trees, roofs, even objects sacred to the fetish; they seize what they fancy, hats and clothes off the spectators, animals and even children, shouting when they have got booty and waving it in the air towards the tomtom with whom they later deposit it. So possessed are they that they roll on the ground, eat earth, turn somersaults and walk on the narrowest coping. The onlookers are in a state of pleasurable terror; the dancers are filled with the spirit of the thunder and must not be opposed in anything they are inspired to do; who can oppose a thunderbolt? They once took my topi, which alarmed me, for I had no other; but the kindly legba returned it when the dance was finished.

While we were at Abomey we saw the public dances of many different fetishes, for the Dahomeyans are pious people and in the numerous villages many rites were held (of course in the town of Abomey they don't dance.

The Nesshoué are always in a very great company and elaborately dressed in many cloths of different but harmonious tones, avoiding all pure colours except blue and green. They wear chased silver daggers at their waists, and on their arms cunningly worked armlets and bracelets in solid silver; the men carry sossyabi with the axe-like blade in silver, the women horse-tails, also mounted on silver. Their dances are mostly slow and undulating, after the character of a river; they dance together so that their varied clothes look like a bed of living flowers, their silver ornaments sparkling like dew. Against the background of the blue sky and the palms, with occasional trees of a deeper green and scarlet fruit, the effect is of the greatest beauty. Sometimes they dance in lines and sometimes in single file but always with the strictest rhythm and co-ordination. There is only one dance which is done individually. Perhaps the most lovely of all their dances is the Selili, or gleaning dance (the river makes the harvest): in a long line they hold their sossyabi and fans parallel with the ground and with one leg stretched behind them they advance with a quick undulating movement, gradually gathering speed till they seem like a sea wave. I deeply regret that I have not the skill to reproduce even faintly the most beautiful spectacle I have ever seen; and a colourless photograph is as dead as the Grecian landscapes without light.

The Fetishist Convents

A convent consists of a collection of huts and courtyards surrounded by a living hedge. The huts differ from ordinary living huts by having the roof much lower; moreover the straw thatch descends to the ground and the only entrance and illumination is a tiny hole in the thatch just wide enough for a person to crawl through. The courtyards are relatively large, for the rites take place in them; the living hedge surrounding the group of buildings is planted with various sacred or magic trees (particularly the leaves of Fa) joined by the commonest surrounding vegetation. These convents are always situated in the bush, usually amidst trees; there is no marked path leading to them and unless you know where they are or unless a drum is playing it is possible to pass a thicket daily without suspecting any building near.

Except for a few guardians the convents have no permanent population. Child fetishers spend three years in them, and all fetishers return to them from time to time; moreover if a fetisher has committed a sin it is in the convents that he must expiate it. The number of convents in existence is probably not known by anybody, and a great deal which goes on in them is completely secret. Even if they are inspected by the local authorities, whether black or white, they have most of them neighbouring hide-outs. Children could very easily be born in them without their existence being known.

In one of the convents women fetishers were preparing for a special rite. The fetishist convent huts, like the temples, are divided into two sections, of which only the second is holy. In the convent I am describing this second portion was filled with women packed so closely that they had barely room to sit. In an area which was certainly less than a hundred square feet there were more than a dozen women. They were all dressed alike with a cap of purple net from which hung long strings threaded with cowries falling to the breast, so thick that they completely hid the face. Across the otherwise naked torso were slings of cowries and purple beads; they had ordinary skirts and anklets of cowries. They were all in very deep trance and completely motionless; all the actions of everyday life, feeding, washing and so on, had to be done for them. They were no longer themselves; they were filled with the power of the fetish. They could no longer speak; only by a certain ritual could the priest make them talk, and then it was no longer the woman but the fetish itself talking through its agent in its own language. In the present instance the women were to be in this state for three weeks, during which except for ceremonies they could not go out of the hut or see the light. The wonderworkers are in this state permanently; if a man is completely filled with the fetish he performs no ordinary actions and never sees the light, nor does he eat any solid food. These wonderworkers are few and live in the most deserted places;

their powers can be controlled because they can only work through the agency of a normally conscious priest.

To call these entranced women out of the hut an elaborate ceremonial is necessary. They can only move to the sound of a special tomtom; when this starts playing the chief fetish priest kneels by the entrance and shakes a rattle while he invokes the fetish with prayers; the other fetishers present prostrate themselves and repeat the prayers, rubbing their hands together. After some time the tomtoms become louder and the fetishers shriek; one of the women has shown her mask at the door. A cockerel is immediately fetched; its legs and wings are broken and its tongue pulled out; its beak is stuffed with special leaves and it is held by its legs; a drop of the blood is let fall on each of the woman's big toes; she comes out and with head downcast starts dancing feverishly, swinging her shoulders with a force which would tire an ordinary person in a few minutes. After the first several more are called out with the same ceremonial; not all that are in the hut, for that can only be left completely empty at the greatest ceremonies. The women dance in a vague circle, but like blind people; they have to be continually guided to prevent them knocking themselves against the buildings. Before they can return to the fetish hut they have to be purified; they are led on to a special mat where their hands and feet are laved in holy water, after which another chicken is mutilated in the same cruel fashion and a drop of blood is allowed to fall from its beak on their thumbs and big toes. They are led back to the hut with prayers and rattles; they enter it backwards, creeping on all fours. This is the essential basis of fetish worship; the body is used as a vessel to be filled with the divine force, no less holy because the owner of the body is unaware of what occurs.

In another convent two women were undergoing penance for sins they had committed; from the priest and Prince Aho I got a short description of their misdoings and the expiations required.

One of the women had gone to her cousin's funeral, against the express command of her fetish. On the following morning she fell into a trance from which she could not be awakened; she stayed in this alarming state for some time, only recovering lucidity for a few moments on the second day during which she said "I have seen my fetish in my sleep; he orders me to go to him. I don't know where," after which she immediately returned to her trance. Considerably alarmed the girl's parents consulted the bokonon; the Fa replied that the girl had sinned and the sin must be discovered and he dictated what sacrifices were to be made for that purpose. The parents followed the prescription exactly but were much alarmed when during the sacrifice a couple of vultures entered the girl's hut. After the first moment of panic however they considered that the vultures might be omens; they offered to the birds some akassa (coarse maize flour) which they ate; this was a sign that the fetish had accepted the sacrifice, which was further confirmed by the girl's awakening and confessing. To expiate this sin the Fa ordered the girl to go to the convent. For seven days she was confined to the fetish house, where she had to sleep on the bare earth; she was not allowed to wash and was given no food except akassa and water. At the end of the seven days the girl was publicly exorcised, and bathed in holy water. This had happened a few days before we visited the convent; the girl was now allowed to walk in the courtyard; she could eat cola and the flesh of white chickens after a drop of their blood had been allowed to fall on her tongue and her forehead. Every day she was laved three times in holy water. This was to continue for a week; on the sixth day the parents were to bring to the convent two white goats, two white chickens and two white pigeons, two measures each of flour and oil and seven parrot feathers. On the evening of the same day her head would be shaved and all her belongings taken from her; she would be given a white pagne to cover herself. On the seventh day all her relations would gather at the convent as well as a number of fetishers. All the sacrificial animals would be killed and the oil and flour made into a paste. The chief fetisher would be dressed entirely in white; he would first of all bless the paste and then return the sinner to her parents, after praying to the fetish to keep all its children from sin. He would then give a portion of the paste to the sinner and after her to all present and would say to the girl "Now you are clean again and can eat with us." After a general dance the girl would return home.

The second woman while travelling with her husband had eaten some antelope, a food taboo to her. She was immediately seized with a belly ache and became completely and immovably constipated; her skin turned "antelope colour." The Fa said that she had eaten some forbidden meat and before the fetish she confessed. (It is possible that she had not known what she was eating.) Her constipation was cured by a decoction of seven sacred leaves and she was then purified in the same manner as the other woman. The only difference was in the final ceremony. The parents had brought with them a white antelope and two white chickens. The priest on his side prepared three packets of sacred leaves. The first packet of leaves was mixed with the saliva and nail parings of the sinner and placed in the antelope's mouth. The antelope was then killed and the heart torn out; the priest touched the sinner's body with it and said "This woman has not given her heart to the antelope but to the fetish." This action and formula, with the necessary variations, was repeated with the head and the tail. The heart, tail and head with the leaves in its mouth were then placed in a jar; the outside of this jar and the body of the sinner were then covered with spots of red and white paint. The jar would be transferred to a spot named by the fetish (probably where three roads met) and shortly after the fetisher would place the second packet of leaves in some water which he would bless and with which the sinner would bathe. The third packet of leaves would be placed in the zenvi (the hole in front of the fetish altar in which offerings and impregnated objects are placed) and the two chickens so killed that all their blood would fall on the leaves. The bodies of the chickens would be buried in front of the altar. This woman was less severely punished than the other because it was possible that her sin had been unconscious; though that did not make it less heinous, or her less dangerous in her unclean state (sinners are a source of contamination), yet the penalty was less severe.

The women in the convent of Lissa (the chameleon) were very similar in behaviour and dress to those of Agassou. There was only one peculiarity: as they danced they changed colour quite noticeably, their skin going through every hue of brown from a dirty white to nearly black. Although there is physiologically nothing inexplicable in this, the effect of half a dozen women with the colour of their skins visibly altering all the time they danced was very extraordinary.

MAYA DEREN
The Goddess of Lust

Voudoun has given woman, in the figure of Erzulie, exclusive title to that which distinguishes humans from all other forms: their capacity to conceive beyond reality, to desire beyond adequacy, to create beyond need. In Erzulie, Voudoun salutes woman as the divinity of the dream, the Goddess of Love, the muse of beauty. It has denied her emphasis as mother of life and of men in order to regard her as mother of man's myth of life—its meaning. In a sense, she is that very principle by which man conceives and creates divinity. Thus, to man himself, she is as mistress.

It is significant that, to the Haitian, she is as important as the loa of the elemental cosmic forces and even more beloved. For the Haitian is not at all a simple, elemental man. Even though (or perhaps precisely because) it is so difficult for him to acquire even those things which are requisite for daily life, he is almost obsessed with the vision of a life which would transcend these, a dream of luxury in which even the essentials of life are refined to appear as indulgences. The lady of that sublime luxury is Erzulie. In her character is reflected all the *élan,* all the excessive pitch with which the dreams of men soar, when, momentarily, they can shake loose the flat weight, the dreary, reiterative demands of necessity; and the details with which the serviteur has surrounded her image reflect the poignant, fantastic misconceptions of luxury which a man who has only known poverty would cherish.

He conceives of Erzulie as fabulously rich, and he neither inquires into nor explains the sources of this limitless wealth, as if by such disinterest he becomes himself freed from concern with sources and means. He shares her impatience with economies, with calculation, even with careful evaluation. Erzulie moves in an atmosphere of infinite luxury, a perfume of refinement, which, from the first moment of her arrival, pervades the very air of the peristyle, and becomes a general expansiveness in which all anxieties, all urgencies vanish. The tempo of movements becomes more leisurely, tensions dissolve and the voices soften, losing whatever aggressive or strident tones they may have had. One has the impression that a fresh, cooling breeze has sprung up somewhere and that the heat has become less intense, less oppressive.

Her first act is to perform an elaborate toilette for which the equipment is always kept in readiness in the hounfor or the private chapel; and it is always the very best that the houngan or serviteur can afford. The enamel basin in which she washes is neither chipped nor discolored; the soap is new, still in its wrapper; there are several towels, probably embroidered; and a special comb, mirror and even tooth-brush have been consecrated to her. She is provided with a fresh white or rose silk handkerchief which she arranges carefully around her hair. Perfume is imperative, and there may be powder as well. A white or rose dress of delicate cloth, with lace or embroidery, has been kept in readiness for her. And, finally, she is brought not one necklace, but several, of gold and pearls, along with ear-rings and bracelets and her three wedding-bands.

It is the elaborate formalism of her every gesture which transforms this toilette from a simple functional activity to a ritual statement. The cleansing with which it begins (and which, as such, would hardly be necessary for the serviteur already at his best for a ceremony) is a ritual of purification.[1] The careful, unhurried accumulation of costume is an act which, step by step, rejects the primitive, the "natural condition," and, step by careful step, instructs the fortunate attendants in the idea of beauty, the sense of form, and, above all, the cumulative painstaking process by which a work of man—be it art or myth—is created. The Goddess examines each article minutely; where alternative choice exists, her considered selection, her indecision are very pointed; each effect is critically scrutinized, often rejected and rearranged. The very process of this creative transformation becomes so significant that whether it is a large audience or a small family who await her, or

[1] Basil leaves, which are understood as a purifying agent, are especially associated with Erzulie and are steeped or rubbed in the water for her bath. Her demand for absolute cleanliness is another of her special traits.

how long they may have to wait, ceases to be of any consequence. What is of consequence is the act itself, and the demonstration of the fact that such an act can transfigure the female into the feminine.

Thus attired, powdered and perfumed, she goes out into the peristyle escorted by several of the more handsome men, her favorites. There she may make the rounds, greeting the men guests effusively, but extending only the little fingers of each hand to those women who are not special devotees. Her voice is a delicate soprano; her every gesture, movement of eyes, and smile, is a masterpiece of beguiling coquetry; with her, human relationship becomes itself significant rather than merely a means to an end. She may visit her altar chamber and be pleased that the flowers are fresh, for flowers are her passion. She may ask for a favorite song, for she loves to dance and is the most graceful of all loa; or she may simply give audience to her admirers, and by her postures and attitudes transform the crude chair in which she sits into a throne. If she is being feasted that day, she eats delicately, of a cuisine that is more exacting than that of any other loa—a just-so blending of seasonings and sauces. Above all, she favors desserts, decorated cakes and confections of all kinds. Or, if she has arrived on an impromptu visit, she may be content with a sip of the *crème de menthe* or the champagne which, theoretically, should always be ready for her appearance.[2]

Admittedly, requirements such as champagne seem an exaggeration in the face of the general poverty. She has even been known to say—when there was no water to sprinkle on the earthern floor to settle the dust and cool the room—"Sprinkle perfume instead!" And if one indulges even such exaggerations, it is, in part, because of the overwhelming innocence with which she proposes them. She is not so much indifferent to the difficulties her requests create for the serviteur, as ignorant of the existence of difficulties; for there are none for her, and she is herself as bounteous as demanding. As

---

[2] Her sense of form extends to a rather strict sense of decorum. She will not countenance any boisterousness or disorder. She punishes those whom she finds unkempt. She will not tolerate the drinking of hard liquor in her presence, and her special devotees respect this prohibition on the days sacred to her, whether she is present or not.

Lady of Luxury, she gives gifts constantly: her own perfume, the handkerchief she wears, the food and money which she conscripts from the houngan and distributes generously. She particularly rewards those who are handsome, or who dance well, or whose personality pleases her. She never neglects one who is devoted to her.

As Lady of Luxury she is, above all, Goddess of Love, that human luxury of the heart which is not essential to the purely physical generation of the body. She is as lavish with that love as she is generous with her gifts. She treats men with such overflowing, such demonstrative affection that it might seem, at times, embarrassing. She will embrace them, and kiss them, caress them, sit with an arm around those to both sides of her. Nothing is meted out or budgeted, there is more than enough; this is her way of loving, this is the divine fecundity of the heart. . . .

In the midst of the gaiety she will inexplicably recall, as women sometimes do, some old, minor disappointment. She will remark the one inadequate detail here among the dozen major achievements. Suddenly it is apparent that imperceptibly she has crossed an invisible threshold where even the most willing reason and the most ready reality cannot follow; and, in another moment, she, who seemed so very close, so real, so warm, is suddenly of another world, beyond this reality, this reason. It is as if below the gaiety a pool had been lying, silently swelling, since the very first moment; and now its dark despair surfaces and engulfs her beyond succor. She who has been loved by all the major loa (and it is not they who were promiscuous) is convinced, by some curious inversion, that they have each betrayed her. She reiterates this complaint, even against the reminder that Ogoun still presses his court and that Agwé still takes care of her in her illnesses. She, who is the wealthiest of the loa, the most frequently gifted with luxurious accoutrement, suffers for not being "served" enough. She, who is the most complimented, most beloved, most often wedded in the sacred marriage of devotee and divinity—she who is Goddess of Love—protests that she is not loved enough.

Inevitably then—and this is a classic stage of Erzulie's possession—she begins to weep. Tenderly they would comfort her, bringing forward still another cake, another jewel, pledging still another promise. But it would seem that nothing in this world would ever, *could* ever, answer those tears. It is because of these tears that the women, who might otherwise resent her, are so gentle. In their real, reasonable world there is no grief like this.

There are times when this sense of all things gone wrong is projected in that combined rage and despair which is Erzulie Ge-Rouge. With her knees drawn up, the fists clenched, the jaw rigid and the tears streaming from her tight-shut eyes, she is the cosmic tantrum—the tantrum not of a spoiled child, but of some cosmic innocence which cannot understand—and *will* not understand—why accident should ever befall what is cherished, or why death should ever come to the beloved. But whether the raging tears of Erzulie Ge-Rouge, or the despairing sobs of Erzulie Maîtresse, this weeping is so inaccessible to reason that one thinks, inevitably, of a child's innocence of reason.

So, Maîtresse Erzulie, weeping, comes to that moment which has been called her paralysis. Just as the hurt of a child mounts and transcends both its own cause and solution, reaching a plateau where it exists as a pure pain, so her articulate complaints cease, even the sobbing; and the body, as if no longer able to endure, abandons the heart to its own infinite grief. Her limbs, her neck, her back go limp. Her arms, stretching across the shoulders of the men who support her on either side, her head tilting, the cheeks wet from tears, the lids closing over eyes turned inward toward some infinite darkness, she presents, as Ogoun did, the precise attitude of the Crucifixion. So she is carried from the stilled, saddened public to some adjacent private chamber. Stretched on the bed, her arms still outflung, she falls asleep as a child might, exhausted by too great a grief. Those who brought her in, and others, who, unreasonably, would still wish to do something for her, stand about quietly, speaking in whispers. They are glad to see that sleep has come, and with it, respite; for they sense that her pain is not only great but perhaps even eternal.

PART 14

War and Peacemaking

HANS STADEN

Killing and Eating One's Enemy in Sixteenth-Century Brazil

On the day following we reached a place not far from the country of my captors, called Occarasu, a great mountain. There we camped for the night, and I went to the hut of Konyan Bebe, the chief king, and asked what he intended to do with the two mamelukes. He replied that they would be eaten, and forbade me to speak with them, for he was very wrath, saying that they should have stayed at home instead of going to fight with his enemies. I begged him to spare their lives and sell them back again to their friends, but he was resolved that they should be eaten.

This same Konyan Bebe had then a great vessel full of human flesh in front of him and was eating a leg which he held to my mouth, asking me to taste it. I replied that even beasts which were without understanding did not eat their own species, and should a man devour his fellow creatures? But he took a bite saying *Jau ware sehe:* "I am a tiger; it tastes well," and with that I left him.

When they first bring home a captive the women and children

set upon him and beat him. Then they decorate him with grey feathers and shave off his eyebrows, and dance around him, having first bound him securely so that he cannot escape. They give him a woman who attends to him and has intercourse with him. If the woman conceives, the child is maintained until it is fully grown. Then, when the mood seizes them, they kill and eat it.

They feed the prisoner well and keep him for a time while they prepare the pots which are to contain their drink. They bake also special pots in which to prepare the mixture wherewith they paint him, and they make tassels to tie to the club with which he is to be killed, as well as a long cord, called Mussurana, to bind him when the time comes. When all is ready they fix the day of his death and invite the savages from the neighbouring villages to be present. The drinking vessels are filled a few days in advance, and before the women make the drink, they bring forth the prisoner once or twice to the place where he is to die and dance round him.

When the guests have assembled, the chief of the huts bids them welcome and desires that they shall help them to eat their enemy. The day before they commence to drink, the cord Mussurana is tied about the victim's neck and on this day also they paint the club called Iwera Pemme with which they intend to kill him.

It is about 6 feet (a fathom) long, and they cover it with a sticky mess, after which they take the eggs of a bird called Mackukawa, which they break up to powder and spread upon the club. Then a woman sits down and scratches figures in the powder, while the other women dance and sing around her. When the club Iwera Pemme is ready decked with tassels and other things, they hang it in an empty hut upon a pole, and sing in front of it all night.

In the same manner they paint the face of the victim, the women singing while another woman paints, and when they begin to drink they take their captive with them and talk to him while he drinks with them. After the drinking bout is over they rest the next day and build a hut on the place of execution, in which the prisoner spends the night under close guard. Then, a good while before daybreak on the day following, they commence to dance and sing before the club, and so they continue until day breaks. After this they take the prisoner from his hut, which they break to pieces and clear away. Then they remove the Mussurana from the prisoner's neck, and tying it round his body they draw it tight on either side so that he stands there bound in the midst of them, while numbers of them hold the two ends of the cord. So they leave him for a time, but they place stones beside him which he throws at the women, who run about mocking him and boasting that they will eat him. These women are painted, and are ready to take his four quarters when he is cut up, and run with them round the huts, a proceeding which causes great amusement to the others.

Then they make a fire about two paces from the prisoner which he has to tend. After this a woman brings the club Iwera Pemme, waving the tassels in the air, shrieking with joy, and running to and fro before the prisoner so that he may see it. Then a man takes the club and standing before the prisoner he shows it to him. Meanwhile he who is going to do the deed withdraws with fourteen or fifteen others, and they all paint their bodies grey with ashes. Then the slayer returns with his companions, and the man who holds the club before the prisoner hands it to the slayer. At this stage the king of the huts approaches, and taking the club he thrusts it once between the slayer's legs which is a sign of great honour. Then the slayer seizes it and thus addresses the victim: "I am he that will kill you, since you and yours have slain and eaten many of my friends." To which the prisoner replies: "When I am dead I shall still have many to avenge my death." Then the slayer strikes from behind and beats out his brains.

The women seize the body at once and carry it to the fire where they scrape off the skin, making the flesh quite white, and stopping up the fundament with a piece of wood so that nothing may be lost. Then a man cuts up the body, removing the legs above the knee and the arms at the trunk, whereupon the four women seize the four limbs and run with them round the huts, making a joyful cry. After this they divide the trunk among themselves, and devour everything that can be eaten.

When this is finished they all depart, each one carrying a piece with him. The slayer takes a fresh name, and the king of the huts scratches him in the upper part of the arm with the tooth of a wild beast. When the wound is healed the scar remains visible, which is a great honour. He must lie all that day in his hammock, but they give him a small bow and an arrow, so that he can amuse himself by shooting into wax, lest his arm should become feeble from the shock of the death-blow.

FATHER PAUL LEJEUNE
Hiroquois Cruelty

Now, as in the wide stretches of territory in this country there are a great many wholly barbarous tribes, so they very often make war upon each other. When we arrived at Tadoussac the Savages were coming back from a war against the Hiroquois, and had taken nine of them; those of Quebec took six, and those of Tadoussac three. Monsieur Emery de Caën went to see the captives, hoping to save the life of the youngest one. I pleaded very earnestly for all three, but was told that great presents were necessary, and I had none. Having arrived at the cabins of the Savages, which are made of poles, clumsily covered with bark, the top left uncovered for the purpose of letting in light and of leaving an opening for the smoke to go out, we entered that of the war Captain, which was long and narrow. There were three fires in the middle, distant from each other five or six feet. Having entered, we sat down here and there on the ground, which was covered with little branches of fir, for they have no other seats. This done, they brought in the prisoners, who sat down beside each other. The eldest was over 60, the second about 30, and the third was a young boy from 15 to 16 years old. They all began to sing, in order to show that they were not at all afraid of death, however cruel it might be. Their singing seemed to me very disagreeable; the cadence always ended with reiterated aspirations, "oh! oh! oh! ah! ah! ah! hem! hem! hem!" *etc.* After singing for some time, they were made to dance, one after the other. The eldest one rose first, and began to walk through the room, entirely naked, except, as I have said, for a piece of fur which covered what nature has hidden. He stamped his feet upon the ground while marching, and sang continuously. This was all the dance; and while it was going on all the other Savages in the hut clapped their hands, or beat their thighs, drawing this aspiration from the depths of their stomachs, "a—ah, a—ah, a—ah"; and then when the prisoner stopped they cried, "o—oh, o—oh, o—oh"; and, when the one reseated himself, the other took up the dance. Monsieur de Caën asked when they would be killed. "To-morrow," they answered. I went to see them again, and I found three wooden stakes erected where they were to be executed; but news came from Quebec that a treaty of peace was being negotiated with the Hiroquois, and it would perhaps be necessary to surrender the prisoners, and thus their death was delayed. There is no cruelty comparable to that which they practice on their enemies. As soon as the captives are taken, they brutally tear off their nails with their teeth; I saw the fingers of these poor creatures, and was filled with pity, also I saw a large hole in the arm of one of them; I was told that it was a bite of the Savage who had captured him; the other had a part of a finger torn off, and I asked him if the fire had done that, as I thought it was a burn. He made a sign to show me that it had been taken off by the teeth. I noticed the same cruelty among the girls and women, when these poor prisoners were dancing; for, as they passed before the fire, the women blew and drove the flame over in their direction to burn them. When the hour comes to kill their captives, they are fastened to a stake; then the girls, as well as the men, apply hot and flaming brands to those portions of the body which are the most sensitive, to the ribs, thighs, chest, and several other places. They raise the scalp from the head, and then throw burning sand upon the skull, or uncovered place. They pierce the arms at the wrists with sharp sticks, and pull the nerves out through these holes. In short, they make them suffer all that cruelty that the Devil can suggest. At last, as a final horror, they eat and devour them almost raw. If we were captured by the Hiroquois, perhaps we would be obliged to suffer this ordeal, inasmuch as we live with the Montagnards, their enemies. So enraged are they against every one who does them an injury, that they eat the lice and other vermin that they find upon themselves,—not because they like them, but only, they say, to avenge themselves and to eat those that eat them.

FATHER BARTHELEMY VIMONT
Hiroquois Cruelty

These poor Algonquins were in their own country, living in huts in the depths of their great forests, in a place where, in all probability, no Hiroquois had even been. That is why they thought of nothing but their hunting, and not of defending themselves against those Barbarians. When the latter came upon the tracks of the hunters, they crept upon them stealthily, to massacre them in their first sleep. When night began to conceal trees and men with its darkness, and to wrap most of these good people in slumber, a woman called out as she was about to lie down: "It is all over with us; the Hiroquois are killing us." I know not by what instinct she uttered those words; be that as it may, at the same time those tigers entered their cabin, with arms in their hands, and seized them, some by the hair and others about the body. Some who were awakened by the noise, and who tried to defend themselves, were at once slaughtered. The fight was soon over, and the Hiroquois finding the poor people already overcome by sleep and fright, bound them with strong cords,—men, women, and children; and, in less than an hour, were masters of their lives, of their little wealth, and of their cabins. Seeing themselves victorious, they prepared their supper in the house of the vanquished. Some brought wood, and others went for water. Great kettles were placed over the fire. The shambles were not far away. They dismembered those whom they had just slaughtered, cut them in pieces, and threw the feet, legs, arms, and heads into the pot, which they set to boil with joy as great as the sorrow felt by the poor captives who remained alive, when they saw their countrymen serving as the quarry of these Werewolves. The women and children wept bitterly, and those half Demons took pleasure in hearing their doleful chants. When the supper was cooked, these wolves devoured their prey; one seized a thigh, another a breast; some sucked the marrow from the bones; others broke open the skulls, to extract the brains. In a word, they ate the flesh of men with as much appetite as, and with more pleasure than, hunters eat that of a Boar or of a Stag.

Daylight had approached during this fine feast. When those wolves had gorged themselves on a meat that they consider delicate, they took away their prisoners. A woman named Kicheuigoukwe, who was unable to keep up with the band, was at once knocked on the head. Many men and women envied her good fortune, for she had escaped from her misery very easily. "As for me," said she who told the story, "if I had been baptized, I would have considered it a mercy to die thus; my eyes would not have been forced to see the horrible sights and unnatural cruelties that they have witnessed.

"Among all the captive women, we were three who had each a little child, about two months old. We had not journeyed far before those wretches robbed us of them. Ah, my Father," she said, "be not surprised if I weep now. I shed many tears when they tore from my bosom my poor little son. But alas! if I did not know that thou wilt have compassion on us, I would say no more. They took our little children, placed them on spits, held them to a fire, and roasted them before our eyes. Did I not hope that you Frenchmen will wreak vengeance for such cruelties, I would be unable to speak. Those poor little ones knew not as yet the fire, when they felt its heat. They looked at us, and cried with all their might. Our hearts were broken when we saw them roasting, all naked, before a slow fire. We tried to drag them away, but in vain, for our bonds and those Barbarians prevented us. "O! kill them," we cried, "kill them, wretches that you are. What have these poor little innocents done to you?" They had no ears, no pity; they laughed at our tears, and at our fruitless efforts. They are not men; they are wolves. After they had put the poor little babes to death by fire, they drew them off the spit to which they were fastened, threw them into their kettles, boiled them, and ate them in our presence." "I confess," says the Father who has written to us of this tragedy, "that when I saw the tears shed by that poor mother and listened to such unheard-of cruelties, *Commota sunt viscera mea.* I was touched to the heart." But let us continue our journey; let us follow these prisoners, and see what reception awaits them in the Hiroquois villages.

When the dismal band reached the great Falls of the Chaudière,—this is a river which suddenly falls into the River of the three meadows, above Montreal,—a captive woman, observing a spot where the stream was not entirely frozen over, cast herself into it in her despair, preferring to perish in the water rather than to die by fire. At first the rapidity of the current threw her out. The Hiroquois ran up, wishing to save her from a precipice in order to cast her into an abyss. But when they saw her at the last extremity, they clubbed her to death and cut off her head, taking her scalp. It would occupy too much time to relate all the incidents that occurred on the way. Let us hasten.

While victors and vanquished pursued their route, two young men went on in advance, to convey the news of the victory. A great many persons came at once to meet them a full day's journey. The women brought Indian corn and other food, which they offered to the warriors who had come to a halt on the arrival of these vivandières. The prisoners, both men and women, were made to dance, and the night passed amid shouts of rejoicing.

On the following day, as they approached a Village, they found a large cabin all prepared; it was furnished with fires and fireplaces, prepared in various places. Some Demons were waiting there for the captives, who were brought in triumph, tied and bound like poor victims of death. A crowd of men, women, and little children surrounded them, rending the air with sounds as dismal to the vanquished as they were pleasant to the victors. When they entered this Hell, they were received with heavy blows from sticks; cords were tied around their wrists, which the strongest among their foes tightened with enraged fury. The pain of this is very severe. Their arms were slashed; their backs and shoulders were gashed; their fingers were cut off,—on some, many; on others, few,—not with knives, but with scales of fishes, so that the torture might be more cruel, more lasting, and more painful. The poor creature who escaped, had both her thumbs cut, or rather hacked off. "When they had cut them off," she said, "they wished to force me to eat them; but I put them on my lap, and told them that they could kill me if they liked, but that I could not obey them."

After this first reception, food was brought to them, to give them

new strength,—in order to torment them longer, and to make them their playthings, as the Demons do with the souls of the damned. They ordered the men to sing, and the women to dance. "They tore and pulled off our garments," said this poor creature; "they exposed us, entirely naked, to the jeers and howls of all their Villages. They made us dance in that condition, to the voices and songs of our countrymen." *Musica in luctu importuna narratio.* Alas! what joy can a heart feel in a dance amid Demons?

The night passed amid joy and sorrow. In the early morning, the poor sufferers were made to ascend a large scaffold erected for the purpose, so that they might be seen by all the people, and that no one, either great or small, should fail to witness the new cruelties that they should be made to endure. Those Demons armed themselves with torches and firebrands. The smallest among them applied these to the soles of the feet of the unfortunates, through openings in the scaffold, while the others applied them to their thighs and sides,—in a word, to the most sensitive parts of the body. The captive women were ordered to burn their husbands and their countrymen. They replied that they would not. There was only the daughter of one Awessenipin—called by the French "the coal"—who burned the captive men and women indifferently. She imagined that such cruel conduct would save her life; but, on the contrary, it brought on her a more painful death than on the others. One of the prisoners manifested not the least sign of pain, in the height of his torments and sufferings. The Hiroquois were furious with rage on observing this firmness, which they consider an evil augury —for they believe that the souls of the warriors who despise them will make them pay dearly for the death of their bodies; seeing, I say, such firmness, they asked him why he did not cry out. "I do," he replied, "what you could not, if you were treated with the same cruelty that you show me. The iron and the fire that you apply to my body would make you cry out very loud, and weep like children, while I do not flinch." On hearing these words, those tigers threw themselves on their half-consumed victim, tore off his scalp, and cast sand, heated red-hot and burning with fire, on his bleeding skull. They threw him off the scaffold, and dragged him around the cabins. In that condition he looked like a monster; he had only blood and hot sand for hair; his eyes and his entire face were covered with fire and gore; his body was all slashed and roasted; his hands were fingerless,—in a word, *non erat vulneri locus.* The wounds overlapped one another. Such a sight, which would have caused horror to men, rejoiced those Demons, who, as their final act of cruelty, cut open the breasts of those whom they wish to kill, tear out their hearts and their livers, which they roast; they cut off their feet and their hands, which they cook partly under the embers, partly on a spit before the fire; in short, they roast and boil them, and then they eat them with delighted rage. *Homo homini lupus;* man becomes a wolf to other men, when he allows himself to be governed by Demons. Alas! can it be possible that the Father and the Frenchmen, of whom I will soon speak, have been treated in like manner by the Barbarians who have recently taken and carried them off to their country?

I learn that they killed only the men and the more aged women, sparing about thirty of the younger ones in order that they might dwell in their country, and marry as if they had been born there. The two who escaped expected the same torture that they saw the others suffer; but they were told that they should not die,—that their foes would rest satisfied after having burned them with torches, and gashed their bodies all over.

The fury of those lions being appeased with the blood of their enemies, these poor women remained with their wounds and their burns, without putting on any plaster or applying any other remedy but patience. They passed the Winter in suffering and sorrow, as wretched slaves, daily hearing the bluster of those Barbarians against the French and Algonquins, whom they wish to exterminate completely, so they say, knowing that they are supported and armed by the Dutch.

JAMES R. MURIE

A Pawnee War Party

There was a fixed ritual for the control of a war party, which when organized for a foray was for the time being a kind of wolf society (araris taka, society of the white wolf). Its mythological basis is quite fundamental, being that part of the creation myth in which a wolf pursued man and deceived him. In any event, the god of war is a mythical wolf and it was directed that a wolfskin should always be placed at the top of a bundle and that the Skidí were to be the wolf people, as the name implies. Hence, to become a real warrior one must follow the ways of the wolf. One who does so can go to the keeper of a bundle and borrow the war clothing therein together with the pipe. The wolfskin remains in the bundle, but the objects he takes away carry with them the power of the wolf. By their association with the bundle, these war clothes represent the powers of the west and when the borrower is so clothed these powers are with him. He can now organize and lead a war party, but he himself must not imitate the wolf, that is left to his followers. Thus, they become like the wolf first placed upon the earth and may have power to steal upon the enemy and get away without being discovered.

Before setting out upon a foray a ceremony is held in the village in which as in all else the borrower of the regalia from the bundle is the leader. An altar is made and the bundle from which the regalia are to be borrowed is brought in and placed before the leader. Upon it is the wolfskin and in the minds of the warriors the wolf is present and, hence, always with them upon the way. A buffalo skull rests upon the altar.

The war regalia of the bundle are usually a pipe, a collar, a lariat rope, a hawkskin, an ear of corn (Mother Corn), some red paint, down feathers, and a leader's feathers.

As the bundle is present there must be a north and south side and two leaders. On the march they go abreast with the others behind in order of their rank. A four-day ceremony follows, before setting out. On the way, their organization is for each side, or line: a leader, two scouts, two soldiers, the warriors, and the inexperienced assistants. The four scouts are really charged with the responsibility of the movement and may be said to be in command though the leaders stand for the highest authority. They scout about in the early hours of the day and at all times on the journey. Their signals are made as wolf cries. When a scout has anything to report, he tells it privately to the leader of his side. At the proper time the leader announces the import of the report in a formal ritualistic manner. They never approach or in fact go anywhere in a direct line, but follow an ever-changing course. The members of the party paint their faces and robes heavily with white clay, which is the war paint of the Pawnee and symbolizes the wolf. The scouts also wear two white eagle feathers in the hair so set as to resemble the ears of the wolf.

Thus when one looked over the crest of a hill, he would appear as a wolf. Wolfskin caps were often worn by these scouts to heighten the illusion. Since in course of time other Indians knew the wolf cry signals, different animals were imitated according to orders of the leader.

When the enemy has been located, the leaders conduct the party into a thicket and hold a ceremony. The inexperienced members of the party (youths) gather the wood and act as servants. One young man goes out to cut the drumsticks, these he rolls up in his robe and with wolf cries runs into camp, placing the sticks before those who are to be singers. The rolled up robe he also places there for them to beat upon. A small circular altar is made by clearing the sod and exposing fresh earth. The ear of corn, the otterskin collar, the pipe and the hawkskin taken from the bundle at the start, are placed in position. All then arrange themselves in two sides as in the regular ceremony. One goes out and hunts up a buffalo skull which also has a place upon the altar. The ceremony is opened with the regular smoke offering. The leader sends one to cut a number of small sticks, at least one for each member of the party. With these sticks, offerings are to be made for which each member brought certain trinkets. These offerings are formally dedicated to all the powers of the earth, sky, etc. Each ties his present to a stick and plants it at the altar. The offerings for the powers above are set up vertically and the others in corresponding positions. The drumsticks are then taken up for beating upon a robe and singing and dancing follow. The four soldiers drive out the dancers and keep them dancing around the fire.

The songs are largely derisive of those who stayed at home. The members also sing of their sweethearts. All these songs have a peculiar rhythm and end with wolf calls, from which they take the name of wolf songs. On the journey no one is permitted to speak of home and relations with women, lest he lose heart.

At the close a council is held to develop the plan of action. Thus, it is decided as to whether they will simply run off horses by stealth, or make an attack. If the enemy seems numerous, the former is most desirable. In this case a few men are selected to go for the horses while the others wait. Usually the scouts and the soldiers are sent on this mission, temporary soldiers being appointed to hold the men in camp. The scouts endeavor to drive out the horses toward the main body who catch what they can and mounting, drive off at high speed. The leader rides ahead, the others hold the flanks of the loose horses while the scouts and soldiers bring up the rear. They ride almost continuously for three days, or until exhaustion, and then camp in a sheltered place. Some hunt, others guard the horses. When the first buffalo meat is brought in an altar is made, as before stated, and the regular smoke offering performed. Two men are then chosen by the leader to divide the spoils. They divide the horses according to the ranks of the members, inexperienced men getting but one horse. After the division the name-changing ceremony is performed for the young men on their first war party.

After sufficient rest, they set out for home. As they approach their village they set the grass afire at intervals so that their people may know that a war party is returning. When near the village they paint their faces black or dot over with black the white paint of the warpath. When in sight they signal the result of the expedition and are met by the chiefs who triumphantly conduct them into the village. Feasting and jollifying then follow. If coups have been counted or scalps taken, a victory dance will be held.

After an interval the leader of the party calls the members together and any of those formerly in a party who now constitute a kind of society of the wolves. The altar is again constructed and the ceremony performed. Two of the captured horses are brought out and loaded with presents, the objects from the bundle are also placed there and the horses led to the keeper of the bundle where they are received by the priest. They are then returned to the bundle and the keeper goes at once to the place of ceremony; he stands by the altar and gives them his blessing.

On the warpath a man may vow to give one horse to the mother corn, in which case a horse is given to the keeper of the main bundle, who also gives his blessing.

With these acts the true wolf dance begins. In the dance all the young men may join, who hope to go out with the next war party, and as they dance the old men sit around and ridicule their ardor. With this ceremony and the return of the sacred objects to the bundle, the war party ceases to exist.

W. LLOYD WARNER

Causes of War in Australia

Of seventy-two recorded battles of the last twenty years in which members of Murngin factions were killed, fifty were for blood revenge—the desire to avenge the killing of a relative, usually a clansman, by members of another clan. Of these, fifteen were deliberate killings, against the tradition of what is fair cause for a war, and because it was felt that the enemies had killed the wrong people. Ten killings were due to stealing or obtaining by illegal means a woman who belonged to another clan. Five supposedly guilty magicians were killed by the clan members of victims of black magic. Five men were slain for looking at a totemic emblem under improper circumstances and thereby insulting the owning clan and endangering the clan's spiritual strength.

The idea underlying most Murngin warfare is that the same injury should be inflicted upon the enemy group that one's own group has suffered. This accomplished, a clan feels satisfied; otherwise, there is a constant compulsion toward vengeance, causing a continuous restlessness among those who are out to "buy back" the killing of one of their clansmen. The stealing of a woman provokes the same spirit, since the group feels itself injured; and only the return of the woman and a ceremonial fight, or the stealing of another woman, will satisfy the hurt to its self-esteem, unless the clan has retaliated by killing or wounding one of the enemy clansmen. The same feeling is instigated by the improper viewing of the totem—an insult and an injury to the entire clan.

Any of the above causes for war may be given deliberately or by accident, but in either case warfare is a certain consequence. If a young man chances upon an old man engaged in making a totemic emblem, the former is killed; or if a man is accidentally killed in a fight by a member of a friendly group, the dead man's people retaliate. There is, nevertheless, considerable feeling that an accident should not cause open hostilities, but it has small influence upon the public opinion of those who believe themselves injured.

There are a number of forms of ritualistic injury. If women look at a totemic emblem they are killed by their own group, with the help of any other group that has been offended by their actions. The clan to which they belong is not held responsible except in a minor way. Some years ago the Liagaomir clan was holding a totemic ceremony, using its carpet snake totemic emblems (painted wooden trumpets). Two women stole up to the ceremonial ground and watched the men blowing the trumpet, went back to the women's camp and told them what they had seen. When the men came back to camp and heard of their behavior, Yanindja, the leader, said, "When will we kill them?"

Everyone replied, "Immediately."

The two women were instantly put to death by members of their own clan with the help of the men from the other group.

Maritja, one of the most conventional men in the society, was making a shark totemic emblem. He had hidden it in a hollow tree near the border of the men's ceremonial grounds. Some women belonging to the visiting Burera tribe had walked near it. This had been established by the identification of their footprints by Maritja and his brothers. Maritja went down to the Burera camp and said to the assembled group, "You all know I never make trouble unless there is very good cause for it. You know I look for peace, but your women have done my people a great wrong. They have walked near the place where I had my totem hidden. I shall be sick and maybe I'll die."

The Burera men said, "You are right. If they have done this you may kill them if you wish." Nothing further was done since it was not considered a very great wrong; but had the women actually looked at his totemic emblem he could have killed them, and their clan would not have retaliated.

Munyiryir's wife was burning a patch of brush while hunting for bandicoot. The husband had hidden the string for his totemic emblem in the bushes. The fire destroyed it. The string belonged to the Daiuror clan. They tried to kill her and would have succeeded, but she escaped to the mission with the help of her husband. He was felt to have done wrong in helping her.

A young Warumeri clansman illicitly viewed a stone totemic emblem that is situated on Elcho Island. The men of the clan followed his footsteps and saw what he had done. When they caught him they immediately killed him.

A Mandelpui boy came upon two old Liaalaomir men making a totemic emblem. When they saw him they said, "Come look," and with smiles and gestures indicated their approval of his having a closer view of their totem. This was to put him off his guard; a few days later they ambushed and killed him.

PERCY AMAURY TALBOT

The Conduct of Oronn Warfare

Before warriors start on the war-path, it is customary to offer a sacrifice to the chief fetish of the town. All the inhabitants join in this ceremony, and afterwards each of the chosen band submits himself to the "Shot and Matchet Juju," the principal rites of which consist in the priest rubbing magic leaves over the whole body of the warrior, in order to render him invulnerable, and a black Juju powder over his face to make him invisible to his opponents. When each had been protected in this way, another ceremony was performed. A great "medicine" was made and a fresh sacrifice offered, during the slaying of which the priest called upon the "soul names" of the strongest and most famous warriors among the enemy, adjuring these to leave their bodies and come at his bidding; so that in the day of battle they might be soulless, and therefore powerless to fight.

In the war-shed at Ikot Ibiuk, a village near Eket, may be seen a section of tree-trunk, hollowed bowl-wise, some three feet in diameter and encircled by a string of buffalo skulls. Medicines mixed, according to my informant, of magic leaves, human blood and that of buffaloes—the latter regarded hereabouts as the symbol of brute strength—was poured therein, and of this potion each warrior was given to drink before starting out for the scene of action.

On the conclusion of the rites, the band of fighting men form into line, and without word spoken, start straight for the enemy's town. From necks and wrists hang many charms: leopard claws in chains or pendants to give courage and skill, and little bags containing magic roots and leaves to act as an additional talisman against bullets. Fish-eagle feathers, too, are sometimes worn by chiefs, as a means of acquiring the strength and keen vision of these sacred birds.

As the band of warriors march through the town, they must pass along without saluting any woman whom they chance to meet. Neither may they look backwards, nor still less return, even a few steps, on any pretext whatever. The tabu on food is recorded in the last chapter; here, therefore, it is enough to say that, as among the Dyaks,[1] so Ibibio warriors never eat "soft food," such as pumpkin or soup, and, while on the march, must avoid the dwelling-place of any woman. Neither may they pass through water which women use either as a bathing or washing place; but, if it is impossible to avoid this altogether by making a détour, must march for a considerable distance up stream before crossing.

While on the road no one may touch any part of a warrior's body, lest contact with another under the protection of a different "medicine" should counteract the effect of his own. Here, however, there is no law against a man himself touching his head or indeed

[1] Haddon, *Magic and Fetishism*. London, 1910, p. 10.

any limb. If bitten by insects, or suffering irritation from skin disease or other cause, it is forbidden to scratch the part, "lest even so small a sound should betray your presence to an enemy. All that is permitted is to lay a hand softly upon the spot."

So soon as the first shots are heard, it is allowable, as an extra safeguard, to chew some of the magic roots or leaves with which the little wallet-shaped amulets are filled; but this must on no account be done before the firing starts, otherwise the transgressor will go mad and lose himself amid his enemies. When the smoke of the battle grows so dense that it is no longer possible to see the foe clearly from a distance, men drop their guns and rush into the thick of the fight, armed only with sword or matchet, but secure that no harm can befall them since the Juju has made them invulnerable.

Should a man become wounded in spite of all safeguards, the misfortune is explained by a supposed breach of Juju law inadvertently committed, or by the superior power of the enemy's magic. In such a case, instead of washing the wound with hot water as was the usual custom, the native doctor used to go into the bush and cut a stick the size of the gash. This substitute was washed and tended as though it were the real wound, until by sympathetic magic the injured flesh grew whole.

At times, instead of a stick another part of the body was treated as if the wound were there; for instance, should a gash have been made in the thigh an arm would probably be chosen for attention.

Not long ago, at 'Ndiya, one of the Juju Images slashed at the head of a woman named Adiaha Udaw Anwa, cutting it twice in the form of a rough cross. The native doctor tried to cure her, for the injury was very grave. To do this he first tied a soft rope round her forehead; then dipped a cloth in hot water and held it to the base of the back and pit of the stomach. Medicine was also rubbed upon her neck. The real wound was left untouched, save that occasionally a feather was dipped in oil and drawn lightly over the dried blood to soften it.[2] The woman was healed but the scars are clearly to be seen.

---

[2] Cf. *A late Discourse . . . by Sir Kenelm Digby, Kt., Touching the Cure of Wounds by the Power of Sympathy* (1658).

Before an engagement, scouts are sometimes sent forward, secretly, to a place through which the enemy is expected to pass. Arrived there, they sprinkle "medicine" upon the leaves and ground, and so soon as this comes in contact with the skin of the hostile warriors, even the bravest and most hardened begin to shout and howl with pain. Men are said to have gone mad from the irritation thus produced.

Perhaps it may be well to mention here a personal experience which seems to show the possibility of such a measure. During my first tour in Africa, while I served as Assistant Commissioner on the Anglo-Liberian Boundary Commission, our way took us through thick bush in the as yet unexplored interior. Some strange-looking fruits hung from a liane not far from the line of march, and I picked one in order to examine it. Hardly had this been done than my gun-boy flung everything down, and seizing my arm, shook it so suddenly and violently that the fruit dropped from my grasp. Others hurried up and, as I did not understand their language, made signs that I must wash. It was growing late and I wished to press on, so thought that it would be better to wait till we came to the next stream rather than go back to one passed a few minutes before. The men, however, positively dragged me back, and even before the brink was reached, the reason of their solicitude was made plain. My hand began to burn and smart unendurably, and I was glad enough to thrust it into the water. The attendants took up handfuls of sand from the bed and violently scrubbed the palm, afterwards binding it up in cool wet leaves. This treatment probably saved the hand and possibly the arm also, for when we reached camp I was told that the poison was so virulent that hand and arm would have become inflamed, and had there been the least scratch might even have mortified. This may have been an exaggeration, but certainly there was no doubt as to the intense irritation produced by handling the fruit.

According to Chief Daniel Henshaw the Oronn method of warfare differs somewhat from that of neighbouring tribes. "In 1880," he said, "fighting broke out between the towns of Afaha Esuk and Ikonor, and this continued till 1902 when Government sent an Expedition to stop them. Sometimes for weeks not a gun was fired on either side. A favourite method of attack was to choose out some compound at a distance from all others. A path was then cut through the thick bush, almost up to the house but screened from it. There a small force of the enemy waited until one of the male inhabitants was seen to leave his dwelling. Sometimes a chief went forth to bathe in the stream near by. A gun sounded from out the bush, and he fell dead, while the enemy ran away by the secret path they had made, knowing that the townsfolk were not likely to find this unless they stumbled upon it by accident. Often after such a catastrophe the dead man's kin would gather weeping round the corpse, and thus give their foes a further chance to shoot. No women were killed during war-time, so it was customary for the wives of a chief to surround him in a protective ring, whether sitting or sleeping in his house, or going to farm.

"A favourite plan for obtaining intelligence was to bribe some neutral town by means of money or cattle to bring news should they hear that any of the chief foemen were likely to be coming along a certain road on a fixed date. Then, on the homeward way, shots would ring out from a hidden enemy, and their town would welcome them no more.

"In the night time, too, a small band would often creep up to a house, the inmates of which all lay sleeping, and start to pour water at a certain spot upon the mud wall of one of the outside rooms. When this had been done they were able to dig away the soft clay with their fingers, soundlessly and little by little, until a hole was made large enough to look through and find out where the head of that particular family lay. After ascertaining this, they inserted the muzzle of a gun and fired. It is to guard against such a fate that even now, when Oronn Chiefs build a compound, they usually make the principal sleeping-room right in the centre, with thick, low, mud walls built as a protection on either side of the couch."

To guard a path in war-time, the hand and arm of an enemy were usually cut off and suspended from a tree at the junction with the main thoroughfare. People did not venture along a road thus guarded. A further protection was to hew down big branches and lay these across the entrance. Occasionally a cut stone was borne from the Juju-house and erected in the middle of the path, with round ones at its base. Goats were then sacrificed and their blood poured over the stones, while the names of dead members of the principal "societies" of the village or settlement to be guarded were called upon to act as sentinels.

When one town decides to make war upon another, the inhabitants send two men to lay a plantain leaf upon the road before the enemy's town. On this, little piles of powder, shot, and caps are laid as a declaration of hostilities. During our last tour a similar intimation, with the addition of a small gun, carved from wood, was sent to the Commissioner in charge of a neighbouring District, as a sign that a section of his people declared war upon him.

Along the Cross River, kola nuts, salt, and pepper were all used as warnings of the outbreak of danger. Hereabouts kola nuts are usually formed in four sections, one of which is called the "head" and another the "tail." Should a man threatened by some peril come to the house of a friend who has been bound by oath not to disclose the danger, the host, in presenting the usual offering of kola nuts, holds them in his outstretched hand—the "head" towards the wrist, the "tail" towards the fingers, thus pointing in the direction of the visitor, and the other two sections cross-wise, one on each side.

"When the guest is a wise man, he looks carefully at such an offering and notices which way the nuts lie. Should they be placed as described above, he calls to mind that the dead are always borne feet first, so grasps the meaning of the sign. In such a case he at once hurries home along a different road from that by which he came, so as to avoid the enemies lurking to kill him on his return journey.

"Often women born of a hostile town or family fear to give their husbands a direct warning as to threatened danger lest they might later be accused of so doing by their own people and be unable to clear themselves of the charge by swearing the contrary on their native Juju, and so escaping vengeance. In such a case a wife cooks for her husband but puts *no salt* in the food. When the man eats, he sometimes gets annoyed and says: 'You have forgotten to put salt in my chop! Go and bring this at once.' The woman stands with folded arms, saying nothing, but looking very fixedly upon her mate, and not making the least motion to obey.

"Then, if the husband is a clever man, he will read the meaning of her behaviour; but if not, he will call again, more angrily: 'Do you not hear? I tell you to bring salt!' Slowly, slowly, the woman fetches it, but will not put it in; so the man is forced to do this for himself. Should she sleep with him that night, sometimes she sighs softly through the darkness: 'Did I ever forget to put salt in your chop before?' Then at length, if he is in the least wise, he will understand; but if not, on the morrow, she brings saltless food again. After this, unless he is unusually stupid, he will see that it means: 'Danger threatens. Flee away.'

"Such, among our people, is the sign of the salt. Should a man be very fond of pepper, this is sometimes omitted in the same way and with like meaning."

So long as fighting continued, the old people left at home came out daily upon their verandahs and there made the "war juju of the aged"; praying all the time for the success of their warriors. Till peace had been proclaimed, no old man might partake of any food left over from the day before, but this tabu did not apply to women.

Save among the North-eastern Ibibio, where no notice was usually given, fighting generally started at the boundary on a day fixed by the two parties. All men taken were killed and their heads struck off and carried home. In most regions on the capture of a town it was sacked and burnt, and the children were seized and often sold into slavery, while the women usually experienced the same fate.

The weapons in common use were Dane guns and matchets; in addition the Eket and Northern Ibibio employed spears, and some of the latter bows and unpoisoned arrows.

When one of the parties wished to make peace, they sent some friend from a neutral town, or one of their own men, clothed in palm-leaves and white baft, and holding "Alligator" peppers in his hand, to the enemy. If the proposal was accepted, both sides met on the boundary and sacrificed a goat and dog and sometimes a cow. A chief from another town often divided a palm-leaf among the parties. As a rule women were not allowed to be present on such an occasion.

The old rule of a life for a life still holds good among Ibibio, and so firmly do they believe in the right of the relatives of a man who has been killed to exact the death of some member of the slayer's family, that they speak of it in open court as though even white man's law and justice must concede them this.

Such a case came before me at Idua Oronn on August 12, 1913. During the course of the trial Ekkpoikwaw of Edikpo stated on oath, in substance, as follows:

"There was a land case between my family and that of Okong 'Nye Utip. The matter was taken to the Supreme Court, but before the case was decided one side went to cut palm trees on the disputed land. So fighting began. Accused's brother was wounded and afterwards died. This was about five years ago. The other side came and reported to the District Commissioner that our people had killed a man, and they therefore claimed one to kill in exchange, or goods to the same value, according to custom. The District Commissioner refused their request. About two months ago accused again said he wanted to kill a man in our family. So we have brought the case before you."

Okong 'Nye Utip stated:

"I called upon plaintiff's family to supply us with a girl to marry into our family. It was not we who waked up the case again. The other side sent a message to Chief Ekpe Eyo of Eyo Udaw to ask him to say to my family: 'Towns used to fight together and then make peace. How much more so when one family fought another!' We sent to them saying: 'Before we make peace, you must send us a girl.' According to old custom when such an one was sent, so soon as she had grown up, she was married to one of the family. Then her son was given the name of the dead man and succeeded to all his property. When, however, prosecutor's family heard our request, they answered: 'You may send us to heaven above before we give you a girl!' More also they said: 'We are ready to take any oath that it was not we who killed your brother.' "

A very celebrated warrior medicine man, about whose brave deeds many legends have arisen, was Akanam of Ikot Udaw Ede. So strong was this hero reported to be, that it is said he could lay his hands upon a palm tree by the water-side and bend it till the crown of leaves swept the ground. After performing this feat, Akanam would take a stone and pour over it the blood of a white fowl and of a bush squirrel. He then laid the stone in running water near to the bank. Then when a band of the enemy passed by, the tree would spring up, scattering death and destruction among them.

The rule as to the conduct of Oronn warfare was much like that regulating a game, for peace was not supposed to be concluded until exactly the same number of people had been killed on both sides. "The reason why the fight between Ikonor and Afaha Esuk went on so long was that the first-named town killed so many enemies during the first skirmishes, and the longer the fight continued more and more fell to their guns. When Government tried to bring about the cessation of hostilities, the men of Afaha Esuk answered stubbornly: 'No! Not until an equal number have been slain on their side.' If one of the parties failed to inflict the same loss upon the enemy, peace could only be bought by paying heavy compensation. When a town was taken it was either burnt or razed to the ground, while all women and children were sold into slavery. Even the land on which to build a new town had to be ransomed back from the conquerors.

"For the peace ceremony both sides brought a goat and a dog in sacrifice. The head of the first was struck off, but a sharpened stake was driven through the dog's jaws from beneath. The goat's head was then transfixed on the same stick, which was thereupon hung up so that the wretched dog died by slow torture.

"Medicine leaves were spread upon the ground. Upon this bed a quantity of eggs were laid and the blood of the goats sprinkled over all. The chief men from both parties then came forward and bending down on opposite sides of the barrier, crushed eggs, leaves, and blood together in their hands, and with the mixture smeared the faces of their whilom foes, saying: 'To-day we make peace together. We must not see one another's blood any more.'

"After this they divided the flesh of the goats and many other things which had been cooked meantime. Then they ate, drank, sang and were glad because the war was over."

After such a ceremony each warrior went back to his town bearing the heads of those whom he had slain. At every stream which he crossed on the way home, he had to pause and bathe, then rub medicine over himself "to stay the avenging power of the blood which was shed." Without conforming to this purification, he might neither enter his house nor approach any of his wives.

Blood itself is supposed to have strange efficacy, reminding one of that dread libation guarded by the sword of mighty Odysseus, from which the wraiths of friends and companions, long dead, drew force and voice with which to speak to him. Blood is the great strength-giver, the great fertiliser. When Ibeno youths of good family came to man's estate it was customary until quite late years to kill a slave and place the severed head in the hands of the young heir, that he might lick up the fresh-flowing blood.

In olden days human blood, as the greatest of all fertilisers, was shed in floods at the time of the new yam planting. Now that human victims are forbidden, and only the lives of animals may be taken for this purpose, many a strange observance has been substituted. For instance, not long ago a rich husbandman, named Ishi, cut a small piece from the lobe of a poor man's ear and drew therefrom a few drops of blood to pour out before the god of the new farms. The man was well paid for the slight mutilation, and seemed more than content.

With regard to this latter point it may perhaps be worth mentioning that among the Juju objects of a celebrated fetish priest condemned to penal servitude at the Assizes for an attempt on my life a little lustre jug was found. All lustre ware, according to Mary Kingsley, was set apart as sacred to "Juju," and this particular vessel was said to have been dipped in the blood of each fresh victim and then left to dry. It was never cleaned, and only after hours of soaking, followed by vigorous scrubbing, could the many layers be removed and the original surface be brought to view.

When Ibibio men are wounded, whether in fighting or otherwise, tradition bids them hide the flow of blood from the eyes of any woman, that none of these may see strength ebb away from the dominant male. After the wound has dried over, it does not matter so much for a woman to see it. There is no reason why men should not witness the lifeblood flow from the veins of a woman, however. All things feminine are, comparatively, of such little account that it cannot matter for a man to behold one of this inferior sex reduced to the utmost point of weakness and feebleness.

Human blood is looked upon as a great protection both from poison and from ghosts. The best way of using it is to mix it with Juju medicine and then rub this into a small cut made in the body of the man seeking safety. Thus guarded, whether he walks by day or night, neither poisons nor ghosts have power to harm him. With the same intent blood is mixed with the ghost-powder which is rubbed on the forehead, slightly above the junction of the brows, and also between the thumb and first finger of each hand.

As a general rule sacrificial animals are killed by having their throats cut. The body is then dragged round so that the blood sprinkles all the ground. In the case of a goat, two men usually swing and shake it so that the blood falls not only upon the earth but is splashed over the fetish itself.

Before most Jujus to which prayers for health are made, some of the blood of the fowls sacrificed is poured upon the head of the petitioner with the words, "Efera fi" (Be cold), *i.e.* "May you be free from fever!" During some rites the blood of the sacrifices is also sprinkled over the feet of the spectators.

Those warriors who play the Ekong (war) play before setting forth for battle pour goat's blood into a bowl and drink it, because by so doing they hope to imbibe new strength and valour; while, as already described, the most solemn oaths are sworn upon the 'Mbiam Juju, part of the ceremony of which consists in drinking palm-wine into which a few drops of blood from each of the contracting parties has been poured. This oath is often administered to a band of warriors before setting forth for battle in order to guard against treason in their ranks.

On return from a successful campaign, Efik used to bury the skulls of slain enemies in the black mud and ooze of some swamp, then set a sign to mark the spot. After several months had passed by, they went back and dug up the gruesome trophies, washed them clean and brought them home to the town.

To celebrate this a great play was given: guns were fired, and there was much singing and rejoicing. Each woman carried a piece of chalk, and, as a warrior drew near, he held out his arms to her.

the hands straight and palms downward. With the chalk she drew a line from shoulder to finger-tips, calling out "Ekong Umioko!" *i.e.* "The war is finished!" to show her joy at the home-coming. The man repeated "Umioko!" "It is finished!"

Among other Ibibio it was usual to boil the heads of slain enemies in a pot, then scrape off all flesh and keep the skull in the house as a trophy of valour, to be set, in the end, upon the grave of the victor. Many such trophies are to be seen near Itak.

Head-hunting is common over the greater part of Central and Eastern Nigeria, and there can be little doubt that the youthful desire to join the club of the Ubio Owo, or men-killers, which in some regions, especially among the Eastern Ibo, possessed a greater prestige than any other, was the cause of many "wars."

A skull was also necessary for membership in the principal secret societies. So valuable are they that where a grave is not considered safe against desecration, it is carefully hidden.

Among most Ibibio a war dance and play were given as soon as the skulls had been cleaned; sacrifices were made to the latter, apparently as an inducement to the slain warrior to bring his friends, in order that they might meet the same fate. In the north-west, however, no offering was made to the skull till the death of its owner.

Should the slayer find that the ghost of the slain is very strong and is haunting him to his hurt, he offers a dog to the manes of his foe. If this sacrifice proves unavailing, he catches a male lizard, and, with this carefully caged, goes to a place where cross-roads meet. There, by the wayside, he makes a tiny gallows, and taking out the substitute from its prison, passes it three times round his head, crying: "Here I give you a man instead of me. Take him and leave me free." After this he places a thin loop of tie-tie round the neck of the lizard and hangs it upon the miniature gallows.

RAFAEL KARSTEN

The Head Trophy of the Jibaro Indians

The Jibaros never make trophies of the heads of such enemies as belong to their own tribe; that is, with whom they reckon blood relationship. An Indian who did this would run the risk of being himself killed by his tribesmen, even by those neutral before. On the other hand, it is the rule that when a victory has been attained over a foreign tribe, the heads of the slain enemies are taken. Most Jibaro warriors would consider any victory over such an enemy incomplete, and the whole war expedition more or less a failure, unless they returned with one or several head trophies. It, of course, not seldom happens that the Jibaro is able to kill an enemy but not to take his head, because his comrades are able to secure the dead body and perhaps to defeat the slayers. In such a case there can not be a real victory feast. It occurs, however, sometimes, than an enthusiastic Jibaro warrior invites his friends and celebrates a small feast, consisting in drinking bouts and dancing, although he has not been able to capture a trophy but only to kill his enemy.

Contrariwise, it may happen in exceptional cases that a Jibaro, although he has acquired a trophy, does not care to celebrate a feast with it, either because he considers himself too poor to procure the great supply of food necessary for the many guests at such a feast or because he has not enough people in his house to prepare it or friends to invite to it. Thus the great Jibaro chief Nayapi, of Pastaza, has killed about 20 enemies, but has not celebrated a single *tsantsa* feast, evidently in part because his many enemies have not given him the peace and tranquillity necessary for preparing such a feast.

The rule is, however, among the Jibaros that a warrior who has captured a head (*tsantsa*) should celebrate a feast. The head feast for the Jibaro opens the road to honor and fame, to material wealth, to new victories over enemies, and a long life. It is the great mystery feast of the Jibaro Indians; as will presently be seen, it in part has a purely religious significance, inasmuch as the Jibaro through the ceremonies thereby performed believes he acquires the same benefits as most other savage peoples try to acquire by cult actions of different kinds.

As soon as a Jibaro warrior has killed an enemy of another tribe he at once tries to secure his head, which he cuts off as close to the trunk as possible. The warrior who has cut off the head (*muka tsupikma*) is the "lord of the head" (*muka heindinyu*) and the first who, when the victors are many, has the right to celebrate a feast with it. When several Indians in union have killed one enemy it is customary for each of them in turn to celebrate a victory feast with the trophy, which in this case is taken from one house to another.

During the speedy return which generally follows upon a successful attack there is not always time for the victors to at once begin with the preparation of the trophy. They at first have to put themselves in safety from the eventually pursuing enemy. Thus it occurs that they carry the bloody head with them during a couple of days before they get an opportunity to "skin" it (*muka sukurtinyu*). In this work only those warriors engage who have taken part in the killing of the enemy. If the victors are many, and they have been able to acquire only one head, it happens that some of them separate themselves from the rest, saying: "We go off to kill other enemies and to capture our own heads."

Those who remain now start to take off the scalp from the head. At first the following small ceremony takes place: The head is placed upon a large leaf on the ground. Upon the head there is placed another leaf of the forest which the Jibaros call *pingi nuka,* and to which certain magical virtues are ascribed. The warrior who cuts off the head now seats himself on this "seat" and receives juice of tobacco mixed with saliva from the chief, who blows it in through his nose. Then another of the slayers takes his seat on the head and receives juice of tobacco through the nose, etc., until all have partaken. This is the first of a series of ceremonies which have for their object the protection of the slayers against the revengeful spirit of the killed enemy.

The *tsantsa* is now prepared in the following way: Along the back side of the head, from the apex downward, a long cut is made with a knife, whereupon the scalp and the skin of the face is slowly and carefully drawn off from the skull, in much the same way as is done with the hides of animals for stuffing. The skinning of the face is said to be the most difficult part of this work, for here the skin does not loosen by merely drawing it off, but has to be cut from the flesh with a sharp knife. The skull and all fleshy parts that adhere to it are thrown away and the scalp obtained is further prepared. It is attached to a vine and immersed in a pot of boiling water, where it is left for a while. By boiling the scalp it is freed from microbes, contracts a little, and gets more consistence. It is then taken out of the pot and put on the top of a stick, fixed in the ground, where it is left for a while until it has cooled.

A ring is formed of a vine which the Jibaros call *câpi,* of the same size as the circumference of the ready-made *tsantsa* at the neck opening, and this ring is attached to the trophy, at first provisionally, and later, in the same degree as the latter assumes its final size through reduction, more firmly. By means of a needle and a thread consisting of a chambira fiber, that part of the scalp which, for the purpose of the skinning of the head, had been cut open, is sewn together.

The reduction of the trophy now should begin. What at first is done with it, however, rather has the character of some sort of magical ceremony. At the bank of the river three small round stones are looked for, which are heated at the fire. By means of a cleft stick one of the heated stones is taken up from the fire and put into the head through the opening at the neck. This is done by the first slayer (he who cuts off the head of the enemy), whose hand is held by the chief or an old warrior. The head is kept in motion so that the heated stone rolls to and fro within it, burning off a part of the blood and flesh which is still attached to the scalp. The stone is subsequently taken out and again put in the fire. The same procedure is repeated with the second stone, and lastly with the third stone. The stones used are each time put back on the fire, where they are left.

Since a similar procedure is afterwards undertaken with heated sand, the use of the three small stones seems somewhat superfluous. Probably the object of this treatment is only to mortify the soul of the killed enemy, attached to the scalp, and to keep it at bay. This explanation is made more probable by the fact that the ceremony with the three stones is repeated later, at the great feast, and obviously without practical aim.

The proper reduction of the trophy is brought about by means of hot sand. Some fine sand is taken from the river bank and heated at the fire in a piece of broken clay pot (*hakáchi*). When the sand is sufficiently hot it is poured into the head so as to more than half fill it. The head is kept in motion so that the sand acts uniformly upon all its parts. The object of this procedure is to remove the flesh still attached to the skin, to make the scalp thinner, and to reduce the whole trophy. This is attained by the procedure with the hot sand being repeated many times. As soon as the sand has cooled it is taken out of the head, reheated at the fire in the broken clay pot, and again poured into the head. Each time, after taking out the sand from the head, the scalp is scraped inside with a knife in order to remove from it what the sand has burned off. As the trophy dries and shrinks through this treatment the head, and especially the face, is cleverly molded with the fingers, so that it retains its human features, becoming like the head of a small dwarf. This work is continued during the whole return from the war, eventually even at home, consequently during several days or even weeks, the same sand and the same broken clay vessel being always used. These things are always kept and carried on the march by the first slayer, whose duty it is, as soon as the party arrives at a camping place, to collocate the clay pot on the fire and heat sand for the molding of the trophy.

Numbuimartinyu, "The Washing of the Blood"

Immediately after their return the victor or victors have to pass through the purification procedure, connected with a small feast, which the Jibaros call *numbuimartinyu* (from *númba,* blood, and *mártinyu,* to paint, to coat), the principal ceremony of which consists in their legs being coated with chicken's blood. If the victors are many, this ceremony is at first performed with the one who cut the head of the enemy, and thereafter by turns with each of those who took part in the killing. Before the victors, who travel slowly and stop in various houses on the way, arrive home, a message has been sent that the warriors are coming, that a head has been captured and that the preparations for the feast *numbuimartinyu* should begin at once. This feast therefore always has a more or less improvised character.

The first slayer stops in the house of some relations in the neighborhood of his home until the trophy is definitely prepared. It is not until then that his solemn entrance into his own house can take place. He is in the dress of a penitent, has his hair untied, and wears no body-painting or other ornaments. At his side stands the chief or some other old warrior, who will lead the ceremonies at the following feasts and in this capacity is called *whuéa*. Behind these two men the rest of the warriors arrange themselves in a row. The *whuéa* at first gives the slayer juice of tobacco through the nose. Thereafter the latter disengages the trophy from the cloth in which it has been enveloped and with the aid of the old man hangs it round his neck, over the breast. Followed by the rest of the men, he now slowly and ceremoniously, and continually smoothing the hair of the trophy with the hand, proceeds toward the house, stopping outside the door. From within all the women come to meet him, arranged in a row and holding each other by the hands, all in festive dresses and with rattles of snail's shells around the cinctures. On each side of the women the men arrange themselves in two rows inside the house. The introductory dance with the trophy which is called *ihiámbrama,* and which is performed by the victor together with the women, now takes place. From among the women two step forth who have been standing at the head of the rest. Those are the wife and daughter of the victor. For the following dance the daughter grasps him from behind at the cincture with both hands; the wife gives him her hand, standing at the head of the other women. The slayer again seizes the *tsantsa* with the right hand, holding it up with the arm stretched out; with the left he grasps the hand of his wife. All now pass, dancing or hopping with the side foremost, into the interior of the house, to the accompaniment of drums and the rattles of the women, and immediately return to the entrance. The same maneuver is repeated twice more. Each time the slayer, led by the women, returns to the entrance of the house. The aim of this dance is to paralyze the danger threatening the victor from the spirit of the murdered enemy at the first entrance into the house, which is regarded as particularly critical.

The slayer now takes off the *tsantsa* and the latter is tied to a chonta lance which is fixed in the ground close to the door at the inner side. The lance must be made of the hard wood of the chonta palm, to which the Indians ascribe a supernatural power. Another kind of lance, for instance one having an iron point, would not do. In this way the *tsantsa* is kept even at the following feasts during the time it is not needed for the ceremonies. The trophy being tied to the chonta lance, the spirit of the enemy attached to it is mortified and kept at bay.

The *whuéa* lays his hand upon the shoulder of the slayer and takes him round in the house as if to manifest that he can now move about there without danger.

Meanwhile, close to the lance with the *tsantsa* tied to it, two small vessels have been placed. One is a piece of an old broken clay pot (*hakáchi*) containing a little chicken's blood, the other an ordinary small pot with a solution of genipa (*sua*). These three objects, the lance with the trophy tied to it, the piece of the clay pot containing chicken's blood, and the small pot with genipa, seem to be sacred; no unauthorized person may touch them or even come near them.

If among the warriors who took part in the killing of the enemy two or more are from the same house, being for instance two brothers or a father with his sons, a special broken clay vessel with chicken's blood and a special small pot with genipa must be placed at the lance for each of them. The ceremony *numbuimartinyu,* thus, must be performed separately with each slayer from the same house.

The "washing of the blood" now takes place. The slayer takes his seat upon a small round bank close to the vessel with the chicken's blood and the *whuéa* places himself at his side. Around them the women form a semicircle, having their rattles around the cincture as before. They are led by an old woman, called *oháha,* who at the feasts directs all those ceremonies at which the women play the main part. The *whuéa* at first gives the slayer juice of tobacco through the nose. Then he grasps him by the hand, brings it down to the vessel containing the chicken's blood, lets him dip the index finger into it, and subsequently with the blood draw a broad line 2 or 3 inches in length along the front side of one of his legs, from beneath upward. Thereafter the slayer, with the aid of the *whuéa,* applies a similar stroke with the blood to his other leg. While this is being done the women, led by the *oháha,* dance in a ring around them, singing a sort of conjuration, which mainly consists of the following phrase:

Whuéa heingi ikäski numbimarmai ihambratinyu; that is, "The *whuéa,* together with the *oháha* (*ikäski*), paint you with blood to start the fasting."

As we shall see, the ceremony *numbuimartinyu* introduces a time of very strict fasting for the slayer.

The slayer now in his turn does the *whuéa* the same service, drawing with his index finger two streaks with the chicken's blood upon both his legs.

The blood-painting ceremony having been finished, the piece of broken clay vessel, together with the blood left in it, is immediately thrown away into the forest. It is an impure and harmful substance which need no longer be kept.

The *whuéa* asks the wife of the slayer for water, and she brings it in a clay dish (*pininga*). The old man takes a little water from the dish with his hand and puts it upon the head of the slayer. Thereafter he does the same with the wife and daughter of the slayer, putting with his hand a little water upon their heads. All three are subsequently sent down to the river to bathe.

If the slayer has two wives they generally assist at the dance mentioned. If he is quite a young man, who has not yet married, it is considered obligatory that he should look for a bride for the feast. The part of the other woman in this case is played by some near female relative of his.

In the river the slayer carefully washes his whole body, as well as his clothing, soiled with blood in the battle, and lastly his weapons, the still bloody lance and knife. Together with his wife and daughter, who have also washed themselves, he then returns to the house.

On the way they break some twigs of guayusa (*Ilex* sp.), called *weisa* by the Jibaros, a tree the leaves of which are used for the preparation of an aromatic and tonic drink, with which the Jibaros wash their mouths every morning. This drink has now to be prepared. The slayer as well as his wife and daughter together grasp a small clay pot, called *yukúnda,* pour water into it from a larger vessel, and together place it on the fire. As soon as the drink has boiled the *whuéa* takes a little of it in a small gourd, mutters an incantation over it, and passes it to the slayer who washes his mouth with it without swallowing much of it. Thereafter the *whuéa* in the same way gives of the drink to the wife and the daughter of the slayer, who likewise wash their mouths with it. The small clay pot is then taken off the fire and laid aside. The three persons are now properly purified for breaking the fast.

The wife of the slayer goes to fetch the edible top of a small palm which the Jibaros call *tingími,* which is put on the fire to be roasted, exactly on the same place where the guayusa pot had lain. At another fire in the house beans have before been cooked, and at a third manioc, afterwards mashed, a dish called *nauma.* As soon as the palm top is sufficiently roasted the women move over to this fire, take a dish with beans, and another dish with boiled manioc (*nauma*). The three principal persons, the slayer himself and his wife and daughter, now have to break the fast after the "washing of the blood." The *whuéa* at first gives juice of tobacco to the slayer through the nose. Then with two fingers he takes a little of the palm top (*tingími*), spits on the ground, mutters an incantation over it and puts it directly into the mouth of the slayer, who swallows it. Then with two fingers he takes a few beans, and lastly also a small piece of boiled manioc together with a little salt and a little pimiento or Indian pepper, and gives them to the slayer with the same ceremony. Exactly the same action is repeated with his wife and his daughter, each of whom likewise receives a little of the dishes mentioned. The vessels with the food are subsequently carried away by the other women.

Meanwhile food has also been cooked for the guests in the women's department of the house. This food essentially consists of boiled chicken. If there are swine in the house, one is also slaughtered and prepared, but according to old tradition boiled chicken is the main dish at the feast *numbuimartinyu.*

A general banquet now commences, at which the guests eat chicken and manioc, whereas the slayer, his wife, and daughter eat the palm top *tingími,* beans, and manioc.

After the banquet the last ceremony takes place, which consists in the slayer being painted with genipa (*sua*). The slayer seats himself on a bank in front of the pot containing the black dye, and the *whuéa* places himself at his side, grasps his hand, makes him dip his index finger in the solution and apply a broad stroke with it over the mouth so that both lips are painted black.. Thereafter the old man draws a similar black stroke over his own mouth. The women simultaneously dance around the two men, singing an incantation. The pot containing the genipa is now carried away and kept.

The *whuéa* at last addresses the slayer with a sort of speech wherein he points out that he himself has now fulfilled his mission to wash off the blood from the slayer, but that the latter has now to prepare himself for the celebration of the final great victory feast. He has to breed swine and chickens to be slaughtered at the feast; he must plant fields of manioc and plantain; he must in his life carefully observe certain rules of abstinence from eating certain kinds of food, etc.

When darkness sets in, or about 6 o'clock in the evening, a general dance commences, which takes place at all great feasts and is called *hantsēmáta*. This dance will be described later in connection with the *tsantsa* feast proper. The slayer himself takes part in the dance with the trophy hanging on his back. It has to be continued during the whole night until dawn. That night no one in the house is allowed to sleep, and especially not the slayer himself.

Suamartinyu, "The Feast of Painting with Genipa

The principal ceremony at this feast is the washing of the trophy in a magical solution, through which the spirit of the slain enemy is supposed to become the slave and will-less instrument of the victor. Then follows the ceremonial slaughtering of the swine, and the final ceremony when the *whuéa* or priest helps the slayer to dress himself, cuts his hair, makes him break the fast, and lastly paints his face, breast, stomach, arms, and legs with *sua*. The feast *suamartinyu* lasts three or four days.

At the painting of the slayer's body with genipa the Jibaros formerly used a special instrument consisting of a cylindrical object, made of a special kind of very hard clay, into which certain circle-formed ornaments were incised. The instrument was dipped into the genipa solution and rolled along the cheeks, arms, legs, etc., of the slayer, the ornaments incised in the instrument being thereby stamped upon his body. This instrument, which is called *payánga,* is still known, but it is no longer made of clay, but of a kind of wood.

The object of the feast *suamartinyu* is partly to give the slayer renewed protection against the spirit of the killed enemy, partly to favorably prepare the trophy for what is its proper aim, namely, to promote the material wealth of the slayer, especially for the period immediately following the feast *numbuimartinyu.* In the first respect the feast is of significance for him in so far that he need no longer observe the same anxious caution and strict abstinence in his mode of life that was his obligation formerly. Thus he may again dress completely, tie his hair in pigtails, wear face painting and ornaments, manage lances and other weapons, go hunting and fishing, take part in feasts, sleep with his wife, etc. In one word, he can in the main return to his former normal life with the exception that he is obliged to continue keeping diet. Even in this respect he has however, far more liberty than before. With regard to food he has to observe the following rules: The slayer must absolutely abstain from eating pork and chicken. He is allowed to eat all fruits cultivated by the Jibaros, the manioc, however, only boiled, but not roasted. He must not eat the flesh of the tapir (*pamá*), of the great wild hog (*unta pakki*), of the paca (*Cœlogenys paca,* called *kashai* by the Jibaros), or of any kind of monkey. Of birds he must not eat the toucan, the wild turkey, the paugi, or other larger birds commonly hunted by the Jibaros, but only such small forest birds as are shot by blowpipe and nonpoisoned arrows. On the other hand, he is recommended to eat the small peccary (*yankipi*) and the rodent guatusa or agouti (*Dasyprocta aguti*). Of fish he is recommended to eat the large *nápi* (Spanish, *bagre*), and the *wámbi* (Spanish, *bocachupa*), but is forbidden to eat the *kanga* (Spanish, *bocachico*), the commonest fish in the South American rivers. He may also eat small fish or sardines (*chumakai*). If he infringes these rules he runs the risk of falling ill and dying, and the object of the whole feast will fail.

LEWIS H. MORGAN

The Iroquois Faith in Treaties

To the faith of treaties the Iroquois adhered with unwavering fidelity. Having endured the severest trials of political disaster, this faith furnishes one of the proudest monuments of their national integrity. They held fast to the "covenant chain" with the British until they were themselves deserted, and their entire country became the forfeit of their fidelity. In their numerous transactions with the several provinces formed out of their ancient territories, no serious cause of complaint was found against them for the nonfulfilment of treaty stipulations, although they were shorn of their possessions by treaty after treaty, and oftentimes made the victims of deception and fraud. In their intercourse with Indian nations, they frequently entered into treaties, sometimes of amity and alliance, sometimes of protection only, and in some instances for special purposes. All of these national compacts were "talked into" strings of wampum, to use the Indian expression, after which these were delivered into the custody of *Ho-no-we-nă'-to,* the Onondaga sachem, who was made hereditary keeper of the Wampum, at the institution of the League; and from him and his successors, was to be sought their interpretation from generation to generation. Hence the expression—"This belt preserves my words," so frequently met with at the close of Indian speeches, on the presentation of a belt. Indian nations, after treating, always exchanged belts, which were not only the ratification, but the memorandum of the compact.

There was an ancient treaty between the Senecas and the *Gä-quä-ga'-o-no,* or Eries, who resided upon the southern shore of Lake Erie, to the effect that the Genesee river should be the boundary between them, and that when a hostile band of either nation re-crossed this river into its own territories, it should be safe from further pursuit. An infraction of this treaty was one of the reasons of the long-cherished animosity of the Iroquois against them. A similar compact was once made with the *O-ya-dä'-go-o-no*[1] or Cherokees, by which the Tennessee river was the limit of pursuit. If a war-party of the latter had returned and re-crossed the Tennessee before they were overtaken by the pursuing Iroquois, they were as safe from their attack, as if intrenched behind an impregnable rampart. The Iroquois band could still invade, if disposed, the territory of the enemy, but they passed the camp of the retreating war-party without offering the slightest molestation.

[1] *O-ya-dä'-go-o-no,* the Iroquois name of the Cherokees, signifies "The people who dwell in caves."

T

ALFRED REGINALD RADCLIFFE-BROWN

Andaman Peacemaking

In the North Andaman, and possibly in the South also, there was a ceremony by which two hostile local groups made peace with one another. When the two groups have agreed to make friends and bring their quarrel to an end, arrangements are made for this ceremony. The arrangements are made through the women of the two parties. A day is fixed for the ceremony, which takes place in the country of the group that made the last attack. In the village of this group the dancing ground is prepared, and across it is erected what is called a *koro-čop*. Posts are put up in a line, to the tops of these is attached a length of strong cane, and from the cane are suspended bundles of shredded palm-leaf (*koro*). The women of the camp keep a look-out for the approach of the visitors. When they are known to be near the camp, the women sit down on one side of the dancing ground, and the men take up positions in front of the decorated cane. Each man stands with his back against the *koro-čop,* with his arms stretched out sideways along the top of it. None of them has any weapons.

The visitors, who are, if we may so put it, the forgiving party, while the home party are those who have committed the last act of hostility, advance into the camp dancing, the step being that of the ordinary dance. The women of the home party mark the time of the dance by clapping their hands on their thighs. I was told that the visitors carry their weapons with them, but when the dance was performed at my request the dancers were without weapons. The visitors dance forward in front of the men standing at the *koro-čop,* and then, still dancing all the time, pass backwards and forwards between the standing men, bending their heads as they pass beneath the suspended cane. The dancers make threatening gestures at the men standing at the *koro-čop,* and every now and then break into a shrill shout. The men at the *koro* stand silent and motionless, and are expected to show no sign of fear.

After they have been dancing thus for a little time, the leader of the dancers approaches the man at one end of the *koro* and, taking him by the shoulders from the front, leaps vigorously up and down to the time of the dance, thus giving the man he holds a good shaking. The leader then passes on to the next man in the row while another of the dancers goes through the same performance with the first man. This is continued until each of the dancers has "shaken" each of the standing men. The dancers then pass under the *koro* and shake their enemies in the same manner from the back. After a little more dancing the dancers retire, and the women of the visiting group come forward and dance in much the same way that the men have done, each woman giving each of the men of the other group a good shaking.

When the women have been through their dance the two parties of men and women sit down and weep together.

The two groups remain camped together for a few days, spending the time in hunting and dancing together. Presents are exchanged, as at the ordinary meetings of different groups. The men of the two groups exchange bows with one another.

PART 15

Death

MARTIN DOBRIZHOFFER

On the Confines of Life and Death

Death is dreadful to most mortals, but particularly so to the Abipones. They cannot even bear the sight of a dying person. Hence, whenever any one's life is despaired of, his fellow inmates immediately forsake the house, or are driven away by the old women who remain to take care of the sick, lest they should be so affected by the mournful spectacle, that fear of death should make them shrink from endangering their lives in battle. They are, therefore, obliged to pass many nights in another person's tent, or in the open air. As they have very little experience of persons dying a natural death, they do not know the signs of it when it draws near. A short abstinence from food, unusual silence, or sleeplessness, makes them presage approaching dissolution. As soon as a report is spread that a man is dying, the old women, who are either related to the person, or famed for medical skill, flock to his house. They stand in a row round the sick man's bed, with dishevelled hair and bare shoulders, striking a gourd, the mournful sound of which they accompany with violent motion of the feet and arms, and loud vociferations. She who excels the rest in age, or fame for medical skill, stands nearest to the dying man's head, and strikes an immense military drum, which returns a horrible bellowing. Another, who is appointed to watch the sick man, removes every now and then the bull's hide with which he is covered, examines his face, and if he seems yet to breathe, sprinkles him plentifully with cold water, a jug of which is placed under the bed. When I first witnessed these things, I pitied the fate of the sick man, who, I feared, would be killed, if not by the disease, at any rate by the howling of the women and the noise of the drum, or else smothered by the weight of the hide, with which the whole body is covered, and which is as hard and as heavy as a board. Under the pretext of compassion, they use all this cruelty to the departing soul, that the women may be spared the sight of his last agonies, and the hearing of his groans.

If the respiration of the dying man be not heard at a distance like a pair of bellows in Vulcan's workshop, and if his breath stop even for a moment, they proclaim with a Stentorian voice, that he has given up the ghost. A great crowd assembles on all sides, exclaiming, he is dead, he is no more. All the married women and widows of the town crowd to the mourning, attired as I have described before, and whilst they are filling the streets with confused wailings, with the rattling of gourds and beating of pans covered with stags' skins, a sudden shout is often heard announcing, that the man whom they mourn for as dead is come to life again. The joyous exclamation, he is revived, is instantly substituted for the mournful howling of the women, some of whom return home, whilst others hasten to the miserable mortal on the confines of life and death, and torment him with their dreadful yellings, till at last they deprive him of life. After his death, the first business of the bystanders is to pull out the heart and tongue of the deceased, boil them, and give them to a dog to devour, that the author of his death may soon die also. The corpse, while yet warm, is clothed according to the fashion of his country, wrapped in a hide, and bound with leathern thongs, the head being covered with a cloth, or any garment at hand. The savage Abipones will not endure the body of a dead man to remain long in the house; while yet warm, it is conveyed on ready horses to the grave. Women are appointed to go forward on swift steeds, to dig the grave, and honour the funeral with lamentations. What, if we say that many of the Abipones are buried because they are thought dead, but that in reality they die, because they are buried? It is not unlikely that these poor wretches are suffocated, either by the hide with which they are bound, or by the earth which is heaped over them. But as they pull out the heart and tongue of the deceased, it cannot be doubted that they are dead when they are buried; though I strongly suspect that the heart is sometimes cut out when they are half alive, and would perhaps revive were they not prematurely deprived of this necessary instrument of life. The savages, who hasten the burying of their dead so much, presumed to censure us for keeping the Christian Indians out of their graves many hours after their decease.

FATHER PAUL LE JEUNE
Killing the Old Mother

On the second day of January, I saw a number of Savages trying to cross the great river St. Lawrence in their canoes. Usually this river does not freeze in the middle; it drifts or floats immense pieces of ice; according to the course and movement of the current. These poor fellows approached large pieces of the floating ice, sounded them with their paddles, then mounted them, and drew their canoes up after them, crossing over to reach the water on the other side of the ice. Nimble as they are, not infrequently some of them are drowned.

I saw a Savage dragging his mother behind him over the snow. The coaches and wagons of this country are sledges made of bark or wood, the horses are the men who draw them. Now this poor old woman was tied upon one of these sleighs; and her son, being unable, conveniently, to take her down by the common path of a mountain which borders the river along which he was going, let her roll down the steepest place to the bottom, and then went by another route to find her. As I could not bear this act of impiety, I said so to some of the Savages who were near me. They answered:

"What wouldst thou have him do with her? She is going to die any way; take her and kill her, since thou hast pity for her; thou wilt do her a service, because she will not suffer so much; perhaps her son will leave her in the midst of the woods, às he is unable either to cure her or to drag her after him, if he does not find something to eat." This is the way they take care of the sick that they think are going to die. They hasten death by a blow from a club or an axe, when they have a long journey to make, and do this through compassion.

PETER FREUCHEN

Burying the Mother Alive in a Snow House

This certainly was a happy home, and nobody was upset at all that Orsokidok had not come back yet. He had not returned to Mala after following a wounded reindeer. But he would find his way back to the sledge all right. After all, it was only the orphan who was missing, a boy without any family. He was just a little assistant who happened to be around.

Orsokidok arrived the next day at noon. He was hungry and tired. He had not killed an animal, and for two days he had gone hungry. He was in poor humor when he returned but when the others laughed—why shouldn't he join in? Wasn't it funny that there were people who just lay around eating lots of meat while others stayed away simply because they did not want to return? It was the old story that he who tries to get more, in the end gets nothing at all. Finally Orsokidok was given a whole pot of meat which he ate with relish.

They did not continue their journey that day, sleeping instead. Old Naterk was grateful for the rest, for her old legs often hurt her now, and when she breathed there was a rattling noise in her windpipe.

For a little while she walked beside the sledge, half leaning against it for support. Soon, however, she could not keep up with the dogs at all. They had to stop and wait for her. When she finally caught up with them, her face was as red as if she had run a race on a hot summer's day.

"Sit on the sledge and rest," Mala said.

"As if the sledge were not hard enough for the dogs to pull and for you to steer. It is always best for a human being to walk."

Again she stumbled on ahead of the team as was her wont. Mala now saw to it that the dogs did not run too fast. Each time there was a stop he would make it his business to examine the runners very thoroughly and smooth the ice that covered them. He always took so long that Old Naterk, for the greater part of the day, succeeded in keeping well ahead of the sledge. However, she was too weak to find any satisfaction in this feat. The exertion was altogether too great for her. Mala stopped early that day, out of consideration for his brave, old mother.

During the evening, Old Naterk had no appetite; she just lay around, panting heavily like a walrus rising to the surface of the sea.

Puala took a marrow bone which Mala had broken open for him, picked out the marrow, which was not unlike a long, fat worm. Holding the delicacy in front of his grandmother's mouth, he smeared her lips with the choice morsel.

"Eat," he encouraged her. "I shall go out and kill a big reindeer for you."

Old Naterk was touched and told him he was a great hunter who brought his grandmother wonderful things.

"No, I am not," objected Puala, "but I want you to eat when everybody else is eating. If one does not eat, one can't be happy."

"Good, then your old grandmother will eat some of your prey."

Old Naterk could find no rest while the others slept soundly. Her head was hot, there was that rattling noise whenever she took a breath, and she had aches and pains all over her body. She put a few pieces of snow on her forehead and concentrated on some formulas of powerful magic which had helped her frequently before. But the magic words brought no relief. Perhaps she shouldn't have mumbled them while the others were around. She was afraid that she would wake them if she got up now and left the snow hut. So she stayed where she was but somehow could not sleep. She remembered all the amusing nonsense that men had told her when she was young and they were making love to her. Simply everything crowded into her head. She was glad when morning came and the others awoke.

Old Naterk needed a good long time to dress Upik in his clothes, his shoes and mittens. It was even harder for her to get into her own furs and crawl out into the fresh air. How her back ached, when she tried to raise herself! Slowly she walked up a little knoll, sat down and looked around. Then, loosening her belt, she tied the strap around her left foot. There Old Naterk sat, with nobody near her, summoning the spirits to ascertain her fate. She tried to invoke the spirit that had guided her feet and had always solved her problems before. Today, however, the spirit would not respond. One must be strong minded and convinced of one's power to commune with these spirits, otherwise they simply will not come.

She returned just as Mala was preparing the sledge for an early departure.

"I have something to say to you and it is important too," Naterk said.

Mala understood that his mother had something on her mind that was more than the usual woman's talk. Her eyes had an expression that made him feel once more like a little boy. He bowed his head and listened.

"I am tired and I am old. You must build me a snow house because I shall go on a very long journey all alone."

"Please do not speak like that, mother. We all wish to see your face among us always. I shall certainly not build a snow house for you. Let us hurry down to the white men and the ships, where we can get tea and tobacco."

"Oh, Mala my son, but I am tired and must have rest."

"Remember the children, mother. How badly they will miss you. They are sure to cry. Iva always needs your help and good advice. And I—have I not always had you with me? I could not do without you, mother."

Old Naterk did not answer. She mumbled a few words and stared at the horizon. In the far distance, she perceived the bare mountains where the Great Spirit inhaled reindeer through his nostrils whenever he breathed. Here she had lived as long as she could remember.

"Give me my stick," she ordered. "I shall go ahead."

Mala rushed over to the pot, sucked his mouth full of water from it, and squirted it against the runners of the sledge for a new ice coating. Nobody must see how his mother's words affected him. He was dirty with soot because each time he took a mouthful of water the lampblack smudged his face.

Old Naterk stumbled on as well as she could and it took the others quite long before they finally caught up with her. There were so many obstacles to surmount that day!

In the middle of the day, Naterk tired once more. Mala, being the leader of the party, demanded that she ride on the sledge. There she sat and shivered while the others pulled her along and Iva alone broke the path for the dogs.

During the night, Naterk complained that her old back bothered her and that she had severe pains in her whole body. She did not stir when Iva lighted the lamp. Perspiration ran down her wrinkled face; she had strange thoughts and mumbled strange words which nobody understood.

Iva dressed, sat down next to Naterk and spoke to her. But Naterk would not answer. Iva finally pulled a strand of hair from Naterk's head. She threw it into the fire so that the smell of the burning hair might chase away the evil spirits and the root of the disease might be destroyed in the flames. This magic really helped. Old Naterk's thoughts were orderly once more. She took a couple of pieces of dried reindeer meat left over from last year. The pieces were all mouldy but she cleaned them with her finger nails and handed them to the children.

Next morning the sun shone brightly and the journey was continued. But in the course of the day, Naterk put up her fur hood and waited for Mala to come abreast of her.

"My son," she addressed him. "I have firm words to say to you and you must not make any objection. I have lived many years and my legs are tired. Build me a snow hut. When I asked this favor of you before you would not listen to me. Don't wait until it will be necessary for me to command my son to do what his mother bids him."

She busied herself with the load and brushed some snow off Upik who had fallen while playing.

Mala did not answer this time. He took his stick, probed the snow and started to build a house.

"Are we resting for the day already?" the children asked.

"Yes," answered Iva. "That is what father has decided to do."

Thus Mala built a house.

As usual the two women unloaded the sledge, filled in the cracks between the blocks and covered the whole structure with loose snow. The boys took a seal's skin, tied a strap to it and used it for a sledge. As Puala, being a big boy already, wanted to help his father with the building, Upik was left alone. He wanted to play and called to his grandmother.

"Come, grandmother, and pull me. I want to go asledging."

The old woman came.

"You must run quickly."

But her old legs were too weak. Suddenly, her lips quivering, she stopped and tears streamed down her cheeks.

"Grandmother is crying. It's no fun to play with her when she is crying." Upik decided he would rather play alone after all.

When they came in later on, Old Naterk started to get busy on a pair of mittens for the little one. Upik lost so many of them.

Mala went outside and built another igloo. Nobody helped him and he did not ask for any assistance either. Orsokidok had gone with bow and arrows to look for some likely prey. When Mala had finished the house he came in and brushed the snow off his clothes.

"Has anything happened?" Iva asked.

"Nothing at all. I've built a house, that's all." He turned away quickly and walked over to a little mound to look around for Orsokidok.

The old woman collected her belongings. She took one skin after the other, scrutinized it and put it aside. Finally she picked an old, almost hairless skin, rolled it up and was ready to leave the hut. Then she stopped and looked around. Emotion almost overcame her. She stepped over to the sleeping children, put her mouth to their noses and sucked. There was a squirting noise and Puala awoke. What was that for? He was no little boy any more. He could blow his nose himself! But grandmother was so strange today and so rough. She pulled off the boys' hoods, exposing their left shoulders. Right there she dug her teeth in, because the bite of an old woman is a lucky omen for children. Although it did not hurt much, as grandmother's teeth were dull from chewing skins for years and years, the two boys were thoroughly aroused by now and they cried without restraint.

Grandmother was certainly acting strangely today. And there were new mittens and new pants at her place. But she did not speak about it.

"The time to leave has arrived," she said simply, and took her old skin and departed.

"Are you going outside?" asked Iva but she kept on sewing.

The boys lay down and quickly fell asleep again. Life inside the snow hut was just as it had been before.

Outside, the old woman first looked around. The world was beautiful, but her back was so tired and, oh, how she longed to rest her weary bones. Then she crawled into the house built for her and quietly stretched herself out on the old skin.

Soon Mala came. He had seen her enter the hut. He now took his knife, cut a block of snow and walled up the entrance with it. There was not one word spoken when Mala closed up Old Naterk's last house.

There, then, the old woman reposed, waiting for death. She seemingly never tired of thinking. She listened to the children come out of the other house and ask questions about her snow hut. She heard the father tell the children that they must not go into grandmother's hut. She heard Orsokidok come home. He had killed a reindeer, a young calf, a mere yearling. Naterk always used to get a piece of tongue. Tongue of a yearling was soft and easy to chew for old teeth. But why should she think of that now? And then again she heard the boys playing with the sledge they had fashioned from skins. Once the children came so near the hut that she could hear the snow crunching under their little feet. Upik fell down and hurt himself; he set up a great wail.

"I'm hurt, I'm bleeding, oh, mother, grandmother!"

How hard it was to play dead. But Old Naterk was no longer to be reckoned among the living. To the others she had passed on; she was gone. Iva came out and called: "Come in for your food. I have nice boiled meat for you."

"Where is grandmother?" Puala inquired. "Isn't grandmother coming to eat with us?"

Tears welled in Naterk's eyes and her mouth watered. Now she was lying here prostrate. Life, surely, was much more wearisome than death. But the most wearisome thing of all was this slow transition from life to death.

She was still tossing sleeplessly on her hairless skin when dawn came. She listened intently when she heard Mala getting the sledge ready. In her thoughts, Old Naterk followed their every movement: Now the dogs would rush into the deserted hut to fight for the bones left there. Now the load was strapped on the sledge; now the children inquired whether grandmother would walk ahead as usual.—Then the travelers departed and everything became quiet.

Alas, they had started and left her all alone. Perhaps, after all, Mala should not have permitted her to remain behind. He, who was always so good a son—had he really deserted her now? Naterk arose and tried to leave the house but her old limbs were too weak to carry her. She wanted to follow the others and she wanted to stay behind.

Darkness came, spreading its sheltering wings over her. Old Naterk, once born into this world, had lived her full life.—Now she was no more.

In the evening it was very quiet in Mala's snow house; gaiety had fled. Little Upik wanted to know why they were building a house before grandmother had caught up with them. Iva told him to keep still, and nobody said one word more that night than was absolutely necessary. Upik finally cried himself to sleep. Next day they rested and this day and the succeeding days, Mala went hunting but he did not go far; he stayed right in the proximity of the house. The boys became impatient and wanted to know whether they would not soon get down to the ships.

At last Mala went back to the spot where his old mother had gone into her last house. Drifting snow had covered the igloo. No animal had approached it; all around was the silence of death. Mala took his knife and cut a hole in the roof of the house so that Old Naterk's soul could depart.

Returning to Iva, he did not bring any prey that night. He told her that he had come from a visit that grieved him terribly.

"I opened the roof," was all he said and he sat down silently without taking a bite of food.

The children were not permitted to play; they were not even allowed to talk. Iva herself cut snow for drinking water and it was she, too, who cut the meat for the pot—just as if she were a man. Mala did not stir. His hood put up, he sat inside the house all night long, fully dressed. The children, too, were not undressed. Everything seemed so strange.

"The lice are eating me, the lice are eating me," the boys whimpered during the night and scratched themselves furiously. But they were not permitted to take off their furs.

After five days had passed, the children were left alone. The others went back to Naterk's snow house. Mala went ahead and the others followed in his tracks. He cut a hole through the rear of the hut, and they entered Old Naterk's last abode. There she lay in a huddled heap, her pelt hood over her face, her knees pulled up. Mala suddenly remembered when his mother was a young woman and he a little boy. She had always so much to tell him about the men who were ready to fight for her but had never won her. What a splendid mother she had been, what a brave mother—and now—

They dragged the body out of the house to a nearby spot. Where loose stones were scattered over a mighty rock they prepared Old Naterk's grave. She, who had lived, was now dead, and her name must nevermore be mentioned by any living soul. Only those who still breathe are human, and only in their company may one abide. Because they had touched the corpse, they took off their mittens and stuffed them between the stones.

On the way home, they were careful to step into the tracks they had made before. They held their hands close to their bodies so they would not freeze. Now and then Mala would turn back, effacing their tracks with his knife, so that Death should not follow them.

It was evening when they returned. Iva at once took two bags with new clothes and they put on new garments. As Orsokidok had no suit to spare, he just turned his fur coat inside out. All the old clothes were packed up in a bundle and next morning Mala returned to the grave with it. He stayed away a long time and when he retraced his steps, he took care to obliterate his tracks.

At last they journeyed on. Every day they painstakingly wiped out their tracks. Eventually they forgot about it in their eagerness to make quick progress. Ships and the white men beckoned to them and spring was almost upon them. Eider ducks winged their way inland, sea swallows arrived, and big flocks of wild geese, screeching madly overhead, made for the north.

LORIMER FISON and A. W. HOWITT

Funeral Ceremonies in Australia

When an individual of the Kŭrnai tribe died, the relatives rolled the corpse up in an opossum rug, enclosed it in a sheet of bark, and corded it tightly. A hut was built over it, and in this the bereaved and mourning relatives and friends collected. The corpse lay in the centre, and as many of the mourners as could manage to find room lay on the ground with their heads upon the ghastly pillow. There they lay lamenting their loss. They would cry, "Why did you go? Why did you leave us?" Now and then the grief would be intensified by the wife uttering an ear-piercing wail—"Penning i tŭrn!" (my spouse is dead); or the mother—"Lit i tŭrn!" (my child is dead). All the others would join in, using the proper term of relationship; and they would cut and gash themselves with sharp instruments, until their heads and bodies streamed with blood. This bitter wailing and weeping would continue all night; the less closely related persons and the friends alone rousing themselves to eat, until the following day. This would go on for two or three days, when the corpse would be unrolled for the survivors to look at and renew their grief. If by this time the hair had become loose, it would be carefully plucked off the whole body and preserved by the father, mother, or sisters in small bags of opossum skin. They then again rolled up the body, and it was not opened until it was so far decomposed that the survivors could anoint themselves with "oil" which had exuded from it.[1] The only explanation which the Kŭrnai can give me of this horrible custom is, as they say, "to make them remember their relative or friend." Sometimes the body would be opened, the intestines removed and buried, in order that the corpse might dry more rapidly. The ghastly relique, in its bark cerements, was carried with the family in its migrations, and was the special charge of the father and mother, of the wife, or of other near relatives or connections. Finally, the body having, after years, become merely a bag of bones, would be buried, or put into some hollow tree. Sometimes the father or mother carried the lower jaw of the deceased as a memento.

The most remarkable custom in connection with the dead was that of the "Brett" or hand. Soon after death the hand, or both the hands, were cut off, wrapped in grass, and dried. A string of twisted opossum hair was attached so that it could be hung round the neck and worn in contact with the bare skin under the left arm. It was carried by the parent or child, brother or sister. The belief of the Kŭrnai was, and even, I think, still in many cases is that such a hand on the approach of an enemy would pinch, or push the wearer. The signal being given, the hand would be taken from the neck and suspended in front of the face; the string being held between the finger and thumb. The person would then say, "Which way are they coming?" [2] If the hand remained at rest, the question would be again put, but now facing another point of the horizon, and so on. The response was by the hand vibrating in some direc-

---

[1] This horrible anointing is practised at Drummond Island, also in the Kingsmill group.

[2] In one case "Mūnjū! Mūnjū! Wūnman? Mūnjū! tūnamŭn nganjū—brappūrna ma banja!" Mūnjū = there, wūnman = where, tūnamŭn = speak to, nganjū = me, brappŭrna = to throw, ma = to, ban = wild dog; or "Speak! Where are they? Or I throw you to the wild dogs."

tion, and it was thence that the danger was supposed to be approaching. My informants tell me that the vibrations were often so violent that the hand would almost "come over on to the holder."

From what I have said as to the community in food, the community in the right to hunt (with a narrow limitation), and from the community in personal property, which is evidenced by the rapidity with which clothes and other articles pass from member to member of the group, we should expect to find that the personal property of the deceased might become the property of his kin. It is difficult to collect evidence on this head. In the first place, the personality is very limited in extent, and in reality can only include weapons, implements, and garments. But the garments, and very often the weapons and implements of the deceased, were rolled up with his corpse or buried, from a reluctance on the part of his relatives to have constantly before them, after the funeral ceremonies, anything which might recall his loss and their grief.[3]

CHARLES KINGSLEY MEEK

The Death and Burial of a Sudanese King

According to Jukun tradition the Jukun king was only allowed to rule for a period of seven years, being put to death at any convenient time after he had reached this allotted span. No reason is given for the limitation of the period of years to seven. The number seven is apparently a sacred number in all Jukun communities, based perhaps on an ancient Moon cult. But possibly the choice of seven is due to the observation that famines seem to occur roughly at intervals of seven years in the Northern Provinces of Nigeria. Some Jukun, however, state that in former times the allotted span was no more than two years. The Jukun period of two years was subsequently extended to seven, it being said (after the extension) that if the king were killed before that time his ghost would pursue

[3] It seems difficult to reconcile this feeling with the practice of carrying the deceased about with them.

his slayers, but that if he were killed at any later time his slayers had nothing to fear.

We have seen that there were rites performed some six or seven years after the king had been crowned, the object of which was to advance the king to a higher degree of sovereignty, or in other words to secure a prolongation of his period of office. Kings might, therefore, reign for more than seven years and if any credit can be attached to the chronology of the lists of kings in the various Jukun communities it would not appear that the septennial rule was enforced during the last two hundred years. Further if we are to believe the concurrent tradition that a king who fell sick was put to death it must have been permissible to kill the king before the completion of seven years. It may be assumed generally that a popular king was allowed to remain in office so long as he was able to carry out the daily liturgy and as long as the harvests were satisfactory, but that at the end of seven years he was subjected to an ordeal which obtained for him a further probationary period. It is possible that an unsatisfactory king met his death during the ordeal, i.e. during the Ando ku rites.

It is not possible to give full and accurate details of the ritual of the killing and burial of the king, as these are only known to a few officials; or it might be more correct to say that parts of the ritual are known to particular officials, and parts to other particular officials, it being taboo and dangerous for one official to breathe to another a single syllable of the secret duty pertaining to his office. Even the king himself is ignorant of some parts at least of the procedure. The following account is based partly on hearsay and partly on such details as were revealed by persons who had official or accidental knowledge of the ritual.

When the king became sick, or infirm, or broke any of the royal taboos, or proved himself unfortunate, he was secretly put to death. Whether any king was, in the olden days, permitted to die a natural death cannot now be known, but it is noteworthy that many Jukun kings are said to have reached a hoary old age, so that mere old age was not in itself considered a sufficient cause for the ritual murder of the king. The mode of killing was by strangulation with a string or piece of cloth. It is never suggested that the Jukun kings were invited to commit suicide, but it is possible that the stories of Jukun kings calling on trees or the earth to open and swallow them is to be interpreted in this way. Those appointed to commit the murder entered the palace at night having previously suborned the Akû Nako, Katô and Iche to assist, if not to take the principal part in the murder. The two executioners tied a noose of cloth round the neck of the sleeping king, and going off in different directions pulled the cloth until the king was strangled. It is said that if the king woke up and attempted to summon assistance the executioners reminded him that they were but performing the ancestral custom and that it behoved the king to behave quietly, as his royal ancestors had done before him. Another method was for the conspirators to bore a hole in the wall of the king's sleeping apartment and pass a noose through to the king's wife, who fastened it round his neck, the conspirators then pulling on the noose from outside. The king could only be killed by strangulation for two reasons: (*a*) that the executioners might not look into the king's eyes as he died, for if they did his departing soul would slay them; and (*b*) that the king's blood might not be spilt. It is also said that no one who had a claim to the throne might be present at the king's execution.

The king's demise was and is kept a close secret, and is not, in fact, revealed until many months afterwards, when the body is formally buried. Various reasons are assigned for this secrecy such as that the counsellors may have time to choose a successor, that bloody contests between aspirants for the throne may be avoided, or that the royal slaves and wives may not run away. But the real reason would seem to depend on the belief that the king is the crops. If he dies between March and December an announcement of his death would be tantamount to a repudiation of the central feature of Jukun religion, viz. the identification of the king with the annual corn; or to say that he had "returned to the skies" would be the same thing as saying that there would be no harvest that year. It would in fact be an invitation to the crops to wither up. His body is, therefore, kept preserved until after the harvest. Even at the present time, when it is no longer possible to preserve for long the secret of the king's death, it is believed that the crops harvested after his death are the late king's "seed" [1] If he dies in the dry season it might be supposed that his death could be announced with safety, his functions being handed over to his successor; but even in this case the normal rule is observed, though the ensuing crop is regarded as being that of his successor.

As the continued non-appearance of the king would excite suspicion among the people, especially the women of the palace, an announcement is made that the king is unwell. But he is never so unwell that he is unable to perform the daily rites. The palace officials, therefore, assemble every morning as usual and are served with beer, and one of the officials, viz. the Ajifî, personates the king. The same official also summons occasionally one or other of the late king's wives, and, speaking from behind a mat, intimates that he does not wish to see them for some considerable time. The secret is, however, revealed to the late king's principal wife. The Abô takes immediate charge of the late king's property, and it is said that an unscrupulous Abô turns the occasion handsomely to his own advantage, extracting even from the king's widows any loans he may have made to them under a pretence that he was acting at the king's request.

The body of the king is, immediately after death, taken from the sleeping apartments to one of the huts of the king's *bieko* and is there handed over to those special officials[2] whose duty it is to carry out the desiccation rites. It is laid on a platform of wooden planks or guinea-corn stalks. A frontal abdominal incision is made, and the heart is removed and placed on a pointed stick beside a fire. When it is thoroughly dried it is ground into a powder which is handed over to the Akû Nako that it may be secretly and periodically inserted into the food of the king's successor.

The disembowelled body is sewn up, smeared with butter and salt, massaged and bandaged tightly with strips of cloth. It is then placed in an erect position in a hole in the ground, being supported

[1] In Ancient Egypt grain was called the seed of Osiris. See Budge, *Osiris,* vol. i, p. 15.

[2] The Katô Puje and Iche Puje are said to be the officials primarily responsible.

by forked branches set under the shoulders and chin. A log fire is kept constantly burning all round the corpse. If the corpse is seen to swell up in any part an incision is made so as to permit the fluid to escape. It is said that the fat which exudes is collected in a pot and is, like the powdered heart, inserted by the Akû Nako into the food of the king's successor.

The body of the Jukun king is tended day and night by the various Katô acting under the orders of the Katô Puje and Iche Puje. It is their business to see that the fire is not allowed to go out, to drive off flies and burn various kinds of leaves and roots so as to allay the odour from the corpse. For this purpose raw meat may even be thrown on the fire during the early stages of desiccation. The period of fumigation varies from four to ten months, according to the time of the year at which the king had died. Being the personification of the life of the crops he cannot be buried during the dry season. Otherwise the crops would die for ever. He is usually buried at the beginning of the wet season when the bulrush-millet crop has attained a height of about one foot.

A week or so after the death of the Jukun king the Katô Tûwo is sent to the Nani To, the head of the Ba-Nando kindred which is responsible for the carrying out of the royal burial rites, with a gift of five pieces of cloth and a message that the king is ill. The Nani To demands to know the cause of the illness, and when the Katô professes ignorance the Nani To replies that medicine must be administered so that the king's health may be speedily restored. Some months later the Katô again betakes himself to the Nani To with further gifts of cloth and says, "This illness is an illness indeed and passes our strength." The Nani To replies, "Well, if that is so you must bring my son to me" (the Ba-Nando being regarded as the "grandfathers" of all Jukun kings). In due course the Katô, accompanied this time by the seniors and numerous pieces of cloth, go to the Nani To and announce that the king's illness had proved too much. The Nani To makes a pretence of wrath and charges the senior men with the murder of his "son," but they say that the thing came from Chidô and had nought to do with them. The Nani To persists that they are responsible, and the senior men thereupon go down on their knees and throw dust on their shoulders, professing repentance. A day is appointed for the burial at Nando, and the Nani To, who is himself a priest, performs rites at his private shrine which permit him to go from Wukari to Nando, where he performs further rites which permit him to receive the body of the king. He and his followers then set about the construction of the burial enclosure. Meanwhile a public announcement is made at Wukari that the king is no more. His decease is expressed euphemistically by saying, "The Earth has broken my tooth," or by saying merely that the king has gone away. It is thought that he has returned to the skies because of the irreligiousness of men. On the other hand there is in some Jukun communities the Osiris-like conception that the deceased king becomes a Judge of the Dead in Kindo, i.e. the Lower World, for it was stated at Gwana that the ruler and judge of Kindo is Jirkar, the founder of the line of Gwana chiefs.

Several hours before sunrise on the appointed day the king's body is transferred secretly to the sacred enclosure at Puje, and later in the day large crowds assemble, each group of relatives and officials taking up the positions occupied by them during the Puje festival. About 2 p.m. a form of ritual is carried out, which, according to Captain Best, who was present outside the enclosure at the burial of the late king, is "punctuated by sounds reminiscent of the responses of a choir in a vestry." This ceremony lasts half an hour, and after a further pause of twenty minutes a special chant is beaten on a drum, while a fiddler strikes up the tune which normally signalizes the out-coming of the king from his palace. A section of the matting at the north-east corner of the enclosure is then undone and an unsaddled horse appears, ridden by one of the Akû (the Akû nguhwi or Adati) with the body of the king sitting astride behind him. The body is clothed in the royal coat decorated with red birds and scorpions, and the head is covered with a veil of white cloth which is sewn on to the neck and is surmounted by two red cloth topknots. The hands are also veiled with white cloth, and the legs are either swathed in close-fitting white cloth or covered with riding-boots. The body is kept in position by two strips of cloth passed under the shoulders of the corpse and the horseman, and is supported at either side by footmen.[3] The horseman himself is bareheaded and wears a gown of blue cloth, but all the attendant Jukun are clothed, as always at religious ceremonies or in the presence of the king, in cloths rolled at the waist, the upper part of the body being kept bare. The horseman first faces south, then proceeds some paces north, then goes west and then returns eastward to begin the journey to the rising sun. At this stage all the people burst into loud lamentation, throwing themselves on the ground and crying out, "Our lord (*achindoi*), whither are you going? Return, oh return! In whose hands have you left us? Our Corn, our Beans, our Ground-nuts!" The horseman wheels the horse and a drummer plays a chant and sings, calling on the names of former kings and saying that the king whom they know is leaving them; may those who have gone before receive him well, and may he salute his ancestors on behalf of the people. The horseman again wheels his horse as though to go, and again the people break into lamentation. The Angwu Tsi falls on the ground saying, "And are you going off thus and leaving us destitute of rain and corn?" At this the horseman discharges some millet from the dead king's hand, and some water from a flask. Then, having bidden a final farewell to the Angwu Tsi and to the Abakwariga official who had conferred on the king one of the royal titles and now demands its return, the horseman rides off, accompanied by the senior officials and members of the royal family. These proceed as far as a small hamlet where the Kû Za or priest of the corn bars their progress with a demand for the return of the seed which had been conferred on the king at his coronation. A few seeds are handed to the priest who declares that they are worthless as they have been fully used. The Kinda protests that this is not their fault but is the doing of Chidô. They pray the priest to have patience and to allow them to spend the night there. On the following morning they proceed to the hamlet of the Kû Vi, who had conferred the kingship on the king, and there the progress of the party is again barred by a demand for the return of the royal coat, cap and whip. The priestly official known as the Katsô also demands the return of the rain-making cloth. The king is thus

[3] The footmen are the Ahwo, Kû Shâ, Kû Njâ, Kôtsî, Kumba, and Kuju.

divested of his kingship and now becomes merely a corpse. He is given a new personal name and under this name the body is finally handed to the Ba-Nandȯ.

At this stage (i.e. at the hamlet of Avi) all are compelled to retire save the Kinda Achuwo (who is solely responsible for the safe delivery of the body to the Ba-Nando) and the grooms. In former times there remained also four slaves and a second horse, two of the slaves and one horse to be used for sacrificial purposes, and the remaining slaves and horse to become the property of the Nani To. The reduced party, having crossed the marsh which separates the hamlet of Avi from Nando, is met by the Ba-Nando, headed by the Nani To.

The latter at first refuses to accept custody of the corpse, saying, "What is this? Take it away: I know nothing of it." But the Kinda and other officials fall on the ground, and, throwing dust on their shoulders, beseech him, with gifts of pieces of cloth, to receive his "son." Reluctantly the Nani To consents, and then with a flourish of sticks the Ba-Nando drive off the officials and withdraw to Nando with the corpse, slaves, and horses. The corpse is carried into the burial hut and laid on a bier which is covered with mats and with the royal rug known as *biewi*. Numerous cloths are laid over the corpse and beside it is placed the bag containing the late king's nail-parings and the hair which had been shaven from his head during his reign. The space between the bier and the walls of the hut is tightly packed with strips of cloth, the floor and walls of the hut having been first liberally coated with charcoal as a protection from termites. The doorway of the hut is then sealed up from the outside. The hut is entirely made of woven grass and is surrounded on the outside by a stockade made of the branches of the *Gardenia thunbergii* tree with the object of protecting the hut from wild animals.

Close to the burial hut a horse with its legs tied by ropes is tossed on the ground and killed with clubs. In former times two slaves, male and female, were killed by having their necks twisted, their bodies being left near the doorway of the royal tomb.[4] The

[4] Some say that in former times the Wakuku, the king's principal wife was also put to death.

king's spear was set in the right hand of the male slave, being kept in position by a binding of cloth. The horse's halter and the sickle used for cutting grass were laid by his head: for the dead slave was to look after the king's horse in the underworld. The female slave, an old woman, was laid in a reclining position with her right hand raised to the water pot beside her head.

It is said that in bygone days the favourite slave of a king would frequently himself express the wish to accompany his master to the other world. For a favourite slave was treated like the king's own son and fared royally. He could appropriate anything he liked, and if he committed a public offence was generally absolved by his master. On the death of his master he knew well that the days of his prosperity were finished and that if he remained alive there would be numerous persons ready and anxious to wreak their vengeance. If, however, a favourite slave did not offer himself the slaves themselves proceeded to choose one from among their number. It is said that when the slaves heard of their master's death some ran away and hid until the "election" was over. A runaway slave of a deceased king could seek asylum in the compound of the Nani To whose property he then became. The slave chosen for sacrifice was given plenty to eat and drink and was clothed sumptuously. He may have suspected his fate and tried to escape or, well pleased with the pleasures of the moment, have accepted his fate philosophically. The slave selected was known as *Abanuza,* i.e. the attendant of "The Corn." After death he became one of the slave ghosts whose cult is in the hands of the Ba-Nando. These ghosts are propitiated; and in times of drought, or when the harmattan wind is delayed, sacrifice may be offered to them, should the divining apparatus declare that the failure of the rain or wind was due to them, the king providing the sacrificial gifts.

When the Nani To and his assistants have completed their duties they carefully wash their bodies and perform rites at the shrine of Kenjo with libations of bulrush-millet beer and the blood of a black goat. The officiant says, "To-day we have brought to you your grandchild;[5] do you receive him, and grant that we may have health of body and grain in abundance." The grave is guarded for

[5] For this expression compare Roscoe's *The Baganda,* p. 109.

a period of seven days in order that the bodies of the slaves and horses may not be seized by wild animals. Thereafter the Nani To and his assistants return to Wukari and receive the thanks of all. The hut over the king's grave is not, nowadays, kept in repair, but in former times it was rethatched when rites were occasionally offered on behalf of the living king. The occasions for such rites would be when a drought threatened and the divining apparatus had indicated that the rains were being withheld by the former king. Two slaves, provided by the king, were sacrificed, their necks being broken and the blood which exuded from the mouth and nostrils being caught in a calabash and poured on the top of the grave of that king who had been declared to be inhibiting the rains. The formula used was: "Your grandchild has given you this offering. If it is you who are withholding the rains then accept the offering and send us rain that we may harvest our crops and make libations to you."

It is not absolutely certain that at Wukari the favourite wife and the acolytes of the enclosure were put to death and buried with the king, but there can be little doubt that in former times this was the custom. For at Kona it was stated that the chief's favourite wife was strangled with string and placed in a grave beside the chief, and that a young enclosure-attendant was also killed that the chief might not lack someone to spread his mat for him in Kindo. This was the custom also at Pindiga.

There is no formal post-burial mourning for a Jukun king; but on the day on which the body is taken to Puje all Jukun shave their hair-locks and beards, and remain unshaven until the coronation of the new king. They then allow their hair to grow again, and the sprouting of the beard is likened to the sprouting of the new crops.

During the interregnum no pounding of corn in mortars is allowed; the corn has to be beaten with sticks, and it is said that the people suffer considerable discomfort owing to this rough method of preparing the flour. The conception underlying this practice would seem to be that the late king, who has now become an Osiris, has gone away with the corn, and that the people are left destitute until the new king arrives from the skies to play the part of Horus. That year's harvest is regarded as belonging to the dead king, so that the new king may be said, like Horus, to "reap the barley of his father."

JOHN ROSCOE
Human Beings Killed to Invigorate the King

When the King had reigned for two or three months, he went to hunt a leopard. After the animal had been killed, the carcass was brought to the royal enclosure and left in a house for the night. The next morning the King came and tied two cowry-shells on its paws, and poured a little beer into its mouth, and blew over the carcass; the *Kasuju* then took the animal and skinned it, and prepared the skin for the royal rug. The flesh of the leopard was eagerly sought by the people, who boiled it for the sake of obtaining the fat, which was supposed to be of great medicinal value when mixed with certain herbs; this was used for outward application only. The skin was prepared by the chief's *Kasiri* (who had the care of the throne) and *Kiyukyeru* of the Civet Clan under the directions of the *Kasuju*. When it was ready it was returned to the King, who then had it stitched to a lion's skin; this formed the royal rug, upon which he stood on state occasions. It was upon this rug that the heirs of any chief placed their cowry-shells or beads, when they came to thank the King for confirming them in the office. Both chiefs and peasants, when they entered into the King's presence, knelt to address him, and no one was ever allowed to step on the royal rug or over it; to have done so would have merited the punishment of instant death.

After the leopard hunt the King had either to go himself or to send the *Kago* his representative, to hunt a bushbuck. After the animal had been killed, the *Kago* caught a man and took him before the King by night; the King speared him slightly, and he was then strangled; his body was thrown into a papyrus swamp, so that it might never be discovered. Another ceremony performed about this time to confirm the King in his kingdom was to catch a man, bind him, and bring him before the King; the latter wounded him slightly with a spear, and he was then put to death. These men were killed to invigorate the King. Commoners were required to spear an ox, which was killed and eaten, when they became heirs to valuable property.

When the King had reigned for two or three years, two men were brought before him. One of these he speared, the other was spared. The wounded man was killed outside the enclosure by the main entrance; the other man became assistant to the chief of the body-guard, and his first duty after his appointment was to take the body of the man who had been killed, and throw it into the nearest river.

The next important event in the life of the King was his visit to *Nankere* for the purpose of prolonging his life. *Nankere* was a chief of the Lung-fish Clan who lived to the north of the Busiro district; he was never permitted to see the King, except on the occasion when he performed the ceremony for the prolongation of the King's life. When the time had been fixed for the ceremony, *Nankere* selected one of his own sons or, if he had no son, a near relation, who was then fed and clothed and treated in all respects as a prince, and was taken to live in a special house near the place to which the King had to go for the ceremony. After the youth had been guarded and feasted for a month, the King set out from the capital; on the way he stopped at a temple of Mukasa, where he changed his clothing, leaving that which he was wearing in the temple; he also left behind all his anklets, and did not put on any others until he obtained new ones from *Nankere*. When the King arrived at his destination, *Nankere* met him and handed him a gourd of beer, the King giving *Nankere* a gourd in exchange. The King's Mother was present to see her Son for the last time. *Nankere* addressed them both; first, he told the King's Mother to go and build her house, for she was no longer to hold communication with her Son, since he was now of age; next he turned to the King and said: "You are now of age; go and live longer than your forefathers." *Nankere's* son was now brought in; *Nankere* took him by the hand and presented him to the King, who passed him on to the body-guard; they took him outside, and killed him by beating him with their closed fists. The muscles from the back of the body of the murdered youth were removed and made into two anklets for the King, and a piece of skin was cut from the body to make into a whip, which was kept in the royal enclosure for special feasts. The body was thrown upon waste land, and guarded against wild beasts, but not buried. When the ceremony was concluded the King returned to a chief *Walusimbi* in Busiro; on the way thither he stopped at Baka, seated himself under a large tree, and played a game of spinning the stones from the fruit of a wild fruit-tree. This game is usually played by two children, who spread a plantain-leaf on the ground to obtain a smooth surface, and spin their stones at the same time; the stone which strikes the other and knocks it down, without falling itself, is called the winner. On this particular occasion the King played the game with one of his attendants. After the King had played the game for a time, food was announced; the King then went to Busuju, had his meal, and then mounted a rock to survey the country from the top. When he descended, he crossed the stream Nakibibe, where he was met by a chief *Kidu* of the Mushroom Clan who conducted him to his wife *Naku.* Here the King planted a plantain-tree, and cut some grass, which he handed to his wife *Naku,* who was a member of his party; and *Naku* told some of her maids to make a basket from it, while they were on the way to the chief *Walusimbi.* A little further on they were met by the chief *Gunju,* from whom they inquired the way to *Walusimbi's* house, and he conducted them thither. When they reached their destination, they approached the house from the back; *Walusimbi* called out: "Who is passing at the back of my house?" and the King answered, in a meek voice, "I was doing so." He had to pay *Walusimbi* nine women, nine cows, nine goats, and nine loads of bark-cloths for the error of passing by the back premises. *Walusimbi,* who had been warned of the King's approach, and was prepared for his coming, had placed a stool outside his fence, and had covered it with a rug made of a lion's and a leopard's skin; he had also placed a second similar rug on the ground, upon which he stood, while waiting for the King. The King saluted him, and they exchanged drinking cups; this done, the rest of the party returned to Baka, while the King again played the spinning-game, this time with

Walusimbi. In the evening the King was conducted to a house in a garden, named *Kimogo,* where he spent the night; the chiefs *Kasuju, Namyago,* and *Gunju* brought a stone each for the fire-place, and a sacred meal of millet was cooked and eaten there. In the morning the King returned to the tree near *Walusimbi's* house, to play the game again; he would call for the fruit stones to play with, and whoever ran to bring them would be caught and speared to death on the spot, with the object of giving the King long life. The King next went again to the rock, mentioned above, seated himself on it, and called for someone to bring fire. The fire was kindled, and the King cast cowry-shells into it, as though they were fuel; two chiefs, the *Mugema* and the *Mubaja,* also threw cowry-shells into the fire, until the chief *Nabuwama* came, and snatched them away, saying: "What do you mean by burning cowry-shells?" The King then moved on to Kibibi. Some boys had been sent on in advance with the cooking-pots which had been used on the previous night for perparing the royal food. As soon as the King saw them, he asked: "What do you mean by carrying pots in front of me and soiling my path with soot from pots?" His attendants at once ran after the boys, dashed the pots to the ground and broke them, and killed as many of the boys as they caught. The King and his train passed on to the princess *Naluwembi,* where the King stopped until the anklets made from the muscles of *Nankere's* murdered son were ready for him to wear; it was the princess *Naluwembi* who had to superintend the making of them. When they were finished, they were put on the King, and the party then proceeded to Kibibi, where the King took his stand upon a hillock, saying: "I want a hut built here, go and cut the grass and bring the materials." The man who first arrived with grass was caught and killed, and his head was placed upon the top of the hut. The King entered the hut when it was ready, and his wife *Naku* cooked him a meal there. The hut was called *Naku's* hut, and was afterwards kept as a fetich shrine during the King's lifetime. During the time that the King was on the road from *Nankere* to Kibbi he constantly sent messages to his Mother whom he had left behind; he now sent a farewell-message to her from Kibibi, as he was not expected to meet her again. From Kibibi he returned to his court.

From time to time it was customary for the King to give a feast to his people to commemorate his accession. After he had been engaged in the *Nankere* ceremony, he made a feast on a much larger scale than any previous one. During this feast, *Mutebi,* a priest, went about carrying under his mantle the whip which had been made from the skin of *Nankere's* murdered son; any person whom he struck with it had to pay either nine or ninety cowry-shells (according to his ability) to the goddess Namulondo, to prevent sickness and death from falling upon him. When a person who had been struck with the whip went to pay the cowry-shells to *Mutebi,* the latter struck him on the shoulder with his hand, and by this means removed a curse which the whip had laid upon him and which deprived him of generative powers. At the end of the feast the keepers of the drums removed all the drums but one, *Busemba,* which they left as though they had forgotten it. Someone in the crowd would notice the apparent over-sight, and would bring the drum after the dummers, saying: "You have left one behind"; this person was caught and killed, and the bones from his upper arm were made into drum-sticks for that particular drum. The custom is said to have its origin in the following story: King Tembo killed Kimera in the forest, and the ghost haunted the King and wished to be avenged on him. To appease the ghost, Tembo made a drum, and directed that the sticks used for beating it should be the bones of a human being, and the story adds that, when the bones had been provided, the ghost of Kimera was quieted. The ceremony of leaving the drum behind, and slaying the man who fetched it, was called "The remembrance of *Busemba.*" This particular drum was only brought out once during the reign of a king, and was kept covered from the time it was used until the next king's reign. *Mutebi* occasionally went into the King's presence dressed in a mantle of cow-hide, which covered his body from neck to foot. Under his robe he concealed at such times the arm-bones of the man who had been killed for *Busemba.* As he stepped before the King, he quickly produced the bones, and shook them before the King, then quickly hid them again. He repeated this action, and then walked slowly away, and restored the bones to their proper place. They were decorated with cowry-shells and small bells, which sounded as he shook them.

WILLIAM MARINER

The Sacrifice of a Child

It has already been mentioned more than once, that places which have been consecrated, either by express declaration, or by the burial of great chiefs, are forbidden to be the scene of war, and that it would be highly sacrilegious to attack an enemy, or spill his blood within their confines. This circumstance, however, occurred a few days after the dispute about the female prisoners; the particulars of it are as follow:—Palavali (brother of the warrior Havili) went out one day on a foraging party with six men in two small canoes, and landed near a consecrated inclosure, called Gnacao, one of the most fertile places in the whole island. Here they met with four of the enemy, who, perceiving their inferiority, made an endeavour to get into the consecrated place, where they would have been perfectly safe. Palavali, however, seeing their intention, got between them and the fencing, when one of the enemy made a bold push to pass his antagonist, and scramble over the reed-work, and had actually got one leg over, when Palavali struck him a furious blow on the head, and felled him dead within the place. Seeing now what he had done, he was struck with fear, and ran away to the canoes, followed by his men. As soon as he arrived at the fortress, he communicated to Finow what had passed, saying, in his defence, that he was so eager in pursuit, as to be out of all self-command. The king immediately ordered cava to be taken to the priest of his own tutelar god, that the divinity might be consulted as to what atonement was proper to be made for so heinous a sacrilege. The priest being inspired, made answer, that it was necessary a child should be strangled to appease the anger of the gods.[1] The chiefs then held a consultation, and came to the determination of sacrificing a child

[1] This is perfectly consistent with the Tonga custom, whenever the divinities are supposed to be exceedingly offended. It is a piece of superstition far from being uncommon in the history of mankind. Unpleasant truths, as well as agreeable ones, must be sought out and related, if we wish to arrive at a true knowledge of our own nature.

of Toobo Toa, by one of his female attendants.[2] Toobo Toa was present, and gave his consent that his child (about two years old) should be immolated to appease the anger of the gods, and turn aside their vengeance for the sacrilegious crime committed. The child was accordingly sought for; but its mother, thinking *her* child might be demanded, had concealed it. Being at length found by one of the men who were in search of it, he took it up in his arms, smiling with delight at being taken notice of. Its poor mother wanted to follow, but was held back by those about her. On hearing its mother's voice, it began to cry; but, when it arrived at the fatal place of execution, it was pleased and delighted with the band of *gnatoo* that was put round its neck, and, looking up into the face of the man who was about to destroy it, displayed in its beautiful countenance a smile of ineffable pleasure. Such a sight inspired pity in the breast of every one; but veneration and fear of the gods was a sentiment superior to every other, and its destroyer could not help exclaiming, as he put on the fatal bandage, *O iaooé chi vale!* (poor little innocent!). Two men then tightened the cord by pulling at each end, and the guiltless and unsuspecting victim was quickly relieved of its painful struggles. The body was then placed upon a sort of hand-barrow, supported upon the shoulders of four men, and carried in a procession of priests, chiefs, and matabooles clothed in mats, with wreaths of green leaves round their necks. In this manner it was conveyed to various houses consecrated to different gods, before each of which it was placed on the ground, all the company sitting behind it, except one priest, who sat beside it, and prayed aloud to the god that he would be pleased to accept of this sacrifice as an atonement for the heinous sacrilege committed, and that punishment might accordingly be withheld from the people. When this had been done before all the consecrated houses in the fortress, the body was given up to its relations, to be buried in the usual manner.

[2] On such occasions, the child of a male chief is always chosen, as being worthier than others, and a child by an inferior female attendant, because it is not a chief;—only those children being chiefs whose mothers are chiefs.

The Funeral of the King's Daughter and the Death of the King

It must be here noticed, that the king had determined, in the event of his daughter's death, not to bury her exactly after the Tonga fashion, but partly according to that, partly agreeably to the custom of Hamoa, and partly according to a fancy of his own. After the body was washed and anointed with oil, it was wrapped up in fourteen or fifteen yards of fine East India embroidered muslin, which had formerly belonged to one of the officers of the Port au Prince. It was next laid in a large cedar chest, which had been made on board the same ship, for the use of Mr Brown, out of some cedar planks taken in a prize. Over the body were strewed wreaths of flowers, made for the purpose by her female attendants. Orders were now issued by Finow, that nobody should wear mats, although it was customary on such solemn occasions, but should dress themselves in new tapas (this is the Hamoa custom); and instead of *ifi* leaves round their necks, he ordered that they should wear wreaths of flowers (this was an idea of his own), as if dressed for some occasion of rejoicing. The chest was placed on two large bales of *gnatoo,* in the middle of the house, and the body lay thus in state for the space of twenty days; during which time Mooónga Toobó, Finow's principal wife, and all her female attendants, remained constantly with the body. In the course of the first night the mourners broke out in a kind of recitative, like that on occasion of the death of Toobó Nuha, but in a very imperfect way, because Finow had ordered that no appearance of sorrow or sound of lamentation should be made; but, in spite of this injunction, they occasionally could not restrain their grief, beating their breasts with every mark of deepfelt anguish. It is difficult to conceive the reason of Finow's whimsical conduct on this occasion, unless it were (as generally interpreted) an impious and revengeful endeavour to insult the gods, by ordering those ceremonies not to be performed which were considered objects of religious duty on such sacred occasions. Every morning and evening provisions and cava were brought for the entertainment of those who attended on the body. On the nineteenth day it was removed from the cedar chest, and deposited in the model of a canoe, about three feet and a half long, made for the express purpose, and nicely polished by one of Finow's carpenters (this is the Hamoa custom). By this time the body had become much inflated, and extremely offensive; but the office of removing it was performed by some foreigners, natives of Hamoa, who were accustomed to such tasks. During the whole of this day, and the following night, the body enclosed in the canoe, with the lid closely fastened down, remained in the house. In the mean time Finow issued orders for a general assembly of *all* the inhabitants of the island, to take place the ensuing morning, and nobody to be absent under any pretext whatsoever, not even that of illness. Early the following day all the people accordingly assembled before the house, where there was a large supply of provisions and cava for the conclusion of the ceremony. In the mean time the body was conveyed to the Fytóca, where it was deposited inside the house, without any pomp or form, not within the grave, but on the top of it, that Finow might see the coffin whenever he pleased, and take it away with him whenever he went to a distance.

On this extraordinary occasion, which the caprice of Finow rendered a scene of rejoicing rather than of mourning, after the provisions and cava were shared out, they began the entertainments of wrestling and boxing as usual at festivals. After the men had shown their strength and dexterity in these feats by single engagements, the king gave orders that all the women who resided north of the *mooa* should arrange themselves on one side, ready to combat all the women who resided south of the *mooa,* who were to arrange themselves on the other. It was not a very rare occurrence for women to fight in pairs on occasions of rejoicing; but a general engagement like this, with about fifteen hundred women on each side, was a thing altogether new, and beyond all precedent, and quite unexpected at a funeral ceremony. The women, however, readily engaged, and kept up the contest, with obstinate bravery, for about an hour, without a foot of ground being lost or gained on either side: Nor would the battle have subsided then, if Finow, seeing the persevering courage of these heroines, had not ordered them to desist, the battle having cost them several sprained ancles and broken arms. They fought with a great deal of steadiness, and gave fair hits, without pulling one another's hair. The men now divided themselves in like manner into two parties, and began a general engagement, which was persisted in a considerable time with much fury, till at length that party which belonged to the side of the island on which Finow dwelt began to give way. Instantly he rushed from the house in which he was seated, to reanimate his men by his presence and exertions, which he effected to such a degree, that the opposite party in their turn fell back, and were completely beaten off the ground.

This contest being now ended, the company dispersed, each to his respective home, whilst Finow retired to a small house, which had been built since his daughter's death, near Böóno (the large house on the *malái*); and there, feeling himself much exhausted, he laid down to rest from his fatigue. He had not been long in this posture, before he found himself very ill: his respiration became difficult; he turned himself repeatedly from side to side; his lips became purple, and his under jaw seemed convulsed. From time to time he groaned deeply and most horribly, and the bystanders were much affected. The women shed a profusion of tears, and the men were occupied no doubt with the thoughts of what commotion might happen in the event of his death, what blood might be spilt, and what battles lost and won. The king, in the meanwhile, seemed perfectly sensible of his situation. He attempted to speak, but the power of utterance was almost denied him. One word alone could be clearly distinguished, *fonnood* (land or country): Hence it was supposed that he meant to express his anxiety respecting the mischiefs and disturbances that might happen to the country in the event of his death. After waiting a little time, finding he did not get better, the prince, and a young chief named Voogi, went out to procure one of Finow's children by a female attendant, to sacrifice it to the gods, that their anger might be appeased, and the health of its father restored. They found the child in a neighbouring house, unconsciously sleeping in its mother's lap. They took it away by force, and retiring with it behind an adjacent Fytóca, strangled it as quickly as possible with a band of *gnatoo*. They then carried it with all speed before two consecrated houses and a grave, at each place hurrying over a short but appropriate prayer to the god to interfere with the other gods in behalf of Finow, and to accept of this sacrifice as an atonement for his crimes. They now returned to the place where Finow lay, but found him with scarcely any signs of life, speechless and motionless: his heart, however, could be just felt to beat. In the mean while he was placed on a sort of hand-barrow, which had been just made on purpose, fancying there were still some hopes of his recovery, and carried to different consecrated houses, although he had, almost beyond a doubt, breathed his last with violent struggles ten minutes before. He was first carried to the house dedicated to Tali-y-Toobó, where an appropriate prayer to the god was hurried over, the corpse (for it was now perhaps nothing more) was then conveyed to the house of the god *Toói-foóa-Bolótoo,* where a similar prayer was preferred. Not contented with this, they next carried it to the grave of a female chief named Chinitacala, whose spirit was in like manner invoked. Some hope still remaining, the body was at last carried a mile and a half up the country, on the road towards Felletoa, to the residence of Tooitonga, their great divine chief, at Nioo Lolo. Having arrived here, it was conveyed to Tooitonga's cook-house, and placed over the hole in the ground where the fire is lighted: this being thought acceptable to the gods, as a mark of extreme humiliation, that the great chief of all the Hapai Islands, and Vavaoo, should be laid where the meanest class of mankind were accustomed to operate. All this time Tooitonga remained in his own house, for his high character, as a descendant of the gods, rendered it altogether unnecessary, and even degrading and improper, that he should interfere in this matter.

ALICE C. FLETCHER

A Ghost Lodge for the Dead Child

The ceremonies here described were witnessed among the Ogallala Indians in 1882. The old men of the tribe told me that formerly a period of two years was necessary to fulfil the requirements of this rite. Now six months or a year will suffice.

These Indians entertain the belief that after death the soul will linger near the body so long as it is preserved or any part of it kept intact, particularly if not exposed to the air. The clothing too, which was needful to the comfort of the body, partakes of the individuality of the person and the spirit will linger about these articles. On account of this belief the personal belongings are always placed with the body of the dead, and an Indian will never consciously wear any article of clothing which has been used by one who is deceased. This idea that the soul lingers near any part of the body which is carefully preserved is closely connected with the Shadow or Ghost Lodge. The name was explained as referring to the soul being like a shadow continually with the body and at death gradually fading away.

A ghost lodge is usually kept for a child. The rites are initiated by the father who is the principal actor and responsible person in all the ceremonies. It is creditable to have kept a lodge of this character, and the public consideration seems to arise from the general respect paid to any especial honoring of the dead, as giving proof of family faithfulness and affection, as well as the accumulation of wealth by the father, and the characteristic disposition of it. It is by such deeds that a man gains tribal distinction, and favors his advance to public office. These preferments are won from the tribe by an Indian proving his devotion to the religious ceremonies and traditions of his fathers, by a faithful fulfilment of certain rites, as well as by showing prowess in action and wisdom in counsel.

If, on the death of a child, the father desires to keep a ghost lodge, he speedily sends for a holy or "wakan-man," who on his arrival at the father's tent, takes a pipe, which is handed him, and fills it chanting a ritual suitable to the occasion. One of the criers of the camp is called and he receives the pipe and starts for the tent of a man who has successfully kept a ghost lodge. As the crier enters the tent he says in an intoning voice:[1]

---

[1] The prayers and rituals are chanted or intoned. When the latter is used the breath is audibly inhaled, something as it is during ceremonial smoking. All ceremonial addresses and announcements by the criers are given in a key

"The one who sends me wishes to keep a ghost lodge," and offers the pipe. The man addressed accepts the pipe, lights it, and smokes it in silence. When it is finished he goes to the father's tent where the child lies dead.

After entering the tent and observing a brief silence the man sent for walks over to where the child lies dressed in its best clothing, its face painted red, and taking a knife cuts off a lock of hair just above the forehead. He then hands the hair to the mother, who takes it, wraps it in a piece of new cloth, and lays it away, where it remains undisturbed for four days. Skin was formerly used in place of cloth.

Four yards of red cloth are divided into two parts. One part is carried out beyond the camp, to an elevation if possible, and buried in a hole about three feet deep. This is an offering to the earth, and the chanted prayer asks that the life, or power in the earth, will help the father in keeping successfully all the requirements of the ghost lodge. The other part of the red cloth is lifted and offered to the buffalo, with a prayer that good may be granted to the father during the period of the lodge-keeping. After this ceremony the cloth is cut into eight strips and given to eight men who have successfully kept a ghost lodge. This is a request for their good will and help. Formerly a deerskin, well tanned and painted red, was thus offered. These ceremonies are performed by the wakan-man and the man who cut the child's hair.

The dancing society to which the father belongs present him with horses, and friends make gifts; these are all treasured against the day of final ceremonies. After these preliminaries the body of the child is put away with the usual burial rites.

The duties of the father begin at the time the hair is cut and continue until the closing ceremonies, six months or a year afterwards. During this interval he cannot eat dog meat or any flesh scraped from the skin or hide of an animal. He cannot cut open the head of any animal to get the brains, strike or break any ribs or do any butchering. He cannot take a gun, pistol, arrows, or any weapon in his hand. He cannot run, go in swimming, make any vio-

---

differing from the natural tone of voice. This is the conventional manner, and is often unconsciously adopted on ordinary occasions.

lent movement, shake a blanket, his clothing, or in any way disturb the air. No one must pass before him or touch him, and to prevent this disaster a coal of fire is always kept about two feet in front of him as he sits in the tent. Although he remains with his family he must live apart from his wife, and on no account take a child in his arms, for if he should so forget himself the child would surely die.[2]

During the four days the hair is laid away the mother and sisters, or the near female relatives, make a small buckskin bag in which the hair is to be placed. A pack of the same material or cloth is prepared, having buckskin thongs with which to tie it. A new tent is pitched not far from the father's tent, the opening toward the east. Formerly this tent for the ghost lodge was set a little within the tribal circle or open space, out from the line of living tents.

On the fourth day the wakan-man, and the man who had cut the hair from the child, repair to the tent set apart for the lodge, and make up the pack into a roll about six inches in diameter and two feet long, enclosing the buckskin bag containing the lock of hair cut from the child, and the pipe which had been filled by the wakan-man and sent out by the father. To these are added any other articles which the parents may choose to contribute. Three crotched sticks had been cut by a male relative, and for the honor of doing this he had given away the value of a horse. On these sticks the pack is tied.

---

[2] An Indian who was keeping a ghost lodge attended the sun dance. One day while there he forgot the duties of the ghost lodge and suffered his six year old daughter to approach him, and took her in his arms. Too late he recalled the penalty he had incurred. A fortnight later when I entered his tent, where he was sitting with the coal of fire before him, I saw the little girl lying sick unto death, on the opposite side of the fire. Bending over the child it was evident that she was beyond any medical aid. Her father accepted her fate as a punishment he had merited. Her mother was equally hopeless and sat without, working on moccasins to be given away on the approaching final ceremonies, while her brothers and sisters were racing over the hills pictures of careless health. It was a striking scene. To every inquiry I made as to the cause of the child's illness, cold, fever, or the like, the invariable answer given by relative or acquaintance was: "Her father forgot and took her in his arms." It was impossible to present to the people any natural cause for the child's illness, from that which was so clearly another evidence, supernaturally given, of the sanctity and power of their religious ceremonies. Next day the child died, leaving her parents full sore at heart.

No woman but the mother of the child is allowed to enter this tent. She has charge of the pack, but can only pass into the tent when performing some duty incident to the lodge-keeping. When entering the tent she turns to the left and makes the entire circle, always going behind the pack and passing out by the right. This mode of entering and leaving is observed by all who enter the tent. No one may pass between the pack and the symbol drawn on the ground, or between that and the fire.[3] Nor can any one turn back on his passage round the tent, for one must always move in a continuous circle from left to right. On clear sunny days, when the wind does not blow, the mother carries the crotched sticks, with the pack tied to them, outside the tent, setting them up about four or five feet in front of the entrance. As the sun declines she returns the pack to its place in the tent. When it thunders, or if a gun should be fired, or any unwonted noise should be heard, she must hasten to cover the pack. If, when the pack is out of doors, a sudden wind should rise, the mother must instantly take the pack into the tent. Thus her constant care is necessary.

Every day the father of the child enters the ghost lodge tent and the mother, soon after, sets kettles of food inside the tent door. The father loosens the dish from the pack, a small quantity of the food is placed in it, and the dish set down near the pack. The father then takes a bit of the food from the dish with his fingers and, lifting it, says: "We offer this food that you may help us, that we may escape ill fortune. We ask you to help us to avoid any sickness or misfortune that may lie in our path." [4] The offering is then dropped upon the mellowed earth and buried in it. During this ceremony persons of the male sex may be present. It is usual for orphans, the aged, or any one in need of food, to repair to the ghost lodge to share in this daily feast given by the father as a religious hospitality.

In the tent certain rules must be observed; the mode of entering, moving about and leaving have been already mentioned. No one

[3] The spaces here mentioned are always considered as consecrated or set apart in every ceremony I have witnessed or learned about, and this applies to many tribes.

[4] This is the usual form of asking a blessing. This ceremony takes place at every feast, dance or ritual observance where food is eaten. The father does not address the ghost pack, but the deity or life of the animal food.

may blow the fire with his mouth. When it needs to be livened one may gently fan it with the wing of a bird, but in no other way: no one may spit toward the centre of the tent, but if he needs to cast anything from his mouth, he must turn his head and throw the saliva behind him. No tales of fighting, nor any quarrelsome words, nor any subject which is "bad" must be spoken in a ghost lodge. Quietness and friendliness must pervade the tent.

If at any time during the period of keeping the lodge the father should by accident hear of any violent words or deeds, he must at once perform certain rites which will avert the evil consequences to him and his family. He must take a few coals of fire, and lay on them a bunch of sweet grass, or sprays of cedar. As the smoke rises he must crouch over the coals bringing his blanket close about his body, drawing it over his head and face so as completely to shut him in with the smoke; sitting thus while the aromatic fumes circle his entire person, he thinks of the duty of carefully fulfilling the ritual of the religious ceremony and by his faithfulness arresting disaster and securing good fortune for his kin.

During the months occupied with these duties the man can do little more than fulfill them. As he is debarred from hunting and providing food and raiment, his needs are supplied by his kindred. It is not enough that his avocations should be peaceful but it is his duty to relinquish any hard feeling he has had and forget old injuries. The keeping of a ghost lodge is a signal of peace and cancels all grudges between parties. The father may not smoke with any one lest he should consort with a man who was at enmity with some other person. The Indians in explanation pointed out that it was for the purpose of enforcing peace in a man's actions and thoughts that he was forbidden to take weapons in his hand; and the coal of fire placed before him while sitting in his tent was indicative of his setting himself apart for this religious duty, "the coal being like a partition between the father and all the world."

During these intermediate months, the family are busily employed making eagle war bonnets, embroidering moccasins, tobacco pouches, tobacco boards, fashioning pipes and ornamenting clothing and gathering together a large amount of possessions to be given away at the closing ceremonies. After a ghost lodge a family are often left in poverty, but with the Indians it is not accumulation and hoarding, but the record of that which a man has given away which entitles him to greatness and influence.

Any one of the same gens[5] as the father, who had lost a child, after the ghost lodge had been inaugurated and who desired to join in the ceremony, could prepare a similar pack, and tie it to the one in the ghost lodge. Each family thus represented must contribute its quota of gifts at the final day.

As that time draws near word is sent abroad, inviting members of other gens, and even of other tribes, to be present and participate in the feast. Four days the crier proclaims the opening of the packs and distribution of the gifts, and during these days the families are busy preparing for the coming feast. A man who has successfully kept a ghost lodge is invited to take charge of the proceedings. For this service he receives large presents from the parents represented in the lodge. To give an idea of this payment the following list of articles was received by the man having charge of the ghost lodge herein described.

Four garnished buffalo robes embroidered with porcupine quills, four woven sashes, four calico shirts, four pipes, four plugs of tobacco, four hatchets, six pairs of moccasins, six dishes, six tin pans, seven yards of calico (a dress pattern), ten butcher knives, two pairs of leggings, two strings of bells, two curtains (strips of tent cloth used to protect the sleeping place), two comforters (bed quilts), one lariat, one hoe, one bed made of reeds, one steer, two or three ponies.

Among the articles given away, the following were counted.

Thirty-two ponies, one hundred pairs of moccasins, ten shawls, seven buffalo robes, three war bonnets (eagle feathers), eight calico dresses (made up), besides numerous tin pails and cups, knives, coffee pots, tin pans, looking glasses such as the young men wear, embroidered beaded dresses, knife cases, match pockets, bows and arrows, wooden bowls, balls, shinny sticks embroidered with beads, a quantity of dried cherries, squash, pounded meat and other things.

---

[5] It was only the Indians of one gens or clan who joined in this ghost lodge. Further investigation will prove whether this is always the rule among tribes which hold similar lodges.

From early morning to well on toward noon the women were engaged carrying these gifts singly, in packs made of raw hide, or in wooden trunks, and placing them at the door of the new tent set up to receive them. On this final day all signs of mourning are put away, for the first time since the death occurred the immediate relatives braid their hair, and every one is in gala dress. Over 800 people gathered to the feast, and were scattered over the grass. Forty-two great kettles hung from crotched sticks, the beef soup and dog stew flavored with dried cherries or turnips sent up fumes of steam. The sticks used to stir these viands were forked, having the end ornamented with beads and ribbons. Young girls were bringing water from the creek, the older ones grinding coffee, and all busy preparing for the great crowd of guests. The abrupt outline of the buttes, dark evergreens marking the gullies, the narrow valley through which flowed the clear rapid creek with its border of shrubs and large graceful trees, the green bottom lands dotted with white tents, while a few were scattered over the hills that rose in terraces to the east, together with the vast throngs of gayly dressed Indians, combined to make a picture full of color, spirit, and a wild beauty all its own, bearing no familiar lines to eastern civilized eyes.

The new tent set up for the reception of the gifts is placed near the ghost lodge tent, the door facing the east. Near the centre a fire is kindled, an oval figure drawn on the ground similar to that cut on the floor of the ghost lodge. The sod is removed from within the figure, the earth mellowed, four live coals laid on the mellowed earth and sweet grass dropped on them. Outside the figure eight coals are placed, four on each side, and sweet grass laid on to smoulder.[6] On the north and south side a buffalo chip is set. Back of the oval figure the sod is removed so as to leave a narrow, oblong figure in the earth on which sprays of Artemisia are spread like a mat; behind this the presents are arranged in piles, one pile for each ghost represented in the lodge.

After this arrangement is completed a feast is given and while that is in progress the women set a row of crotched sticks in front

[6] The protective purification and consecration, secured by fire and sweet or aromatic smoke is noticeable throughout this ceremonial, and the number of small fires and their positions seem to indicate a connection with the worship of the four quarters or winds.

of the tent, laying on poles to form a framework, on which they spread for exhibition the gifts they had previously made into piles at the back of the tent. When the feast is concluded, the master of ceremonies distributes these gifts, reserving those which are to be given away in the ghost lodge tent. Visitors and the poor are remembered in the lavish bestowal.

The interior of the ghost lodge is rearranged in the following manner. The space occupied by the packs is marked off in an oblong, the sod removed and the ground spread with Artemisia. The figure having the mellowed earth in which the offerings of food have been buried each day, is covered with a red cloth. On the centre is laid a disk of shell; eight live coals, four on each side, are arranged outside the figure, and sweet grass laid on them. Four buffalo chips are outside of these at the four corners. The different packs are loosened from the initial pack and each one fastened to sticks about four feet long. There were nine packs, three belonging to young men, three to boys, two to girls and one to a woman. The sticks are bound with hide, and an oblong piece of hide, ornamented and having on it a face rudely outlined in paint, is hung in front of each pack. Upon the packs belonging to the young men are fastened eagle feather war bonnets. These effigies are arranged in a semicircle on the south side of the tent, the sticks being thrust in the ground, and the gifts contributed by the relations of the dead person piled about his effigy.

Only men who have kept a ghost lodge are entitled to sit in this tent, and join in smoking the pipe which had been filled with the appropriate ritual. The man in charge of the ceremonies distributes the gifts which rest about the effigies to the men present. In so doing he is particular so to dispose of the articles as, for instance, to avoid giving an eagle war bonnet to a man who had received one on a previous and similar occasion. Such items are well remembered in an Indian camp, for it is in this way that possessions change hands. The men who receive at this time will save up their treasures and give them away at some future religious or secular festival.

When all the gifts are distributed the packs are opened, the pipes are given to poor men, and the hair once more handed back to the mother who either keeps it, or buries it, and the soul of the child, which has been supposed to linger about the pack, is now free to depart.

The shadows were gathering in the valley and the last glow fading from the buttes, as the tents fell and the poles were gathered and carried off by their possessors, for not an article used in this strange ceremonial remained in the possession of the parents who had thus paid to the full their tribute of affection for the dead, and proved themselves faithful to the custom of their ancestors. The stars came out and shone over the silent plains, for the men, women and children had vanished with the day.

PART 16

Immortality

LAURA WATSON BENEDICT

People Who Have Two Souls

Like other Malay peoples, the Bagobo have a great body of myth and of folklore concerning the behavior of the souls of man, events connected with death, and the nature of future existence. Inhabiting every individual, two souls called *gimokud* are recognized—shadowy, ethereal personalities, that dominate the body more or less completely. The right-hand soul, known in Bagobo terminology as the *Gimokud Takawanan,* is the so-called "good soul" that manifests itself as the shadow on the right-hand side of one's path. The left-hand soul, called *Gimokud Tebang,* is said to be a "bad soul" and shows itself as the shadow on the left side of the path. The name for either shadow is *alung*. The takawanan is associated, in native thinking, with those factors of existence that stand for life, health, activity, joy; while the tebang is associated with factors that tend toward death, sickness, sluggishness, pain. The left-hand soul often departs from the human body and does unlooked-for things that have an unhappy influence on the body: it undertakes alarming exploits; it wanders about as a dream-spirit, thus producing nightmare, or, at least, horrible mental images during sleep. The right-hand soul, on the contrary, is associated with the normal continuity of existence, for it never leaves the body from birth until death, except to lie, at times, as the right-hand shadow, still attached clingingly to the physical frame. Death is the simple fact of the passing of the right-hand soul out from the body, and becoming permanently separated from it. But the stream of individual existence is not checked by death, for the takawanan goes at once to the Great Country below the earth, and there continues to live, in much the same manner as on earth, except for the non-corporeal and ghostly appearance that characterizes all of its activities.

Right-hand Soul or Gimokud Takawanan

Brown in color like a Bagobo, they say the takawanan would look, could one but clearly glimpse it, and in all other characteristics, it is like the living Bagobo, except for its tenuous substance. It is identified with the activities and the life itself of the body, and hence remains in the body throughout life; for the event of its removing itself to a distance would spell death. I have heard the opinion hazarded by a Bagobo youth that the takawanan might go away for just a little while without the body dying, but this idea may have been suggested by observing his shadow, and fancying that it might move away from him. The customary concept of the takawanan, as well as the conduct observed at a deathbed, implies that this soul inhabits the human body perpetually, or as a shadow remains closely attached to it, until death.

Signs of death. The beating of the pulse at the wrist and the pulsations that are to be felt "on top of the head" are signs of the presence of the gimokud takawanan in the living body. When a Bagobo is mortally sick and death is imminent, an attendant holds the wrist of the patient, with the index and the middle fingers at the dorsal side, and the thumb on the pulse, in order to note whether the gimokud is still there. When the pulse ceases to throb, the gimokud is ready to take leave of the body, but, since it cannot find an exit through the wrist or the finger-tips, it passes up to the head of the dying man and goes out through that point in the crown where a pulsation is apparent (probably the anterior fontanelle). Somebody lays fingers or palm of the hand on top of the head to ascertain the exact moment when gimokud takes its flight. The cessation of heart-beat, *laginawa,* is often noted also. The signs of death are therefore three: (*a*) The stilling of the pulse; (*b*) The cessation of throbbing on the skullcap; (*c*) The stopping of heart-beat.

Sometimes they make efforts to detain the takawanan in the body: they seize and shake the arms of the dying man; they grasp his head and make it wag to and fro, in the hope of checking the spirit's departure; but as the sure signs of death become apparent they cease all efforts to hold the gimokud.

Summons to the living. Between the time of death and burial it is still possible for the right-hand soul to communicate with the living, and this it does on a vast scale. Immediately after leaving the body, it is customary for the spirit to give notice of its last journey, and at the same time try to secure a companion, by visiting in the form of an insect every house in the world. The entire series of visits is supposed to be made during the short period—say, from twenty-four to thirty-six hours—that elapses between death and burial. The insect enters a house and sings in a small voice that is like the chirp of a cricket, or the soft tinkling of a little bell called *korung-korung*. Nobody can see the gimokud, but at night when "the bug with the sweet voice chirps on the wall" one knows that somebody is dead. Then the person listening must say: "Who are you? my brother? my sister?" If the singing stops immediately, it is a sign that a near relative is dead, but if the sound keeps on it indicates that some other family has been bereaved.

Sometimes the chirping is interpreted as a summons to some friend or relative to follow the dead one, who asks for a fellow traveler to the lower world. Fearful of sickness and death coming upon him, the listener quickly replies: "You can come here no more because you are now going to the Great City. You have still a little love (*diluk ginawa*) for me; do not bring me sickness." This formula is usually potent enough to banish the importunate spirit. It is said that when a gimokud is very insistent for a companion, a friend may die within a day or two, an example quoted being that of Adela, the Bagobo wife of a Visayan. Of her, they narrate that she caused a woman friend to die one or two days after herself, because she feared to journey alone to the lower world.

This form of spiritual manipulation is considered quite proper for a timid person or for a youth, but there is a feeling among the Bagobo that a gimokud who is strong and brave will not wait around for a friend to die, but will start alone for the Great City. A boy of fourteen, nephew of Adela, confided to me his fears of the gruesome journey.

> "If a gimokud is not brave, he waits for a companion to die. I am afraid to go alone to the Great City. When I am dead, my spirit will wait near my friend, Karlos, and will say to his spirit: 'I want you to go with me to the One City.' Then my friend will get a sickness and die, and I shall have a companion; but if he does not want to go with me, I do not force him, but I ask other friends—many."

After the burial, the ghost-bug can sing no more, for the spirit has started for Gimokudan, and can never again disturb the living by chirping at night. The gimokud is now known also as *Kayung*.

A rain lasting several days, or even a week, is a phenomenon very significant when it occurs immediately after the death of a Bagobo, for it is caused by the tears of the dead gimokud, who is lingering about, waiting for a friend to accompany him. A magical rite must then be performed to still the lamentations of the spirit. Suppose that showers fall incessantly after the death of a boy. Forthwith, his father places a few areca-nuts and betel-leaves, with perhaps a little tobacco, on the ground as an offering to the gimokud, and cajoles him with words like these: "Do not cry any more, for you know you do not love your father; you would rather go to the Great City." The spell is efficacious; the rain ceases; the gimokud stops its weeping and starts alone on the last journey. This case does not appear to be reconcilable with the belief that the soul leaves the earth for Gimokudan immediately after the funeral, for in the tropics a body cannot be kept for several days unless embalmed, while the metaphorical showers may last for a week. A Malay, however, does not think in exact dialectic, and perhaps would not be conscious of the contradiction.

Left-hand Soul or Gimokud Tebang

Diametrically opposed to the takawanan, as regards its character and its final fate, is that other soul of man, the Gimokud Tebang, which shows itself as a shadow on the left side of one's path, and appears also as the reflection in the water. This left-hand soul is hurtful to the body it inhabits, and is the direct cause of many a pain and sickness.

When a Bagobo catches sight of his reflection in a clear stream, he must look at it soberly; he must not betray any feeling of pleasure or of amusement. If he laughs at his image in the water, he will die (presumably because he has mocked his left-hand soul).

Dream exploits. It is the left-hand soul which leaves the body at night and goes flying about the world, where it encounters various dangers. All these adventures, with their accompanying sensations, are experienced by the Bagobo in his dreams. As a Bagobo youth explained to me: "When I dream at night, my gimokud tebang is flying and the buso is catching me, or I am falling from a cliff. I dream that I am riding on a boat and fishing in the sea. Many ships I see there that the buso are riding. They look like men with ugly faces and coarse black hair all over their bodies, and some have wings. Then I try to run away."

There is an element of real danger in these dream exploits of the left-hand soul, for it is stated that if the tebang should be caught and eaten by a buso, the human body to which it belongs must die, for the buso, having swallowed the soul, instantly goes in search of the body itself.

One startling exploit of the left-hand soul, that has become known to the Bagobo in dreams, is an attempt to reach the Great City and there join the good spirits in their pleasant home. The tebang gets as far as the City of the Black River, but there is stopped by Mebuyan, who asks, "Are you alive?" The tebang replies, "Yes, Lady," and then Mebuyan dismisses him with the words: "Go back to where you came from." Now, if the left-hand soul still persists in forcing an entrance, and tries to bathe his joints in the dark river, like the more fortunate right-hand soul, he gets wet feet and becomes very sick, and is obliged to return to earth.

Closely connected with dreams, are the delusions experienced in trance by diseased or neurotic individuals, who, on waking, describe frightful visions in graphic detail. I quote from a story given by the boy, Islao.

"There are two kinds of dreams: the tagenup and the orup. In the orup, you see nothing; you hear nothing. You will die. The Buso will kill you, if you have no companion to waken you. The orup is making noise without words. A man who wakens from orup tells about it: he says his body is heavy; all the time he hears a sound like the leaves moving in the wind, or like the noise in your ears when you swim. He sees a big man with one eye holding him; the eye looks like a great bowl in the middle of his forehead. Many men who wake up from orup say this. The big man is a buso who wants to carry him off and eat him."

Thus we have the ordinary adventure dream, called *Tagenup;* and the trance or the delirium accompanying a pathological condition, called *orup*. In both cases, the left-hand soul is supposed to absent itself from the body, and to become an actor in situations that imperil the body, and that are remembered on waking.

Yet not alone in nightmare and in delusions, is a malign influence exerted over the body when this evil soul escapes from it; for other forms of suffering are connected, sympathetically, with the varied exploits of Gimokud Tebang. He swims in the deep sea and sends shivers through the person to whom he belongs; he strikes his foot on a sharp stone and drives pains through the material foot; he drinks poison, thus causing agony in the stomach; and, by various other sorts of behavior, he brings about a corresponding condition in the body which he dominates.

At the moment of death, the tebang leaves the body for the last time, now to become a buso-ghost, and to join the innumerable company of buso that haunt graves and tall trees and lonely places. Now he is lonely, they say, and wants a companion to prowl around with him at night, everywhere. Like the right-hand soul, he lingers about until the body is buried, in a gruesome attempt to give a summons to some living friend. Folklore tells us that the tebang wanders alone through the forests until he finds an old rotten tree, to which he puts the question: "Can you kill me?" and to this the dead tree answers, "No." Then the tebang bunts his head against the weak and hollow trunk, and instantly the old tree comes crashing to the ground. This means that somebody is going to die soon. Therefore, when one hears at night the sound of a tree cracking and breaking down, when there is no man near to fell it, one knows, straightway, that the left-hand soul is thrusting his head against the trunk, for a signal to some companion. It is a sign of death.

GEORGE GREY
The Reincarnated Son

After we had tethered the horses, and made ourselves tolerably comfortable, we heard loud voices from the hills above us: the effect was fine,—for they really almost appeared to float in the air; and as the wild cries of the women, who knew not our exact position, came by upon the wind, I thought it was well worth a little trouble to hear these savage sounds under such circumstances. Our guides shouted in return, and gradually the approaching cries came nearer and nearer.

I was, however, wholly unprepared for the scene that was about to take place. A sort of procession came up, headed by two women, down whose cheeks tears were streaming. The eldest of these came up to me, and looking for a moment at me, said,—"Gwa, gwa, bundo bal,"—"Yes, yes, in truth it is him"; and then throwing her arms round me, cried bitterly, her head resting on my breast; and although I was totally ignorant of what their meaning was, from mere motives of compassion, I offered no resistance to her caresses, however disagreeable they might be, for she was old, ugly, and filthily dirty; the other younger one knelt at my feet, also crying. At last the old lady, emboldened by my submission, deliberately kissed me on each cheek, just in the manner a French woman would have done; she then cried a little more, and at length relieving me, assured me that I was the ghost of her son, who had some time before been killed by a spear-wound in his breast. The younger female was my sister; but she, whether from motives of delicacy, or from any imagined backwardness on my part, did not think proper to kiss me.

My new mother expressed almost as much delight at my return to my family, as my real mother would have done, had I been unexpectedly restored to her. As soon as she left me, my brothers, and father (the old man who had previously been so frightened), came up and embraced me after their manner,—that is, they threw their arms round my waist, placed their right knee against my right knee, and their breast against my breast, holding me in this way for several minutes. During the time that the ceremony lasted, I, according to the native custom, preserved a grave and mournful expression of countenance.

This belief, that white people are the souls of departed blacks, is by no means an uncommon superstition amongst them; they themselves never having an idea of quitting their own land, cannot imagine others doing it;—and thus, when they see white people suddenly appear in their country, and settling themselves down in particular spots, they imagine that they must have formed an attachment for this land in some other state of existence; and hence conclude the settlers were at one period black men, and their own relations. Likenesses, either real or imagined, complete the delusion; and from the manner of the old woman I have just alluded to, from her many tears, and from her warm caresses, I feel firmly convinced that she really believed I was her son, whose first thought, upon his return to earth, had been to re-visit his old mother, and bring her a present. I will go still farther, and say, that although I did not encourage this illusion, I had not the heart to try to undeceive the old creature, and to dispel her dream of happiness. Could I have remained long enough to have replaced this vain impression by a consoling faith, I would gladly have done it; but I did not like to destroy this belief, and leave her no other in the place of it.

The men next proceeded to embrace their relation, Jen-na, in the same manner they had before done me; and this part of the ceremony was now concluded.

The women, who had retired after having welcomed me, again came in from behind some bushes, where the children all yet remained, and bringing several of them up to me insisted on my hugging them. The little things screamed and kicked most lustily, being evidently frightened out of their wits; but the men seized on and dragged them up. I took the youngest ones in my arms, and by caresses soon calmed their fears; so that those who were brought afterwards cried to reach me first, instead of crying to be taken away.

A considerable time had been occupied by these various occurrences, which to me had been most interesting; but one of a more painful character was now to follow. It appears that a sister of the native Jen-na had been speared and killed by a man, who at present was resident with this tribe; and although most of them were on friendly terms with this native, they conceived that Jen-na was bound to revenge her death in fair and open fight. The old lady (my mother) went up to him, and seizing his merro, or throwing-stick, told him, that the man who had killed his sister was at a little distance; "and if," said she, "you are not a man, and know not how to use this, let a woman's hand try what it can do," at the same time trying to force it from him. All the time that she was thus pretending to wrench his merro away, she indulged in a most eloquent speech, to endeavour to rouse his courage. I do not know enough of the language to translate it with proper spirit or effect, as I only caught the general meaning: it had, however, a great effect on Jen-na; and some young ladies coming in at the conclusion, his mind was instantly made up; indeed, the certainty that bright eyes were to look upon his deeds, appeared to have much the same effect upon him that it had upon the knights of old,—and jumping up, he selected three good spears (all the men being willing to lend him theirs), and hurried off to an open space, where his antagonist was waiting for him.

The combats, one of which was now about to take place, much resemble the ancient tournaments. They are conducted with perfect fairness. The combatants fight in an open space, their friends all standing by to see fair play, and all the preliminaries, as to what blows are to be considered foul or fair, are arranged beforehand, sometimes with much ceremony.

Taking into account the fantastic ornaments and paintings of the natives, the graceful attitudes they throw themselves into either when trying to avoid the spears of their enemy, or about to throw their own; and the loud cries and wild motions with which they attempt to confuse and terrify their adversaries, I must confess that if any exhibition of this nature can be considered showy or attractive, this has no ordinary claims to admiration.

MOTOLINÍA (TORIBIO DE BONAVENTE)
(Died 1568)

So That the Sun Might Rise Again

Very noteworthy ceremonies and festivals were held on the last day of those fifty-two years and on the first day which began the new year and "olympiad."[1] On the last day of the last year at the hour of vespers, in Mexico and all its territory, and in Tetzcoco and its provinces, at the order of the temple ministers, all fires were extinguished with water in the temples of the devils as well as in private houses. Even in certain places where fire was kept perpetually burning, it was extinguished on that day. Then certain ministers of the temples of Mexico went out two leagues to a place that is called Ixtlapalapa and ascended a hill upon which stood a temple of the devil held in great reverence and devotion by Moteuczoma, the great lord of Mexico. In that place, then, at midnight, which was the beginning of the year of the following "hebdomad," these ministers kindled new fire with a stick which was known as the fire stick.[2] Then they lighted a torch, and before anyone kindled a fire

---

[1] The occasion was considered as especially dangerous to mortal men, since it was feared that the sun might fail to rise, and the Tzitzimimé demons would descend from the first heaven to destroy mankind and so bring about the end of the world. The principal feature of the ceremonies was the production of new fire by means of the ceremonial fire sticks, and it was upon the successful performance of this operation that the rising of the sun was supposed to depend. On the eve of the new year all fires were extinguished.—From Thomas A. Joyce's *Mexican Archeology,* 1914.

[2] According to Sahagún (vol. II, p. 269) the new fire was kindled on the breast of a captive who had been taken in war. As soon as the fire was kindled the captive was sacrificed. Torquemada (vol. II, p. 294) says that the fire was kindled on the breast of *a freshly sacrificed captive,* "en la misma herida." Motolinía does not mention the captive, and Gómara explicitly states that the sticks used for kindling the fire are placed on the ground. Gómara's information is mostly second-hand and much less to be relied upon than Sahagún's.

for private use, they bore it with great zeal and haste to the principal temple in Mexico. There they placed the fire before the idols, and then brought a captive taken in war and, sacrificing him before the new fire, they cut out his heart, and the chief minister sprinkled the fire with blood as a sort of benediction. When this ceremony was finished and the fire was, as it were, blessed, there were people from many places waiting there to carry new fire to the temples of their towns. This they did, first asking permission of the great Mexican prince or pontiff, who was a sort of pope; and they bore it with great zeal and speed. Although the town might be many leagues away, they went so fast that they very shortly brought the fire there. They performed the same ceremony in the provinces far distant from Mexico, and it was performed everywhere with great joy and rejoicing. As soon as the day dawned a great festival was held in all the land, but principally in Mexico, and in Mexico alone they sacrificed four hundred men.

MARGARET MEAD
Re-Creation

When there is to be a great cremation in which many casteless people will share in the great ceremonials for a Brahman priest or a member of the prince's household, people prepare for weeks, making thousands of prescribed offerings and selling everything that they have in order to spend more on the ceremony. Because of the great number of guests who come to cremations, it is impossible to predict the cost, and this weight of rising and unguessable expenditures adds to the anxiety. Cremations are regarded as work by those whose responsibility they are, but they provide a festival for the surrounding villages.

The weeks of laborious preparation culminate in three days of ceremonial. The graves are first covered with human clothes, then opened, and the bones are dug up and assembled. They are dressed again and laid out in a little town built in the cemetery. Delicate little dolls which represent the souls of the dead are carried home from the cemetery to the houses where they lived on earth, there to receive food and drink, to pray to the ancestors, and finally to ask leave to depart. These little "souls" are then carried back to the cemetery and placed inside the bundles of dressed-up bones. Thus the person is again re-created. On the next day, a new set of "souls" is taken to the priest's house and blessed, and the "bones" are later given a second laying-out as if they were corpses. On the third day the bones are burned in coffins shaped like animals appropriate to each caste, but the cremation fires are no sooner out than the people are poking among the ashes, gathering the small bits of specified bones and again re-creating a body upon which the little cornucopia-shaped prayer leaves are laid, so as to define again all the sacred anatomical points. Representative samples of this re-created body are then ground to dust in a mortar, each close relative taking a hand at the grinding, and the dust is placed in still another human replica and finally carried to the sea. It is thrown into the sea, but only to be re-created again in a new replica at stated periods thereafter. When someone dies, people may insure themselves by buying a special holy water, which permits them to wait twenty-five years before undertaking this elaborate, expensive, and demanding ritual. After each phase in the death ceremonial—after the real death, after the cremation, after the disposal of later re-creations of the body of the dead—comes the ceremony of *mepegat,* in which the souls, carried in the arms of members of the family like the babies which they will again become, ceremonially break the tie which binds them to the living—but only for a little while.

BIBLIOGRAPHY

Bateson, Gregory: *Naven*. Cambridge University Press, 1936

——— and Margaret Mead: *Balinese Character*, a Photographic Analysis, New York Academy of Sciences, 1952 (Special Publication)

Benedict, Laura Watson: "A Study of Bagolo Ceremonial, Magic and Myth," *Annals of the New York Academy of Sciences*, vol. XXV, 1916

Benedict, Ruth: "Configuration of Culture in North America," *American Anthropologist*, New Series, No. 1, 1932

Boas, Franz: "The Social Organization and the Secret Societies of the Kwakiutl Indians," *U. S. National Museum, Annual Report*, 1894-1895, Washington, 1897

Bogoras, Waldemar: "The Chuckchee," *American Museum of Natural History, Monographs*, vol. VII. New York, Leiden, 1904

Bunzel, Ruth L.: "The Pueblo Potter," *Columbia University Contributions to Anthropology*, vol. VIII, 1929

Callaway, Rev. Canon, Henry: *The Religious System of the Amazulu*, translated from the Amazulu. Trubner & Co. London, 1870

Catlin, George: *Illustration of the Manners, Customs, and Conditions of the North American*, in a Series of Letters and Notes Written during Eight Years of Travel and Adventure among the Wildest and Most Remarkable Tribes Now Existing, 2 vol. Seventh Edit. H. G. Bohn, London, 1848

Crawley, Ernest: *The Mystic Rose*. Boni & Liveright, New York, 1927

Codrington, Robert Henry: *The Melanesians*. Clarendon Press, Oxford, 1891

Crowell, Samuel: "The Dog Sacrifice of the Senecas," *The Indian Miscellany* (edit. by William Wallace Beach), Albany, 1877

Cushing, Frank Hamilton: "Zuni Breadstuff," *Indian Notes and Monographs*, vol. VIII, Museum of the American Indian, Heye Foundation, 1920

David-Neel, Alexandra: *Magic and Mystery in Tibet*. Crown Publishers, New York, 1937

Deren, Maya: *Divine Horsemen*, Thames and Hudson, London, New York, 1953

Devereux, George: "Institutionalized Homosexuality of the Mohave Indians," *Human Biology*, vol. IX, 1937, Johns Hopkins Press, Baltimore, Maryland

Deacon, Arthur Bernard: *Malekula*, a Vanishing People in the New Hebrides, edited by Camilla H. Wedgwood. George Routledge and Sons Ltd., London, 1934

Dixon, Roland B.: "The Shasta," The Huntington California Expedition, *American Museum of Natural History, Bulletin*, vol. XVII, New York, 1907

Dobrizhoffer, Martin: *An account of the Abipones*, an Equestrian People of Paraguay, translated from the Latin by Sara Loleridge. John Murray, London, 1922

Dorr, Herbert C.: "A Ride with the Apaches," *The Indian Miscellany* (edited by William Wallace Beach) Albany, 1877

Doughty, Charles M.: *Travels in Arabia Deserta.* Jonathan Cape Ltd., London, 1927

Elwin, Verrier: *The Muria and Their Ghotul.* Oxford University Press, London, 1947

Emmons, G. T.: "Native Account of the Meeting between La Perouse and the Tlingit," *American Anthropologist, New Series,* vol. XIII, Lancaster, Penn., 1911

Engels, Friedrich: *The Origin of the Family, Private Property, and the State,* in the Light of the Researches of Lewis Morgan. International Publishers, New York, 1942

Erikson, Erik H.: *Childhood and Society.* W. W. Norton & Co. Inc., New York, 1950

Evans-Pritchard, Edward Evan: *The Nuer,* a Description of the Modes of Livelihood and Political Institutions of a Nilotic People. Clarendon Press, Oxford, 1940

Fortune, R. F.: *Sorcerers of the Dobu,* the Social Anthropology of the Dobu Islanders of the Western Pacific. E. P. Dutton and Co., New York, 1932

Freuchen, Peter: *Eskimo,* translated by Albrecht Paul Maerker-Branden and Elsa Branden. Grosset and Dunlap, New York, 1931

Fison, Lorimer and A. W. Howitt: Kamilaroi and Kurnai. George Robertson, Melbourne, Sidney, 1880

Fletcher, Alice C.: "Indian Ceremonies," *Peabody Museum of American Archeology and Ethnology, The XVIth Report,* Cambridge, Mass., 1883, Salem Press, Salem, Mass., 1884

Freud, Sigmund: *The Basic Writings,* translated and edited by A. A. Brill. The Modern Library, New York, 1938

Gide, André: *Travels in the Congo,* translated by Dorothy Bussy. Knopf, New York, 1929

Gorer, Geoffrey: *Africa Dances,* a Book about West African Negroes. Faber and Faber, London, 1935

Grey, George: *Journals of Two Expeditions of Discovery in North Western and Western Australia during the Years 1837, '38 and '39.* T. and W. Boone, London, 1841

Grinnell, George Bird: *The Cheyenne Indians.* Yale University Press, New Haven, 1923

Harrisson, Tom: *Savage Civilization.* Knopf, 1937

Henry, Alexander: *Manuscript Journals of Henry, Alexander and Thompson, David,* edited by Elliot Coues. Francis P. Haroer, New York, 1897

Herodotus: *History,* translated by George Rawlinson. J. M. Dent and Sons Ltd., London and Toronto, 1924

Herskovits, Melville J. and Frances S.: *Rebel Destiny.* Whittlesey House, New York, 1934

Hose, Charles: *Natural Man,* a Record from Borneo. Macmillan and Co. London, 1926

Hubert, H. and M. Mauss: "The Nature and Significance of the Ceremony of Sacrifice," Open Court, Chicago, 1926

Junod, Henri A.: *The Life of a South African Tribe.* David Nutt, London, 1912

Karsten, Rafael: "Blood Revenge, War and Victory Feasts among the Jibaro Indians of Eastern Ecuador," *United States American Ethnology Bureau, Bulletin 79,* Washington, 1923

Kidd, Dudley: *Savage Childhood,* a Study of Kafir Children. Adam and Charles Black, London, 1906

Kroeber, Alfred L.: "The Arapaho," *American Museum of Natural His-*

tory Bulletin, vol. XVIII, 1902, New York, 1904

Landtman, Gunnar: *The Kiwai Papuans of British New Guinea.* Macmillan and Co., London, 1927

Lawrence, David Herbert: *Kangaroo.* Martin Secker, London, 1923

Lee, Dorothy: "Being and Value in Primitive Culture," *The Journal of Philosophy,* vol. XLVI, No. 13, June 23, 1949

LeJeune, Father Paul: *The Jesuit Relations and Allied Documents,* Travels and Explorations of the Jesuit Missionaries in New France, 1610-1791, edited by Thwaites, Reuben, Gold, vol. V. The Burrows Bros. & Co., Cleveland, 1901

Levy-Bruhl, Lucien: *Primitive Mentality,* translated by Lilian A. Clare. Macmillan, London and New York, 1923

———: *How Natives Think,* translated by Lilian A. Clare. Knopf, New York, 1926

Malinowski, Bronislaw: *Argonauts of the Western Pacific,* an Account of Native Enterprise and Adventure in the Archipelagoes of Melanesian New Guinea. George Routledge and Sons, Ltd., London, E. P. Dutton and Co., New York, 1922

Maning, a Pakeha Maori: *Old New Zealand,* a Tale of Good Old Times. Richard Bentley and Son, London, 1876

Marett, R. R.: *Anthropology.* Henry Holt, New York, 1911

Mariner, William: *An Account of the Natives of the Tonga Islands in the South Pacific Ocean,* Compiled and Arranged from the Extensive Communications of Mr. Mariner by John Martin. Constable and Co., London, 1827

Mead, Margaret: *Coming of Age in Samoa,* a Psychological Study of Primitive Youth for Western Civilization. W. Morrow and Co., New York, 1928

———: *Sex and Temperament,* in Three Primitive Societies. W. Morrow and Co., New York, 1938

Meek, Charles Kingsley: *A Sudanese Kingdom,* An Ethnological Study of the Jukun-speaking people of Nigeria, 2 volumes. Kegan Paul, Trench, Trubner, London, 1931

Melville, Herman: *Typee,* Narrative of a Four Months' Residence among the Natives of a Valley of the Marquesas Islands. John Murray, London, 1846

Mooney, James: "The Ghost Dance Religion and the Sioux Outbreak of 1890," *United States Bureau of Ethnology, Fourteenth Annual Report,* 1892-1893, part 2, Washington, 1896

Morgan, Lewis H.: *League of the Ho-Do-No-Sau-Nee or Iroquois.* Dodd, Mead and Co., New York, 1904

Motolinia: *History of the Indians of New Spain,* translated by Elizabeth Andros Foster, The Cortes Society, printed by the University of New Mexico, 1950

Murie, James R.: "Pawnee Indian Societies," *American Museum of Natural History, Anthropological Papers,* vol. XI, part 7, 1914

Nadel, S. F.: *A Black Byzantium,* the Kingdom of Nupe in Nigeria, published for the International Institute of African Languages and Cultures. Oxford University Press, London, New York, 1942

Nietzsche, Friedrich Wilhelm: *The Genealogy of Morals,* translated by Horace B. Samuel. The Macmillan Co., New York, 1929

Radin, Paul: *Primitive Man as Philosopher.* D. Appleton and Co., New York, 1927

Radcliffe-Brown, Alfred Reginald: *The Andaman Islanders.* Cambridge University Press, 1933

———: "The Social Organization of Australian Tribes," *The Oceania Monographs,* No. 1, Melbourne, Macmillan and Co., London, 1931

Reik, Theodore: "Ritual, Psychoanalytical Studies," translated from the second German edition by Douglas Bryan, *The International Psychoanalytical Library,* No. 19. Hogarth Press and the Institute of Psychoanalysis, 1931

Roheim, Geza: "Psychoanalysis of Primitive Cultural Types," *The International Journal of Psychoanalysis,* vol. XIII Jan.-Apr. 1932. Published for the Institute of Psychoanalysis, by Bailliere, Tindall and Cox, London

Roscoe, Rev. John: *The Baganda,* an Account of Their Native Customs and Beliefs. Macmillan, London, 1911

Rousseau, Jean-Jacques: *The Social Contract,* translated by G. D. H. Cole. J. M. Dent and Son Ltd., London, 1938

Roth, Walter E.: "An Inquiry into the Animism and Folklore of the Guiana Indians," *United States Bureau of American Ethnology, Thirtieth Annual Report,* 1908-1909, Washington, 1915

Sahagun, Fray Bernardino de: *A History of Ancient Mexico,* translated by Fanny R. Bandelier, vol. 1. Fisk University Press, Nashville

Sapir, Edward: *Selected Writings,* edited by David G. Mandelbaum. University of California Press, Berkeley and Los Angeles, 1949

Shirokogoroff, S. M.: *Psychomental Complex of the Tungus.* Kegan Paul, Trench, Trubner and Co., London, 1935

Spencer, Baldwin and Frances Jones Gillen: *The Native Tribes of Central Australia.* Macmillan, London, 1899

Staden, Hans: *The True History of His Captivity, 1557,* translated from the German and edited by Malcolm Letts. George Routledge and Son, Ltd., London, 1928

Stevenson, Matilda Coxe: "The Zuni Indians," *United States Bureau of American Ethnology, Twenty-Third Annual Report,* 1901-1902, Washington, 1904

Strabo: *Geography,* translated by Jones, volume 7. Putnam's Sons, New York, 1930

Tacitus: "Germany and Its Tribes" in *The Complete Works,* translated by A. J. Church and W. J. Brodribb. The Modern Library, 1942

Talbot, Percy Amaury: *Life in Southern Nigeria.* Macmillan, London, 1923

Trumbull, H. Clay: *The Blood Covenant,* a Primitive Rite and Its Bearing on Scripture. John D. Wattles, Philadelphia, 1893

Tylor, Edward B.: *Primitive Culture.* John Murray, London, 1871

Vimont, Father Barthelemy: *The Jesuit Relations and Allied Documents,* Travels and Explorations of the Jesuit Missionaries in New France, 1610-1791, edited by Thwaites, Reuben, Gold, vol. XXII. The Burrows Bros. and Co., Cleveland, 1901

Warner, W. Lloyd: *A Black Civilization,* a Social Study of an Australian Tribe. Harper and Bros., New York, 1937

Wissler, Clark: "Ceremonial Bundles of the Black Foot Indians," *American Museum of Natural History, Anthropological Papers,* vol. VIII, part 2, New York, 1912